BUSINESS ENGLISH

R. Gupta

PUSTAK MAHAL®

Publishers
Pustak Mahal®

Administrative office and sale centre

J-3/16 , Daryaganj, New Delhi-110002
☎ 23276539, 23272783, 23272784 • ***Fax:*** 011-23260518
E-mail: info@pustakmahal.com • ***Website:*** www.pustakmahal.com

Branches

Bengaluru: ☎ 080-22234025 • ***Telefax:*** 080-22240209
E-mail: pustakmahalblr@gmail.com
Mumbai: ☎ 022-22010941, 022-22053387
E-mail: unicornbooksmumbai@gmail.com

ISBN 978-81-223-1630-8

Edition: 2017

Printed at: Ar Emm International, New Delhi

PREFACE

"The quality of your relationships and results will be determined by the quality and quantity of your communication with other people."

—Ronnie Morris

Central Area Vice President
Coca Cola Bottling Company of North Texas

Almost all business activities are envisioned, planned, implemented and analysed in some way or the other with the written word. Public and private entities rely upon business-writing to communicate important information, both externally and internally, concerned with the conduct of their business. It is basically important that any writing concerning business is written in clear, unambicious and concise manner.

Poorly written business documents produce undesired results and lead to disastrous consequences. Carefully chosen, properly organized and well written words enhance the probability of effective business communication.

The purpose of business-writing is to convey information or request for information in clear manner. A lot of writing for business is poorly written, disorganized and incomplete and leads to ineffective business running.

Whether writing for a sales proposal, sending e-mails or preparing an instruction manual, there are certain steps you need to follow for creative business-writing. You need to:

a) organize the ideas and information to be communicated;
b) consider the audience to be addressed;
c) write with clarity;
d) proofread;
e) edit your text.

Whatever has been written in this book is based on the experiences gained during service and interactions with participants of training programmes conducted by me. I have also taken liberty to draw upon the relevant literature.

I hope this book will help readers in making their writing clear, concise as well as effective.

—Author

Contents

SECTION - I

Business-english

SECTION - II

Job-applications

SECTION - III

Business-letters

SECTION - IV

Legal Templates

SECTION - V

Classified Vocabulary

General Business Vocabulary

SECTION - VI

English Thesaurus

SECTION - I

Business-english

Chapter

1

Business-writing: 6 Reasons for its Importance

Writing is concerned with putting thoughts on paper. It helps in creating and organising ideas, views, feelings, opinions and attitudes, and makes comprehension easy and effective. For an idea and opinion to be expressed effectively, it requires to be further processed and developed properly.

Advances in communication technology have reduced the need for writing. You can transmit messages orally over the telephone quickly and easily. Computerised communication through e-mail and voice-mail and holding teleconferences are in vogue. Nevertheless, no business can function without the written word. Important reasons for business-writing are as follows:

1. **Aid to Career Advancement** – Generally, people are judged by the way they use their language in expressings to their ideas in writing. You may have meaningful ideas, but that is not enough. Effective expression of ideas instil confidence in readers and motivates them to accept the writer's views. If your reader is your boss, effective writing is persuasive. If he is your subordinate, such writing is educative. Always remember that outstanding leaders in any field of activity have been effective communicators. With excellent convincing abilities, therefore, the skill to write effectively is one of the most important communication skills for advancement in one's career.

2. **Aid to Decision-making** – Employers need people with effective writing skills. They search for persons who can report quickly and effectively on the activities and the requirements of their large, complex organizations. Why? This is because they want concise, timely and accurate information – not a mass of undigested data – for decision-making. Such information can be provided by skilled writers who have the ability to think clearly and precisely – to analyse data, to appreciate the intrecacies of problems, to examine facts objectively, to weigh alternatives in a more detached way and help make sound recommendations or decisions.

3. **Acquisition of Power** – An organization requires employees with rich communication skills for writing letters, speeches, drafting memos and reports for their superiors. The easy access to their bosses and interactions with them give the impression that they wield considerable influence. They also earn a great deal of credit as well as respect their superiors and colleagues and they may encash it to acquire more power in the organization.

4. **Growth in Business** – For better planning, its implementation and for achieving goals, in this way, it becomes necessary to possess effective communication writing skills, lasting impression and better business results may be obtained.

5. **Better Public Relation Results** – It is important for any organization to have a good Public Relation (PR) person to handle its publicity arena and who with his judicious planning and execution of tasks fetch a good image to the company.

   Best public relation results can be obtained by simply focussing on two directives. First your communication efforts should follow a specific plan and secondly this communucation plan should be aligned with the strategy of your company. Thus, a good written proposal will not only bring success in one's professional career but also earn him/her a good reputation and growth orientation in the company.

6. **Improves Credibility** – A poorly written document or proposal might not just fail but it could end up being a black mark on the company's name. Grammatically weak business-writings can never attract the reader. They can neither inform, nor entertain and hence they do not promote result-oriented action. Thus, a well-written proposal or presentation improves the credibility of the organization.

Chapter 2

16 Business areas where Business-writing is Required

In the first place, a written docoment serves as a powerful witness. So disputes and ambiguities are avoided in the future. In other words, business oral communication alone is inadequate to transmit complex information. A written document serves as an aid to memory and understanding. Besides, there are countless situations in which a business may require a written document for the smooth conduct of its numerous activities. Following are the situations where business-writings are important.

- To correspond with clients, customers, suppliers, employees or their unions, government agencies or professional bodies to convey, explain or exchange information;
- To write notes to explain a case, to suggest courses of action and to obtain or convey decisions;
- To prepare précis and briefs to explain complex cases or present information in voluminous documents;
- To write inter-office notes or memos to exchange information or obtain concurrence;
- To issue directions to comply with decisions of the management;
- To prepare annual reports;
- To make plans, monitor them and evaluate their outcomes;
- To prepare feasibility reports of projects and evaluate their performances.
- To make proposals and justify them;
- To prepare agendas for meetings and conferences, record minutes and prepare action taken reports;
- To prepare position papers, status report or other business and technical reports;
- To evaluate performance of employees, products and processes;
- To award contracts, monitor them and evaluate them;
- To prepare procedure manuals and training materials for improving;
- To prepare reports of study tours;
- To announce news and changes in the organization.

Chapter 3

11 Rules of Effective Business-writing

At every level and type of business, clear and efficient writing is important. If the information is complicated or inaccurate, it may create misunderstandings and extra effort may be required to interpret it correctly and get clarifications. Poorly-written and badly-organized documents would harm the image of the organization. Employers expect clear, concise, complete and correct writing, so that sound decisions may be made quickly and clear instructions issued. In other words, effective writing is a must.

Effective writing is a prized skill. This skill is required at all levels, but its importance increases as one moves up in the organizational hierarchy.

As with other skills, one can become an accomplished writer if one practises long enough. We will discuss in this chapter some principles which, if correctly followed, will help you become a skilled writer. In order to become an accomplished writer, following points should be considered:

1. Focus on the Reader

Before you start writing, you should be clear about what you want to state and convey. You can then only decide better what information you should give, whether it is complete and how best you can present it. The more you concentrate on your readers and their needs, the better chance you have to get the response you hope for. Your understanding of these aspects will decide your tone, the content, the vocabulary and the format of your document. Therefore, you should focus your attention on your readers and try to find answers to the following questions:

- **Purpose:** Why are you writing this document? Do you want to explain an idea or provide information? Do you want to convince others about your viewpoint or persuade them to accept it? Do you want to describe in detail a new procedure? Do you want to request or motivate them to accept your suggestions? Do you want to announce, analyse or report findings?
- **Target Readers:** Who will be the prospective readers? Your boss? Your subordinates? Your customers, clients or suppliers? Government agencies? Your employees or their unions? Political leaders? Environmental groups? What information does the reader already have and what more is required to be given and explained? Are the readers familiar with the jargons which you propose to use? What roles are they expected to play? Does the reader have a veto power? Can they put obstacles in the ongoing

scheme? What may be their likely response? Are they likely to be receptive, indifferent or hostile? How would different groups of readers react to a similar text? Whether any unpleasant information could be conveyed to the readers? Should it be mentioned subtly or the writer depending upon his waiting skills follow an assertive approach?

- **Main Points:** What are the main points? Are they too many? (Remember, too many points may deflect the focus from the main ones and readers may lose interest in your writing.) So focus on the central thesis only that governs and unifies the writing in your document.
- **Timing:** Should you send the document now or later? Are there any resource constraints which may make your proposal unacceptable at this time? Are you late in sending the proposal whose need is already over? If somebody else is also simultaneously sending similar information, should you check whether there is any contradiction or overlapping in the information being sent from the other sources?

2. Use Conversational Style

The key to effective writing is to use conversational style. You 'talk' to your readers imagining that they are in front of you and then write those words that you would use in your 'talk.' While using conversational style, one should use the appropriate words, not jargons which may unfamiliar a good number of readers.

To 'talk' on paper:

- **Use simple, short, familiar words** as we use in the spoken language, such as 'try' instead of 'endeavour' and 'guess' instead of 'surmise'.
- **Use a variety of punctuation marks.** Not only the full stop and comma, but also semi-colon, colon, dash, question mark and apostrophe, as may be necessary. Punctuation marks replace hand gestures and voice inflection in oral conversation. As hand gestures and voice inflection relieve monotony of a speech, so also punctuation marks relieve the monotony of reading and make it more interesting with the right kind of pauses for emphasis.
- **Use more personal pronouns** as we use in normal conversation. Generally, in office writing, personal pronouns are not used so that writing is kept formal and objective. This is an outdated approach as writing is becoming more personal and informal that establishes a rapport with the readers.
- **Use contractions** occasionally to give an informal tone to your writing as it proves very helpful. Basically, It depends upon the target readers. If you want to be formal and maintain an objective distance, the writing may be without contractions.

3. Make Your Message Complete

The message will be complete if it contains all the information that readers may need for getting the desired response. A complete message saves time and effort that may be needed for clarifications of avoidable doubts and questions that may arise on account of incomplete information. It also helps in building goodwill.

Whether you are writing a note, a draft of a communication, a report or are replying to an enquiry try to answer all questions – stated or unstated. Similarly, when making a proposal, try to answer all the questions that may normally arise while examining it. Even if some unpleasant or unfavourable information is to be given, give it with tact and honesty, without hurting the emotions of the readers.

Answers to the six questions – What, Why, When, Where, Who and How—will cover almost all aspects of the subject matter and help you in making your message complete as well as informative.

4. Maintain Clarity in Your Writing

Clear writing reflects clear thinking. Clarity means that your sentences are straight forward, clear, direct and precise.

To achieve clarity:

- **Use simple, short and familiar words**. These are easy to understand and are unlikely to be misinterpreted or misunderstood. Avoid technical or business jargon whenever you are writing to a person who is unfamiliar with such words. For example:

Avoid	Use
accompany	*go with*
accordingly	*therefore, so*
applicable	*apply to*
acquire	*get, gain*
advise	*tell*
encourage	*urge*
supplement	*add to*
assist	*help*
commence	*begin*
complete	fill out, finish

- **Put only one idea in a sentence** and keep the sentence length to 15 or 20 words. Write additional sentences to express other ideas. Remember that long sentences are difficult to write, read and comprehend correctly.
- **Achieve appropriate readability** by keeping word-and-sentence lengths at the readers' educational level. Also, use difficult words - words with three or more syllables - to the minimum. To keep readers interested, sentences should be varied. These can be a mix of short, medium and long sentences together with a mix of simple (35 per cent), complex (50 per cent) and compound (15 per cent) sentences.
- **Activate your sentences by using active voice verbs** as much as possible. Sentences with active voice verbs are generally more straightforward and informative; they are also briefer. Liberal use of personal pronouns may help you in using active voice verb more frequently.

For example:

For	Say
• The demand for the release of confiscated goods was not accepted by the Customs authorities.	• The Customs authorities refused to release the confiscated goods.
• The result was announced by the Commission on Saturday.	• The Commission announced the result on Saturday.
• A farewell function has been planned by us in honour of Mr Mirdha.	• We have planned a farewell function in honour of Mr Mirdha.
• These figures were checked by the Finance Department.	• The Finance Department checked these figures.

- **Use concrete expressions instead of abstract ones**. Abstract writing is vague and general. It leads to uncertainty, misunderstanding and confusion. Readers would be at cross-roads as such expressions in sentences creat ambiguity, leaving no scope for a right comprehension. Such writing loses its effectiveness. Therefore, use concrete expressions that create a vivid picture in the readers' mind, use concrete nouns, accurate verbs and significant modifiers (adjectives and adverbs) that may relate to the senses of sight, sound, touch and smell. Also, wherever possible, use anecdotes and examples to clarify your point and maintain the readers' interest.

5. Be Concise

Conciseness means that you express your ideas in a few words. Conciseness is an outstanding virtue. Be brief and to the point and weed out empty words - unnecessary words and phrases that do not contribute to the readers' understanding. Conciseness adds to emphasis and gives writing a sense of preciseness. By removing redundant expressions you help important ideas stand out. A long-winded document may be clear to you but too demanding of the readers' time and attention.

Do not confuse between conciseness and brevity. A concise document is full of substance about the main theme; it says much in a few words. On the contrary, a document may be brief, yet not concise; it may not suffice to provide the information required.

To achieve conciseness:

- **Use single-word substitutes, instead of phrases**, wherever possible, without changing the meaning. Remove wordy expressions that do not add to the meaning. For example:

Avoid	*Use*	**Avoid**	*Use*
are of the opinion	*believe*	*in an effort to*	*to*
are prepared to admit	*have admitted*	*in the case of*	*if*
at this point of time	*now*	*in the event that*	*if*
along the lines of	*like*	*in the majority of instances*	*usually*
at the present time	*now*	*in the matter of*	*in*
by means of	*with; by*	*in the nature of*	*like*
close proximity	*near*	*in the near future*	*soon*
consensus of opinion	*consensus*	*in the neighbourhood of*	*about*

For	Say	For	Say
due to the fact that	*because*	*in terms of*	*in, for*
during the course of	*during*	*in the time of*	*during*
engaged in the study of	*studying*	*in view of the reason/*	*because, fact*
few in number	*few*	*that since*	*as*
for the purpose of	*for*	*limited number*	*a few*
for the reason that	*since, because*	*meet together*	*meet*
for amount of		*more specifically*	*for instance,*
from the point of view of	*for*	*for example*	*such as*
has the capability	*can*	*on a few occasions*	*occasionally*
herewith is	*here is*	*on a weekly basis*	*weekly*
in addition	*besides, also*	*on behalf of*	*from*
in favour of	*for, to*	*on the basis of*	*by*
in order to	*to*	*on the grounds that*	*since, because*
in accordance with	*by, under*	*on the occasion of*	*when*
in a number of cases	*in many cases*	*point of view*	*aspect, option*
in connection with	*about*	*that is to say*	*in other words*
incumbent upon	*must*	*until such time as*	*until*
in lieu of	*instead of*	*we would like to ask*	*please*
in regard to	*about,*	*with a view to*	*to*
concerning		*with reference to*	*about*
in relation to		*with regard to*	*about*
in spite of the fact that	*although*	*with the result that*	*so that*

- **Omit which and that clauses, wherever possible.** For example:

For	Say
• The manager bought desks that are of executive type.	• The manager bought executive type desks.

- **Avoid overusing It is, It was, There is, There was, There are, There were** at the beginning of a sentence. This gives the sentences a sense of immediacy and crispness. For example:

For	Say
a. It was decided by the Board that the applications for membership would be considered at the next meeting.	a. The Board decided to consider applications for membership at its next meeting.
b. There has been no increase in passenger fare in the rail budget 2016-17 presented by the railway minister.	b. The railway minister has not increased the passenger fare in his rail-budget 2016-17.

- **Include only relevant statements in your writing.** Stick to the purpose of the message, omit irrelevant words and rambling sentences; omit unnecessary information. Avoid long introductions, unnecessary explanations, pompous words and excessive politeness. Use adjectives and prepositions sparingly. Avoid verbosity.

- **Avoid the use of expressions** like "It is appreciated," "It should be noted," "In this connection," which are often superfluous.
- **Avoid unnecessary repetition.** Repitition leads to emphasis, but not always. Use shorter name after you have mentioned the long one once; use pronouns or initials instead of repeating long names; cut out all needless repetition of words, phrases and sentences.

6. Be Coherent

Coherence means linking sentences and paragraphs with transition words and connectors that show a logical relationship between sentences and paragraph, so that ideas clearly express the intended meaning. If you put your ideas logically, they will not be spread across the document, thereby convincing the readers about the intended message.

To achieve coherence:

★ Stick to one idea for each paragraph.

★ Use transitions and connectors.

★ Use reference words and repeat key words.

In a paragraph, each sentence should be relevant to the main idea expressed in the topic sentence. By rambling from idea to idea, the readers will lose their interest as well as attention. Most readers prefer to handle one idea at a time. They depend on paragraph breaks to signal the completion of one idea and the beginning of the next.

Transition words and phrases such as **therefore, meanwhile,** and **however** help point out the way from one sentence to another. They lead readers from one paragraph to another. These are signposts that help them to follow your logic and flow of ideas. Transition words must be aptly chosen to mark a clear relationship between and within sentences.

Some transition words and phrases that can be used to create relationships are given below:

Contrast —

however	***However**, since ideas are building tools, one cannot build a successful business without them, as one could not build a house without bricks.*
although	***Although** he was tired, he stayed up late completing his pending work.*
but	*We have had nothing in the office **but** trouble with the printer.*
conversely	*"All bubblegum contain rubber. **Conversely** not all things which contain rubber are bubblegum."*
nevertheless	*Many people disagreed with her. **Nevertheless**, her colleagues supported her.*
yet	*He is a college professor, **yet** he acts childishly with his friends.*

still	*Are you **still** working for the same company?*
on the other hand	*The job was not interesting, **on the other hand** it was well-paid.*
in contrast	***In contrast,** cash flows are not always a direct measure of a company's performance.*

Time —

now	***Now** that you have sketched out your marketing and product service approaches, you are ready to tackle sales.*
later	*He shall speak to you **later**.*
after (that)	*We first played tennis **after** that we went to our office.*
before (that)	*I apologised to him **before** he could scold me.*
meanwhile	*Prayag was drafting a letter in office. Tarun, **meanwhile**, was out with his friend for an important work.*
following	*He became ill on Sunday and was hospitalised the **following** day.*
(since) then	*I have been working in a bank ever **since** I left school.*

Comparison —

similarly	***Similarly**, people who deal with power holders must appeal to the deference that is expected.*
likewise	*Some have little power to do good and have **likewise** little strength to resist evil.*
in the same way	***In the same way** you judge others, you will be judged by your standard of behaviour.*

Cause and Effect —

as a result	*Ravi was a beginner in his new business. He worked very hard, **as a result of which** he achieved his goal and became a successful man in his business.*
therefore	***Therefore**, to ensure survival, entrepreneurs should carefully pick their type of business, adjust to market needs, define birth size and work hard to achieve growth.*
consequently	*The company ran out of funds, **consequently**, none of the employees or creditors could be paid.*
thus	*He exposed the fraudulent documents and **thus** prevented the merger of the companies.*
so	*India must increase exports **so** that foreign exchange could be earned.*
because	*Many workers were laid off **because** of the recession.*
hence	*I worked very hard from morning till night, **hence** I found myself extremly tired.*

Example —

for instance	*There are many types of sentence,* ***for instance****, assertive, interrogative, imperative, etc.* ***For instance*** *-*
for example	***For example****, one new manufacturer developed a new electronic temperature measuring instrument and he was unsure of how to price it.*
specifically	*She* ***specifically*** *stated she did not want to be contacted by phone.*

Addition —

moreover	*He set a new record in this race.* ***Moreover****, he is an excellent athelete.*
besides	***Besides*** *being difficult, grammar can be confusing. No one besides me can understand it.*
in addition	***In addition****, it is often the case that a corporation is formed under the laws of one State while operating in another.*
also	*He completed the report and* ***also*** *finished the worksheet.*
too	*He was* ***too*** *tired to continue his work. He likes to take a short walk in his garden.*
furthermore	***Furthermore****, having the best ideas first by no means guarantees success.*

Sequence —

first	*He was standing* ***first*** *in the line.*
next	*The* ***next*** *name in the list was Sarita's.*
then	*I spoke to him on Wednesday, but I haven't seen him since* ***then****.*
last	*Arvind was the* ***last*** *to arrive home.*
finally	***Finally,*** *the editor had abridged the massive book by removing the boring parts.*
to begin with	***To begin with****, it is probably not contemplated by any of those persons that their stock will be freely transferable and that 'new partners' may be imposed upon them by a selling stockholder.*
further	*I have nothing* ***further*** *to say on the subject.*

Use coordinating conjunctions – and, but, yet, or, nor, to connect ideas within sentences.

Use reference words like – this, that, these, those and other pronouns to join new ideas with points made earlier.

Repeat key words in different forms using synonyms to emphasise the ideas in the topic sentence.

7. Be Correct

Correctness means:

- Facts, figures and words are correct;
- No grammatical errors;
- Use of correct punctuation.

Absolute accuracy in regard to the contents

- **Facts and figures are presented to make a point.** No reader would like to spend time in computing the meaning out of facts and figures. Therefore, the writer should make sure that they are explained before presenting them.

  The writer should maintain accuracy in presenting facts and figures, thereby leaving no space for doubt about the content in the mind of readers. Also, some words may be similar in form but different in meaning or similar or almost similar in sound when pronounced, but different in meaning or mean the same as another word but which are used in a different sense. Therefore, exercise care and choose the right word to convey your message, lest it should be misinterpreted or misunderstood.

  Some pairs of words are given below:

(a)	*Eminent* *Imminent*	*Respectful and distinguished; notable; outstanding.* *(Esp. of unpleasant event) about to happen; likely to happen soon.*
(b)	*Forego* *Forgo*	*Precede in place or time.* *Go without (something).*
(c)	*Precede* *Proceed*	*To come or go before in time order or position.* *To begin a course of action; carry on or continue; move forward.*
(d)	*Spacious* *Specious*	*Having plenty of space.* *Superficially plausible but actually wrong; misleadingly attractive.*
(e)	*Band* *Banned*	*Group of people who have a common interest or purpose.* *Something that is not allowed or illegal.*
(f)	*Complement* *Compliment*	*The number of quantity that makes something complete.* *A polite expression of praise.*
(g)	*Flair* *Flare*	*A natural ability or talent.* *A sudden brief burst of flame or light.*
(h)	*Plain* *Plane*	*Simple & ordinary, easy to understand.* *A flat surface, a level of existence or thought.*

- **Be careful in spellings.** Misspelled words are a complete NO. Errors of transposition ('nad' instead of 'and' or 'recieve' instead of 'receive') are also errors that show carelessness. Thus, it is highly advisable to proofread the document not once but many times before sending the final draft.
- **Use correct punctuation marks for variety and clarity.** All good writings begin with the understanding of grammatical rules, which should be followed rigorously, leaving no space for errors not even of punctuation marks.

✐ **You should particularly avoid errors** such as dangling modifiers, subject and verb agreement, logical comparison and parallelism:

(a) ***Dangling modifier*** is a participle intended to modify a noun or pronoun (called **subject of reference**) but it is left dangling (hanging) because it is not related to the subject of reference. For example:

Entering the room, the light was quite dazzling. (Here, the subject is light, but the participle **Entering** does not relate to it.

Revised: *When I entered the room, I found the light quite dazzling.*)

(b) **Subject and verb agreement** means that the subject and the verb in a sentence must agree (be the same) in person (first, second or third) and in number (singular or plural). For example:

The state of his affairs were such as to cause anxiety to his creditors. (Here, the verb **were** does not agree with the subject **state**. It should be replaced by the verb **is**).

(c) **Logical comparison** means that the things being compared are of the same kind and are actually comparable. For example:

Our health benefits are different from our competitor. (**benefits** and **competitor** are not comparable. Revised : Our health benefits are different from the benefits of our competitor.

(d) **Parallelism** means all units in a sentence are parallel or identical in grammatical construction and they harmonise with each other. In other words, each unit must have the same grammatical form as all the others. For example:

Her skills for the job included researching organization and writing lenthly reports. (The sentence has two participles (**researching** and **writing**) and a noun (**organization**). A harmonious construction requires all the three as participles. Revised: Her skills for the job included researching, organizing and writing long reports.)

8. Maintain Courtesy

The tone of writing reflects upon courtesy employed by the writer. Courtesy, in general terms, implies politeness with the right choice of words and right medium of expression. Words play a significant role in showing a serious, critical or warm mood of the writer. The writer should make a coscious effort of avoiding any unpleasantness, which might embarrass him later or give a wrong image in the organization.

Words like “please” and “thank you” will have enhanced effect if following points are considered:

★ be sincerely tactful, thoughtful and courteous;

★ omit expressions that irritate, hurt or belittle;

Courtesy is an attitude of mind which is reflected in whatever you write. If you use abrupt or blunt expressions because of a mistaken idea of conciseness or because of your negative personal attitude, you are being discourteous. You should consciously make effort to omit abrupt, blunt or discourteous expressions from your writing. For example,

Avoid	Use
• Your letter is not clear to me. I cannot understand it.	• If I understand your letter correctly, it is what you want.
• Do not overspend or exceed budget allocation.	• Exercise economy in expenditure.
• It is obvious that you have already forgotten what I wrote to you two weeks ago.	• As mentioned in my letter of ..... (data) to you .....

- **Show your thoughtfulness and appreciation** by sending cordial, courteous messages of congratulation and appreciation to your clients or colleagues, whenever an occasion arises.
- **Always promptly attend to enquiries or requests** of your clients and your colleagues.
- **Avoid expressions** like "*I do not agree with you*," or "*You probably do not know...*"
- **Adopt informal and straightforward approach.** The polite formality of the past is considered coldness or snobbishness. The friendlier and more "real" you sound, the better is the chance to relate to your readers. Therefore, avoid excessive formality or politeness but also taking care of the right choice of words.
- **Express yourself positively** and show that you are always cheerful, self-assured and optimistic. Emphasise positive facts; it is always more persuasive to suggest what you want than what you don't want. For example:

Avoid	Use
Perhaps you won't object to my suggestions...	I am sure you'll agree with my suggestions.
Without careful preparation, we won't be able to win the contract.	With careful preparation, we will be able to win the contract.
Don't waste energy.	Conserve energy.
Do you want any help, write to me.	Should you require further asistance please don't hesitate to write to me.

9. Organize Your Writing

- **Put your ideas clearly and logically to organize your writing skill** and in the best order for effect. Even an excellent piece of grammatically correct writing will fail to convince readers if it shows confused and disorganized thinking. For impact, your writing should follow a logical sequence, keeping in view how your readers will receive your document.

Two main ways to organize the topics are:

- ★ from the most important to the least important one and;
- ★ from the least important to the most important one.

Few other ways to organize documents are:

- ★ in a chronological order;
- ★ geographically or location wise;
- ★ process or product wise and;
- ★ by making comparison or contrast.

✐ **Arrange the topics alphabatically (name of client or customer) from the most to the least important point.** In such cases, the opening statement should emphasise on the theme of the content, depending upon the receptivity of the reader. The opening paragraph should convey to the reader as what is to be covered in your document and its conclusions, recommendations or requests.

For example, if you propose action to improve the efficiency in your department, the topics may be organized in the following manner:

- ★ What is the present method?
- ★ Why is it proving unsatisfactory?
- ★ What do you suggest to change in the present setup?
- ★ Why do you think these changes are necessary?
- ★ How would these changes benefit the organization?
- ★ Is the change in method feasible?
- ★ What follow-up action will be needed to implement the change?

✐ **Never begin the document with your main point** if readers are hostile or if your suggestion, request or conclusion is controversial. The writer should show thoughtfulness to convey unpleasant news by leading readers step by step through the arguments. Give appealing and persuasive information at the beginning, help readers to understand your position and lead them to your conclusion. For example, if a new system to record attendance is to be introduced and this is likely to be opposed by the affected persons, the approach can be:

- ★ Why is the change needed?
- ★ What is the proposed new system to be introduced?
- ★ What are the benefits of the new system?
- ★ How will the new system be operated?
- ★ When will the new system be introduced?
- ★ When will a meeting be arranged to explain the new system and clarify the doubts and objections, if any?

If your readers are several persons, some of whom are receptive and others are resistant, treat all readers amiably and present the information accordingly.

- **Chronological order of organizing a document** may be used to emphasise the order of sequence of events when describing the history of a product or presenting a report. Even in this arrangement, detailed chronology need not be given at the beginning; start with presenting important facts, so that readers can have a quick view of the contents of your document and then follow with details in the required chronological order.
- **Geographical or locational order is suitable when dealing with developments** in different locations. For example, you may prepare tour reports or present statistics about sales or production in different locations or report performance of units at different places.
- **Process or product order is suitable when you are preparing instructions** about a process, machinery or equipment or preparing training or procedure manuals or reporting the results of some studies according to products.
- **Comparison/Contrast order may be used in evaluating two or more machines, processes or proposals.** Comparison is used for emphasising similarities among two or more things and contrast is used for emphasising differences. In this method, do not mix statements of similarities and differences or advantages and disadvantages in the same section. The proper approach will be to discuss similarities or advantages of the things being compared in one section and differences or disadvantages in another section. For example, if two proposals A and B are being evaluated, present their advantages and disadvantages in the following way:
    - ★ Advantages – Proposal A and Proposal B
    - ★ Disadvantages – Proposal A and Proposal B
- **All ideas in the document may not be of equal importance.** Some ideas will be more important than others. The importance of an idea is reflected by the coverage it receives and the place it is located in the document. If the idea is important, it will be dealt with in adequate detail and located prominently either at the beginning or at the end of the document and not interspersed with several less important ideas. If a less important idea is given more coverage and prominence, the readers may feel misled or may become indifferent or resistant to your ideas.

10. Presentation of Your Document

Presentation of your document should be able to fetch a visual impact. It should be easy to read and the key points should be such that can catch readers' attention quickly. Your document will then stand out of hundreds of documents that are received in offices every day.

For a good visual impact:

- ★ Use headings liberally;
- ★ Keep paragraphs short;

- ★ Use bold letters to highlight key words;
- ★ Use bullets or other lists;
- ★ Allow plenty of white space;
- ★ Use different typeface to call attention to important steps, dates, deadlines or to highlight important information.

✎ **Use headings** which are like road signs that guide the readers on through the document. Readers can have an overview of the document by going through the headings. Thus, headings speed up reading of the document; repetition helping readers skip through the document and focus attention, where desired.

Headings also help in arranging the document into blocks of information in paragraphs rather than scattering ideas throughout the document.

It is not necessary that each paragraph should have a heading; use sub heads where there are more than one paragraph under one heading.

Start each block by conveying main point. If the heading is a question, begin the block by answering that question. Supporting details can be given in bulleted lists or numbered lists.

Five levels (or styles) of headings are used to present information in a meaningful way:

Level 1. Centred, bold face, upper / lower case.

Level 2. Left aligned, bold face, upper / lower case.

Level 3. Indented bold face, lowercase with a period. Begin text after period.

Level 4. Indented bold face, italicized, lower case with period. Begin after period.

Level 5. Indented, italicized, lower case with period. Text after period.

If your document has only two levels, use the first and the third level.

If the document has only one level, all styles would work. However, preferably the third one should be used as this is easier to read and readers' eyes return naturally to the left margin; they are more likely to read a heading on the left-hand side.

The order of headings shows the importance of the idea. The principle is that you move from ideas of major to ideas of minor importance.

The order of headings should be consistent in the writing. If you use headings in different ways in the same document, you are likely to confuse readers. Once you decide what style of headings you prefer, follow it throughout the document.

Headings and sub-headings should be identified by using italics or bold type fonts.

✎ **Always start with a short paragraph.** A short paragraph should contain only a few sentences. With long paragraphs, writing appears unfriendly, reading becomes difficult and comprehension drops.

The opening sentence of the paragraph should, generally, contain your main point (called 'the topic sentence') and subsequent sentences should expand on this point.

Such a presentation will enable the readers to get the needed information quickly.

If sub-ideas in a paragraph are indented, readers will get a visual signal that you are supporting a key point with data that explains or expands it.

For effect, an idea may be written in a sentence. It may follow with a longer paragraph explaining the sentence. The technique should not be used too often as it may lead to distraction.

The writer should make sure that there is only one idea in a paragraph.The writer's aim is to make the writing clear in comprehension rather than confusing the readers by including too many ideas in one paragraph.

If a major idea has several sub themes, more than one paragraph can be written to explain these several sub-ideas under a major paragraph heading.

Bullets can be used for single words, phrases, sentences or even paragraphs. They isolate information and present it with plenty of white space.

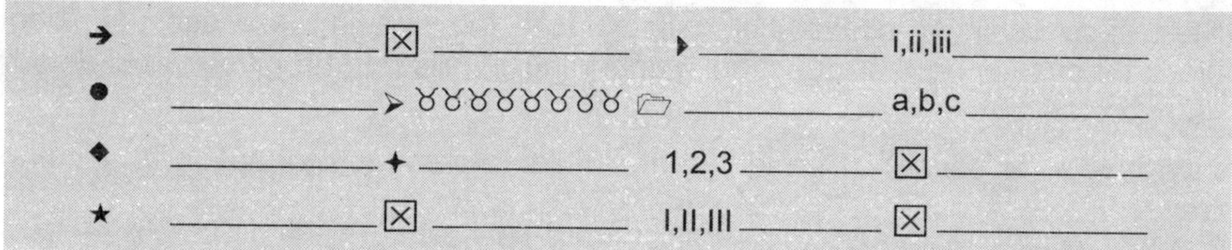

Punctuation in bulleted paragraphs should be as in normal paragraphs. In bulleted lists, if the listed item is a sentence, start with a capital letter and put a full-stop at the end. If the listed item is not a sentence, don't start with a capital letter nor put a full–stop at the end of the item.

Do not have some items that are full sentences and some items that are not. Set up a pattern for a list and stick to it – either all full sentences or all only phrases.

When your document is to list some information, use bullets or hyphens for each item in a list. It will show organization of information within a paragraph. Or, instead of bullets or hyphen, you may use asterisks, small boxes, checkmarks, squiggles and graphic art.

When items in a list have some priority or order, use numbers instead of bullets.

If lists within paragraphs are indented, your writing will be more effective. Indented lists attract the readers' attention and the information in the list can also be quickly grasped. Such lists add to the white space and make the document easily readable and well presented.

Use White space– It is the space between paragraphs and sections, between headings and text, between text and items in the indented list as well as between the items and in the margin– top, bottom, left and right. It gives readers a visual break from the dense look of the text. Such writing appears uncluttered and inviting, gives a clear visual impression of organization of your ideas to the readers and improves the readability of the writing. If too much material is packed on a sheet of paper, the white space gets reduced and the text gives a cluttered and messy look. Such a presentation makes reading difficult, causes eye fatigue and gives readers a poor impression of the writing.

Use different typefaces– such as bold, italics, all capitals– to draw attention to important action steps, dates, deadlines or to draw attention to a specific word, phrase or sentence. Headings and sub-headings are also identified by these devices:

B - Bold	Aa - Small Caps
I - Italic	A^A - Superscript
U - Underline	A_A - Subscript
AA - All Caps	~~A~~ - Strikethrough

During conversation, we put emphasis on words or phrases by raising or lowering our voice, by gestures and pauses, stress and intonation. Similarly, typefaces facilitate giving emphasis and stress while writing.

Conclusion

Writing is an essential activity in business. If it is effective, it will speed up business, avoid backtracking, get rid of confusion and create goodwill. Therefore, try to make your document complete, clear, concise, correct, coherent, courteous, well-organized and attractively presented. Such a document will attract readers; they would also form favourable image about the organization and the message the document seeks to convey. It also shows to them that the writer and the organization have shown consideration not only for the message, but for the readers as well.

Learning and loving business-writing skills can have a positive impact on an individual's career advancement. Professional quality writing sent through effective channels of communication helps in the smooth functioning of the organization and improves productivity and the ability of all functional areas to work together; all the more in an increasingly global workplace, where team spirit is the norm.

Getting promoted is also facilitated by writing skills. Good writing skills communicate intelligence, professionalism and competency.

Chapter
4

Bring Clarity in Your Writing

Introduction

The purpose of writing is to get across your message to the readers. Clarity in writing will help you to achieve this purpose and get the desired outcome from the readers.

Face to face communication helps in quickly clarifying doubt, which is not possible in the case of written communication. Therefore, your writing should be such that it can be understood without your presence and no scope is left for any confusion. Clarity in writing also helps in building trust with the writer. You should put yourself in your readers' position and see whether they will understand or interpret your words and sentences with the same meaning you have in your mind.

1. Use Short, Simple, Familiar Word

Words give shape to our thoughts, feelings and experiences, they are also the means of communication. They let us speak out our minds and make our identity understandable to others. They are the building blocks of written or spoken communication.

Formal communication, whether written or spoken depends upon the apt choice of appropriate words. Thoughtfully selected words help conveying the message in the right sense. They will also improve readability and show our competence in using the language. Words should, therefore, be chosen with great precision for correct interpretation.

Short, simple, familiar words are generally more accurate and direct, such words are unlikely to be misinterpreted or misunderstood. They are also easier to understand and do not put strain on our memory. In contrast, long, unfamiliar words tax our memory and force us to slow down. For example, it is easier to understand the short word **begin** than the word **commence** or **so** instead of **consequently**. If you use short, simple and familiar words, your document will be more appealing in terms of simplicity and efficiency and at the same time convey the correct sense of your message.

A short list of some long, unfamiliar words and their simple equivalents is given below:

Long, unfamiliar word	Short, simple, more familiar word
accelerate	*speed up, move faster*
accompany	*go with*
accomplish	*do*
accordingly	*so, therefore*
acquaint	*say, tell*
acquire	*get, gain*
advert	*refer*
advise	*tell, recommend*
afford an opportunity	*let*
aforementioned	*these*
anticipate	*expect*
apprise	*inform, tell*
applicable	*apply to*
approximately	*about*
ascertain	*find out*
assist	*help*
assistance	*help*
attributable	*due*
augment	*increase, add*
commence	*begin*
communicate	*write, inform*
compensate	*pay*
conclude	*end*
concerning	*about*
concur	*agree*
consequently	*so, therefore, as a result*
converse	*talk*
cooperate	*help*
deem	*think*
demonstrate	*show, prove*
desire	*want*
determine	*decide, find out*
detrimental	*harmful*
disclose	*tell, show*

Long, unfamiliar word	Short, simple, more familiar word
endeavour	*try, effort*
ensue	*follow*
ensure	*make sure*
exhibit	*show*
facilitate	*help*
forward	*send, mail*
furnish	*supply, provide*
furthermore	*also*
incorporate	*include*
identical	*same*
implement	*carry out, do*
in addition	*also*
indicate	*show, state briefly*
inform	*say*
initial	*first*
initially	*at first*
initiate	*start*
insufficient	*not enough*
liquidate	*pay off*
locate	*find*
location	*place*
maintain	*keep, support*
modify	*change*
monitor	*check, watch*
numerous	*many*
nevertheless	*but*
observe	*see*
obtain	*get*
personnel	*people (staff)*
pertaining to	*about*
presently	*soon, now*
prior to	*before*
prohibit	*forbid, prevent*
provided that	*if*
purchase	*buy*

regarding	*about*	*sufficient*	*enough*
relating to	*about*	*supplement*	*add to*
remuneration	*payment, reward*	*supply*	*send*
request	*ask*	*surmise*	*guess*
require	*need*	*terminate*	*end, stop*
reside	*live*	*time period*	*time*
residence	*home*	*transmit*	*send*
respecting	*about*	*transpire*	*happen*
retain	*keep*	*utilisation*	*use*
reveal	*show*	*utilise*	*use*
review	*check, go over*	*viable*	*workable, practical*
(to) state	*(to) say*	*visualise*	*see, form a mental picture*
submitted	*sent*		
subsequent	*later, next*	*whereas*	*since*
subsequently	*afterwards*	*witnessed*	*saw*

Techinical jargons should be avoided for better comprehension of the text. The writer in a bid to impress ends up using ostentatious or unfamiliar words and phrases. The purpose of writing is to get the message across, which in itself creates a lasting impression. The choice of short, simple and familiar words also takes out the stiffness from the writing.

When you write, you have to search for the right words more thoroughly and carefully. Some words have only literal, primary meaning – **denotation**. But some words invoke ideas or feelings in addition to their primary meaning – **connotation**. You should, therefore, be aware of all the meanings of words you use so that you convey the message accurately. Choose words that you think people will understand in the same way as you want them to. You may consult a dictionary as well as a thesaurus to check denotative and connotative meanings of words you choose in your writing.

2. Keep Your Sentences Short and to the Point

There is no fixed limit for the sentence length. Depending on the context, sentences can be short or long. Unnecessary use of short and simple sentences makes the writing appear amateurish. Whereas too many long, complex and compound sentences will make your writing difficult to understand and assimilate and will make your readers confused.

A long sentence can be split into short sentences by changing a comma into a full-stop and using a capital letter to begin the next sentence. Sometimes, a few words may be changed to restore proper grammar after the split. For example:

(a) ABC Ltd. has requested the installation of an additional terminal at Chandraprabha Building for the purpose of providing access to the Rashtriya Informatics Centre's time-sharing computer system.

(**Rewritten:** *ABC Ltd. has requested for the installation of an additional terminal at Chandraprabha Building. It will provide access to the Rashtriya Informatics Centre's time-sharing computer system.)*

(b) If the construction of flats and houses continues at its present rate in this locality as our Planning Department has forecast, present traffic facilities will be inadequate in three years.

(**Rewritten:** *Our Planning Department has forecast that construction of flats and houses will continue at the present rate in this locality. If this is so, present traffic facilities will be inadequate within the next three years.)*

Try to keep the sentence length between 15 to 20 words by putting only one major idea in a sentence. When a sentence exceeds 40 words, try to rewrite it in more than one sentence.

Variety in sentence length may keep readers alert and interested. You may achieve variety by a mix of sentences - short/long/long/short/medium/long/medium. They may also be a mix of simple (say, 35%), complex (say, 50%) and compound (say, 15%) sentences.

3. Achieve Appropriate Readability

Appropriate readability means that words and sentences in the writing should be easily understood by readers. Reading and comprehension levels are roughly equivalent to the level of one's education. A high level of education increases one's vocabulary. The reader's general education level should be kept in mind while writing the document.

One way to find appropriate readability is to check the writing with reference to the **Gunning Fog Index**. This index was developed by Robert Gunning to find out how hard a piece of writing is. According to Gunning, hard writing makes the ideas unclear. The Fog Index checks the writing with reference to the word-length and sentence-length of the written piece. The ratio of word-length and sentence-length corresponds to the number of years of formal education a reader of average intelligence would need to read and understand at that level of word-and-sentence load.

According to the Gunning Fog Index

(a) an index of 10 corresponds to readers who are about 10 years of age or have left school at that age, plus or minus a year or so,

(b) a range of 11 to 13 implies a senior school level standard,

(c) a range of 14 to 16 goes with a university educated reader or a reader who has equivalent practice with fairly difficult books,

(d) range of 16 to 17 is a marginal case,

(e) an index beyond 17 shows the reading is too hard.

If it is over 17, it will not be suitable for prolonged reading. For a readable writing, the ideal index is between 10 and 12 that requires the reading skills of a 10th or 12th grade student. But the writing may range between 8 and 14, below 8 it will look amateurish and over 14 it will make reading heavy.

The Gunning Fox Index is easy to work out. Take a sample of about 100 words from a typical passage. (Count the exact number of words in the passage – it is better if it is around 100 words). Then follow these three steps:

Step 1: Find out the average number of words per sentence. Also, count the total number of sentences. Now, work out the average sentence–length by dividing the number of words in the passage by the number of sentences. Sometimes two grammatical sentences may be joined by a semi-colon. Use your judgment, but you should generally count them as two sentences.

Step 2: Find out the percentage of hard or polysyllabic words (words with three or more syllables). But there are three exceptions:

- ★ Proper nouns, capitalised names of people, places, companies, products, even though they are polysyllabics,
- ★ Combination of words which are made of smaller words, like **well-being, firefighting,**
- ★ Words made up of three syllables by the addition of-ed, -es, -ing, such as **appointed, confesses, harbouring, etc.**

Words of these three exceptions are counted as easy words, although they are polysyllabics.

Step 3: Add the average sentence-length and the percentage of hard or polysyllabic words and multiply the sum by 0.4. This will give the Fog Index of the passage.

- ★ For example, a passage of five sentences has 100 words. The average sentence-length is 20 (100/5). If 10 of these words are hard or polysyllabic, the percentage of hard words is 10 per cent. The sum of the two numbers is 30 (20+10). Multiplied by 0.4, the Fog Index of the passage is 12 (30x0.4).

A combination of average sentence–length and percentage of polysyllables of 25 (Fog Index 10) or 30 (Fog Index 12) will generally be acceptable. You may give your readers any of the following combinations:

- ★ 15 words per sentence and 15% polysyllables or
- ★ 22 words per sentence and 8% polysyllable or
- ★ 25 words per sentence and 5% polysyllables or
- ★ 5 words per sentence and 25% polysyllables.

At 25 words per sentence and 5% polysyllables, readers will receive easy information in large doses. At 5 words per sentence and 25% polysyllables, they will receive heavy information in small doses.

Usually, a ratio of 20/10 (20 words per sentence and 10% polysyllables) is workable. Technical writing may need more polysyllables and a ratio of 15/15 may be all right.

Sometimes it may not be possible to control the vocabulary word-load. But you can always control sentence-length. If heavy vocabulary is used, write short sentences so that your readers may understand your ideas.

The Fog Index only measures HOW you write, not WHAT you write. It only shows how difficult the sentences are, it can't measure whether the ideas progress logically from sentence to sentence. It measures how hard the words are, but it can't measure whether they are the right words. The index can be used as a tool to analyse the strength and weakness of your writing and can point out the approaches for improving it.

4. Prefer Active Voice Verbs

Every sentence that you write has an implied or expressed verb. It is the verb that carries the action, the movement, the force of your ideas. This verb can be in **active voice** or **passive voice.**

Active voice verbs show that the subject in a sentence is the doer of the action. When the subject receives the action of the verb, it is in passive voice. The passive voice is made up of a form of the verb plus the past participle (e.g. **is given, was given, are given, had given, have been given, had been given, etc.).**

The use of active voice makes your sentences come alive. This form is briefer, it is also more straightforward and informative. On the other hand, passive voice sounds weak and ineffectual, it also shows that the subject is unwilling to take responsibility for the action:

Active voice also gives a sense of immediacy to the content.

A young journalist sent me this story. (Active voice – 7 words)

This story was sent to me by a young journalist. (Passive voice – 10 words)

Although active voice is the preferable form to use in your writing, in some cases the use of passive voice may be more appropriate. For example, passive voice may be used when:

(a) The actor is unknown or unimportant:

★ *The legislator was re-elected.*

★ *The expressway will be completed in the next six months.*

(b) The emphasis is on the object or the act rather than the actor:

★ *What happened to the school? It was granted recognition.*

(c) Blunt expressions are to be avoided:

★ *Your request for more funds has not been accepted by the government.*

★ *You are requested to attend the meeting.*

5. Use Concrete Expressions

The words you write may be clear to you and precise in the meaning. But they may not be so to the readers. If, however, you can refer specifically to the thing you are talking about, they will find it easier to know your meaning. Such concrete words give lucidity and grace to your writing. Concrete words refer specifically to the thing the writer is talking about and makes it easier for the reader to understand the message, adding lucidity and grace to your writing.

Abstract writing is vague and general. It may lead to uncertainty, misunderstanding and confusion and can lose its effectiveness. Besides, it is open to many interpretations and is potentially inaccurate. Concrete expressions, on the other hand, are specific, definite, vivid and rightfully solve the purpose of effective communication. Therefore, use concrete expressions to convey your ideas.

The best way to be precise is to rely as much as possible on concrete nouns, accurate verbs and significant modifiers which relate to the senses of sight, sound, hear, touch and smell and create an image in the reader's mind. A concrete noun is a noun that refers to a specific object. For example, when you say **'desk'**, you are using a concrete word that refers to a specific piece of furniture. But if you say **'furniture'**, you do not clearly tell readers about which specific piece of furniture you are referring to and they will be left guessing what you mean. An accurate verb describes the action as specifically as possible. For example, if a person is going to catch a bus, tell readers whether he is **walking, running, jogging**, **striding** or **galloping**. A significant modifier is an adjective or adverb that names specific quality or manner. For example, a **green** house, a **dilapidated** building, moving **lazily.** The writer's statements should be backed by facts and figures and used precisely and accurately.

Anecdote is yet another way to write concrete expressions. Anecdotes or examples support better understanding of a complex and abstract idea, whereby the reader gets persuaded.

For	Say
• A majority of respondents believe that many road accidents are caused by faulty driving.	• 55 per cent of respondents believe that 75 per cent road accidents are caused by faulty driving.
• The State machinery should provide immediate relief to the victims of natural catastrophic events.	• The State machinery should provide immediate relief to the victims of natural catastrophic events, such as organize rescue operations and channelise available human power into areas where they can be used more effectively.

Conclusion

Clarity in writing is an essential element of effective writing. It is vital for conveying your message correctly to readers and saving the extra effort that may be required to clarify your points later.

Chapter

5

Writing: Do's and Don'ts

Introduction

Effective writing structures and crystallises one's thoughts, thereby inspires learning. It has a logical flow of ideas and is cohesive. It holds together well as there are links between sentences and paragraphs. Effective writing is crisp, brief, clear and courteous. It seeks to tell as much as possible, as clearly as possible, with as few words as possible. You can make your writing crisp by acquiring a good writing style, cultivating sound practices and omitting "empty" words that do not contribute to meaning, clarity or courtesy. Cohesive writing is easy to follow as it works like a unified whole. It uses language effectively to maintain a focus and the reader is kept on track. Your writing will have these attributes if you guard against five 'sins' in writing - **circumlocution, tautology, gobbledygook, jargon and clichés.**

1. Circumlocution

Circumlocution is the use of too many words where fewer would do. *Circumlocution is also called circumvolution or periphrasis or ambage. It refers to an ambiguous or roundabout figure of speech*. It is often used by early learners, where in the absence of a word, the subject could be simply described.

A short list of commonly used lengthy phrases is given below, with suggested substitutes:

Phrase	Suggested substitute
after very careful consideration	*after considering*
along the lines of	*like*
another one	*another*
apart from the fact that	*but, except*
are of the opinion	*believe*
as a consequence of	*because of, consequently*
at all times	*always*
at an early date	*soon*

attached please find herewith	*attached*
at the earliest possible moment	*immediately, soon*
at the time of writing	*now, at present*
at the present time	*now*
at this moment	*now, at present*
at this point of time	*now, at present*
at your earliest convenience	*soon*
because of the fact that	*because*
be of assistance	*assist*
both of them	*both*
by means of	*by, with*
can't be possible	*can't be*
consensus of opinion	*consensus*
depreciate in value	*depreciate*
despite the fact that	*although*
due to the fact that	*because*
during the course of	*during*
enclosed herewith please find	*enclosed*
few in number	*few*
for a period of a month	*for a month*
for the purpose of	*for, to*
for the reason that	*since, because*
fullest possible extent	*fully*
give encouragement to	*encourage*
give consideration to	*consider*
has a requirement for	*requires*
have need for	*need*
I am of the opinion that	*I think, I believe*
I beg to disagree	*I disagree*
in actual fact	*actually*
in addition to	*besides*
in a majority of cases	*usually*
in all probability	*probably*
in a most careful manner	*carefully*
in a most satisfactory manner	*satisfactorily*

in as much as	*since, because*
in association with	*with*
in close proximity to	*near*
in compliance with your request	*as you requested*
in connection with	*about*
in less than no time	*soon, quickly*
in more than one instance	*more than once*
in order to	*to*
in regard to	*about*
in spite of the fact that	*although, even though*
in the event that	*if*
in the near future	*soon*
in the light of the fact that	*because*
in the majority of cases/ occasions/instances	*usually*
in the near future	*soon*
in the neighbourhood of	*near, about*
in the recent past	*recently*
in view of the fact that	*because, since*
irrespective of the fact that	*although*
it is my intention to	*I intend*
make use of	*use*
meet together	*meet*
notwithstanding the fact that	*even if, although*
on a few occasions	*occasionally*
on a temporary basis	*temporary, temporarily*
on behalf of	*for*
on the occasion of	*when*
prior to	*before*
provide a contribution to	*help*
report to the effect that	*report that*
subsequent to	*after*
succeed in making	*make*
take into consideration	*consider*
there can be little doubt that	*clearly*
this is to thank you	*thank you*

this time	*now*
until such time as	*until*
we would like to ask	*please*
with a view to	*to*
with regard to	*about, concerning*
with reference to	*about*
with the exception of	*except*

2. Tautology

Tautology is unnecessary repetition within a statement of the same idea in different words. Such repetition adds redundant words in your document. Redundancy should be avoided to make the writing crisp. It is a needless repitition of a thought or an idea, which is done especially in words other than those of the immediate content. It does not give additional force or clarity. Some redundant expressions are given below. (The words in bold are redundant and may be dropped.):

Note: While this is genertally true, it is relevant to remember that Tautology is essential when we wish to add weight and stress as well as give importance on what we wish to express.

A

absolute guarantee
absolutely certain
absolutely essential
absolutely necessary
actual fact
actual truth
added bonus
adding **together**
advanced ahead
advance reservation
advance warning
after **the end of**
all **and sundry**
all meet **together**
alongside **of**
already existing
and moreover
attached **hereto**
ATM **machine**
audible click
awkward predicament

B

bald**-headed**
basic essentials/fundamentals
blend **together**
both **together**
brief **in duration**
brief moment
but however
but nevertheless

C

came **at a time** when
cancel **out**
chief protagonist
clearly obvious
climb **up**
close proximity
close scrutiny
collaborate **together**
combine **into one**
combine **together**
commute **back and forth**
complete monopoly
completely destroyed
completely empty
completely filled
completely random
consensus **of opinion**
continue **on**
continue to remain
cooperate **together**
currently **today**

D

decorative garnish
descend **down**
direct confrontation
dwindled **down**
deep chasm
different varieties
drop **down**
definitely decided
difficult dilemma
during **the course of**

E

each **and every one**
empty space
enter **in**
estimated **at about**
evil fiend
early beginnings
enclosed **herein**
equal **to one another**
estimated **roughly at**
exact duplicate
earlier **in time**
end result
established fact
every now and then
exact opposites

F

fake copy
fellow teammates
final conclusion
first **and foremost**
first **of all**
for **a period of** six months
foreign imports
foundered **and sank**
fake pretences
few **in number**
final completion/ending
first began
first started
for **the purpose of**
forever **and ever**
free gift/pass
fellow classmates
filled **to capacity**
final outcome
first introduction
follow **after**
foreign exports
forward planning
future prospects

G

gather **together**
good benefits
glowing ember
had done **previously**
good bargains

H

harmful injury
honest truth
hopeful optimism

I

I **myself personally**
important essentials
introduced **for the first time**
if **and when**
in **close** proximity
important breakthrough
intense fury

J

joined **together**
just recently/exactly
invited guests

K

kneel **down**

L

last **of all**
look back **in retrospect**
lift **up**
lonely isolation

M

major breakthrough
merge **together**
mix **together**
may/might **possibly**
mesh **together**
mutual cooperation
mental telepathy
midway between

N

natural instinct
new beginning
new recruit
now pending
necessary requisite
new innovation
no trespassing **allowed**
null **and void**
never **at any time**
new invention
none **at all**

O

old cliché
originally created
old proverb
over **and done with**
opening introduction
over- exaggerate

P

pair of twins
past experiences
past records
permeate **throughout**
personally believe
positively true
pre-recorded
proceed **ahead**
proven facts
parched **dry**
past history
penetrate **into**
personal friend
plan **in advance**
possibly might
present incumbent
protest **against**
passing fads
past memories
perfect ideal
personal opinion
poisonous venom
postponed **until a later time**
probed **into**
protrude **out**

R

raise **up**
reduce **down**
relic **of the past**
revert **back**
reason **why**
refer **back**
repeat/resume **again**
round **in shape**
reflect **back**
reply **back**

S

safe haven
saw **with my own eyes**
senseless mistakes
since **the time when**
solemn vow
still continues
strangled **to death**
sufficient **enough**
surrounding circumstances
sad tragedy
seemed **to be**
share **together**
sincerely mean it
spelled out **in detail**
still persists
stupid fool
sum total
sworn affidavit
same **identical**
seems **apparent**
short **in length**
skipped **over**
stacked **on top of each other**
still remains/continues
suddenly exploded
summer **season**

T

temporary recess
thoughtful deliberation
true fact
temporary reprieve
totally eliminated
thoughtful contemplation
totally finished

U

ultimate conclusion/end
usual custom/habit
unexpected surprise
utter annihilation
unintentional mistake

V

very/absolutely unique
viable alternative

W

ways **and means**	**well-known old** adage	when **and if**
whether **or not**	widow **woman**	written **down**

3. Gobbledygook

Gobbledygook is the use of meaningless or unintelligible language which not only confuses readers but also fails to enlighten them. It includes speech sounds that are not actual words or forms such as highly specialised jargon that appears non-sensible to outsiders. The term 'gobbledygook' is used in politics since long. It was used by a US Congressman, Maury Maverick in 1944 to describe the pompous bureaucratic language. To avoid this, you should ask yourself three questions:

★ Do I fully understand what I'm writing about?

★ Have I expressed in writing exactly what I wanted to say?

★ Will all my readers understand what I'm saying?

Some pompous, meaningless phrases are given below:

★ All things being equal;

★ As of right now;

★ In a manner of speaking;

★ It goes without saying;

★ Of necessity;

★ To all intents and purposes;

★ Within the foreseeable future.

4. Jargon

The word 'jargon' is defined as a specialised language of a particular trade, profession or specific group of activities.

But all jargons are not pretentious rubbish. The terms often used in any business and profession will be understood by those who belong to that field. In such a case, it is a form of time-saving professional shorthand, designed for accurate and efficient communication between members of a particular group of persons. Jargon is a technical terminology or characteristic idiom of a special activity or a group of persons.

The philosopher Bonnot de Condillac observed in 1782 that "every science requires a special language because every science has its own ideas."

A short list of such words and phrases and their jargon-free alternatives is given below:

Jargon	Alternative	Jargon	Alternative
accentuate	stress	accomplish	finish, complete
axiomatic	obvious	bullish	recentful
come on stream	start working	core	basic
end of the day	in the end	funded	paid for
generate	make, produce	hidden agenda	disguised purpose
implement	fulfill, carry out	put on the back burner	postponed, delayed
ongoing	continuing, constant	input	ideas,investment
state of the art	latest, newest	take on board	consider, accept
track record	experience	user-friendly	easy to use
a large number	many	disburse	pay, distribute
a member of	part	disseminate	spread
a variety of	different, varied	domiciled	living
advantageous	helpful, favourable	ducidate	explain
acquiesce	agree	envisage	expect
below	beneath	hitherto	until now
		ouster	break through

A sub-class of jargon is empty words. These words are redundant and the use of such words puts unnecessary strain to read and retain in the brain. Such empty words are "nature", "factor", "facet", "character", "aspect", feature", "condition". For example:

★ **It looked *like a tool of useful nature*.** (It looks like a useful tool.)

★ ***The time factor* will keep him from attending the conference.** (Lack of time will prevent him from attending the conference.)

★ **Those remarks were *of a decidedly unpleasant character*.** (Those were unpleasant remarks.)

Sometimes, we use pedantic, technical and pseudo-technical expressions which are difficult and appear high-brow. Use of such words should also be avoided. For example:

consume (eat)	impecunious (poor)
corpulent (fat)	interface (coordinate)
crave (ask)	patronise (to support)
divulge (disclose)	peruse (to follow)
evince (show)	replicate (repeat)
gratis (free)	transpire (happen)

5. Clichés

A cliché is a word, phrase, clause or sentence that has been over-used and shows a lack of original thought. Clichés appear to be colourful or impressive. But they make the writing sound stale, because these expressions are seen again and again and have been repeatedly used. You should avoid such expressions, as far as possible and make your writing much fresh and original as far as possible.

In phraseology, the term 'cliche' takes on a more technical meaning, which refers to an expression imposed by conventionalised linguistic usage. The term is frequently being used in modern times to explain an idea or action which is predictable and based on an event that has already occured. It has its origin in the French language. The use of cliches in speech, argument or writing is generally regarded on account of being unable to find a better word or expression.

A short list of clichés is given below:

A

above and beyond the call of duty
accident waiting to happen
acid test
add insult to injury
after all is said and done
a gift from god
a little learning is dangerous
all's well that ends well
all in all
a pillar of society
as luck would have it
at arm's length
as luck would have it
a sight for sore eyes

B

back in the saddle
a step in the right direction
at a loss of words
back on track
backseat driver
ball is in your court
be an open book
barking up the wrong tree
be your own worst enemy
beat a dead horse
beggars can't be choosers
be an open book
believe me
better late than never
bird's eye view
bitter end
bone of contention
broaden one's horizon
bundle of nerves
both sides of the coin
bury the hatchet
by and large

C

call his bluff
can't judge a book by its cover
cold as ice
centre of attention
cloak and dagger policy
come full circle
conspicuous by his absence
count your blessings
counting on you
crossing the line

D

dead wrong
dog-eat-dog
done to death
down in the dumps
down and out
due in large measure to
easier said than done
duly noted

E

easy come, easy go
easy target

F

face the music
fair and square
fall from grace
far and away
far reaching consequences
few and far between
fit as a fiddle
fly in the ointment
for all intents and purposes
free as a bird
from the frying pan into the fire
from time immemorial

G

game plan
get down to brass tacks
get to the bottom of it
give a damn
give rise to
go for the kill
go it alone
go the extra mile
go to pieces
goes without saying
good for nothing
green with envy
grist for the mill

H

have run their course
head over heals
have had their day
hammer out details
hedge the bet
hit the nail on the head
heated argument
hit the ceiling
hour of need

I

icing on the cake
in hot water
I couldn't care less
increasingly apparent
in due course
in a nutshell
in the driver's seat
in seventh heaven
in the final analysis
in the nick of time

K

keep your fingers crossed

L

last but not the least
let the cat out of the bag
learning curve
leave no stone unturned
light at the end of the tunnel
lie low
like a bull in the china shop
little does he know
live it up
lock, stock and barrel

M

make the blood boil
make ends meet
making the supreme sacrifice
method in madness
mince words
millstone around the neck
more than meets the eye
moment of truth

N

naked truth
nearing the finishing line
nip in the bud
needle in a haystack
needs no introduction
no strings attached

O

on cloud nine
on top of the world
off the cuff
out of the woods
over-riding importance

P

pass the buck
powers that be
proud as a peacock
pulling the leg
pull the rug from under the feet
put words in one's mouth
put on hold

R

rags to riches
ripe old age
rule the roost

S

sell like hot cakes
shooting oneself in the foot
shot in the arm
sitting duck
skeleton in the closet
smooth sailing
spill the beans
steal the limelight
stem the tide
stick to your guns
stick your neck out
strike a balance
strange bedfellows
suffice it to say

T

take on board
take one's word for
take the liberty of
the die is cast
the order of the day
think outside the box
tighten your belt
through thick and thin
throw caution to the wind
to each his own
to avoid like plague
to fall between two stools

U

unfairly courteous
upset the applecart

V

vicious circle

W

whole nine yards
where angels fear to tread
where there is smoke, there is fire
wild goose chase
welcome with open arms
wipe the slate clean
wishful thinkinq
with belated breath
without further delay
woefully inadequate
words fail me
wreck havoc

Conclusion

Learning and loving business-writing skills can have a positive impact on an individual's career advancement. Professional quality writing when sent through effective channels of communication improves productivity and the capability of all functional areas to work cohesively, specially in an increased global workplace where the norm is collaboration.

Excellent writing is sure to earn respect. It improves the effectiveness of the person's word usage in both oral speech and written form. The person's writing helps in forming the reader's opinion about the writer's abilities. For such writing, you should ensure that these pitfalls and blunders – circumlocution, tautology, gobbledygook, jargon and clichés – do not find a place in your writing in order to make them clear and unambiguous.

Chapter

6

Confusing Words

Introduction

Some words in English can cause trouble for speakers and writers as these words share similar pronunciation, spelling or meaning with another word. These words are commonly called 'Homophones' or Confusing words. These words may sound alike when spoken, but carry entirely different usage and meaning. You may be clear about all the meanings of a word. But if the word has different meanings, you may not be sure that the readers will understand the word in the same way as you intend them to. Therefore, malaprops should be used to convey the right message without being misunderstood.

A list of sets of such words is given below to help you choose the right word and save yourself from being ambiguous. It is advisable to use dictionary, when in doubt and use them correctly.

1. **Ability** – skill or talent, possession of means or skills to do something.
   Capacity – the ability or power to do something.
2. **Abstain** – restrain oneself from doing something, formally decline to vote.
   Refrain – stop oneself from doing something, repeated lines in a poem or song.
3. **Accede** – assent or agree to.
   Exceed – be greater in number or size than, go beyond what is allowed, be better than, surpass.
   Concede – finally admit that something is true, surrender or yield (a possession, advantage or right).
4. **Accent** – a particular way of pronouncing the different words of a language, an emphasis given to a syllable, area or class.
   Ascent – to climb the summit of a mountain, a rise in status.
   Assent – the expression of approval or agreement, official sanction.
5. **Accept** – consent to receive or undertake (something offered), believe to be valid or correct, take.
   Except – not including, other than the one just made.
6. **Access** – the means or opportunity to approach or enter a place, the right or opportunity to use something or see someone, retrieval of information stored in a computer memory.
   Excess – an amount that is more than necessary, permitted or desirable.
7. **Accessory** – a thing which can be added to something else in order to make it more useful, versatile or attractive, a small article carried or worn to complement a garment,
   Accessory – a person who assists the perpetrator of a crime.

8. **Adapt** – to change or adjust to a different situation, make suitable for a new use or purpose.
Adopt – to choose to take up or follow (an option or course of action), formally approve or accept.
Adept – very skilled or proficient expert in something.

9. **Admit** – accept as valid, allow to enter, confess to or acknowledge (a crime, fault or failure).
Confess – acknowledge reluctantly, admit to a crime or wrongdoing.
Acknowledge – accept or admit the existence or truth, confirm receipt of or gratitude for, greet with words or gestures.

10. **Advice** (n) – guidance or recommendations offered about future action.
Advise (v) – recommend, offer advice to, inform about a fact or situation.

11. **Affect** (v) – make a difference, have an effect on, pretend to have or feel.
Effect (n) – result, a change as result of an action, impression produced in a person's mind.

12. **All together** – all in one place or in a group.
Altogether – completely, in total, on the whole.

13. **Alter** – change in character or appearance or composition.
Change – make or become different, take or use another instead of.

14. **Alternative** – available as another possibility, (of two things)) mutually exclusive.
Alternate – occur or do in turn, change repeatedly between two contrasting conditions, every other.

15. **Allow** – let (someone) have or do something, admit as legal or acceptable, provide or set aside for a purpose, admit the truth of.
Permit – to grant permission to do something, to consent to or to tolerate, an official certificate or document granting authorisation, licence.

16. **Allusion** – an indirect implicit reference.
Illusion – a false idea or belief, a deceptive appearance or impression.

17. **Amiable** – friendly and pleasant in manner. (usually used to describe people)
Amicable – behaviour characterised by friendliness and absence of discord. (used to describe actions, gestures, etc.)

18. **Among** – indicating a division, choice or differentiation involving three or more parties.
Between – at, into or across the space separating two objects, places or points, indicating a connection or relationship involving two parties.

19. **Answer** – something said, written or done as a reaction to a question.
Reply – say or write something in response to something said or written, respond by a similar action, the action of replying, a spoken or written response.

20. **Anxious** – expressing worry, nervousness or unease, very eager and concerned to do something or for something to happen, impatient, keen.
Eager – strongly wanting to do or have something, keenly expectant or interested.

21. **Anyone** – any person or people.
Any one – any single person or thing.

22. **Anyway** – in any case, at any rate, nevertheless.
Any way – in any manner, by any means.

23. **Apathy** – lack of interest or enthusiasm.
Antipathy – a deep-seated feeling of aversion.

24. **Apposite** – very appropriate.
Opposite – situated on the other or further side, facing.

25. **Appraise** – assess the value, quality or performance.
Apprise – inform or tell someone of something.

26. **Apt** – appropriate, suitable, quick to learn.
Likely – such as well might happen or be true, promising, probably.

27. **Artistic** – having or revealing natural creative skill, relating to or characteristic of art or artists.
Artificial – made as a copy of something natural, contrived or false.

28. **Avenge** – inflict harm in return for (an injury or wrong), inflict retribution on behalf of (a wronged person).
Revenge – retaliation for an injury or wrong, desire to repay an injury or wrong.

29. **Beneficial** – causing a good result, advantageous.
Beneficent – charitable, generous.

30. **Capable** – having the ability or quality necessary to do something, competent (person).
Capacious – having a lot of space inside, roomy.

31. **Cease** – come or bring to an end, stop.
Seize – take hold of suddenly and forcibly, take (an opportunity) eagerly and decisively.

32. **Ceremonial** – relating to or used for ceremonies, a role or post involving ceremonies.
Ceremonious – relating or appropriate to grand formal occasions.

33. **Character** – mental and moral qualities distinctive to an individual.
Conduct (n) – the manner in which a person behaves, the directing or managing something.
Conduct (v) – organize and carry out, guide to and around a place.

34. **Childish** – immature, silly, foolish
Childlike – having the good qualities, such as innocence, associated with a child.

35. **Cite** – quote (a book or author) as evidence for an argument, mention as an example.
Site – an area of ground on which something is located, a place where something has occurred.
Sight – faculty or power of seeing, place of interest to tourist or other visitors, vision.

36. **Coarse** – rough or harsh in texture, unrefined.
Course – a procedure adopted to deal with a situation, a series of lectures or lessons in a particular subject, route or direction followed by a ship, aircraft, road or river.

37. **Command** – give an authoritative order, the ability to use or control something.
Commend – praise formally or officially, recommend, present as suitable or good.

38. **Common** – occurring, found or done often, not rare.
Mutual – experienced or done by each of two or more parties, shared by two or more parties.

39. **Complacent** – uncritically satisfied with oneself or one's self or one's achievements.
Complaisant – willing to please others, courteous, obliging.

40. **Complement** – a thing that contributes extra features to something to enhance or improve it.
Compliment – a polite expression of praise or admiration, formal greetings sent as a message.

41. **Comprehensive** – including or dealing with all or nearly all aspects of something.
Comprehensible – able to be understood, intelligible.

42. **Confident** – feeling certainty about something.
Confidant – a person to whom one confides, reliable, trustworthy.

43. **Considerable** – notably large, having merit or distinction.
Considerate – careful not to harm or inconvenience others.

44. **Conscience** – a person's moral sense of right and wrong.
Conscious – aware of responding to one's surroundings, aware, deliberate and intentional.

45. **Consistently** – acting or done in the same way over time, unchanging in standard or time, compatible or in agreement.
Constantly – occurring continuously, remaining the same.

46. **Contagious** – spread by direct or indirect contact of people or organisms, likely to affect others.
Contiguous – sharing a common border.

47. **Contemptible** – deserving or worthy of contempt, despicable, mean.
Contemptuous – showing or feeling contempt, scornful, disdainful.

48. **Continual** – constantly or frequently occurring with intervals in between.
Continuous – without interruption, forming a series with no exceptions or reversals.

49. **Credible** – able to be believed, convincing.
Creditable – deserving public acknowledgement and praise but not necessarily outstanding.

50. **Council** – a body elected to manage the affairs of a city, county, country or a society.
Counsel – advice, a legal adviser.

51. **Custom** – traditional and widely accepted way of behaving or doing something.
Habit – a tendency or disposition to act in a particular way, mental disposition or attitude.

52. **Decent** – appropriate, of acceptable standard, satisfactory, conforming with generally accepted standards of morality or respectability.
Descent – a downward slope, a person's origin or nationality.
Dissent – express disagreement with a prevailing view or official decision.

53. **Deny** – refuse to admit the truth or existence of, refuse to give (something).
Refuse – indicate unwillingness to do something, indicate unwillingness to accept or grant (something offered or requested).

54. **Dependant** – a person who relies on another, especially a family member, for financial support.
Dependent – contingent on or determined by, relying on something or someone for support.

55. **Desert** – callously or treacherously abandon, leave (a place), a waterless landmass or area, desolate area of land with little or no vegetation.
Dessert – the sweet course eaten at the end of a meal.

56. **Device** (n) – a thing made or adapted for a particular purpose, a plan, scheme or trick.
Devise (v) – plan or invent a complex procedure or mechanism.

57. **Discreet** – careful and prudent, so as to avoid giving offence or attracting attention.
Discrete – individually separate and distinct.

58. **Doubt** – feeling of uncertainty or lack of conviction, feel uncertain about.
Suspect – believe (something) to be probable or possible, believe (someone) to be guilty of a crime or offence, without a certain proof, doubt the genuineness or truth of.

59. **Economic** – relating to economics or economy, justified in terms of profitability.
Economical – giving a good value or return in relation to the resources or money expended, sparing in the use of resources or money.

60. **Effective** – producing a desired or intended result.
Efficacious – capable of or successful in producing an intended result over a long time.

61. **Elicit** – evoke or draw out (a response or answer).
Illicit – forbidden by law, rule or custom.

62. **Elusive** – difficult to find, catch or achieve.
Illusive – deceptive, based on false idea or belief.

63. **Emigrate** – leave one's own country in order to settle permanently in another.
Immigrate – come to live in a foreign country.

64. **Eminent** – respectful and distinguished within a particular sphere, notable, outstanding.
Imminent – (esp. of unpleasant events) about to happen, likely to happen very soon.

65. **Empathy** – the ability to understand and share the feelings of another.
Sympathy – feeling of pity and sorrow for someone else's misfortune, understanding between people, a favourable attitude.

66. **Envy** – discontented or resentful longing aroused by another's possessions, qualities or luck.
Jealousy – envious of someone else's possessions, achievements or advantages, suspicious or fearful of being displaced by a rival.

67. **Error** – a mistake or inaccuracy, as in action or speech, an incorrect belief or wrong judgment.
Mistake – an act or judgment that is misguided or wrong, misconception or misunderstanding.
Blunder – an error of action which brings shame or causes a stupid or careless mistake.

68. **Especial** – notable, for or belonging to chiefly to one person, unusual, exceptional, specific.
Special – set apart for a particular purpose, better, greater or otherwise different from what is usual, designed or organized for a particular occasion or purpose.

69. **Excite** – cause to feel very enthusiastic and eager, give rise to (a feeling or reaction).
Incite – encourage or stir up (violent or unlawful behaviour), urge or persuade to act in a violent or unlawful way.

70. **Exhausting** – tiring out completely, using up (resources or reserves) completely.
Exhaustive – fully comprehensive.

71. **Expect** – regard as likely to happen, do or be the case, suppose or assume, require as appropriate or rightfully due, require (someone) to fulfil an obligation.
Hope – a feeling of desire for something and confidence in the possibility of its behaviour, a thing, situation or event that is desired, to wish for something good or welcome.

72. **Finally** – at last, in conclusion.
Finely – delicate or intricate workmanship.

73. **Flair** – natural ability or talent, stylishness and originality.
Flare – sudden brief burst of flame or light, a sudden burst of strong emotions.

74. **Forceful** – powerful, assertive, vigorous.
Forcible – done by force.

75. **Forego** – precede in place or time.
Forgo – go without (something desirable).

76. **Formally** – in accordance with rules, in a proper, polite or official manner.
Formerly – in the past, previously, in earlier times.

77. **Graceful** – having or showing elegance of movement, courteous goodwill.
Gracious – courteous, kind and pleasant, showing the elegance and comfort brought by wealth.

78. **Guess** – estimate or suppose (something) without sufficient information to be sure.

Suppose – think or assume that something is true or probable, but without proof, assume or think that something is the case as a precondition.

Think – have a particular opinion, belief or idea about something or someone, use one's mind actively to form connected ideas about someone or something, have a particular mental attitude.

79. **Hate** – feel intense dislike for or a strong aversion towards, intense dislike.

Dislike -- feel distaste for or hostility towards someone or something.

80. **Hear** – perceive (a sound) with the ear, be told or informed of.

Listen – to concentrate on hearing something, to take heed, pay attention.

81. **Hoard** – a secret stock or store, a store of money or valued objects or information.

Horde – a large group of people (used in a derogatory sense).

82. **Human** – relating to or characteristic of humankind, relating or characteristic of people as opposed to God or animals or machines.

Humane – compassionate or benevolent, intended to have a civilized effect.

83. **Idle** – not working or in use, having no purpose or basis, avoiding work.

Lazy – unwilling to work or use energy, showing a lack of effort or care, slow-moving.

84. **Incredible** – impossible to believe, difficult to believe, extraordinary, amazingly good.

Incredulous – unwilling or unable to believe something.

85. **Imperative** – of vital importance, giving an authoritative command, an essential or urgent thing.

Imperious – arrogant and domineering.

86. **Imply** – to suggest a meaning.

Infer – to draw meaning from something.

87. **Industrial** – of, used in or characterised by industry.

Industrious – diligent and hardworking.

88. **Ingenious** – clever, original and inventive.

Ingenuous – innocent and unsuspecting.

89. **Insure** – arrange for compensation in the event of damage to or loss of property, life of a person.

Ensure – make certain that (something) will occur, make sure that (a problem) does not recur.

90. **Judicial** – relating to administration of justice, appropriate to a law court or judge.

Judicious – using good judgment, sensible.

91. **Jealous** – envious of someone else's possessions, achievements or advantages, fiercely protective or vigilant of one's rights or possessions.

Zealous – having or showing great energy or enthusiasm for a cause or objective.

92. **Lay** – put something down gently or carefully, put down and set in position for use.

Lie – be in or assume a horizontal or resting position on a supporting surface, exist or be found.

93. **Later** – afterwards, at a time in the near future.

Latter – denoting the second or second – mentioned of two people or things.

94. **Loose** (adj) – not firmly in place or tied up, careless and indiscreet.

Lose (v) – no longer have or retain, become unable to find,

95. **Meat** – flesh of an animal.

Meet – come face to face with, come together formally for discussion, etc., fulfil or satisfy.

Mete – dispense or allot justice, punishment, etc.

96. **Moral** (adj) – concerned with the principles of right and wrong behaviour.

Morale (n) – the confidence and feeling of well-being of a person or group at a particular time.

97. **Necessity** – an indispensable thing.

Need – a thing that is wanted or required, a requirement.

98. **Negligent** – failure to take proper care over something.

Negligible – insignificant, so small or unimportant as to be not worth considering.

99. **Ordinance** – an authoritative order.

Ordnance – mounted guns, cannons,department of an army looking after its supplies.

100. **Passed** – moved or caused to move in a specified direction, left behind or on one side in proceeding.

Past – gone by in time and no longer existing.

101. **Peace** – freedom from disturbance or war, tranquility.

Piece – a portion of an object or of material produced by cutting, tearing or breaking the whole, an instance or example.

102. **Persecute** – subject to prolonged hostility and ill-treatment.

Prosecute – institute or conduct legal proceedings against, continue with a view to completion.

103. **Personal** – affecting or belonging to a particular person, involving the presence or action of a particular person.

Personnel – people employed in an organization, persons engaged in an undertaking.

104. **Possible** – capable of existing, happening or being achieved, that may exist or happen but that is not certain or probable.

Probable – likely to happen or be the case.

105. **Precede** – to come or go before in time, order or position.

Proceed – to begin a course of action, go on to do something, carry on or continue, move forward.

106. **Preposition** – (grammar) a word governing and usually preceding a noun or pronoun and expressing a relationship to another word or element.

Proposition – statement expressing a judgment or opinion, a statement expressing concept that can be true or false.

107. **Prescribe** – advise and authorise the use of (a medicine or treatment), recommend as beneficial, state authoritatively that (something) should be done in a particular way.

Proscribe – condemn or forbid, especially by law.

108. **Prevaricate** – speak or act evasively.

Procrastinate – put off doing something, delay or postpone action.

109. **Principal** – first in order of importance, main.

Principle – fundamental truth or proposition serving as foundation for belief or action, a rule or belief governing one's personal behaviour, morally correct behaviour and attitude.

110. **Quite** – fairly, moderately, to a partial extent, somewhat.

Quiet – making little or no noise, undisturbed, uninterrupted, discreet, moderate or restrained.

Quit – leave, especially permanently, resign from (a job), stop or discontinue.

111. **Raise** (v) – lift or move to a higher position or level, set upright, increase the amount, level or strength of, cause to occur or to be considered, collect or levy (money or resources), bring up a child.

Raise (n) – an increase in salary, an act of raising a stake or bid.

Raze – tear down and destroy (a building or town, etc.).

112. **Respectable** – regarded by society as being proper, correct and good, of some merit or importance, adequate or acceptable in number, size or amount.

Respective – belonging or relating separately to each of two or more people or things.

113. **Right** – appropriate, suitable, fitting or proper, correct or true, morally justified, good or acceptable, in accordance with facts.

Rite – a religious or other solemn ceremony or act.

Write – mark (letters, words or other symbols) on a surface with a pen, pencil or similar instrument.

114. **Root** – the essential, fundamental or primary part or nature of something, established deeply and firmly.

Route – a way taken or planned to get from one place to another.

Rout – disorderly retreat of defeated troops, a decisive defeat.

115. **Safety** – the condition of being or feeling secure, denoting something designed to prevent injury or damage.

Security – the state of being or feeling secure, assured freedom from poverty or wants, the caution taken against theft, espionage, etc.

116. **See** – perceive with the eyes, experience or witness (an event or situation).

Look – direct one's gaze in a particular direction, search for or try to find something or somebody.

Observe – watch attentively, notice, say, remark, fulfil or comply (with an obligation).

117. **Servitude** – state of being a slave or completely subject to someone more powerful.

Servility – excessive willingness to serve or please others.

118. **Spacious** – having plenty of space.

Specious – superficially plausible, but actually wrong, misleadingly attractive in appearance.

119. **Stationary** – not moving, not changing in quantity or condition.

Stationery – paper or other material used for writing.

120. **Tamper** – interfere with (something) without authority so as to cause damage.

Temper – a person's state of mind in terms of being angry or calm, a tendency to become angry easily, a sudden outburst of anger.

121. **Thorough** – complete about every detail, performed with or showing great care and completeness.

Through – moving in one side and out of the other side of (an opening or location), occupying or visiting several points scattered around in (an area) as a result of, by means of.

122. **Transient** – lasting only for a short time, staying or working in a place for a short time.

Transitory – not permanent, short-lived.

123. **Vacant** – not filled or occupied, showing no sign of thought or intelligence, blank.

Empty – having nothing inside, with nobody in it.

124. **Value** – the regard that something is held to deserve, importance or worth.

Price – the amount of money expected, required or given in payment for something, something expended or endured in order to achieve an objective.

125. **Variation** – a change or slight difference in condition, amount or level, a different or distinct form or version.

Variance – the fact or quality of being different or inconsistent, the state of disagreeing or quarrelling.

126. **Virtual** – almost or nearly as described, but not completely or according to strict definition, (computing) not physically existing but made by software to appear to do so.

Virtuous – having or showing high moral standards.

127. **Wary** – suspicious.

Weary – tired.

128. **Watch** – look attentively, keep under careful, protective observation, exercise care, caution or restraint about.

Witness – a person who sees an event take place, evidence, proof.

129. **Weather** – the state of the atmosphere at a place and time as regards temperature, wind, rain, etc, (v.) come safely through.

Whether – experiencing a doubt or choice between alternatives, expressing an enquiry or investigation.

130. **Wilful** – intentional, deliberate, stubborn and determined.

Willing – ready, eager or prepared to do something, given or done readily.

131. **Wreck** – the destruction of a ship at sea, a building, vehicle,etc., that has been destroyed or badly damaged.

Wreak – cause (a large amount of damage or harm), inflict (revenge).

Conclusion

Words give shape to your ideas, feelings and attitudes. A wrong word may destroy any goodwill that you may have developed over a period of time. Therefore, choice of correct words which truly reflect what you want to convey is essential for effective writing. Experienced writers know that careful word selection and its usage can lead to refined and polished work. Just as a mason uses bricks to build durable homes, writers should use words to produce effective writing.

ଔଷ

Chapter

7

Use of Contractions

Introduction

A contraction is made when two words are squeezed to form one word. One or more letters which are left out from the original two words are replaced by an apostrophe ('). This apostrophe is put in place of the missing letter or letters.

The use of contractions gives an informal and friendlier look to your writing. You look natural and closer to your reader. Of course, if you want to be formal, as in official documents, you may not use contractions. Since we frequently use contractions while speaking, it is surely acceptable to use them in our daily business-writing. Business-writing has become less formal than it was a decade ago mainly because of the influence of email. Many people use email as an alternative to face-to-face conversation where informality could be the key.

A list of contractions commonly used is given below. Make use of this list in your writing.

Contraction	Full form
can't	cannot
didn't	did not
don't	do not
hasn't	has not
hadn't	had not
he'd	he would, he had
here's	here is, here has
I'm	I am
I'll	I will, I shall
ain't	I am not
shan't	shall not
it'll	it will
it's	it is, it has
let's	let us
mustn't	must not
she'll	she will
she'd	she would, she had

Contraction	Full form
couldn't	could not
doesn't	does not
haven't	have not
he's	he is, he has
he'll	he will
I'd	I would, I had
it'd	it would, it had
I've	I have
isn't	is not
ma'am	madam
she's	she is, she has
shouldn't	should not

that'll	that will	they'll	they will
that'd	that would/had	that's	that is, that has
they'd	they would/had	they've	they have
they're	they are	there's	there is, there has
there'd	there would, there had	there'll	there will
there've	there have	that's	that is, that has
wasn't	was not	weren't	were not
we've	we have	we'll	we will
we're	we are	we'd	we would, we had
what's	what is, what has		
who'd	who would/had	who's	who is, who has
won't	will not	wouldn't	would not
you'll	you will	you'd	you would/ had
you've	you have	you're	you are

Conclusion

Contractions are not an essential part of effective writing. You may use them or write without them and the writing will not become harder. But contractions do give an informal tone to writing. If you want to be closer to your readers, use contractions. But if you want to be formal and maintain distance, you may write without them.

Remember that though it is acceptable to use contractions in business-writing, it is not always preferable. Therefore, when the writer wants to emphasise a particular idea or point, using two wcrds is a better choice.

Chapter

8

Rules of Grammar

Introduction

A language is made up of words which are put together in the form of sentences. These sentences must convey sense and meaning and must follow the rules of grammar. These rules tell us how a language works. They tell us how we can make our writing error-free, to the best of possibility. Error-free writing keeps the reader engrossed and conveys the right message. One should avoid being liberal in the use of words to avoid any misinterpretation of language and message.

Grammar is a very old field of discipline. It lays down the rules and regulations as well as the manner in which that language is to be written and spoken.The sentence was first divided into subject and verb by Plato, the famous philosopher from ancient Greece. This was about 2,400 years ago when Plato and other Greek philosophers of ancient Greece formulated the basic rules of grammar for the Greek language which were in later years incorporated into the English grammar. Since then, students across the world find it indispensable to study the rules of grammar and make their English expressive. By following the rules of grammar, you should be able to write with precision, brevity and elegance, develop a critical look at the language and write effectively.

- Sentences: Their Kinds, Elements and Structure
- Phrases and Clauses
- Nouns
- Pronouns
- Verb
- Voice
- Mood
- Infinitives
- Gerund
- Participle
- Adjectives
- Adverbs
- Determiners
- Prepositions
- Conjunctions

Common Sentence Errors: Comma faults, subject and verb agreement, dangling modifiers, misplaced modifiers, squinting modifiers, parallelism, logical comparison, etc.

1. Sentences: Kinds, Elements and Structure

What is a Sentence?

A sentence is *a group of words that follows a proper order and makes a complete sense*. It begins with a capital letter and ends with a full stop **(.)** or its equivalent such as a question mark **(?)** or an exclamation mark **(!)**.

A sentence should express a single idea or thought related to that idea. It should be complete in thought and complete in construction. It should be clear, unambiguous, logical in expression and be grammatically correct.

A sentence may be as long as necessary to express the idea. But it should neither be too long, nor too short as to look jerky. There should be variety in the length of sentences – such as short-long/long-short/medium-long/medium and a mix of simple sentences (say, 35%), complex sentences (say, 50%) and compound sentences (say, 15%) -- so that readers may remain alert and interested. Rambling, unclear and long-winded sentences should be avoided, and irrelevant matter should not be allowed to cloud the intent and meaning of a sentence.

Sometimes a group of words begins with a capital letter and has a punctuation mark at the end, but it has neither the subject nor the main verb. Such sentences are called **fragments**. Such sentences may be made complete by putting in the subject and the verb.

Sometimes, run-on sentences are used. These are really two or more sentences (or independent clauses) that run together without the proper punctuation to join them. Such sentences may be rewritten by joining the two sentences with a comma and a conjunction or by joining the two sentences with a semi-colon or by making two separate sentences. For example:

1.	Two volumes of this work are now complete the first will be published next year. Two volumes of this work are now complete, the first will be published next year. or, **Revised:** Two volumes of this work are now complete and the first one will be published next year. or, Two volumes of this work are now complete. The first one will be published next year.
2.	We agree with your goals. Although we do not agree with your methods. **Revised:** Although, we do not agree with your methods, yet we agree with your goals. or We agree with your goals. We do not, however, agree with your methods.

Sometimes, single-word sentences or sentences with a few words are used for emphasis. These are called **irregular sentences.** Sentences that express a complete, independent thought are called **regular sentences.**

Kinds of Regular Sentences

Regular sentences are of four kinds: **Declarative** or **Assertive, Interrogative, Imperative, and Exclamatory.**

A **Declarative** or **Assertive sentence** makes a statement:

★ *People become entrepreneurs because there is a challenge that excites them.*

★ *The survey makes a distinction between a user and a connection of mobile phones.*

★ *Jim worked hard everyday, therefore, he expected a raise at the end of the year.*

An **Interrogative sentence** asks a question:

★ *Why has India lacked in the area of research and development?*

★ *Is your house ready for visitors?*

★ *Should I call or email you?*

An **Imperative Sentence** directs or makes a request or gives a command:

★ *Don't talk so loudly.*

★ *Complete that job and report to me.*

★ *Go away.*

★ *Be there at 5 this evening.*

Note: The subject of an imperative sentence is 'You', because the speaker or the writer is giving you an order or making a request. But the word 'You' is not usually spoken or written in the sentence. The listener or the reader has to understand it.

An **Exclamatory Sentence** expresses strong feelings and emotions; such as excitement, horror, shock, surprise, pain, anger, disgust, etc.

★ *How sad, my plans should come to this end!*

★ *Water, water all around, but not a drop to drink!*

★ *I can't believe it! Reading and writing actually paid off!*

★ *If only God would give me some clear sign!*

Sentences can express thoughts or actions positively or negatively. *A **negative** sentence gives the impression that something is **not***, rather than that something **is**. Most negative words begin with **n** and **not** is one of the most frequently used negative words. The contraction for **not** is **n't**. So any contraction that ends in **n't** is a negative word. Other negative words are **hardly**, **scarcely** and **barely.**

If there are too many negatives in the writing, the overall effect will be negative and depressing. Therefore, it is better to express thoughts and actions in a positive way, as far as possible. For example:

★ *Nobody was absent. (Negative)*

★ *Everybody was present. (Positive)*

★ *There was no one present in the meeting who did not appreciate the manager's performance. (Negative)*

★ *Everyone present in the meeting appreciated the manager's performance. (Positive)*

Elements of a Sentence

The main elements of a sentence are its **subject** and **predicate**.

The subject tells us something about a person, a thing, a place or an idea. It may be a noun or a noun equivalent, such as a pronoun, a noun clause, a gerund or an infinitive. It tells us who or what the subject does or is about. It may be a **simple subject,** a **compound subject** or a **complete subject.**

A simple subject is the main noun or noun equivalent that names the subject. It is usually one word, except that when some name has more than one word, all the words in the name are a simple subject. For example:

★ **Exporters** are struggling to ink new contracts.

A compound subject is two or more simple subjects joined by a conjunction (**and or):**

★ **Coal and power** are the two mainstays of the Indian energy sector.

A complete subject is the simple or the compound subject and all the words that go with it – a noun, a pronoun, an adjective or the equivalent of an adjective which modifies it.

★ **Nervous exporters** are struggling to ink new contracts.

The predicate tells us that the subject is performing an action or it states the condition of the subject. The most important part of the predicate is the verb.:

★ The decline in exports *requires* efforts.

The predicate may be a **simple, a compound** or **a complete predicate.**

A simple predicate is the verb in the complete predicate:

★ Every job **has** its ups and downs.

A compound predicate is two or more verbs joined by a conjunction (**and or, but**):

★ The company **manufactures and distributes** its products most economically.

A complete predicate is everything in the sentence that is not the complete subject. It consists of other words that are related to the verb, such as objects, complements and modifiers:

★ The decline in exports **requires concerted efforts by exporters.**

Objects may be **direct** or **indirect**. A direct object of a verb is a noun or noun equivalent that is needed to complete the statement. It answers the question **what** or **whom** after the verb:

★ Anxious contestants often falter in their **responses**.

★ The winners have decided to go on a **picnic**.

★ The winners could not decide what they should do with the **prize money**.

An indirect object receives the action of the verb indirectly and comes before the direct object. It answers the question **to whom** or **what** or **for whom** or **what**. It is used with verbs of **telling**, **asking**, **giving, receiving** and so on and names the receiver of the message or gift, etc. But in prepositional phrases it comes after the direct object:

★ He gave the *mission* a new orientation.

★ He gave a new orientation to the *mission*. (Prepositional phrase)

Complement is a noun or an adjective in the predicate which follows a linking verb **be** in its various forms such as **am, is, are was, were, has been, being, might be** or other linking verbs like **seem, appear, feel, grow, act, look, smell, remain, become, taste** and **sound.**

Complement is related to the subject rather than to the verb and expresses a condition rather than direct action. A noun used as complement is called a **predicate noun** and an adjective used as a complement is called a **predicate adjective.**

★ Ramen is a skilled *pilot*. (Predicate noun)

★ The pilot seemed a little *uncertain*. (Predicate adjective)

Modifiers are words that describe, limit or make more exact the meaning of main elements (subject-verb-object or subject-linking verb-complement) of a sentence. They may be single words, phrases and clauses, which qualify or expand a simple statement. Single words used as modifiers may be adjectives or adverbs. Adjectives relate to nouns and are usually placed before the words they modify or come immediately after them. Adverbs usually stand close to a particular word (verb, adjective or adverb) they modify:

★ It was a *painful, difficult* journey. (Modifies the noun **journey)**

★ A number of potholes in the road made the journey *painful* and *difficult*. (Modifies the noun **journey)**

★ They *specifically* desired to visit the site of the accident. (Modifies the verb **desired)**

★ The enemy crossed the border *silently*. (Modifies the verb **crossed**)

★ He finished the given task too soon. (Modifies the adverb **soon)**

Structure of Sentences

The three basic sentence structures are:

1. Simple **2. Complex** **3. Compound**

A **simple** sentence makes one statement. It is made up of one complete subject and one complete predicate:

★ *Luck is the outcome of hard work.*

★ *The competition among mobile operators will only grow.*

*A **complex** sentence has an independent clause* and one or more dependent clauses***, such as a conditional clause beginning with **if** or a relative clause introduced by **which** or **who**:

★ *If you want to be competitive, you have to show that you love technology and processes.*

(*An independent clause is a group of words in a sentence that has a subject and a predicate and can stand alone as a sentence.

**A dependent or subordinate clause is a group of words that is used with an independent clause to express a related idea.)

Note: In a complex sentence, either the independent or the dependent clause may come first.

A **compound** sentence is made up of two or more independent clauses. These independent clauses are joined by a comma and a conjunction **(and or, yet, but**) or by a semi-colon. It doesn't have a dependent clause.

★ *The component industry is the backbone of the automobile sector and the loss of production does not augur well for anybody.*

A **compound-complex** sentence contains two or more independent clauses and one or more subordinate clauses:

Because the candidates have been so argumentative (subordinate clause), **some voters are confused (**independent clause**) and many have become disinterested** (independent clause).

2. Phrases and Clauses

(a) A phrase is *a group of words connected as a unit to a sentence*. It has no subject or predicate. It can be used as a noun, an adjective or an adverb and may be a noun* phrase, a prepositional** phrase or a verbal*** phrase.

(*A noun is the name of a person, a place, an object, an animal, an idea, a concept, an action or a quality.

**A preposition is a word that shows location, movement or direction.

***A verbal phrase is a verb used in sentences as a noun or as a modifier.)

(b) A phrase made up of a noun and its modifiers is called **a noun phrase.**

★ ***The star-studded event*** won a loud applause.

★ ***The teaching and medical professions*** are becoming ***gender friendly*.**

A **prepositional** phrase begins with a preposition **(at, from, by, in, with, on, for, under, etc.)** followed by a noun or a noun equivalent (called the **object of preposition**) and all the words in between. It can be used as an adjective or as an adverb depending on what element it modifies. When it functions like an adjective, it is called an **Adjective phrase**. When it functions as an adverb, it is called an **Adverb phrase**:

★ Nobody likes a person *with a bad temper*. (Adjective phrase - modifies the noun, 'a person')

★ He came *from a small town in the north-east of India.* (Adverb phrase - modifies the verb 'came')

★ The plane *with an extra man on board* got a bit slow. (Adjective phrase - modifies the noun 'plane')

★ Sachin persevered in the face of many obstacles. He seems to have acted *with great alacrity*. (Adverb phrase - modifies the verb 'acted')

★ The accused received punishment *with a smile*. (Adjective phrase - modifies the noun 'accused')

★ Prices of essential commodities are increasing *at a very rapid rate.* (Adverb phrase - modifies the verb 'are increasing')

(d) A **verbal** phrase consists of a participle*, a gerund** or an infinitive*** plus its objects or complement and modifiers.

(e) A **participial verbal phrase** functions as an adjective and modifies nouns and pronouns.

★ India, ***now advancing towards economic recovery***, has still a long way to go. (Participial phrase used as an adjective modifying the noun **India)**

(f) A **gerund verbal phrase** works as a noun.

★ ***A decaying society*** needs to be kicked awake in every sector. (Gerund verbal phrase used as a noun)

★ ***Thinking good thoughts*** precedes good action. (Gerund verbal phrase used a noun)

(g) An **infinitive verbal phrase** can serve either as a noun, an adjective or an adverb.

★ Good managers like to ***help their fellow employees***. (Infinitive verbal phrase used as a noun)

★ **Vikram's ambition** to ***become a doctor*** **was fulfilled**. (Infinitive verbal phrase used as an adjective modifying the noun **ambition**)

★ The respected leader lived *to see* his projects materialise. (Infinitive verbal phrase used as an adverb modifying the verb **lived**)

(h) A **clause is** *a group of words that has a subject and a predicate*. It may be an **independent** or **main clause** or a **dependent** or **subordinate clause.**

(i) **An independent** or **main** clause is a complete expression and can stand alone as a sentence. A compound sentence has more than one independent clause:

★ *You will never know failure unless you try and you'll never know success until you experience failure.*

(j) The connection between two independent clauses may be of four kinds:

(i) **Cumulative** or **copulative**, where the two independent clauses are joined together by a coordinate conjunction, such as **and, both--and, also, as well as, not only – but also, moreover, besides, further, likewise, well:**

★ The innocents were punished ***as well as the guilty***. (Meaning, the guilty were also punished.)

(*A participle is that form of the verb which shares the qualities of both verb and adjective.

A gerund is a noun derived from a verb which ends in '–ing**'.

***An infinitive is the preposition **'to'** followed by a verb.)

(ii) **Alternative** or **disjointed**, where the two independent clauses are disjointed in meaning and a choice between them is offered for acceptance. These are joined by coordinate conjunctions, such as **either—or, neither—nor, otherwise, else**:

★ Walk quickly, ***else you will be left behind.***

(iii) **Contrast** or **adversative**, where the two clauses are opposed in meaning to each other and are joined by conjunctions, such as **but, nevertheless, however, whereas, while, only, now, on the one hand, etc.**

★ He is slow, ***but he is sure.***

(iv) **Inference**, where the second independent clause draws an inference from the first. These clauses are joined by conjunctions, such as **therefore, then, for, consequently, hence, so, etc.**

★ He is unwell, ***so*** he could not complete the assignment.

Notes:

(1) Sometimes a subordinate conjunction (relative pronoun or relative adverb) is used to join the independent clauses of a compound sentence:

★ *I walked with him to the station,* **where** (and there) *we parted.*

★ *I shall see you tomorrow,* **when** (and then) *we can complete the discussion.*

(2) Compared sentences are often contracted when the independent clauses have a common subject or a common verb:

★ *He chided their wanderings, but relieved their pain.* (He chided their wanderings, but he relieved their pain)

★ *Some praise the workers and some the architect.* (Some praise the workers and some praise the architect)

(3) Sometimes no connecting word is used to join the coordinate clauses in a compound sentence and the connecting word is replaced by a semi-colon(;) .

★ *The image that you give is that of someone who slogs late into the night; the quality of the work done is not reckoned here.*

(k) A **dependent** or **subordinate** clause functions as a part of the sentence. It is related to the independent or main clause by a connecting word that shows its subordinate relationship, either as a **relative pronoun (when, who, which, that, whose, what, etc.)** or a **relative adverb (where, when, etc.)** or a **subordinate conjunction (because, although, since, after, if,)** etc.

★ The project, ***which will cost Rs.80 crores,*** will include systems for irrigation and lighting.

★ ***When we talk of industries,*** all the industries are somehow related to pollution.

(l) Subordinate clauses are used like nouns – **Noun Clause**, like adjectives – **Adjective Clause** or like adverbs – **Adverb Clause**.

(m) The **noun clause** can be a subject of a verb, the object of a transitive verb, the object of a preposition or of an infinitive, the complement to a verb or in apposition to a noun or pronoun:

- ★ ***Why he came to see the minister,*** is still a secret. (Subject in a noun clause)
- ★ Be attentive ***to what he says***. (Object of the preposition '**to**' in a noun clause)
- ★ The doctor wanted to know ***why the patient had taken sleeping pills.*** (Object of the infinitive '**to know**')
- ★ The witness confessed ***that his information was wrong***. (Object of the verb **'confessed'**)
- ★ It is good ***that he has come back***. (Complement of the verb '**is**')
- ★ The general agreement was ***that your company would not contest the award.*** (Complement of the verb **'was')**
- ★ It is a well-known fact ***that plants should get direct sunlight***. (Apposition to the noun '**fact**')

Note: A word or a noun clause in apposition is a noun or noun equivalent placed besides another noun to complement or supplement its meaning.

(n) The adjective clause is connected by a relative pronoun (**who, which, whom, whose, that, as, but)** or a relative adverb **(when, where, why, whence, whither, wherein, how**)

- ★ Such men, ***as are false***, set a bad example.

(o) The adjective clause may be **restrictive** or **non-restrictive**. A restrictive adjective clause identifies or defines the antecedents that it qualifies and gives essential information about it. It is introduced by **that, which, who** or **whose** and is not normally separated by commas. A non-restrictive adjective clause gives more information about its antecedent that could be left out without affecting the structure or meaning of the sentence. It is separated by commas.

- ★ A system ***that involves a degree of cost-sharing between the end-user and the payer*** – the government or insurance companies – would encourage responsible utilisation of health benefits. (Restrictive adjective clause)
- ★ People ***who become famous*** pass through many hardships. (Restrictive adjective clause)
- ★ All kinds of migration, ***as plenty of evidence in our cities shows,*** do not bring benefits for migrants. (Non-restrictive adjective clause)

(p) The adverb clause does the work of an adverb and can have any of the following functions:

(i) Time (when, as soon as, while, before, until, after, as, by the time, everytime, once, whenever, next or last time, first time, since, whenever, so long as, just as, till, etc.):

- ★ He left the office ***after*** completing the assignment.
- ★ We shall ***now*** begin to work.

(ii) Place (where, whence, whither, whereas, wherever, etc.):

- ★ They can stay ***where they are.***

(iii) Purpose (that, lest, so that, in order that, etc.):

★ He worked very hard ***so that*** he could get promoted as a manager.

(iv) Condition (if, whether, unless, in case, as if, even if, only if, in the event, etc.):

★ ***Whether you like or not*** you have to complete the work by the evening.

(v) Cause or Reason (as, since, because, that, due to the fact that, as long as, in order that, so (that), now that ,etc.):

★ ***Since*** you promise to work hard, you will be promoted.

★ ***As long as*** he works for this company, he can't learn anything worthwhile.

(vi) Manner (as, so far as, according to, etc.):

★ Do unto others ***as*** you wish to be done by.

(vii) Comparison (as, as much as, no less than, than):

★ He hates smoking ***as much as*** he hates gambling.

(viii) Result or Effect (that – it should be preceded by so or such in the independent clause):

★ He rose in the career *so* fast ***that*** he left behind all his colleagues.

(ix) Supposition or Contrast (though, although, even though, whereas, even if, as, notwithstanding this, all the same, however, whatever, etc.):

★ ***However innocent you may be,*** you will have to pay the penalty.

(q) Sometimes clauses of a few words are included in sentences. These clauses have no relationship with independent clause or any other clause in the sentence. These are called parenthetical clauses:

★ These are the very reports which ***you thought*** were lost.

Other examples of such clauses are:

★ If I am not mistaken ★ It is true.

★ As it were ★ I think .

(r) **An elliptical clause** implies both a subject and a predicate, even though both these elements do not in fact appear in the clause. Such clauses avoid excessive wordiness, preserve a sense of variety and add to the rhythm of the text:

★ ***While on a tour to Mumbai,*** the officer received word of his promotion. (The elliptical clause implies 'While the officer was on a tour to Mumbai')

3. Nouns

A noun is a word that names a person, a place, an object, an animal, an idea, a concept, an action or a quality.

Nouns can be classified as Proper Noun and **Common Noun.**

A proper noun is the name of some particular person, thing or place (**Rahul, Sachin, Delhi, Chennai, Mount Everest, etc.**). A common noun is the name shared by all entities of the same class or kind **(author, owner, friend, etc.)**

Common nouns can further be classified as:

(i) **Collective noun** – The name of a number (i.e. collection) of persons, things, or animals, taken together: **audience, crowd, family, flock, club, school, team, bunch, colony, etc.**

(ii) **Concrete noun** – The name of a person, place, animal, or things that we can see or touch: **earth, sky, window, cloud, fire, stapler, lake, etc.**

(iii) **Abstract noun** – The name of something intangible which we cannot see or touch: an idea, feeling, emotion, concept, action or quality: **beauty, happiness, ability, anger, bravery, honesty, laughter, hatred, disappointment or assistance.**

Nouns can also be classified as:

(i) **Countable** – Names of objects, people, etc., which can be counted like **book, brother, apple**, etc.

(ii) **Uncountable** – Names of things or attributes which cannot be counted: **milk, sugar, gold, honesty**, etc.

Notes:

★ Countable nouns have singular and plural forms, uncountable nouns do not have plural forms.

★ Proper nouns always begin with a capital letter.

★ Proper nouns are sometimes used as common nouns:
Kalidas is often called the Shakespeare (the greatest dramatist) of India.

★ A collective noun is treated as a singular entity when it refers to the group as a whole. When the members of the group act individually, it is treated as a plural.

★ A, an, the are special words called articles. They are noun signals which tip off that there's a noun coming up in the sentence.

Gender of Nouns

A noun that denotes the sex of a being as male is called the **masculine** gender: **boy, lion, hero, etc**.

If it denotes the sex as female, it is called the **feminine** gender: **girl, lioness, heroine, etc.**

A noun that denotes either a male or a female is said to be the **common** gender: **parent, child, person, relation, neighbour, etc**.

A noun that denotes a thing that is without life is said to be the **neuter** gender: **book, pen**.

Objects are often personified, i.e. spoken of as if they were living beings. They are of masculine gender if they are remarkable for their strength and violence (**Sun, Summer, Time**) and of feminine gender, if they are remarkable for their beauty, gentleness and gracefulness (**Moon, Earth, Nature**).

Number of Nouns

A noun can be in **singular number** or in **plural number**. A noun that denotes one person, place, or thing is said to be in the singular number. If it denotes more than one person, place, or thing, it is said to in the plural number:

Singular – **boy, tree, pen, book**
Plural – **boys, trees, pens, books**

Note: The spelling of a singular noun almost always changes when it becomes a plural. Most plurals can be formed by adding –s or –es. But many nouns do not follow this format:

★ **bench – benches, leaf – leaves, woman – women, party – parties.**

Letters, figures and other symbols are made plural by adding an apostrophe and **–s**:

★ **Dot your i's and cross your t's.**

★ **Add two 5's and four 2's.**

Abstract nouns are uncountable and have no plurals. When such words are made plurals and used as countable, their meaning changes:

Provocation (singular), **Provocations** (cases of provocation).

Names of substances are also uncountable, but when used as plurals, their meaning changes:

Copper (singular) **Coppers** (copper coins)
Iron (singular) **Irons** (fetters)

Some nouns have the same form in both singular and plural:

★ **sheep, deer, species, fish, cattle, furniture**

Some nouns are used only in plural:

★ **scissors, spectacles, jeans, shorts, trousers**

Some nouns look plural, but are in fact singular:

★ **physics, mathematics, accounts, acoustics, athletics, gymnastics, measles, headquarters, vegetables**

Case:

When a noun (or pronoun) is used as a subject, it is said to be in the **Nominative** Case. When a noun (or pronoun) is used as an object, it is said to be in the **Objective** or **Accusative** Case:

★ ***Karan*** was promoted yesterday. (Nominative case)

★ ***We are*** the largest manufacturer in this area. (Nominative case)

★ The Chairman will sign the ***contract*** next week. (Objective case)

Note: The nominative generally comes before the verb and the objective after the verb. To find the nominative case, put who? or what? before the verb. To find the objective case, put whom? or what? before the verb and its subject.

When the form of a noun shows ownership or possession, it is in the **possessive** case. In singular nouns, the possessive case is formed by adding an apostrophe, and **–s**:

★ The Secretary's *skills* were exemplary.

A plural noun that ends in **–s**, add an apostrophe to form the possessive case. But if the plural noun does not end in **–s**, add an apostrophe and an **-s**:

★ Manufacturers' lobby ★ Children's park ★ Men's apparel

When a noun or a title consists of several words, the possessive sign is attached to the last word:

★ The Prime Minister of ***Bhutan's*** speech

★ The commander-in-***chief's*** personal staff

When two nouns are in apposition, the possessive sign is put to the latter only:

★ This is Tagore, the ***poet's*** house.

When two nouns are closely connected (i.e. two or more nouns possess the same thing together), the possessive sign is put to the latter:

★ Manoj and ***Anju's*** boutique

When two or more connected nouns imply separate possession (i.e. the same type of things but separately and distinctly), the possessive sign is put to each of them:

★ Raja ***Rao's*** and R .K. ***Narayan's*** novels

Possessive case is chiefly used with the names of living beings. Ex: **Minister's statement**, but **cover of the book** (and not **the book's cover**).

Possessive case is used:

(i) with the names of personified objects: **nature's laws, duty's call**

(ii) with nouns denoting time, space, weight: **a day's work, a foot's length**

As a general rule, the possessive case is used to denote possession or ownership:

★ ***the defeat of the enemy,*** not ***the enemy's defeat***

★ ***the execution of the spy,*** not ***the spy's execution***

Sometimes a noun in the possessive case has a different meaning from a noun used with a preposition:

★ ***The Minister's reception*** (reception hosted by the Minister) ***was well attended.***

★ ***The reception of the Minister*** (reception of the Minister hosted by a host) ***was held in his constituency.***

4. Pronouns

The word 'pronoun' means 'for a noun' and it comes in place of it. It functions as a noun but it does not specifically name a person, thing, animal, place or an idea. It is used as a substitute for a previously mentioned noun or a noun phrase (called its antecedent) and thus avoids repetition of noun in the writing as well as in speaking.

The antecedent of a pronoun should be clearly stated, not merely implied and the pronoun must specifically refer to this antecedent. The antecedent should not be a noun used as a modifier or a noun in possessive form. Also, the same pronoun should not be used for different antecedents in the same sentence.

Kinds of Pronoun

Pronouns are of eight kinds: **Personal, Demonstrative, Indefinite, Reflexive, Intensive, Interrogative, Relative and Reciprocal**. Of these, personal pronouns are used the most.

Personal pronouns refer to specific people and things. They are of three kinds:

(i) First Person (which includes the person or persons doing the speaking or writing): **I, me, us, my, mine, our, ours, we**.

(ii) Second person (which includes those who are being addressed or spoken to): **you, your, yours**.

(iii) Third Person (all the others about whom something is being said): **he, she, him, his, her, hers, it, its, they, them, their, theirs**.

Personal pronouns are used as subjects, objects or in possessive case and as singular or plural. Here is a chart that shows personal pronouns by case, number and person:

Persons/case	1st person		2nd person		3rd person	
	Singular	*Plural*	*Singular*	*Plural*	*Singular*	*Plural*
nominative case	*I*	*we*	*you*	*you*	*he, she, it*	*they*
Object Case	*me*	*us*	*you*	*you*	*him, her, it*	*them*
Possessive	*my, mine*	*our, ours*	*your, yours*	*your, yours*	*his, her, hers,*	*their, theirs*

Pronouns used for nouns in subject position should be used as subjects and pronouns used for nouns in object position should be used as objects. Subject pronouns should not be used in objective position; similarly, object pronouns should not be used in subjective positions:

Incorrect	Correct
Ask the secretary and ***I*** for any further information that you may need. You and ***me*** are going to be late.	Ask the secretary and ***me*** for any further information that you may need. You and ***I*** are going to be late.

Personal pronouns in the possessive case (my, mine, our, your, her, their, his) have two forms – one is used as an adjective before a noun (***my*** project, ***her*** proposals) and the other is used by itself or in a phrase after a noun (that project is ***mine***). A mix of these two forms should be avoided:

Incorrect:	Correct:
• The group presented ***her*** and ***mine*** proposals before the Board.	• The group presented ***her*** proposal along with ***my*** proposal before the Board.

Notes:–

1. Possessive pronouns used as adjectives are: my, our, your, his, her, its, their, whose.
2. A possessive pronoun never has an apostrophe. The word 'it's' is the contraction of 'it is' or 'it has' and the possessive form of it is 'its'.

Personal pronouns have both singular and plural forms. A personal pronoun referring to a singular antecedent should be singular, the one referring to a plural antecedent should be plural. Also, the gender and person must be the same as the noun for which it is used. Do not shift from singular to plural form or from we to you or one.

Incorrect	Correct
• When ***an employee*** has spent a lot of time on his project, ***they*** are likely to feel discouraged if ***they*** are criticised for wasting their time.	• When ***an employee*** has spent a lot of time on his project, ***he*** is likely to feel discouraged if ***he*** is criticised for wasting time.
• When ***a person*** has worked for a year in Mumbai, one is reluctant to relocate in a small town.	• When ***a person*** has worked for a year in Mumbai, ***he*** (or, ***she***) is reluctant to relocate to a small town.

Or

Demonstrative pronouns point out (demonstrate) specific persons, animals, places, things and ideas. These are: **this, that, these, those:**

★ ***These*** are your project reports. **That** is her car.

This refers to what is close at hand and nearest to the thought or person of the speaker, while that refers to what is over there farther away and more remote:

★ ***This*** is better than ***that.***

That, with its plural '**those**', is used to avoid the repetition of a preceding noun:

★ Our offer was better than ***that*** of the competitor.

When two things which have already been mentioned are referred to, this refers to the latter thing, last mentioned, 'that' to the former thing, first mentioned:

★ Virtue and vice offer themselves for your choice: ***this*** (i.e. vice) leads to misery, ***that*** (i.e. virtue) to happiness.

Indefinite pronouns refer to nouns in a general, indefinite way:

★ ***Everyone*** is talking about the problem of global warming.

★ ***Some*** people escaped with minor injuries in the train accidents.

Indefinite pronouns are:

all	*another*	*any*	*anybody*	*anyone*
anything	*both*	*each*	*either*	*every*
everybody	*everyone*	*everything*	*few*	*least*
less	*little*	*many*	*more*	*most*
much	*neither*	*nobody*	*none*	*nothing*
no one	*one*	*other*	*others*	*plenty*
several	*some*	*somebody*	*someone*	*something*

Each, either, neither are also called **Distributive** pronouns, because they refer to one person or thing at a time. These words are followed by the verb of singular form.

Either and **neither** should be used when speaking of two persons or things. When more than one is spoken of **any**, **no one** or **none** should be used.

If **one** is used as a personal pronoun, ensure that you maintain consistency by following through with **one's** (for my, our), **oneself** (for myself) and not mixing it with pronouns such as **my, you, our,** etc.

Some indefinite pronouns **(all, any, both, each, few, one, several, some)** can also be used as adjectives. When these words are adjectives, they have nouns after them, when they are used as indefinite pronouns, they have no nouns after them.

Some indefinite pronouns **(little, less, some, none, more)** tell us about portions, not numbers and therefore should be used only for uncountable nouns.

Each, everybody, everyone, one, either, neither, someone, somebody, anyone, no one, nobody and something are always singular and should be used when their antecedents are also in the singular form.

Any, all, some, most, none, may be singular or plural, depending on the particular reference.

- ★ If ***any*** of these ***books*** are yours, let me know. (The noun **books** is plural)
- ★ ***Most*** of the ***guests had*** already gone. (The noun **guests** is plural)
- ★ ***Most*** of the ***donation*** has already been distributed. (The noun **donation** is singular)

If an indefinite pronoun is used with a verb or a personal pronoun in a sentence, it should match with the number of the verb and the personal pronoun.

- ★ ***Each one*** of us ***has*** problems.
- ★ ***Few*** of the contestants ***are*** likely to turn up today.
- ★ ***Neither*** of the protestors could explain what his /her grievance ***is***.

Reflexive pronouns refer back to the subject in an expression where the doer and the recipient of an act are the same. When a reflexive pronoun emphasises a noun or another pronoun, it is called intensive (emphatic) pronoun. Reflexive and intensive pronouns are formed by adding the singular form –self or the plural form -selves to some personal pronouns:

Singular	Plural
herself, himself, itself, myself, yourself	**ourselves, themselves, yourselves**

Reflexive pronoun	Intensive pronoun
With their casual play, the team let ***themselves*** down.	The Director ***himself*** gave this information to the press.

Note: The reflexive form is not used as the subject or as a substitute for me.

Interrogative pronouns ask questions. These pronouns are: **what, which, who, whom, whose.**

★ **What** will all the people say?

★ ***Which*** of the reports, you think, is correct?

Relative pronouns introduce relative clauses that act as nouns. These are: **that, which, who, whom, whose, whatever, whoever, whomever:**

★ I think I know ***whose*** carelessness has caused this accident.

★ He is free to do ***whatever*** he likes.

To prevent ambiguity, relative pronouns should be placed as near as possible to their antecedents.

Notes: –

(1) **Who** has different forms for the objective case and the possessive case:

who -- Nominative case, **whom** – Objective case, **whose** – Possessive case.

(2) **Who** refers to persons, '**which'** generally refers to things without life and for animals, '**that**' refers to either person or things. **Which** is often used to refer to impersonal organization of people, like groups, clubs, companies, etc.

(3) **That** usually introduces restrictive adjective clauses. **Who** and **which** are used both restrictively and non-restrictively.

(4) **Who** and **whoever** are subject pronouns, **whom** and **whomever** are object pronouns. These words should be used to match similar subject and object nouns.

(5) **That** defines the meaning or intention of the preceding phrase or clause, **which** is used when the identifying information is already supplied in the sentence.

(6) When **which** introduces a non-restrictive adjective clause giving additional information, this clause is separated by commas.

(7) **That** is used in preference to **who** or **which**:

(i) after adjectives in the superlative degree:

★ He was the ***most*** eloquent speaker ***that*** I ever heard.

(ii) after the words **all, same, any, none, nothing, (the) only:**

★ ***All*** is not gold ***that*** glitters.

★ It is the ***same*** report ***that*** he has been searching.

★ There is nothing in this book that can fetch readers' attention.

(iii) after the interrogative pronouns, who, what:

★ ***What*** is it ***that*** has been giving you so much trouble?

Reciprocal pronouns express a mutual give and take relationship. These are: **each other** and **one another**. **Each other** refers to two persons or things, **one another** usually refer to more than two.

- ★ The two companies were in competition with ***each other***.
- ★ They all gave evidence against ***one another.***

5. Verb

Action or Main or Basic Verb

An **action** or **main** or **basic** verb is a word that describes an action. Action does not mean just physical action ***(go, scream, climb, throw, manufacture),*** it also means quiet, peaceful actions, both physical and mental ***(think, listen, sit, write)***, condition or state of being ***(feel, sleep, dream, hear, wonder)***. Normally, it is the most important word in a clause or a sentence.

- ★ Time *changes* all things.
- ★ When we *know* very little about a problem, we *tend* to worry about the worst-case scenario.

A verb is **transitive** (it means *passing over*) when action passes over from the doer (subject) to a person or thing (object). It is **intransitive** (it means *not passing over*) when there is no object or which expresses a state or being.

- ★ Our teams ***visit*** all our customers personally. (Transitive)
- ★ The Managing Director ***thinks*** highly of the new Executive Director. (Transitive)
- ★ Migrant unskilled workers ***keep*** most urban households running. (Transitive)
- ★ Migrant labour ***comes*** from distant places. (Intransitive – action)
- ★ This guard ***sleeps*** while on duty. (Intransitive – state)
- ★ Investing in innovation ***is*** like sowing the seeds of an institution. (Intransitive – being)

Notes:

(1) Most transitive verbs take a single object. But such transitive verbs as **give, ask, offer, promise, tell,** etc. take two objects after them -- an indirect object which denotes the person to whom something is given or for whom something is done. A direct object is usually the name of something, such as:

- ★ The contests offer to the ***players*** (Indirect object) a great ***joy***. (direct object).
- ★ The manager shared with ***Mukesh*** (Indirect object) a closely guarded ***secret***. (direct object)

(2) Some verbs e.g. **come, go, fall, die, sleep, lie** denote actions which cannot be passed over. They can, therefore, never be used transitively.

Parts of a Verb

A verb has three main parts:

(i) The **present**, which is used by itself for the present tense and with the auxiliary verb **will** for the **future** tense. It forms the **present participle** with auxiliary verbs by adding **–ing** to the basic verb: **I go**. (Present tense), **I will go**. (Future tense), **I am going**. (Present Participle).

(ii) The **past**, which is used for the past tense: **I went.**

(iii) The **past participle** which is used with the auxiliary verbs **have, has** or **had** to form the three perfect tenses: **I have gone**. (Present Perfect), **I had gone**. (Past Perfect), **I will have gone**. (Future Perfect)

Note: The past participle cannot be used alone as a full verb in the past tense.

Tense

In grammar, **Tense** means or refers to time. Action verbs express that someone is doing something at the present time (i.e. action is taking place now) – **Present Tense**; was doing in the time that has passed (i.e. action has taken place sometime before now) – **Past Tense** or will do something in the future time (i.e. action has not yet started but may happen any time after now) – **Future Tense**. These are the three basic tenses which help us to express the relationship between the action and the time of its occurrence.

★ Many problems in the education field ***arise*** from incompetent management of resources. (Present)

★ Many problems in the education field ***arose*** from incompetent management of resources. (Past)

★ Many problems in the education field ***will arise*** from incompetent management of resources. (Future)

Note: In clauses with **if, unless, when, while, as (while) before, after, till, until, by the time** and **as soon as,** present tense is used for future tense:

★ We won't go for a picnic ***if*** it rains.

★ Let' wait ***till*** he finishes his work.

★ Please ring me up ***as soon as*** you arrive at the factory.

Apart from these basic tenses, verbs can be used to express a wide range of actions through:

(i) **Present Continuous Tense** that shows that the action is incomplete or is continuing, i.e. it is still going on.

★ The Assistant ***is searching*** the missing file.

(ii) **Present Perfect Tense** is formed with the word 'has' or 'have'. It shows that the action began in the past and was completed at the present time:

★ The Assistant ***has searched*** for the missing file.

(iii) **Present Perfect Continuous Tense** that shows the action is going on continuously and not completed at the present moment:

★ The Assistant ***has been searching*** for the missing file.

(iv) **Past Continuous Tense** that shows an action going on at sometime in the past:

★ The audience ***was listening*** to the Chairman's speech.

(v) **Past Perfect Tense** is formed with the word 'had'. It describes an action completed before a certain moment in the past:

★ The audience ***had heard*** the Chairman last year also.

(vi) **Past Perfect Continuous Tense** shows an action which began before a certain point of time in the past and continued in the present time:

★ The Chairman ***had been explaining*** this plan in the previous meetings also.

(vii) **Future Continuous Tense** tells us about actions which will be in progress at a time in the future. This tense also tells us about actions in the future which are already planned or which are expected to happen in the normal course of time:

★ This time tomorrow the team of experts ***will be visiting the site of the*** accident.

★ The President of the company ***will be meeting*** the employees next week.

★ The mail ***will be coming*** soon.

(viii) **Future Perfect Tense** is formed with the words 'will have'. It tells about actions that will be completed by a certain future time:

★ By the end of this month, I ***will have worked*** in this company for five years.

(ix) **Future Perfect Continuous Tense** tells about actions which will be in progress over a period of time that will end in the future:

★ By next month this company ***will have been doing*** business here for three years.

Regular and Irregular Verbs

Verbs are divided into two groups – **regular** or **weak** verbs and **irregular** or **strong** verbs. Regular verbs follow a pattern – the basic form of the verb simply adds an **–s, –es,--ing or –ed** to express a different time or mood.

Irregular verbs form their past tenses and past participles in an irregular manner. Here are some irregular verbs used in everyday speech and writing:

Present	Past	Past Participle
arise	*arose*	*arisen*
bear	*bore*	*borne*
begin	*began*	*begun*
bind	*bound*	*bound*
blow	*blew*	*blown*
bring	*brought*	*brought*
buy	*bought*	*bought*
choose	*chose*	*chosen*
come	*came*	*come*
deal	*dealt*	*dealt*
dive	*dived/dove*	*dived*
drag	*dragged*	*dragged*
dream	*dreamed/ dreamt*	*dreamed/ dreamt*
drive	*drove*	*driven*
fall	*fell*	*fallen*
flee	*fled*	*fled*
fly	*flew*	*flown*
forget	*forgot*	*forgotten*
freeze	*froze*	*frozen*
give	*gave*	*given*
grow	*grew*	*grown*
hang(person)	*hanged/hung*	*hanged/hung*
hold	*held*	*held*
kneel	*knelt*	*knelt*
lay(place)	*laid*	*laid*
leave	*left*	*left*
lie(recline)	*lay*	*lain*
lose	*lost*	*lost*
meet	*met*	*met*
pay	*paid*	*paid*
quit	*quit/quitted*	*quit/quitted*
rid	*rid*	*rid*
ring	*rang*	*rung*
run	*ran*	*run*
see	*saw*	*seen*
shake	*shook*	*shaken*
shoot	*shot*	*shot*
shrink	*shrank/shrunk*	*shrunk*
sink	*sank/sunk*	*sunk/sunken*
slay	*slew*	*slain*
speak	*spoke*	*spoken*
spring	*sprang*	*sprung*

Present	Past	Past Participle
awake	*awoke*	*awoke/awaken*
beat	*beat*	*beat*
bid	*bade*	*bidden*
bite	*bit*	*bit/bitten*
break	*broke*	*broken*
burst	*burst*	*burst*
catch	*caught*	*caught*
cling	*clung*	*clung*
cut	*cut*	*cut*
dig	*dug*	*dug*
do	*did*	*done*
draw	*drew*	*drawn*
drink	*drank*	*drunk*
eat	*ate*	*eaten*
fight	*fought*	*fought*
fling	*flung*	*flung*
forbid	*forbade*	*forbidden*
forgive	*forgave*	*forgiven*
get	*got*	*got/gotten*
go	*went*	*gone*
hang(thing)	*hung*	*hung*
hide	*hid*	*hid/hidden*
keep	*kept*	*kept*
know	*knew*	*known*
lead	*led*	*led*
lend	*lent*	*lent*
lie(untruth)	*lied*	*lied*
light	*lighted/lit*	*lighted/lit*
mistake	*mistook*	*mistaken*
prove	*proved*	*proved/proven*
read	*read*	*read*
ride	*rode*	*ridden*
rise	*rose*	*risen*
say	*said*	*said*
set	*set*	*set*
shine(sun)	*shone*	*shone*
show	*showed*	*shown/showed*
sing	*sang*	*sung*
sit	*sat*	*sat*
slide	*slid*	*slid*
spin	*spun*	*spun*
stand	*stood*	*stood*

steal	stole	stolen	sting	stung	stung
stink	stank	stunk	stride	strode	stridden
strike	struck	struck	strive	strove	striven
swear	swore	sworn	swim	swam	swum
swing	swung	swung	take	took	taken
teach	taught	taught	tear	tore	torn
tell	told	told	think	thought	thought
thrive	thrived	thrived	throw	threw	thrown
tread	trod	trod/trodden	undergo	underwent	undergone
wake	woke/waked	woken	wear	wore	worn
wring	wrung	wrung	write	wrote	written

Note: If a verb has more than one choice for a principal part, you can use whichever one sounds better to you.

You will notice that some irregular verbs are the same for all the three forms, some in which two of the three forms are the same and some in which all the three forms are different.

Auxiliaries

Auxiliaries means 'helpers'. It adds to basic verbs. There are two kinds of auxiliaries: **primary** auxiliaries: **be** (and its forms **am**, **is, are, was, were**), **has** (and its forms **have, had**) and **do** (and its forms **does, did**) and **modal** auxiliaries: **can, could, may, might, must, shall, should, will, would, ought to.**

Primary auxiliaries are used to make tenses, passive forms, questions and negatives. Modal auxiliaries are used before basic verbs and express meanings such as permission, possibility, certainty and necessity. Sometimes, **used (to), need a**nd **dare** are also used as modal auxiliaries:

- ★ Migrant workers ***are helping*** the construction boom. (Present continuous tense)
- ★ The factory gate ***was opened*** by the police. (Passive form)
- ★ ***Does*** the government ***realise*** that migration is driven by the people's need to improve their lives? (Question)
- ★ Talent ***does not find*** entry into politics very smooth. (Negative)
- ★ ***May*** the company import more raw material to meet the rising demands of its products? (Permission)
- ★ The workers ***will not work*** in this organization any more. (Possibility)
- ★ Living in crowded urban areas ***must*** be difficult. (Certainty)
- ★ Banks ***ought to*** lead the move towards financial inclusion. (Necessity)

6. Voice

Voice is that *form of the verb which shows whether the subject does something or has something done to it*. A verb is in the **Active Voice** when its form shows that the subject does something, i.e., is the doer of the action. A verb is in the **Passive Voice** when it shows that something is done to the person or the thing denoted by the subject. The passive consists of a form of 'be' plus the past participle and the subject is introduced using the preposition by or with:

(Active)	(Passive)
• The Commission ***announced*** the result on Saturday.	• Guidelines regulating constructions ***have been diluted*** by the authorities.
• Mr. Agarwal has written the delivery notes.	• The delivery notes have been written by Mr. Agarwal.
• Rohan coordinated the meeting in Shyam's absence.	• The meeting was coordinated by Rohan in Shyam's absence.

Active voice is used when the doer of the action is to be made prominent. Passive voice is used when you do not know the doer, when the doer is unimportant, when emphasis is not on the doer but on the object or the act or when you want to avoid personal blunt accusations or commands. It is also used for impersonal instructions.

★ ***It is felt*** that your complaint arises from a misunderstanding.

★ The sentence was written yesterday by one of my technical persons.

Combining an active and a passive verb in the same sentence will be awkward:

Awkward	Revised
• The country *needs* more money to build new schools and it *will be raised* through a bond issue.	• The country *needs* more money to build new schools and *will raise* it through a bond issue.

7. Mood

Mood shows the attitude or purpose of the action denoted by the verb. There are three moods:

Types of Mood

1. Indicative 2. Imperative 3. Subjunctive

1. When a verb makes a statement of fact or asks a question or expresses a supposition which is assumed as a fact, it is in the **indicative** mood. For example:

   ★ *Entrepreneurship largely depends on innovation and the way you think.*

   ★ *Can integrating with global biggies become a challenge to Indian companies?*

   ★ *If innovation is a social process then it needs to be managed as such.*

2. A verb which expresses a command, an exhortation, an entreaty or prayer is in the imperative mood. For example:

   ★ *Bring the file immediately.*

   ★ *Do noble deeds, not dream them all day.*

Note: The subject of a verb in the imperative mood is you, but it is not spoken to.

3. The **subjunctive** mood scarcely exists in present-day English:

(a) The Present subjunctive mood occurs when it expresses a wish, a hope, a desire, an intention, a possibility or a resolution:

★ *God bless you!*

★ *We propose to increase the subscription by one thousand rupees.*

★ *It was suggested that he wait till the next morning.*

(b) The Past subjunctive is used after the verb **wish**, to indicate a situation which is unreal or contrary to fact:

★ *I wish I knew more about this company.* (I am sorry I don't know more about it)

(c) after **if**, to express improbability or unreality in the present:

If we started now, we would be in time. (but we cannot start now)

(d) after **as if/as though/unless**, in hypothetical conditions:

★ *He ordered Krishna about as if he were the boss.* (but he is not)

(e) after **it is time**+subject, to imply that it is late:

★ *It is time we started.*

(f) after **would rather**+subject to indicate preference:

★ *I would rather you went by air.* (I should prefer you to go by air)

(g) when **be** or **were** are used at the beginning of a clause:

★ *All books, be that fiction or non-fiction, should provide entertainment in some form or the other.*

(h) in certain fixed expressions and phrases:

★ *Be that as it may !* ★ *Come what may !* ★ *So be it !*

8. Infinitives

Infinitive is the *preposition* ***'to'*** *followed by a verb*. For example:

★ Many men desire ***to make*** money quickly.

★ Kamala wants **to study** with her friends.

★ She did not hesitate **to tell** the boss that some employees were stealing office stationary.

★ We want to visit all the historical places.

Infinitive is a verbal which is a kind of noun with certain features of the verb, especially that of taking an object (when the verb is transitive) and adverbial qualifiers. It can function as a noun, an adjective or an adverb.

Noun	Adjective	Adverb
To steal is a crime. ***To live*** *a happy life is everyone's deepest desire.*	*She always brings a book* ***to read.*** Those are words ***to remember***.	The hill is too steep ***to climb.*** *I stopped in order* ***to stroke.***

The **'to'** is frequently used with the infinitive, but it is omitted:

(i) after the auxiliary verbs **will, would, shall, should, do, did, may, might, can, could, must;**

(ii) after the phrases **had better, had rather, would rather, sooner than, rather than**;

(iii) after **dare** and **need** in negative or interrogative forms:

★ *I need not say how grateful I feel.*

★ *How dare you speak like this?*

(iv) after the verbs **bid, let, make, feel, see, hear, behold, watch, know** in the active voice;

★ *I felt his heart beat.*

★ *The police let him go.*

(v) after **but** and **than**, if the verb **do** (or one of its form) is used before it.

★ *He did nothing but complain against the boss.*

★ *He did no more than wish him good luck*

When many verbs in the infinitive are joined together by **and, 'to'** is used only before the first:

★ The Managing Director asked him *to come* and *motivate* the employees.

Uses of Infinitives

The infinitive is used as:

(i) subject of a verb

★ **To change** India, the old orthodoxy of hierarchy and hero worship must change.

(ii) object of transitive verb

★ He likes **to play** cricket.

(iii) complement of a verb

★ A doctor's greatest happiness is **to serve** the sick.

(iv) object of a preposition

★ The culprit had no choice but **to surrender**.

(v) an objective complement

★ We saw him **to go**.

The infinitive is also used:

(i) as an adverb qualifying a verb, usually to express a purpose—

★ The great man lived ***to serve*** the poor.

(ii) to qualify an adjective—

★ This medicine is pleasant ***to take.***

(iii) as an adjective qualifying a noun

★ Only when a supply chain manager gets a chance ***to sell*** directly to the consumer does the company have the full incentive ***to scale*** up its operations.

(iv) as qualifying a sentence:

★ ***To be*** a powerful country, India must be in the forefront of knowledge and technology worlds.

Sometimes, the infinitive is split or separated by placing an adverb or an adverbial phrase between **'to'** and the verb. This should generally be avoided and sentence should be rephrased:

★ **Split infinitive:** We request you *to kindly come* and *preside* over the function.

★ **Revised:** We request you *kindly to come* and *preside* over the function.

9. Gerund

Gerund is that *form of the verb which ends in **–ing** and is used as a noun*:

★ What was most ***striking*** in Asia, was how few people held doors open for us.

A compound gerund is formed by placing past participle after the gerund of have and be:

★ I have heard of Kunal ***having won*** the contract.

★ He is desirous of ***being praised***.

Uses of Gerund

The gerund is used as—

(i) subject of a verb:

★ ***Improving*** energy efficiency is a way to reduce generation cost of electricity.

(ii) object of a transitive verb:

★ I like ***reading*** poetry.

(iii) object of a preposition:

★ The team leader must work at ***giving*** his team a sense of security.

(iv) complement of a verb:

★ The pursuit of truth seemed higher ***calling.***

A gerund and not an infinitive, is used after the verbs; like **hinder, prevent, prohibit, persist, succeed, fond, despair, think:**

Incorrect	Correct
• Do not prevent him ***to play***.	• Do not prevent him ***playing***.
• I like ***to read*** poetry.	• I like ***reading*** poetry.
• ***To give*** is better than **to receive**.	• ***Giving*** is better than receiving.
• Teach me ***to swim***.	• Teach me ***swimming***.
• ***To see*** is ***to believe***.	• ***Seeing*** is ***believing***.

10. Participle

Participle *is that form of the verb which has the quality of both a verb and an adjective*:

- ★ ***Hearing*** the noise, the guard woke up.
- ★ We met a girl ***carrying*** a basket of flowers.
- ★ He rushed into the field and foremost ***fighting*** fell.
- ★ The girl, ***thinking*** all was safe, attempted to cross the road.

Notes:

A participle is a verbal phrase when it acts as an adjective:

- ★ We live on a ***winding*** road.

Participle may be:

(i) Present participle, which ends in **-ing** and represents an action which is going on or incomplete or imperfect:

★ ***Being*** occupied with important matters, the chief had no time to meet the visitors.

(ii) Past participle, which usually ends in **–ed, -d, -st, -en or –n** and represents a completed action or state of the thing spoken of.

- ★ ***Blinded*** by a dust storm, the army fell into disorder.
- ★ ***Driven*** by hunger, he stole a piece of bread.

Participle is used:

(i) attributively:	A rolling stone gathers no mass.
(ii) predicatively:	The man seemed worried. (modifying the subject man) The receptionist kept the visitor waiting. (modifying the object visitor)
(iii) absolutely with a noun or pronoun going before:	God willing, we shall have another good monsoon. Weather permitting, there will be a picnic tomorrow.

11. Adjectives

Adjective is a word that *tells us more about a noun or a pronoun by describing or modifying* it. It can precede a noun or follow one. It can follow a number of verbs (**is, are, was, were, am, being, been, look, seem, become, stay,** etc.). It can follow pronouns.

An adjective usually answers three questions about a noun or a pronoun:

- ★ What kind of? (**A cheerful** smile),
- ★ How many? (**Two** projects),
- ★ Which one? (**This** car).

1. Kinds of Adjective

Adjectives may be divided into the following classes:

(i) **Adjectives of Quality** (Descriptive adjectives), which show the kind or quality of a person or thing: ***honest*** man, ***large*** city, ***old*** man, **foolish old** crow, etc.

(ii) **Proper Adjectives** which are formed from Proper Nouns. They are always capitalised. All proper nouns can be made or used as proper adjectives: ***Indian*** tea, ***French*** wines, **Indian** tobacco, **Muglai** chicken, **Rajisthani** tea, etc.

(iii) **Adjectives of Quantity,** which show how much of a thing is meant: ***some*** rice, ***enough*** exercise, ***no*** sense, ***little*** intelligence, ***much*** patience, ***enough*** food, ***any*** rice, ***great*** care, ***half*** share, ***sufficient*** rain, ***whole*** sum, etc.

(iv) **Adjectives of Number (Numeral** adjectives), which show how many persons or things are meant or in what order a person or thing stands, ***five*** books, ***several*** mistakes.

Numeral adjectives are of three kinds:

(a) **Definite Numeral Adjectives,** which denote an exact number – **Cardinals** which show how many (**one, two, three,** etc.) and **Ordinals** which show the order of things in a series (**first, second, third,** etc.).

(b) **Indefinite Numeral Adjectives,** which do not denote an exact number **(all, no, many, few, some, any, certain, several, sundry).**

(c) **Distributive Numeral Adjectives** which refer to each one of a number (**each, every, either, neither**).

(v) **Demonstrative Adjectives** point out (demonstrate) which person or thing is meant: ***This*** car, ***That*** car, ***These*** books, ***Those*** books.

Note: These adjectives can also act as demonstrative pronouns. But demonstrative pronouns are not followed by nouns as demonstrative adjectives are.

(vi) **Interrogative Adjectives,** which are used with nouns to ask questions: ***What*** manner? ***Which*** way? ***Whose*** book?

2. Degrees of Comparison

Comparison can be expressed in three ways (called degrees):

Positive (or simple form of modifier) shows no comparison
Comparative (comparing two things)
Superlative (comparing three or more things)

Generally, **-er** and **–est** forms are used with words of one syllable and **more, most** with words of more than one syllable:

Positive	Comparative	Superlative
great	greater	greatest
disgusting	more disgusting	most disgusting

When the positive ends in **-e,** only **–r** and **–st** are added: **fine, finer, finest.**

When the positive ends in **–y,** preceded by a consonant, the **–y** is changed into **–i** and **-er** or **–est** are added: **happy, happier, happiest.**

When the positive is a the word of one syllable and ends in a single consonant, preceded by a vowel this consonant is doubled before adding **–er** and **–est**: **big, bigger, biggest.**

Some adjectives form the comparative and the superlative degrees irregularly i.e. their comparative and superlative are not formed from the positive: **bad, worse, worst.**

The following words have lost their comparative meaning and are used as positive: **former, latter, elder, upper, inner, outer, utter**.

Example: Mohan is my ***elder*** brother.

The following comparatives have no comparative or superlative degrees. They are used as positive adjectives: **interior, exterior, ulterior, major, minor.**

Example: He is still a ***minor***, so he can't be allowed to cast vote.

The following words are used as comparatives, but are followed by **to** instead of **than: inferior, superior, prior, anterior, posterior, senior, junior.**

Exmaple: He is ***junior*** to me.

12. Adverbs

An **adverb** is a word that *describes or modifies a verb, an adjective or another adverb*.

Kinds of Adverb

Adverbs are of three kinds:

1. **Simple adverbs** (Govind reads ***quite*** clearly.)
2. **Interrogative adverbs** (***When*** did you come?)
3. **Relative adverbs** (This is the reason ***why*** I left)

Simple adverbs may be divided into the following classes according to their meanings:

time	**before, immediately, sometimes, daily, late, soon, periodically, lately, suddenly, eventually, never, then, finally, now, today, first, tomorrow, already, formerly, ago, forever, tonight, yesterday, yet, early**.
frequency	**often, again, rarely, frequently, once, seldom, always, twice, never, usually, generally**.

place	**above, down, inside, anywhere, everywhere, outside, away, here, there, within, backward, near, out, up, in, below**.
manner	**badly, fast, stupidly, brilliantly, loudly, gracefully, carefully, cleverly, quietly, vigorously, eagerly, skilfully, well, quickly, easily, slowly, wildly, soundly, clearly, thus, sadly, bravely, calmly, hard, so, agreeably, heavily, slowly**.
degree or quantity	**so** (glad)**, as** (tall as)**, quite** (wrong)**, rather** (busy)**, partly** (night) **so** (quickly)**, too** (quickly)**, very** (quickly)**, quite** (quickly)**, rather** (quickly)**, really** (quickly)**, awfully** (quickly)**, somewhat** (quickly)**, extremely** (quickly)**, amazingly** (quickly)**, fully** (prepared)**, exceedingly**(polite)**, extraordinarily**(smart)**,almost**(right)**, strangely** (enough)**, altogether** (mistaken)**, no better** (things)**, any** (better)**, pretty** (well)**, partly** (right).
affirmation and negation	**surely, certainly, not**
reason	**hence, therefore, so, consequently, wherefore, accordingly**

Interrogative adverb not only modifies some word, but also introduces a question:

★ ***Why*** are you so late?

Relative adverb not only modifies some word, but also refers back to some antecedent. It introduces a subordinate clause:

★ I remember the university ***where*** I had studied.

Comparison of adverbs

Adverbs of manner, degree and time have three degrees of comparison (like adjectives):

Positive (or simple)	Comparative	Superlative
early	earlier	earliest
soon	sooner	soonest
hard	harder	hardest
fast	faster	fastest
rapidly	more rapidly	most rapidly
skillfully	more skillfully	most skillfully

Notes:

1. Adverbs ending in **–ly** form the comparative by adding **more** and superlative by adding **most**.
2. **Some** adverbs **(now, then, where, there, once)** cannot be compared.

Some adverbs form their comparative and superlative degrees irregularly:

Positive	Comparative	Superlative
ill/bad	worse	worst
little	less	least
much/many	more	most
well	better	best
late	later	latest

13. Determiners

***Determiners** are articles, demonstratives, possessives and indefinite adjectives which precede the noun they modify*. They are also called **'fixing'** words which help to identify or limit the nouns or noun phrases which they precede. Determiners determine the **number (one or many), place (this or that), possession (my, our, your) or quantity (some, much, little, few):**

★ ***This*** Institute has ***an*** Ethics Reviewer.

★ ***A*** bonus issue has a positive impact on ***the*** market.

The difference between a determiner and a pronoun is that a determiner precedes the noun it modifies, but a pronoun is used in place of the noun and stands alone.

Kinds of Determiner

Determiners are of two kinds: **Definite** and **Indefinite**.

Definite determiners refer to something specific. These determiners are:

(a) **Definite article: the ('The doctor'-** indicates some particular doctor.)

(b) **Possessive: my, his, your, her, our, their.**

(c) **Demonstrative: this, that, these, those.**

Indefinite determiners refer to the unspecified, abstract and impersonal entities.
Example: **A car** it could be one of a million cars.

Indefinite determiners are:

(a) **Indefinite article: a, an. ('A doctor'** - means any doctor)

(b) **Quantifier: every, most, several, each, any, either, some, few, much, many, little, both, another, more, neither, enough, all.**

(c) **Exclamatory: what, such.**

(d) **Interrogative: which, whose.**

The choice between the articles **a** and **an** is determined by sound. **A** is used before a word beginning with consonant sound: **a** book**, a** house, **a** company, **a** university, **a** union.

An is used before a word beginning with a vowel sound: **an** enemy, **an** umbrella, **an** hour, **an** honest client.

Notes:

1. In **hour** and **honest,** the initial consonant is not pronounced and the word is pronounced with a vowel sound.
2. In **university** and **union, a** is used because these words begin with a vowel, but sound **yu**.

Two determiners are not used together. We do not say: *I will buy the a car.*

Use of definite article 'the'

The definite article **the** is used:

- when we talk of a particular person or thing or one already referred to:
  - ★ **The** book you want is out of print.
- when a singular noun is meant to represent a whole class:
  - ★ **The** rose is **the** sweetest of all flowers.
- before some proper nouns which are place-names:
  - ★ **Oceans and seas:** ***the*** Black Sea, ***the*** Pacific Ocean.
  - ★ **Rivers:** ***the*** Ganga, ***the*** Nile.
  - ★ **Canals:** ***the*** Suez Canal, ***the*** Panama Canal.
  - ★ **Deserts:** ***the*** Sahara desert.
  - ★ **Group of islands*:* *the*** West Indies, ***the*** Bahamas, ***the*** Andaman & Nicobar Islands.
  - ★ **Mountain ranges:** ***the*** Himalayas, ***the*** Andese, ***the*** Alaska, ***the*** K2.
- before the names of communities and nations: ***the*** British***,*** ***the*** Chinese, ***the*** Indian.
- before the names of some books: ***the*** Ramayana, ***the*** Vedas, ***the*** Puranas.
- before the names of things unique of their kind*:* ***the*** sky, ***the*** ocean, ***the*** earth.
- before a proper noun when it is qualified by an adjective or an adjectival phrase: ***the*** great Caesar**,** ***the*** immortal Shakespeare.
- with superlatives: **the** darkest cloud, ***the*** best book.
- with ordinals: ***the*** first man, ***the*** fourth chapter, ***the*** ninth paragraph.

Use of Indefinite Article a/an

The indefinite article is used:

- In its original numerical sense of one: Twelve inches make ***a*** foot.
- in the vague sense of 'certain': ***an*** applicant, ***a*** witness.
- in the sense of any to single out an individual as the representative of a class:
  - ★ **A** patient should follow his doctor's advice.
- to make a common noun of a proper noun:
  - ★ **A** Daniel comes to judgment ('Daniel' means a very wise man).

- in phrases like: **a** few, **a** little, **a** lot.
- to refer to a person known only as a name:
  - ★ **A** Mr Kannan is presiding over the meeting.

Omission of the Article

The article is omitted:

- before names of substances and abstract nouns (i.e. uncountable nouns):
  - ★ Gold is a precious metal.
  - ★ Honesty is the best policy.
- before plural uncountable nouns used in a general sense:
  - ★ Computers are used in many offices.
- before most proper nouns, i.e., names of people, names of continents, countries, cities, etc. and names of individual mountains: Asia, Europe, Nagpur, Mount Everest.
- names of meals used in a general sense:
  - ★ When will you like to have *dinner*?
- before languages: English, Hindi, French.
- before school, college, university, hospital, prison, bed, when these places are visited or used for their primary purpose:
  - ★ We learnt computers at *school.*
  - ★ The patient is still in *hospital.*
  - ★ He stays in *bed* till late in the morning.
- before the names of relations and of cook and nurse:
  - ★ *Father* has returned from tour.
  - ★ *Nurse* has given notice to quit.
- before predicative nouns denoting a unique position:
  - ★ He was elected Chairman of the Board.
- in certain phrases containing a preposition followed by its object: at sunset, by train.

14. Prepositions

Preposition is a word that *shows the relationship between a noun or a pronoun, (which is its object) to another word in the sentence*. The word preposition means 'that which comes before.' Prepositions have nouns or pronouns following them. But sometimes prepositions are put after the subject they govern.

★ Which case are you talking of?

Prepositions tell us where something is **(location – in, on, near, under, inside, outside)**, where something is going **(direction – to, around, towards, through, past, beside)**, when something happens **(time – until, during, till, since, before, at, in, after, past)** and the **relationship** between a noun or a pronoun and another word **(with, by)**.

Compound prepositions are two or more words, working together like a one-word preposition: **according to, ahead of, along with, as far as, as for, as to, aside from, away from, apart from, as per, close to, due to, instead of, because of, but for, by means of, by way of, contrary to, due to, except for, in addition to, in back of, in case of, in front of, in lieu of, in place of, in regard to, in spite of, instead of, on account of, on behalf of, out of, prior to, thanks to, up to, with respect to, with the exception of,** etc.

The prepositions **for, from, in, on,** are omitted before nouns of place or time:

★ Wait (for) a minute.

★ He did it (in) last week.

The following words do not take prepositions after them: **barring, concerning, considering, notwithstanding, order, pending, regarding, respecting, touching.**

Incorrect	Correct
• Considering about the quality, the price is not high. • I have ordered for his dismissal.	• Considering the quality, the price is not high. • I have ordered his dismissal.

Some one-word prepositions are given below:

aboard	*about*	*above*	*across*	*after*	*against*	*along*
alongside	*amid*	*among*	*around*	*as*	*at*	*before*
behind	*below*	*beneath*	*beside*	*besides*	*between*	*beyond*
but	*by*	*concerning*	*despite*	*down*	*during*	*except*
for	*from*	*in*	*inside*	*into*	*like*	*near*
of	*off*	*on*	*onto*		*out*	*outside*
over	*past*	*regarding*	*round*	*throughout*	*since*	*through*
till	*to*	*toward*	*under*	*underneath*	*unlike*	*until*
up	*upon*	*with*	*within*	*without*		

The words **persist, insist, refrain, prohibit, prevent, confident, intent, assist, hinder, expert, fond** require a preposition followed by a gerund:

Incorrect	Correct
He persisted to say this.	He persisted in saying this.

Note: Many words used as prepositions may be used as other parts of speech:

(preposition)	(adverb)
• The closest village is ***over*** that hill. • I told no one ***but*** my boss. • His father arrived soon ***after***. • I have not slept ***since*** yesterday.	• He leaned ***over*** and whispered in her ear. • He is nothing **but** a shadow of his former self. • ***After*** a month, he returned. • I have not seen him ***since***.

15. Conjunctions

Conjunction is a word (or a unit of words) that *connects words, phrases, clauses or sentences*.

★ The scheme opened today, ***but*** no one came forward to subscribe for the plan.

★ God made the country ***and*** man made the town.

Kinds of Conjunction

Conjunctions can be classified into four categories:

1. Coordinating Conjunctions;
2. Correlative Conjunctions;
3. Adverbial Conjunctions;
4. Subordinating Conjunctions.

Coordinating Conjunctions (also, and, but, for, neither, nor, only, either, or, so, still, yet) join words, phrases, (independent) clauses or sentences together. The sentence contains two independent statements or two statements of equal rank or importance. Hence, the coordinating conjunctions join these two statements or clauses of equal rank. For example,

★ We must give of ourselves ***and*** the world will open its arms to us.

Coordinating conjunctions may further be classified as:

(i) **Cumulative conjunction** (and) **adds** one clause to the other.

★ We carved not a line a***nd*** we raised not a stone.

(ii) **Adversative conjunctions** (but, yet, still) **contrast** two statements or bring in an opposing factor to the first statement:

★ Failure is a wonderful teacher, ***but*** one should not wait for it to improve oneself.

★ He was poor, **yet** honest.

(iii) **Alternative conjunctions** (either or, neither, nor) express a choice between two alternatives:

★ ***Either*** he is mad o***r*** he feigns madness.

(iv) **Illative conjunctions** (for, so, therefore) express an inference:

★ Something certainly fell in, ***for*** I heard a splash.

(v) **Compound conjunctions** (in order that, on condition that, even if, so that, provided that, as though, as much as, as well as, as soon as, as if, rather than, except that, excepting that, as long as, as to) take the role of coordinating conjunctions:

★ The notification was published ***in order that*** all might know the new regulations.

Note: Any of the coordinating conjunctions, with the exception of **or, nor,** may be omitted and replaced by a comma, semi-colon or colon:

★ Coming up with ideas is not the difficult bit, implementation is what requires extra effort.

Correlative Conjunctions (both...and, either...or, neither...nor, whether...or, just as... so, not only...but also, though...yet) are used in pairs to join the units or thoughts that have a mutual relationship. But the pair is split up by other words. As with coordinating conjunctions, the units they join should be of the same grammatical class: nouns and nouns, adverbs and adverbs, verbs and verbs, phrases and phrases, clauses and clauses, sentences and sentences.

★ He was driving ***not only*** recklessly, ***but also*** without licence.

★ ***Either*** you go ***or*** I go.

It is incorrect to say: *Their dog is neither quiet nor obeys simple commands*, because the pair of correlative conjunctions (neither....nor) is being used to connect adjective **quiet** to the verb phrase obeys simple commands. The sentence must be reworded to make the grammatical ranks match:

★ Their dog is neither quiet nor obedient,

or

★ Their dog neither stays quiet nor obeys simple commands.

Adverbial Conjunctions/ Conjunctive Adverbs (accordingly, consequently, moreover, hence, however, nevertheless, therefore, furthermore, likewise, additionally, in the same way, similarly) join clauses of equal value.

★ They knew that the story has been lifted from another magazine, ***moreover*** they knew who had written it.

Subordinating Conjunctions introduce subordinate clauses that function like nouns, adjectives or adverbs. These conjunctions are classified according to their meaning:

(i) **Time** (before, after, until, till, since, as soon as, when, whenever, while):

★ No nation can be perfectly governed ***till*** it is competent to govern itself.

(ii) **Cause or reason** (because, as, for)

★ He may enter the club, ***as*** he is a member.

(iii) **Purpose** (so that, so as to, lest, in order that)

★ India must increase exports ***so that*** more foreign exchange could be earned.

(iv) **Result or consequence** (so, so that, such, that)

★ He was ***so*** tired ***that*** he could scarcely stand.

(v) **Condition** (if, unless or, as long as, provided that)

★ Grievances cannot be redressed ***unless*** they are known.

(vi) **Concession** (although, though, even though, but, however, yet, in spite of)

★ A book is a book ***although*** there is nothing in it.

(vii) **Comparison** (as, than, like, as if, as though)

★ America is stronger ***than*** India.

(viii) **Place** (where, wherever)

★ I will find out ***where*** he comes from.

(ix) **Contrast** (although, while, whereas)

★ In China, the Communist Party derives its legitimacy from delivering growth, ***while*** in India, a government derives its legitimacy from having been voted in.

(x) **Preference** (sooner than, rather than)

★ I would take up this project ***rather than*** remain idle without work.

(xi) **Exception** (except, except that, excepting that, but)

★ He'd play today, ***except*** that he's torn a muscle.

16. Some Common Errors

1. Comma Faults

A comma fault occurs when two or more independent clauses are joined by a comma, rather than by a coordinating conjunction or a semi-colon or are not separated by a full stop:

★ Exports are a worry**,** they have fallen twice as fast as imports during the quarter.

Each of the two clauses in this sentence could stand alone as a simple sentence or the two clauses could be separated by a full stop or joined into a compound sentence by a semi-colon or by an appropriate conjunction:

★ Exports are a worry. They have fallen twice as fast as imports during the quarter.

or

★ Exports are a worry**,** they have fallen twice as fast as imports during the quarter.

or

★ Exports are a worry because they have fallen twice as fast as imports during the quarter.

Putting a full stop is the best solution when the ideas are clearly distinct or when there are many commas in either or both the statements. But correcting a comma fault by putting a full stop between two very short and closely connected statements may result in two weak sentences:

★ *I opened the door noisily, he did not move.* (Here it is preferable to join the two clauses by **but** instead of making each clause a separate sentence)

A comma fault may be corrected by substituting a semi-colon for the comma when the ideas expressed in the two clauses are closely related:

★ *The key problem in the sugar industry has been shortage of sugar cane, farmers have shifted to cultivation of other cash crops.* (Here the comma may be substituted by a semi-colon).

A semi-colon should also be used when adverbial conjunction *(accordingly, moreover, however, consequently, therefore)* appear at the junction of two independent clauses:

★ *The electricity went off during the storm, therefore, we could not read or watch television.* (Here a semi-colon may be put in place of the comma).

A comma which abruptly breaks a sentence should be omitted to correct such a fault:

★ *The idea of PSUs was conceptualised at a time when, India hardly had any industrial infrastructure.* (Here the comma after when is unnecessary and should be omitted).

2. Subject and Verb Agreement

Subject and verb agreement means that the subject and the verb in a sentence must be the same (agree) in person (first, second or third) and in number (singular or plural).

Often, by the 'Error of Proximity', a verb is incorrectly made to agree in number with a noun near it, instead of with its subject:

★ *The state of his affairs were such as to cause anxiety to his creditors.* (Here, the verb **were** should be replaced by the verb **is** or **was**, because the subject **state** is singular.)

A compound subject made up of two or more singular and having different qualities of nouns or pronouns joined by 'and' requires a plural verb:

★ **Gold and silver** are precious metals.

But if the nouns suggest one idea to the mind or refer to the same person or thing, the verb is singular:

★ ***Law and order means*** different things to people with different political opinions.
★ ***Bread and butter is*** his only food.
★ ***My friend and benefactor has*** come.

Words joined to a singular subject by- **with**, **as well as, together with, along with, in addition to**, etc. are parenthetical. The verb should, therefore, be put in the singular:

★ Silver, ***as well as*** cotton, ***has*** fallen in price.
★ The ship, ***with its crew, was*** lost.
★ The treasurer, ***along with*** the president, ***was*** held responsible for the mismanagement of the company.

Two or more singular subjects connected by **or** or **nor** require a singular verb:

★ Our happiness ***or*** our sorrow ***is*** largely due to our own actions.

But when one of the subjects joined by **or** or **nor** is plural, the verb must be plural and the plural subject should be placed near the verb:

★ ***Neither*** the Chairman ***nor*** the Directors ***are*** present.

When the subjects joined by **or** or **nor** are different persons, the verb agrees with the nearer:

★ ***Either*** you ***or*** he ***is*** mistaken.

But it is better to avoid these constructions and write: **You are mistaken or else he is.**

Either, neither, each, everyone, many a, must be followed by a singular verb:

★ **Each** of these substances is found in India.

★ **Many** a man does not know his own good deeds.

Two nouns qualified by **each** and **every** even though connected by **and** require a singular verb:

★ **Every** man and every woman is required to attend the rally.

Some nouns which are plural in form but singular in meaning take a singular verb:

★ The ***news is*** true.

★ The ***wages*** of sin ***is*** death.

'Pains' and **'means'** take either the singular or the plural verb, but the construction must be consistent. For example:

★ Great ***pains have been*** taken to accomplish the task.

★ The ***means*** employed by you ***is*** sufficient to complete the task.

But, in the sense of income, **means** always takes a plural verb. For example:

★ My ***means are*** insufficient to cope with the rising prices.

None, though singular, commonly takes a plural verb:

★ None ***are*** so deaf as those who will not hear.

A collective noun takes a singular verb when the collection is thought of as one whole, plural verb when the individuals of which it is composed of are thought of:

★ The Committee **has** issued its report.

★ The Committee **are** divided on one minor point.

But consistency should be maintained. For example:

★ The Committee **has** appended a note to its **(not their)** report.

When the plural noun is a proper name for some single object or some collective unit, it must be followed by a singular verb. For example:

★ The United States **has** a big navy.

Expressions signifying quantity or extent (kilometres, litres, years, rupees) take a singular verb when the amount or time is considered as a unit:

★ Fifty rupees **is** a big sum.

When the amount or time is considered as a number of individual units, a plural verb is used. For example:

★ The last three months have been the coldest in Delhi's history.

In clauses that begin with **one of those who** (or **that**), the verb is plural.

★ He is **one of those men who** never care how they look. (The verb is plural because **who** refers to **men**, not to **one**.)

But, when **the only** precedes **one of those who,** the verb is singular, since **who** refers to a single person or thing. For example:

★ He is ***the only*** one of those leaders who ***supports*** his followers wholeheartedly.

A verb must agree with its subject, not with its complement or its object. For example:

★ The chief trouble (subject) ***was*** the threats that we received from the terrorists during the trip.

★ The threats (subject) that we received during the trip ***were*** our chief trouble.

When the word order is inverted, the verb agrees with its subject and not with some other word. For example:

★ **Is** any ***one*** (subject) of these pictures for sale?

★ **Are** these **pictures** for sale?

Subjects like **series, portion, part, type,** take singular verbs even when modified by a phrase with plural noun. For example:

★ The most interesting ***part of the investigations*** was the discovery and identification of forged documents.

3. Dangling Modifiers, Misplaced Modifiers, Squinting Modifiers, Absolute Modifiers

A Dangling modifier is an adjectival phrase or clause intended to modify a noun or pronoun (called subject of reference), but it is left 'hanging' because it is not related to its subject of reference. For example:

★ **Arriving** at the station, **the sun** came out. (The subject in the sentence is 'sun', but the participle **'Arriving'** does not modify it.)

★ **Entering** the room, **the light** was quite dazzling. (The subject is 'light', but the participle **'Entering'** does not modify it.)

★ After **descending** through the clouds, **Mumbai** lay beneath us. (The subject is 'Mumbai', but the participle **'descending'** does not modify it.)

The error of dangling modifier can be corrected by:

(a) revising the sentence to make the relationship more accurate; or

(b) adding the name of the 'doer' of the action immediately after the phrase; or

(c) changing the phrase into a subordinate clause.

The three sentences given above may be re-written as follows:

★ After arriving at the station, he saw the sun came out.

★ When I entered the room, I found the light quite dazzling.

★ After we descended through the clouds, Mumbai lay beneath us.

A misplaced modifier is a phrase or clause that is not positioned close enough to the word it is supposed to modify. For example:

Incorrect	Correct
• *I was stopped by a policeman without a driver's licence.* • *The dog was chasing the boy with the spiked collar.*	• *Driving without a licence, I was stopped by a policeman.* • *The dog with the spiked collar was chasing the boy.*

A **squinting modifier** is an adverb placed between two verbs and it is often difficult to determine which verb the adverb is supposed to modify. For example:

Incorrect	Correct
• *The stack of chairs he had arranged carefully collapsed in the wind.* (It is not clear whether the stack of chairs was 'arranged carefully' or whether it 'carefully collapsed')	• *The stack of chairs he had carefully arranged collapsed in the wind.*

Absolute modifiers (Impersonal Absolute) are participial or infinitive phrases that modify the statement as a whole and thus do not need a specific reference word in the main clause. These modifiers are complete and independent, their form does not depend on anything else in the sentence:

★ ***Everything considered***, this plan seems best. ('Everything considered' If one considers everything)

4. Parallelism

Parallelism means all units in a sentence or a bulleted list are parallel or identical in grammatical construction and they harmonise with each other. This *means that each item in the sentence or the list has the same grammatical form as all the others*. If the first item is a noun phrase, every other item in the list should be a noun phrase, if one item begins with an infinitive, every other item must begin with an infinitive, if one item begins in an **-ing** verb, every other item must begin in an **–ing** verb, if one item is a complete sentence, all the other items must be complete sentences. Such constructions appeal because they are rhythmic in nature. They also show care and planning in writing:

★ Her skills for the job included researching ***organization*** and writing long reports. (x)

The first sentence has two participles and a noun. A harmonious construction of all three participles must be grouped. For example:

★ Her skills for the new job included **researching, *organising*** and **writing** long reports.(✓)

Similarly, inharmonious construction in the following sentence needs to be removed For example: ★ He is efficient, thorough and ***has a lot of imagination***. (He is efficient, thorough and ***imaginative.***)

5. Logical Comparison

When using comparisons in your writing, make certain that the things being compared are of the same kind and are actually comparable. For example:

Terms not comparable – *Our health benefits are different from our competitor.* (**benefits** and **competitor** are not comparable).

Terms comparable – *Our health benefits are different from the benefits of our competitor.*

Statements involving comparison should be written in full, particularly if any misunderstanding might arise through shortening one of the terms. For example:

Ambiguous	Clearer
• *I owe him less than you.*	• *I owe him less than I owe you (or, I owe him less than you do.)*
• *The houses and shops I saw in Japan were just like any town in America.*	• *The houses and shops I saw in Japan were just like the houses and shops of any town in America.*
• *My duties were much difficult than my brother.*	• *My duties were more difficult than my brother's duties were.*

Double comparisons with **as....as, if....than,** should be filled out in writing. For example:

Incorrect	Correct
He is as tall if not taller than his brother.	*He is as tall as, if not taller than, his brother.*

Since the **if....than** construction tends to interrupt sentence movement, it is better to complete the first comparison and then add the second, dropping **than**. For example:

★ He is as tall as his brother, if not taller.

Other is used when the comparison involves things of the same class, but not when the things being compared belong to two different classes:

★ He is a better speaker than **any other** men in the group.
★ He speaks better than **any (not any other)** lady in the group.

Other is not used with superlative comparisons. For example:

- ★ The ancient India had attained the highest skill in medicine that had up to that time been achieved by **any nation.**

To introduce a prepositional phrase of comparison, 'like' should be used. For example:

- ★ He looks ***like*** his father.
- ★ Bicycle riding, ***like*** golf, can be enjoyed at almost any age.

Avoid substituting **as** for **like** or **such** as in prepositional phrases like this:

- ★ Some writers **like** (not as) Prem Chand take their material from rural India.

Conclusion

The formal study of the rules of grammar is a crucial part of education for children from the initial building years through advanced learning. A common misconception is that knowledge of grammar is unnecessary and that one can learn the skill of language naturally. While it is true that learning and obeying the rules of grammar will not confer excellence to your writing, but ignoring them will probably create doubts on your ability to write well. The primary focus in grammar has been to prevent the dominance of old and outdated rules in favour of more precise, accurate and competitive ones. Therefore, observe the rules of grammar and improve your communication skills which are vital for success in your professional work.

ଔ

Chapter

9

Rules of Punctuation

Introduction

Punctuation is the use of some symbols or marks in writing to separate sentences and their elements, to clarify their meaning and to indicate how words are related to each other. These marks indicate the aspects of intonation and meaning not otherwise conveyed in the written language. They replace hand gestures and voice inflection which a speaker uses to bring variety in speech and emphasise important points. The use of these marks also improves communication and breaks the monotony of the written word.

In written English, punctuation is important to be clear about the comprehension of words. With the help of punctuation marks, we can know pauses within a sentence, identify direct speech from indirect speech and identify question sentences and exclamatory sentences.

The rules of punctuation differ with language register, location and time and keep developing too. There are two major styles of punctuation in English—

a) American or traditional;

b) British or logical punctuation.

Commonly Used Punctuation Marks

1. Full Stop (.)
2. Comma (,)
3. Semi-colon (;)
4. Colon (:)
5. Dash (–)
6. Hyphen (-)
7. Parenthesis ( )
8. Brackets [ ]
9. Question Mark (?)
10. Exclamation Mark (!)
11. Apostrophe (')

12. Quotation Marks (‘ ’)

13. Capitalisation (**A**nt, **B**ee, **E**gg ....)

14. Syllabication (sa-tis-fac-tory)

We will also consider rules for capitalisation and syllabication.

1. Full Stop (.)

Full stop is also known as ‘period’, ‘point’ or ‘stop.’ It separates one sentence from another and marks the end of a sentence. It is the sign which states that a self-contained utterance has been completed. It usually refers to the longest pause that you make in speech.

Uses of Full Stop:

(i) At the end of a sentence that is not an interrogative* or an exclamatory** sentence:

- ★ Necessity is the mother of invention/ innovation.
- ★ We need to create a skilled workforce in the country.

* an interrogative sentence asks a question.

** an exclamatory sentence expresses strong feelings or emotions.

(ii) Sometimes, at the end of a sentence even though it is not complete:

- ★ What was relevant for the towns of Hazaribagh and Rambagh was irrelevant for villages ***and vice versa.***

(iii) After most initials and abbreviations:

a.m. (Ante Meridien)	**p.m. (Post Meridien)**
etc. (et cetra)	**e.g. (exempli gratia)**

Exceptions: (1) The present trend is not to use full stop after initials of the name.

R C Pathak	**S C Nagpal,**

(2) Many people do not use full stop after those abbreviations which are formed by the first and the last letter of the word.

Mr (Mister)	**Mrs (Mistress)**	**Dr (Doctor)**

(3) Acronyms do not have full stops and they are written in all capital letters.

NASA	**AIIMS**

(4) If the last word in a sentence is an abbreviation with a full stop, do not use another full stop to end the sentence:

- ★ Modems incorporate many features such as electronic mail, banking, travel, reservations, *etc.*

2. Comma (,)

Comma gives detail to the structure of sentences and makes their meaning clear by marking off words that either do or do not belong together. It usually refers to the natural breaks and short pauses that you make in speech.

Uses of Comma

(i) To mark off parts of a sentence that are separated by coordinating conjunctions*that join independent clauses** in a compound sentence***:

★ Cabinet notes should not be unwieldy nor annexures should be voluminous.

*A coordinating conjunction is a word that joins two sentences of equal ranks together. These conjunctions are: **and, but, yet, nor, for, so, or.**

**An independent clause is a group of words in a sentence that has a subject and a predicate and it can stand alone as a sentence.

***A compound sentence is made up of two or more independent clauses.

Exception: Comma may be omitted before conjunctions **and, or, nor** in a compound sentence if the coordinate clauses are short and closely related to the thought.

★ Life is short and time is fleeting.
★ He had to finish his job or his boss would be furious.
★ John didn't like Peter nor did I.

(ii) After a dependent clause* that comes at the beginning of a complex sentence**:

★ ***While migration might be good***, we must also look into the causes that propel 'distress migration'.
★ ***When a communication from a Member of Parliament is addressed to the head of an attached office***, it should be replied to by the addressee himself.

*A dependent or subordinate clause is used with the main clause to express a related idea.

**A complex sentence contains an independent clause and one or more dependent clauses.

(iii) To balance parts of a sentence that balance or complement each other:

★ Do not await the approval of the proposed course of action, but put up a draft simultaneously along with the note.

(iv) To separate a relative (adjective) clause that is non-restrictive*:

★ The consultants, *who have wide experience*, are considered experts for such studies.

*A non-restrictive relative (adjective) clause is a group of words which contains a subject and a predicate of its own and does the work of an adjective. It does not define or qualify the subject.

A restrictive relative (adjective) clause does the work of an adjective and defines or qualifies the subject. It is not separated by commas.

★ Those men ***who had worked all day*** were tired.
★ The questions ***that the speaker did not answer*** were the most interesting ones.

(v) In pairs, to separate elements in a sentence that are asides or not part of the main statement and can be removed without any noticeable effect on the meaning:

★ His excuses, ***to say the least,*** were unbelievable.

★ Computers can, ***of course,*** calculate average satisfactory ratings quickly.

(vi) To introduce direct speech:

★ The leader told the audience, ***'I do what I promise.'***

(vii) For clarity when one expression might be mistaken for another:

★ After he broke his ***hand, writing*** was very difficult for him.

(viii) In front of a direct quotation in the middle of a sentence:

★ The Chairman said his bank had gone for sizeable expansion and added, ***'We need people to facilitate the expansion plans.'***

(ix) At the end of a direct quotation that is a statement (not a question or an exclamation) when it comes at the beginning of a sentence:

★ ***'The pugilist was suspended for unsporting behaviour,'*** the Sports Secretary explained.

(x) After adverbs, phrases and subordinate clauses that come at the beginning of a sentence:

★ ***However,*** the hiring may not be in direct proportion to the number of employees retiring.

★ ***At the global level,*** the recession has led to an increase in the barriers to movement of people across borders.

★ ***If the war breaks out,*** no city in the world will be safe.

★ ***As time passes***, everything is forgotten.

(xi) In pairs to set off adverbs (**however, therefore, consequently, too, also**) when it means **'by contrast'** or **'on the other hand'.**

★ ***However,*** a good deal of discretion is left in the hands of area managers.

(xii) To separate each pair of words connected by **and**:

★ ***High and low, rich and poor, wise and foolish*** — all must use their democratic rights.

(xiii) To separate adjectives which define separate attributes of the same noun:

★ Venkatesh is ***efficient, thorough and imaginative*** in his work.

Exception: Omit comma where adjectives work together to create a single image or when the last adjective has a closer relation to the noun:

★ Everyone works to earn one's ***bread and butter***.

★ The Minister welcomed the ***distinguished foreign visitor***.

(xiv) To separate three or more words or phrases in a list or series:

★ We have to create an environment of ***openness, discussion, debate, pluralism and meritocracy***.

Notes:

A comma is not used after the last item in the list or series.

(xv) To mark two or more adverbs or adverb phrases:

Slowly, steadily, uncomplainingly, the engineer worked till the final completion of the project.

(xvi) To indicate the omission of a verb when its repetition is to be avoided:

★ The Chairman gave Mohan a medal, ***to Krishan, a certificate***.

★ You do your work, ***I, mine.***

(xvii) After introductory words, phrases and clauses at the beginning of a sentence:

★ *No*, you are not allowed to leave office before the closing time.

★ *In the name of justice*, please be fair to that poor man.

(xviii) To set off the person you are speaking to:

★ ***Murthy***, I've been expecting you since Monday.

(xix) After greeting and closing in a letter:

★ **Dear Sir,** (greeting)

★ **Yours faithfully,** (closing)

(xx) To separate proper names from titles and degrees:

★ **Ashutosh Banerji, Director.**

★ **Dr Raghu Raman, M Sc, Ph d**

(xxi) In addresses to separate towns, districts and States:

Lucknow, UP **Chennai, Tamil Nadu** **Mumbai, Maharashtra**

(xxii) Between the day and year in a date:

14th August, 2011

Notes: (1) Do not put a comma in a date if it is only the month and year: **August 2011.**

(2) Do not use only a comma to join clauses of a compound sentence without a conjunction:

★ There has been an impressive increase in the number of primary school ***teachers***, ***the*** imbalance in teacher allocation continues to be a major concern.

(The conjunction **but** should be added after the comma)

(3) Do not separate a subject from its predicate:

★ Those with the lowest incomes and no other ***means, should*** get the most support.

(The comma after the word **means** should be removed.)

(4) Do not separate the verb from its object:

★ The artist ***painted,*** a mountain scene of great beauty.

(The comma after the word **painted** should be removed.)

3. Semi-colon (;)

Semi-colon marks a grammatical separation that is stronger in effect than a comma, but less strong than a full stop. Normally, two parts of a sentence divided by a semi-colon balance each other, rather than leading from one to the other.

Uses of Semi-colon

(i) As a stronger division in a series of three or more items in a sentence that already contains commas:

★ Leaving your own home, community network and identity is not the best option for everyone; it is a difficult choice that one accepts for lack of opportunity and unemployment in the place of origin.

(ii) To join the independent clauses of a compound sentence together when you don't use a comma and a conjunction:

★ When I'm on time, no one notices; when I'm late, the whole office knows.

(iii) In front of some conjunctions (**however, therefore, moreover, consequently**, **nevertheless**) that join together two simple sentences into a compound sentence,

★ This training manual is confusing; moreover, it lacks an index and a table of contents.

(iv) To separate a series of loosely related clauses:

★ Today we love what tomorrow we hate; today we seek what tomorrow we shun; today we desire what tomorrow we fear.

4. Colon (:)

Whereas a semi-colon links two balanced statements, a **colon** leads from the first statement to the second. It is a mark of anticipation, directing attention to what follows. Typically, it links a general or introductory statement to an example, a cause to an effect or a premise to a conclusion.

Uses of Colon

(i) To introduce a list or illustrate a point or explain a statement:

★ Make an outline: headline each paragraph, begin each paragraph with a topic sentence and proof-read for spelling and punctuation.

★ Vacation time increases with the length of service: one week the first year, two weeks the second to the fifth year and three weeks thereafter.

★ No one should drink this water: it is dirty.

(ii) To introduce a quotation or speech:

★ The CEO said: 'Striking the balance between operating costs and adequate reserves drives the retail level distribution.'

Note: Quotation marks are not used with a long quotation. Instead, the quotation is indented both sides from the main text.

(iii) To separate two contrast sentences:

★ To err is human: to forgive divine.

★ Prosperity tries the fortunate: adversity, the great.

(iv) To present a conclusion:

★ The aforesaid analysis leads to the conclusion: Do not pay service charges (or any money) to any agency promising a job, without making inquiries about it.

(v) As a substitute for a conjunction:

★ Alas, this equality is a sham: equality is not possible between those imposing the rules and those imposed upon.

(vi) To introduce a question:

★ The essential point is simply this: did the government fulfil their assurances?

(vii) To introduce sub-titles (if there is any) in a book:

★ Managing Across Borders: The Transnational Solution (by Sumantra Ghoshal)

(viii) In formal footnotes and bibliographies:

★ Senge, PM 1990: *The **Fifth Discipline: The Art and Practice of Learning Organization**,* New York Doubleday/Currency.

(ix) After greeting in a business letter (American style):

Dear Sirs:

(x) between the hour and the minutes when you use numbers to express time:

6:30 am, **8:15 pm**

5. Dash (–)

Dash can be used to show more emphasis, add information or create special effects:

★ With our love for record keeping – doubtless a mark of our business society – the origin of everything is known or easily discoverable.

Uses of Dash

(i) Before and after comments, questions, exclamations or other interrupters that you write into a sentence to give information or add extra emphasis:

★ The paper recycling unit – ***located at Nangal Devat in Vasant Kunj*** – will churn out 3000 sheets of recycled paper each day.

(ii) To introduce a list of items:

★ The government is not under any kind of pressure – ***overt, covert or diplomatic.***

(iii) After an interrupted or unfinished statement or thought:

★ I knew it couldn't possibly be Rohan ***and yet*** ------.

6. Hyphen (-)

In print, a **hyphen** is half the length of a dash, but in writing there is little noticeable difference. While dash is used to separate words and groups of words, hyphen is used to link words and parts of words.

Hyphen is used to join two or more words so as to form a single word (often called a compound word): e.g. **free-for-all, multi-ethnic, right-handed, after-care, punch-drunk, tight-rope, air-conditioner, class-conscious, matter-of-fact**, etc. Straightforward noun compound words are now much more often spelled either as two words (e.g. **boiling point, credit card, focus group)** or as one even when it involves a collision of consonants (e.g. **database, earring, breaststroke).** In American English, compound words are written as two words; in British English, these are often written as one word.

A compound word spelled as two words is made into a hyphenated form or a one-word form:

(a) when a verb phrase such as **hold up** or **back up** is made into a noun e.g. **hold-up, back-up.**

(b) when a noun compound is made into a verb, e.g. **a date stamp** becomes ***to date-stamp***; but do not hyphenate a normal phrasal verb, e.g. **continue *to build up* your pension** and not **continue *to build-up* your pension**.

Uses of Hyphen

(i) To join a prefix ending in a vowel such as **co**- and **neo**- to another word:

co-opt, **neo-impressionism**

although one word forms are becoming more usual e.g. **cooperate, neoclassical**.

(ii) To avoid ambiguity by separating a prefix from the main word. For example: to distinguish ***re-cover*** (provide with a new cover) from ***recover*** and ***re-sign*** (sign again) from ***resign***.

(iii) To join a prefix to a name or designation:

anti-Christian **ex-husband** **ex-employee**

(iv) To stand for a common second element in all but the last word of a list:

two-, three- or four-fold.

(v) To clarify meanings in groups of words which might otherwise be unclear or ambiguous:

Twenty-odd people came to the meeting.

(vi) To clarify the meaning of a noun compound, that is normally spelled as separate words, when it is used before a noun:

★ **An up-do-date record** (normally, the words 'up to date' are written as separate words, e.g. **the record is up to date**).

★ **I have a credit-card debt.** (normally, the words 'credit card' are written as separate words e.g. **I have a credit card**)

(vii) When noun compound is two words, hyphenate any verb derived from it:

★ Compound noun **beta test**, but the verb derived from it **to beta-test.**

Notes: (1) Do not insert a hyphen between an adverb ending in –**ly** and adjective qualified by it, even when they come before a noun:

★ **a highly competitive market (✓); a highly - competitive market (×)**

★ **recently published material (✓); recently - published material (×)**

(2) Compound adjectives such as **well known**, when used predicatively, i.e. after a verb, are generally unhyphenated, but when used attributatively as an adjective, i.e. before a noun, they are generally hyphenated:

★ He is not ***well known, but*** is a ***well-known*** writer.

(viii) in two-part numbers from twenty-one to ninety-nine:

thirty-eight, **two-thirds of a box**

Notes: Nowadays hyphens are no longer used for many words.

7. Parenthesis ( )

Parentheses or **round brackets** have curved marks. These are used to give incidental or explanatory information to the reader.

Uses of Parenthesis

(i) To give details and examples:

★ According to rules ***(F.R. 11),*** the whole time of a government servant is at the disposal of the government.

★ The assessment record sheet allows for repeated assessments every twelve weeks ***(assessing fitness more often than this is a waste of time).***

★ If the communication to be despatched by post is important ***(e.g. a notice cancelling a licence or withdrawing an existing facility),*** it should be sent by registered post.

(ii) Around the abbreviations and acronyms of an organization after you have written its full name:

★ The Insurance Regulatory and Development Authority (IRDA) is taking steps to protect the interests of the common man.

★ Jeewan has applied for joining a course on Creative Writing from the Indira Gandhi National Open University (IGNOU*)*.

(iii) To enclose figures or letters used to enumerate points:

★ The alternatives before us are *(1)* reduce the amount of scholarships, *(2)* reduce the amount of book grants, *(3)* reduce the number of scholarships and book grants but retain the amount as proposed and *(4)* retain the number and amount of scholarships as proposed but reduce the amount of book grant.

(iv) To give incidental remarks such as a statement, a question, a direction or an exclamation:

★ He was an efficient and respected official ***(how unfortunate that we have lost him!)*** who did his work with dedication and devotion.

Note: If parentheses are used in the middle of a sentence, do not put full stop or comma at the end of the expression in parentheses, you can use a question mark or an exclamation mark in such a case. But if the parenthetical statement is a separate sentence, the appropriate end punctuation should be placed inside the closing mark.

8. Brackets [ ]

Brackets or **square brackets** are used to insert words which are not intended to be part of sentence but are interjections by editors or authors.

Uses of Brackets

(i) To set off any insertion in quoted material:

★ At a recent academic marketing conference in the U.S., the central question being debated was 'what is stopping Indian retail from modernising [unsaid: into something that we recognise as familiar], when will kiranas die.'

(ii) To enclose the word **sic**. (meaning: thus or so) to mark an error in spelling, usage or fact that appeared in the original:

★ His narration was of a village boy who had been motivated to kill people to become a big man [sic.].

9. Question Mark (?)

A **question mark** is used after a sentence expressing a direct question. It is also used to show that a statement is approximate or doubtful.

Question mark is not used in a question in an indirect speech, which is really a statement about a question.

Uses of Question Mark

(i) After a sentence, expressing a direct question:

★ The manager asked, 'Where have you put all the documents of this case?'

★ Is teaching a serious career?

★ Do we know what outputs do we get from our system like China does?

Exception: No question mark is put at the end of an indirect question:

★ He asked whether it wouldn't be better for society if the migrants could choose to stay home.

(ii) At the end of a sentence which begins with a statement but ends with a question:

- ★ Many development workers who have worked in conflict zones have raised a legitimate question: why poor people are taking to arms and getting themselves killed?
- ★ People generally better their lot by moving, but should they be compelled to do so?

(iii) Immediately after a question that is included with a sentence:

- ★ You think he is making excuses for his failure, don't you?
- ★ This is the best time to launch the new scheme, isn't it?

Note: (1) Don't use a question mark after a polite request that sounds like a question but really isn't:

- ★ Will you please sign your name here?

(2) When a question mark and a quotation mark occur together, the question mark is placed inside the quotation marks, if the quotation is a question. The question mark is put outside the quotation mark, if the whole sentence is a question.

- ★ 'What do you know about VAT?' the trader asked his customer. 'Just imgaine, what happens if all natural energy resources would finish one day?'.

10. Exclamation Mark (!)

An **exclamation mark** is used after an emphatic interjection and after statements that are genuinely exclamatory:

Congratulations, you finished second!

Uses of Exclamation Mark

(i) After strong interjections (special words that show strong feelings or emotions like excitement, happiness, horror, shock, sadness, pain, anger and disgust):

- ★ Oh, no! That's not my proposal!
- ★ You're out of your mind!
- ★ Ah, such are the joys of small victories in the world of air travel!

(ii) After exclamatory sentences:

- ★ I can't stand this place any more!
- ★ How I wished we could win that contest!

(iii) After a strong imperative sentence:

- ★ Sit down and be quiet, you nut!
- ★ Come here! Right now!

11. Apostrophe (’)

An **apostrophe** is used to write contractions and to indicate possessive case of nouns and some indefinite pronouns.

Singular nouns form possessive case by adding **-’s** (e.g. **Amit’s operation, book’s chapters, room’s temperature**). In plural nouns ending in **-s**, the apostrophe is added after **s** (e.g. **lawyers’ agitation, employees’ welfare)** and when a plural noun ends in a letter other than **-s**, by adding **-’s** (e.g. **men’s aspirations, children’s rights**).

Uses of apostrophe

(i) In contractions:

- ★ can’t cannot
- ★ there’s there is
- ★ ma’am madam
- ★ mustn’t must not

(ii) To indicate possessive case of nouns:

- ★ Newspaper’s claim
- ★ people’s misery
- ★ rival’s tactics
- ★ members’ privileges

(iii) To indicate possessive case of some indefinite pronouns:

- ★ someone’s efforts
- ★ anyone’s guess
- ★ nobody’s responsibility

Note: For names ending in **-s**, add **-’s: Charles’s, Dickens’s, Das’s, Thomas’s**

12. Quotation Marks (‘ ’)

Quotation marks or inverted commas in a piece of writing indicate direct speech and material quoted from other sources. Usually double quotation marks are used, single quotation marks (‘ ’) are used when a quotation is written within another quote. Quotation marks, whether double or single, are always used in pairs before and after the quoted material.

Uses of Quotation Marks

(i) To report actual words spoken in speech or conversation:

- ★ The Chairman explained, “We have an individual ethics and compliance reviewer in each department to handle the compliance queries about the department.”
- ★ The mentor said, “You’re good at making models, you’re intelligent, you could easily do it.”

(ii) To set apart material taken directly from another writer or speaker. (Ensure that you follow the exact wording, spelling, grammar and punctuation of the source):

★ As Confucius said: "In a country well governed, poverty is something to be ashamed of. In a country badly governed, wealth is something to be ashamed of."

Notes: (1) When quoted material is short and included in the body of a paragraph, use quotation marks to set it apart.

(2) When the quoted material is relatively long---more than one full sentence from the original source or more than four lines of your writing, indent the material, but not enclose it in quotation marks.

(3) When quoted material appears with a quotation, use single quotation marks to show such quoted material.

(4) Place commas and full stops inside the quotation marks and semi-colons and colons outside the quotation marks.

(5) Place question marks, exclamation marks and dashes inside the final quotation mark when they apply to the quotation only. These marks should be placed outside the final quotation marks when they apply to the entire statement.

13. Capitalisation

Capitalisation means to begin a word with a capital letter.

Some rules for capitalisation are given below:

(1) The first letter in a sentence is capitalised:

★ ***The*** committee recommended that the system of proxy voting should be discontinued.

(2) The first person singular pronoun **I** is always capitalised.

(3) A proper noun begins with a capital letter: **Subhash, Pankaj, Reena**

(4) A proper adjective begins with a capital letter: ***Indian*** **diplomat,** ***British*** **symphony**.

(5) Titles that show the rank or position of people, when used with their names, begin with a capital letter: **Captain Ganesh**

(6) When a person's title is used in place of his name, the first letter of the title is a capital letter:

★ Congratulations **Commande**r, we have touched the shore!

Note: Do not capitalise a title used without a person's name unless you are addressing the person directly.

(7) All the words in the salutation in a letter should begin with a capital letter:

★ **D**ear **M**ehta, **M**y Dear **R**amesh, **D**ear **S**ir

(8) The first word in the closing of a letter should begin with a capital letter:

★ **W**ith warm regards

(9) The first word in the superscription of a letter should begin with a capital letter:

★ **Y**ours faithfully, **Y**ours sincerely, **T**ruly yours

(10) The days of the week and the names of months should start with a capital letter:

★ **M**onday, **M**ay

(11) The names of important festivals and of national holidays begin with a capital letter:

★ **D**iwali, **C**hristmas, **I**dul-Fitr, **I**ndependence Day, **R**epublic Day

(12) The names of religions, religious groups and political parties should begin with a capital letter:

★ **H**induism, **I**slam, **C**hristianity, **S**ikhism, **I**ndian **N**ational **C**ongress, **C**ommunist **P**arty of **I**ndia, **B**hartiya **J**anta **P**arty.

(13) The words in titles awarded are capitalised:

★ **B**harat **R**atna, **A**shok **C**hakra, **P**adma **V**ibhushan.

(14) The first, last and all the main words in the title of books, movies, poems, songs, plays, magazines, newspapers, essays or television shows begin with a capital letter:

★ **T**he **T**imes of **I**ndia, **T**he **N**ational **G**eographic, **A** **T**rip to the **M**oon.

Note*:* Main words generally means every word except short prepositions, coordinating conjunctions *(***an, but, for, nor or, so, yet)** *or* articles **the, a, an**.

(15) The first letter of a word referring to a family member, when the word stands alone in a sentence without a possessive pronoun or when it is followed by person's name is capitalised:

★ **U**ncle **G**anesh, **A**unt **J**ane.

14. Syllabication (Word-division)

Sometimes it becomes necessary to divide or 'break' a word when the line on the page has run out of space. Such word division is permissible if two conditions are met: (i) the word must be divisible and (ii) the division is at the right place.

Guidelines for Word-division

(1) Avoid dividing the words at the end of more than two or three successive lines. Also, avoid dividing a word at the end of a page or the last word in a paragraph.

(2) When a word is divided, there should be more than one letter on the first line and more than two letters with the last part of the word. For example: re-duced, mili-taries

(3) Each part of the divided word must contain a vowel. For example: **col-leagues, vio-lence**

(4) When a word is divided, a hyphen is attached to its first part, so that the hyphen is at the end of the line. For example:

★ The management decided to take disciplinary action when some absents refused to apologize.

(5) Some words are never divisible. Such words are:

★ one syllable word, e.g., ca**tch, strange, through**

★ contractions, e.g.**; can't, won't, you've**

★ abbreviations, e.g., **NDMA, PURA, Asst., Est.**

★ numbers written as numerals, e.g., **2011, 8,000, 8.30, 0.239**

(6) The correct places for dividing a word are:

★ after a prefix, e.g. **post-pone, pre-pay, un-veil, ir-relevant,**

★ before a suffix that has more than two letters, e.g., **produc-ing, climb-ing**

★ between the main parts of a closed compound, e.g., **inter-national**

★ at the hyphen of a compound, e.g., **over-crowded, self-assessment, part-time**

★ after double consonants if the root word ends in double consonant, e.g., **add-ress-ing, pass-ing, tell-ing**

★ between two consonants, if the final consonant is preceded by a vowel, e.g., **win-ning, mes-sage, plan-ning, min-utes, hun-dred**

(7) It is incorrect to divide a word in the following cases:

★ before a two-letter suffix, e.g. **serious-ly, odd-ly**

★ after the first syllable if it has only one letter, e.g., **a-tomic, a-mend**

★ before the last syllable if it has only one letter, e.g., **mafi-a**

Note: When dividing a word at the end of a line, use a dictionary to check the proper division of the word.

Conclusion

Punctuation helps put spoken words into writing. It facilitates the right kind of expression into writing for which voice intonation, pauses, volume and tone are used while speaking. Appropriate use of punctuation shows that a person has good knowledge of grammar.

Punctuation helps in presenting your ideas clearly and accurately. Writing without punctuation is like a speaker talking in monotone. No audience likes such a speaker. So, good speakers use hand gestures and voice inflection to help their listeners and make their talk interesting. Punctuation marks in writing replace those hand gestures and voice inflection. Use of these marks will make your writing more interesting. You will also be able to bring variety, make your sentences clearer and put emphasis at the right place.

It is very important to know all the punctuation marks, their meaning and significance in order to produce a good piece of writing and more significantly, to convey the correct message.

Chapter

10

Essentials of Effective Correspondence

As an employee goes up in the hierarchy of his career, he has to spend more and more of his time in handling correspondence. It is, therefore, well understood that the success of any organization would largely depend upon its correspondence. Thus, it is obligatory for an executive to learn and master the art of writing effective letters.

The characteristics of effective correspondence are—

- **Simplicity:** It is the polite, personal touch that proves to be more effective rather than the stiff, detached style generally associated with business correspondence.

For example,

Typical expression	Suggested expression
• '....subsequent to your perusal of the documents.'	'....after you have examined the documents.'
• 'we would ask you to be good enough to...'	• 'will you please...'

- **Conversational Style:** Modern executives prefer to use friendly and conversational style rather than stilted, stiff and dull style of correspondence.

Stiff	Conversational
• Thanking you in advance	• I/we sincerely appreciate
• Kindly advise/inform at an early convenient date	• Please let me know soon

- **Clarity of Goal:** The writer's primary goal is to be clear about the information sought or given. Therefore, he must have all the facts and figures about the information. There is no room for ostentatious and ambiguous language in business correspondence.

- **Public Relations Aspect:** Business English has serious concern with the image of the organization in the market. Everybody forms an image about the company through many artefacts and business correspondence is an important factor among them. Letters have the quality of permanence and most of them are kept in files for future reference.

- **Your Attitude:** It is very important that the writer's interest in the receiver is reflected in business correspondence. Correspondence experts, therefore, advise a shift from 'I' and 'we' to 'you' and 'your'.

We Attitude	You Attitude
• We have received your letter on June 20.	• Thank you for your letter of June 20.
• I am happy to report...	• You will be happy to learn...

- **Courtesy:** This involves writing directly to the reader by using expressions like:

  '...as you will agree, Mr. Subhash'

  '...we wish you the best in your endeavour'

- **Sincerity:** This implies that the readers must believe in what is said. The writer should not sound insincere through words of questionable value.

- **Due Emphasis:** An effective letter would highlight the significant point by diligently positioning them in sentences and paragraphs. More significant points are given more space in the body of the letter.

  Emphasis by sentence structure would come in a different way. Short and simple sentences are more emphatic than long ones.

- **Coherence:** Linking words like 'besides', 'therefore', 'likewise' and 'however' and the pronouns like 'this', 'that' and 'there', provide a logical progression to the thought content of the writer. A forceful thrust is achieved by repetition of keywords.

- **Care for Culture:** For international correspondence, the choice of words should be appropriate all the more, to avoid any miscommunication and offend the receiver. The writer should avoid culturally derived words, colloquialisms and slang. Even idioms and phrases should be avoided. Therefore, one must correspond in simple words having universal acceptance.

- **Ethical Standard:** All effective correspondence should uphold a specific ethical standard. The writer, on behalf of the organization, should be clear about the legitimate goals. Persuasion and tact does not imply to be indifferent to ethics. It should reflect in every letter, depending upon the sincerity of our feelings, concern for the receiver and image of the organization.

Chapter

11

Enrich Your Writing

Introduction

English has always been a language open to enrichment from other languages. The adaptation of borrowed vocabulary to the native pattern is a lengthy historical process. We have already dealt with the morphemes and words introduced in the more distant past. Hence, we now turn to a few more decent imports from different languages.

One good sign of foreignness is the preservation of original source–orthography, which is in some way different from the familiar spelling conventions in English. Having a word spelled with an accent mark letters or letter sequences immediately signals that there is something different about the word.

Another possible criterion for 'foreignness' is semantic novelty. Recently borrowed words cover notions that originate elsewhere; they often evoke associations with a specialised field, particular culture, with social phenomenon or customs outside the English-speaking world.

By adopting these words in English, particularly business English, we enrich both our vocabulary and our knowledge of foreign traditions, practices and views.

Foreign words and phrases are often used in speech and writing. Many such terms have become familiar and well-established, but all readers may not be comfortable with them. If such terms are used in writing, they should preferably be set in italics to draw the reader's attention. Also consult a good dictionary to ensure their correct usage and pronunciation.

Some foreign words and phrases commonly used are given below:

FOREIGN TERM	***MEANING***
ab initio	*from the beginning*
ad hoc	*for a particular purpose*
ad infinitum	*endlessly, forever*
ad interim	*for the meantime*
ad nauseam	*to an excessive degree*
ad valorem	*according to value*
aide-de-camp	*a military officer acting as assistant to a senior officer*

conted...

aide memoire	*an aid to memory, diplomatic memorandum*
alter ego	*an intimate friend*
amicus curie	*an impartial advisor to a court of law*
apologia	*an apologetic writing, a formal written defence of one's opinion or conduct*
a priori	*based on theoretical deduction rather than empirical observation*
apropos	*with reference to*
avant-garde	*new, experimental*
bête noire	*a person or thing one particularly dislikes*
bona fides	*in good faith, honesty and sincerity of intention*
carte blanche	*complete freedom to act as one wishes or thinks best*
cause célèbre	*a controversial issue that attracts a great deal of public attention*
contretemps	*a minor dispute or disagreement*
cul-de-sac	*a street or passage closed at one end*
de facto	*holding a position in fact, whether legally or not*
de jure	*by right, in law*
de rigueur	*required by etiquette or current fashion*
detente	*easing of hostility or trained relations between countries*
élan	*energy, style, enthusiasm*
enfant terrible	*a person who behaves in an unconventional or controversial way*
en masse	*all together, in a body*
en route	*on the way*
entente	*friendly understanding, informal alliance between states or factions*
espirit de corps	*a feeling of pride or mutual loyalty within a group*
exempli gratia (e.g.)	*for instance, as an example*
ex officio	*by virtue of one's office*
ex parte	*on one side only*
ex post facto	*with retrospective effect*
faux	*artificial, not genuine*
faux pas	*a social blunder*
hoi polloi	*the common people (derogatory)*
honoris causa	*degree awarded as a mark of esteem*
ibidem (ibid)	*in the same source (referring to previously cited work*
idem	*to indicate an author or work that has been just mentioned*
impasse	*deadlock, insoluble difficulty*
impromptu	*unplanned, unrehearsed*
in camera	*in the private room*
incognito	*concealing one's identity*
in extenso	*in full*

conted...

infra dignitatem (infradig)	*demeaning, below one's dignity*
in limine	*in the beginning*
in re	*with regard to, in the case of*
in situ	*in the original position*
inter alia	*among other things*
inter se	*among themselves*
in toto	*in the whole, entirely*
ipso facto	*by that very fact or act*
laissez faire	*a policy of non-interference, especially abstention by governments in the workings of free markets*
lingua franca	*a common language*
locus standi	*right to appear in a court*
magnum opus	*a great work of art/literature*
mala fides	*in bad faith, intent to deceive*
mea culpa	*an acknowledgement of own fault or error (exclamatory)*
memoralia	*things worth remembering*
mon ami	*my friend*
modus operandi	*mode of operating*
mutatis mutandis	*with necessary alterations*
née	*a married woman's maiden name originally called*
nom de plume	*an assumed name*
non sequitur	*conclusion or statement which does not follow from the previous argument*
nouveau riche	*people who have recently acquired wealth*
obiter dictum	*something said by the way, an incidental remark*
par excellence	*better than all others of the same kind*
pari passu	*side by side, together, equally or equivalently*
per annum	*for each year*
per capita	*for each person*
per diem	*daily, per day*
per se	*by itself*
persona non grata	*a person who is not acceptable*
piece de resistance	*the most remarkable or important feature of a creative work*
prima facie	*on the first view*
pro bono	*legal work undertaken without charge*
pro forma	*according to form*
pronto	*promptly, suddenly, immediately*
pro rata	*in proportion*

conted...

pro tempore	*for the time being*
quid pro quo	*a favour or advantage in return for something*
raison d'être	*important reason or purpose for something*
re	*about, concerning*
résumé	*curriculum vitae, summary*
sanctum sanctorum	*holy of holies*
sangfroid	*coolness or composure under trying circumstances*
sine die	*without a definite day, for an uncertain period*
sine qua non	*absolutely essential*
status quo	*existing state of affairs*
status quo ante	*previous state of affairs*
sub judice	*under judicial consideration*
sub poena	*a writ ordering a person to attend a court*
tete- a- tete	*private conversation between two people*
tour de force	*a feat of strength or skill*
ultimatum	*a final demand of terms*
ultimo	*(dated) of the last month*
ultra vires	*beyond one's legal power*
verbatim	*word for word*
versus	*(v) against, as opposed*
via	*by way of, en route*
via media	*a compromise, a middle course*
vice	*in place of, a substitute for*
vice versa	*the order being reversed, the terms being exchanged*
vide	*see, consult*
vis-a-vis	*as compared with, in relation to*
viva voce	*oral examination*
viz.	*namely, in other words*
voila	*behold, there it is*

Conclusion

Foreign words and phrases are sometimes used to emphasise some point and also to enrich the language used in the writing. Many of these terms have become familiar and well-established in English usage and, therefore, it is not necessary to put them in bold face or italics. But such of the terms that are likely to be unfamiliar to readers should be set in italics or bold face. While occasional use of these terms will be acceptable, frequent use of these terms in the same piece of writing will make the writing unfriendly and should be avoided.

Chapter

12

Speed up Your Writing

Introduction

Abbreviations, acronyms and initials are shortened forms of words. Their use in formal writing is generally avoided. But these are often used to speed up writing.

Abbreviations save space and prevent the distraction of needlessly repeated sentences or words. However, the space saved is so small that the use of abbreviations is basically determined by custom, convenience to the reader and also the appearance of the printed page. There may be numerous variations in the use of abbreviations. Therefore, a good dictionary should be consulted for more thorough guidance on the spelling, capitalisation and punctuation of a specific abbreviation.

1. Abbreviations

Some guidelines for a few types of abbreviations are given below:

Courtesy titles **Dr, Mr, Mrs, Messers** (M/S) are always abbreviated when used with proper names. The courtesy title **Ms**. Is equivalent to Mr. in addressing a woman with regard to her marital status.

Academic degrees are generally abbreviated: **MA., PhD., MD., MS.**

If a government agency or some other organization is known primarily by its initials (or some other shortened name), use familiar abbreviation rather that the full name: **CBI, SBI, BCCI, NIA.**

In ordinary writing, most expressions of time, weight and size are written out: **in a minute** (*not* in a min.), **after one hour** (*not* after one hr.), **a half inch** (not ½ inch or ½').

Note: These units are abbreviated in directions, references and technical writing when they are used with figures: **12 kg., 16 ft.**

Measurements expressed in technical terms are abbreviated when they are used with figures: **18 kmp** (kilometre per hour), **40 rpm** (revolutions per minute).

When an abbreviation is composed of initials, all the initials are capitalised:

- ★ **CBDT** – Central Board of Direct Taxes
- ★ **CMD** – Chairman and Managing Director
- ★ **MBA** – Master of Business Administration
- ★ **IIT** – Indian Institute of Technology

When a lowercased term is abbreviated, the abbreviation is usually lowercased:

- ★ **establishment - est.**
- ★ **assistant - asst.**
- ★ **et cetra - etc.**

An abbreviation that ends in a lowercase letter is no longer followed by a full stop:

- ★ **Captain – Capt**
- ★ **Professor – Prof**
- ★ **Miscellaneous – Misc**

If an unfamiliar expression or the name of an organization, institution etc. is to be used repeatedly, its full name and abbreviation should appear together, the full name first followed by the abbreviation in the parentheses, thereafter, in the text, only the abbreviation may be used:

- ★ Employees Provident Fund Organization **(EPFO)**
- ★ Reserve Bank of India **(RBI)**

If the last word in a sentence is an abbreviation with a full stop, do not use full stop to end the sentence:

- ★ The function ended with cultural programmes, sports, etc.

Some abbreviations commonly used are given below:

ab init	*from the beginning*
a/c	*account, air conditioner*
AC/DC	*alternating /direct current*
ad, advt	*advertisement*
Adj	*Adjective, Adjutant General*
Admn	*Administration*
anon	*Anonymous*
Apt	*Apartment*
assoc	*Association, associate*
Asst	*Assistant*
Aug	*August*
Ave	*Avenue*
bldg	*Building*
Capt	*Captain*
cf	*Compare with*
chap	*chapter*
cm	*Centimetre*
Co	*Company*
Col	*Colonel*
Cpl	*Corporal*
Comdr	*Commander*

contd...

Contd	*Continued*
Dept	*Department*
Do	*Ditto (the same)*
Doz	*Dozen*
ed	*Editor, edition, edited by*
EQ	*Emotional Quotient*
E-mail	*Electronic mailing*
esp	*especially*
et.seq	*and the following*
fig	*figure*
Gen	*General*
Gov	*Governor*
Hon	*Honorable (the word will be spelled out if preceded by the)*
Inc	*Incorporated*
in	*inch*
incl	*inclusive, including, includes*
inf	*information*
jr	*junior*
Kg	*Kilogramme*
kl	*Kilolitre*
km	*Kilometre*
kmp	*Kilometre per hour*
lab	*Laboratory*
lb	*Pound*
Lat	*Latitude*
Long	*Longitude*
Ltd	*Limited*
Maj	*Major*
misc	*miscellaneous*
ml	*millilitre*
msgs	*messages*
Mt	*mountain*
No	*number*
oz	*ounce*
pg or pps	*page, pages*
Pres	*President*
Prof	*Professor*

contd...

pt	*part, pint, point, print*
PTO	*Please Turn Over*
Pvt	*Private*
Rd	*Road*
Rev	*Reverend (the word will be spelled out if preceded by the)*
sec	*section*
Sgt	*Sergeant*
Sr	*Senior, Sister*
St	*Street, Saint*
Subj	*subject*
Supdt	*Super indent*
Univ	*university*
Vol	*Volume*
Vs or v	*Versus, opposing*
wrt	*with reference to*
yd or yds	*yard, yards*

2. Acronyms

An abbreviation that is pronounced as a word is called an **acronym**. It is formed from the initial letters of other words. It does not have a full stop and it is generally written in all capital letters.

Some common acronyms area given below:

AIDS	*Acquired Immune Deficiency Syndrome*
AIIMS	*All India Institute of Medical Sciences*
APEC	*Asia Pacific Economic Cooperation*
ARPANET	*Advanced Research Project Agency Network*
APEDA	*Agriculture and Processed Food Products Export Development Authority*
ASEAN	*Association of South East Asian Nations*
ASSOCHAM	*Association of Chambers of Commerce & Industry in India*
AUM	*Assets Under Management*
AWACS	*Airborne Warning and Control System*
AWOL	*Absent Without Leave*
BASIC	*Brazil, South Africa, India, China – a group of nations formed in 2010 for negotiating climate change*
BIMSTEC	*Bangladesh, India, Myanmar, Sri Lanka, Thailand Economic Cooperation*
BRICS	*Brazil, Russia. India, China, South Africa – a group of nations formed in 2002*
CAPART	*Council for Advancement of People's Action and Rural Technology*
CAT	*Central Administrative Tribunal/Common Admission Test*

contd...

CATE	*Combined Aptitude Test in English*
CIBIL	*Credit Information Bureau of India limited*
COFEPOSA	*Conservation of Foreign Exchange and Prevention of Smuggling Activities Act*
COPRA	*Consumer Protection Act*
CRISIL	*Credit Rating information Services of India Limited*
FIICI	*Federation of Indian Chambers of Commerce & Industry*
GAAP	*Generally Accepted Accounting Practices*
GATE	*Graduate Aptitude Test in Engineering*
GMAT	*Graduate Management Aptitude Test*
HUDCO	*Housing and Urban Development Corporation*
INMAS	*Institute of Nuclear Medicine and Applied Sciences*
IRDA	*Insurance Regulatory and Development Authority*
IBSA	*India. Brazil, South Africa – a group of nations formed in 2003 for emerging Economies*
ICRA	*Investment Information and Credit Agency of India*
ICRISAT	*International Crop Research Institute for Semi Arid Topics*
IIT	*Indian Institute of Technology*
IRDA	*Insurance Regulatory and Development Authority*
ISRO	*Indian Space Research Organization*
LASER	*Light Amplification by Stimulated Emission of Radiation*
MAT	*Management Aptitude Test*
NAC	*National Advisory Council*
NASA	*National Aeronautics and Space Administration/National Academy of Statistical Administration*
NEERI	*National Environmental Engineering Research Institute*
OPEC	*Organization of Petroleum Exporting Countries*
OPERA	*Oscillation Project with Emulsion Tracking Project*
PAN	*Permanent Account Number*
PAR	*Performance Appraisal Report*
PETA	*People for Ethical Treatment of Animals*
PURA	*Provision of Urban Amenities in Rural Areas*
PIN	*Personal/Postal Identification Number*
RADAR	*Radio Detecting and Ranging*
SAARC	*South Asian Association for Regional cooperation*
SCUBA	*Self-contained Underwater Breathing Apparatus*
SEBI	*Securities and Exchange Board of India*
SAT	*Scholastic Aptitude Test*
SEWA	*Self Employed Women's Association*
SIMRAN	*Satellite Imaging for Rail Navigation*
SNAFU	*Situation Normal, All Fouled Up*

contd...

SONAR	*Sound Navigation Ranging*
SWAT	*Special Weapons Action Team or, Special Weapons and Tactics*
TOEFL	*Test of English as a Foreign Language*
UNESCO	*United Nations Education, Scientific and Cultural Organization*
UNICEF	*United Nations International Children's Education Fund*
VAT	*Value Added Tax*

3. Initials

Initials are a kind of abbreviation that is formed by taking the first letter of a name or a word. These are used in place of the whole name or word. Some common initials are given below:

AD	*Anno Domini (any year from 1 on)*
ADB	*Asian Development Bank*
AM or am	*ante meridian (the time from midnight to noon)*
APM	*Administered Price Mechanism*
ASAP	*As soon as possible*
ASLV	*Augmented Satellite Launch Vehicle*
ATM	*Automated Teller Machine*
ATR	*Action Taken Report*
BIFR	*Board of Industrial and Financial Reconstruction*
BIS	*Bureau of Indian Standards*
BOLT	*Build-Operate-Lease-Transfer*
BOT	*Build-Operate-Transfer*
B2B	*Business to Business*
B2C	*Business to Consumer*
CBDT	*Central Board of Direct Taxes*
CBEC	*Central Board of Excise and Custom*
CEO	*Chief Executive Officer*
CERN	*European Centre for Nuclear Research*
CII	*Confederation of Indian Industry*
C-in-C	*Commander in Chief*
CMD	*Chairman and Managing Director*
COD	*Collect (or cash) on Delivery when the package arrives*
E&OE	*Errors and Omission excepted*
EPFO	*Employees Provident Fund Organization*
EQ	*Emotional Quotient*
FAQ	*Frequently Asked Questions*
FCNRA	*Foreign Currency Non-Resident Account*
FCRA	*Foreign Contribution Regulation Act*

contd...

FDI	*Foreign Direct Investment*
FII	*Foreign Institutional Investors*
FM	*Frequency Modulation*
FMCG	*Fast Moving Consumer Goods*
FPB	*Food Products Order*
FSDC	*Financial Stability and Development Council*
GDP	*Gross Domestic Product*
GIS	*Geographical Information System*
GOI	*Government of India*
GPS	*Global Positioning System*
GRE	*Graduate Record Examination*
GST	*Goods and Service Tax*
HNWI	*High Net Worth Individuals*
HQs	*Headquarters*
IASB	*International Accounting Standards Board*
IELTS	*International English Language Testing System*
IMF	*International Monetary Fund*
IPO	*Initial Public Offering*
IPR	*Intellectual Property Right*
IQ	*Intelegence Quotient*
ISBN	*International Standard Book Number*
ISO	*International Standard Organization*
IVRS	*Integrated Voice Response System*
JNNURM	*Jawaharlal Nehru National Urban Renewable Mission*
NDMA	*National Disaster Management Authority*
NMIZ	*National Manufacturing Industrial Zones*
NREGA	*National Rural Employment Guarantee Act*
NTRO	*National Technical Research Organization*
OECD	*Organization for Economic Cooperation and Development*
PDS	*Public Distribution System*
PFRDA	*Pension Fund Regulatory and Development Authority*
PIL	*Public Interest Litigation*
PM or pm	*Post Meridian (noon to midnight)*
PNR	*Passenger Name Recorder*
PPP	*Public Private Partnership*
PTO	*Please Turn Over*
POW	*Prisoner of War*
PS	*Postscript (a note written after the close of a letter)/ Police Station*
RAC	*Reservation against Cancellation*

contd...

RSBY	*Rashtriya Swasthya Bima Yojna*
RSVP	*Please Respond (often put on invitations)*
RTE	*Right to Education*
RTI	*Right to Information*
SEZ	*Special Economic Zone*
SMS	*Short Message Service*
TDSAT	*Telecom Disputes Settlement and Appellate Tribunal*
TRAI	*Telecom Regulatory Authority of India*
UFO	*Unidentified Flying Object*
UIDAI	*Unique Identification Authority of India*
UNO	*United Nations Organization*
UNEP	*United Nations Environment Programme*
VIP	*Very Important Person*
WHO	*World Health Organization*
WPI	*Wholesale Price Index*
WTO	*World Trade Organization*
TDS	*Tax Deducted at Source*

There are some terms (generally indicated by their abbraviations) that find widespread application in business and commercial transaction, especially those related to movement of goods, construction, executioin of projects, etc.

The words and phrases which have evolved over 10 years are regonised and accepted by all countries.

Some such frequently used terms are furnished below with a view to facilitate the work of those engaged in using English for business and commercial purposes:

FOR	*Free on rail*
FOB	*Free on board*
FCA	*Free carrier and delivery upto the place of the buyer*
FAS	*Free along side to ship are the part of shipment to the buyer*
Ex Works	*Delivery of the goods at the works or factory of the seller*
CFR	*Cost and freight*
CIF	*Cost insurance and freight*
JV	*Joint venture*
OEM	*Original equipment manufacturer*
B/L	*Bill of lading*
R/R	*Railway receipt*

contd...

C/N	Consignment note
DAF	Delivery at the frontier
LC	Letter of credit
BE	Bill of exchange

The use of these terms is necessary for determining as welll as assigning the responsibilities of the parties in an agreement or contract so as to avoid disputes during and subsequent to the execution of a business deal since a variety of expected and unexpected factors is involved.

Conclusion

Although in formal writing, abbreviations and initials are generally not used, but acronyms are commonly used. Even otherwise, abbreviations, acronyms and initials are often used to speed up writing, they help in quick reading and, therefore, they do have an important place in the vocabulary of writers.

The rapid advancement of information technology in recent times seems to be the driving force for the usage, as new inventions and concepts with multiword names create a demand for shorter and manageable names.

Acronyms are a crucial and most evolutionary area of the lexicon of many languages.

ଔ

Chapter 13

Ensure Correct Spellings in Writing

Introduction

An essential element of effective writing is that whatever you write must have correct spellings. If you do so, you will show that you care for your readers and for your writing. You will fulfil the expectations of your readers that you follow the conventions of spelling. You will also ensure that your readers understand your writing in the way you want them to. They will not be confused and will not be searching for meaning of what you actually wanted to convey.

Spelling is not simple but understanding its structure makes it easy to decode and does not remain limited to people 'born to spell' to grasp it. Learning to spell helps cement the connection between the letters and their sounds.

With a view to ensuring that your spellings are correct, you should:

(a) learn the spellings of difficult words, look at each such word carefully, notice each syllable and try to fix it in your mind.

(b) use dictionary when in doubt about the spellings of a word.

(c) proof-read carefully, word-by-word, what you have written, you may read each word aloud, pronouncing each word distinctly.

(d) follow some rules of spellings as a guide for correct spellings (of course, there are some exceptions to these rules also!).

Rules of spellings

Plurals of Nouns

Regular plurals are formed by the addition of **–s** and in the case of nouns ending in **–s, -x, -ch or –sh**, by the addition of **–es**:

pens	pens
friend	friends
glass	glasses
rich	riches

book	books
patient	patients
box	boxes
nourish	nourishes

Nouns ending in –**y** following a vowel, form plural by adding **–s:**

ray	rays
boy	boys

toy	toys
play	plays

Nouns ending in –**y** preceded by a consonant, change –**y** to –**i** and add –**es**:

cry	cries
jury	juries

lady	ladies
diary	diaries

Exception: In proper nouns, if **–y** is preceded by a consonant, -**y** is retained and **-s** is added to make plurals:

Shelly	Shellys

Sawhny	Sawhnys

Nouns ending in **–o** preceded by a vowel, form the plural by adding **–s**:

studio	studios
radio	radios

folio	folios
tattoo	tattoos

Exceptions:

cello	cellos
photo	photos

piano	pianos
eskimo	eskimos

If final **–o** is preceded by a consonant, plural is usually formed by adding **–es:**

echo	echoes
hero	heroes

veto	vetoes
embargo	embargoes

In some nouns ending with **–o**, plural is formed by adding –**s** or **–es:**

cargo	cargos, cargoes

zero	zeros, zeroes

Some nouns ending in **–f** or –**fe**, often form plurals by adding **–s**:

belief	beliefs

chief	chiefs

Maximum nouns ending in **–f**, form their plurals by changing **–f** to –**ves:**

half	halves
knife	knives

leaf	leaves
thief	thieves

Exception: In some nouns ending in **–f**, plurals are formed by changing **-f** to **–s** or –**ves**:

elf	elfs, elves
hoof	hoofs, hooves

scarfs	scarfs, scarves
wharf	wharfs, wharves

Some more principles of spelling are discussed below: **Final –e**

(a) In words ending in silent **–e**, drop the –e when **–y** or a suffix beginning with a vowel is added:

argue+ing arguing	value+able valuable	hope+ing hoping
live+ing living	drive+er driver	scare+y scary

(b) Words ending in silent –e generally retain the –e before adding a suffix beginning with a consonant:

arrange+ment arrangement	safe+ty safety	sincere+ly sincerely
require+ment requirement	care+less careless	care+ful careful

Exception: Note that silent –**e** is dropped when adding a suffix beginning with consonant in the following words:

argue+ment argument	awe+ful awful	nine+th ninth
due+ly duly	true+ly truly	five+th fifth

(c) When the suffix –**ing** is added in words ending with –**ie**, -**e** is dropped and **-i** is changed to **–y:**

die+ing dying	lie+ing lying	tie+ing tying

But **-e** is retained before adding a suffix to the words ending with a vowel followed by a consonant to avoid confusion:

dye+ing dyeing (not dying)	**singe+ing singeing** (not singing)

(d) In words ending in –**ce** or –**ge**, retain the final –**e** before adding suffixes beginning with **a, e, i, o** or **u**:

change+able changeable	notice+able noticeable

But in some words, when adding the suffix –**age**, retain –**e**:

acre+age acreage	mile+age mileage

-ie and –**ei**

Write –**i** before –**e**, except after –**c** or when sounding like –**a**, as in **neighbour, weigh**:

achieve	ceiling	beige
believe	conceit	eight
chief	conceited	freight
grief	deceive	reign
retrieve	receive	veil

Exception: Note the following words:

ancient	forfeit	scientist
efficient	heir	seize
counterfeit	height	society
foreign	leisure	weird

Final Consonant

(a) Double the final consonant when adding a suffix that begins with a vowel **(-able**, **-ed, --er, -ing**) to a word of one syllable ending in a single consonant after a single vowel and with words of more than one syllable ending the same way and accented on the last syllable:

bag+age baggage	**begin+ing beginning**	**beg+ed begged**
rob+er robber	**occur+ed occurred**	**control+er controller**

(b) If the accent does not fall on the last syllable, do not double the final consonant:

benefit+ed benefited	**pilot+ed piloted**	**suffer+ing suffering**

(c) In words ending in **–l,** do not drop the **-l** before the addition of **-ly:**

comical+ly comically	**cool+ly coolly**	**local+ly locally**

(d) In words ending with **–n,** do not drop the **–n** before adding the suffix **–ness:**

clean+ness cleanness	**even+ness evenness**	**green+ness greenness**

(e) Do not double the consonant in words with two vowels before the final consonant or in words ending with two consonants:

Daub+ing daubing	**help+ed helped**	**keep+er keeper**
Peck+ing pecking	**spoil+ed spoiled**	**lurk+ing lurking**

Exception: The consonant **–l** is doubled even if the accent does not fall on the last syllable:

quarrel+ed quarrelled	**travel+er traveller**	**signal+ing signalling**

Final –y

(a) A final –**y** preceded by a consonant changes to –**i** before all suffixes except those beginning with –i:

happy+ly happily	**beauty+ful beautiful**	**carry+ed carried**
marry+age marriage	**body+es bodies**	**mercy+ful merciful**
study+ing studying	**marry+ing marrying**	

(b) A final –**y** preceded by a vowel remains unchanged when a suffix is added:

delay+ed delayed	**enjoy+able enjoyable**	**play+ful playful**

Exception: There are a few exceptions:

say+ed said	**day+ly daily**	**pay+ed paid**	**lay+ed laid**

-full as a suffix

When the suffix **–full** is added to a word, drop the second **–l:**

cheer+full cheerful	faith+full faithful	grace+full graceful
harm+full harmful	peace+full peaceful	thank+full thankful

2. Frequently Mis-spelled Words

Some words are frequently mis-spelled in common writing. A short list of such words is given below. Carefully proof-read these words when they come in your writing and prevent spelling mistakes.

इनमें से प्रत्येक Spelling को कॉलम में दिए गए सही Spelling के पहले bracket में (×) चिह्न के साथ व्यवस्थित करें। सही Spellings के बाद bracket में (✓) चिह्न दें और दोनों शब्दों के बीच थोड़ा Gap रखें।

abudence	discription	past-time	superflous
acommodate	disapoint	precison	vengence
alude	garantee	pronounciation	accidentaly
attachd	incesant	reoccurence/reccurence	aggrevate
changable	laborius	recind	atheleties
coinveniance	monotonus	shedule	callus/calous
dependant	oporchunity	symetrical	consious
disappearence	preceeding	vacum/vaccum	delibrate
existance	proceedure	acessible	collegue
imencity	recieve	advantageus/advantegeous	noticable
intrrupt	reprive	appearence	sieze/seige
mislleneous	satelite	boqnet/bouque	dextrous
omited	simutaneus/simuteneous	conscinse	exaggrate
persuation	unweildy	defendent	hindrence
previledge	acceede	develope	insistance
qorum	aquainted	endevor/endevour	managable
relive	anguis	hieght/hight	occurence/occurrance
rouge	benefitted	irresistibel/iresistible	perceptibel
sevarity	consantrate	maintenance	prejudise
tornament	deciet	nusance	quandry
absorbtion	desend	pecuriry/peccuniory	repititioin/repetison
acustomed	embarass	preffered/prefered	resistence
ambigity	haras	propritary	separate
attendence	incidently	refering	simpathy
conceide	lagitimate	resemblence	wholsome/holesome

Frequently Mis-spelled Words

abundance	*absorption*	*accede*	*accessible*	*accidentally*
accommodate	*accustomed*	*acquainted*	*advantageous*	*aggravate*
allude	*ambiguity*	*anguish*	*appearance*	*athletics*
attached	*attendance*	*benefited*	*bouquet*	*callous*
changeable	*concede*	*concentrate*	*conscience*	*conscious*
convenience	*colleague*	*deceit*	*defendant*	*deliberate*
dependent	*description*	*descend*	*develop*	*dexterous*
disappearance	*disappoint*	*embarrass*	*endeavour*	*exaggerate*
existence	*guarantee*	*harass*	*height*	*hindrance*
immensity	*incessant*	*incidentally*	*irresistible*	*insistence*
interrupt	*laborious*	*legitimate*	*maintenance*	*manageable*
miscellaneous	*monotonous*	*noticeable*	*nuisance*	*occurrence*
omitted	*opportunity*	*pastime*	*pecuniary*	*perceptible*
persuasion	*preceding*	*precision*	*preferred*	*prejudice*
privilege	*procedure*	*pronunciation*	*proprietary*	*quandary*
quorum	*receive*	*recurrence*	*referring*	*repetition*
relieve	*reprieve*	*rescind*	*resemblance*	*resistance*
rogue	*satellite*	*schedule*	*seize*	*separate*
severity	*simultaneous*	*symmetrical*	*superfluous*	*sympathy*
tournament	*unwieldy*	*vacuum*	*vengeance*	*wholesome*

Conclusion

The importance of spelling has been questioned in recent years as word processing programmers are equipped with spell checker and some educational reformists have suggested that focusing on spelling holds back the creative processes of writing. Spelling is a precise and difficult process. In order to spell correctly, one must retrieve the letters of the word form.

Chapter 14

Prepare Effective Notes, Precis and Briefs

Introduction

Organizations receive many communications from external sources which include their clients/customers, other organizations, government agencies, shareholders and members of the public. Besides, inter-departmental communications are also generated for seeking advice and concurrence on issues concerning more than one department. These communications become **'cases'** which have to be disposed off after appropriate consideration by the decision-making level.

If the decision-making level is the recipient of the case, he may dispose it off and keep a brief record of the considerations that led to the decision made by him. But, if the recipient of the case needs to have it examined or if he has to obtain approval of higher levels in the organization, the case may have to be put up with a note.

Introduction Note

'**Note**' means remarks recorded on a case to speed up its disposal. It may be an analysis or statement of the questions requiring decision, a précis of previous papers or suggestions regarding the most suitable course of action. The decision made by the competent authority also becomes a part of 'Notes' portion of the case.
The act of recording remarks on a case is called '**Noting.**' Note-taking has been an important part of human history and scientific development. The Ancient Greeks had developed 'hypomnema', which meant 'recording information for personal use on important subjects'.

Why Record Notes?

The need for recording notes arises because the competent authority may not have the time to look into all the aspects of the case or to check any errors or misstatements of facts made in the communication. Sometimes, the information given in the case may be incomplete and gaps may have to be filled up. Or, the background of the case may be unclear and some research may be required for understanding the case. In all such cases, the decisions-making level may take the help of the functionaries dealing with the subject matter and ask them to examine the case thoroughly and put it up. Notes will be required in all such cases.

If the subject matter of the communication is important or if the decision made is likely to create controversy or it may have to be justified later on, it is advisable to keep a record of the case in the form of notes which tell the considerations or circumstances in which a particular decision was made and the level at which it was made.

Importance of Note-taking

(a) It is important for providing necessary evidence to inform and develop one's argument.

(b) It helps in concentrating on and comprehending the information one is reading by helping to summarise the ideas and arguments in the text.

(c) Taking notes help people extend their attention spans and keep them focused on the work at hand.

(d) Note-taking boosts not only comprehension but also retention. People tend to learn more effectively when they are using multiple senses and activities. It helps as it requires both listening and writing skills.

(e) Note-taking helps in selecting important material and discard what is not relevant.

(f) Good notes will provide a gauge about what is significant to the instructor and arrange points in easy-to-view piece of information.

Action before Noting on a Case

Before recording a note, the dealing hand should check that all facts or statements made in the communication are correct and complete information has been given to consider the case. If there is some difference, it should be reconciled. If there are gaps in the information received, these gaps should be got filled up.

Forms of a Note

A note may be in any of these forms:

(a) Brief remarks on a simple or routine case;

(b) A précis of previous papers, in a case in which exchanges of views have been going on for a long period of time and it is necessary to give an overview of the whole case so that a decision may be made;

(c) A statement of the case in which views of other organizations or parties, who were consulted, have been obtained and a decision is now required to be made;

(d) An analysis of questions in a complicated case which has been examined in detail and a decision is now to be made;

(e) Views, comments and suggestions made by persons who have considered the case at different levels in the organization. These views, etc. may include suggestions about alternative courses of action, implications of each such course and recommendations about the most appropriate course of action and

(f) Final orders passed in the case.

Characteristics of a Good Note

Note is a piece of internal communication. It should have the following characteristics:

(1) **Complete,** i.e., it should answer all questions that may have been raised and all the other questions that may arise while considering the case. Answers to questions such as **What? Why? How? When? Where?** and **Who?** will help in making the note complete. Even if some questions have not been asked, but which seem to be relevant for fuller examination of the case, such questions should be raised and answers to such questions should also be given.

(2) **Clear**, i.e., it should be written, as far as possible choosing short, simple familiar words, using short sentences, inactive voice and preferring concrete expressions.

(3) **Concise**, i.e., it should not contain wordy, trite or unnecessary expressions and should include only relevant statements. It should avoid repetition of either words or of ideas.

(4) **Coherent**, i.e., it should be logically arranged, sticking to one idea for each paragraph and sentences and paragraphs should be linked together.

(5) **Correct**, i.e., it should be factually correct, figures should be free from mistakes and the writing should be grammatically correct.

(6) **Courteous**, i.e., it should express ideas tactfully, without hurting anybody's feelings and emphasise positive facts. If apparent errors or incorrect statements or figures in a case are to be pointed out or if an opinion expressed has to be criticised, care should be taken to use courteous and temperate language free from personal remarks.

(7) **Organized properly**, i.e., it should put ideas in the best order for impact, reflecting clear thinking. The first paragraph should state the main points followed by paragraphs giving evidence and discussing it and the final paragraph should contain recommendations.

(8) **Visually attractive**, i.e., it should be made attractive by dividing the note in serially numbered paragraphs, using headings liberally and keeping the paragraphs of six to ten lines each. Where possible or necessary, use bullets and other lists and leave a small margin of about a one inch on all sides (left, right, top and bottom).

Seven-step Approach to a Good Note

After complete information has been collected and the case has been examined, prepare a note following the seven-step approach:

- ★ Identify issues involved.
- ★ State background facts.
- ★ Analyse each issue in the light of facts.
- ★ Consider possible courses of action.
- ★ Examine implications for each course of action.

★ Recommend solution (s) which appears to be the best.
★ Point out the level at which decision may be made.

If the note is lengthy, summarise in the last paragraph the issues involved and the suggestions for consideration and decision.

II – Precis Writing

Introduction

Quite often, busy managers do not have time to go through a mass of documents about a case. But they need to be informed of its important points. This information is made available to them through a précis.

What is a Precis?

*A **précis** is a digest of the important facts of a case.* It gives the main points of a lengthy statement or a bulk of documents lucidly and briefly and saves the reader's time in going through a mass of verbiage.

Précis, Paraphrasing and Summary

Précis should not be confused with paraphrasing or summarising. *A paraphrase reproduces not only the substance of a passage, but also its details* and it can be longer than the original. But a précis must always be shorter than the original.

A précis is not the same thing as a summary. *A summary is a brief statement of the main points of a passage*. While preparing the summary, the order of ideas given in the original need not be followed. But a précis is a clear, short and systematic development of the main idea in the order as given in the original. A summary is briefer than a précis, the ratio of original to précis is 3 to 1 and of the original to summary may be between 20 to 1 and 10 to 1.

Uses of Precis Writing

Précis writing is useful in many ways. It:

- is an excellent exercise in mental discipline that forces you to be attentive while reading so that you do not miss any important fact.
- teaches you to express your thoughts clearly, concisely and effectively. It is a corrective to the common tendency of vague and disorderly thinking and loose and diffused writing.
- a time-saving device for busy managers who want to be informed of the facts of a case without having to go through a mass of documents.

Characteristics of a Good Precis

A précis is prepared to replace another document (or a number of documents) or to reproduce the ideas of someone else. A good précis will, therefore, have the following characteristics:

(i) **Accuracy:** The précis should be a true and faithful presentation of ideas in the original. It should not only give facts, reasons and arguments contained in the original, but should also convey the exact trend and meaning of the main text. It should not distort the original in any way, but must be its brief version. The writer should not add anything, make no comments, nor correct any facts.

(ii) **Impartiality:** The precise should not contain any extraneous matter, nor should the writer express his own views. It should be written in one's own words, in third person, past tense.

(iii) **Conciseness:** The précis should not have any irrelevant and unimportant matter. It should not have unnecessary details or incidental comments. It should not have figures of speech, illustrations and ornamental phrases and expressions. The writer should act as a sieve, separating the necessary from the useless.

(iv) **Clarity:** The précis should be paragraphed, each paragraph dealing with one phase of the subject. Sub-headings of the paragraph are not necessary.

The précis should be grammatically correct, free from colloquial expressions, slangs, circumlocutions and redundancies.

(v) **Logical order:** The précis should contain facts presented in a logical order and the facts should be so grouped as to enable the reader to pass freely from one to another. It is not correct to choose at random a few sentences from the original, join them together by conjunctions or conjunctive adverbs and hand in the resulting patchwork as précis.

(vi) **Brevity:** The précis should not be verbose. The ideas should be expressed as briefly as possible, but telegraphic curtness or such brevity leading to ambiguity of meaning should be avoided.

(vii) **Completeness:** The précis should faithfully represent all the facts in the original. The reader is unaware of the content.

The précis should be self-contained, thus not requiring any reference to the other material. Only the relevant point in the original is to be included in the précis.

How to Prepare a Precis?

The following guidelines for preparing précis will be found useful:

- Read through the document twice, to grasp its general purpose.
- The text should be thoroughly read and the relevant points should be underlined.
- Number on the margin and in logical order, all points thus underlined. Numbering

helps in quick dealing with the main points, while, at the same time, you considerably lessen the chance of omitting some important facts in the draft précis.

- Prepare a rough draft of the précis including all the numbered points.
- Compare the draft with the original to check if anything important has been left out or anything unimportant has been included.
- Give a suitable heading to the précis, conveying its general meaning.
- Give in the opening sentences of the précis a clear idea of what is to follow.
- Do not use abbreviations. Omit such short words as **a, an, in or, of**. Cut down the number of words in the précis by deleting adjectives and adverbs, except those that have a special or technical significance. Use semi-colons for conjunctions, except when deleting conjunctions would affect the grammatical accuracy of the sentence.
- Maintain a sense of proportion in presenting facts. Do not add details of one major fact, with a half-dozen minor ones and leave another major point entirely unexplained.
- Do not try to reduce each paragraph in the original to one-third. It is the over-all length of the précis that should be reduced to one-third of the original.
- It is also not necessary that the précis should have as many paragraphs as in the original. If the original has more than one thought, independent of one another in a paragraph, all of them should be stated separately in separate paragraphs of the précis.
- It becomes important to carefully revise précis and then finally document it. While doing so, check, amend and revise the précis keeping in view the characteristics of a good précis.

III – Preparing Briefs

Introduction

A **brief** is an updated summary of facts of a case. It is prepared to advise senior functionaries so that they may answer questions in a meeting or at a conference in which that case is likely to come up for discussion.

A brief should be prepared keeping in view the principles of effective writing. It should be complete, concise, clear, coherent, correct and courteous presentation of the facts of the case.

How to Prepare a Brief?

A brief should contain the following information (as may be applicable):

- Explain the background of the case.
- What is the policy on the basis of which the case has been handled so far?

- If there are some issues relating to the case, what attempts have been made in the past to resolve them and with what result?
- What are the new developments that require reconsideration of the case?
- What are the different viewpoints that have emerged after consultation with other departments organizations or other knowledgeable persons?
- What other points are likely to be raised now and how can they be answered?
- What are the alternative plans to tackle the issue and what are the implications of each of these plans?
- Which alternative plan appears to be the best and why?

After preparation, the brief should be put in a folder for submission to the functionary.

Conclusion

Preparation of notes, précis and briefs are important functions in an office. Since the work that organizations perform these days has grown enormously in volume, complexity and variety, attention to details in preparing effective notes, précis and briefs will help in making prompt and correct decisions, boost the morale of persons working in the organization and show that the organization is efficient and effective.

SECTION - II

Job Applications

General Job Applications

Here we give certain important points which must be borne in mind while applying for a job

1. Remember that the immediate objective of your application is not to secure the job but to get a chance for an interview.
2. Highlight your qualities briefly.
3. Give complete particulars, as desired by the prospective employer, in a simple and straight forward manner.
4. Avoid using stereotyped sentences like 'hoping for the favour of an early, assuring of my best services!'... etc.
5. Type the application neatly and correctly.
6. The format should be like that of a business letter.
7. Do not send cyclostyled applications, or pre-printed application forms with details filled in.
8. Always send the original typed copy and not the duplicate copy.

Type I : Application which Includes the Details of Resume

Dear Sir,

In response to your advertisement in 'The Hindustan Times' dated May 8, 2017, I wish to apply for the post of Private Secretary to the Managing Director.

I graduated from Delhi University in 1996 securing 76% marks in B.A. (Hons) English.

This was followed by a one year Secretarial Course at the well-known Reliance Secretarial Institute, New Delhi, from where I acquired proficiency in Business Correspondence, Shorthand, Typing, Operating Computer & Secretarial Practice.

At present I am employed with Bright Light Company, New Delhi, as an Office Assistant. The present job calls for handling of routine correspondence besides other Secretarial Work. My shorthand and typing speeds are 120 and 60 w.p.m. respectively.

Having lived in various parts of the country I can speak Hindi, Punjabi and Marathi fluently and have working knowledge of Gujarati and Bengali.

I am 25 years old, excellent in health, and had been a good player of hockey during my college days. My work with the present employer has been highly appreciated (testimonials are attached) but I feel that your job offers greater scope for career growth and use of my potentiality.

I take the job with a great sense of responsibility, enjoy the challenge of new situations, and expect to make a positive contribution to your organization.

Hope to get an interview call from you.

Thanking you,

Yours faithfully,

Encl : Testimonials

Type II: Application with Separate Resume

Dear Sir,

In response to your advertisement in 'The Hindustan Times' dated March 8, 2017, I wish to apply for the post of Private Secretary to the Managing Director.

At present I am employed with Bright Light Company, New Delhi, as an Office Assistant but feel that your job offers greater scope for career growth and use of my abilities.

I take the job with a great sense of responsibility, enjoy the challenge of new situations and expect to make a positive contribution to your organization.

Hope to get an early interview call.

Thanking you,

Yours faithfully,

Encl : Copies of testimonials

Bio-data

Name	:	
Date of Birth	:	April 15, 1976.
Present Address	:	
Permanent Address	:	
Academic and Professional Qualifications	:	B.A. (Hons) English from Delhi University in 1996 securing 76 % marks. Did a one year course of Secretarial Practice at Reliance Secretarial Institute, New Delhi. Acquired proficiency in : Business correspondence, Shorthand, Typing, Operating Computers, & Secretarial Practice. Shorthand/Typing speed : 120 / 60 w.p.m. respectively.

Working Experience	:	Have been working with Bright Light Company, New Delhi, as Office Assistant for 11/2 years. The job involves handling of routine correspondence, filing taking dictation and answering visitors' queries.
General Qualifications	:	Can speak Hindi, Punjabi and Marathi fluently and have working knowledge of Gujarati and Bengali.
Personal Details	:	Excellent health. Have been a good player of hockey during college days.
Present Emoluments	:	
Salary Expected	:	

The present trend is slightly different. Mostly the applicants send a bio-data to the prospective employer along with a Covering Letter. This Covering Letter may be as small as that of two-three sentences, but in the style of a formal letter. A few examples of such letters are given below:

1)

Dear Sir,

With reference to your advertisement in the Times of India dated 22nd March, 2017, for the post of an Executive Secretary, I wish to offer my candidature.

I am enclosing a copy of my bio-data for your perusal and kind consideration.

I hope to hear from you about the date of interview.

Yours Sincerely,

2)

Dear Sir,

In response to your advertisement in the Employment News dated ..., for the position of an Accountant, I would like tc apply for the same.

I am sending herewith a copy of my resume/ curriculum vitae for your consideration.

Could you let me have an interview with you at an early date?

Yours Sincerely,

3)

Dear Sir,

I have come to know through reliable sources that there exists a vacant post of Sales Engineer in your esteemed organization.

Please find enclosed a copy of my resume for your perusal and kind consideration.

Should you require any further information, the same will be provided to you at the time of interview.

Hope to hear from you,

Yours sincerely,

Let us study how to frame a good resume, in the latest style, which is the first interface of a candidate with the potential employer:

- The employer should get an idea by the first glance itself. Thus make it briefer and stick to the points only. Ideally a resume should be of one page or maximum two.
- Sell yourself using friendly language, addressing only the employer's need, without using large paragraphs and repetitions.
- Make the 'experience portion' clearer, mentioning how long, in what capacity, and what you have done for the previous organizations. It has to be specific, measurable, action-oriented and realistic.
- Be candid and unambiguous so that the employers feel comfortable in hiring your services.
- Don't write much about your hobbies and interests, age, height, weight etc. unless it is relevant to the position.
- Make it neat, clean, in good stationery absolutely error-free.
- Avoid using the pronoun 'I' like "I have conducted…etc.". Use only "conducted ….".

The sample resume of a senior level Executive Secretary in the latest style:

K. RAMACHANDRAN PILLAI

17F, Pocket A-I

Mayur Vihar-III

Delhi-110096

Ph. Resi: 91-11-2615270

E-mail: kr.pillai@psinetcs.com

Experience : 15 years of service as Executive Secretary, Personal Secretary, etc. providing support to Senior Management functionaries in large Indian Corporate Houses and Multi-nationals. (Starting from the latest is as below):

- Currently (for last 3 years) attached to the **Managing Director, PSINet Consulting Solutions, a $2 billion multi-national with HQs in US, as Executive Secretary**. Besides routine Secretarial Tasks, work includes coordination, communication with sister companies and counterparts spread across the globe, team-oriented assignments, drafting and editing of key materials, handling MD's personal work, etc.
- 3 ½ years in Xerox as **Secretary to GM-HRD** and then **CEO-Staff Affairs**. Besides Secretarial work, "updated and edited the Company's Personnel Policy Manual; Designed and implemented events and programmes, Arranged residential and non-residential Training Programmes and other Management Development Programmes; handled preparation of Minutes and Training related materials, Maintained interaction and communication with Company's JV partners, excelled in drafting and editing key and critical business related correspondence.
- Six years in **Godrej (an Indian Giant group)** as a **Steno Secretary**, where besides secretarial work, had to handle customers all over the world.
- Three years in **Camphor and Allied Products Ltd. as a Steno-Typist.** Work included inter-company/ departmental coordination and general office work, liaison with import, export and insurance people.

Qualifications : B.Com from the University of Kerala. Pre-Degree Course in the first division and First Rank in the district.

Tech. Qualifications : Kerala Govt. Technical Examination Diploma in **Typewriting & Shorthand**. Speed 60 w.p.m. and 100 w.p.m. respectively.

Software knowledge	:	**MS-Word, Excel, Power Point, e-mail and Internet** and a little exposure to Adobe Page-Maker.
Training Exposure	:	**Have undergone:** ◆ **Five-day Course on TQM**; familiar with Quality Tools and Processes; ◆ A course on Train the Trainer; ◆ Kaizen Principle in work-life; ◆ Six months Banking Training in Canara Bank; ◆ Well exposed to ISO tools and processes.
Merits & Recognition	:	**Won prizes/ Certificates in** English Elocution, Essay Writing, Debates, Many times winner of Long Term Productivity Awards, etc.
Personal	:	Highly interactive, team-oriented & empathic, good in communication, principled, religious, honest, candid and hard-working.

General Job Application

Starting the letter

1. In response to your advertisement in 'The Times of India' dated June 8, 2017, I wish to apply for the post of Office Superintendent in your institution.
2. I have learnt from reliable sources that the post of Labour Welfare Officer in your office has fallen vacant.
3. I am interested in the vacancy you have advertised in 'The Hindustan Times' dated July 8, 2017, for a Sub-editor and wish to offer my services for the same.
4. This is to enquire whether you have a vacancy of an Office Assistant in your office.
5. I understand from Mr. Sunil Kumar, one of your suppliers, that you wish to appoint a Sales Engineer.
6. As Mr. Arun Kishore will be leaving your office on 31st July, I wish to offer my service for the same post.
7. I wish to offer my services for the post of Sales Officer which, as I understand, falls vacant by the end of this month.
8. This is to apply for the post of Sales Manager in your office which you have advertised in 'The Times of India' dated 8th May, 2017.
9. With reference to your advertisement in 'The Statesman' dated 21st August, 2017, I wish to offer my services for the post of Steno-typist in your organization.

10. I have learnt from a reliable source that the post of an Accountant is lying vacant in your office. I wish to offer myself as a candidate for the same.
11. In response to an announcement made in the Employment News on 10th June, 2017, I wish to apply for the post of a Translator (Hindi to English).
12. Going through Employment News, I found that a situation of a lecturer in English is lying vacant in your college. I offer myself as a candidate for the same.
13. Please refer to your advertisement in 'The Times of India' dated 14th May, 2017, for the post of a Law Officer, I wish to offer my services for the same.
14. Having come to know through a monthly bulletin of your Deptt. that you need a travelling Salesman, I offer my services for the same post.
15. Through a circular issued from your office, I have come to know that the post of a Draftsman is lying vacant in your office. I offer my candidature through this application.

Middle portion of the letter is given separately in the forthcoming pages

Closing the letter

16. I look forward to hearing from you.
17. I trust you will consider my application favourably and give me a chance to meet you.
18. I would appreciate an interview with you when I could give you more details about myself.
19. I can come for an interview, at any time convenient to you. I enclose a self-addressed and stamped envelope so that you could respond to me.
20. I look forward to the opportunity of a personal interview.
21. I shall be grateful to you for an interview call at your convenience.

Various Job Applications (Middle portion of the application for all types of jobs)

There are two different types of applications — one containing the particulars in the application itself and the other with a bio-data separately made. Their samples have already been given. You can select anyone of those, according to your requirement.

Here we give particular samples of various types of approaches for different job applications.

Private secretary

1. I completed my education in June this year and have been employed as an Office Assistant with Bhatia Electric company. Although I do not have long experience, I am

hard-working and take the work with great sense of responsibility. I am confident that your Managing Director will find me a competent Private Secretary.

2. For more than two years, I have been working as P. A. to the Sales Manager, India Trading Corporation. I am confident that I would prove to be a competent Personal Secretary to your Managing Director.
3. Although I am working in the same capacity in India Marketing Agency, I am applying for this job as your company is well-established and can offer greater scope for career advancements.
4. I have good knowledge of word processing and can work on MS Office, besides handling eMails and surfing Internet.

Accountant/ Accounts Assistant

1. I am a Commerce Graduate from Mumbai University and have good knowledge of Accountancy, Auditing, income-tax procedure and company Law.
2. I can also draw up Balance Sheets and Profit and Loss Accounts.
3. Apart from my work as Accountant, you may find my knowledge of Secretarial work also useful.
4. Now I have enough experience to take independent charge of maintenance of Accounts, preparation of bills and writing of account books.
5. I am computer literate and friendly with the software Tally.

Cashier

1. I passed B.Com from Delhi University in 1975, securing 52% marks and specialised in Book-keeping and Accounting.
2. I am, therefore, quite well-versed in book keeping and billing, etc.
3. Having worked for three years as a Cashier in the Delhi Textile Emporium, I have the requisite experience for the job.
4. I am computer literate and friendly with the software Tally.
5. If your rules require a security deposit I am willing to do so to a reasonable extent.

Typist-cum-clerk

1. I can type accurately at a speed of 60 w.p.m.
2. I am excellent in word processing on Computer and is familiar with MS Word, Excel and MS-Outlook.
3. I am fairly acquainted with office work such as filing, indexing, etc. and also possess elementary knowledge of book-keeping.
4. I have also been attending short-hand classes for the last six months.
5. I have the ability to work for long hours and can cope with work pressure easily.
6. I take the work with a great sense of responsibility.

Labour welfare officer

1. I have studied Labour Welfare at the Delhi School of Social Studies, and am a registered member of the Labour Welfare Officers' Association.
2. I speak Hindi, Punjabi, Bhojpuri and Bengali fluently, and this enables me to deal easily with labour hailing from different parts of the country.
3. I am well versed in labour and factory legislation and possess the requisite qualifications as provided under the Factories Act.
4. On account of my present job in the textile mill I have adequate experience in handling industrial labour.
5. I have done a short-term course in computer and know its basics.

Librarian

1. I completed my MLISC (Master of Library & Information Science from IGNOU in 1999 securing 60% marks.
2. I am fully conversant with the DEWEY decimal classification systems.
3. I can competently manage all aspects of Library routine, including classifying and cataloguing of books and periodicals.
4. I have worked in computerized environment and am familiar with the relevant software.
5. I am good at various search methods which include CD search and Internate surfing.

Driver

1. During my five years of driving career I have not had any accident.
2. I have never been challaned even for minor violations of the Traffic Rules.
3. I have fairly good knowledge of automobiles and can do minor repairs.
4. I am ready for a trial any time, at your convenience.

Nurse

1. I completed B.Sc. in Nursing from the Delhi University in 1996 and am a registered member of the Trained Nurses' Association of India.
2. I also hold the St.John's Ambulance Certificates of Proficiency in First Aid, Nursing and Hygiene.
3. My work has generally been appreciated by my superiors.
4. I can undertake both medical and surgical nursing and have long experience in handling children and the aged.

Personnel officer

1. I hold an M.A. degree in Social Science from Mumbai University and have also completed a correspondence course in Personnel Management from the London School of Correspondence Courses.

2. I have sound knowledge of modern principles and practices of personnel management, aptitude tests, work incentives, etc.
3. I am also acquainted with the methods of merit rating and performance audit.
4. I have five years' experience as Assistant Personnel Officer in a public sector undertaking.
5. A short-term course on Computer that I have undergone with NIIT, Delhi, has enabled me to improve my productivity during my career.

Stenographer

1. My Short-hand and Typing speeds are 140 and 70 w.p.m. respectively.
2. I have also completed a course on book-keeping and secretarial practice.
3. I am good at English and thus can handle correspondence independently.
4. If required, I can aiso work in the capacity of a Secretary.
5. I am good at MS Office Software like Word, Excel, Power Point and Access, besides handling e-mail and Internet.

Store-keeper

1. I am fully conversant with the theory and practice of store-keeping.
2. Having worked as an Assistant Store-Keeper with Mehta Surgical Company for two years, I have fairly good knowledge of handling and recording stocks.
3. I am fully conversant with all aspects of store-keeping.
4. Since I have also worked on a computerised Store Management System, I could increase my productivity by 200%.
5. On account of my training and experience, I am in a position to discharge efficiently all duties that are assigned to me as a storekeeper.

Telephone operator-receptionist

1. I have good command over spoken English and can also converse fluently in Hindi.
2. I have a pleasing personality and a well modulated voice, and can handle all enquiries on the telephone.
3. I can handle the most modern EPABX and other Voice Storage systems.
4. I have completed a three months course of Telephone Operators and Receptionists from Reliance Commercial Training Institute, New Delhi.
5. I do maintain all my official contacts on computer and am well-versed on how to appropriately manipulate these data.

Private tutor

1. I am a IInd class Commerce Graduate from the Delhi University and have been giving private tuitions for the last ten years.

2. As I have been an English teacher in Delhi Public School for five years, I am familiar with all school requirements.
3. I can coach your son in all subjects and guarantee his progress in the subjects he is weak in, at present.
4. We can, of course, discuss the terms and conditions when we meet.

Typist

1. After completing my SSLC in 1999 with 2nd division I attended the Delhi Typewriting Institute and have now acquired good speed and accuracy in typing.
2. Besides office routine I can do simple invoicing and tabulation work, etc.
3. I can also cut stencils well and can operate any standard duplicating machine.
4. I am very good at Computers and can work on Windows 2007, especially all software on MS-Office.

Salesman

1. Besides being a Commerce Graduate, I have taken a diploma in Business Management and Control and other subjects related to retail sales.
2. For the last three years I have been working as a part-time Salesman for a well-known cosmetic company and my sales, on an average, have exceeded ₹ 50,000/- a month.
3. I am in perfect health and prepared to travel anywhere in India.
4. I have a way with people and know the art of persuading prospective customers into placing orders.

Sub-editor

1. I also have a diploma in Journalism from the Nagpur University.
2. Since June this year I have been working as an apprentice with 'The Hindustan Times' and as a result have become conversant with the process of producing a paper.
3. I am proficient in English and can process data in a computerised environment.
4. I am of good health and prepared to work even in night shifts.

Hotel cook

1. I have got a diploma in catering from the College of Catering, Mumbai University.
2. For two years, I have worked as an Assistant to my father who was the Chief Cook at the famous Leela Vilas Hotel in Shimla for more than 15 years.
3. I can prepare Indian, Continental as well as Chinese dishes.
4. At times, I have prepared meals for more than 100 people at very short notices.

Manager

1. I completed M.B.A. from the College of Business Administration, Hyderabad in 2016, securing 87% marks and have done a one year course on Computers.
2. I have three years experience as Assistant Manager in Bharat Auto Industries, Yamuna Nagar.
3. I can handle matters regarding Accounts, Finance, General Administration and Board Meetings competently.
4. My work with the present employer has been highly appreciated, as I have managed to establish harmonious relation between the staff and the management.

Mechanic

1. I have got a diploma from the Polytechnic Institute, Delhi, specialising in the working of Internal Combustion Engines, Electric Motors and allied subjects.
2. As a trainee at the Polytechnic, I have had the opportunity to dismantle car engines and reassemble them.
3. As an apprentice with Yantra Industries since last year, I have efficiently handled engines of various types and makes.
4. Having worked for some time in a tool manufacturing industry, I have acquired the knowledge of various types of tools required for the repair and servicing of engines and machines.

Technician

1. I have completed a two year diploma in Mechanical Engineering from the Industrial Training Institute, Malviya Nagar, New Delhi.
2. As an apprentice with Pratima TV company, Ghaziabad, I have also acquired fairly good knowledge of electronics.
3. My present job has given me adequate experience in various technical jobs like welding, soldering, wiring, etc.
4. If required I can also deal with customers.

Teacher

1. I completed M.A. History in 1995, from the Mumbai University securing 76% marks. In 1996, I got B.Ed (Bachelor of Education) from the same University securing 78% marks.
2. I have been teaching English and Geography to IX and X classes for the last two years, in a Municipal School in Poona.
3. For more than five years I have been giving private tuitions to high school students.
4. I have an impressive personality and have the knack of handling students well.

Space seller

1. After completing B.Com. in 1978 I have been working as Space Seller on behalf of "Blend", a monthly magazine published from Nagpur, with a circulation of 25,000 copies.
2. The monthly average of advertisement business which I procured for the magazine has always been at least six times of my remuneration.
3. I have been an active campaigner of advertisements for "Perception" a Kolkata monthly, with a circulation of more than 18000 copies and have established good contacts in the advertising circle in Mumbai.

Air hostess

1. Having wide-ranging interests I have sound basic general knowledge.
2. I am fluent in English as well as Hindi and am interested in hospitality industry.
3. As desired by you in the advertisement, I have a pleasing personality and am modest in approach.
4. I am unmarried and prepared to undergo any vocational aptitude and physical tests that may be necessary to prove my suitability for the job.

Apprentice

1. I have been taking keen interest in everything mechanical ever since my childhood.
2. Of late, I have also got exposed to computer applications and am good at CAD.
3. Basically, being interested in mechanical work I have a small workshop at home in which I tinker about. I have also forged certain hand-tools.
4. The stipend you offer during my apprenticeship is acceptable to me.
5. I am of good health and take pride in working with my hands.

Canteen manager

1. I have taken a Diploma in Hotel Management and Catering from the Catering College, Mumbai.
2. I can efficiently supervise a large kitchen equipped with all modern cooking appliances.
3. I have also studied dietetics and nutrition thoroughly and can prepare meals for a big group.
4. For two years I have worked as an Assistant to the Canteen Manager of Messrs. Globe Industries, Faridabad.

Draftsman

1. My work with the present employer has been highly appreciated and I was also sent to West Germany for an advanced course in this line.
2. During my three years of service with Delhi Engineering Company, I have gained valuable experience in structural and mechanical drawings.
3. I am extremely good at all the related software and have worked in a computerised environment.

4. I have also done some architectural sketching and tracing.
5. My plans and blue-prints in the present job have been frequently praised for their accuracy as well as in the overall perspective.

Headmistress of school

1. I am M.A. M.Ed. from the Mumbai University and have specialised in modern methods of education.
2. I have 15 years of experience as a senior teacher and two years experience as an Assistant Headmistress in reputed High Schools in Delhi including St. Francis Public School.
3. I am fully conversant with the administrative functions of a large educational institution.
4. I have a knack for handling children, and along with maintaining discipline, I can win their confidence and love.

Hotel manager

1. I have five years experience as Assistant Manager in the well-known Badshah Hotel of Mumbai.
2. I am conversant with all aspects of hotel management, from daily menus to security and from public relations to arranging conventions.
3. I can fluently speak English, Hindi, Punjabi and Gujarati and also have working knowledge of French.
4. I have the experience of having worked in a computerised environment.
5. I have sufficient experience in handling foreign guests.

Lawyer for industrial concern

1. I have five years experience as Legal Adviser to M/S Delhi Steel Industries.
2. I have passed the L.L.M. examination and have sound knowledge and experience of Industrial Legislation, Factory Act, Labour Law, etc.
3. On a number of occasions, I have represented my Company in legal disputes in the High Court and the Supreme Court.
4. For more than three years I have worked as an Assistant to the reputed legal expert of Mumbai on Industrial Legislation, Mr. F. M. Kanoonwala.
5. I generate most of my documents and affidavits on a computer without depending on a typist.

Publicity officer

1. I have a diploma in Journalism from Nagpur University and have also done a correspondence course in Publicity, Public Relations and Advertising from the London School of Journalism.

2. I have a good knowledge of computer and all related software, expertise in design and lay-out.
3. As an Assistant Publicity Officer for Rose Cosmetics Ltd., Nagpur, I have conducted several successful advertising campaigns, trade fair, road-shows, etc.
4. I am well-versed in printing and production techniques and also conversant with all publicity media like Press, Radio and T.V., etc.

Press reporter

1. I have a Diploma in Journalism from the Punjab University.
2. I am excellent in handling English language besides being good in Hindi and Punjabi.
3. I am a computer literate and can generate reports on computer.
4. I was closely involved in the publishing of the students' news paper brought out by the University Department of Journalism.

Sales manager

1. As an Assistant Sales Manager, I have been able to achieve creditable sales results and exceed the targets.
2. I have a sound knowledge of maintaining accounts and modern business methods specially in sales management.
3. I am known in my field for effectively handling tough sales related problems.
4. I have a good knowledge of modern methods of publicity, public relations and advertising which are prerequisites to sales.
5. I know how to generate spread-sheets and sales statistics on a computer.

Travelling salesman

1. I have five years' experience in door-to-door sales canvassing of various consumer products.
2. I am prepared to travel to any part of the country and find pleasure in meeting people.
3. I am in excellent health which, I believe, is essential for a travelling salesman.
4. I know the art of dealing with the people and can speak English, Hindi, Punjabi, Bengali and Gujarati fluently.

Agent

1. As the sole representative of Gala Cosmetics Ltd., for entire Maharashtra I have built up personal contacts with all major cosmetic dealers in the state.
2. Although I am new to this line I am confident of performing well in the business on account of my old contacts in the city.
3. I am confident that my connections in the trade circle will result in a large turnover for your firm in this region.

4. We could negotiate the agency terms at an early date and I would accept any reasonable offer.

Accounts assistant

1. I have passed B.Com degree examination from the Punjab University with 90% marks in Advanced Accounts.
2. I have been an apprentice with Dena Bank, Karol Bagh, New Delhi, for more than 6 months.
3. I can easily maintain the books of accounts of any type of business.
4. I have a good handwriting and can speedily enter data into a computer. I am also familiar with the software 'Tally'.

Lecturer

1. Apart from having a good academic record I have also published papers in literary journals like Humanities Review, etc.
2. I am a writer and one of my books was chosen for an award by the Maharashtra Literary Conference.
3. I am a good orator and have often compered many cultural programmes during college days.
4. I am fond of teaching and I make it interesting for the students.
5. Despite the fact that I have done M.A. in Hindi, I have also good command over the English language.

Copy-writer in advertising agency

1. I have done a correspondence course in Advertising from the London School of Correspondence Courses.
2. I have made a special study of the 'copies' of leading Indian advertisers, and my paper on this subject has been appreciated by the London School of Advertising.
3. I have a flair for writing and can produce forceful and punch packed 'copy' on any product.
4. I can also visualise advertisements and have working knowledge of lay-outs.
5. My basic knowledge of computers has made my work more productive and speedy.

Engineer

1. I completed my B.E.(Electrical) from I.I.T. Kanpur, in 1994 securing grade A (90% marks).
2. I have worked as an apprentice engineer for 4 years with Hindustan Electric Company, Kolkata, and am very proficient in a computerised environment.
3. I have more than 2 years of experience in working at power generation plants.
4. I have also been designing and making small electrical gadgets for everyday domestic use.

Advertisement manager

1. Over the years I have managed to establish close personal contacts with all major advertising agencies in Delhi.
2. I also have personal contacts with many major advertisers in Kolkata.
3. I have more than 5 years of experience in coordinating the activities of Creative Departments and the Studio. I am very good at presentation software like Adobe, Coreldraw, Photoshop, etc.
4. I also have sound knowledge of block-making, offset printing and various other production techniques.

Shop assistant

1. I have passed the Higher Secondary Examination.
2. I can speak Hindi and English fluently.
3. I have a pleasing personality.
4. I like any job involving public dealings and can be successful at the counter of any commercial establishment.

Proofreader

1. I have a sound knowledge of English and am very good at spellings.
2. I know all the signs of proof-reading and can read proofs without omissions.
3. I have read proofs at home for the New Book Publishing Company, on assignment basis.
4. I am quite used to working on a computer and am very familiar with most of the types/ fonts, designing magazine lay-outs and book pages, etc.

Do's and Don'ts of a Good Resume

Do's

- **Mention your relevant experience**
- **Optimise resume for ATS (Applicant Tracking System)**— ATS is a software which helps employees to sort candidates by relevance. If you have already applied for job, ATS scans you with relevant keywords. So use keywords related to your field of work in your resume.
- **Show numbers**— If you have any achievments, mention them with numbers. Quantify your achievments to help employer know more about you.
- **Include soft skills**— No matter how small your skills are, do mention them. You may leave out childhood skills, like playing basketball, etc.
- **Show your awards**— Do mention the awards you got in life, something really interesting about you.

- **Add keywords in resume—** Keywords, used in Ads, are the things which are going to help you to be tracked by the ATS. So use them necessarily.
- **Show different roles—** If you have wroked in a company in different capacities, do mention them.
- **One page resume—** Try to mention relevant information in one page.
- **Use creative templetes—** Before writing your resume, try to find out how you can make your resume creative.
- **Format—** Your resume format should be latest and not outdated.
- **Dates and Times—** Your work should be in a chronological way. If there is some gap, do mention it.
- **Proof reading—** When you are finished, give it to someone who can proofread if for spelling and factual mistakes.
- **Paper work—** Before typing, make your resume on paper to save time and energy.

Don'ts

- **Impressive background—** If you don't have any impressive background with regard to your experience, don't worry. If you are fresher, or if you want to apply in a field which is new for you, try it.
- **No job ad-wording—** Don't use words used in your job ad. Make it original.
- **No secret data—** Don't mention any secret information in your resume.
- **NO obvious information—** Don't give information which is obvious or common, like net surfing, MS Word, etc.
- **Only few hobbies—** Don't mention all the hobbies since childhood to maturity. Try to mention hobbies which are relevant to your job.
- **Unimportant or irrelevant experience—** Don't mention the experience which is unimportant or irrelevant to the job applied for.
- **Employment gap—** Don't hide it.
- **Don't lie—** No information should be false as the employer may cross check any information anytime.
- **No overloading—** Don't overload your resume with information. Avoid giving unnecessary information.
- **Your own design—** Don't invent your own design or style. Follow the one developed by professionals.
- **Font experiment—** Don't do any experiment with font face.
- **No buzzwords—** Don't use too much buzzwords or technical jargon. If necessary to use, don't use them all at one place, rather across the resume.
- **Spell check—** Never forget to run spell check for any mistake before submission.

SECTION - III

Business-letters

BUSINESS-LETTER

"Good correspondence is the soul of successful business. Without correspondence, there can be no trade. Modern business is the greatest romance of the age. It spins out money which can buy law and life."

A business letter needs a careful drafting because a well-written letter can go a long way in producing desirable results. It may clinch a sale deal, sort out a complaint or fetch a customer. It is a very straight forward document, but, at the same time, friendly and conversational in tone. It is also a substitute for a personal talk or a conversation on telephone.

Let your business letter be a credit to yourself and your firm. Draft the letter in a professional style. If the letter has mistakes and faulty constructions, it can put a question on your business dealings.

However, there is nothing complicated about these letters. In every company, large amount of business and considerable sales are done through mail. Thus, every letter has its bearing on the balance sheet. Every outgoing letter is a spokesman of the company's policy. It is silent but not dumb. It helps to increase the reputation of the firm. It opens markets and outlets for goods and services. It is also a mode of generating profits.

Since the business has become extremely complicated nowadays, the ability to write good business letters is an asset. The correspondence between the head office, branches, production units and sale depots helps the company to run smoothly. Thus, a letter has both internal and external uses and importance.

Considering the fact that a letter gets only a few minutes of the reader's attention, the message must be clear, correct and concise. The letter should be well organised as to perform multiple functions of conveying a message, building goodwill and creating a favourable response. It is difficult to avoid negative ideas but what matters most is how they are used. A skillful correspondent handles the negative attitude with a tactful positive approach. Almost all negative ideas can be put in a positive way, for example,

	Negative	**Positive**
1.	We cannot despatch the consignment until you inform where it is to be delivered.	We shall despatch the consignment as soon as you confirm the address.
2.	We shall not make such delays in future.	We shall take care to ensure prompt delivery in future.
3.	Unless the old dues are cleared, further goods cannot be despatched.	Kindly pay the dues and maintain your goodwill.

Everyone has a style of his own. But, however good it might be, there can always be a scope for further improvement. A good style is an asset to a writer and it can be improved with practice and training. For an effective letter, the correspondent must have a clear knowledge of products, services or subject he is dealing with. He must put all this with a flow of good and impressive language.

For an organisation or a commercial set-up, correspondence has a vital bearing on its relations with customers. Therefore, the message should be clear and precise so that there is no difficulty in understanding it.

Simple and natural language is the key to good business correspondence. The letter should be friendly in tone and content. In your telephonic conversation, you never say, "It is regretted that the goods cannot be delivered today." Rather say, "I am sorry, we cannot deliver the goods today." Thus, the letter should be framed keeping in view what and how the situation demands. Simplicity should never be comprovised.

Some tips for good letter writing

For writing effective business letters, we are giving some useful tips below:

1. While writing a business letter, keep in mind whom you are writing to. Give all the information he needs clearly so that there is no doubt on his part.
2. Catch the attitude of the incoming letter and reply accordingly.
3. Use conversational language in the letter, wherever possible.
4. Be clear, courteous and precise, avoiding ambiguity.
5. Be as polite and dignified as possible.
6. Avoid using high sounding words. If the letter demands, the reply should be elaborate and detailed one.
7. Discard stereotyped language.
8. Use effective phraseology.
9. Avoiding monotony and dryness; introduce variety in the letter.
10. Divide long letter in paragraphs.
11. Make the opening catchy, as it has lasting impact on the reader.
12. Revise the letter before closing it.
13. Avoid repetitions.

Keep the letter reader in mind

This can be best done by keeping the reader's point of view in mind. Anticipate his feelings, requirements and come up with sure and subtle replies. Visualise the letter's impact on yourself. If it is impressive and effective, the job is done.

Catch the attitude

The reply should be in tune with the letter received. Think out the objective clearly and then reply accordingly. Skill, tact and practice are necessary for tackling different queries and approaches.

Use natural and conversational language

The letter's tone should be friendly and natural. It should be simply written to convey a message for impressing the reader. Some examples are given below.

	Avoid	Write
1.	I have pleasure in informing you...	I am pleased to tell you (or to say...)
2.	Please be good enough to advise us...	Please let us know...

Write clear and definite language, avoiding ambiguity

Think before you write. Express yourself in a clear and simple language. It should not leave the reader in doubt, rather should be definite and clear.

Be courteous and considerate

'Courteous' does not mean that unnecessary adjectives should be used. For example, 'Your esteemed order', etc. Your approach should be on the positive side without meaning any disrespect.

Avoid business jargon

Avoid the use of words and phrases which the reader fails to understand easily. Jargons are the words that are specific to a subject and should not be used in general letters. The letter should be short, simple and to the point. Lengthy letters often bore the reader. For example,

	Avoid	Write
1.	We express our regret at being unable to fulfil your order on this occasion with customary promptness.	We regret we cannot meet your present order immediately.
2.	Under active consideration	Being considered
3.	With reference to	About
4.	In connection with	For
5.	It should be noted that	Please note

Discard stereotyped language

Modern business letters do not use old terminology that make letters stereotyped. For example,

	Avoid	Write
1.	Adverting to your letter	Referring to your letter
2.	We beg to acknowledge	We have received
3.	Your esteemed favour to hand	Received your letter
4.	The favour of your early reply will oblige.	An early reply is expected.
5.	Under separate cover	Separately
6.	Your goodself	You
7.	Kindly take into consideration	Please consider
8.	Assuring you of our best attention at all times.	We will pay full attention. / We assure you of the best of our attention.

Use effective phraseology

Use of familiar and easy words is desired, which can be easily understood by the reader. For example,

	Avoid	Write
1.	Communication	Letter
2.	Will you be good enough...	Will you please...
3.	In the near future	Soon/shortly
4.	It gives much pleasure	I am pleased; I am happy/glad
5.	We will execute your order expeditiously.	We will process your order shortly.
6.	We beg to acknowledge receipt of your favour.	Thanks for your enquiry/order.

Introduce variety

Avoid monotony and repetition. Use active voice on the whole but for variety, you may use passive voice as well. For example,

	Avoid	Write
1.	Please let me know at once if you are unable to deliver the goods or not.	If you are unable to deliver the goods, please inform me/us immediately.
2.	We have noted with surprise the contents of your letter.	We surprisingly noted the contents of your letter.
3.	We despatched the goods on 15th.	The goods were despatched on the 15th.
4.	You did not sign the order form.	The order form was not signed/left unsigned.

Opening and closing of effective letter

A. Opening

Although 'Thank you for your letter', 'This refers to your letter', etc., are normally used, yet one can introduce variety with expressions like 'I was glad to receive your letter', 'When I received your letter of…', etc.

B.Closing

	Avoid	Write
1.	We shall deal promptly with any orders you place with us.	Your orders will be dealt with promptly.
2.	Thanking you in anticipation.	Thanking you/Thank you/Thanks and Regards.
3.	Hoping to hear from you soon.	I hope to hear soon from you.
4.	Trusting this meets with your approval.	I trust you will approve of this/ I hope to get your approval to this.

Revising the letter

Check your letter before signing and revise, if required, before mailing it. Also put the following questions to yourself:

1. Is the letter impressive?
2. Is the letter well drafted?
3. Are spellings and punctuation correct?
4. Is the message clear and simple?
5. Does the letter fulfil the reader's needs?
6. How would you react to such a letter?

If all the above questions have a positive reply, your letter is ready to be mailed.

Construction of a Business-letter

A letter is like an organic being, having a head, body and tail. Unlike personal letters, business letters have certain characteristics to observe. Effective correspondence is the mainstay of any business. Success and failure in business also depend on effective communication.

Since a good amount of money is involved in business dealings, the correspondence has to be handled carefully. Everything has to be calculated thoughtfully. A shabby letter may spoil company's image. Be brief, natural, courteous and conversational.

It is abrupt to start a letter with the expression of a regret or remorse. Express pleasure in hearing from the other party. After this, go on to the business aspects of the letter, enlisting the items you want to bring to the reader's notice, in different paragraphs.

As in case of personal letters, the main parts of a letter, apart from the content of the message are *heading, date, inside address, salutation, closing* and *signature.* However, certain variations can be there depending upon the case. The letter must first make a visual impression as the first impression counts.

The appearance of a letter also depends on the quality of paper and print, neatness of the fold, the style of lay-out, etc. In every good company, efficient clerical attention is paid to the make-up of the letter.

Essential parts of a business-letter

1. Letterhead;
2. Date;
3. Inside address;
4. Salutation;
5. Body of the letter;
6. Complimentary closure;
7. Signature and designation;
8. Enclosure reference;
9. P. S. (Post script).

1. Letterhead

Letterhead is the printed heading giving the name and address of the company. Generally, it occupies about six and a half centimetrcs of space from top. Create a moderate size and modern face heading. Simplicity of design is also an essential requirement. The letterhead should have only necessary information and that too in brief. However, it must include:

(i) Name of the company;
(ii) Complete address;
(iii) Nature of business;
(iv) Telephone number, telegraphic address and E-mail address, if any;
(v) Address of Registered Office and branch office, if any;
(vi) Logo of the company, if any.

2. Date

The date should appear on the top, two spaces below the upper margin. It may appear on the right hand or on left hand margin as well. The year is written in full as 2017. The date can be written in any of the following ways:

(i) On the right hand margin, for example,

On the right-hand side top:
2nd August, 2017
or
August 16th, 2017
or
2nd August 2017

(ii) On the left-hand side top, for example,
2nd August, 2017 (or other date styles mentioned above)

3. Inside address

The inside address includes the name and address of the addressee. This is exactly the same address as given on the envelope. The inside address is written on left hand side margin.

Fully-indented style

To

M/s. Universal Book Stall,
Post Box No.540,
New Delhi-12

Blocked style

To,
M/s Universal Book Stall,
Post Box No.540,
New Delhi-110 012

A business letter must have the address of the addressee inside too, because, when the copies of such letters are filed, their identification is necessary.

4. Salutation/ attention line

The salutation is a complimentary term used to begin a letter. A letter addressed to an organisation or a company begins as under:

Sir/Madam
Dear Sir
Dear Sirs
Dear Mr....(Name)*

Originality, of course, pays in business correspondence and equally so in business contacts. If one is writing to somebody familiar, it is preferable to begin the salutation by name, for example,

Dear Mr. Sharma,

* This is in vogue nowadays.

5. Body of the letter

A reference line will help the addressee to understand the subject matter of the letter and refer it to the relevant file. This reference line can go below the salutation.

The body of the letter conveys the main message to the person or firm. If the letter deals with different subjects, they should be put in different paragraphs, in the order of importance.

6. Complimentary close

The complimentary close should be consistent with the salutation and content of the letter. It should express regard and respect for the addressee. A good correspondent uses appropriate words. The pairs of salutations and complimentary closures often used are given below :-

Salutation	**Complimentary close**
Dear Sir(s)/ Dear Madam	Yours truly
Dear Mr.	Yours faithfully*
	Thanks and Regards

7. Signature

There are different styles of putting signatures after the complimentary close. Sometimes, the letter is signed by some junior official on behalf of a senior. In that case, "for"is prefixed before the signature. In case of women 'Miss' or 'Mrs' is put in the parenthesis. Nowadays, 'Ms', is also being used for women who do not tell anything about their marital status. The name and designation of the signatory are typed leaving space for signature.

8. Enclosure reference

Usually the letter is accompanied by some enclosures. It may be a bill, a proforma invoice, a copy of previous reference, a self-addressed envelope, a leaflet, etc. In such a case, it is necessary to mention the number of enclosures so that the despatcher can check the same at a glance. It also helps the addressee to identify the enclosures expected.

9. P.S. (Postscript)

In case of some important omission, it can be mentioned at the bottom of the letter. It should not generally exceed three lines. Sometimes its aim is to get pointed attention of the reader. As it stands at last, it leaves a lasting impression on the leader. For example,

P.S. 1. Don't forget that the sale closes on 9th of this month.

2. How is your new venture in Mumbai coming up?
3. I read your latest article in The Hindustan Times and found it quite interesting and enlightening.

---

* This is the most widely used complimentary close.

10. The address on the envelope

This is invariably the same as the Inside Address. If the address on the envelope is written correctly, it will reach correct destination on time.

The address on the envelope should be typed or neatly written leaving a space of about 4 c.m. on the top. This space can be used for franking the postage mark or affixing the postage stamps.

The address should be broken into 3 or 4 lines as under:

i). The name and designation of the chief executive, for example, Proprietor, Partner, Manager, Managing Director, etc., of the firm or office should be followed by the name of the business organisation.

ii) Locality, Street, Road, etc.

iii) Name of the town/city preferably in bold letters.

iv) Name of the state and pin code, for example,

a) The Sales Manager,
M/s. Leader engineering works,
46, DARYA GANJ,
NEW DELHI -11 00 02.

b) Mr. James T Sobers,
Divisional Manager,
125, Esplanade Road,
WEST BENGAL

Note: Different parts of the address like designation, name of the street, etc., should preferably be used in separate lines. Name of the city or district should preferably be in capital letter.

Streamline Your Letter

General guidelines

1. Gone are the days when the business letters were written by hand. These days, business letters are generally typewritten or computer generated. Handwritten letters can be illegible and thus hamper business dealings. Moreover, they create a negative impression on the receiver.
2. The typist should be efficient. Care should be taken to type letters correctly. Erasers should be avoided. If a letter has too many corrections it should be re-typed. If done on a computer, it can easily be edited. It should be ensured that poor quality paper is not used for typing letters.

3. If the letter is typed on a typewriter, make sure that it is clean and has good quality ribbons. However, computers are the most common medium of letter formation today. A good typist is one who sees to it that:

i) the type is clean;

ii) the touch is even;

iii) the eraser's impressions are unnoticeable;

iv) there is absence of 'strike overs';

v) there are no ink/pencil corrections;

vi) alignment of capital letters with small letters is correct;

vii) spacing of the typed area on paper is correct;

viii) spacing between words and lines is correct;

ix) In case of a computer or electronic typewriter, most of the above are automatically taken care of. A word processor or a computer has innumerable options and facilities to edit, and manipulate a letter or document. In the latest software like MS Office, most of these are menu driven in the system itself.

Forms of indention

A letter may be typed or indented in three different ways:

1. Block format

Block format features all elements of the letter alligned to the left margin of the page. It has a neat and simple appearance. Paragraphs are separated by a double line space.

2. Semi-block format

Semi-block is similar to block but has a more informal appearance. All elements are left-aligned, except for the beginning of each paragraph, which is indented five spaces. Paragraphs are separated by a double line space.

3. Fully indented / Modified block format

Modified block differs from block style in that the date, and signatue lines begin at the centre point of the page line. The beginning of each paragraph is indented five spaces, along with the subject line, if used. Paragraphs may be separated by a single or double line space.

Block Format

Letter-head

May 12th, 2017/12th May, 2017

M/s. Jugal Kishore & Sons,

Main Avenue,

Santa Cruz,

MUMBAI-55

Dear Mr./Ms (name of the addressee),

This letter is in full block form. Every line including the date and the complimentary close, is at the left hand margin. Since there is no indention, letters in this form are typed quickly. It is useful where correspondence is large. It is the latest in styles of lay-out and is now universally popular.

Thanks and regards,

Yours faithfully,

Manager

Semi-Block Format

Letter-head

10th September, 2017

M/s. Sehgal & Sons,

M/s. Industrial Town,

Jalandhar-144001

Dear Sirs,

This is the semi-block form and is quite common in correspondence. Here, the date, complimentary close and signature are written on the right-hand side. It is a modification over the modern Block Form.

Yours truly,

Supervisor

Indented/ Modified Block

10th September, 2017

Dear Mr. Mark,

This letter has used the fully indented style. The recipient's name and address and the paragraphs of the body of the letter are indented five spaces. In few cases more spaces are used. The typists will decide the space level.

The subject of the letter is types just 2 lines below the salutations at the centre. The difference between 2 paragraphs will be 2 lines.

The complimentary closing is typed at the center 2 lines just below the body of the letter. The signature is written five line-spaces below the complimentary closing. Although this style looks beautiful, this style is not widely used these days. Because typing a letter in this style requires many keyboard strokes, this style is avoided.

Yours Sincerely,

Summary of a good business-letter

A good business letter is one which can:

1. Sell goods;
2. Revive old clients/customers;
3. Secure new customers and business;
4. Convince customers;
5. Stimulate dealers;
6. Create goodwill;
7. Collect bad debts;
8. Adjust complaints;
9. Open up new outlets;
10. Influence the balance sheet.

Other points to be remembered

- Investment in correspondence for business pays in the long run.
- A good letter, like a seasoned diplomat, fetches goodwill and business.
- In correspondence, promptness is a must. It enhances the pace of business activities.
- Try to understand all implications of assurances/commitments given in your letter.
- Business calls for action at the right time. Learn to cash it at the right time.
- Every letter should be well-written, well-typed and well-set. The stationery used should be the best possible.

- The language of the letter can do wonders. Be selective in the choice of words and phrases. A good style and expression can make the letter a treat for its reader, eventually bringing benefits to your company as well.

Different Types of Business-letter

A modern businessman has to deal with different kinds of letter in his routine activities. It is not easy to classify all business letters or to give a detailed list of all such letters. Different situations require different approaches. A list of commonly-used business letters is given:

1. Letters of enquiry and replies;
2. Circular letters;
3. Letters containing offers or quotations;
4. Letters ordering goods;
5. Letters acknowledging orders;
6. Follow-up letters;
7. Letters acknowledging goods received and making payments;
8. Letters regarding claims, complaints and adjustments;
9. Insurance letters;
10. Letters regarding forwarding of goods;
11. Export and import trade correspondence;
12. Correspondence with government offices;
13. Banking correspondence.

For every kind of letters, different styles and terminology are used. Care should be taken to understand different forms of letters, their requirements and implications.

1. Letters of enquiry

In today's business world, there are numerous enquiries as there are innumerable products and services offered for sale, which are backed up by massive publicity. Interested parties wish to find out more about the product than what the advertisement informs them. The letter of enquiry asks about specific details about the product. A hotel manager as a user may ask for information about a washing machine while a dealer may be interested to know about the trade terms for retailing the same. Such a letter may include the following points:

a) Request for information with reference to the advertisement; and

b) The purpose for which information is sought.

2. Circular letters

Sometimes, information regarding change of address, opening of a branch office or getting a new telephone connection, etc., is brought to customer's/client's notice through a circular letter. Such a circular letter is either cyclostyled or printed.

3. Letters containing offers or quotations

An offer is in the form of a circular and is meant for the general public including regular customers. Here the intention may be to clear old stock or expand the market. However, a quotation is a specific offer for sale, in response to an enquiry. The language of such a letter should be persuasive in order to win over the customer.

4. Letters ordering goods

While placing an order for goods in a letter, do mention the list of articles required by you. Such a letter must also contain full directions on forwarding, full name, address of the sender, quantity of articles, etc. Lack of information may cause unnecessary delay and misunderstanding at both ends.

5. Letters acknowledging order

All orders should be promptly acknowledged, especially if the order requires some time for its execution. The buyer feels satisfied on getting the acknowledgement. However, the probable date of despatch should also be indicated.

6. Follow-up letters

Follow-up letters are important as they show a continuing interest in the client. The language of the letter must be persuasive to win over the customers. The aim should be to coax the wavering customer into buying the product.

7. Letters acknowledging goods received and making payments

The acknowledgement of goods soon after they are received is an effective business practice. In case there is a delivery note from the sender, it should be signed and returned. The mode of payment may be through a cheque or a bill of exchange. Bill of exchange is used both for internal and foreign trade.

8. Letters regarding claims, complaints and adjustments

Sometimes, the goods are damaged in transit because of careless handling by rail or road transport. This results in complaints. Such a complaint should be firm and polite in tone. A feeling of adjustment and understanding should be exhibited in the complaint.

9. Insurance letters

Often, the exported goods are insured to avoid future complications. The fire and marine insurance are important as they save businessmen from future losses and risks.

10. Letters regarding forwarding of goods

The goods within the country are moved through private carriers and railways. Usually, there is no correspondence while despatching or receiving goods except filling up a few forms. Complaints or claims, however, may crop up on account of delays, losses or damage of goods.

11. Export and import correspondence

This correspondence calls for not only skillful handling but alertness of mind, technique and complete knowledge on the part of the correspondent. Business is usually done through Forwarding Agents/Commission Agents. The Forwarding Agent is responsible for receiving the goods and their safe shipment. Since foreign correspondence is expensive, unnecessary correspondence should be avoided. Email has brought a lot of relief in case of foreign correspondence in terms of cost, accuracy, speed, etc. However, the exported goods should be insured against risks.

12. Correspondence with government offices

Every company has to correspond with a number of government departments. At times, there are proformas to deal with them but correspondence is also necessary on a number of occasions. Some of the government departments with which an ordinary citizen may have regular dealings include Income Tax, Sales Tax, Posts and Telegraphs, CCI & E, DGS & D, etc.

13. Banking correspondence

Banks accept deposits and maintain different types of account with the clients. The services of the bank are many and of varied types, but usually done through printed forms and proformas like cheque, bills, hundis, bills of exchange, etc. However at times, correspondence becomes necessary. Be polite and learn routine bank terminology for effective correspondence.

Business Enquiries

Dealer's First Enquiry from Manufacturer about his Product

Introductory

1. We have come across the advertisements about your domestic appliances in various magazines and newspapers.
2. We have seen your advertisement and have huge interest in buying the products offered by your company.
3. We have come across your advertisement in the "Industrial Journal" and would like to get into business with your reputed firm.
4. Thanks for sharing valuable information on your hardware products.
5. I got to know about your high quality products from one of my customers.

Ask for detailed information about the product

6. Could you provide us with more details about their range, size, quality, prices, etc. and send some samples?

7. Please send us some samples with information about their prices, quality and range, etc.
8. Kindly let us know if the parts used in your machines are indigenous or imported?
9. Please let us know if you manufacture 15 m.m. bolts we have requirement for the same.
10. As we plan to place a huge order, please let us know the maximum quantity you can supply by the end of January, 2018.
11. It would be great if we can have some samples as it is a must before placing any order.
12. We understand that you manufacture silk saris and would supply us 100 pieces within 15 days.
13. Can you please confirm the time period you require to deliver the goods as per our order? We would prefer the supply within 15 days.
14. What is the mode of transport to send the goods at the earliest? We want to place an early order and get the supplies within a week.
15. Kindly confirm the required time frame for the supply of goods.

Give information about yourself

16. We are one of the largest dealers in quality bolts in this area and we wish to expand our range of stocks.
17. We are one of the biggest dealers of electrical gadgets in Bilaspur, and we would like to stock the latest items of similar type.
18. We deal in all types of hand-tool and wish to get regular updates about new products.
19. We are one of the biggest furniture suppliers to the government agencies in our area.
20. We have direct approach to the industries and they always look to us for the supply. Find enclosed our company brochure for reference.
21. We have recently acquired the dealership of Escorts Tractors and want to stock the ancillaries.

Ask about trade terms

22. Kindly let us know the general and product-specific terms and conditions.
23. Will you please share the terms and best price on which you can supply goods to us?
24. Please state in your reply about the terms of payment as well as best possible trade discount.
25. Please let us know about the extra charges for the transportation of goods.
26. I request you to clearly mention the discount on goods and terms of payment.
27. Can you please arrange to insure the goods before despatch?

Any other enquiry

28. Will you be able to manufacture the items if we specify the size, shape, weight, colour and range?
29. Do you have any dealer in our district?
30. Will you please confirm in detail about the manufacturing services offered by your company?

Mention your own specialities, if any

31. We are eagerly waiting for an early response from you.
32. Payments will be done online through our bankers, Bank of India, as mentioned in the letter.
33. We have a practice of making payments within a week after the arrival of goods.
34. We have been dealing in hand-tools for the last 10 years.
35. We have regard for the business relationship once created. We hope we will have a lasting business association.

Mention other conditions, if so desired

36. Prices quoted should be f.o.b or f.o.r.
37. We shall require delivery of the material at our plant in Faridabad.
38. Payment of goods received is made through our bankers within a week after delivery.

Close of the letter

39. If the goods are up to our satisfaction, we wish to have a long-term business relationship with you.
40. As the matter is urgent, we would appreciate an early reply, preferably within a week.
41. As our expansion plans are afoot, we require the information at the earliest.

Enquiry about Advertised Goods

Referring to the advertisement

1. We have recently seen the advertisement of your ball-point pen on television.
2. For quite some time, we have been watching your advertisement of cooking-ranges in newspapers, magazines and television.
3. We got to know about your range of cosmetics through an advertisement film.
4. We are interested in the latest hair tonic introduced in your advertisement.
5. We have seen your advertisement in The Times of India and will be grateful if you could send us particulars of the television you have advertised.

6. We shall feel obliged if you could furnish us with more details about your cooking range, advertised in CookeryPlus recently.

Asking for more information

7. The advertisement, however, does not give sufficient information.
8. Although the advertisement gives the price, yet other details like size, shape, quality and discount offers are missing.
9. The advertisement, however, is too brief to get fair idea about the product.
10. Your short advertisement on television gives insufficient information about the product.
11. A newspaper advertisement, however, gives only a rough idea of colour and shape of the product.
12. We would, therefore, appreciate more details about the product.
13. Since we are highly interested in this product, please let us know from where and how we can buy it.
14. Kindly share printed literature about the product.
15. We would, therefore, request you to send us the catalogue, price list and other printed material having the details about the product.
16. As I shall not be available in the country next week, I request you to please share complete product details at the earliest.
17. As we want to buy it in bulk, we would appreciate more information about the same.

Closing the letter

18. Samples would be particularly welcome.
19. Can you please arrange a demonstration of the product at our office location or at some other place convenient to both of us?
20. We would appreciate a call from your representative soon.
21. We would, in fact, appreciate a personal meeting with your Marketing Manager.
22. We hope this is the beginning of a lasting business relationship.
23. We usually make huge purchases. So we would like to get the relevant information about the products before hand.
24. Thus, please, send us complete information about your products.
25. We deal in steel furniture and often have similar product requirements. We sincerely hope for a lasting business relationship between us.
26. We are sure you will find dealing with us a pleasure.
27. We hope to get a quick response from you.

Request for Catalogues, Price-List and Samples

1. I saw one of your executive tables in one of my friend's office and found it quite impressive/elegant.
2. I have a large domestic appliance retail business and am interested in the electric ovens you have been advertising on television.
3. A friend of mine has recently bought electric shavers from you for his retail shop. I'm also interested in buying them.
4. Your firm has been recommended to us by M/s. Kala Mandal Centre who happen to be our regular customers.
5. The other day I came across a demonstration of your CD player in our market and found it quite attractive and handy.
6. We shall feel obliged if you could send us the samples and price list of your new range of shirting material by post, courier or through your salesman.
7. We are interested in buying fancy table-cloths being manufactured by you.
8. We have seen your advertisement on Star TV and would be thankful to receive your catalogue for the new ball, recently introduced.
9. We have a good demand for neckties in our market. Thus, we would really appreciate if you could send us your price-list at the earliest.
10. Your advertisement for the sewing machine interests us. Please send us complete details of the product as soon as possible.
11. I am particularly interested in furniture suitable for a small office. Kindly share the price and discount details at the quickest.
12. As we have an advertising agency, we are particularly interested in art material like painting brushes, poster and pastel colours, etc.
13. I need a similar machine, but smaller in size, for small-scale printing.
14. With our large sales network, we hope to give you a substantial annual business.
15. As we are an export house, we shall help you to introduce your products in foreign markets too.
16. So, could you please share a copy of the catalogue and price-list of your new VCP collection along with the leaflets to be given to our prospective customers?
17. Kindly share a copy of your detailed catalogue to us.
18. So, please send us a copy of your catalogue and other important information so that we can make the best choice.
19. Please let us know what discount do you normally give on bulk purchases?
20. As we are planning an expansion of our business soon, we would like to have this information at the earliest.
21. We would appreciate an early reply with latest information on the discussed product.

22. When replying, please specify your delivery schedule as well.
23. As we have urgent requirement, please let us know if you can supply the goods from stock before end of this week.
24. We shall appreciate if you could offer special discount on bulk purchases.

Request for Quotations

Give your introduction first

1. We have recently started rnanufacturing transistor radio sets and will be in need of bulk supplies of dry batteries.
2. We are large-scale fabricators of children's garments and now propose to diversify into men's wear as well.
3. We will be shortly opening a crockery shop at main Chandni Chowk and wish to stock a wide range of China and glassware you offer.
4. We are the wholesale dealers in all types of cotton fabric.
5. We undertake contract for door-to-door sales of consumer products.

Now make further enquiries from seller

6. We have seen the samples of the battery-cell through your representative recetly.
7. As you manufacture a wide range of men's shirtings, we hope you will be able to meet our requirements in terms of quality and quantity.
8. As you are a major quality manufacturer of glassware and crockery in the region, we would like to receive stocks from you.
9. Your range of cosmetics will add to our variety.
10. The new soap developed by your company is likely to be a saleable item in our list of products. It appears to be a profitable proposition.

Tell about your requirements

11. We are looking for reasonably-priced quality cells from you so as to order them in bulk, around 5000 or more at one time.
12. However, at present, we propose to place a trial order to you.
13. We are planning to stock goods in bulk and thus need an acceptable quote from you.
14. We deal exclusively with wholesale dealers and, hence, we shall need huge and regular supply of the products.
15. We are government suppliers/exporters and thus require high quality material.

Request for quotations

16. Could you please send at the earliest the best quotation for 10,000 dry batteries to be delivered over a period of one year?
17. We, therefore, look forward to your quotations for one thousand bone china tea-sets along with the terms and time of delivery.
18. Can you please send us best quotations for the following items of crockery?
19. It is, therefore, requested that you send us quotations for bulk supply of this raw material along with your terms and conditions.
20. Please share your current best and confirmed offers, along with the delivery schedule. We want urgent deliveries.

Brief instructions

21. We want to place an order of 500 toddler baby frocks. Please send a quote for the same along with delivery time, discounts and other details.
22. To start with, please send us best quotation for 1000-metre fine cotton shirting material. If we feel the demand, we shall place a bigger order soon.
23. Thus, please send quotations for the supply of 1000 pairs of nylon socks at the earliest.
24. Can we have samples and best quotation for 2000-metres of curtain material from you?
25. Our decision relies not only on quotations but also on samples. Therefore, we request you to please share both of them as soon as possible.
26. We need a sample before finalising the deal. So please send one tea set so that we can evaluate the product and place orders accordingly.
27. Are you in a position to manufacture customised dress material? If so, we shall send the specifications and thereafter have the quotations for the same from you.

Close

28. A prompt reply would be appreciated/is expected.
29. We hope your quotation is favourable enough to start a long-term business relationship between us.
30. The tenders will be opened on 21st December at 3.00 p.m. in the office of the Chief Administrator.
31. We emphasise more on quality rather than price. So please keep this criterion in mind.
32. If you offer us a really competitive quotation, we would like to place a large order.
33. If your price is unmatchable as compared to other suppliers, we shall place an immediate order with you. Hence, please share the best possible rates with us.

Enquiry about Raw Material Supply

Introduction

1. We are large scale distributors of kitchenware and now propose to manufacture a variety of crockery and other modern kitchenware.
2. We are leading steel utensil makers of north India and also are importers of steel sheets from West Germany.
3. We are leading manufactures of synthetic cloth of different varieties and require large quantities of nylon and terene yarn for the purpose.
4. We have recently started manufacturing of small rubber items like rubber bands, erasers and floaters. We curretly require natural rubber in bulk.
5. At present we are manufacturing men's wear. We regularly require fabrics of diverse qualities and designs in bulk.

Enquiry about supplies

6. Please let us know at the earliest if you could supply extruded raw plastic to meet our requirements.
7. As we plan to go in for import substitution shortly, please confirm if you can meet our heavy demand of steel sheets with the following specifications.
8. Will you be able to supply yarn as per our requirements?
9. To what extent can you meet our requirements? Our requirement details are given below.
10. Kindly send us samples of your production range with price and other important details.
11. Kindly state your supply capacity along with the general terms and conditions of your company.

Close

12. On getting your positive response, we shall share our requirements and other particulars to you.
13. If you can meet our requirements, please do share your terms and conditions regarding prices, trade-discount, delivery schedule, etc.
14. We hope your terms and conditions are reasonable and we get into strong business relationship.
15. Before despatching the consignment, do inform us how you are sending it so that we can track accordingly.

General Enquiries

Beginning

1. Please let us know the terms and conditions on which you can supply 100 boxes of full size nylon socks.
2. We have come to know that you are a reputed dealer in electrical goods. Can you supply 100 tube-lights within a couple of days? The requirement is urgent.
3. We come to know that you are among the leading manufacturers of stainless-steel utensils. We would like to know if you can supply 100 plates from the ready stock at the factory price.
4. This is to enquire if you supply zinc appliances in bulk. The list of the products required by us is enclosed herewith.
5. We request you to supply us with photographic material immediately, in a day or two maximum. The list of items required is enclosed with this.
6. We recently came to know about your plastic material business. We would like to know if you supply the raw material in small fraction also.

Closing

7. We look forward to hearing from you soon.
8. As the matter is urgent, we shall appreciate an early reply from you.
9. If the material matches our requirements, we would like to place regular bulk orders.
10. We rely on you for standard material and, therefore, expect you to be prompt to our enquiries.
11. As we have got increased demand now, earliest possible supply will be appreciated.
12. We would like to hear soon from you. Our enquiries may turn into big orders, if the terms and prices are found satisfactory.
13. We will appreciate an early reply.
14. Please get back to us at the earliest.

Sample Letters

Dealer's first enquiry

Dear Sir,

We have come across the advertisements about your domestic appliances in various magazines and newspapers.[1] Please send us some samples with information about their prices, quality, range, etc.[7] We have direct approach to the industries and they always look to us for the supply. Find enclosed our company brochure for reference.[20] Kindly let us know the general and product-specific terms and conditions.[22] We are eagerly waiting for an early response from you.[31] Payment of goods received is made through our bankers within a week after delivery.[38] If the goods are up to your satisfaction, we wish to have a long-term business relationship with you.[39]

Thanking you,

Yours faithfully,

Enquiry about advertised goods

Dear Sir,

We have recently seen the advertisement of your ball-point pen on television.[1] Although the advertisement gives the price, yet other details like size, shape, quality and discount offers are missing.[8] As we want to buy them in bulk, we would appreciate more information about the same.[17] We hope this is the beginning of a lasting business relationship.[22]

Thanking you,

Yours faithfully,

Request for catalogue, price-list and samples

Dear Sir,

I saw one of your executive office tables in one of my friend's office and found it quite impressive/elegant.[1] I am particularly interested in furniture suitable for a small office. Kindly share the price and discount details at the quickest.[11]

Thanking you,

Yours faithfully,

General enquiries

Dear Sir,

We have come to know that you are a reputed dealer in electrical goods. Can you supply 100 tube-lights within a couple of days? This requirement is urgent.[2] We look forward to hearing from you soon.[7]

Thanking you,
Yours faithfully,

Business-replies

It costs considerable efforts to get a prospective buyer encouraged to enquire about your product and be your customer. Thus, a reply to his query has to be cleverly and politely drafted.

It is just like a customer being attracted by a window display. It is then the job of the salesman to sell something to him by tempting him with product features, etc. Similarly, your responsibility as a sales person is heavy. Smart handling on your part may result in getting the enquiry turned into an order. Remember, the prospective buyer wants to know how he can get benefit from the deal; hence you have to focus on this only. For the enquirer's convenience, you can always attach a list of goods along with benefits and attractive features. They can be ticked by the customer for the placing of order.

At times, the order cannot be immediately met because of lack of fresh stocks. In such cases, the order should be acknowledged and the customer should be assured of prompt delivery.

Reply to Dealer's First Enquiry from Manufacturer about His Product

Convey pleasure on receiving the enquiry

1. Thank you for your letter dated May 23, 2017 enquiring about our domestic appliance range.
2. We are pleased to see your interest in the corduroy we have recently introduced in the market.
3. We are happy to learn that you are interested in our plastic crockery.
4. We are honoured with your interest shown in our product.
5. We are glad to receive your letter regarding the information required on our electronic appliances.

6. We are thankful to you for sending your representative to enquire about our readymade garments.
7. We are privileged to have your letter enquiring about bulk purchase of our cosmetic items.
8. Since our goods are of high quality, our wholesale rates are a bit higher than the market rates.
9. We believe in quality and honest bargains, so we assure you of best services and fairest deal.
10. Although we give f.o.r. up to the destination, we do charge for packing and local transportation.
11. We offer six-month guarantee on the goods and therefore you may exchange them during this period, in case there is any manufacturing defect.
12. We send goods by road transport as we believe in prompt service.
13. If desired by you, we can insure the goods at your expenses.
14. All money transactions will be made through our authorised bank, Punjab National Bank.

Express hope of mutual goodwill

15. We shall be pleased to furnish any other information you may need.
16. We hope you will be able to place an order with us soon.
17. We shall deal promptly with any order you send us.
18. We assure you of a long lasting business relationship.
19. Although at the moment we have many orders in hand, yet we will try our best to execute yours at the earliest.
20. We have enough stocks to comply with your orders immediately.
21. We have the items in stock which you enquired of and can deliver as soon as we receive your orders.
22. We are confident that you will be satisfied with the quality of our goods and will associate only with us for your future requirements.
23. We assure you of our fullest co-operation and services in future too.

Reply to Enquiry about Advertised Goods

Express pleasure on customer's having marked the advertisement

1. We are happy to learn that you have noticed our advertisement in last week's newspapers.
2. We are delighted to learn that you have taken interest in our commercial programme on Star TV.
3. We are pleased to know that you have seen our advertisement on television and are interested in the hair-tonic manufacture.
4. It's been a pleasure to know that you have seen our short telefilm on our latest tooth paste product.
5. We are pleased to know that our advertisements about Mopeds on FM and television have been impressing our customers and we are getting healthy response from them.
6. We are quite satisfied with the positive response to our advertisements.
7. We feel that our advertisements have served the purpose and are happy to find that you interested in our goods.

Give more details

8. As the advertisement does not carry all the details, we enclose a printed folder enlisting our new line of products and their prices.
9. We hope that the literature attached herewith would give you all required information about the product, its range and price.
10. We have plans to diversify into ladies garments soon.
11. We are sending you details about our goods with further reference to our advertisements.

Give information about the goods

12. We hope the enclosed list is sufficient to have clear understanding as it contains detailed information about the advertised goods.
13. Our products are of high quality and will be up to your satisfaction.
14. The catalogue will indicate the variety of sizes and colours of this popular product.
15. We are sure that in addition to the advertised items there are many other products illustrated with details in the folder which might interest you.
16. In fact, we are a Company set up with German collaboration and you can completely rely on our quality.
17. Our goods are always the same as advertised. We are sure to satisfy you through our dealings.

Close the letter with a hope of getting the order

18. We hope that the rates would appeal you and prompt you to place an early order with us.
19. If you place an early order with us, you can expect a delivery within a week.
20. We can arrange for a demonstration of our sewing machine at a place convenient to you.
21. We are sure that the high quality of our products and attractive trade terms will encourage you to stock these fast-selling items.
22. If you want any other information before placing an order, our representative would be happy to call you as per your convenience.
23. If you place a bulk order, we'll give discount. The discount terms are enclosed herewith.

Reply to Request for Catalogues, Price-list and Samples

Express pleasure on receiving the letter

1. We are pleased to receive your letter of April 8, 2017 in response to our advertisement for mixers.
2. Thank you for the telephonic enquiry last Tuesday regarding our various transistors.
3. As requested in your letter dated 10th September 2017, we enclose a catalogue in respect of our different products.
4. This is in response of your enquiry dated 4th January 2017.
5. We are obliged for your enquiry of 3rd July regarding the prices of different items.

Fulfil the request

6. As requested by you, we enclose a copy of our detailed catalogue.
7. Please find enclosed the catalogue of our domestic appliances.
8. As per your enquiry, I am enclosing a catalogue with current price list of our mixers.
9. We are enclosing a few photographs and arranging to send you some of our samples so as to give you fair idea of our range of products.
10. Our salesmen are soon going to conduct a door-to-door campaigning in your area next week. They will give samples to you as well. A price-list, however, is enclosed for now.
11. We are sure you will find our enclosed price list reasonable enough to move on with the deal.
12. The catalogue lists cost of different items. These are our latest and best prices.
13. This is our latest catalogue with revised prices and features.
14. It's our pleasure to share a copy of our illustrated catalogue/latest price list you've asked for in your letter of 23rd May.

15. We are pleased to receive your enquiry last week and thus enclose our catalogue with the endorsing letter for you.
16. On account of Diwali, we offer 15% discount on all items purchased. Please do not let this golden opportunity pass on and place an order immediately for the best offers.
17. We will arrange to send samples of our shirting material soon. If in case, any of your representatives comes to our new market showroom, he may collect them from there too.
18. Samples of our shirting range, which you have asked for in your letter of 15th March, are being sent to you today through our representative. Hope you would like them.

Give details of the catalogue

19. We feel, you may be particularly interested in our No.3 mixer. In fact, this is our latest and the most economical model so far.
20. Our terms and conditions are printed on the back-cover of the catalogue.
21. The catalogue has been devised keeping in view all the relevant information the buyer might require.
22. You will find particulars of the electric kettle and its illustration on page 10 of the catalogue.

Give details of the product

23. Without any increase in fuel consumption, it gives out just 15% more heat than the earlier models.
24. We feel the item illustrated on page 4 of the catalogue is ideal for your current requirement.
25. All our current models are shock-proof, efficient in operation and more economical in fuel consumption.
26. As evident from the illustrated catalogue, all our new models come in elegant cases.
27. In case you want a smaller size, there are many suitable ones listed on page 12 of the catalogue.
28. Considering your current requirement, we recommend you to choose any of the items given from page 14 to 16.

Close the letter with the hope of getting the order

29. We look forward to getting a trial order, which will convince you of our product quality.
30. In case you want a demonstration before placing an order, we shall be happy to welcome you to our show-room any time throughout the business hours. We are open from 10 a.m. till 7 p.m.
31. You will surely get a chance to explore the variety of items if you call on us.

32. We sincerely hope that our price-list enables you to place orders and establish trade relations with us.
33. We hope the samples reach you safely and you place an order with us soon.
34. We wish to hear from you very soon and expect your multiple orders.
35. Feel free to place an order in bulk and avail of our discount offers.
36. We trust you will not miss the chance of our current offer and will place an early order.
37. On account of Diwali festival, we have come up with special benefits to customers who place orders before the end of this month.

Reply to Request for Quotations

Beginning

1. Thank you for your enquiry of August 3, regarding quotation for 100 'Executive' model office tables.
2. This is with reference to your enquiry put on November 5, 2016. As per your request, we shall be supplying you nylon socks at the rate of ₹ 15/- per pair.
3. In response to your letter received last Monday, we are happy to send the following quotation for the goods you have indicated.
4. As per your request, the prices of the items required by you are as given below.
5. Please find herewith our rates for all the items required by you. Kindly send your approval to proceed.

Closure

6. We hope you will find our rates reasonable and place an early order with us.
7. Please let us know by return of post if we may book your order at the prices quoted.
8. As our stocks of these goods are limited, we strongly recommend you to take early advantage of this opportunity.
9. As the prices quoted are exceptionally low and are likely to rise soon, in view of the imminent hike in the raw material price, we would advise you to place your order without delay.
10. You may find our rates a little higher than other manufacturers, but our quality is incomparable.

Reply to Enquiry about Raw Material Supply

Beginning

1. We are pleased to learn that you are a large-scale distributor of plastic crockery and plan to expand your business.
2. Thank you for the enquiry of April 2, 2017, for the purchase of steel sheets in bulk.
3. We are pleased to learn that you require nylon and terene yarn for the manufacture of synthetic cloth.

Closure

4. We will be glad to supply extruded raw plastic as per your requirement.
5. We have enough stock of steel sheets and can deliver whenever you require.
6. We are a big stockist of nylon and terene yarn and can supply the required quantity within a week of the request made.
7. You may please let us know your requirement for a number of frocks required, and we shall be fulfilling the same at the earliest.

Reply to General Enquiries

Beginning

1. We are pleased to receive your enquiry of January 3, 2017 about the multi-purpose electric iron marketed by us.
2. We are glad to learn that you are interested in our preserved food items.
3. It is nice to know that you are interested in a large variety of paper material, which we manufacture. We would like to know more about your requirement.
4. It is a pleasure to see your interest in stocking our entire range of electronic instruments.
5. Thank you for the interest you have shown in our fabrics.

Closure

6. We will be happy to furnish any further information you may require.
7. We are looking forward to your order.
8. We have a reputation for being prompt and efficiency is our watchword.
9. Any order you may like to place with us can be met immediately from the ready stock.
10. We have the items in stock and can deliver them as soon as we receive your order.
11. We are confident that you will be satisfied with the quality of our goods.
12. We hope to have a long lasting relationship with you.
13. We assure you of our fullest co-operation in business.

14. We shall be providing you the best after-sale services.
15. Trust our services and be sure about best quality and pricing.

Letter Rejecting Quotation

First thank the seller for sending quotation

1. Thank you for sending your quotation for the proposed purchase of 1000 yards of handloom cloth by us.
2. You were good enough to quote on 19th August for 100 electric heaters we proposed to buy from you.
3. I appreciate the quick response from you on the quotation requirement by us.
4. In response to our enquiry dated 8th June, we have received your quote for 200 plastic buckets along with the sample.
5. I am glad on receiving prompt quotation for 200 pairs of suede jackets I had proposed to purchase from you.

Express regret giving reasons

6. Their quality is definitely good but the prices are rather on the higher side. We have been purchasing the same kind of jackets at a much lower price till now.
7. Although the goods suit our requirements, their prices are much higher than we had expected.
8. The quality and prices of the fabric suit our requirements but your quotation reached us rather late. In the mean time, we had placed an order with some other manufacturer.
9. Although your prices are quite competitive, yet the sample does not meet our specifications.
10. We surely found the quality of your samples good, but your quote seems to be non-competitive.

Close on a positive note

11. We have asked for more quotations from other manufacturers. We shall take a final decision after taking their products' quality and prices into consideration.
12. However, next time we shall again invite quotations from you and hope that you will be prompt in replying.
13. If you are able to supply us better quality material on the same price, we can think over it.
14. I shall now seek quotations from other dealers, but may find it necessary to refer to you again if their prices are not an improvement over yours.
15. We have reviewed samples and prices of other manufacturers as well and found your quotation on a higher side. We shall come back to you, as and when required.

Sample Letters

(Reply to dealer's first enquiry)

Dear Sir,

Thank you for your letter dated May 23, 2017 enquiring about our domestic appliance range.[1] We believe in quality and honest bargains, so we assure you of best services and fairest deal.[9] We have enough stocks to comply with your orders immediately.[20]

Thanking you,
Yours faithfully,

(Reply to enquiry about advertised goods)

Dear Sir,

We are happy to learn that you have noticed our advertisement in last week's newspapers.[1] As the advertisement does not carry all the details, we enclose a printed folder enlisting our new line of products and their prices.[8] We hope the enclosed list is sufficient to have clear understanding as it contains detailed information about the advertised goods.[12] If you place an early order with us, you can expect a delivery within a week.[19]

Thanking you,
Yours faithfully,

(Reply to request for catalogue)

Dear Sir,

We are pleased to receive your letter of April 8, 2017 in response to our advertisement for mixers.[1] As requested by you, we enclose a copy of our detailed catalogue.[6] We feel, you may be particularly interested in our No.3 mixer. In fact, this is our latest and the most economical model so far.[19] On account of Diwali festival, we have come up with special benefits to customers who place orders before the end of this month.[37]

Thanking you,
Yours faithfully,

(Reply to requests for quotations)

Dear Sir,

Thank you for your enquiry of August 3, regarding quotation for 100 'Executive' model office tables.[1] Please let us know by return of post if we may book your order at the process quoted.[7]

Thanking you,
Yours faithfully,

(Reply to enquiry about raw material supply)

Dear Sir,

Thank you for your enquiry of August 3, regarding quotation for 100 'Executive' model office tables.[1] Please let us know by return of post if we may book your order at the process quoted.[7]

Thanking you,
Yours faithfully,

(Reply to general enquiries)

Dear Sir,

We are pleased to receive your enquiry of January 3, 2017 about the multi-purpose electric iron marketed by us.[1] We have the items in stock and can deliver them as soon as we receive your order.[10] We are looking forward to your order.[7]

Thanking you,
Yours faithfully,

(Reply to letter rejecting quotation)

Dear Sir,

Thank you for sending your quotation for the proposed purchase of 1000 yards of handloom cloth by us.[1] Although your prices are quite competitive, yet the samples do not meet our specifications.[9] If you are able to supply better quality material on the same price, we can think over it again.[13]

Thanking you,
Yours faithfully,

Business-letters promoting goodwill

Apart from winning customers, business letters promote goodwill too. These are letters which are written when apparently there is no dire need for doing so. Writing such letters is a part of official routine. However, special care should be taken to understand customers' requirements, because customer deserves the best.

Goodwill letters should be courteous and cordial. A slight personal touch can work wonders. These letters should be precise.

Those engaged in sales promotion realise the real worth of correspondence building up goodwill. The best way to achieve customer's goodwill is to offer best and up-to-date services. Very often, customer' letters of complaints are overlooked, which should not be the case. It must be noted that goodwill letters promote mutual understanding and are of considerable help, in times of fierce competition. One has to have a constructive approach towards business. Such letters are handy when important customers plan an expansion of their existing premises or seek a foreign collaboration. Additional services with friendly approach can win many customers. For instance, an offer of credit in the event of a fire in customer's warehouse can win his long-term trust in your company. These letters should always be written by responsible officers of the company.

Manufacturer's Goodwill-letter

First of all, express pleasure over customer's enquiries

1. Thank you for your enquiry dated May 10, 2017.
2. We are pleased to receive your letter dated August 8, 2017, enquiring about our hardware products.
3. Sincere thanks for sending a letter seeking information about a variety of our plastic products.
4. Thanks for showing interest in our cosmetic products.
5. We are obliged to have received your letter of enquiry dated July 22, 2017.
6. It gives us immense pleasure to know that you are interested in our computer hardware products.
7. We are glad to have received your note enquiring about the nature of polish used on our stoves.
8. We have got your letter dated July 23, 2017 expressing interest in our goods and we thank you for the same.

Now come to the point

9. As per your request, we enclose our catalogue and price-list.
10. Accordingly, we are enclosing pamphlets of our various products herewith.
11. Please find attached our latest catalogue with features addition.

12. This is our latest price-list and we hope you would find it competitive in prices.
13. Our representative will shortly deliver a sample of our latest soap prepared by our manufacturing division.
14. The prices and particulars about various items mentioned in the enclosed catalogue and pamphlets will certainly answer all your product-related queries.

Now suggest some business aspects promoting goodwill

15. You are most welcome to visit our factory whenever you are there in Mumbai.
16. We hope you would pay a visit to our factory so that we could show our high-quality raw materials and excellent workmanship to you.
17. If you find it convenient, please join us for a seminar on the "Changing Patterns of Automotive Industry" hosted by the company at Ashoka Hotel on April 8, 2017 at 10 a.m.
18. We sincerely feel that the information you would collect on a visit to our factory would prove interesting as well as useful for placing orders in future.
19. If you visit the current Trade-Fair at New Delhi, please do not forget to call at our stall. You can contact us at 9999999999.

Close the letter offering your extra services

20. If there is anything more we could do for you, please do not hesitate to write to us.
21. Please let us know how we can extend our services to you.
22. Feel free to contact for any other assistance from us.
23. Do not hesitate to contact us for any other concern.
24. We are soon going to celebrate the silver jubilee of the company's inception. We would wish you to join us on the happy occasion. A formal invitation will be sent to you soon.

Letter Explaining Late Reply

Begin with a slight touch of regret for delay

1. I am extremely sorry for the delay in sending the catalogue and price-list requested by you in your letter dated October 8, 2017.
2. I am extremely sorry for the delay in replying to your letter of August 8, 2017.
3. I regret for the delay in replying to you.
4. Sincere apologies for delayed reply to your request of April 8, 2017 for a demonstration of our photocopier.
5. It is a lapse on our part that we could not respond promptly to your enquiry of May 9.
6. We are really sorry for the delay in replying to enquiries as per your letter of July 2017.
7. I am sorry, I could not reply to you earlier.

Give reasons for delay

8. The delay was caused as our company's auditing was going on and I was completely tied up there.
9. The delay has occurred as I was on tour last week and could not attend to your request.
10. We have unexpectedly run out of samples, and as soon as they are replenished, we shall despatch you the ones you have asked for.
11. Our Technical Representative, who gives the demonstration, has reported sick last week. So, we could not arrange an early demonstration to you.
12. On account of some labour problem, the work was disrupted and hence I could not attend to your request earlier.
13. There were some technical issues in our production department and I was caught up in resolving that.

Apologise again while closing the letter

14. I hope you will bear with us for this short period of delay.
15. We hope you do not mind this delay on our part which will not recur.
16. I regret the inconvenience this delay has caused you.
17. We shall make sure that this delay doesn't happen again.
18. I honestly hold the responsibility for this delay, but request you to take it in good spirits.
19. This is the first occasion that we were late in replying. So we hope you will not mind it.
20. It is, of course, a lapse on our part but we assure that we will take care to meet on queries promptly in future.

Letter of Regret

Begin with conveying your pleasure

1. Thank you for submitting your manuscript of "Business Letter Writing" to me.
2. Thank you indeed for the sample of your new cheese you have sent us.
3. I am grateful to you for the sample 'copy' you have prepared for the advertisement we plan to release soon.
4. You were certainly prompt in despatching the catalogue and price-list in response to our enquiry.
5. We appreciate your promptness in sending your representative for demonstration of washing machine.
6. Thanks for the sample of new detergent powder which you sent to us last week.

Express genuine regrets/ inability

7. I am, of course, impressed with the care with which you have written the book and I would have certainly accepted it for publication had we not released a book on a similar subject only last month.
8. It is definitely a fine product but unfortunately does not meet our requirements at the moment.
9. The advertisement 'copy' is definitely a sincere effort, but this is not the type of advertising we have in mind.
10. Your catalogue and price-list are surely informative but rather on the higher side and not suitable for the market in which we operate.
11. The demonstration performed by your representative was quite satisfactory, but we have postponed the project for the time being. I am sorry for our present inability to move on with this deal.
12. Thank you for the promptness in attending to our enquiries but in view of certain unforeseen expenditure, I am sorry, at present we are unable to place the order.

Close the letter with a touch of regret

13. I am, therefore, most regretfully returning your manuscript.
14. I am sorry but we won't be able to proceed with the deal for now.
15. Sincere aplogies but I am not in a position to utilise your services at the moment, but, I will definitely get in touch with you some time next month.
16. We regret but we are not yet equipped to sell your fine product.
17. I hope our inability to place orders for your goods at present, will not disturb our good business relations.
18. I am sure we will continue to have business deals in future, despite this temporary gap.
19. We have filed your catalogue and hope to place orders at some appropriate time in future.

Letter of Regret for Oversight

Refer to the oversight

1. It has come to our notice that the consignment sent to you on 5th of the month has fifteen garments less than mentioned in our despatch letter.
2. We regret to inform you that the curtain material sent to you on the 8th of this month is not the quality to what you had ordered for.
3. This is to inform you of a mistake in the despatch of ten bone china tea-sets on the 10th of this month.
4. We regret to inform you that 20 electric kettles despatched to you on 5th June are of the "medium" size while you had ordered for "large" size.

5. We are sorry but we have just been informed by our sales person that wrong order has been delivered at your place.

Express regret or concern

6. We are extremely sorry for this oversight.
7. In fact, because of the oversight of the despatcher, the lables of address on the boxes got changed.
8. Actually, our sales department followed instructions given in your earlier letter and, by mistake, your second letter was overlooked.
9. There were few other orders for the same location, and the salesman got confused in addresses. The mistake, however, is definitely at our end.

Now, talk of amends

10. However, we have instructed our sales department to prepare a fresh consignment and despatch it to you at the earliest. I hope you will receive it within a week.
11. Please arrange to return the earlier goods at our expenses. The replacements will be despatched tomorrow.
12. We assure you that in future we shall not give you any cause to complain. For now, we are sending the correct order today and request you to kindly return the wrong one.

Sample Letters

(Manufacturer's goodwill letter)

Dear Sir,

We are pleased to receive your letter dated August 8, 2017, enquiring about our hardware products.[2] As per your request, we enclose our catalogue and price list.[9] We hope you would pay a visit to our factory so that we could show our high-quality raw materials and excellent workmanship to you.[16]

Thanking you,
Yours faithfully,

(Letter explaining late reply)

Dear Sir,

I am extremely sorry for the delay in sending the catalogue and price-list requested by you in your letter dated October 8, 2016.[1] The delay was caused as our company's auditing was going on and I was completely tied up there.[8] I hope you will bear with us for this short period of delay.[14]

Thanking you,
Yours faithfully,

(Letter of regret)

Dear Sir,

Thank you for submitting your manuscript of 'Business Letter Writing' to me.[1] I am, of course, impressed with the care with which you have written the book and I would have certainly accepted it for publication had we not released a book on a similar subject only last month.[7] I am, therefore, most regretfully returning your manuscript.[13]

Thanking you,
Yours faithfully,

(Letter of regret for oversight)

Dear Sir,

It has come to our notice that the consignment sent to you on 5th of the month has fifteen garments less than mentioned in our despatch letter.[1] We are extremely sorry for this oversight.[5] However, we have instructed our sales department to prepare a fresh consignment and despatch it to you at the earliest. I hope you will receive it within a week.[9]

Thanking you,
Yours faithfully,

Business-letters of Thanks

Business relations often call for letters of thanks and appreciation. Such letters enlarge areas of influence and are profitable in the long run. The content has to weigh more in spirit than in letter. The art of writing a truly concise letter is a difficult one. One has to infuse the letter with a touch of goodwill, cordiality and friendship. This can be done in the opening paragraphs. Here are a few examples.

Opening paragraphs

1. We received with thanks your order No… dated…
2. We acknowledge with thanks the receipt of your order No…
3. This is to thank you for your enquiry/ order No…
4. Thank you for your Order No… dated…
5. It gives great pleasure to receive your order…
6. We are delighted to receive your order...

Some occasions for letters of thanks

1. Getting an order from a new customer;
2. Getting large orders from old customers;
3. Getting prompt payments/ remittances;
4. Getting useful promotional suggestions.

Getting an order from a new customer

1. When you get first order from a new customer, send a personal letter of appreciation immediately. Such a letter should be written by a senior official. This will fetch a lasting goodwill.
2. Mention a definite date for executing the order so as to win customer's trust for long-term.
3. Close the letter with a note of appreciation/goodwill and express your pleasure in serving your customer.

Getting large orders from old customers

The old trade relations and customers are as important as the new ones. Due attention and recognition should be paid to their letters and timely execution of orders. Here also, you can follow same methods as above, besides the following:

1. Stimulate old customer's interest in your products by including some sales talk and selling points of the goods ordered by him.
2. Suggest the profits he can make from the sale of goods ordered by him.
3. Expectations of fresh orders should be given at the close of letter.

Getting prompt payments remittance

Getting prompt payments are as important as getting orders. This keeps the business run smoothly. Therefore, it is necessary to express appreciation/gratitude over prompt realisation of money.

Getting useful promotional suggestions

These are the wholesale dealers or retailers who come in direct touch with the customers. As customers are the best judges of a product's quality, their reactions go a long way in reviewing and improving a product. Letters of suggestions, thus, should be acknowledged with appreciation.

Letter of Thanks for the First Order

Begin your letter with thanks

1. Thank you for your order dated May 8, 2017. Please note that your order of 100 woollen blankets will be despatched on next Monday, i.e., 23rd May, 2017.
2. We acknowledge with thanks your order dated 13th November. We despatched the crockery yesterday at your mentioned address. Please find enclosed our invoice No. 4321 for the same order.
3. We are pleased to inform you that the glassware you had ordered on May 15, 2017, has been couriered to you today and shall reach you by 25th May. Courier slip has been attached for your reference.
4. Thank you for your order dated July 8, 2017, for 200 Oxford pocket dictionaries. The books will be despatched by the beginning of next week.
5. We thank you for placing an order with us. For your information, you will be receiving the ordered goods by next Monday definitely. We have despatched them through Kangaru Transport yesterday.
6. We feel proud to serve you for the first time and hope to establish good relations in future.
7. I am obliged for the opportunity you have given us, to have business transactions with you for the first time. I sincerely hope for a lasting business relation with you.

While closing the letter, expect your customer to be satisfied

8. We wish you will find the crockery up to the mark in every respect and perfectly matching to your requirements.
9. We wish the goods will reach you safely and in time and that you will be satisfied with their quality.
10. We hope you'll like the product quality and will share further orders with us soon.
11. We look forward to serving you contentedly, in future too.
12. We hope the goods quality will meet your requirements and we can have pleasant and lasting business connections with you.
13. Please acknowledge the receipt. Hope you find the goods up to your expectations.
14. May we hope that this order is a promising beginning of a pleasant and fruitful business relationship between us in the long-run?
15. We trust this order will go a long way in creating an era of healthy business relations with your reputed company.

Letter of Thanks for Large Orders

Begin the letter with your appreciation/ gratitude

1. We appreciate the unusually large order for 'Weekend' shoes and thank you for your continued confidence in us.
2. Thanks for the large order of dry battery cells you have placed with us. We will make sure that your confidence remains with us for long-term.
3. We are grateful for your large order dated 8th October for 'Deluxe' office tables. We feel extremely honoured at your confidence in us.
4. We are thankful to you for such a substantial order of transistor sets and the trust you have maintained in us.
5. Our sales team is jubilant over the large order of 9th July for bed sheets that you have placed with us. We assure you of our prompt compliance of the same.
6. Your large order for vegetable oil with us shows your good confidence reposed in us. Thanks a lot for this.

Discuss prospects of good business relations

7. We have always valued our esteemed relationship built over years and we will do our best to maintain it.
8. Our relationship with your firm has always been a matter of great asset for us, and we will do everything to strengthen it.
9. You have always been our esteemed customer. We hope our relationship, built over years of mutual confidence, will grow further in coming days.
10. We assure our full co-operation in growing business relations between us.
11. We assure that we shall never let your confidence in us go down and that there would never be any complications in our business relations.
12. We have, in fact, always counted on you for big supplies. We hope it goes for long-term.

While closing the letter, convey your gratitude again

13. It has always been a great pleasure to deal with you.
14. Very soon we are planning a diversification of our business into hosiery industry and will despatch samples for review to you soon.
15. Thank you again for this fine expression of your continued trust in us.
16. We once again extend our thanks for relying upon our prompt service and credit.

Thanks for Prompt Settlement of Accounts

Start the letter with thanks and a cheerful note

1. This is to thank you for the prompt settlement of our accounts during the preceding year.
2. This is to express our sincere thanks for settling our bill promptly.
3. Thank you for the prompt settlement of our accounts during the preceding financial year.
4. We thank you for your quick settling of all our outstanding bills.
5. Ever since you have started business association with us, you have always been making timely settlements of our accounts. We are extremely thankful to you.

Mention utility of swiftness in payments

6. It has eased our financial burdens as a number of bills were pending with us.
7. Your payment has been of great help to us at a time when we ourselves were facing heavy commitments connected with the development of our business.
8. The timely payment by you is indeed a proof of your professional business ethics.
9. Quick payment has come in handy as we had been planning to make some bulk purchases this week.
10. Swiftness in settling the accounts is, of course, a sign of your high reputation in this business market.

Expectations for lasting cordial relations may be touched upon at the close of the letter

11. We hope you will continue to give us the opportunity to serve you.
12. This is a positive indication of our growing cordial relations.
13. It has always been a matter of great pleasure for us to serve you.
14. We sincerely hope that our business relationship will continue to grow in future, irrespective of the unintentional slips on our part.
15. I am sure we can count upon such good co-operation from you in future too.
16. Your co-operation will go a long way in establishing smooth and lasting relationships with your suppliers.

Thanks for a Service Performed

Begin your letter with thanks

1. Thanks for returning the draft of the catalogue along with your detailed comments on it.
2. We sincerely thank you for your enlightening suggestions concerning the publicity folder we intend to publish soon.

3. Please accept our sincere thanks for your valuable suggestions for improvement of our products' quality.
4. Thank you for contacting the transporter on our behalf.
5. Your tips for the boost of our sales will definitely help us modify and improve the quality of our product.

Discuss the services rendered

6. We are indeed grateful to you for the trouble you have taken for us.
7. I realise how busy you are. And despite your pre-occupations, you have taken time for our job.
8. Your detailed examination of our proposal would be extremely useful to us.
9. I am sure your valuable suggestions will help us a lot in giving a thrust to our business activities.
10. The modifications you have suggested will certainly make our product more useful and popular in the market.

Repeat your appreciation again at the close

11. Thank you again for your highly useful suggestions.
12. Please accept our thanks once again for your kind service.
13. I hope we will be able to compensate for your valuable services in some way.
14. We again thank you for your valuable feedback.
15. Your ideas have indeed taken our publicity department by storm. Thanks once again.
16. Perhaps, I will never be able to pay for the valuable services you have rendered to us.

Sample Letters

(Letter of thanks for the first order)

Dear Sir,

Thank you for your order dated October 8, 2017. Please note that your order of 100 woollen blankets will be despatched on next Monday, i.e., 23rd November, 2017.[1] We wish the goods will reach you safely and in time and that you will be satisfied with their quality.[9]

Thanking you,
Yours faithfully,

(Letter of thanks for large order)

Dear Sir,

Thanks for the large order of dry battery cells you have placed with us. We will make sure that your confidence remains with us for long-term.[2] We have always valued our esteemed relationship built over years and we will do our best to maintain it.[7] It has always been a great pleasure to deal with you.[13]

Thanking you,
Yours faithfully,

(Thanks for quick settlement of accounts)

Dear Sir,

This is to thank you for the prompt settlement of our accounts during the preceding year.[1] It has eased our financial burdens as a number of bills were pending with us.[6] We hope you will continue to give us the opportunity to serve you.[11]

Thanking you,
Yours faithfully,

(Thanks for a service performed)

Dear Sir,

Thanks for returning the draft of the catalogue along with your detailed comments on it.[1] We are indeed grateful to you for the trouble you have taken for us.[6] I hope we will be able to compensate for your valuable services in some way.[13]

Thanking you,
Yours faithfully,

Sales-letters of Promotion

Sales promotion calls for the basic knowledge of the product being marketed, the particular areas of its wide acceptance, effective distribution networks, smart and active representatives, flexible and competent management and good knowledge of the market conditions. No product can be successful just on the basis of publicity. Quality is a must. It is, therefore, imperative that the person handling sales correspondence is competent and keeps all these factors in mind. He must have a deep understanding of all the involvements and implications of his approach in handling sensitive correspondence. A letter, of course, can make or mark entire prospects of an upcoming business.

A good letter may cover the following points:

1. Stimulate interest;
2. Create the buying impulse;
3. Build confidence about the product;
4. Clinch the bargain.

An effective sales letter should be easy to read and understand. The contents should be divided in short paragraphs. One should see to it that typing and stationery are clean. Certified and updated mailing lists for announcements and business circulars are also essential parts of a progressive business house. The letter should be well-drafted and posted on time.

Any mistake in the letter can have an adverse effect on company's sales and reputation. A businessman is no writer or journalist, but he is certainly expected to be able to express himself well. The ability to choose the right words and use them skillfully is essential for a good and effective correspondent. Punctuation, spellings, grammar, effective phrases and above all their meticulous use, make a world of difference in business sales promotion.

Introducing a New Product

Begin with an introduction about the new product

1. We take this opportunity to introduce you to our new can-opener/motor-cycle/filter, which we have launched in the market recently.
2. This is to keep you updated about our new revolutionary concept in safety locks, which have been recently marketed.
3. It is the result of painstaking research and exhaustive laboratory tests that we are able to launch this never-before easy-to-wash fabric in the market.
4. It is a major breakthrough that our engineers have achieved in automobile technology.
5. We are sure that the great utility and superb finish of the new product will convince you of its ready saleability.
6. Today, it is the best motor-cycle in the market in this price range.

Now build up confidence

7. We have sent you a sample of the product for your valuable comments and reactions.
8. We have sent a sample of this product to you and would welcome if you would put it to test.
9. We will soon be despatching its sample and hope you will approve of its quality.
10. We have full confidence that your inspection and testing of the product would let you know about the high quality of this product. For this purpose, you may please feel free to come to our office anytime between 10.00 a.m. and 2.00 p.m.

Discuss price range and business terms

11. The enclosed folder is indicative of its competitive price.
12. We are giving 20% discount on orders of ₹ 50,000 and above.
13. We can offer special terms even for your trial orders provided the orders reach us before the end of this month.
14. We give regular trade discount on a trial order too, if in case it is a big one.

Close the letter with an invitation for a trial order

15. We hope to get a positive response from you soon.
16. Request you to please send us a word in mail.
17. When you call for an order, please ask for me. I shall be there to assist you with the best offer.
18. As you wanted something of this kind, we hope you will soon place an order with us.
19. We request you to place a trial order with us so that we can prove our efficiency.
20. Place a trial order with us and we're sure you'll like the quality and service we offer.

Soliciting a Customer for a Product

Begin with asking customer's choice/ selection

1. Would you like to buy best summer fabric at an unmatched price?
2. Would you like to have a complete cooking machine that would save you time and energy by half?
3. Would you like to become popular with friends? Do you have an inferiority complex? Are you suffering from a chronic disease?
4. Do you want to buy the latest exquisite variety of the best south Indian silk saris?
5. Are you on the lookout for exquisite bone china crockery at a price never heard before?
6. Do you want your dinner party to be a super success?
7. Do you plan to go on a vacation but would need stress-free travel arrangements?

Mention your services/ products

8. The New Style Clothing will meet all your needs.
9. Then our 'Cook Master' is what you are looking for.
10. Become a knowledge master just by getting hold of our 'Treasure House of General Knowledge'.
11. Visit our 'Silkalaya' Emporium and have a look on all of them at one place.
12. Our exquisite, 50-piece dinner set is the one for you.

13. All you have to do is to read our 'Fabulous Recipes'.
14. You can leave everything to us and just relax on your trip.

Give more details of available services

15. Manufactured with the latest machinery, this fabric is launched with a lot of colour varieties.
16. Pure Product's butter is the proud owner of F.P.O mark of quality.
17. This unique domestic appliance is easy to handle and economical in power consumption.
18. At present, it is in heavy demand and if you don't order for it fast, you may be delayed in delivery.
19. This fascinating digest brings you facts from all over the world to enrich your knowledge.
20. If you are looking for a treasure of knowledge in one place, this is the book made for you.
21. All these saris are equally beautiful, if you can make a choice.
22. Nowhere else will you find such exquisite saris at such reasonable prices.
23. The dinner set will win all your guests' admiration and speak well of your taste.
24. In these exquisite pieces, art of the potter and painter has come together in all its perfection.
25. The book is a real treat for all book-lovers.
26. If you want to find international masterpieces of the culinary art at one place, this unique cookery book is what you are looking for.
27. We assure royal treatment for you and will plan each and every detail of your holiday carefully.
28. Reservations, bookings, entertainment, tickets—we take care of everything.
29. You may easily rely on us for a memorable tour that you will cherish throughout your life.

Close your letter by insisting on definite business

30. Do not be late. Please register with us by filling and posting us the enclosed form.
31. You are cordially invited to a demonstration of the machine at our factory, at your convenient date and time.
32. We could let you have a copy on approval basis.
33. Just one visit is all you need to be fascinated.
34. You are most welcome to visit our shop any time and test our statement.
35. Book your copy before it is too late.
36. So, why don't you drop in at our office for a chat and get all the details?
37. Hurry and grab the offer before it ends!

Soliciting a Customer for a Service

Begin your letter with a clear understanding of customer's requirements

1. We have been informed by M/s Vishal Bharat Suppliers Ltd., that you are looking out for competent agents for clearing and forwarding of consignments.
2. It has been brought to our notice that you propose to publish a number of books next year and that you are looking out for a good offset printing press.
3. I have been told by my friend. Mr. Suresh Jain, who is your Chartered Accountant that you are on the look-out for a representative with good contacts to handle your liaison work with the Government Departments in Delhi.
4. We understand from our client. Mr. Ramesh Gupta, that you require the services of a tax consultant for filing of your tax returns regularly.
5. I have been informed by one of your employees, Amit Chopra, that you are looking out for a good part-time accountant.

Begin your letter with a clear understanding of customer's requirements

6. It is our pleasure to introduce our services at your disposal and provide you with the best facilities.
7. This is to inform you that our large printing establishment is capable of handling your publication programme.
8. You will be glad to know that I have been a liaison-officer with DCM for more than 10 years. I am sure you can entrust me with your Delhi work.
9. I have been a practising tax-consultant for more than 20 years now, and it would be my pleasure to assist you.
10. I assure prompt and efficient service to you.
11. Our experience in this line has been of more than 20 years and we have been handling accounts of S.Kumars and Gopinath & Sons for the last 10 years.
12. Our staff is well-versed with the relevant procedures and all the work entrusted to us will be carried out timely and efficiently.
13. Enclosed are the details of our handling charges which are extremely competitive.
14. We have successfully handled similar work for other publishers too and it has been highly appreciated.
15. We also have modern computer typesetting facilities in our press.
16. Our rate list for various types of printing jobs is enclosed herewith, which is highly reasonable as compared to the market.
17. My contacts in this field have been profitably used by many leading business concerns.

18. For my professional experience and competence, you can please refer to M/s. Machine Makers Pvt.Ltd., and M/s. Rang Nirman Pvt. Ltd., for whom I have done similar work for many years.
19. I wish to inform you that several big and reputed concerns have appointed me as their Tax Consultant so far.
20. I have 20 years experience to my credit as an accountant in various concerns.
21. Timeliness and quality service are my specialities and if you hire my services, I guarantee both of them to you.

While closing, express expectations of positive response

23. We look forward to hearing from you.
24. I am sure you will be satisfied with our work.
25. I hope you will entrust this responsibility to me.
26. So, may I have the confidence that our association would prove to be mutually beneficial?
27. I would very much appreciate a trial of my services.

Manufacturer's Offer to Retailers

Begin with alluring offers

1. Here is a fabulous offer. Research has now enabled us to offer you a large range of toilet soaps at highly reduced rates.
2. We are happy to announce that our increased production capacity has now enabled us to offer you our quality cosmetics at reduced rates for large orders.
3. Our researchers have recently developed a new high quality detergent powder, which is much cheaper than the ones available in the market.
4. We have removed certain existing faults from our transistor-kits, which were brought to our notice by our customers and have now come up with updated kits with special discounts.
5. We are sure you will like our recently-developed cloth material, which is tested through a technical process.

Give details of goods offered

6. The details of price reduction along with the list of goods are enclosed for your reference.
7. Looking at our quoted price, you will agree that they are much below than those of other manufacturers in the market.
8. Moreover, we are offering flat 10% discount on purchase of ₹ 25,000 and above.
9. You can easily find the increased rates of discount proportionate to the purchasing amount. We also give guarantee for one year for proper functioning of the appliance.

10. Though there has been a slight hike in our prices, our quality has also improved accordingly.

Other Relevant Topics

11. The quality of our products, of course, remains unchanged.
12. You will see for yourself that the quality of our product has considerably improved.
13. Immediate despatch is guaranteed, as we have ample of stocks.
14. In fact, these are the additional accessories which have somewhat pushed up its price.
15. You will find a slight rise in prices but it is due to the high cost of raw material and improved product quality.

Expectations of getting business

16. We appreciate your confidence in us and look forward to serve you again.
17. We are sure that the new given prices will motivate you to place early and big orders with us.
18. We hope this new offer will put our relationship on a firmer footing.
19. We hope you will utilise this reduction to the maximum extent.
20. We look forward to a big order from you as we feel our new product's quality speaks for itself.
21. We sincerely hope that you'll give a big order to us soon.

Notifying Price Increase to Retailers

Announce the new prices and give reasons for the increased prices

1. With effect from the 1st of next month, the prices of all our products are being raised by 10%. This is due to even better quality production now.
2. We regret to announce that on account of the hike in power rates, we are compelled to raise the prices of our plasticware.
3. On account of the increase in overheads, we have most reluctantly decided to raise the prices of our electric wires by 5% from the 15th of this month.
4. We are compelled to raise the prices of our items by 10% from the 1st of next month due to increased electricity charges.
5. Our new consignment will have an increase of 15%, due to the increased cost of raw materials and excise duty.
6. We apologise for the price hike but we do not have any other option as we have received a directive from the All India Metal Product Manufacturers' Association for the same.
7. Please note that we have to go for products' price increase, which is due to a steep rise in the essential raw material's cost.

8. We would certainly not have taken this step, had the Government not subjected our raw material to heavy duty in the new budget.
9. This increase has become unavoidable because of the rising cost of labour, raw material and electricity.
10. This hike is the direct impact of the heavy import duty recently imposed by the Government on our raw materials.

Assure good quality products

11. However, please rest assured that there will be no change in the high quality of our products.
12. We guarantee that with increased prices, the quality of all products will be even better and not worse.
13. With increased product rates, you can be sure of good quality and better services from our end.
14. You can rely without any doubt on our superior quality of goods, which has its own image in the market.
15. You can always return the goods if they are not up to your satisfaction, though we are sure we'll never give such a possibility to you.

Express hope of cordial business relations

16. Our new price-list is under preparation and will be sent to you along with special offers.
17. However, we are giving concessions to our old customers and you're certainly among them. We will charge 5% less rates to what have been mentioned in the enclosed list for you.
18. We hope that our business relationship continues to be as cordial as before and the slight increase in price hike cause no reason for any annoyance.
19. We assure you of the same prompt service as we have been rendering in the past.
20. We hope that this slight increase in prices will not make any difference to our good business relations.

General Sales-letter

Opening

1. We are large scale manufacturers of leaf-springs and coil-springs and are taking the liberty of sending you a copy of our latest catalogue and price-list.
2. As you are our regular customer, we wish to give a special offer to you.
3. We hope you will be interested in the latest plastic goods we have introduced in the market on the terms and conditions mentioned in the catalogue.

4. We would like to offer some exclusive ready shirts with guarantee to you at prices never seen before.
5. We have recently bought a large quantity of antique pieces at very attractive terms. We offer them to you at very reasonable prices with hopes that you would love the quality and beauty of these pieces.

Closing

6. We hope you would definitely not like to skip this exceptional offer.
7. We look forward to a large order from you soon.
8. We are offering you articles of the highest quality at a very reasonable price and hope you will take the opportunity to try it out.
9. We know that heavy demand of our books exists in the market, thus, you will find an easy market for them. So do not miss the opportunity.
10. We shall be pleased to send our representative to you on receipt of the enclosed enquiry form duly filled in.
11. We shall be pleased to welcome you to our showroom at any time to give you a demonstration. For any other assistance in this regard, you may please call us anytime between 10 a.m. to 6 p.m. (Monday-Saturday).

Visits by Salesmen

Marketing salesmen are an asset to any company. They help to give a boost to the sales and popularise company's products. Very often, they go out of station to explore markets. Thus, it is advisable that their visits are preceded by letters of introduction or details intimating about their visits.

Sometimes even senior officers of the company make business trips to enhance business interests. In this context, letters acquire even greater significance.

Sample Letters

(Introducing a new product)

Dear Sir,

This is to keep you updated about our new revolutionary concept in safety locks, which have been recently marketed.[2] We have sent you a sample of the product for your valuable comments and reactions.[7] The enclosed folder is indicative of its competitive price.[11] We hope to get a positive response from you soon.[15]

Thanking you,
Yours faithfully,

(Soliciting a customer for a product)

Dear Sir,

Would you like to buy best summer fabric at an unmatched price? The New Style Clothing will meet all your needs.[8] Manufactured with the latest machinery, this fabric is launched with a lot of colour varieties.[15] Just one visit is all you need to be fascinated.[33]

Thanking you,
Yours faithfully,

(Soliciting a customer for a service)

Dear Sir,

It is our pleasure to introduce our services at your disposal and provide you with the best facilities.[1] Our staff is well-versed with the relevant procedures and all the work entrusted to us will be carried out timely and efficiently.[7] We look forward to hearing from you.[17]

Thanking you,
Yours faithfully,

(Manufacturer's offer to retailers)

Dear Sir,

Here is a fabulous offer. Research has now enabled us to offer you a large range of toilet soaps at highly reduced rates.[1] The details of price reduction along with the list of goods are enclosed for your reference.[6] You will see for yourself that the quality of our product has considerably improved.[12]

Thanking you,
Yours faithfully,

(Notifying price increase to retailers)

Dear Sir,

We regret to announce that on account of the hike in power rates, we are compelled to raise the prices of our plasticware.[2] However, please rest assured that there will be no change in the high quality of our products.[11] Our new price list is under construction and will be sent to you along with special offers.[16]

Thanking you,
Yours faithfully,

(General sales letter)

Dear Sir,
As you are our regular customer, we wish to give a special offer to you.[2] We know that heavy demand of our books exists in the market, thus, you will find an easy market for them. So do not miss the opportunity. We hope you would definitely not like to skip this offer.[6]
Thanking you,
Yours faithfully,

(Buyer's request for company's salesman to call)

Dear Sir,
We have read with interest your advertisement of plastic goods like toys, buckets, etc. in the latest issue of Femina. We are general merchants dealing in household items and feel that a market exists for their sale in our district. Therefore, please ask your representative to contact us when he visits this area. Also, please send your company brochure along with some good selection of samples.

With thanks,

Yours faithfully,

(Reply to letter requesting salesman's visit)

Dear Sir,
We are pleased to receive your letter dated March 9, 1982, and have arranged for Mr. Bharat Bhushan, our Sales Officer, to call you in the beginning of the next month. You will be glad to learn that our plastic buckets and tiffin-boxes have been highly appreciated by our customers and are constantly in demand. Once you have examined the samples, we are sure that you will like them as their quality speaks for themselves. As our products are in huge demand, we have been generally finding it difficult to meet quick requirements. Thus, we suggest you to place an early order (at least three weeks before) of the goods. We hope this is the beginning of a lasting relationship between us.

Thanking you,

Yours faithfully,

Orders for Goods

When an order for goods is placed, its various aspects must be kept in mind so as to avoid delay and complications in delivery. Details of goods must be mentioned very clearly. There should be no confusion about the specifications, quantity, mode of payment and transportation. The instructions are elaborated here for you.

1. Article, its quantity and quality

If the product line is long it is advisable to mention numbers on the catalogue referring to your requirements. However, if there is no catalogue attached, one can clearly mention the specifications like size, colour, and quantity.

2. Packaging

For packaging, special instructions are a must. Different types of products come in different packings for convenience in transportation. For instance, glassware and many chemicals call for a very thorough and specialised packing. Be sure which type of packing should be done for your required goods. If you are new to a product, you may ask for suggestions from manufacturer.

3. Delivery

Do give clear instructions about the delivery of goods. They can be sent through any convenient mode of transport like road, air or sea. The point of destination and date of delivery are again important points to be included. All these details are generally printed in a tabulated form to enable an easy and quick placing of order. Do make sure that there is no printing mistake in address and date, else, it will result in unwanted delay or blunder. Even the companies make suitable indenting forms or list of articles for easy placing of orders. It eliminates possibilities of omissions of important details.

General Letter for Placing Orders

1. We thank you for your letter dated 25th October, 1982 in response to our enquiry for the supply of 300 tea-cups. Kindly place the order for the following goods (list enclosed).
2. This is to confirm our telephonic conversation this morning regarding the purchase of 15 portable Remington typewriters. We enclose an order for the same.
3. Thank you for sending your new price-list on 1st May. Hereby, we would like to place an order for the items listed below:

   200 White bed sheets @ ₹ 100 per item

   300 Pillow covers @ ₹ 40 per item
4. As these items are urgently required by our customers, we will appreciate an immediate delivery.
5. We agree to the prices you have quoted in your letter yesterday and hereby request you to send the mentioned list of goods immediately.

6. Please let us know if your offer of 15% reduction on these items still stands or not.
7. Kindly let us know if we can expect goods' delivery by 15th November as they are quite urgently required.
8. Please send them by Kangaroo Transport, which has an office in your city.
9. We hope to receive your advice of delivery by return post.
10. Please note that we would not be able to accept the goods if delivered after 15th of next month as our customer shall be leaving for abroad then.
11. We shall be obliged for prompt delivery as the goods are needed urgently.
12. Since the crockery is a fragile item, please see to it that packaging is done properly and with utmost care.
13. A prompt execution of our order is solicited.
14. They can be sent through any goods train, bound for Delhi.
15. We request you to please confirm the expected delivery date of all listed items.

Placing Order from Catalogue

First indicate your requirements

1. Please send the following machine tools by V.P.P.
2. Thank you for sending the catalogue. We have marked for the goods urgently required by us.
3. I have gone through your latest catalogue and request you to send the items listed against the following numbers.
4. The printed date of catalogue is June 2017. Please confirm if this is the latest one.
5. We need immediate delivery of the following items, as per your new catalogue.
6. We are sending our delivery boy tomorrow between 9-11 a.m. for a spot delivery of 200 electric shavers. He will carry the catalogue which is marked for the size and shape of the items.
7. Kindly share the latest catalogue so that we can place early orders.

Refer to delivery and payment

8. Enclosed herewith is the cheque of ₹ 5000/- towards the total payment/advance mentioned in your letter.
9. I am enclosing herewith a crossed cheque of ₹ 5000/- towards the part payment of goods.
10. Please acknowledge the receipt of this advance payment and despatch us the parcel.
11. Please let me know the mode of payment.

12. Our payments are exclusively through cheques or drafts. What is your preference?
13. We are very prompt in making the payments but only through banks. Our banker is Oriental Bank of Commerce.
14. We shall appreciate your giving prompt attention to this order.
15. Please note that our payments are very prompt so you do not have to worry on that.
16. Please despatch the goods on receipt of this order.
17. Since we need the goods immediately, please do not delay further.
18. We are making the payments in advance just to facilitate your sending the consignment at the earliest. We know you have a tremendous regard for your old customers.
19. In case there is any hitch in the supply, please let us know immediately. We have an urgent requirement right now.
20. Please rest assured for timely payments from us.

Placing Order for Advertised Goods

Make a mention of the advertisement

1. I have seen your new tape recorder advertisement in Hindustan Times of August 4, and would like to place an order for five pieces.
2. I have listened with keen interest to your advertisement of "Rapidex English Speaking Course" on radio. Please send me two copies by V.P.P.
3. I have come across your advertisement of 'Kitchen Master' and hereby wish to place an order for one.
4. Advertisement of your detergent powder on the Delhi Television has convinced us about its good quality. Please supply the same as per our order below. Also, please clarify the payment terms and conditions.
5. We are impressed with the demonstration of your "Knit Master" in a television advertisement. I am placing order for five pieces.

Give details of delivery

6. Kindly send the books at the address given below.
7. Please despatch the article to the above address by or before the end of this week.
8. One of the two pieces is to be sent to my address given above and the other to the following name and address.
9. The address of the person, this is to be delivered, is as follows.
10. The moment you receive the advance payment of the item, please send it directly to the address given below.
11. Kindly execute this order immediately as I have to go out of station by next week.

12. Please find attached the advance payment cheque and attend to this order urgently.
13. We can arrange for our truck to collect the goods from your Delhi office anytime it is convenient to you. Advance payment cheque for the said order is attached with this.
14. I would appreciate your promptness in sending the items mentioned in the order letter. As discussed earlier, rest of the payment will be done as soon as the goods are delivered.
15. Please let me know about the launch of your new products, as and when you introduce something new.
16. Please send the ordered goods by 20th of this month and keep me informed about the new offers and discounts.

Acknowledgement of an Order

Convey pleasure on getting the order

1. We are pleased to have received your order No.123 for 20 immersion type water heaters.
2. We thank you for your order for 50 wall paintings (No.4B in our catalogue).
3. This is to acknowledge with thanks the receipt of your order for two dozen 'Constellation' neckties and matching hand kerchiefs.
4. Thank you for placing the order of ten sewing machines with us. We hereby acknowledge the receipt.
5. We have received the order no. 256 for 25 pairs of sports shoe and we sincerely thank you for the same.

Letter regarding execution of the order

6. It is an honour for us to get a chance to serve you. We shall be delivering the goods at your place within the said time.
7. We thank you for this fresh order for our new items. We feel proud that you have appreciated our previous services.
8. As all the items were in stock, we have despatched them to you today by the passenger train. Details of the despatch attached.
9. Our workers are busy on your order and we hope the job will be completed well before the stipulated time. We hope to serve you better this time.
10. The goods are being packed on a priority basis and will reach you within the next week.

Above details can be summed up as under

11. The goods have already been despatched as per your orders. These have been sent by Mercury Transport and will reach you on Monday. The transport slip for details has been attached herewith.

12. As per your request, the goods are being flown to you by air. Details of the flight are mentioned below.
13. We acknowledge with thanks your order of 5th May 2017. Please find enclosed our Invoice No. PL. 840.
14. We are just awaiting a green signal from the shipping corporation. As soon as that comes, we shall despatch the consignment.
15. Since your order was small, we have sent it through our representative Mr. Kishan Kumar and you will get the consignment by Tuesday.
16. We are pleased to inform you that goods against your order No. B-401 have been sent by goods train today.
17. Please note that the goods which you have ordered on May 5, 2017 are now ready for despatch. We are awaiting your instructions to proceed.
18. We have instructed Messrs. Bharat Goods Movers to forward the under-mentioned consignment to you by rail. It will reach you by August 25th surely.
19. There is a slight change in the flight for your ordered goods. We are planning to fly goods to you by Indian Airlines now due to unforeseen strike of Spice Jet Airlines. We shall intimate the date of their departure soon.
20. The goods were sent to you this afternoon by express railway parcel.
21. To avoid the risk of breakage of glassware, we have sent them by the road transport.

Close the letter with expectations of securing more orders

22. We hope the goods will reach you in time and you will place more orders with us in future too.
23. Hope you'll be satisfied with the quality of goods and have a lasting business relationship with us.
24. We guarantee the goods quality and hope to give you even better quality and features next time.
25. We trust the goods will reach you safely and on time.
26. We have despatched the goods as per your instructions. However, we request you place an early order with us next time. Else, we'll have to transport them through flight.
27. We hope you will be pleased with the goods quality and we'll continue sharing smooth business relationship with you.
28. Kindly stay informed that the goods have been despatched today and will reach you by Wednesday.

Intimation of Goods Despatched

Advise despatch

1. Please note that the 25 dozen sweaters you have ordered on 14th October, will be despatched to Mumbai tomorrow by rail for shipment on S.S. Indian Trader, which leaves for Colombo on 3rd December.
2. Enclosed herewith is our invoice for 500 pieces of woollen blankets ordered on 6th February, 2017 by you. The goods have been despatched to you by Kangaroo Transports yesterday. I request you to make timely payment.
3. The garments you had ordered on 25th April have been despatched today by goods train to reach Mumbai on 2nd of next month. Enclosed herewith is the copy of invoice and railway receipt.
4. In compliance with your order of 7th March, we have dispatched the parcel of goods by passenger train today and have forwarded the documents through your bankers, the Bank of India.
5. The crockery is being transported today by our truck and shall be there with you by tomorrow noon. Enclosed herewith is a copy of the bill.
6. We are glad to inform you that we have sent the following goods as per your order by V.V.P. today. Kindly confirm in mail once you receive them.

Mention the documents enclosed or sent

7. Enclosed herewith is our invoice for order no. 251 and, we shall present shipping documents and our draft for acceptance through the Chartered Bank, as agreed.
8. Please find enclosed our invoice and draft of ₹ 12,000 in favour of your company at 60 days' sight.
9. R/R No.508352 dated March 5, 2017 with a copy of your invoice No.158 has been sent to your Mumbai office.
10. The R/R has been forwarded through Punjab National Bank, Karol Bagh, New Delhi. It may be collected from its Head Office in Mumbai.
11. The documents have been forwarded to you through your bankers and a copy of the invoice is enclosed herewith for your reference.
12. Please honour the documents on presentation.
13. The remaining amount may please be paid on receipt of V.V.P.
14. Our bill No.541 for ₹ 200198/- is sent herewith, in duplicate.
15. Please collect the R/R against payment.
16. As per our agreement, we have surrendered the documents to the Chartered Bank, Connaught Place, New Delhi, who have accepted our draft for ₹ 2,00,000/- at 60 days' sight.

Mention about the special features of consignment

17. These sweaters have been manufactured from the finest lamb's wool especially for you. And we are sure you will find them worth the price.
18. Since the glassware are fragile items extreme care has been taken to pack them in straw and paper chippings.
19. The goods have been packed in four special cases lined inside with waterproof cloth.
20. The machines are as per your specifications and are securely packed in strong wooden boxes.
21. Each sewing machine has been carefully tested and carries five years' warranty.
22. Our technical representatives in Mumbai will be pleased to advise you on any point of fitting or maintenance. They also hold an adequate stock of spare parts.
23. We are sure the goods will reach you intact.
24. If you find any manufacturing defect in any of the pieces, you may kindly return them immediately.
25. We trust that the goods will reach you in excellent condition.

Closing the letter

26. And we hope this is the beginning of a lasting business relationship between us.
27. We appreciate your trust in us and inclination to further business dealings.
28. We assure you with similar care and attention to all further orders you would place with us.

Delay in Execution of Order

Begin by acknowledging the order and give reasons for delayed execution

1. Thank you for your order for Mixers, dated November 8, 2016. We are sorry for the delay caused in the execution of the order on account of labour strike in the factory.
2. We are thankful to you for your order of 500 pieces of item no.3 in our catalogue. However, we regret to inform that there might be some delay in executing it because of its exceptionally heavy demand in the market currently.
3. We are thankful to you for your order dated May 4, 2017 for 500 plastic buckets. However, we regret to inform you that we might not be able to supply them by the end of the month as desired by you due to heavy power cuts in the area.
4. Thanks a lot for your order for 800 electric irons. We are really sorry but we cannot supply them immediately due to a recent fire which has extensively damaged our factory.

5. We are glad to receive your order of 2nd December, but very much regret that at present the product you have ordered is out of stock. Hence, there will be some delay in fulfilling your order.
6. Much to our regret, a strike of transport companies in Delhi is causing some delay in the despatch of a number of consignments, and the goods you ordered on 5th August are among those held up.

Requesting for more time for execution of order

7. However, the work will resume in the factory very soon and we will be in a position to meet the demand.
8. We are, however, taking urgent steps to execute your order and shall be able to deliver the goods in not more than 15 days' time.
9. However, we hope to make the delivery in three weeks time and hope you will bear with us till then.
10. We have ordered heavy generators to stand the power cuts and shall be ready with your order within next 15 days. Please bear the delay with us.

Expecting the order to stand

11. Please intimate if the delay is acceptable to you.
12. We hope the delay will not cause too much inconvenience to you.
13. We would be grateful if you confirm your order as per the revised schedule.
14. We deeply regret this delay, but are helpless in this regard.
15. Meanwhile, we apologize for the delay and trust it will not cause you much inconvenience.
16. As a new thermal plant is coming up in the district, we hope the power supply will soon become regular, thus enabling us to meet orders regularly without delay.
17. We deeply regret the delay and hope this will not affect our business relations.

Inability to Execute an Order

Begin with thankful acknowledgement

1. Thank you for your order dated 8th May for 50 "Executive" leather sofa sets.
2. This is to express our thanks for your order dated 8th October, for 20 pieces of our "Tiptop" cooking tables.
3. We thank you for your order dated 9th September, for 500 "Toddler" baby frocks in assorted sizes and colours, with a request to deliver them by 14th of this month.
4. We are in due receipt of your order dated 2nd December, for 10 "Majestic" transistors/100 dinner sets.
5. This is to confirm your order dated 8th November, for the delivery of 1000 embroidered frocks.

Regrets over inability

6. We have to express our inability in supplying the goods because of our earlier heavy commitments.
7. We are extremely sorry to admit that the tables/chairs requested by you are out of stocks.
8. However, we regret to inform you that we are unable to supply the requested goods as we have stopped manufacturing this make.
9. We regret to comply with your orders for being put in short supply of raw materials.
10. We apologise but we cannot supply the items as our production has suffered heavily on account of labour problems and we have many prior commitments.

Suggest alternatives

11. But we could supply the same number of our 'Comfort' type sofa sets, if you find them suitable.
12. However, plain glass dinner sets of very high quality are available in case they meet your requirements.
13. Perhaps, we can get your order ready in case you can wait for a month.
14. However, we can import your required product from our abroad links in case you are willing to pay the excise duty.
15. However, we could probably meet your order after a few months.

Close the letter with the hope of repeat performances

16. We sincerely hope you will give us another opportunity to be of some service to you.
17. However, we are sure the situation will improve soon and we will be in a position to meet your future orders on time.
18. We trust this will not deter you from placing further orders with us in future.
19. However, despite this, we look forward to a long and lasting relationship in future.

Offer of Goods on Approval

Begin with reference to earlier talks

1. Confirming our telephonic conversation of this morning,...
2. As per request by your Business Representative, Mr. Kamal Kishore, after discussions with our sales officer, Mr. Prem Gulati on the 3rd of this month,...
3. As per instructions in your letter of 5th December...
4. This follows the demonstration of our new electric toaster in front of your purchase officer.
5. After your talks with our representative and our samples test,...

Advice letter

6. As per your approval, we are sending one toaster with the retail price of ₹ 525/- only.
7. ... we have despatched a parcel of 10 pairs of 'Nylotex' socks at the rate of ₹ 19.50/- per pair.
8. ... we have despatched to you by goods train two lemon sets of our latest 'Royal Blue' variety.
9. We are shortly sending you 10 'Majestic' transistors through our representative.
10. We are despatching five welding appliances at your place.

Give reference of earlier talks/ correspondence

11. As agreed, we have arranged to leave the piece with you for a period of two weeks, and if by then you do not find a customer for it, it is understood that you may either return it to us at our expense or retain it at 30% discount on the retail price.
12. In case you retain the piece for more than a month, we will consider it sold at our end.
13. It is agreed that in case you are unable to sell these in one month from today, you can send them back at our expenses.
14. Please note that the goods sent on approval can be accepted back only if received in good condition and within the stipulated time.
15. As per our agreement, if unsold, the goods will only be exchanged for other goods and not returned.

Request for Extension of Delivery Period

Express regrets over delayed delivery and give reasons

1. This refers to your order No.314/52 dated 15th August, for supply of 500 sewing machines.
2. We very much regiet to say that presently we are not in a position to execute your order within a week, as per your stipulation.
3. We reluctuantly request you to extend the delivery period of your order No.63/4 of April 1, for supply of 500 'Sharp' ball-point pens, for at least a month.
4. We shall feel obliged if you could extend the delivery period by just one week.
5. Kindly allow us to send your anticipated goods next weekend instead of this weekend.
6. In fact, recent transporters' strike has badly disrupted our deliveries and we are quite helpless in this regard.
7. Sudden strike by transporters is causing unnecessary delay from our end. We request you to allow 7 days' time for delivery.

8. The extension has become necessary because there is a temporary halt in our production due to the installation of new machinery. You know we never cause any delay otherwise.

At the closing, apologize again

9. We once again deeply apologise for this delay, though it is not in our hands.
10. We shall be grateful if you bear with us for this time.
11. We are, however, confident that we shall be able to affect the delivery by 15th of next month and hope that this schedule will meet with your approval.
12. We are once again very sorry for this delay and hope that you will understand our situation.
13. We hope you understand that the delay is due to circumstances completely beyond our control and we shall very much appreciate if you allow us this additional time.

Substitute for Supplier's Order

Acknowledge order with a feeling of pleasure

1. We are glad to learn from your letter dated 8th May that you wish to place order for 500 lace handkerchiefs/50 'Hi-Mod' T-shirts.
2. Thank you for your letter of 11th April, enclosing your order for 50 sky blue terene readymade shirts/'Blue Bird' T-shirts.
3. This is to thank you for your order for 50 'Playmouth' toy cars.
4. We are glad to receive your valuable orders for our plastic buckets.

Give reasons for offering alternate goods

5. But, we are sorry to say that handkerchiefs ordered by you have been 'out of stock' after we quoted for them. It will take around four weeks before we can get them ready.
6. We apologise but on account of constantly changing fashions, we have discontinued the manufacturing of this dress material.
7. However, we can supply the new dresses created by our designers, which have been highly appreciated by importers.
8. We have now new designs in readymade T-shirts, which we can supply if you wish so. Two samples are being sent to you for review.
9. You, of course, understand that in this fast changing world, we have to keep pace with it by bringing new designs and shapes.
10. As you required urgent execution of order, we have taken the liberty of substituting them with white cambric handkerchiefs of similar quality.
11. If you find it all right, we can supply you blue shade in the same material.

12. We, therefore, suggest that this product could be of greater interest to your clients and we can supply it in adequate quantities at short notice.
13. We can, of course, replace the toys cars by our new battery operated automatic 'flying car'. There is not much difference in the cost.
14. These new handkerchiefs have become very popular in our home markets.
15. The new transistors have been improved by our research and are much superior to the earlier ones.
16. These new toy cars are not only more attractive but are built to last longer.
17. At the rate of ₹ 80/- a metre, this dress material is much cheaper than terene and is equally attractive in finish.
18. If you want the new longer lasting tools we can supply them to you. The price is a little more than the earlier one but they are built to last.

Closing the letter

19. We hope that this substitution is acceptable to you and will bring you more business.
20. We hope you can wait till then.
21. In case, however, you do not find it suitable you can return it at our expense.
22. However, if you are not satisfied with this substitute, we shall certainly take it back at our expense and replace it with your original requirement as and when it is available.
23. We are sorry for this change and hope you do not mind it.
24. We are looking forward to your appreciation of our new item.
25. We trust you would like the new design and quality of material.

Refusal to Reduce Price

Express regret and give reasons

1. We have carefully considered your counter-proposal of 5th July to our offer of children's woolen knitwear/glassware/decorative pieces but regret that we cannot accept it.
2. This refers to your request dated 8th July for reduction in our prices of stainless steel utensils.
3. Having given due thought to your proposal of 23rd April regarding a reduction in our prices for clutch-plates, we regret to say that the proposal is unacceptable by us.
4. This is to express our inability to reduce our printing charges, in view of high cost of labour and printing machines.
5. I am sorry to say that our prices are fixed as the quality is maintained. Therefore, we are unable to negotiate on the prices.
6. The steep rise in the cost of raw materials has left us with no alternative but to slightly raise our rates.

7. The prices we have quoted in our letter of 3rd June leave us with only minimum margin. Hence, we will not be able to negotiate the prices further.
8. Our prices are in fact much lower than those available in the market.
9. The cloth we use undergoes a special process that prevents shrinkage and increases durability. As our cost of production is quite high, we will not be able to negotiate on our quoted prices.
10. In fact, we are unable to compromise on the question of prices and quality. As a result, you may find our rates slightly higher than the market rates.
11. As we have already agreed to a large discount, a further reduction is not possible from our end.
12. As you know that these ivory pieces call for special workmanship, it is not possible to cut down their prices.

Expectations of maintaining cordial relations

13. If you are interested in our original offer, please feel free to drop us a line.
14. We shall always be glad to hear from you and consider any proposal that might lead to business between us.
15. We hope this inability on our part to reduce prices does not affect our future business relationship.
16. We, however, look forward to your co-operation in future.
17. We hope you will understand our helplessness in this regard and give us an opportunity to serve you.
18. However, we will be always glad to serve you.
19. Please confirm if you would like to proceed with the current deal.

Cancelling an Order

Begin with giving reference of the order placed

1. Please refer to our letter dated 30th June, placing an order for 15 medium-sized steel almirahs/steel sheets/picture-tubes.
2. Your Delhi representative, Mr. Arun Kumar, must have informed you about our order to buy 10 dozen brass belt-buckles listed as "Deluxe" in your catalogue.
3. We had given you an order for supplying us 10 barrels of mustard oil at ₹ 88/- per kg by the 30th of this month.
4. This refers to my telephonic conversation with your sales manager regarding purchase of 20 reams of lucky parchment.
5. Please refer to our order placed with your representative, Mr. Man Mohan, on the 1st of this month for the supply of 100 ink bottles of 800 millilitres.

Reasons for cancelling order

6. Kindly consider the order as cancelled as the labour has gone on a lightning strike and at the moment we do not need the raw material.
7. I regret to inform you that the order now stands cancelled as per this letter.
8. We regret sending this email to you cancelling the order as the delivery date has expired long ago.
9. We are compelled to cancel our order for 10 television picture-tubes as you are not in a position to meet our specifications.
10. The cancellation has become necessary because the delivery schedule suggested is not acceptable to us.
11. The necessity for cancelling the order had arisen in view of the sheer oversight of our store-keeper who missed to register five dozen beit-buckles received by us last month.
12. It is because till now we have not received the goods or any reply from you and the stipulated time of delivery has expired.
13. As we have got a much lower quotation from some other company for the same quality of almirahs, we would like to cancel this order.
14. However, we have got stocks of an outgoing concern at much lower rates immediately and at the same time you have expressed inability to begin supplies till next month.
15. We have been compelled to take this decision in view of the latest market reports about fall in prices of this oil as a result of heavy import of a substitute.

Apologies and assurance for maintaining cordiality

16. However, in three months' time, we are likely to require replenishment of our stock and then we shall endeavour to make good the loss.
17. We shall send you our instructions for other supplies in due course.
18. We again apologise for the inconvenience caused to you and assure you of further orders from us.
19. In case you have incurred any loss on this account, you may please debit it against our next bill.
20. Should you incur any loss on this account, we will arrange to reimburse the same as early as possible.
21. In order to compensate the loss sustained by you on this account, we shall favour you shortly with an order for other items required by us.
22. Please, again accept our apologies.
23. We shall get back to you with another order, as and when required by us.

Request for Forwarding Instructions

Indicate about the position of order

1. We are pleased to confirm that 25 portable "Deluxe" typewriters you had ordered on 18th April, are ready for despatch.
2. Please note that 2 tonnes of tea you had ordered on 2nd February, is ready for the delivery.
3. We are happy to inform you that 200 yards of rayon you had ordered on 8th July are ready for despatch.

Now request for instructions from buyer

4. At the time of placing the order, you have asked us for fast delivery and we are happy to inform that we are able to accomplish your instructions.
5. Now, we are waiting for your shipping instructions to despatch the goods.
6. The arrangements have already been made for their despatch by passenger train. We are just awaiting your instructions.
7. Arrangements for shipment c.i.f. Hong Kong, have already been made with Modern Shipping Corporation. We will dispatch the order once we receive green signal from you.
8. We shall arrange for the shipping documents to be sent through Chartered Bank against our draft for acceptance, as agreed earlier.

Now closing hoping for a lasting business relationship

9. We hope the goods reach you in perfect condition and in time.
10. As soon as we receive a mail confirmation from you, we shall despatch the goods.
11. Thus, please inform us at the earliest regarding further action.
12. We appreciate this opportunity to serve you and look forward to do more business with you.

Sample Letters

(General letter for placing order)

Dear Sir,
We thank you for your letter dated 25th October, 2017 in response to our enquiry for the supply of 300 tea-cups. Kindly place the order for the following goods (list enclosed).[1] Kindly let us know if we can expect goods' delivery by 15th November as they are quite urgently required.[7]

Thanking you,
Yours faithfully,

(Placing order from catalogue)

Dear Sir,
Thank you for sending the catalogue. We had marked it for the goods urgently required by us. We shall appreciate your prompt attention to this order.

With thanks,
Yours faithfully,

(Placing order for advertised goods)

Dear Sir,
I have seen your new CD Player's advertisement in 'Hindustan Times' of August 4, and would like to place an order for five pieces.[1] Kindly execute this order immediately as I have to go out of station by next week.[11]

Thanking you,
Yours faithfully,

(Acknowledgement of an order)

Dear Sir,
We are pleased to have received your order No. 123 for 20 immersion type water heaters.[1] It is an honour for us to get a chance to serve you. We shall be delivering the goods at your place within the said time.[6] The goods have already been despatched as per your orders. These have been sent by Mercury Transport and will reach you on Monday. The transport slip for details has been attached herewith.[11]

With thanks,
Yours faithfully,

(Intimation of goods despatched)

Dear Sir,
Please note that the 25 dozen sweaters you have ordered on 14th October, will be despatched to Mumbai tomorrow by rail for shipment on S.S. Indian Trader, which leaves for Colombo on 3rd December.[1] Enclosed herewith is our invoice for order no. 251 and we shall present shipping documents and our draft for acceptance through the Chartered Bank, as agreed.[7] These sweaters have been manufactured from the finest lamb's wool especially for you. We are sure you will find them worth the price.[17] We appreciate your trust in us and inclination to further business dealings.[27]

With thanks,
Yours faithfully,

(Delay in execution of order)

Dear Sir,
We are thankful to your order of 500 pieces of item no. 3 in our catalogue. However, we regret to inform that there might be some delay in executing it because of its exceptionally heavy demand in the market currently.[2] We are, however, taking urgent steps to execute your order and shall be able to deliver the goods in not more than 15 days' time.[8] We hope the delay will not cause too much inconvenience to you.[12]

Thanking you,
Yours faithfully,

(Inability to execute an order)

Dear Sir,
Thank you for your order dated 8th May for 50 'Executive' leather sofa sets.[1] We have to express our inability in supplying the goods because of our earlier heavy commitments.[6] But we could supply the same number of our 'Comfort' type sofa sets, if you find them suitable.[11] We sincerely hope you will give us another opportunity to be of some service to you.[16]

With regret,

Yours faithfully,

(Offer of goods on approval)

Dear Sir,
This follows the demonstration of our new electric toaster in front of your purchase officer.[4] As per your approval, we are sending one toaster with the retails price of ₹ 1525/- only.[6] As agreed, we have arranged to leave the piece with you for a period of two weeks, and if by then you do not find a customer for it, it is understood that you may either return it to us at our expense or retain it at 30% discount on the retail price.[11]

Thanking you,
Yours faithfully,

(Request for extension of delivery period)

Dear Sir,
This refers to your order No. 314/52 dated 15th August, for supply of 500 sewing machines.[1] We very much regret to say that presently we are not in a position to execute your order within a week, as per your stipulation.[2] We shall be grateful if you bear with us for this time.[10]

With regret,
Yours faithfully,

(Substitute for suppliers' order)

Dear Sir,
This is to thank you for your order for 50 'Playmouth' toy cars.[3] You, of course, understand that in the fast changing world, we have to keep pace with it by bringing new designs and shapes.[9] We hope this substitution is acceptable to you and will bring you more business.[19]

Thanking you,
Yours faithfully,

(Refusal to reduce price)

Dear Sir,
We have carefully considered your counter-proposal of 5th July, to our offer of children's woollen knitwear/glassware/ decorative pieces but regret that we cannot accept it.[1] If you are interested in our original offer, please feel free to drop us a line.[13]

Thanking you,
Yours faithfully,

(Cancelling an order)

Dear Sir,
Please refer to our letter dated 30th June, placing an order for 15 medium sized steel almirahs/steel sheets/picture-tubes.[1] We regret sending this email to you cancelling the order as the delivery date has expired long ago.[8]

With regret,
Yours faithfully,

(Request for more information)

Dear Sir,
Thank you for your order of 22nd February for the supply of 20 pairs of "Weekend" shoes of size 8. The shoes are in our stock but before their despatch, we would like to know about the colour you wish to have. They are available in three colours, namely beige, light brown and dark brown. As soon as we receive your instructions, we shall despatch the goods.

Thanking you,
Yours faithfully,

(Request for forwarding instructions)

Dear Sir,

We are pleased to confirm that 25 portable "Deluxe" typewriters you had ordered on 18th April, are ready for despatch.[1] At the time of placing the order, you have asked us for fast delivery and we are happy to inform that we are able to accomplish your instructions.[4] We hope the goods will reach you in perfect condition and in time.[9]

Thanking you,

Yours faithfully,

Letter of Complaints and Adjustments

Every business has problems to tackle and difficulties to overcome. These problems may be complaints which come from different sections. They can be about poor services, damaged goods, billing mistakes, undue delay in supply, discourteous treatment and so on.

As in business one cannot afford to lose temper, the complaints call for tactful and polite handling. The letter should be well-worded and smack of good manners.

Thus, while writing a letter of complaint or adjustment, the information about dates, order numbers, invoice numbers, and description of goods and quantities must be specific. One must check ones' reference properly. Unpleasant words like dishonest, careless, unfair, false, etc., should be avoided. Confine your complaint to statement of facts and a polite enquiry as to what your supplier proposes to do about it.

Some occasions for writing complaints making claims are

1. Delayed delivery of goods upsetting sales plans.
2. Arrival of goods in damaged condition.
3. Receiving wrong order.
4. Difference in quantity/quality from what was ordered.
5. Price charged higher than quoted.
6. Unsatisfactory service.
7. Goods delivered at the wrong place.
8. Discourtesy shown by the staff of shop/office.
9. Mistakes in a bill.
10. Breach of other terms and conditions.

Points to be remembered while complaining

1. Promptness in making complaint.
2. Cause of complaint and your concern about it.
3. Details of order number, invoice number and other relevant details.
4. Asking for cause of delay and your further instructions about acceptance/cancellation.
5. Any inconvenience caused to you.
6. Your suggestions for adjustments, making up the loss or damage in transit, etc.

(Letter of complaint)

M.M. Gupta,
45, D.N. Road,
Mumbai-400 002
25th April, 2017

M/s. Modern Furniture Company,
6671, M.G. Road,
Kolkata.

Dear Sir,

Please refer to my letter dated 20th February, placing an order for a walnut table with six chairs. I am sorry that despite your promise to supply it within three weeks, I have not yet received it. In case the delivery is not made within two weeks, I will be compelled to cancel the order.

Please let me know on highest priority whether you will be able to deliver the furniture by the specified time.

Thanking you,

Yours faithfully,

M.M. Gupta

(Reply to complaint)

Modern Furniture Company
6671, M.G. Road
Kolkata.

28th April, 2017
Mr. M.M. Gupta,
45, D.N. Road,
Mumbai-400002.

Dear Mr. Gupta,

We received this morning your letter of April 25. I am sorry to learn that the dining table and chairs have not been delivered to you yet and regret the inconvenience caused to you.

The furniture was despatched by a truck of Rajput Transport on March 28 and should have been delivered latest by 8th April. I feel the delay is because of some transit problems.

I have checked with the transporters and have been assured that the furniture will reach you anyhow within a week. Please accept our apologies for the delay and our appreciation for bringing the matter to the notice. We request you to please bear this undue delay.

Thanking you,

Yours faithfully,

(G.Malhotra)
Manager

Complaint to Supplier about Non-delivery

Begin with reference to order number and its date, etc.

1. I sent you an order for 50 copies of "Rapidex Professional Secretary's Course" on 5th June.
2. Please refer to our letter dated 3rd July, placing an order for two dozen Kashmiri silk saris.
3. In our letter No.B-14 dated 27th August, we had placed an order for 50 velvet cushion covers of standard size in four colours — blue, red, pink and orange.
4. This refers to our order No. C-18, dated 3rd September, 2017 for 100 battery eliminators.
5. We had sent you a letter requesting for supply of 25 'Super Tone' transistor sets on 11th August.
6. While placing the order, we had stressed upon immediate delivery of books as the new sessions start on 2nd July.
7. We had ordered for them as we planned to participate in a sari exhibition at Grand Hotel here.
8. As we were expecting to receive them in a week's time, we had made commitments to our retailers accordingly.

9. As per our letter dated 1st July with order no CA 1114, this order is for a friend settled abroad who is currently here and plans to leave the country within a month.
10. Referring to our letter dated 29th September with order no. MH 1184, we believed that you would send the material within the stipulated time.

Give information about non-delivery of goods

11. We are sorry to say that we received neither the books nor any intimation regarding the delay.
12. But, till today we have not received the goods.
13. So far, we have not received any information from you regarding the supply of the material.
14. Despite our regular reminders, we have not received the supply which is highly disappointing.
15. We are sorry to inform you that we have not heard anything from you about the order we placed with you last week.
16. We are compelled to write that we have waited long enough for the ordered goods but failed to receive them so far.

Write about the inconvenience caused due to non-delivery

17. As the session is about to start, the non-availability of books is going to cause great inconvenience.
18. As these items are urgently required, the delay will result in potential loss of business to us.
19. If the saris do not reach us within ten days, we will not be able to participate in the exhibition.
20. A lot of important work has been held up because of the non-delivery of this essential equipment.
21. As he is going to leave the country soon, I request an immediate delivery of the goods.
22. However, we are prepared to wait till 15th January by which date we must receive the delivery of goods in full.
23. Please ensure a fast delivery to enable us to keep our commitments and maintain our image in the market.
24. As the goods have to be shipped, we must receive them within a weeks' time. In case of non-delivery, the order will stand cancelled.
25. This delay has caused us a lot of inconvenience, wherein we have to give many awkward explanations to our customers.
26. We would like to inform you that the goods are for export and the last date of shipment on the L/C is 3rd July, 2017. We hope you understand the urgency now.

Request for an early reply

27. We request you to take an urgent step in this regard.
28. So, please let us know by return post by which date our order will be executed.
29. If we do not receive any intimation from you regarding delivery, we will consider it as cancelled.
30. Be kind to inform us immediately about the delivery of goods.
31. We expect to get a note from you on the supply position.
32. As the order is extremely urgent, we are expecting an urgent action to it.

Complaint to Carrier about Non-delivery

Advice of non-delivery of goods

1. We regret to inform you that the consignment of three packages of woollen blankets sent through you and addressed to M/S. Sunil Kumar & Co., Connaught Place has not yet been delivered.
2. This is to inform you that two packages of printed books from M/s Pustak Mahal were booked from Delhi by Frontier Mail bound for Mumbai Central on 5th March, 2017, vide R/R No.383349. Despite a lapse of one week, they have not reached the destination.
3. Our consignors, M/s. Yantra Machine Works, Mumbai, had booked two boxes containing machinery parts at Patna by Tinsukia Mail bound for Delhi. But, your parcel office at Delhi informs us that the goods have not yet been received.
4. We are sorry to say that the goods sent from Mumbai to Delhi have not reached so far. The details are as given under.
5. On 5th March, 2017, we had booked goods with your Delhi Transport Office vide order No.B-18, but, they have not reached their destination yet.

Details of goods despatched

6. The packages were delivered at your office on 2nd February for despatch by Passenger Train and should have been delivered at its destination by 5th February. The receipt No. is 2453.
7. The R/R against which the goods were booked bears No. DA/22456.
8. The parcels were duly booked at your booking office, New Delhi Railway Station, on 15th November, as per R/R No. RB/22068 dated 15th November, 2016.
9. Our sales representative, Mr. Sudhir Malhotra had booked the consignment with your Operation Incharge, Mr. Bal Kishore, on 8th April. The booking order No. is CA/8242.
10. Refer to your R/R No.972816 dated 2nd August, 2016, regarding the material booked for Lucknow.

Request for tracing the goods

11. Since we urgently need the goods, please try to trace them as soon as possible.
12. Thus, please check up the whereabouts of the goods and inform us at the earliest.
13. As we require the goods within a week for distribution, please locate them immediately so that we can go ahead with our programme.
14. Kindly find out the reasons for non-delivery of the goods and inform us on priority.
15. Our important sales have been held up because of this non-delivery. Please take action in this regard at once.

Complaint regarding Late Delivery

Inform about delayed delivery

1. This is to bring to your notice the late delivery of ten 20 kg boxes of Assam tea ordered on 3rd August.
2. Although you had promised the delivery of jeans by 5th of this month, we received the supply only on 30th.
3. We had learnt from your representative that our order, placed with him, would be executed positively in the first week of this month, but we received the goods only today, at the end of the second week.
4. This refers to our order for 200 neckties, placed with you on 8th April. Please note that the supply has been received today after one month.
5. We had ordered for 10 dozen 'Sharp' ball-point pens on 8th May and requested for their supply within a week. However, we have received them today, on 2nd June.
6. I regret to inform you that the goods reached us four weeks after the stipulated date of supply.

Write about similar delays in the past also

7. Unfortunately, there have been similar delays from your end in the past also.
8. I am sorry to point out that this is not the first delay we have faced in your services.
9. We have noticed that of late, such delays on your part have become more and more frequent.

Discuss the extent of loss due to delay

10. This compels us to say that if such circumstances prevail, it will be difficult for us to have business dealings with you.
11. Under these circumstances, it may not be possible for us to continue our business with you.

12. The goods have arrived after our customer has cancelled the order. As a result, we have incurred substantial loss.
13. Please understand that the delay in delivery has been eroding our customers' faith in us.
14. Our own reliability in respect of deliveries of goods to our customers depends upon the punctuality of our suppliers like you.
15. We are sorry to inform you that delays are losing our trust in your services.

At the close of the letter, lay stress on time-bound order again

16. We hope you will understand our position. Now onwards, we will rely only on punctual supply of the orders.
17. We hope you will be more careful in future, stick to delivery schedules and give us no more cause for complaints.
18. We hope we would not get another occasion to complain, in future.
19. We shall be glad if you look into the matter at once and let us know the reasons for the delay.
20. Please note the order stands cancelled if the goods do not reach us by the end of the next week.
21. Kindly let us know the exact reasons behind this undue delay.

Report on Damaged Goods

Begin by informing about the damage noticed

1. We received a consignment of three packages of woollen blankets from you on 2nd March, as per our order. But, at least four blankets are found in damaged condition.
2. We are sorry to inform you that in the parcel of nylon socks you sent on 15th of this month, 10 pairs were soiled and partially torn.
3. On 15th of this month, we received 200 glass tumblers from you. However, the improper/ careless packing has damaged at least 40 of them in transit.
4. This refers to your delivery of 50 cricket bats on 14th April. The handles of 9 of them are coming off.
5. We are sorry to report that package No. 15 containing glassware/Hydrogen peroxide despatched under our instructions of 15th March was received in a badly damaged condition.
6. As we found the waterproof covering of the package torn, six blankets got soiled. We have to get them dry-cleaned before we can sell them.
7. As a result of careless packing, some of the chemical solution has spilled in the package.

8. Although the package containing the goods appeared to be in perfect condition, when unpacked, some of them were found broken. I am sure that this damage is the result of rough handling in transit.

Then ask for replacement or compensation

9. Will you, please arrange to send replacement immediately and charge to our account?
10. As the sweaters were bought on 'ex-works' terms, we realise that the responsibility for damage is ours and we have taken up the matter of compensation with the railway authorities.
11. So please despatch the replacements soon at your cost and take up the matter with your transporters.
12. Please fix the responsibility for this damage and let us have immediate replacements.
13. We assume you will take up the matter with the transporter at your end.
14. Alongwith this letter, we are sending you back the damaged socks.
15. Meanwhile, I have kept the damaged tumbler aside, in case you need them to support your claim with the railways for compensation.
16. We have also registered a complaint with the transporter and he has promised to settle the issue with you.
17. Upon learning the extent of damage, we will write to you again.
18. Since this chemical solution calls for skilled packing, please be careful in its packing next time.
19. We will appreciate if you send us credit note for the value of the damaged items.
20. We feel we can share the value of damage amongst ourselves.

Complaint regarding Inferior Quality

Begin by informing about the inferior quality of goods supplied

1. This refers to our order for 500 clutch plates/cardigans/hand-tools/electric heaters, dated 25th July.
2. We have received the delivery but are disappointed with its quality.
3. We feel there has been some mistake in despatch on your part.
4. The clutch plates you have sent, are not of our specification.
5. We regret to inform you that the quality of your consignment of nylon threads of the 6th January, has not been satisfactory at all.
6. The goods appear to be sturdy but their finish is very poor.
7. When we examined the goods received against our order No.583 of 3rd June, we found that their finish was not at all as per our expectations.

8. Many customers have complained to us about the poor quality of fountain pens supplied by you on 25th July.
9. It is really unfortunate to have received such material in a trial order.
10. We are disappointed to receive such inferior material for our order.

Discuss inconvenience caused due to inferior quality of goods

11. As a result, we are not in a position to offer these goods for sale.
12. It is not in accordance with our business standards to sell such inferior goods.

Mention further suggestions

13. Consequently, we are left with no other alternative but to ask you to take the goods back and replace them with those of required quality.
14. If you cannot accept the goods back, we may not be able to continue business with you.
15. We are returning herewith the defective items and expect you to send us faultless items.
16. If you get us the replacement, we can extend the delivery period by two weeks.
17. In view of our long business relationship we hope you will be prepared to make some allowance for the inferior quality, so that we push them at the discounted rates. Our credibility will hurt if we despatch this quality of goods. Goods sent by you, being of poor quality, is likely to be returned by our customers.
18. We are sure, you will adopt an accommodating approach towards this and replace the goods/accept the goods back.
19. We hope we will not get another reason to complain you again.

Complaint regarding Short Supply

Beginning

1. We thank you for the prompt execution of our order No.L.314 dated 20th April. But while we had ordered for 20 immersion rod heaters, we have received only 10 in the package delivered to us.
2. On 20th of this month, we got the supply of 20 pairs of socks against our order No.SVT/ADT/M-20, whereas we had ordered for 30 pairs.
3. Thank you for sending the shirting material. However, we have found on measurement that it is only 30 metres in length and not 35, as we required, vide our order No. M-14 of 23rd February.
4. I would like to point out that some articles, as per our order, are not found in the package delivered to us today.
5. Moreover, we have not received any intimation about the short supply.

Ask reasons for short supply

6. Please let us know the reason for such short supply.
7. Your transporter was unable to explain this short supply. So, kindly clarify the reason behind it.
8. The consignment is not accompanied with an explanation from you.
9. Please intimate when we might get the rest of the supply.
10. Please be informed that the cost of the missing articles will be deducted from the next payment.

Request for making up the deficiency

11. We still need the rest of the goods. Please let us know how fast you can send them.
12. You are, therefore, requested to make up for the shortage at the earliest.
13. As our customer is soon leaving for abroad, please deliver us rest of the goods at the earliest.
14. We will feel obliged if you can supply the missing articles at once or issue a credit note.
15. Thus, could you please find out the reasons for this short supply and compensate us?

Complaint against Incomplete Work/ Poor Services

Start the complaint giving a few facts

1. On 8th July, I received my Philips cassette recorder sent to you for repairs last month.
2. Last Monday, your Service Engineer, Mr. Gopal Sharma came to check up the faults in our Kelvinator refrigerator.
3. On 5th July, I left my defective CD player at your shop for repair.

Now complain about unsatisfactory work

4. Since he could not rectify the defect on account of lack of equipment, he left with a promise to come the next day.
5. When I played the recorder yesterday, I found that the same defect was still persisting. The recorder often produces a strange sound and the tape gets struck on its head.
6. At that time, I had explained to your service engineer the defects in detail. Yesterday, I received its delivery and surprisingly it has gone from bad to worse.

Refer to further complications, if any

7. Since then, the refrigerator has been lying like that and it is causing us great inconvenience.
8. Earlier, its recorder had been running though at a low volume. But now, even the disc refuses to move.

Request for a prompt action in this regard

9. I would request you to take an immediate action in this regard and send your engineer at the earliest.
10. Since the defect has not been rectified, please arrange to pick it up from my place and do the needful.
11. I shall drop it at your shop at my convenience and request you to mend it by an early date.
12. I hope you'll take a prompt action for this fault and get it corrected on priority.

Sample Letters

(Complaint to supplier about non-delivery)

Dear Sir,

I sent you an order for 50 copies of "Rapidex Professional secretary's Course" on 5th June.[1] We are sorry to say that we received neither the books nor any information regarding the delay.[11] As the session is about to start, the non availability of books is going to cause great inconvenience.[17] We request you to take urgent step in this regard.[27]

With thanks,
Yours faithfully,

(Complaint to carrier about non-delivery)

Dear Sir,

We regret to inform you that the consignment of three packages of woollen blankets sent through you and addressed to M/S Sunil Kumar & Co., Connaught Place has not yet been delivered.[1] The packages were delivered at your office on 2nd February for despatch by Passenger Train and should have been delivered at its destination by 5th February. The receipt No. is 2453.[6] Since we urgently need the goods, please try to trace them as soon as possible.[11]

With thanks,
Yours faithfully,

(Complaint regarding late delivery)

Dear Sir,

This is to bring to your notice the late delivery of ten 20 kg boxes of Assam tea ordered on 3rd August.[1] Unfortunately, there have been similar delays from your end in the past also.[7] This compels us to say that if such circumstances prevail, it will be difficult for us to have business dealings with you.[10]

With regret,
Yours faithfully,

(Report of damaged goods)

Dear Sir,

We received a consignment of three packages of woollen blankets from you on 2nd March, as per our order. But, at least four blankets are found in damaged condition.[1] Will you please arrange to send replacement immediately and charge to our account?[9]

With thanks,
Yours faithfully,

(Complaint regarding inferior quality)

Dear Sir,

This refers to our order for 500 clutch plates/cardigans/hand-tools/electric heaters, dated 25th July.[1] We have received the delivery but are disappointed with its quality.[2] As a result, we are not in a position to offer these goods for sale.[9] If you get us replacement, we can extend the delivery period by two weeks.[16]

With regret,
Yours faithfully,

(Complaint regarding short supply)

Dear Sir,

We thank you for the prompt execution of our order No.L.314 dated 20th April. But while we had ordered for 20 immersion rod heaters, we have received only 10 in the package delivered to us.[1] Please let us know the reason for such short supply.[6] As our customer is soon leaving for abroad, please deliver us rest of the goods at the earliest.[13]

With regret,
Yours faithfully,

(Complaint against incomplete work/poor services)

Dear Sir,

On 8th July, I received my Phillips cassette recorder sent to you for repairs last month.[1] When I played the recorder yesterday, I found that the same defect was still persisting. The recorder often produces a strange sound and the tape gets stuck on its head.[5] Earlier its recorder had been running though at a low volume. But now, the disc refuses to move.[8] Since the defect has not been rectified, please arrange to pick it up from my place and do the needful.[10]

Thanking you,
Yours faithfully,

Replies to Complaints: Adjustment-letters

Since nothing is perfect, complaints about one's products or services should not be taken with a frown. A large business is a complex network of various departments and people. There can always be a lapse somewhere which might lead to complaint by customers. At the same time, a complaint from a customer cannot be ignored. If it happens, it might have repercussions on the business in the long run. One must keep one's customers satisfied. In some western countries, various companies invite criticism of their products. They even circulate printed forms for the customer to tick off the points regarding flaws in the goods. These help them to better their products' quality. All professional businessmen are keen to introduce reforms in the business. This gives more credibility to their business. Thus, a prompt action on a complaint is a must.

Some Don'ts while Handling Complaints

Tact, sincerity and patience are required in handling letters of complaints

1. Do not express surprise over customer's complaint. This undermines his assessment. However, to say that such an error did not occur earlier is to justify him.
2. Do not be too apologetic. He expects your sincere approach to his problem and will be satisfied if you show concern.
3. While making adjustment, do not give the feeling that you are doing him a great favour.
4. Do not shift the blame to a junior member of the staff or make someone else a scapegoat of it.
5. Do not repeat the details of faults.
6. Do not try to sound unethical by saying 'our rules do not allow it', 'company's policy does not allow it', etc. The customer is above these internal definitions. He has the right to get satisfactory service.

Purpose/ Function of a Good Adjustment-letter

Whatever decision one might take in regard to complaints, a definite set of rules has to be followed. A proper attitude and frame of mind are essential for handling delicate situations. One must try to realise the position of the customer adjustments valuing customer's feelings. Make sure that customer's shaken confidence in the company and its make is restored. This can only be done by a right attitude to the mistake pointed out by the customer. Thus, the businessman must be able to locate the source of error, control it and forgive it. Proper human relations with employees are conducive to better business relations.

Some Do's while Handling Complaint

1. Empathise with customer and listen to his complaint carefully. Console the customer that he will get refund or replacement for the loss.
2. Sometimes apart from the inconvenience, loss of money is also involved.
3. Use polite tone as in such circumstances, the tone is more important than the content.
4. Show courteous attitude as it will get a favourable response.
5. Sometimes the customer is only half correct and not fully justified. Still, be helpful, sympathetic and courteous.

Types of Adjustment-letter

Here, a few important points have to be kept in mind, such as responsibility for the fault, business relations with the customer and his earlier record of dealings. Adjustment letters can be grouped as follows:

1. Letters of apology owning error and granting adjustments.
2. Letters explaining non-acceptance of complaint and refusing adjustment.
3. Letters offering a compromise.
4. Letters requesting the customer to wait while matters are under consideration.
5. Letters of partial compromise according to the extent of error owned/admitted.

Reply to Complaint regarding Non-delivery

Acknowledge the letter informing of non-delivery of goods

1. This refers to your letter concerning non-delivery of hand-tools booked vide your order No.AS/2448 of 5th May.
2. We regret to learn from your letter that the lipsticks ordered by you in the beginning of this month have not yet reached you.
3. We are surprised to learn from your representative today that the shirts you had ordered on 23rd October, have not yet reached you.
4. It was quite surprising to know that the consignment of 20 tea-sets despatched to you, as per your order No.SL/2881 of 10th November, has not reached you so far.
5. We are totally in dark about their whereabouts.

Give proof of delivering goods in time

6. We assure you that your order was executed on the same day it was received. Here is the execution slip for your reference.
7. It is surprising as we had despatched the goods to our transporter the next day itself.

8. We confirm that your consignment was delivered in time to the Parcel Booking Office at Mumbai Central Railway Station for onward despatch by passenger train.
9. Our transporter informed us that the goods were delayed a little. And we feel that they must have reached you by now.
10. We feel very much concerned about the non-receipt of the goods by you. It was sent through registered post parcel. We are attaching the postal receipt of the same.

Close the letter indicating future action

11. On receipt of your letter, we have immediatley taken up the matter with the railway authorities/our transporters here.
12. We will let you know about the developments this side as soon as possible.
13. We think it would be advisable that you also make enquiries at your end.
14. We are getting in touch with the transport company and will let you know about their reply very soon.
15. We are complaining about the matter to the postal authorities and hope to advise you shortly.

Reply to Complaint regarding Late Delivery

Convey regrets in the beginning of your reply

1. We have received your letter dated 8th January and regret the delay in despatching 20 reams of sunlit bond-paper you ordered on 30th December last year.
2. Your letter dated 2nd May regarding the supply of 20 easy-chairs has been received by us and we sincerely regret the delay in delivery of goods.
3. We are sorry to learn from your representative that you have not received the consignment of 20 dozen cotton-shirts we had despatched to you as per schedule.
4. Your letter dated 8th August, complaining about delay in delivery has come as a surprise. We had despatched the goods to you on the next day of receiving your order.
5. We are writing this letter reference to your letter dated 2nd June complaining about the delivery of twenty 160 litre refrigerators on 29th May instead of 14th.
6. We are sorry to learn about the delay in delivery of the neckties that you ordered on 30th September.
7. We are surprised to know from your representative about the delayed delivery of lunch boxes.

Explain the cause of delay and its non-recurrence

8. We admit that an unexpected rush of activities caused a slight delay in executing your order but we assure you that we are doing our utmost to expedite delivery.
9. We had already sent you a telegram informing the late despatch of your consignment which we hope you might have received by now.

10. In fact, a heavy demand of electric heaters this season somehow delayed the delivery.
11. This delay has occurred because of the fact that our plant is not working full-time on account of regular power-cuts.
12. A recent labour strike had stalled the work for some time. Now, the workers have resumed the duty and we assure you that there will not be any delay in future.
13. We are the only manufacturers of these goods and our resources have been overtaxed.
14. Our transporters were heavily booked and so they could not deliver the goods in time.
15. It is our usual practice to send goods well in advance of delivery dates and the consignment of toys which you refer to was despatched on the 3rd of this month. We believe the delay was caused at the transporter's end.
16. We are very much concerned that our efforts to give punctual delivery are disturbed by delays in transit.

Give adequate assurance for future dealings

17. We are taking up the matter of delay with the transport company, in all seriousness.
18. We are sure we shall be able to supply the goods in time in the future.
19. Till the recent rush, we have never failed in delivering the goods within the scheduled time. We hope you will take a favourable view of the recent delay.
20. The power problems have eased off and our production has become normal. So, in future, we shall be able to supply the goods in time.
21. We assure you that every effort will be made in future to guarantee the delivery in time.
22. We assure you that we are doing all we can to speed up delivery and apologise for the inconvenience caused to you.
23. Our transporter has assured us that in future they will make the deliveries in time and will not give us a chance to complain.

Reply to Complaint regarding Damaged Goods

Begin by conveying your sincere apologies

1. We are sorry to learn from your letter dated 3rd August that some of the glass tumblers were received by you in broken/damaged condition.
2. This is with deep regret to your complaint dated 3rd August about the damaged parcel of socks.
3. Your complaint of 2nd October concerning the damaged cotton bed-sheets has caused us great concern.
4. We are sorry to learn that some of the tea-sets despatched to you on 8th April were found damaged.
5. We are surprised to learn that despite our tremendous care, knitwears have reached you in a soiled condition.

Give assurance of more alertness in future transactions

6. To avoid inconvenience and annoyance to our customers , we have now employed a packaging specialist.
7. We have now started ordering for special packing cases to ensure safe delivery of goods.
8. We have to especially reinforce all future consignments by rail and we hope this will prevent any damage in future.
9. We have decided to switch over to 'Modern Transport' for despatch of goods. This will hopefully ensure safe deliveries.
10. We are ready to meet half the cost of the damage occurred during transit.

Suggestions to rectify loss

11. You need not return the broken tumblers. They can be further destroyed. Replacements are following soon.
12. We realise the need to reduce your selling price for the damaged sweaters and are ready to allow a special allowance of 10%, which you have suggested.
13. You can return the soiled blankets through our representative, Mr. Ashok Kumar, who will be visiting your area on 10th March. We shall replace them with new ones.
14. We take the responsibility of the damaged goods and shall adjust its cost in our next transaction.
15. Kindly send the estimate of the damaged goods. We shall deduct the amount in our next bill.

Reply to Complaint regarding Inferior Goods

Convey regrets at the beginning of your letter

1. We regret to learn from your letter dated 29th May that you are not satisfied with the pens/books shirts supplied as per your order No.SL/7824.
2. This refers to your complaint of 29th May expressing dissatisfaction over the neckties' quality supplied to you on 2nd May.
3. We are sorry for the inconvenience caused to you due to dissatisfactory supply of lunch boxes.
4. Your letter of 3rd April complaining about the quality of ball-point refills supplied as per your order No.265, has caused a great deal of concern in us.
5. We are very much disturbed at your complaint of 2nd May regarding the quality of the electric heaters supplied against your order of 28th March.
6. This is to express our concern over your complaint about the quality of shirting material supplied to you on the 3rd of this month.

Show gratitude on bringing the error to your notice

7. We are glad that you have brought the matter to our notice.
8. At the same time, we are thankful to you for pointing it out.
9. Still, we thank you for promptly reporting this to us.
10. We really appreciate your frankness in the matter.

Give explanation, if possible

11. We assure your satisfaction in future regarding the quality of the material.
12. We ourselves have tested the heaters and found them not up to the mark. Our technicians are advising ways to improve their quality.
13. We have inspected the goods from the same batch and agree that they do not tally with your specifications.
14. In fact, there had been some mistake by our despatch department.
15. We admit that it has been a lapse on our part and we are taking steps to avoid such mistakes in future.
16. Since the goods you had ordered for were out of stocks, our sales department took the liberty of substituting them with those of a different quality.

Indicate steps taken to rectify errors

17. The defects in the goods have been traced to a fault in one of the machines, and it is being rectified now.
18. We are arranging to replace 50% (i.e., 200 pens) of your unsold stock.
19. We shall soon meet your order for terene shirts in place of the cotton ones you received, and these are at present being fabricated.
20. As soon as fresh supply is ready, we shall replace the goods.
21. We have arranged for immediate despatch of replacements.

Give suggestions for clearance of defective goods

22. If it is not too much of inconvenience to sell the cloth already supplied, we can send you a credit note for the difference, as soon as we hear from you.
23. The defective books may kindly be returned at our expenses.
24. If you can keep the books for sale, we are ready to give 5% discount on them.
25. Please return the defective pens to us as soon as you receive the replacement from us.

Express hopes of satisfying the complaint by your above action

26. We trust the replacements we are sending now, will be upto your satisfaction.
27. We sincerely apologise for the trouble caused to you, and will take all possible steps to ensure that such a mistake does not recur.
28. We are ensuring stricter quality control tests and assure you that such a mistake will not take place again.
29. We admit our drawback and promise you our best of services in future.

Indicate if complaints are not acceptable

30. We have investigated your complaint and regret to say that we could not find any justification for it.
31. We have gone through your complaint but regret to say that we are unable to entertain as we find it unjustified.

Explain reasons of non-acceptance and talk of future action

32. As all our fountain pens are of the finest quality and subjected to a variety of quality control tests, we fail to understand your complaint.
33. All our products are thoroughly examined before passing into store and we have their government quality licence.
34. Since we have proof of their quality, we are sorry to say that we cannot entertain your request.
35. Since our manufacturer refuses to take back the goods once sold, we express our helplessness in this regard.
36. Therefore, we shall have no option but to refuse to accept the goods, if returned.

Closure of a letter not accepting the complaint

37. We hope you will take it as a fair and reasonable solution to the matter.
38. You will appreciate that no other course is open to us, under the circumstances.
39. We do understand your point of view but are helpless in this regard.

Closure for the ordinary reply

40. We hope this will now settle the matter to your complete satisfaction.
41. We trust you will have no further cause to complain.
42. We regret the trouble caused to you.
43. Please feel free to express your opinion in future too in case of any such problem.

Reply to Complaint for Mistake

Beginning

1. Thank you for your letter of 14th June. It has given us the opportunity to set right the mistake regarding the address of your factory.
2. We are sorry but we have not received the circular you issued notifying the change of address.
3. We are grateful to you for pointing out the mistake regarding the despatch of an old paid bill.
4. The mistake you pointed out was indeed inadvertent but unfortunate.
5. We are thankful to you that you have given us a chance to mend our errors.

Closure

6. We apologise for the trouble our mistake may have caused you.
7. We assure you that we shall be careful not to repeat such mistakes in future.
8. We deeply regret having given you a cause to complain and assure you that we shall make sure that the matter is resolved at the earliest.
9. We are sorry that you have suffered our mistake. It will never happen again.
10. Kindly excuse for the undesirable happening. We assure you that it will not be repeated.

Reply to Complaint for Poor Services

Begin by acknowledging the letter

1. We are in receipt of your letter dated 9th September and apologise for the carelessness of our service engineer.
2. We have received your CD player, which according to your complaint, has not been properly repaired.
3. We regret to learn from your letter dated 8th October that the defect of the VCP you had sent to us has not been rectified.
4. We are sorry to learn from your letter dated 19th September that our service engineer has not yet visited you.

Give explanation, if possible

5. In fact, our engineer who visited you on last Monday has reported sick since then.
6. We have made enquiries at our end and found that because of the absence of one of our senior supervisors, the system was delivered without proper checking. We admit our mistake and are sorry for the same.

7. As far as we are aware, nothing leaves our workshop without a thorough check-up. There is a possibility that during transit, the recorder has got damaged.

Now assure of full co-operation

8. However, we are instructing Mr. Krishan Kumar to visit you tomorrow and rectify the defect in your refrigerator.
9. We are arranging for transfer of your system to our workshop and assure you that it will be mended to your satisfaction this time.
10. We apologise for the inconvenience caused and assure you that next time you will not have an occasion to complain.
11. We are arranging for an immediate repair of your system and hope that it will satisfy you.
12. We look forward to extending our services to you in future.
13. We hope you will ignore this lapse on our part and give us a chance to serve you in future too. We commit not to repeat such service failures.

Sample Letters

(Reply to complaint for non-delivery)

Dear Sir,
We regret to learn from your letter that the lipsticks ordered by you in the beginning of this month have not yet reached you.[2] We assure you that your order was executed on the same day it was received.[6] We are getting in touch with the transport company and will let you know about their reply soon.[14]

With regret,
Yours faithfully,

(Reply to complaint regarding late delivery)

Dear Sir,
Your letter dated 2nd May regarding the supply of 20 easy-chairs has been received by us and we sincerely regret the delay in delivery of goods.[2] We admit that an unexpected rush of activities caused a slight delay in executing your order but we assure you that we are doing our utmost to expedite delivery.[8] We are sure we shall be able to supply the goods in time in the future.[18]

Thanking you,
Yours faithfully,

(Reply to complaint regarding damaged goods)

Dear Sir,

This is with deep regret to your complaint dated 3rd August about the damaged parcel of socks.[2] We have now started ordering for special packing cases to ensure safe delivery of goods.[7] We take the responsibility of damaged goods and shall adjust its cost in our next transaction.[14]

Assuring you of full cooperation,
Yours faithfully,

(Reply to complaint regarding inferior goods)

Dear Sir,

We regret to learn from your letter dated 29th May that you are not satisfied with the pens/books/shirts supplied as per your order No.SL/7824.[1] We are glad that you have brought the matter to our notice.[7] In fact, there had been some mistake from our despatch department.[14] We are arranging to replace 50% (i.e., 200 pens) of your unsold stock.[18] Please return the defective pens to us as soon as you receive the replacements from us.[25] We trust the replacements we are sending now, will be up to your satisfaction.[26]

Assuring you of prompt action,
Yours faithfully,

(Reply to complaint for mistake)

Dear Sir,
Thank you for your letter of 13th June. It has given us the opportunity to set right the mistake regarding the address of your factory.[1] We are sorry but we have not received the circular you issued notifying the change of address.[2] We apologise for the trouble our mistake may have caused you.[6]

Thanking you,
Yours faithfully,

(Reply to complaint for poor services)

Dear Sir,

We regret to learn from your letter dated 8th October that the defect of the VCP you had sent to us has not been rectified.[3] We have made enquiries at our end and found that because of the absence of one of our senior supervisors, the system was delivered without proper checking. We admit our mistake and are sorry for the same.[6] We are arranging for transfer of your system to our workshop and assure you that it will be mended to your satisfaction this time.[9]

With regret,
Yours faithfully,

Letters regarding Transport of Goods

There are four modes of transportation available to us—road, rail, air and sea. In all big cities and towns, there are agents to book goods for such transportation. Not just that, there are many independent agencies too who undertake the task of despatching goods. These agencies are fully conversant with legal formalities and transporting techniques. They even have printed material for replies and queries. However, at times, need arises for letters too.

Letter to Shipping Company regarding Freight Rates

Begin the letter by giving goods' details and asking tariffs

1. We shall soon have 20 cases of crockery ready for shipment to Kandy, Ceylon from Chennai. Each case weighs 70kg and measures 1 ¼ x 1 ¼ x 1m.
2. So, will you please send us details of present freight charges for despatch of these goods?
3. As we wish to send a consignment of leather garments in 10 wooden cases, each weighing 20kg from Mumbai to Dubai, we would feel obliged if you could send us your freight rates.
4. Kindly inform us about the freight rates for packaged handicrafts from Chennai to Port Louis, Mauritius. The consignment will consist of 4 wooden cases, each weighing 15kg and measuring 1 ½ x 1 x 1m.
5. We wish to enquire about the freight rates for shipment of packaged woollen garments from Mumbai to London. These goods will be in 8 wooden cases, each weighing 10kg and measuring 1½ x 1 ½ x 1m.

Enquire about the actual shipment

6. You may also inform us of the frequency of your sailing and the duration of the voyage.
7. Please also let us know about the sailing schedule and voyage's duration.
8. We understand that S.S. Ratnagiri is due to sail on 20th July but we would like an earlier sailing if possible.
9. As our customer has been pressing for the goods, please let us know when they can be shipped at the earliest.
10. Please inform us if we have to book the consignment in advance or not.

Enquiry of Freight Rates from Road Transport Company

Describe your goods

1. We wish to send books in 25 wooden boxes measuring 50cm x 50cm x 25cm to Mumbai early next month.
2. Will you please quote your freight charges to Mumbai for 10 wooden cases containing glass tumblers. The size of the boxes is 50cm x 30cm x 20cm.
3. We propose to despatch 10 cardboard cartons of readymade garments measuring 1 x 1 x 0.25m to Mumbai on the 1st of the month.

Make specific enquiries

4. So please furnish the following information per return.
5. Therefore, please let us know about the following details at the earliest.
6. Can you arrange to collect the goods from our office at the above address?
7. Do we have to deliver the goods at your office or could you please arrange to pick them up from here?
8. How long will the goods take to reach Mumbai?
9. What would be the freight and other charges, if any?
10. Are the insurance charges included in the freight or do we have to pay them separately?
11. We shall feel obliged if you send us detailed information about the freight rates, time taken to cover the distance and the mode of lifting the goods.

Letter to Airlines regarding Transport of Goods

Describe the goods first

1. We are sending through our representative, Mr. Devendra Kumar, 100 cases of mangoes for despatch to London.

2. We wish to send by air 50 baskets of Mangoes to London.
3. Through the bearer of this letter we are sending 100 rose buds packed in cellophane bags for air freight to London.
4. We intend to send 100 cases of transistors to Port Louis (Mauritius) from Delhi.
5. We are a Handicraft Unit and plan to send by air handicrafts from Delhi to Paris.

Indicate the documents

6. All papers, duly completed, are enclosed.
7. Enclosed please find all necessary documents, duly completed. Please let us know if any other documents are required or not.
8. We have completed all the papers which are enclosed.
9. All the formalities are over. The necessary documents are enclosed with the letter.

Mention about the invoice

10. The freight bill for these cases may be sent to us in duplicate for payment.
11. Please let us know if you would require part payment in advance or full payment after the delivery.
12. You are requested to submit the freight bill for this cargo in duplicate for settlement.
13. To promote goodwill, we can make the payment in advance.

Letter to Forwarding Agent

Begin your letter with important points involved

1. Our company has been operating a large network of parcel despatch service.
2. We receive and despatch large volume of parcel everyday.
3. Our business involves handling of large amount of parcel despatches.

Discuss your requirements

4. We shall appreciate if you could send your representative to apprise us of your services and charges for the same.
5. So please let us know if you could handle this business as our Clearing Agent and intimate your charges for the same.
6. Could you act as our forwarding agents? If so, please let us know about the details of your services.

Letter from Forwarding Agent regarding Terms

Begin your letter with reference to the letter received/visit of the representative

1. Thank you for your letter of 7th July.
2. This is to thank you for your letter dated 7th July, 2017.
3. This has reference to the visit of your representative, Mr. Kumar to our office on 4th May.
4. This has reference to the meeting between your agent and our partner Mr. Rao.
5. We are glad to have had talks with your agent on Monday, the 10th July.

Indicate your trade terms

6. We are pleased to state our terms which are as follows.
7. Please note our terms as given below.
8. We will collect all the goods from your factory for onward transportation by road or rail.
9. For transportation of goods from your godown to the transporter's or railways, we will charge extra. The rates are given below:
10. A sum of ₹ 50/- will be charged for our services for each inward and outward parcel, subject to a minimum of 200 parcels every month.
11. We deal in insured goods only.
12. All bills submitted by us should be paid within 30 days.
13. All our bills should be payable on the 1st of every month.
14. We shall keep on sending our revised rates from time to time.
15. The validity period of these terms will be subject to negotiation.

Close the letter hoping for favourable reply

16. We hope you find our terms favourable and will have regular business deals with us.
17. We hope these terms will be acceptable to you.
18. Please confirm whether these terms are acceptable to you.
19. I am quite sure that you would accept these reasonable terms.
20. We look forward to a long and fruitful relationship with you.

Letter to Railway for Giving Open Delivery

Begin your letter giving reasons for taking open delivery

1. Our representative Mr. Kulbhushan Kapoor, visited you on 18th August for taking delivery of two parcels of books against PWB No.226801 and found that they were badly damaged.
2. This is to report the damage to our packages containing glass tumblers. The damage was noticed by our representative, Mr. Shastri, when he went to your office on 18th April to take their delivery.
3. We regret to inform you that the parcel of woollen goods sent to us was found damaged and torn when our representative Mr. Manmohan, visited your office to take its delivery against PWB No.384983.
4. On 8th July, when our representative, Mr. Suresh Virmani, went to your office to take delivery of the parcel of garments addressed to us, he found it damaged and some of the pieces missing.
5. This is to inform you that the crockery packages despatched to us were very much damaged. Please refer to PWB No.14568 and note the extent of damage which is as under: (I) Handles of two tea pots broken, (ii) Three cups broken.

Now, request to take open delivery

6. We, therefore, request you to give us open delivery of the parcels.
7. It is, therefore, requested that an open delivery of the said parcels be given to us.
8. So please give an open delivery of the damaged consignment. Our representative can call on you whenever you find it convenient.

Letter to Carrier to Release Goods from Customs

Mention details of documents

1. Enclosed please find a letter from British Airways with invoice for 2 cases of readymade garments despatched from London on 8th May, 2017.
2. Please find enclosed a letter from Singapore Airlines with invoice for a case of dress material despatched from the United States on April 2, 2017.
3. Please find enclosed a letter from Air India along with an invoice for 5 cases of dry fruits despatched from Kabul on May 9, 2017.

Advice for delivery of goods

4. Please arrange to collect the same and deliver it to us at our office.
5. Kindly make arrangements to collect and deliver it at our office at the given address.

6. Please make arrangements to transport to us the luggage in the next two-three days.
7. Please receive these papers and arrange the delivery. Details are given in the letter.
8. Kindly acknowledge this letter sent through the bearer and manage to send the articles to our godown at the given address.

Sample Letters

(Letter to shipping company for freight rates)

Dear Sir,

We shall soon have 20 cases of crockery ready for shipment to Kandy, Ceylon, from Chennai. Each case weighs 70kg and measures 1 ¼ x 1 ¼ x 1m.[1] So, will you please send us details of present freight charges for despatch of these goods.[2] You may also inform us of the frequency of your sailings and the duration of the voyage.[6]

Thanking you,

Yours faithfully,

(Enquiry of freight rates from road transport co.)

Dear Sir,

We propose to despatch 10 cardboard cartons of readymade garments, measuring 1 x 1 x 0.25m to Mumbai on the 1st of the next month.[3] We shall feel obliged if you send us detailed information about the freight rates, time taken to cover the distance and the mode of lifting the goods.[11]

With thanks,

Yours faithfully,

(Letter to airlines re. transport of goods)

Dear Sir,

We are sending through our representative, Mr. Devendra Kumar, 100 cases of mangoes for despatch to London.[1] All papers duly completed, are enclosed.[6] The freight bill for these cases may be sent to us in duplicate for payment.[10]

Thanking you,

Yours faithfully,

(Letter to forwarding agent)

Dear Sir,

Our company has been operating a large network of parcel despatch service.[1] We shall appreciate if you could send your representative to apprise us of your services and charges for the same.[4]

Thanking you,

Yours faithfully,

(Letter from forwarding agent re. terms)

Dear Sir,

Thank you for your letter of 7th July. We are pleased to state our terms as follows.[6] All our bills should be payable on the 1st of every month.[13] Please confirm whether these terms are acceptable to you.[18]

Thanking you,

Yours faithfully,

(Letter to railway for giving open delivery)

Dear Sir,

Our representative Mr. Kulbhushan Kapoor had visited you on 18th August for taking delivery of two parcels of books against PWB No.226801 and found that they were badly damaged.[1] We, therefore, request you to give us open delivery of the parcels.[6]

Thanking you,

Yours faithfully,

(Letter to carrier to release goods from customs)

Dear Sir,

Please find enclosed a letter from Air India along with an invoice for 5 cases of dry fruits despatched from Kabul on May 9, 2017.[3] Please arrange to collect the same and deliver it to us at our office.[4]

Thanking you,

Yours faithfully,

Collection-letters

One of the primary issues of any commercial establishment is to keep the books of accounts in good order. This can only be done if firms' bills are paid in time, but, at times, the credit customers fail to make payments within the stipulated time. In that case one has to send reminders to customers. Such customers may be of three types.

1. Good credit customers

The ones who pay up promptly and do not keep their suppliers waiting for money. These customer scarcely need any reminders.

2. Fair credit customers

They fall behind in payments at times and await a few reminders before clearing dues. With them it becomes a kind of habit. However, after a few reminders they pay up.

3. Poor credit customers

These are difficult to tackle. They make it a habit not to pay up until they are reminded repeatedly and they cannot delay any further. They require regular reminders until the money is realized.

After the bill, collection procedure starts with the monthly statements. Reminders are sent periodically to realise uncleared dues. Without them, of course, a company cannot run.

Usual/ Formal Collection-letter

Formal reminder

1. Our records show that you have yet to clear your account No.L/123 dated 15th December, 2017.
2. May we remind you that the above account has not yet been cleared?
3. This is to remind you that we have not received payment of the above account already a month overdue.
4. According to the enclosed statements, the outstanding amount due from you is ₹ 5000/- only.
5. You have always been very prompt in settling your accounts; and we hope this bill also receives a similar response.
6. The outstanding sum, according to our books, amounts to ₹ 5,000/- only.

Request for early response

7. We hope that you will settle the account at the earliest.
8. An early settlement of the account will be appreciated.
9. We would request you to settle this account at the earliest.
10. We have always been very earnest in our dealings and hence we hope that our outstanding bill for ₹ 2500/- will soon be cleared.
11. As we have received another order from your agent we would appreciate an early settlement of this account.
12. In view of our cordial business relations, it is necessary to get our previous accounts settled.

First Collection-letter

Begin with a friendly approach and tone

***In case the account No. is given at the top, do not write it again in the letter.**

1. As you are usually quite prompt in settling the accounts, we wonder if there is any special reason for delay this time.

2. May we call your attention to our outstanding account for ₹ 5250/- settlement of which is now overdue for more than a month?
3. We shall be glad if you pay attention to our statement of account dated 5th March 2017, which still remains unpaid.
4. We wish to draw your attention to our invoice No.PN/2041 for ₹ 3,550/- which we have not yet received.
5. We have noted that your account, which was due for payment on the 15th of last month, is still outstanding.
6. We may remind you that you had promised for an immediate settlement of the account at the time of the delivery of goods.
7. While checking our accounts we have found that there is a balance of ₹ 6220/- due from you for the purchases made in April 2017.
8. We regret to remind you that despite our letter of 8th November enclosing an invoice ₹ 8,500/- only, payable on 28 November, we have not received any communication from you.
9. While going through your account, we have noticed that a balance of ₹ 1045/- is still outstanding against your name.
10. It seems you have inadvertently overlooked our invoices of February and March, or there is some other reason for the delay in payment.
11. We very much regret to inform you that we have not yet received the payment of our hundi which fell due on 12th May, 2017.
12. Our accounts department has been waiting for more than a week for the settlement of our account of December for ₹ 25,000/-.
13. We regret to remind you that you have not yet paid the balance of ₹ 7100.50 due on our statement dated 3rd December, 2017.
14. We hope you must have received the statement of account, dated 28th February, showing the balance of ₹ 1500.00.
15. As our auditors have to balance the accounts by the end of this month, we request for a prompt settlement of our bill.
16. To expedite the matter, we are sending our representative with a copy of the invoice. Kindly make payments of our bill.
17. For ready reference, we enclose a copy of the statement of March. These accounts are now overdue.

Request for early payment

18. We shall be glad if you take an immediate action in this regard and settle our accounts.
19. We look forward to your remittance by return mail.
20. We hope to receive the amount overdue/cheque within the next few days.

21. We hope you will settle the account expeditiously.
22. As the financial year is coming to a close we request you to make immediate payment of the bill.
23. Please let us know at the earliest when can we have the payment.
24. We will appreciate your making the payment at the earliest. If you cannot, please let us know the reasons.
25. We shall be pleased to receive your cheque in settlement of this account.
26. Kindly help us to bring your account up-to-date by paying the outstanding amount.
27. Please let us know the date when you retired the hundi so that we could write to your bankers for payment.

Second Collection-letter

Write a courteous but firm letter

1. We regret to say that an amount of ₹ 5195.50 is still outstanding against your name, and we have not received the payment despite a reminder dated 4th February.
2. On 17th January we sent you a letter reminding that on 3rd December we had sent you our statement for November 2017, showing an outstanding balance of ₹ 2205.50 due for payment by 31st December 2016.
3. Despite our reminder dated 24th May for an outstanding payment of ₹ 2800/- we have not heard from you.
4. We regret to inform you that despite our request dated 3rd September for the settlement of the amount due on our invoice No.P.241 of 24th July, we have not heard anything from you.
5. This is to request you again for the payment of ₹ 8851/- outstanding against your account. We had reminded you that your account, already more than a month overdue, had not been settled.
6. We are at a loss to understand why we have had no reply to our letter dated 27th May requesting you to settle the amount outstanding on our March statement.
7. We regret to remind you again of our unpaid bill for ₹ 8805.15, now nearly three months overdue.
8. We are sorry to draw your attention to your unpaid balance of ₹ 6640/- which has not been paid despite the reminder sent through our representative last month.

Ask for reasons for delay and request for early payment

9. No doubt there might be some special reason for this delay in payment. We shall welcome an explanation for the same and hope for the clearance within a week.
10. As this amount is overdue for more than two months, we must ask you either to send us your remittance within the next few days or at least offer an explanation for the delay.

11. We have not so far pressed you for a settlement because of your good past record.
12. For a regular customer like you, our terms of payment are 3% for one month. We hope you will not withhold payment any longer and thus compel us to revise these terms to your disadvantage.
13. You will understand that a prompt payment is in the best interests of a cordial relations.
14. We trust you will now attend to this matter without any further delay.
15. We are sorry to inform you that it is not possible for us to give you any further credit.
16. We regret to press for an immediate payment of the outstanding amount.
17. We hope you will give a positive response to our representative who is the bearer of this letter.
18. As the amount owing is considerably overdue, we shall be grateful to receive your cheque at your earliest.
19. Kindly send us the remittance immediately or explain any reason for further delay.
20. As we have to settle certain important bills, we must insist on the immediate clearance of our account.

Third Collection-letter

Mention earlier reference of letters

1. We do not appear to have received any reply to our previous requests dated 4th and 17th August for payment of ₹ 1,110.35 which has been outstanding against your name for more than four months.
2. We fail to understand why we have not received your reply to our two reminders dated 17th March and 4th April requesting you to pay ₹ 2895.10/- due on our January 2016 statement.
3. We are surprised and disappointed not to have received any reply from you despite our two reminders dated 8th April and 5th May 2016 for payment of ₹ 2,050/-.
4. We note with surprise and disappointment that we have not received any replies to our two previous reminders for payment of ₹ 3000/- due on your account.
5. We have sent you two reminders earlier dated 2nd July and 24th July requesting you to pay us the amount of our invoice No.125/023.
6. We regret to inform you that we haven't had any reply to our previous requests for payment due on our statement of October.
7. Despite our two reminders of your delinquent account, we have not heard anything from you regarding the payment of ₹ 5000/- due on our invoice No.DL/489.
8. Your balance of ₹ 5750/- which dates back to November 2016 is still unpaid in spite of our two reminders.

Request for payment clearance by a specified date

9. We regret to inform you that now we must press for immediate payment.
10. I hope you will understand our position and will not delay the payment any more.
11. As we would not like to harm your credit and reputation we propose to give you time till the end of this month to clear your account.
12. As our dealings over many years have been satisfactory we are giving you ten more days to settle this overdue account.
13. We still hope you will discharge this account without any further delay.
14. Unless we receive the payment in full settlement by the end of this month,...
15. Unless we receive the payment in full settlement by 23rd of this month...

Indicate legal implications

16. If you fail to stick to this date we will be left with no other choice but to resort to legal action.
17. I regret to inform you that this is the last reminder and if the payment does not come forth, we'll be left with no other option but to stop our business dealings with you and take recourse to law.
18. We shall have to consider seriously further steps to recover the amount.
19. We shall instruct our lawyers to recover the amount due to us.
20. We shall have to take legal action.
21. We hope you will prevent the matter from going to court and thereby avoid inconvenience and heavy expenditure on both the sides.
22. We shall be compelled to hand-over this matter to our attorneys.
23. We hope you will not compel us to take the unpleasant step of handing over the matter to our solicitors.
24. We shall pass the matter on to our legal advisers for necessary action.
25. We shall be constrained to resort to legal action at your cost and risk.

Sample Letters

(Usual/formal collection letter)

Dear Sirs,

Our records show that you have yet to clear your account No.L/123 dated 5th December, 2017.[1] We hope that you will settle the account at the earliest.[7]

Awaiting an early response,

Yours faithfully,

(First collection letter)

Dear Sirs,

As you are usually quite prompt in settling the accounts, we wonder if there is any special reason for delay this time.[1] As our auditors have to balance the accounts by the end of this month, we request for a prompt settlement of our bill.[15] We shall be glad if you take an immediate action in this regard and settle our accounts.[18]

Awaiting an early reply,

Yours faithfully,

(Second collection letter)

Dear Sirs,

We regret to remind you again of our unpaid bill of ₹ 8805.15, now nearly three months overdue.[7] We are sure there might be some special reason for this delay in payment. We shall welcome an explanation for the same and hope for the clearance within a week.[9]

Yours faithfully,

(Third collection letter)

Dear Sirs,

We do not appear to have received any reply to our previous requests dated 4th and 17th August for payment of ₹ 1110.35 which has been outstanding against your name for more than four months now. As we would not like to harm your credit and reputation we propose to give you time till the end of this month to clear your account.[11] If you fail to stick to this date we will be left with no other choice but to resort to legal action.[16]

Yours faithfully,

Remittance-letters

The modern methods in accounting, new electronic devices and computers etc. have up to a large extent, eliminated the need for letters of transmittal with payments. However, still in the local business transactions such letters are used. Moreover, in most of the cases today the business houses use printed letters.

Such a letter must specify the amount and nature of enclosure (cheque/draft/postal order/ etc.) and should give the date and number of the bill being paid. An expression of appreciation for service rendered is in good taste.

However, sometimes payments cannot be made because of certain errors in bills or statements of account or noncompliance with the terms settled earlier. On such occasions, letters should be written promptly referring to delay in payment. These letters should be courteous in tone and tactfully written.

Acknowledgement of remittance

A letter acknowledging receipt of the payment is not as necessary as the letter of transmittal. It can be sent as a matter of routine, token of appreciation or referring to further business orders.

Billing errors

Claims of errors in billing should be carefully investigated and acknowledged as soon as possible. If the error is proved, admit it, apologise for it and offer adjustments. Send a corrected bill with a covering letter as soon as possible.

Stopping payment of cheque

If it is necessary to ask a bank to stop payment of a cheque, it should be done promptly either by telephone/telegram or letter.

Letters regarding Remittance for Goods Received

Give details of remittances

1. Please find enclosed cheque No.568350 HB dated 28th August 2016 for ₹ 2000/- drawn on the Punjab National Bank in full settlement of your invoice No.3942 dated 14th August 2017.
2. We are pleased to enclose the cheque No.SB 829421 dated 10th April 2016 for ₹ 5000/- drawn on the Punjab National Bank, in full settlement of your invoice No.3428.
3. Enclosed is our cheque No.AB 408212 drawn on Grindlays Bank, Connaught Place for ₹ 5250/- in full settlement of your invoice No.12 dated the 1st of this month.
4. We are finally settling all due accounts on our part and sending the amount of ₹ 5682/- through cheque No.AB428641 drawn on the Syndicate Bank, Greater Kailash, New Delhi and regret any inconvenience caused to you.
5. With this cheque for ₹ 3507/- you will find you have nothing due on us now.

Request for official receipts

6. Kindly/please acknowledge the receipt.
7. You can send your acknowledgement in the normal course.
8. Receipt of the cheque/amount may be kindly acknowledged.
9. Please confirm the receipt of the cheque by return mail.
10. We hope to send a cheque for the balance (₹ 2320/- only) next month.

11. Kindly bear with us for the remainder amount till the next month.
12. We hope it is not too much of inconvenience to you if we send the balance amount (i.e., ₹ 5800/-) next month.
13. The rest of the amount will be remitted to you positively next week.
14. The balance will be sent to you next month after we have gone through the details of the account.

Acknowledgement of Remittance

Convey thanks

1. This is to thank you for your cheque for ₹ 12000/- in full settlement of our invoice No.3942 dated 14th August 2017.
2. We are in receipt of your cheque for ₹ 1850.75 in full settlement of our invoice No.521 dated May 7, 2017.
3. Thank you for your cheque for ₹ 5750.50 sent in full settlement of our invoice No.150 of 15th March 2017.
4. We express our thanks on receiving the cheque for ₹ 3540/- against bill No... of...
5. We are thankful to you for the immediate payment of ₹ 5000/- through cheque against our recent supplies.

Also send the receipt

6. Enclosed is the receipt for the cheque.
7. Please find enclosed our receipt for the same.
8. Our receipt for the amount is enclosed.
9. For your records, we are sending the receipt for the amount.

Express expectations for more flow of business

10. We hope, now, you will place fresh orders with us.
11. May we now expect that you will favour us with further order?
12. We hope that our promptness in dealing with you will encourage you to place fresh orders with us.
13. We are sure you will entrust us with more orders as our accounts are cleared.

Letters Disputing an Account

Give reasons for non-acceptance of bill

1. We have received your statement for October, 2017 but are returning it herewith, as it is at variance with our account books.

2. Kindly find herewith your statement for July 2017, which we are returning, as it does not tally with our account books.
3. We regret we have to return herewith your statement for May, 2017 as it does not agree with our books.

Indicate details of errors in bill

4. You have charged us for four dozen pens while we had purchased only three dozens.
5. Your statement shows that you have charged us for twenty pairs of kurta-pyjamas while we had ordered and received only fifteen.
6. While you had agreed to give us 15% discount on the purchase initially, you have not done so.

Ask for an amended bill

7. We shall be obliged if you could look into this matter and let us have the modified statement.
8. Kindly make necessary corrections in the statement and we will pay it immediately.
9. Please check up at your end and let us have the amended statement for payment.
10. If you feel there has been some misunderstanding and there is no mistake on your part, please clarify.

Sample Letters

(Letter regarding remittance for goods received)

Dear Sirs,
Please find enclosed the cheque No.568350 HB dated... for ₹5000/- drawn on the Punjab National Bank in full settlement of your invoice No.3942 dated 14th August 2017. You could send your acknowledgement in the normal course.[7]

Thanking you,

Yours faithfully,

(Acknowledgement of remittance)

Dear Sirs,
This is to thank you for your cheque for ₹12000/- in full settlement of our invoice No.3942 dated 14th August 2017.[1] We hope, now, you will place fresh orders with us.[10]

Thanking you,

Yours faithfully,

(Letter disputing an account)

Dear Sirs,

Kindly find herewith your statement for July, 2017 which we are returning as it does not tally with our account books.[2] You have charged us for four dozen pens while we had purchased only three dozens.[4] We shall be obliged if you could look into this matter and let us have the modified statement.[7]

Thanking you,

Yours faithfully,

Business-circulars

Business circulars are meant for providing information about any change taking place in a particular commercial establishment. The general public can be informed through the media. But, the clients or customers have to be informed individually. Thus, the circular contains information which the customer would be glad to know. The inside address is given on each circular separately before it is mailed. Like other letters the circulars also should be effective and friendly in tone having a proper lay-out.

Circulars can be sent on several occasions-(I) expansion of a business (ii) introducing new product line (iii) opening a new branch (iv) shifting to other premises (v) repairs (vi) lockout or some other trouble (vii) clearance sales (viii) change of business terms or bankers, etc.

Shrewd business circulars also carry a sales message with them. In fact, the big business thrives on flashing different types of circulars from time to time.

Example of a circular on the opening of a new branch

Dear customer,

We are glad to announce the opening of a new branch in Calcutta for the convenience of and service to our growing customers in the city and its upcountry towns. Our branch address is as under:-

Pustak Mahal
405, Mahatma Gandhi Road,
Kolkata-1 (W.B).

The new building that also accommodates other departmental stores is located in the heart of the new fashionable market which has come up on this prestigious road. Mr. Gupta, our salesman from Delhi will be incharge of this new branch. You are cordially invited to visit us on its inaugural ceremony on November 1, 2017.

We take this opportunity to express our thanks for your continued patronage over the last so many years and shall endeavour to provide our best service to you in future too.

Yours faithfully,
For M/s Pustak Mahal.

Circular Announcing Opening of New Business

Announce the new business

1. We are pleased to announce the opening of a general store at the above address on the coming Diwali.
2. We take great pleasure in announcing the opening of a T.V repair shop in your colony's market (shop no.617) on the auspicious day of Janmashtami.
3. We are glad to inform you about the opening of a Refrigerator repair shop at No.5 Laxmi Road, Delhi on the New Year day.
4. This is to gladly announce that we are opening a book shop at 3145, Nai Sarak on the 14th August, 2017.
5. We take great pleasure in announcing the opening of Super Sari Emporium at 15, Ajmal Khan Road, Karol Bagh on the eve of ensuing Diwali festival.

Give introduction about yourself

6. We have been in this line of business now for more than ten years and our product knowledge is extremely good.
7. My experience in this trade as a representative of M/s India Sales Corporation is of more than ten years. Therefore, it will help me a great deal to serve customers efficiently and meet their requirements promptly.
8. As technical supervisor for Fairview Television Company I have competently handled and repaired all kinds of T.V. sets.
9. We have been in this line for a long time. Wide and varied experience will help us to mobilise the business and satisfy the customers.
10. This has been our family business for three generations. Thus, we are well versed in cloth trade.

Make a mention about new premises

11. The store's timing will be from 10 a.m. to 7 p.m.
12. The opening ceremony of the centre will take place in the morning at 10 o'clock on the above day.
13. We are offering 5 per cent inauguration discount on all first day purchases.
14. Attractive gifts will be offered on all first day purchases of more than ₹ 500/-.

Extend invitation

15. We look forward to your patronage.
16. We hope you will grace the occasion with your presence on the opening day.
17. May I invite you to avail of the inauguration discount?
18. You are cordially invited.

Circular regarding New Branch

Announce the opening of a new branch

1. We take great pleasure in announcing that on 1st August 2017, we are opening a new branch of readymade garments at 15 Nehru Place, New Delhi.
2. We are pleased to inform you that as part of our expansion plans we have opened a new branch of our saree store in your colony.
3. Owing to the large increase in the volume of our trade in North Mumbai we have decided to open a branch in Dadar.
4. We are pleased to inform you that our new store at No.7 South Extension Market, New Delhi will be officially inaugurated by the Minister of Tourism on Sunday the 9th July, 2017.

Give reasons for opening a new branch

5. The new branch is just the expression of customers' growing faith in our products.
6. Although we have so far served you efficiently, you deserve still better services that await you.
7. Now with a branch in your locality we have virtually come to your door steps.

Give details about the new branch

8. Mr. Sunil Kumar, our Manager for the last 20 years, will be in-charge at the new branch.
9. The new branch will be opened on 15th April, 2017. Therefore, from that date all orders and enquiries may be sent to Mr. Sunil Kumar at 18 Laxmi Road, Puna, instead of sending them to our Mumbai office.
10. This branch is managed by some of the best salesmen of the line who will take pleasure in providing excellent service.
11. Mr. Prem Prakash who has been in charge of the wholesale division at our head office for the last 15 years will head the new branch.
12. Mr. K.L. Sharma will represent us in this new branch. His dealings with customers have always been highly appreciated.

Express hope for closer business patronage

13. We take this opportunity to thank our customers and are sure that our services will further improve with this new arrangement.
14. We welcome a visit by you to our new branch.
15. We eagerly look forward to provide you with more extensive services.
16. At this new branch we hope to receive your orders as usual for prompt delivery.
17. Our association has been long lasting and we hope that it will continue likewise.

18. So in future please send your enquiries and orders to our Agra branch instead of sending them directly to our Head Office in New Delhi.

Circular regarding Acquisition of a Firm

Inform about acquisition

1. It is our pleasure to inform you that M/s Beauty Products Co., has been acquired by us from the 1st of this month.
2. We have recently purchased the sole interests in the silk sari business of M/s Mysore Sari Emporium, 15 Main Road, Shahdara.
3. We have pleasure in informing you that M/s Cosmetic Corner, Sunder Market, has been acquired by us from 1st May, 2017.
4. We take pleasure to intimate you that Modern General Stores, 14 Kamla Market, has been purchased by us. We shall start transactions from 2nd August, 2017.
5. It is our pleasure to inform you that we have taken possession of 'Fashion House', 28-A, Shaktinagar, and from 15th August, 2017, we are starting a retail sale.

Give self introduction

6. You will be pleased to know that we have been in this line for more than two decades.
7. Our long experience in this line and substantial investment place us in a position to offer better goods to the customers.
8. Being new in this line of business, we have hired highly professional and competent staff.
9. We are well-known in the market in this trade and hope to fully satisfy the public.
10. We have been veterans in this field. Thus you can rely on us for quality products.
11. We shall not only continue to trade under the old name but also make every effort to adhere to our predecessor's policy of sound services on which the goodwill of the firm has been built.
12. The business will be transferred to a new department in our main store in Connaught Circus, New Delhi, with Mr. Sushil Kumar as the Manager.
13. Mr. Sushil Kumar was the General Manager of the old firm and his deep knowledge of the readymade garments business, acquired during a lifetime spent in the trade, will continue to be at your disposal.
14. Mr. L. Kahyap who will be in charge of Fashion House is an expert designer and well versed in this trade.
15. We have completely renovated the premises and have spent a considerable amount on the décor.

16. In order to get acquainted with our prospective customers we are hosting a lunch at 2 p.m. on 8th August. You are cordially invited.
17. We propose to offer the old stock in a bargain sale next week on very attractive terms.
18. We have reduced prices by 10% on every item of old stock and, thus, we hope to get better acquainted with you.

Extend invitation for visit

19. We hope you will be kind enough to extend your usual co-operation.
20. We can assure you of the best of our services. Please pay us a visit and see for yourself.
21. We are sure that even under the new management this firm will continue to receive your generous support.
22. We hope we shall build a lasting relationship with you.

Notice of Change of Address

Inform about shifting of premises

1. We take pleasure in informing you that we have shifted to larger premises at Nav Niwas colony from 1st August, 2017.
2. We have pleasure in informing you that the offices of Gorgeous Garment Company, Ajmeri Gate, Delhi, have been shifted to 5/6 WEA Ajmal Khan Road, Karol Bagh, New Delhi, w.e.f. July 19, 2017.
3. This is to inform you that we have shifted our offices to the new commercial complex at Kalyan Puri, New Delhi.
4. The new address of our firm is Nirmal Cheap Silk Store, 25 Ajmal Khan Road, Karol Bagh, New Delhi.
5. From 1st June 2017, we will be functioning from 15 Shri D.B. Gupta Road, Karol Bagh.

Give details of the new premises

6. The need for larger premises on account of steady expansion has warranted this shift.
7. The place is centrally located and will facilitate prompt deliveries.
8. The new premises also provide scope for better methods of production that will increase output besides improving the quality of our products further.
9. The new site is in the heart of the city and within easy reach by rail and road.
10. At the new place transport has now become easier ensuring prompt deliveries.

Give assurance for better services

11. We hope to serve you better with these improvements.
12. Although the new premises are on the outskirts of the city, we hope to meet deliveries promptly.
13. We are sure of serving you better from this place.
14. We can assure you of efficient services.

Announcement regarding Clearance-sale

Make announcement of sales

1. This is to advise you that we are holding a clearance sale from 15th March. We enclose a catalogue.
2. We take great pleasure in informing you that we are holding a clearance sale from February 14 to 19, 2017.
3. We are holding a clearance sale of our old stocks for a week commencing from Monday, February 14, 2017.
4. We are going to have a clearance sale for a week at very reduced prices from 1st June 2017 to 6th June, 2017, at Janpath Hotel, New Delhi.
5. As the winter is coming we are holding a clearance sale of our cotton clothes, starting from March 2, 2017.

Refer to attractions of sale

6. All stocks will be cleared regardless of cost.
7. Attractive discount is being offered on all articles ranging from 10% to 40%.
8. Prices have been reduced in some cases by over 50% and in all departments exceptional opportunities are being offered to obtain high class goods at prices far below the cost.
9. The goods offered for sale are new and of high quality.
10. Stocks to be cleared are excellent, both in terms of variety and quality.

Extend invitation to sales

11. As we expect heavy rush we suggest that you visit the shop in the morning hours when it is going to be more comfortable.
12. During the first few days of the sale you will find many bargains at very low prices.
13. We hope you will be able to pay us a visit during the sale and make your selections.
14. In case you are unable to visit we shall be happy to reserve for you any goods that you order from the catalogue, to be despatched on February 1, 2017.
15. Assuring you of the best and most efficient services.

Circular regarding Retirement of a Partner

Start with main information

1. We regret to inform you that our senior partner Mr. Rajaram Shastri has decided to retire from 31st March this year.
2. We regret to inform you that our senior partner Mr. Dharm Dutt Shastri has decided to retire from the firm.
3. We are sorry to announce the retirement of our valued partner, Mr. Man Mohan from this firm.
4. We are sorry to inform that our partner, Mr. K. Sharma, has opted to proceed on retirement from 3rd December, 2017.
5. This is to inform you that our partner, Mr. M.N. Gupta, has withdrawn his share from the company and thus he ceases to be our partner any longer.

Mention something about the outgoing partner

6. He has sought this retirement on account of ill health.
7. Shri Das will, however, continue to act in an advisory capacity.
8. His absence, of course, will leave a gap which would be difficult to fill.
9. Mr. Verma has had to take this decision on account of old age and continuing ill-health.
10. Mr. Sharma has cut his share by 50% and appointed his son, Rajat Sharma, as partner in his place.
11. The withdrawal of capital by Mr. Shastri will be made good by the continuing partners. As a result the volume of firm's capital will remain unchanged.
12. The firm will continue to function under its present name of Shastri Kumar & Co., and there will be no change in its established policy.
13. The business will be conducted as it has been in the past.
14. In consequence of the withdrawal of capital by the retiring partner, we have applied for a loan from Industrial Finance Corporation and it has been sanctioned.
15. No further change will be made in the constitution of the firm, its name or its policy.

Express hope for cordial relations

16. We hope that the new arrangements will not affect our long business relationship and you will continue to repose your faith in us.
17. We will ensure that the firm's present standard of service is maintained.
18. With the induction of young blood like his son, we hope to make our services more efficient.
19. We take this opportunity to thank you for your co-operation in the past and hope we can count on your continued support.

20. I take this opportunity to again remind you of our continuing cordial relationship and wish that it becomes better in the years to come.
21. We assure you of the same care and prompt attention to your orders as in the past.

Circular regarding Admission of New Partner

Make announcement about new partner

1. We take pleasure in announcing the induction of Mr. Bharat Bhushan as a partner in our firm.
2. We are pleased to inform you that Mr. Ram Prasad Gupta, our esteemed partner, has inducted his son, Mr. Ramesh Gupta, as the fifth partner of our firm.
3. We are pleased to inform you that we have now admitted Mr. Ramanath as a partner w.e.f. 8th July, 2017.
4. It is our pleasure to inform you that we have just taken Shri Raj Kishore, an experienced mechanical engineer, into partnership of the firm.
5. We are glad to inform you that with effect from July 1, 2017, Mr. Bhaskar Rao, our General Manager, will become a partner of this firm.

Tell the necessity for taking new partner

6. This was, in fact, necessitated following the death of our friend and partner, Mr. Dhan Raj.
7. In fact, the substantial increase in the volume of business made it imperative for inclusion of another partner.
8. We were compelled to add a new partner because of our workload and business expansion.
9. His inclusion has come in view of the proposed expansion of our business.
10. Entry of a new partner was necessary as one of our former partners had shifted his interests to some foreign concern.

Give introduction of the new partner

11. Mr. Prakash has been our General Manager for the past ten years and is well acquainted with every aspect of the firm's business.
12. Although Mr. Gupta is young, he is dynamic and has a lot of drive.
13. He has worked as Sales Manager with Telco for more than 10 years.
14. We are sure his experience will come in handy and further boost our business.
15. A specimen of Mr. Bharat Bhushan's signature is given below.
16. Our dealings will not be affected in any way on account of this new admission.
17. We are sure to do better under his expert guidance.

Circular regarding Conversion of Partnership into a Private Ltd. Company

Change in constitution of business

1. We take great pleasure in informing you that our company has become a Private Limited Company w.e.f. July 1, 2017.
2. We are pleased to inform you that we have decided to convert our firm into a Private Limited Company with a view to raise the necessary capital for the proposed expansion and diversification of our business.
3. It is our pleasure to inform you that we are converting our business into a private company so that we could serve you still better.

Advice about new name

4. Additional capital for the expansion of company's activities has necessitated this step.
5. The new company has been registered with limited liability under the name of "Patel & Desai Pvt. Ltd."
6. Our company, thus, has been renamed as "Fashion Wear Co. (P) Ltd".

Assurance for good future dealings

7. Although the constitution of the company has changed, we assure all our customers the same co-operation and attention.
8. The nature of business will remain exactly as before and there will be no change in business policy.
9. It goes without saying that this will not, in any way, affect our healthy relationship with our customers.
10. We shall constantly endeavour to meet our business commitments with complete customer satisfaction.
11. We assure that our customers' interests will remain quite safe in our hands.
12. We take this opportunity to assure you that you will receive the same care and attention as in the past in the execution of your orders.
13. We hope the new arrangements will not affect our business relationship in any way but will continue to grow.

Sample Letters

(Circular Announcing Opening of New Business)

Dear Sirs,
We take great pleasure in announcing the opening of a T.V. repair shop in your colony's market (Shop No.617) on the auspicious day of Janmashtami.[2] As technical supervisor for Fairview Television company, I have competently handled and repaired all kinds of T.V. sets.[8] The opening ceremony of the centre will take place in the morning at 10 o' clock on 4th September, 2017. You are cordially invited.[18]

Thanking you,

Yours faithfully,

(Circular regarding new branch)

Dear Sirs,
We take great pleasure in announcing that on 1st of August, 2017, we are opening a new branch of readymade garments at 15 Nehru Place, New Delhi.[1] Although we have so far served you efficiently, you deserve still better services that await you.[6] Mr. Sunil Kumar, our Manager, for the last 20 years, will be in-charge of the new branch.[8] We welcome a visit by you to our new branch.[14]

With thanks,

Yours faithfully,

(Circular regarding acquisition of a firm)

Dear Sirs,
We have recently purchased the sole interests in the silk sari business of M/s Mysore Sari Emporium, 15 Main Road, Shahdara.[2] Our long experience in this line and substantial investment place us in a position to offer better goods to the customers.[7] We shall not only continue to trade under the old name but also make every effort to adhere to our predecessor's policy of sound service on which the goodwill of the firm has been built.[11] We propose to offer the old stock in a bargain sale next week on very attractive terms.[17] We hope you will be kind enough to extend your usual co-operation.[19]

Thanking you,

Yours faithfully,

(Notice of change of address)

Dear Sirs,

We take great pleasure in informing you that we have shifted to larger premises at Nav Niwas Colony from 1st August, 2017.[1] The new site is in the heart of the city and within easy reach by rail and road.[9] We are sure of serving you better from this place.[13]

With thanks,

Yours faithfully,

(Announcement regarding clearance sale)

Dear Sirs,

We take great pleasure in informing you that we are holding a clearance sale from February 14 to 19, 2017.[2] Attractive discount is being offered on all articles, ranging from 10% to 40%. In case you are unable to visit we shall be happy to reserve for you any goods that you order from the catalogue, to be despatched on February 1, 2017.[14]

With thanks,

Yours faithfully,

(Circular regarding retirement of a partner)

Dear Sirs,

We are sorry to announce the retirement of our valued partner Mr. Man Mohan from this firm.[3] He has sought this retirement on account of ill-health.[6] We assure you of the same care and prompt attention to your orders as in the past.[21]

With thanks,

Yours faithfully,

(Circular regarding admission of a new partner)

Dear Sirs,

We take pleasure in announcing the induction of Mr. Bharat Bhushan as a partner in our firm.[1] This was, in fact, necessitated following the death of our friend and partner Mr. Dhan Raj.[6] A specimen of Mr. Bharat Bhushan's signature is given below.[15]

With thanks,

Yours faithfully,

(Circular regarding conversion of partnership to a private ltd. co.)

Dear Sirs,

We take great pleasure in informing you that our company has become a Private Limited Company w.e.f. July 1, 2017.[1] Our company thus, has been renamed as "Fashion Wear Co. (P) Ltd."[6] The nature of business will remain exactly as before and there will be no change in business policy.[8]

With thanks,

Yours faithfully,

Agency Correspondence

Any growing business calls for wider markets. And, it is not possible for every company to open branches at all the places where it has markets. Thus, it has to rely on agents – a practice widely accepted all over the world. An agency can be set up on the initiative of the principal or the agent himself. In such an arrangement, both parties have to be extremely cautious because the reputation and goodwill of both affect each other's business.

While having such an arrangement, both parties keep a number of factors in mind. The agent has to see whether a potential market for the particular product exists or not and whether it can be easily developed. On the other hand, the manufacturer/principal must make sure about the financial soundness of the agent, technical skill to handle the product, his market connections, effectiveness of sales organisation, and the nature and extent of the other agencies he might hold. The supplier/principal can negotiate terms of business/agency commission keeping in view all these matters. He, of course, has to take into account the market possibilities, his own production capacity, interest and policies for promoting the business in a particular area. Now, whether such an arrangement finally comes through or not depends mainly on the requirements or preferences of the principal or the agent.

General Application for an Agency

Beginning

1. We shall be glad if you would consider our application to act as agents for the sale of your footwear/spark plugs.
2. We are the agents of a number of Mumbai based publishers and wish to procure agency for your books also.
3. We take this opportunity to offer our services as agents for the sale of your glassware in our city, Delhi.
4. We understand from M/s Vohra and Sons that you are looking for agents in Bulandshahr.
5. Given a chance, we shall feel privileged to work for and on behalf of your company.

6. We take this opportunity to offer ourselves as your representatives in the city.
7. Being in this field for a long time we have extremely good connections in the city.
8. Till recently, we had been acting as agents of M/s. New Star Publications. But as they have now opened their own office in the city they don't need our services. We are, therefore, free to offer our services to any other firm.
9. Our reputation in the auto industry is well-known and we are already dealers for Suzuki and LML scooters.
10. We have a well-furnished showroom on the prestigious Mahatma Gandhi Road.
11. On account of our prompt and excellent service, our clientele has grown steadily ever since we established our firm.
12. We hope to hear favourably from you and feel sure that we will have no difficulty in reaching agreeable business terms.
13. If desired, we can give you several first rate references.
14. We anticipate no problem in settling the terms and conditions for such business.

Appointment of Local Agent

Inform about granting the agency

1. We thank you for your letter of 5th October and are pleased to inform you that we have decided to appoint you our agent for Delhi.
2. We take pleasure in informing you that following your discussions with our representative, Mr. I.K. Mundra, who visited you last week, we have appointed you our agent for Bangalore from the 1st of next month.
3. Having carefully taken into consideration the agency terms you have offered and the references you have provided, we are pleased to appoint you our agent for Mathura for a trial period of one year.
4. We are pleased to inform you that our Directors have approved your application for agency with effect from 1st January 2017.

Terms and conditions of agency

5. We have decided to put you on a trial period of three months initially. During this period, we shall pay 7% commission on all the sales.
6. If the terms of the said agreement meet your approval, we request you to return us the duplicate copy duly signed by you.
7. We shall be sending our representative, Mr. B.J. Kapoor, next week with a formal agreement of terms and conditions, to be signed by you.
8. Kindly go through the terms and conditions sent separately and return them duly signed.
9. Your appointment as our agent is, of course, subject to your approval of our terms and conditions, a copy of which is enclosed.

Close of the letter

10. We hope the enclosed agreement will receive your consent and we quote our present prices which are as follows.
11. We have already had business relations with a couple of firms in your city whom we are now intimating about your appointment as our agent.
12. If you agree to these terms, we shall send a formal agreement to be signed by you.
13. Now, will you please let us have your plans and programme to organize sales in your district during the first six months.
14. As soon as we hear from you, we shall arrange to despatch the goods for the first three months.

Acceptance of Agency

Convey acceptance

1. We thank you for your letter of 9th March along with copies of your standard form of agency agreement and are happy to convey our acceptance of your agency.
2. We have received your form of agency agreement and are happy to return it duly signed by our Managing Director, Mr. M.R. Aggarwal.
3. We have gone through your terms of agreement and are pleased to intimate you that we accept your offer.
4. Thank you for your letter of 3rd October, offering us the sole agency for your milk products in Haryana.
5. We thank you for offering us the agency for your sarees in Bangalore and appreciate the confidence you have reposed in us.

Other important things

6. We have also received your catalogue which covers an extensive range of interesting titles.
7. Your publications are in big demand because they are ideally suited to the High School and under graduate courses.
8. We are prepared to incur an initial expenditure of ₹ 50,000/- on advertising and will back it up with active campaign through our sales-staff.
9. We are now sending a circular to prospective customers in this region informing them of our appointment as your agents.

Closure

10. Thank you for giving us the first opportunity to take your agency here.
11. As desired by you, we enclose a copy of the contract duly signed by our Managing Director, Mr. K.P. Gulati.

12. We now look forward to a mutually beneficial business relationship with you.
13. We already represent several other manufacturers and assure you of our best services.
14. We accept your terms and conditions as set out in the draft agreement and look forward to a happy and successful working relationship with you.

Enquiry for Sole Agency

Begin with your offer

1. We have recently read with interest your advertisement in 'The Times of India' offering the sole agency of your brassware.
2. We have seen your machine tools in the International Trade Fair at Delhi this year and have found them of high quality.
3. We have been impressed with the high quality and reasonable prices of your photographic material demonstrated in the International Exhibition in Mumbai.
4. Having had a discussion with your partner, we have become interested in representing you in Chandigarh.
5. Having had an opportunity to visit your hardware stall in the 'Trade Fair 99', we are inclined to have a sole agency for the same.

Give your credentials

6. As a leading distributor of high fashion garments with more than ten years' standing in the market, we are well acquainted with the market conditions in the region.
7. Through an active sales organisation, we have established good contacts with leading retailers.
8. Although we handle several other agencies, they are in non-competing lines.
9. You would, of course, be interested in knowing about us. And for this, we would refer you to Bharat Sales Emporium, Delhi and Bank of India, Connaught Place, New Delhi.
10. We are well-known distributors with over fifteen years' standing and branches in most of the principal towns of Gujarat. You can refer to Punjab National Bank, Main street, Ahmedabad, to know more about us.
11. We are well acquainted with the local market conditions and have a wide experience in the trade.

Express expectations of good business

12. We have seen your catalogue and are convinced that there is a promising market for these products in Karnataka.
13. We are sure your products will have good sales in these areas.
14. We are sure that we will be able to give a boost to the sales of your products.

15. We are confident that with the high quality of your products and our selling experience, we can make a grand success of achieving the sales target for this year.
16. Since we are experts in the field, we are sure of bringing you a good margin of profit.
17. We are confident of bringing you huge profits because of our wide-ranging contacts in the field.

Close the letter on a bright note

18. We firmly believe that such an arrangement will be of mutual benefit to both of us.
19. We assure you that our handling of your products, as sole agents for the territory of Maharashtra, will be of advantage to both of us.
20. We look forward to your acceptance.
21. We are sure of getting you unexpected profit if we become your sole agent here in Poona.

Reply to Enquiry for the Sole Agency

Convey thanks on receiving enquiry

1. We thank you for your letter of 22nd November and are pleased to learn that you are interested in promoting the sales of our products.
2. We are happy to learn that, in your opinion, there are good prospects for the sale of our products in your State.
3. Thank you for your letter dt. 8th April and we are pleased to learn that you like our kitchen appliances.
4. We thank you for your letter of 25th November, expressing your interest in our hand-tools.
5. We feel pleased to acknowledge your interest in our electronic products advertisements which you have noticed in the national press.

Ask details about terms and prospects regarding the sole agency

6. We have not yet decided about giving agency for Maharashtra but if your representative calls on us when he is in Delhi next we would be glad to discuss with him the possibility of coming to some agreement with you.
7. Although we have not taken any decision regarding the agency, yet we have advised our representative Mr. Jugal Kishore to visit you next week.
8. A rough estimate of the amount of stock you could hold, at a given time, would be welcome.
9. We are a growing company and wish to develop trade in your region.
10. We would certainly like to get in touch with your representative, when he is in town, to discuss the prospects in detail regarding the Sole Agency which you have asked for.
11. Meanwhile, we take pleasure in sending you our catalogue and price-list giving details of discount.

Tell about your immediate programme

12. In the meantime, your representative can visit us whenever he is in town. He can see for himself the excellent quality of raw material and the manufacturing technology at our factory.
13. Meanwhile, we would be pleased to supply you with an initial order at the prices quoted against a sight draft at 30 days, after booking of the order.
14. Meanwhile, could you please send us the detailed record of your sales performance for the past two years.
15. In the mean time, we are ready to supply you the initial order at the maximum discount and free transportation.

Agent's Request for More Commission

Ask for more Commission

1. We would be glad if you consider some upward revision, in your present rate of commission to the wholesale dealers.
2. We write this letter to request you to increase our commission.
3. We trust you will agree with us that the present condition of the sale justifies an increase in the percentage of commission we receive from you.
4. In view of the prevailing competitive condition in the market, we have to request you to increase our rate of commission.
5. Since we have recently brought huge orders and incurred heavy expenses, we have to request you to increase our rate of commission.

Express why it is necessary to increase commission

6. In fact, because of the latest trends in the market, it has become more difficult to market your goods.
7. Ever since we have taken your agency many competitors have entered the market and established themselves.
8. As a result of increased competition we have been able to hold our sales only by driving our salesmen hard and increasing our publicity budget.
9. And this, of course, calls for compensation from the manufacturer.
10. In order to compete effectively, we would request you to increase the rate of commission.
11. Although your garments are modern and stylish, in view of the fact that many other competitors are already established firmly in the line, it is providing difficult to make a dent on the market.
12. As my sales efforts for your products will now mean additional expenditure on advertisement, I must request you to bear part of the increased costs.

Close with expectation of more Commission

13. We feel the compensation from your side could be in the form of an increase in commission, say by 10%.
14. We suggest this figure after carefully calculating the increase in our advertising budget/ selling costs.
15. Under the circumstances we sincerely hope you will revise the commission.
16. As is evident from the present scenario, we are left with no option but to ask for a raise of 2 ½% in the rate of commission.
17. I shall be pleased to hear what you have to suggest as regards the increase in commission.
18. Considering our old established relations, we hope you would take a favourable decision on our request.
19. We hope you would consider our present request with understanding and sympathy.
20. We trust you will take a favourable view of the circumstances and allow an increase in the rate of commission.

Manufacturer's Reply to Agent's Request for More Commission

First acknowledge the letter

1. Thank you for your letter of 21st July.
2. We are in receipt of your letter dated February 2, 2017.
3. Thank you for your letter dt. 8th July on...
4. We confirm receipt of your letter dated 2nd May, 2017.
5. We thank you for your letter dated 5th April, 2017.

Agree to the agent's proposal

6. We have noted with utmost concern the problems presented by our competitors in your city.
7. We are pleased to learn the extra efforts you have put to meet the new challenge.
8. Although we are sure that our products, in long run, will stand the test of time, we realise that the growing competition must be met by more active advertising.
9. We agree that it would not be reasonable to expect you to bear the full cost.
10. We realise your difficulty in meeting the challenging situation in the market.

Give information for future programme

11. However, to increase the commission at this stage would be difficult, as our prices leave us with a very small margin.
12. Instead, we propose to allow you an advertising credit of ₹ 1,000/- in the current year towards your additional costs.
13. However, in view of the very small margin of our profit, we can increase your commission by 2% only.
14. Thus, we have accepted your proposal but can allow only 2% increase as a short term measure for 6 months, on account of the current market situation.
15. We hope you will be happy with the alternative arrangement we have suggested.
16. With due appreciation of your efforts to maintain the sales of our products, we regret we will not be in a position to increase your commission for another six months.

Sample Letters

(General application for agency)

Dear Sirs,

We shall be glad if you would consider our application to act as agents for the sale of your spark plugs.[1] Our reputation in the auto industry is well known and we are already dealers for Suzuki and LML scooters.[9] We anticipate no problem in settling the terms and conditions for such business.[14]

Thanking you,

Yours faithfully,

(Appointment of local agent)

Dear Sirs,

We are pleased to inform you that our Directors have approved your application for agency with effect from 1st January, 2017.[4] Kindly go through the terms and conditions sent separately and return them duly signed.[8] We hope the enclosed agreement will receive your consent and quote our present prices, which are as follows.[10]

With thanks,

Yours faithfully,

(Acceptance of agency)

Dear Sirs,

We thank you for your letter of 9th March, along with copies of your standard form of agency agreement and are happy to convey our acceptance of your agency.[1] We have also received your catalogue which covers an extensive range of interesting titles.[6] Thank you for giving us the first opportunity to take up your agency here.[10]

With thanks,

Sincerely yours,

(Enquiry for sole agency)

Dear Sirs,

We have recently read with interest your advertisement in 'The Times of India' offering the sole agency of your brassware.[1] We are well-known distributors with over fifteen years' standing and branches in most of the principal towns of Gujarat. You can refer to Punjab National Bank, Main Street, Ahmedabad, to know more about us.[10] We are sure your products will have good sales in these areas.[13]

Thanking you,

Yours faithfully,

(Reply to enquiry for the sole agency)

Dear Sirs,

We thank you for your letter of 22nd November, and are pleased to learn that you are interested in promoting the sales of our products.[1] Meanwhile could your please send us the detailed records of your sales performance for the past two years.[14] Although we have not taken any decision regarding the agency, we have advised our representative Mr. Jugal Kishore to visit your city next week.[7]

With best wishes,

Faithfully yours,

(Agent's request for more commission)

Dear Sirs,

We trust you will agree with us that the present condition of the sale justifies an increase in the percentage of commission we receive from you.[3] Ever since, we have taken your agency many competitors have entered the market and have established themselves.[7] Under the circumstances we sincerely hope you will revise the commission.[15]

Thanking you,

Yours faithfully,

(Manufacturer's reply to agent's request for more commission)

Dear Sirs,

Thank you for your letter of 21st July.[1] We have noted with utmost concern the problems presented by our competitors in your city.[6] We realise your difficulty in meeting the challenging situation in the market.[10] Thus, we have accepted your proposal but can allow only 2% increase as a short term measure for 6 months, on account of the current market situation.[14]

Yours faithfully,

Trade Reference and Status Enquiry

When the goods are sold for cash, there is no need for the seller to enquire into the financial standing of the buyer. But when they are sold on credit, as is the common business practice nowadays, the seller has to make sure about the financial credit-worthiness of the buyer. He must know whether the customer can make the payment in time or not. He can obtain this information from various sources, namely (i) trade references supplied by the buyer himself (ii) the buyer's banker or (iii) various trade associations.

However, the credit through bank is taken against Hundi. The 'Hundi' can be of any duration varying from 30 days to 180 days. This credit is safe since Hundi has legal validity and is accepted as a sure evidence in the civil court.

Supplier's Request for References

Ask for trade references

1. We shall be glad to take in hand your order dt. 3rd February, for immediate delivery if you send us the customary trade references.
2. We thank you for your order No.L503 for the supply of 100 'medium' hockey sticks.

3. We are pleased to receive your order of 15th May. But since it is your first order we shall be glad to consider credit terms if you kindly provide us with the usual trade references.
4. We are happy to receive your order of 2nd November for 100 Banarasi silk saris. We could, of course, extend the required credit, if you kindly send us the name and address of your bankers.
5. Thank you for your order of 10th June for 100 'Deluxe' dining-tables. However, we would like to inform you that since it is your first dealing with us we require references.
6. We thank you for your order of 4th November, but since this is your first order with us, and as it is customary in our business, we would appreciate your giving us trade reference of a party with whom you have had dealings for the last few years.
7. Will you, therefore, please send us the names and addresses of two other suppliers with whom you have dealings?

Give assurance of business cooperation

8. As soon as we hear from the reference we shall despatch the goods. Your order is under processing.
9. You will appreciate that this is a normal practice and trust you won't mind our insisting on it.
10. When opening new accounts it is customary to ask for trade references.Therefore, will you please send names and addresses of the referees?
11. So, to enable us to take up the execution of orders we would be glad if you furnish the names of two firms with whom you have had regular dealings.
12. Please send us the name and address of your bankers for the usual trade references.

References Supplied by the Dealer

Begin the letter in this way

1. Thank you for your letter of 5th April. As we hope to place further orders with you, we would like to avail of your credit facilities.
2. As requested in your letter of 7th August, we are furnishing below the names of two dealers to whom you may refer.
3. In response to your letter dt. 4th January we suggest you to refer to our bankers...
4. We thank you for your letter of 8th July and quite understand the need for references. We have completed and are now returning you credit application in which we have listed the names and addresses of our bankers and also of two well-known firms with whom we have had dealings for many years.
5. In response to your enquiry of 18th November, we would like to say that you may take up references with the following firms with whom we have had dealings for many years.
6. We thank you for your letter of 5th June, 2017 and give the names of the following firms as references for you to enquire into our financial standing.

7. We thank you for your letter of 5th October and are happy to inform you that we have been dealing with M/s Modern Utilities Company of your town for the last five years. Our bankers, Central Bank of India, Parliament Street, New Delhi can also be referred to this purpose.

Write about other important matters

8. We now have pleasure in sending you our first order for five "Madhur" pocket transistors at your listed price of ₹ 570/- less 25% on your usual monthly terms.
9. We note that we may expect delivery of the goods ordered last month and look forward to receiving them in time.
10. We now look forward to getting into a large volume of business with you on a regular basis.
11. Now, we hope to get a prompt delivery of the goods ordered by us.
12. Now that the formalities are over, we hope to receive our ordered goods at the earliest.
13. Now we hope this will lead to a long and fruitful business relationship.
14. Here we give the names and addresses of two firms who are our regular suppliers for more than 10 years.
15. For information on our financial standing, we refer you to our bankers...
16. Should you wish to take up references, the following firms will be pleased to answer your enquiries.

Supplier Takes up References

Starting the letter

1. M/s. Fancy Footwear of Baroda wish to open an account with us and have given us your name as reference.
2. We have today received an order for ₹ 50,000/- for stainless steel utensils from Cookwell Kitchen Stores, Faridabad, who have given us your name as reference.
3. Mr. Anil Kumar of 13, Nehru Road, Agra, has referred us to you for information concerning his credit standing.
4. We have received a large order from M/s. Welcome Garments Stores, New Delhi, and shall be grateful to you for any information you could give us concerning their reliability.
5. M/s. Modern Cosmetics Company, New Delhi, have referred us to you for information regarding their credit standing, as they wish to open an account with us.
6. M/s. Tyre-Tube Traders of Ghaziabad have requested us to supply them 100 truck tubes. Since they wish us to supply the goods on credit they have given us your name as reference.

Asking for reference

7. We would be grateful if you could provide us with reliable information concerning his firm's credit-worthiness.
8. We would be grateful if you give us the information you can about the firm's general standing.
9. Please confirm whether, in your opinion, this company is reliable for credit upto ₹ 50,000/- and whether they settle their accounts promptly.
10. We wish to know about the general standing of the firm and if they are likely to be reliable for credit upto ₹ 1,00,000/-.
11. We shall be grateful for any information you could give us about this firm.
12. We shall take it as a favour if you could kindly tell us whether you have found this company reliable in dealings and prompt in settling their accounts.
13. We gather that the credit requirements of this firm may go up to ₹ 50,000/- per month. We will be grateful for your opinion about their ability to meet commitments of this size.
14. We shall also welcome any other information you could supply us about the firm.

Keeping the information confidential

15. We assure you that any information supplied by you will be treated in strict confidence.
16. We shall, of course, treat any advice you give us in this regard as strictly confidential.
17. Your reply will naturally be treated in strict confidence.
18. Needless to say that any information you supply us, shall be treated in strict confidence.
19. We shall be equally glad to render you a similar service, should the need arise.
20. We would perform a similar service to you, if an opportunity ever arises.
21. We shall be equally pleased to perform a similar service to you, if ever you require of us.

Expressing thanks

22. We shall indeed be grateful for your co-operation.
23. Please accept in advance our thanks for any assistance you can give us.
24. Any information you could give us will be greatly appreciated.
25. We shall feel obliged to receive any information in this regard from you.
26. This is something which we need to have business and we will feel thankful for the same.

Enclosing reply envelope

27. We enclose a self-addressed stamped envelope for your reply.
28. Please find enclosed a self-addressed stamped envelope for your kind reply.

29. Please find herewith a stamped, self-addressed envelope for an early reply.
30. Just to save your time, we are enclosing a stamped and self-addressed envelope.

Replies to References

Express your opinion

1. We are pleased to state that though the firm referred to in your letter of 3rd June is a small one, it is well known and has been established in this town for more than 25 years.
2. The company M/s. Greatway Footwear, Model Town, which you have referred to us, is a well-established firm and is very fair in its dealings.
3. We must express surprise that the company you have named has given our name for reference.
4. As far as we know, it is a reputed firm, but we have no definite knowledge of its financial standing.
5. Although they have often placed orders with us, they have been of very small amounts.
6. In response to your letter of 5th March, we are glad to report favourably on M/s. Gorgeous Garment Company, Delhi.
7. In reply to your letter of 17th September, we regret to say that we are unable to express a definite opinion about M/s. Gopinath & Co., Churiwalan, Delhi.
8. We regret that the firm about which you enquired in your letter of 15th July is not well known to us.
9. Concerning the firm mentioned in your letter of 28th February, we recommend a policy of caution.
10. We must regret our inability to extend any assistance regarding the information you desired about M/s. Ashok Brothers, New Delhi.

Give details of your opinion

11. We ourselves have been doing business with this firm for more than five years on credit terms and they have always been regular and timely in settling their accounts.
12. The company you have referred to has been dealing with us for more than 15 years.
13. The account of this firm with us is on quarterly settlement terms, but we have never allowed it to reach the sum you mentioned in your letter.
14. We have had only occasional and small dealings with this firm and even then accounts were not always settled in time.
15. And so, we feel, caution is necessary in this case.

Request for keeping the matter confidential

16. We hope this information will be helpful and that you will treat it as confidential.
17. We accept your assurance that this information will be treated in strict confidence and regret that we cannot be more helpful in this regard.
18. This information is given to you in confidence and without any legal responsibility on our part.
19. We regret we do not know this firm so closely as to express any opinion about it and that we cannot be of any help to you in this respect.

Sample Letters

(Supplier's request for references)

Dear Sirs,
We are pleased to receive your order of 15th May. But since it is your first order we shall be glad to consider credit terms if you kindly provide us with the usual trade references.[3] As soon as we hear from the referees we shall despatch the goods. Your order is under processing.[8]

With best wishes,

Yours faithfully,

(References supplied by the dealer)

Dear Sirs,
We thank you for your letter of 5th October and are happy to inform you that we have been dealing with M/s. Modern Utilities Company of your town for the last five years. Our bankers, Central Bank of India, Parliament Street, New Delhi, can also be referred to for this purpose.[7]

With best wishes,

Yours faithfully,

(Supplier takes up references)

Dear Sirs,
Mr. Anil Kumar of 13, Nehru Road, Agra, has referred us to you for information concerning his credit standing.[3] We would be grateful if you could provide us with reliable information concerning his firm's credit-worthiness.[7] We assure you that any information supplied by you will be treated in strict confidence.[15] We shall, indeed, be grateful for your co-operation.[22]

With thanks,

Yours faithfully,

(Replies to references)

Dear Sirs,

We are pleased to state that though the firm referred to in your letter of 3rd June is a small one, it is well known and has been established in this town for more than 25 years.[1] We ourselves have been doing business with this firm for more than five years on credit terms and they have always been regular and timely in settling their accounts.[11] We hope this information will be helpful and you will treat it as confidential.[16]

With thanks,

Yours faithfully,

Trade Letter with Foreign Buyers

Export and import trade involves complex procedures and documents. There are certain international traditions and conventions accepted all over the world, in this regard. International trade letters are in many respects, similar to the inland trade letters. Enquiries are made, orders placed, goods received are acknowledged and paid for. Generally foreign trade is carried on the basis of agency system but direct trade relations can also develop.

An exporter normally prefers to send the goods to a known importer in a foreign country. He may appoint his own agent or conduct business through a recognised exporting agent whose function is to collect different goods from different manufacturers. The agents may also look after the packing, and forward, insure and ship the goods. In this, he may be carrying out the instructions of his principal or acting on his own. On the other hand, the importing agent takes care of unloading, customs, warehousing, etc. These formalities being over, he also sells the product through familiar trade channels. Strict government control is exercised in each country on all import/export trade. An order sent by an importer to an exporter is called an indent. It contains all necessary details of the articles required, important instructions for packing, marking, numbering and collection of payments, etc. Packing of overseas goods is carefully and methodically done. It is more or less standardised these days. The marking and numbering help the clearing agent to identify parcels/packets and arrange for distribution or delivery to the concerned.

Sample Letter

M/s. Small Business Publications,
Roop Nagar,
DELHI-110007.

Dear Sirs,

Your Technology books are becoming extremely popular in our country. Of late, there has been a growing demand for them. So, please despatch us 5 dozen sets at the earliest. The books should be securely packed in wooden boxes of 50 kg each and shipped by S.S. Kumargiri. The packages should be marked B-S-P and numbered. Please also arrange for the insurance. Invoice value of the books should not be more than $500.00.

We are willing to honour drafts through the Indian Overseas Bank, Singapore. We shall be placing more orders if the books are accepted by the Technical Institutions and industrial houses.

Thanking you,

Yours faithfully,

In a bid to advance its economy, every country is keen to promote its foreign trade. In India, there are may corporations like State Trading Corporation, Food Corporation, Export Promotion Council, etc., to promote export business. However, in addition to these, there are many companies with sound financial backing which are recognised by the Government as exporting houses.

Advice Note

When goods are exported, the buyer is informed of the shipment by the exporter. This letter is called Advice Note. It contains details of goods sent, their prices, name of the ship, its probable date of arrival, etc. Generally, the shipping documents are handed over to the Bank for collection of the bill, but sometimes they are directly forwarded to the buyer if the relations are old and well established.

Bill of Lading

A port/ports in each country may have outlets to different parts of the globe. When goods are received on the ship, the commander issues a receipt called Mate's Receipt. In turn, the owner of the ship gives a Bill of Lading on getting the Mate's Receipt and freight charges of the cargo. The B.L. contains details of exporter's name, number of packages, identity marks, importer's name and the country to which they are shipped. This document is sent to the importer through the bank and authorises the importer to take delivery of the goods after clearing customs and other dues.

Original Invoice

The first copy of the invoice is called original invoice. It is sent by the exporter to the importer and contains value and description of the goods including markings on packages, etc.

Bill of Exchange

This is an instrument for transfer of money from the buyer to the supplier. The importer of goods pays the stated amount at sight or after sight as agreed upon in business terms.

All the concerned documents are sent to the bank by the exporter in his own town. The bank sends them to the importer's bank in his country. The payment is made forthwith (at sight) or by signing an acceptance (after sight).

From Seller to Buyer Abroad

Inform about the invoice value

1. In confirmation of our letter of 2nd March, we are pleased to inform you that we verified your account for the consignment of shoes by S.S. Jal Vihar and advise you that we have drawn on you today for $200 at two month's sight.
2. We are pleased to inform you that with reference to your letter of 2nd March, we have verified your account for the consignment of readymade garments and have today drawn on you for $200 at two month's sight, as agreed.
3. Confirming our letter of 2nd March, we are glad to say that having verified your account for the Rice consignment by S.S. Jal Seva, we have drawn on you for $200 at two month's sight, as agreed.
4. We confirm having drawn on you a Bill of Exchange for US $500.00 against goods despatched to you by AWB No... and under our invoice No... dt... (AWB-Air Way Bill).

Request for acceptance of draft

5. We hope the draft will be honoured on presentation and our account credited accordingly.
6. Kindly honour the draft when presented and debit our account accordingly.
7. We hope you will accept the draft to the debit of our accounts on presentation.
8. Kindly honour the draft as and when presented and debit it to our accounts.

Letter Accepting Draft

Acknowledge honouring the draft

1. With reference to your letter of 15th April, we are pleased to inform you that we have accepted your draft for $200.
2. We are pleased to inform you that in reply to your letter of 21st March we have accepted your draft of $200 at 20 days' sight, as agreed.

3. In response to your letter of 18th December we are glad to inform you that we have accepted your draft of $125.
4. Please refer to your letter of 1st April 2017 regarding the draft for ₹ 25,550/- which we have accepted.
5. We are glad to inform you that your draft for ₹ 20,225/- has been accepted by us as per your letter dated 12th July, 2017.
6. We have duly presented the draft and honoured it, debiting the same to your account.
7. Draft has been presented and honoured by us and recorded in your accounts.
8. We have received your draft No. SL 58208 and are pleased to inform that we have duly presented and debited to your account as per your instructions.

Letter regarding Draft from Buyer to Seller

Inform about the goods sold

1. We are pleased to inform you that, as indicated in our sales account, we have been able to dispose of your readymade garments for ₹ 25,550/-. After allowing for expenses and commission there remains a balance of ₹ 20,400/- in your favour.
2. We are pleased to report as per Sales Account enclosed that we could dispose of your supply of hardware for ₹ 20,500/-. Out of this sale, a balance of ₹ 15000/- remains in your favour after deducting expenses and commission.
3. As you will observe from the accompanying Sales Account, we have been able to dispose of your plastic buckets for ₹ 10,000/-. Out of this sale a balance of ₹ 7,750/- remains in your favour after allowing for expenses and commission.
4. So you could kindly draw on us at 30 days' sight, as agreed.
5. So, kindly draw on us for this amount at thirty days, under advice to us, when we shall be happy to honour your draft.
6. You are, therefore, requested to draw on us under advice for this sum.

Reply to Letter regarding Draft

Express thanks for getting details of sales

1. We thank you for your letter of 3rd April containing details of Sales Account.
2. Thank you for the Sales Account that you have sent with your letter of 13th August.
3. We are pleased to acknowledge your letter of 5th May along with the Sales Account.
4. We have received your letter dated 6th August containing details of Sales Account.
5. It has been examined properly and found it in order.
6. We have examined it and found it in order.

7. On examination, the documents have been found in order.
8. The details of Sales Account were found correct.
9. We have accordingly drawn on you through Dena Bank, Arya Samaj Road, New Delhi for ₹ 5,500/- at thirty days' sight, as suggested by you.
10. Accordingly we have drawn on you for an amount of ₹ 7,750/- through the Central Bank of India, at 30 days' as agreed earlier.
11. So, please be advised that we have drawn on you through Bank of India, G Block, Connaught Place, New Delhi, for the sum of ₹ 10,900/- at 30 days' sight.

Letter regarding Bill for Collection

Give details of draft

1. We are pleased to enclose the following drafts for favour of collection:

   ₹ 5,550/- at sight on Rao & Co.

   ₹ 3,300/- for 25th May on Shastri Brothers.

   ₹ 7,700/- for 6th August on Soni & Sons.

   ₹ 11,500/- payable in Mumbai.
2. Kindly find enclosed the following drafts for favour of collection.
3. We are sending herewith the drafts as per details given below for favour of collection.
4. We shall be obliged if you would credit the proceeds to our accounts and advise us of the receipt in due course.
5. Kindly credit the proceeds to our account and intimate receipt by return post.
6. Kindly credit the proceeds to our accounts and inform accordingly.

Sample Letters

(Bill of exchange: from seller to buyer abroad)

Dear Sirs,
In confirmation of our letter of 2nd March, we are pleased to inform you that we have verified your account for the consignment of shoes by S.S. Jal Vihar and advise you that we have drawn on you today for $200 at two months's sight.[1] We hope the draft will be honoured on presentation and our account credited accordingly.[5]

With thanks,

Yours faithfully,

(Letter accepting draft)

Dear Sirs,
We are pleased to inform you that in reply to your letter of 21st March, we have accepted your draft of $200 at 20 days' sight, as agreed.[2]
With thanks,
Yours faithfully,

(Letter regarding draft from buyer to seller)

Dear Sirs,
As you will observe from the accompanying Account Sales, we have been able to dispose of your plastic buckets for ₹ 10,000/-. Out of this sale a balance of ₹ 7,750/- remains in your favour after allowing for expenses and commission.[3] You are, therefore, requested to draw on us under advice for this sum.[6]

With thanks,

Yours faithfully,

(reply to letter regarding draft)

Dear Sirs,
Thank you for the Sales Account that you have sent with your letter of 13th August.[2] The documents have been found in order.[7] So, please be advised that we have drawn on you through Bank of India, G Block, Connaught Place, New Delhi for the sum of ₹10,900/- at 30 days' sight.[11]

Thanking you,

Yours faithfully,

(Letter regarding bill for collection)

Dear Sirs,
We are pleased to enclose the following drafts for favour of collection: ₹5,550/- at sight on Rao & Co. We shall be obliged if you would credit the proceeds to our account and advise us of the receipt in due course.[4]

Thanking you,

Yours faithfully,

Export-Import Correspondence

George Bernard Shaw, the famous British dramatist of 20th century, had once remarked, "The universal regard for money is the one hopeful fact in our civilization." It is, of course, true that money is a very important aspect of our life. In the modern times, due to the quick modes of communication and transportation the world is becoming shorter and people of different places are coming closer. As a result, foreign trade is becoming the most important of all trades. It is, therefore, necessary to have sufficient knowledge of correspondence dealing with foreign trade, foreign exchange regulations and foreign banking.

Because of the involvement of a second country in this case, correspondence has more facets and intricacies to it than that of the internal trade correspondence. Different kinds of letters and proformas are used for handling this correspondence. The main features of this correspondence are clarity, courtesy and completeness. This job must be assigned to a person who is fully capable of conveying the business policies of the firm within the framework of foreign exchange rules and regulations. His understanding of the clients on the other side, his own thinking and interest of the foreign trade must synchronize.

Exporter's Enquiry from Manufacturer

Apprise the manufacturer of foreign demand of goods

1. We are pleased to inform you that one of our clients in Europe is interested in large scale purchase of silk shirts.
2. You will be pleased to learn that one of our clients in Italy wishes to make large scale purchase of Indian handicraft goods.
3. It will be of interest to you to learn that a reputed foreign dealer in imitation jewellery wishes to introduce Indian fashions in his market.
4. We are glad to inform you that a foreign firm is interested in making huge purchases of Indian silk saris.
5. It may be of interest to you to note that a foreign firm is very keen in making purchase of 'Televista' television sets for supply to Kenya.

Now ask the manufacturer about his supply position

6. Therefore, we wish to know if you are in a position to supply us adequate quantity of high quality shirts of the material.
7. Consequently, we are interested in knowing if you can undertake to supply such goods of export quality.
8. So could you please send us details and specifications of articles available with you which you can supply in bulk at short notice.
9. We are specially interested in small carved pieces of rosewood and ivory.

10. We are basically interested in fabrics printed essentially with Indian motifs.
11. Our client is particularly interested in sandalwood articles.

Suggest competitive price

12. This is a competitive quotation and is likely to open up a very good avenue for your products in the western Europe.
13. We need not tell you that a really competitive quotation can mean excellent future prospects to you.
14. This is with the assumption that our price would be within certain definite limits which our customer has in mind.

Close your letter with a note about making the best of the opportunity

15. Our trial order will convince you of the promising prospects of this deal.
16. It will be clear to you that supplying a genuine product could bring you huge profits in the form of regular orders.
17. We hardly need to mention that this is an excellent opportunity for you to enter the export market in a big way, provided, the quality of your products meets the high western standards.

Manufacturer's Reply to Exporter

Express thanks for enquiry

1. We are obliged for your enquiry of 4th August.
2. Thank you for your letter of enquiry dated 4th August, 2017.
3. We are thankful to you for your kind enquiry vide your letter of 4th August, 2017.
4. Thank you for your letter of enquiry dt. 5th April.

Reply to the points of enquiry

5. We are prepared to supply you the required goods at the quoted prices less 10% discount with free delivery at destination.
6. We hope you will agree with us that our prices are quite competitive. Catalogue is enclosed.
7. We are offering a special reduction of 10% in the prices of your items in view of the size of your order.
8. We assure you that our quotations for both large and small orders will be extremely competitive.
9. We are quite confident of meeting your delivery schedule.
10. We have a large production unit and can meet your order for any reasonable delivery date.

Write about the supply position of your products

11. Our imitation jewellery is widely exported and has good demand throughout Europe.
12. Our products have been becoming more and more popular in western Europe and have, recently, been introduced into the USA too.
13. We are sending herewith a few samples of the same.
14. Under separate cover, we are sending you some samples for your inspection.
15. You will be pleased to know that we are already a pioneer in this trade.

Express hope for good future business

16. We now look forward to receiving further instructions from you.
17. Looking forward to receiving your order…
18. We trust you find our terms attractive enough for placing an immediate order.
19. We hope now you will place an early order with us.

An Indent

Give information about sending the indent

1. We are enclosing indent No.345 for 150 pairs of nylon socks of different colours and designs.
2. Please find herewith our indent No.123 for 50 Kanchipuram silk saris of various shades and colours.
3. With this letter we are sending you our indent No.689 for 200 handwoven scarves of three colours, namely purple, orange and blue.

Give information regarding quality of goods

4. Please see to it that the sarees are of high quality with attractive prints.
5. Please make sure that the goods are of high standard in order to make a dent in the sophisticated markets of the West.
6. Kindly ensure that all pieces are of high export quality.
7. While executing this order please see to it that only colours going with the spring seasons are used.
8. Please note that only autumn colours are to be used for this lot.
9. Please make sure that the goods meet the high standards of quality laid down by the Textile Committee.

Also give instructions regarding transactions

10. We shall be thankful to you if you could attend to the insurance formalities at your end.
11. You may draw on us through our bankers, the Mercantile Bank, at 60 days' sight.

12. We would like you to get the necessary insurance coverage yourself.
13. Please send the consignment with the freight prepaid.

Reply to Indent

Acknowledge the indent

1. We thank you for your letter of 5th June, 2017 and your indent No.432.
2. This is to acknowledge with thanks receipt of your letter of 5th June along with your indent No.432.
3. We have received your indent No.432 along with your letter dated June 5, 2017.

Write about the progress of execution of indent

4. We have booked this indent and have forwarded it to your friend in Singapore.
5. The said indent has been booked and forwarded to your party in Tokyo.
6. We have been very prompt in completing the formalities of booking the indent and have forwarded it to your party in London.

Close the letter like this

7. We shall shortly be informing you of its acceptance after hearing from him.
8. We shall get in touch with you on hearing about the party's acceptance.
9. We shall, soon, be in a position to advise you on hearing from the party about its acceptance.
10. Immediately on getting a communication from the party, we shall contact you.

Intimation regarding Execution of Export-order

Advise about export-despatch

1. We are pleased to inform you of the despatch of 1000 Chennai check cotton shirts shipped today by S.S. Jal Bharat.
2. We are glad to advise you that 1000 kg of Tajmahal tea as per your order No. Ex.P/401 of July 21, 2017 has been despatched by S.S. Jal Vihar which left Mumbai for London today.
3. We are pleased to inform you of the despatch of your goods by S.S. Neel Sagar leaving Calcutta today for Singapore.
4. We trust that the goods will reach you in good condition and in time.
5. We hope the consignment reaches you safely.

6. We are pleased to inform you that we have today shipped all the goods as per your order No.421 dated... under AWB No… dated… and our invoice No is … dated…

Give information about documents

7. We have surrendered, as agreed, the shipping documents to the Mumbai Bank at 60 days' sight.
8. We trust you will accept on presentation and take delivery of the shipping documents, viz., Bill of Lading, Invoice and Certificate of Origin.
9. We hope you will find all the documents in order.
10. We enclose the bill of lading and shipping documents and hope you will have no difficulty in disposing of the goods.
11. A copy of our invoice No... the original of the GSP Form A and packing list are enclosed to your reference.

Close the letter in this way

12. We look forward to hearing that you have been able to obtain satisfactory prices.
13. We hope to have more opportunities to serve you.
14. We hope this is the beginning of a long fruitful relationship between us.
15. We are sure our efficient service will fetch further business.
16. We look forward to further enquiries and orders from you.

Some more common sentences

17. We are sending you a consignment of Kashmir shawls by S.S. Delhi Darbar, for sale on our account.
18. We regret that we cannot handle your goods on our own account, but would be willing to take them on a consignment basis.
19. We have, today, sent to you a consignment of 100 bags of Dehra Dun rice by S.S. Jal Bharat for which we enclose bill of lading and our invoice.
20. We are delighted to learn that the consignment of 100 Banarasi silk sarees by S.S. Ratnagiri, has fetched you good price.
21. We enclose the bill of lading for goods which will shortly reach you by S.S. Jal Jawahar that left Mumbai on 15th October, 2016.
22. Thank you for your letter of 13th February notifying shipment of 200 boxes of nylon shirts by S.S. White Queen.
23. Thank you for your advice of despatch and the bill of lading for the consignment shipped by S.S. Europa.
24. Thank you for your consignment of 200 high quality ivory pieces which have fetched very good price.

25. We are delighted to learn that the consignment of brown leather shoes sent by S.S. Jal Sagar has brought good profits.

Closing sentences

26. We enclose the bill of lading alongwith shipping documents and hope you will have no difficulty in the collection of the goods.
27. You will, of course, credit our account with the amount due.
28. We look forward to hearing that you have been able to obtain satisfactory profits.
29. We shall send you the proceeds as soon as the goods are sold.
30. We hope the sales will fetch you good profits and we shall have more business with you.
31. We note your instructions concerning the proceeds of the sale and will credit your account with the net amount due.
32. We enclose our account of sales and shall be glad if you draw on us at two months for the amount due.
33. We hope you will be satisfied with the profit of the present consignment and that you will give us further opportunities to handle your consignments.

Exporter Informing Foreign Customer about Executing Order

Thanking and advising about despatching goods

1. We thank you for your order of 3rd April and would like to inform you that we lost no time in approaching the manufacturers for immediate supply of your goods.
2. Thank you for your order of 100 Kashmiri paper-mache table lamps. We are pleased to inform you that as a result of our prompt contact with the manufacturer, we have been able to arrange for the shipment of consignment by S.S. Neel Sagar, due to leave Mumbai on 8th August, 2017.
3. We are grateful to you for your order No. PL-390 of 2nd March, 2017. As soon as we received it, we got in touch with the manufacturers.
4. We are thankful to you for your order No.345 of May 15, 2017 and have pleasure in informing you that we have contacted the manufacturers for supply of goods required by you.
5. We have been able to ship your goods in time by S.S. Jal Seva, as desired by you.

Give detailed information

6. The goods despatched are exactly as per your specifications and we are confident that they are upto your satisfaction.
7. We are confident of having provided you with exactly what your customers require.

8. There is, of course, no compromise as far as the quality is concerned. And so, we are sure the goods will become popular with your customers.

Instructions for transactions

9. We have instructed our bankers, the Llyods Bank, Connaught Place, New Delhi, to surrender the goods against payment of our draft of ₹ 75,000/- for which an invoice is enclosed.
10. This is, of course, the standard procedure with us for the new customers.
11. We could relax our payment procedure on receiving satisfactory references.

Expectation for more business

12. We are confident that our handling of your first order will place our relationship on a firm footing.
13. Now we look forward to obtaining a permanent agency for the supply of brassware.
14. We look forward to many repeat orders, to our mutual benefit.
15. We look forward to establishing a lasting and fruitful relationship with you.

Importer Informing Broker about Imported Goods

Inform the broker about receipt of imported goods

1. We have just received from a leading British house a consignment of 50 boxes of woollen sweaters to which we request you to devote your very best attention.
2. We have very recently received 100 high quality tape-recorder-cum-transistor sets, from a reputed West German firm and invite your attention to these goods.
3. We have recently received fifty world class, complete cosmetic sets from the famous Gala of London, and we would like to bring this to your notice.

Make arrangements for the sale of goods

4. The commission offered in this case represents an excellent opportunity for working up a most desirable connection with this firm which is a big exporter of sweaters.
5. If this arrangement works out well, we shall be entrusting you with future orders also.
6. Most likely the initial commission of 5% would be maintained.
7. In our view this is an excellent opportunity for establishing a profitable business connection with this firm which is a large exporter of many makes of blades.

Close the letter in this way

8. We shall be glad if you avail yourselves of the sampling order immediately.
9. Considering the quality of the goods, we are sure you will avail of the golden opportunity by immediately placing a sample order for these products.

10. We expect you will like to order these quality products for your own market.
11. We are confident of getting your order for these rare items of durable quality.

Importer's Letter regarding Receipt of Imported Goods

Acknowledging the documents

1. We thank you for your Advice Note and the B.L (Bill of Lading) covering machine tools despatched by S.S. Blue Queen, on August 8, 2016.
2. We are pleased to acknowledge the receipts of your Advice as well as Bill of Lading, covering the woollen garments despatched by S.S. Thames Trader.
3. We are glad to intimate that we have received your Advice and also the B.L. regarding the sports goods that you desired by S.S. Jal Bharat.

Write about goods

4. The packing of the goods was perfect and they have arrived in sound condition.
5. We are pleased to inform that the consignment of tea packets has reached us in good condition.
6. It is a pleasure for us to report that the 200 pieces of handicraft goods despatched by you on 8th August, 2000, have reached us.
7. We hope to market these goods at the best profitable price.
8. We assure you that all efforts will be made to place the consignment at the best possible price.

Instructions for remitting proceeds

9. The proceeds will, of course, be forwarded to you without delay.
10. We shall, of course, forward to you the proceeds at the earliest.
11. We shall remit the proceeds at our earliest.
12. We have a reputation for being prompt in clearing the proceeds of the goods.
13. We are prompt in clearing the proceeds of the goods.

Broker's Letter to Importer regarding Sale of Imported Goods

Information about sales

1. We are pleased to state that the 100 boxes of nylon socks entrusted to us have realised a very attractive sum of ₹ 60,000/-.
2. We are happy to inform you that the 50 boxes of imported blades supplied by you on April 8, 2017, have all been sold for a total price of ₹ 20,000/-.

3. We are pleased to report that your consignment of tape-recorder-cum-transistor sets has been readily disposed of for ₹ 25,000/-.
4. On account of painstaking efforts of our salesmen we have been able to sell off your consignment of woollen garments within a fortnight.
5. Our contacts with the business magnates here have enabled us to dispose off the goods fast at a profit of 30%.

Instructions regarding payment

6. We enclose for this sum our cheque No.234/B on the Bank of Baroda, Parliament Street, New Delhi.
7. You are, therefore, requested to credit our account with ₹ 3000/- due to us as commission.
8. Enclosed please find a cheque for this amount drawn on Bank of Mumbai, Church Gate, Mumbai.
9. A sum of ₹ 5,550/- may kindly be credited to our account as commission.
10. We request you to remit the payment of our commission on this account which works out to ₹ 5,050/-.

Prospects for more business

11. We look forward to receiving further orders from you.
12. We trust your suppliers will be satisfied with the profits of this consignment.
13. We hope this will be the beginning of a long and fruitful relationship between us.

Importer's Letter to Foreign Supplier re: Payment-procedure

Beginning

1. We have received your invoice No.LP-340 and agree to accept your draft at 60 days' for the amount due.
2. Thank you for your letter of 17th November. We should be glad if you agree to draw on us at 30 days' documents against acceptance.
3. As requested in your letter of 3rd June, 2017, we have instructed our bankers, the Bank of Baroda, Parliament Street, New Delhi, to give a credit of ₹ 1,00,000/- in your favour.
4. We regret to inform you that because of certain constraints we have to ask for an extension of one month on the term of your bill dated July 25, 2017.
5. I regret that at the moment I cannot meet my commitment in full which is due for payment on 23rd December.

Close

6. Please let us know whether it will be possible for you to give us the credit terms.
7. Please draw on us for the amount due and attach the shipping documents to your draft.
8. We would like to pay by bill of exchange 60 days after sight and shall appreciate if you agree to this.
9. As requested, we shall arrange to open an irrevocable letter of credit in your favour.
10. Our acknowledgement will be given upon acceptance of the bill at Bank of Baroda's London branch at Strand.

Exporter's Letter to Foreign Buyer regarding Payment-procedure

Beginning

1. We have favourably considered your letter of 25th May and are pleased to grant the credit terms asked for.
2. As requested in your letter of 5th August, we have drawn on you for the amount of our April account at three months from today.
3. As agreed earlier we have drawn on you for the amount of the invoice enclosed.
4. We enclose our invoice No.385 and, as requested, have drawn on you at 60 days' for the amount due.
5. As per our agreement, we have drawn on you at 30 day's sight for the amount of the invoice enclosed.

Close

6. Kindly accept the draft and return it as soon as you can.
7. Kindly honour our draft when presented by your bankers.
8. As desired by you we can put your account on a documents against acceptance basis.
9. We have asked our bank to part with the shipping documents against payment of our draft.
10. Shipping documents and our draft for acceptance have been passed on to the Punjab National Bank, Parliament Street, New Delhi-110 001.
11. As agreed earlier, we have instructed our bank to surrender the documents against payment of our draft.
12. As soon as the credit is confirmed, we shall ship the consignment.
13. Your terms of payment on D.P. basis are acceptable to us and we have instructed our bankers, accordingly.

Sample Letters

(Exporter's enquiry from manufacturer)

Dear Sirs,

We are pleased to inform you that one of our clients in Europe is interested in large-scale purchase of silk shirts.[1] Therefore, we wish to know if you are in a position to supply us adequate quantity of high quality shirts of this material.[6] We are basically interested in fabrics printed with essentially Indian motifs.[10] We need not tell you that a really competitive quotation can mean excellent future prospects to you.[13] Our trial order will convince you of the promising prospects of this deal.[15]

Thanking you,

Yours faithfully,

(Manufacturer's reply to exporter)

Dear Sirs,

Thank you for your letter of enquiry dated 4th August, 2017.[2] We have a large production unit and can meet your order for any reasonable delivery date.[10] We are sending herewith a few samples of the same.[13] We hope now you will place an early order with us.[19]

Thanking you,

Yours faithfully,

(An indent by exporter to manufacturer)

Dear Sirs,

We are enclosing Indent No.345 for 150 pairs of nylon socks of different colours and designs.[1] Kindly ensure that the goods are of high standard in order to make a dent in the sophisticated markets of the West.[5] Please send the consignment with the freight prepaid.[13]

With thanks,

Sincerely yours,

(Reply to indent)

Dear Sirs,

We thank you for your letter of 5th June, 2017 and your Indent No.432.[1] We have booked this indent and have forwarded it to your friend in Singapore. We shall shortly be informing you of its acceptance after hearing from him.[7]

With thanks,

Yours faithfully,

(Intimation regarding execution of export order)

Dear Sirs,
We are pleased to inform you of the despatch of 1000 Chennai check cotton shirts shipped today by S.S. Jal Bharat.[1] We have surrendered, as agreed, the shipping documents to the Mumbai Bank at 60 days' sight.[7] We hope to have more opportunities to serve you.[13]

Thanking you,

Yours faithfully,

(Exporter informing foreign customer about executing order)

Dear Sirs,
We thank you for your order of 3rd April and would like to inform you that we lost no time in approaching the manufacturers for immediate supply of your goods.[1] The goods despatched are exactly as per your specifications and we are confident that they are upto your satisfaction.[6] We have instructed our bankers, the Llyods Bank, Connaught Place, New Delhi, to surrender the goods against payment of our draft of ₹75,000/- for which an invoice is enclosed.[9] We are confident that our handling of your first order will place our relationship on a firm footing.[12]

Thanking you,

Yours faithfully,

(Importer informing broker about imported goods)

Dear Sirs,
We have very recently received 100 high quality tape-recorder-cum-transistor sets from a reputed West German firm and invite your attention to these goods.[2] We expect you will like to order these high quality products for your own market.[10] If this arrangement works out well, we shall be entrusting you with future orders also.[5]

Thanking you,

Yours faithfully,

(Importer's letter regarding receipt of imported goods)

Dear Sirs,

We thank you for your Advice Note and B.L. covering machine tools despatched by S.S. Blue Queen on August 8, 2016.[1] The packing of the goods was perfect and they have arrived in sound condition.[4] The proceeds will, of course, be forwarded to you without delay.[9]

Thanking you,

Yours faithfully,

(Broker's letter to importer reg. sale of imported goods)

Dear Sirs,

We are pleased to state that the 100 boxes of nylon socks entrusted to us have realised a very attractive sum of ₹60000/-.[1] We enclose for this sum our cheque No.234/B on the Bank of Baroda, Parliament Street, New Delhi.[6] We hope this will be the beginning of a long and fruitful relationship between us.[13]

Thanking you,

Sincerely yours,

(Importer's letter to foreign supplier regarding payment procedure)

Dear Sirs,

As requested in your letter of 3rd June, 2017, we have instructed our bankers the Bank of Baroda, Parliament Street, New Delhi., to give a credit of ₹100,000/- in your favour.[3] Our acknowledgement will be given upon acceptance of the bill at the Bank of Baroda's London branch at Strand.[10]

With thanks,

Yours faithfully,

(Exporter's letter to foreign buyer regarding payment procedure)

Dear Sirs,

We have favourably considered your letter of 25th May, and are pleased to grant the credit terms asked for.[1] As desired by you, we can put your account on a documents against acceptance basis.[8]

With thanks,

Yours faithfully,

Correspondence with Banks

Nothing moves without money. And in the modern civilization, on account of the growing commercialisation, it has come to acquire paramount importance. The banking industry controls this power in almost every part of the world – backward or modern. Disturbance in this industry throws the economy out of gear. Banking correspondence and its techniques, therefore, occupy a pivotal position in modern business and industry. And so, banking procedures and practices have become a full-time subject in modern education.

Such correspondence should be complete, correct and elegant. Every letter has monetary significance as it gives momentum to financial machinery in one direction or the other. So one cannot afford to be careless in this regard. The letters also call for careful drafting and proper despatching.

Patience, care and a proper grasp of the fundamentals of the subject would enable a correspondent to handle this ticklish part of business activity. Proper educational background coupled with experience goes a long way in making one a good letter writer.

Request to Bank for Overdraft

Seek Permission and give details of required overdraft

1. We thank you for permitting us to overdraw our account up to ₹ 50,000/- in the period from October 15 to December 15, 2017, as discussed yesterday and agreed in the meeting between our Branch Manager, Mr, Bhism Narain Gupta, and your Deputy Manager, Mr. R.K. Gulati,.
2. With reference to our discussion with you on 15th May, we request you to permit us an overdraft on our account to the tune of ₹ 75000/- during the period from October 15 to December 15, 2017.
3. As I explained to you earlier, I would be grateful if you could allow me to overdraw my account up to a limit of ₹ 73,000/- only between October 15 and December 15, 2017.
4. As per our discussions yesterday, we request you to kindly allow us to overdraw our account (No.12346) up to ₹ 75,000/- during the period between 1st July,1999 and 6th October, 2017.
5. Certain financial constraints have compelled us to approach you for a concession to overdraw on our account up to the sum of ₹ 1,00,000/- from 3rd January to 4th March, 2017.

Give reasons for requesting overdraft

6. As already explained we need this facility to meet certain immediate financial requirements on account for our expansion programmes.
7. As explained in the meetings, during this period we have to meet certain heavy expenses for augmenting and updating our stocks.

8. As I have already explained to you I require the additional funds to conduct a publicity campaign immediately.
9. In the event of the special sale campaign, unexpected expenditure may have to be incurred during this period.
10. As we plan to disburse bonus to our employees during this month we require additional funds.

Give assurance for meeting the overdraft

11. Once the festival season starts I hope to receive considerable amount of funds from my customers.
12. The impact of our expansion will certainly be felt by the end of this period, as large payments are falling due from our clients abroad.
13. By the end of this period we hope to get high returns on our publicity campaign.
14. This facility will enable us to invest the money in the campaigns. We are sure to get the returns in the latter half of aforesaid period.
15. We have good reasons to expect heavy returns within the stipulated period.

Ask if a security is required

16. As desired by you we can deposit savings certificates worth ₹ 50,000/- as security.
17. I have an insurance policy of ₹ 50,000/- which I am prepared to deposit as security.
18. We have debentures worth ₹ 75,000/- and an insurance policy of an equal amount, which we shall deposit as security.
19. Our past commitments regarding overdraft have always been honoured and hence there is nothing for you to negate our proposal.
20. Ever since the inception of our business we have been depending on our bankers for finance and have a good record in this regard.

Express hope for favourable response

21. We hope it will not be difficult for you to accede to our request.
22. Hoping for a favourable response...
23. We shall very much appreciate your sympathetic consideration of this request.
24. Expecting a favourable consideration,
25. We hope for an early sanction of the same.

Providing a Guarantor for Overdraft

Beginning

1. I note with regret from your letter of 8th June that you are not prepared to allow me an advance against personal surety.
2. I regret to learn from your letter of yesterday that you cannot allow me an overdraft of ₹ 50,000/- against personal guarantee as requested by me in our meeting on 8th July, 2017.
3. I have received your letter of 2nd January and am sorry to learn that you are unable to allow me any overdraft against personal guarantee.
4. I regret to learn from your letter of 8th July about your inability to allow me an overdraft of ₹ 80,000/- against personal surety.
5. I am sorry to learn from your letter of yesterday that my personal guarantee would not get me the facility of overdraft.

Citing some other guarantee

6. However, I appreciate your position and as desired by you enclose a letter of guarantee duly signed and stamped from M/s. Suraj Kumar & Sons.
7. As a result, I have now obtained a letter of guarantee from Shri Prem Prakash, duly signed and stamped and submit herewith the same.
8. Therefore, please find enclosed a letter of guarantee from M/s. M.L. Rao, duly signed and stamped.
9. Therefore, I am furnishing a guarantee letter from M/s. Kumar & Sons (P) Ltd., 6, Darayganj, New Delhi.
10. Hence we are enclosing a guarantee letter from M/s. Shiv Kumar & Brothers, 6 Shakti Nagar, New Delhi.

Acceptance of the guarantors

11. I understand that the guarantors are well known to you.
12. I understand that you know them well and their guarantee is acceptable to you.
13. I am told that the party providing guarantee is your old client.
14. The party proposed as the guarantor is of good repute and must be well known to you.
15. The guarantor is an old firm and must be in your good books.

Requesting for the overdraft

16. I trust that now you will be prepared to accept the surety offered and finance me to the extent of ₹ 50,000 /-.

17. I hope this guarantee is acceptable to you and now you can allow me the overdraft facilities upto ₹ 75,000/-.
18. I hope you will find this guarantee acceptable and can allow me the advance I require for this period on your usual terms.
19. Now I hope to get the overdraft to the tune of ₹ 1,00,000/- for the said period.
20. Having fulfilled your terms and conditions, we now expect the facility for overdraft to the required amount of ₹ 80,000/-.

Request to Bank for Opening Current Account

Request for opening a current account

1. I have recently moved to Chandigarh and opened a drug store by the above name.
2. This is to request you to open a current account in the name of our firm.
3. Recently we have registered our Garments Export Company in the name 'Ashok Impex (Pvt) Ltd.
4. Please allow us to open a current account with you in the name of our firm.
5. So, we wish to open a current account with you in the company's name.

Send initial deposit

6. Enclosed please find the specimen signatures of our Managing Director, who alone is authorised to sign cheques on behalf of the concern.
7. The account will be operated by our Managing Director, Shri Ganga Prasad only, and his specimen signatures are enclosed.
8. As both the partners will sign cheques on behalf of the firm, their specimen signatures are enclosed.
9. A cheque for the amount of ₹ 50,000/- drawn on the Canara Bank, Connaught Place, New Delhi is sent herewith to be deposited with the opening of our account.
10. We also send herewith a sum of ₹ 50,000/- as our initial deposit.
11. Also, please find enclosed a cheque for ₹ 50,000/- with which we wish to open our account.

Request to Bank for Credit

Tell why the credit is required

1. On account of our steel pipes heavy demand in Iraq our export is increasing at a fast pace and we are not able to finance this trade which has been hitherto depending solely on our capital investment.
2. As we have gone in for an expansion of our glassware business it has put a heavy burden on our resources.

3. A considerable increase in our turnover recently encourages us to install new facilities at our steel rolling plant but we cannot do so within our present means.
4. Having booked heavy orders beyond our expectations, we are finding it difficult to execute and finance them on our account.
5. To meet the increasing demand of plastic goods in the market, we have planned to enlarge our sales network.
6. Therefore, we request you to grant us credit upto 50% of the value of our overseas order of 10th August, on production of the Invoice and Bill of Lading.
7. The new facilities are expected to cost ₹ 5 lakh.
8. So, could you please extend us a loan to the extent of 50% of their expected cost, for a period of six months ?
9. I shall be most grateful if you could grant the credit asked for.
10. I hope the foregoing explanation will enable you to grant the credit requested.
11. I shall be glad if you could see your way to grant me a loan of ₹ 75,000/- for a period of nine months.
12. Please let us know your charges for rendering us this service.
13. We would request you to intimate us your charges for performing this service.

Sending Sight Draft to Bank

Send sight draft and related documents

1. We enclose our sight draft on M/s. India Handicrafts Ltd. of London and attach the Bill of Lading as evidence of our shipment and other documents as listed below:
2. Please find herewith our sight draft on M/s. India Emporium, New York, as well as other documents listed below, including the Bill of Lading supporting its shipment.
3. We are sending herewith our sight draft on M/s. India Sari Centre, Singapore and also the Bill of Lading as evidence of our shipping . Also enclosed are the following documents related to the said transaction.

Instruct to give documents after payment for the draft

4. Kindly deliver these documents to the party named above against payment of the draft.
5. The payment received from the party may be credited to our account after deducting your commission.
6. The documents may be handed over to the party named above on the payment of the enclosed draft.
7. Please credit our account with the amount received after deducting your commission.
8. You may, please, hand over the documents to the party after they pay for the draft.
9. The payment received for the draft may be credited to our account after deduction of your commission.

Instructions to Bank Abroad

Give details of goods

1. Today we have despatched by S.S. Jal Moti to the Singapore office of the Shipping Corporation of India, a consignment of 100 silk saris to be held at your disposal.
2. We have to inform you that 100 pieces of 8' x 10' Kashmiri carpets have been despatched by S.S. Jal Sagar which left Mumbai on 7th November, 2016 for Hong Kong. This is in execution of the order from M/s. Govind Ramani & Co., Hong Kong.
3. We have today sent a consignemnt of 200 lamb's wool sweaters to the Hong Kong office of India Shipping Company by S.S. Motihar.
4. Shipped on an order from M/s. Fancy Warmwear of your city, this consignment is to be held at your disposal.
5. Please note that we have yesterday despatched 100 packets of readymade garments to International Traders, Sydney in execution of an order from M/s. Greatway Garments (Pvt) Ltd.

Tell the status of the party

6. However, we have very little knowledge about this party.
7. However, it being a foreign party, we know little about them.
8. But we know little about the ordering party.

Tell the bank what to do under the circumstances

9. Under the circumstances, we think it would be rather unwise to surrender the shipping documents against mere acceptance of the Bill of Exchange.
10. Under the circumstances, we would not like to surrender the shipping documents just on the acceptance of the Bill of Exchange.
11. We, accordingly, enclose a sight draft on them, together with the Bill of Lading.
12. We are, therefore, sending you a sight draft on them, as also the Bill of Lading.
13. So, we must ask you to obtain payment of all that is due, before you allow them to take possession of the goods.
14. So, kindly insist on full payment of the dues before you part with the goods.
15. So, these goods are to be transferred to the party concerned only after all the dues are settled.
16. You will, of course, debit our account with all necessary expenses.
17. Kindly debit your expenses in this regard to our account.
18. Please surrender the enclosed documents to M/s. Hayward & Co. of London when they accept the enclosed draft.

19. Kindly release the documents only on payment of our sight draft for ₹ 75,000/-.
20. So, kindly obtain acceptance of this draft before handing over the shipping documents.
21. Please present the bill for acceptance and then discount it for the credit of our account.
22. Please present this bill for acceptance of the payment and credit us with the proceeds.
23. As a result, the letter of consent for clearing of goods may be released only on payment of sight draft.

Importer's Letter to Bank regarding Imported Goods

Beginning

1. I enclose the accepted bill, drawn on me by M/s. John & James of London and should now be glad to receive the shipping documents.
2. Please accept the following draft for me, pay them and at maturity debit them to my account.
3. Please arrange with your correspondent in London to open a credit in favour of our firm.
4. Please find herewith a draft in my name and credit the amount to my account later on.
5. Kindly instruct your representative in Kathmandu to open a credit in favour of our firm.

Close

6. Please accept the amount draft for me and debit your charges to my account.
7. Will you please state the amount of your charges for arranging the necessary credits ?
8. Kindly also let us know about your charges for arranging the required credits.
9. After deducting your commission, please credit the amount to my account.
10. Please also let us know about your commission charges at an early date.

General Banking Matters

1. We are surprised to learn from your letter of 15th April that M/s. Comfort Shoe Company have refused to accept our draft which was duly advised.
2. We cannot account for M/s. Good Garments Corporation's refusal to accept our draft despite the fact that it was duly advised.
3. Could you please oblige us by presenting the bill again?
4. Please present the bill once again.
5. If acceptance is again refused, please return the draft to us.
6. In the event of its being refused again, the bill may kindly be returned to us.

Payment instructions

7. Please transfer the Rupee equivalent of $ 2000 to James & Jones, Manchester, in favour of Bonny Baby Good Products, London EC-2.
8. This sum represents payment for costs incurred by that firm on our behalf.

Special Instructions

9. Thank you for advising us of receipt of $ 1000 from the Indian Overseas Bank, on behalf of M/s. Ready Food Exports of London.
10. Kindly credit this sum to our account No.24348.
11. Please let us know after making the necessary transfer.
12. This is to confirm my telephonic message of this morning requesting you to stop payment of cheque No.SB 508352 of 3rd March, 2017 for ₹ 1,00,000/-.
13. Please arrange to buy for me the following securities within the price range given below.
14. Should you require a guarantor, Mr. Sunil Kumar of Kumar Enterprises, New Delhi, has kindly consented to act in this capacity.

On dishonouring the cheque

15. We are surprised to learn that you have dishonoured our cheque No.82453 of the 2nd April for ₹ 73,400/- in favour of M/s. Pretty Plastic Products with the remarks 'Funds not sufficient'.
16. And this is despite the fact that we had submitted a local cheque for ₹ 84,000/- for collection nearly two weeks back and there was ample time to credit this sum to our account.
17. So, kindly inform us of your reasons for dishonouring the cheque as it would affect our reputation.
18. We regret to learn that you have dishonoured our cheque No.W 23507 for an amount of ₹ 50,000/-. Since we have good amount in the bank, we fail to understand the reason for this.
19. On our cheque being dishonoured we lose our image in the market. Kindly furnish the reasons at the earliest.

Sample Letters

(Request to bank for overdraft)

Dear Sirs,

As I explained to you earlier, I would be grateful if you could allow me to overdraw my account upto a limit of ₹73,000/- only between October 15 and December 15, 2017.[3] As I have already explained to you I require the additional funds to conduct a publicity campaign immediately.[8] Once the festival season starts, I shall receive considerable amount of funds from my customers.[11] As desired by you we can deposit savings certificates worth ₹50,00/- as security.[16] We hope it will not be difficult for you to accede to our request.[21]

Thanking you,

Yours faithfully,

(Providing a guarantor for overdraft)

Dear Sirs,

I note with regret from your letter of 8th June that you are not prepared to allow me an advance against personal surety.[1] However, I appreciate your position and as desired by you enclose a letter of guarantee from M/s. Suraj Kumar & Sons, duly signed and stamped.[6] I understand that the guarantors are well known to you. I trust that now you will be prepared to accept the surety offered and finance me to the extent of ₹50,000/-.[16]

With thanks,

Yours faithfully,

(Request to bank for opening current account)

Dear Sirs,

I have recently moved to Chandigarh and opened a drug store by the above name.[1] Please allow us to open a current account with you in the name of our firm.[4] Also, please find enclosed a cheque for ₹50,000/- with which we wish to open our account.[11]

With thanks,

Yours faithfully,

(Request to bank for credit)

Dear Sirs,

On account of our steel pipe's heavy demand in Iraq our export is increasing at a fast pace and we are not able to finance this trade which has been hitherto depending solely on our capital investment.[1] Therefore, we request you to grant us credit upto 50% of the value of our overseas order of 10th August on production of the invoice and Bill of Lading.[6] Please let us know your charges for rendering us this service.[12]

Thanking you,

Yours faithfully,

(Sending sight draft to bank)

Dear Sirs,

Please find herewith our sight draft on M/s. India Emporium, New York, as well as other documents listed below including the Bill of Lading supporting its shipment. Please credit our account with the amount received after deducting your commission.[7]

Thanking you,

Yours faithfully,

(Instruction to bank abroad)

Dear Sirs,

Today we have despatched by S.S. Jal Moti to the Singapore office of the Shipping Corporation of India, a consignment of 100 silk saris to be held at your disposal.[1] However, we have very little knowledge about this party.[6] We, accordingly, enclose a sight draft on them together with the Bill of Lading.[11]

With thanks,

Yours faithfully,

(Importer's letter to bank reg. imported goods)

Dear Sirs,

Please arrange with your correspondents in London to open a credit in favour of our firm.[3] Kindly also let us know about your charges for arranging the required credits.[8]

With thanks,

Yours faithfully,

(General banking matters)

Dear Sirs,

We are surprised to learn from your letter of 15th April that M/s. Comfort Shoe Company have refused to accept our draft which was duly advised.[1] Could you please oblige us by presenting the bill again.[3]

With thanks,

Yours faithfully,

(On transferring the amount)

Dear Sirs,

Please transfer the Rupee equivalent of $2000 to James & Jones, Manchester in favour of Bonny Baby Food Products, London EC-2.[7] This sum represents payment for costs incurred by that firm on our behalf.[8] Please let us know after making the necessary transfer.[11]

Thanking you,

Yours faithfully,

(On dishonouring the cheque)

Dear Sirs,

We are surprised to learn that you have dishonoured our cheque No.82453 of the 2nd April for ₹73,400/- in favour of M/s. Pretty Plastic Products with the remarks "Funds not sufficient".[15] And this is despite the fact that we had submitted a local cheque for ₹84,000/- for collection nearly two weeks back and there was ample time to credit this sum to our account.[16] So kindly inform us of your reasons for dishonouring the cheque as it would affect our reputation.[17]

Thanking you,

Yours faithfully,

Correspondence with Insurance Companies

In the modern times there are different kinds of Insurance companies which cover a variety of risks. Personal life is covered against accidents and death and businesses are covered against damage, fire, loss, theft etc. In India today there are two different types of Insurance companies-Life Insurance and General Insurance. Under the Life Insurance scheme, a person can get himself insured for 20-25 years for a certain amount. During this period, he has to pay the Insurance Company a regular instalment which is called premium. At the end of the period he gets the full amount for which he was insured plus some other benefits. In case he dies during this period, his nominee gets the full amount before the maturity of the Insurance Policy. However, in the case of General Insurance, goods are covered under various schemes. In case of loss, damage, fire etc., the Insurance Company pays the client the amount for which a particular article was insured. Therefore, practice prevails in all big businesses to take an insurance cover for goods despatched and even for goods stored in godowns and warehouses. At a nominal expenditure, the risk of loss is covered and the trader can rest assured on this account.

However, here we are generally concerned with insurance coverage of articles and goods during their transit from one place to another whether by post office, rail or road, air or sea. Let us examine some such cases.

Request for Insurance of Goods in Transit

Beginning

1. Please quote your lowest All-Risk rates for shipment of 100 cases of hand-tools to Singapore from Mumbai. The invoice value of the consignment is ₹ 1,00,000/-.
2. Please hold us covered under insurance for the cosignment referred to below.
3. We shall be glad if you provide cover for 100 boxes of shoes valued at ₹ 50,000/- in transit from Mumbai to Singapore.
4. We wish to renew the above policy for the same amount and on the same terms as before to cover our assets at our office at No.4, Shastri Road.
5. Will you please arrange to take out an all-risk insurance for us on the following consignment of woollen garments from our factory at the above address to Colombo-100 bags of woollen garments by S.S. Ratnagiri due to leave Chennai on 8th August. The invoice value of the consignment is ₹ 1,00,000/-.
6. Please let us know at the earliest on what terms and conditions this insurance can be arranged.
7. Please send us the necessary proposal form.
8. We leave the details to you, but wish to have the consignment covered against all risks.
9. The consignment is covered by our open policy No. NB-675554 and we shall be glad to receive your certificate of insurance.
10. We request you to send us the insurance charges from Chennai to Colombo for the said insurance

Intimation to Insurance Co. regarding Damage by Fire

Give Information about fire

1. We regret to inform you that a fire broke out in our godown last night at 11.30 p.m.
2. We are sorry to inform you that last night around 10 o'clock, a large part of our bookshop was gutted by fire.
3. We are sorry to inform you that yesterday afternoon a fire broke out in our godwon at 4 Nehru Road and caused extensive damage to the stocks.
4. We regret to inform you that a fire broke out in our factory premises at Ballabgarh last night at 11.30 p.m. and as the fire brigade reached late nothing could be saved.
5. It seems to have occurred of short circuit in power supply.

Then send the details of the loss estimate

6. In our rough estimation, the damage is to the extent of ₹ 50,000/-.
7. We assess the damage caused by this fire at around ₹ 50,000/-.
8. According to our calculations the extent of the damage is about ₹ 50,000/-.
9. Having gone through the details, we estimated the demages roughly at ₹ 5,00,000/-

Give further instructions

10. However, please send your representatives as early as possible to survey the loss.
11. So, please send your assessors at the earliest.
12. Kindly let us know what are the particulars to be furnished for making a claim for the loss.
13. We shall be grateful to you for letting us know the procedure we have to follow for making our claim for compensation.
14. We are ready to produce evidence to enable your agent to estimate the loss.
15. Kindly send your representative to estimate the ioss and complete formalities.

Insurance Claim

Inform the loss first

1. Yesterday night a burglary took place at our house and a number of jewellery articles were stolen.
2. This morning my car No.XYZ 1234 was stolen from the parking lot opposite Regal Cinema, Connaught Circus, New Delhi.
3. This is to report that some time during last night the boot of my car, parked opposite my residence was forced open and certain new spare parts of the car were stolen.
4. I regret to report the theft of my car No.DHC 583 insured with you under the above policy.

5. I regret to report that a fire broke out in my house at the above address last night and extensively damaged one of my bedrooms.

Now give details

6. The jewellery consisted of a pearl necklace, four gold bangles and a diamond ring. So, the estimate of total loss is around ₹ 2,50,000/-.
7. The car, as mentioned in insurance papers, is a sky-blue Maruti 800, of 1995 model. Its registration number is…
8. It is a 1995 model Fiat of blue colour.
9. Our rough estimate of the total damage is around ₹ 1,05,000/-.
10. The car is brown 1994 model bearing No…
11. A complaint to this effect has also been lodged with the nearest police station, at Gokhale Marg.
12. We have, of course, immediately informed the police about the burglary.
13. A report of the theft has also been lodged at the nearest police station at Tilak Marg.
14. We have lodged F.I.R with the nearest police station at Sarojini Nagar.
15. An F.I.R. of the theft was immediately lodged with the nearest police station at Bangalow Road.

Write about the claim

16. Would you please send me a Claim-Form so that I can make a formal claim under the policy?
17. Please let me know how I should proceed for making a claim under my insurance policy.
18. Kindly advise me the claim procedure.
19. Please let us know at the earliest how we should go about making the claim.
20. Please find enclosed the form of claim for the loss of my car…

Request for Reduction in Insurance Rates

Non-acceptance of rates

1. We regret to state that we are not satisfied with your rate of 15 paise per cent quoted for the insurance of our premises at the above address against fire.
2. We regret to say that your rate of 15 paise per cent for fire insurance of our premises at the address given above is not acceptable to us.
3. We regret to inform you that the rate of 15 paise per cent that you have quoted for insurance of our premises at the address given above against the risk of fire, is on the higher side.

4. We are sorry to state that your insurance charges are not acceptable to us as they are quite high.
5. We are surprised to see your high rates for insurance coverage of my workshop.

Reasons for non-acceptance

6. There appears to be no justification for this rate as other companies are prepared to cover on identical conditions at 10 paise per cent.
7. We do not think this rate is justified as other companies charge 10 paise per cent for providing insurance cover under the same terms and conditions.
8. This high rate seems to be unjustified because other companies have been charging 10 paise per cent to provide such insurance.
9. As a matter of fact, we still hold policies at 10 paise per cent and it is only our desire to distribute the risk over many companies that prompted us to accept your quotations.
10. We actually have insurance cover at the lower rate, but wish to distribute the risk.
11. We, therefore, request you to cover us to the extent of ₹ 1,00,000/- only.
12. In view of your high rates, we request you to cover us to the extent of ₹ 85,000/- only.
13. However, please note that at this stage we could considerably increase this amount if your rates are reduced to 10 paise per cent.

Tell that reduced rates may fetch more cash amount

14. Still we would like to point out to you that a reduction in your rate could increase the risk amount to a considerable extent.
15. We shall highly appreciate your final reply to our proposal at your earliest convenience.
16. We would be happy to have your response to our proposal by return of post.

General Insurance Matters

Insurance of goods sent by railway

1. We shall be despatching 50 bicycles from Faridabad to Mumbai by passenger train on 6th March, 2017.
2. The total value of these bicycles is ₹ 40,000/-.
3. We wish this consignment to be covered from our godown at the above address to our client's godown in Mumbai.
4. Please let us know the total amount of premium payable for insuring the above goods against all risks.

Insurance of goods shipped

5. Please take out an all-risk policy for five cases of superior cotton shirts valued at ₹ 50,000/- and to be shipped to Singapore by S.S. Jal Vihar, sailing from Mumbai on 8th February.
6. The shipment is for M/s. Indian Fashion Centre, Singapore.
7. We wish to take out an all-risk policy for 10 cases of woollen garments valued at ₹ 1,00,000/-. The consignment is to leave Mumbai for Singapore by S.S. Neel Sagar on 10th August.

Information about damaged goods

8. Please find herewith a copy of the report of the customs authorities regarding medicine bottles worth ₹ 5,000/- which we received in a damaged condition.
9. This consignment was sent by our agent in Tokyo, by S.S. Jal Sagar.
10. As the consignment was fully insured against all risks, we request you to please assess our loss and make an early payment.

Renewal of policy

11. With reference to policy No.234, which expires on 14th May, 2017 we are enclosing a cheque for ₹ 8,810/- for renewing the same for a further period of one year.
12. The value of stock and assets being the same, we have sent the amount as per last year's premium.
13. Please confirm the renewal and send your official receipt by return post.

Sample Letters

(Request for insurance of goods in transit)

Dear Sirs,

Please quote your lowest all-risk rates for shipment of 100 cases of hand tools for Singapore from Mumbai. The invoice value of the consignment is ₹1,00,000/-.[1] Please let us know at the earliest on what terms and conditions this insurance can be arranged.[6]

Thanking you,

Yours faithfully,

(Intimation to insurance co. reg. damage by fire)

Dear Sirs,

We regret to inform you that a fire broke out in our godown last night at 11.30 p.m.[1] In our rough estimation the damage is to the extent of ₹50,000/-.[6] However, please send your representative as early as possible to survey the loss.[10]

Thanking you,

Yours faithfully,

(Insurance claim)

Dear Sirs,

This morning my car No.XYZ 1234 was stolen from the parking lot opposite Regal Cinema, Connaught Circus, New Delhi.[2] It is a 1995 model Fiat of blue colour.[8] A complaint to this effect has also been lodged with the nearest police station, at Gokhale Marg.[11] Would you please send me a Claim Form so that I can make claim under the policy?[16]

Thanking you,

Yours faithfully,

(Request for reduction in insurance rates)

Dear Sirs,

We regret to state that we are not satisfied with your rate of 15 paise per cent quoted for the insurance of our premises at the above address against fire.[1] There appears to be no justification for this rate, as other companies are prepared to cover on identical conditions at 10 paise per cent.[6] We, therefore, request you to cover us to the extent of ₹1,00,000/- only.[11] Still we would like to point out to you that the reduction in your rate could increase the risk amount to a considerable extent.[14]

Thanking you,

Yours faithfully,

General Insurance Matters

(Goods sent by railway)

Dear Sirs,

We shall be despatching 50 bicylces from Faridabad to Mumbai by passenger train on 6th March, 2017. The total value of these bicycles is ₹ 40,000/-.[2] We wish this consignment to be covered from our godown at the above address to our client's godown in Mumbai.[3] Please let us know the total amount of premium payable for insuring the above goods against all risk.[4]

Thanking you,

Yours faithfully,

(Goods sent by ship)

Dear Sirs,

Please take out an all-risk policy for five cases of superior cotton shirts valued at ₹50,000/- to be shipped to Singapore by S.S. Jal Vihar, sailing from Mumbai on 8th February.[5] The shipment is for M/s. Indian Fashion Centre, Singapore.[6]

Thanking you,

Yours faithfully,

(Renewal of policy)

Dear Sirs,

With reference to policy No.234 which expires on 14th May, 2017, we are enclosing a cheque for ₹8,810/- for renewing the same for a further period of one year.[1] The value of stock and assets being the same, we have sent the amount as per last year's premium.[12] Please confirm the renewal and send your official receipt by return post.[13]

Thanking you,

Yours faithfully,

Correspondence with the Post Office

Postal network is an important means of communication throughout the world today. While for the common man it means ordinary delivery of letters and parcels, for the bigger establishment, its role is much more significant. On account of its efficient delivery system, business establishments have come to depend heavily on it. Normally correspondence with the post office is done on the printed stationery provided by the post office. But at times, there are occasions when general letters have to be written. In such letters, necessary details about dates and reference numbers must be mentioned. Here are a few sample letters.

Applying to Post Office for V.P.P. Journal

Beginning of the letter

1. Please note that our daily average of V.P.P. articles has gone up to 50 from 15th November.
2. We take this opportunity to inform you that the number of V.P.P. articles sent by us daily on an average has now reached fifty.
3. This is to inform you that the daily average of our V.P.P. despatches has now reached 50.

Closing of the letter

4. So, we would request you to issue a special V.P.P. Journal in our name.
5. Kindly, therefore, issue us a special V.P.P. Journal.
6. Therefore, please issue us a special V.P.P. Journal.
7. As our daily average of V.P.P. has now reached 50, we hereby request you to please give us a special V.P.P. Journal.

Applying to Post Office for Business Reply Permit

Reasons for application

1. In order to expand our business further, we wish to send Reply-Paid envelops to our clients.
2. We wish to extend the facility of Reply-Paid envelopes to our customers in the interest of expanding our business.
3. In the interest of our expanding business we wish to extend the Reply-Paid card facility to our customers.
4. We wish to provide the facility of Reply-Paid envelopes to our customers.

Note: Close of this letter is similar to the above letter of the V.P.P Journal.

Complaint regarding Non-receipt of V.P.P. Money/Article

Details of articles/V.P.P. M.O.

1. We had sent a V.P.P dated 5th May, 2017, for ₹ 250/- through your post office to M/s. K.L. Rao and Sons, 14, Mylapore, Chennai.
2. On 14th March, 2017, we had sent V.P.P. No.245 for ₹ 175/- through your post office to M/s. Book House, Gohkale Road, Dadar, Mumbai.
3. We wish to inform you that V.P.P. No.0821 dated 11th January, 2017 for an amount of ₹ 410/- had been sent through your post office to M/s. Shastri & Sons, Shivaji Road, Baroda.

Further information

4. Although more than two months have passed since then we have neither received the payment nor the V.P.P back.
5. Although more than one month has passed, we don't have any information about it. We have neither received the payment nor the article back.
6. It has been more than two months since the V.P.P. was sent, but we have received neither the payment for it nor the article back.

7. It is surprising that we don't have any intimation about it nor did we receive back the amount for the said V.P.P even after a lapse of two months.
8. Could you please let us know the reasons for this at the earliest?

Request for tracing out the goods

9. We shall appreciate your looking into the matter immediately.
10. So, please find out without any further delay what happened to it?
11. Please, therefore, make immediate enquiries and let us know the position.

Sample Letters

(Applying to post office for V.P.P. journal)

Dear Sirs,

This is to inform you that the daily average of our V.P.P. despatches has now reached 50.[3] So, we would request you to issue a special V.P.P Journal in our name.[4]

With thanks,

Yours faithfully,

(Applying to post office for business reply permit)

Dear Sir,

We wish to extend the facility of Reply-Paid envelops to our customers in the interest of expanding our business.[2] Kindly, therefore, issue us a permit for Reply-Paid envelops.

Thanking you,

Yours faithfully,

(Complaint reg. non-receipt of V.P.P. money/article)

Dear Sir,

We had sent a V.P.P dated 5th May, 2017, for ₹250/- through your post office to M/s. K.L. Rao, 14 Mylapore, Chennai.[1] It is surprising that we don't have any information about it nor did we receive back the amount for the said V.P.P. even after a lapse of two months.[7]

We shall appreciate your looking into the matter immediately.[9]

With thanks,

Yours faithfully,

Personnel Correspondence

The letters dealing with interviews, appointments, termination of services, resignations, requests for testimonials and references etc, are handled by the personnel department of an office. These are, thus, called personnel letters. Like other commercial letters, these are also specialised letters with a definite style and format.

Call for interview

When a post is advertised a number of applications are received in response. A prospective employer cannot call all the applicants. He has to be selective, keeping in view the educational qualifications and experience of the applicants.

However, while inviting the applicants for the interview various important points have to be kept in mind. Normally, certificates and testimonials are asked for. But in certain interview, it becomes desirable to personally study the specimens of the candidate's professional work. So, one may also ask for them in the interview letter.

If more than one candidate is to be invited not all of them should be called at the same time. Keeping in view the average time one would take with a candidate, one can give different times to the candidates. Sometimes the candidates are called on different days. If required, the candidate can also be asked to confirm whether he would attend the interview or not.

It is also desirable to adopt a personal and friendly tone to put the applicant at ease.

Appointment letters

Normally, in companies two types of appointment letters are issued-provisional and confirmatory. The provisional letters put the candidate on a probation for a certain period. Only after satisfactory completion of the probationary period the employee is confirmed in the job.

Sometimes the terms and conditions of appointment are mentioned in the letter itself and at times separately. Whatever be the case, it should state clearly the salary and other conditions of appointment and also a reference to the duties to be carried out. If the appointment is made verbally at the time of interview, it is desirable that it is confirmed by a letter afterwards.

References and testimonials

It is advisable that testimonials are obtained directly from the referees, because when they are handed over to the candidates, they normally do not certify unfavourably. However, open testimonials for further use should be issued only in very special cases concerning persons of proven ability over a long period of time. Courtesy demands that before giving any names, prior permission should be obtained from the referees.

If you are writing to obtain a testimonial you should give your particulars in detail. These would enable the referee to identify you and know about the job you are applying for.

It is not legally binding on anyone to give testimonial. But if it is written one should be careful to give authentic information. Otherwise the writer may find himself legally liable either to the applicant, or to the employer if the information is 'optimistically misleading'. As a precaution, such envelopes should be sealed and marked as 'private' or 'confidential'.

Terminating the services

At the time of appointment, an employee is recruited on certain terms and conditions. And so his services can be terminated in accordance with the original agreement. On the other hand, he himself can leave the job, fulfilling the conditions initially agreed upon.

Call for Interview

Acknowledge the application and mention the date of interview

1. Please refer to your application for the post of Sales Engineer. You are requested to call at our office at 11.30 a.m. on 8th October. When you call please ask for the Marketing Manager, Mr. Praveen Kumar.
2. With reference to your application for the post of Private Secretary to our General Manager, please call on the undersigned on Monday, the 24th January, between 10.00 a.m. and 4.00 p.m.
3. In response to your application for the post of Marketing Manager, you are requested to call on our General Manager, Mr. Virendra Walia, on 10th August at 11.00 a.m.
4. In response to your application for the post of an Executive Secretary in our company, you are requested to come for an interview and test on July 5, at 3.00 p.m.

Mention, if testimonials etc. are required

5. Our Resident Editor, Mr. Gopal Bhandari, has asked me to acknowledge your application dated October 8, 2017 for the post of sub-editor. You are requested to contact his P.A. Mr. Subhash Saxena anytime between 10.00 a.m. and 4.00 p.m. and ask for an appointment with Mr. Bhandari.
6. Please refer to your application dated September, 5 for the post of Store-keeper in our organisation. You are requested to call on our Personal Manager, Mr. Debu Chaudhary at 3.30 p.m. on 10th September.
7. Please bring with you the testimonials and some specimens of your work.
8. Kindly also bring copies of relevant certificates with you.
9. Please bring with you attested copies of your testimonials and a character certificate.
10. Along with your certificates, please also bring at least two testimonials from your former employers.

11. Please confirm either by telephone or through a letter whether you will be able to come.
12. Please note that you will not be entitled to any T.A. or D.A. for attending the aforesaid interview.
13. As per company rules, you will be entitled to one-side second class fare from your town.

Sample Letter

(Letter for call for interview)

Dear Sir,

Our Resident Editor, Mr. Gopal Bhandari has asked me to acknowledge your application dated October 8, 2017, for the post of sub-editor. You are requested to contact his P.A. Mr. Subhash Saxena anytime between 10.00 a.m. and 4.00 p.m. and ask for an appointment with Mr. Bhandari.[5] Please bring with you the testimonials and some specimens of your work.[7] Please note that you will not be entitled to any T.A or D.A for attending the aforesaid interview.[12]

Thanking you,

Yours faithfully,

Appointment-letters

Starting the letter

1. Further to your interview with our General Manager, Mr. Kanti Ghosh, I am pleased to appoint you on the post of Sales Engineer in our firm.
2. With reference to your interview held on last Tuesday with our Managing Director, I am pleased to offer you the position of Publicity Officer in our company.
3. I am pleased to offer you the post of Personal Assistant to our Legal Adviser, Mr. Man Mohan Gupta.
4. This is to confirm the offer we made to you when you called on us on Monday.
5. I am pleased to inform you of your selection for the post of Assistant Manager in our organisation.

Close

6. I am writing to confirm the offer we made to you when you called yesterday.

Terms and conditions

7. Your duties will be as explained to you at the time of interview, but more particularly you will be directly answerable to the Divisional Manager.
8. Your appointment carries a salary of ₹ 7500/- p.m. during the probation period. After the satisfactory completion of this period, we may consider a further raise in the salary.
9. The office hours are 9.30 a.m. to 6.00 p.m. The atmosphere is pleasant and it offers better prospects for the right candidate.
10. You will be entitled to four week's leave every year.
11. The appointment may be terminated at any time by either side giving two months' notice.
12. The engagement is for one year initially which can be renewed by mutual arrangement for further periods subject to three month's notice on either side.
13. Please confirm immediately your acceptance of this appointment on the terms enclosed and let us know if you can join your duties from the 1st of the next month.
14. Should you decide to accept the appointment, please attend the office at 10.00 a.m on Monday and report to Mr. Prem Kumar.
15. Kindly confirm your acceptance of this offer immediately.
16. Please acknowledge and confirm your acceptance to our offer.

(Appointment letter)

Dear Sir,

I am pleased to inform you of your selection for the post of Assistant Manager in our organisation.[5] Your duties will be as explained at the time of interview, but more particularly you will be directly answerable to the Divisional Manager.[7] Your appointment carries a salary of ₹ 7500/- p.m. during the probation period. After the satisfactory completion of this period, we may consider a further raise in the salary.[8]
You will be entitled to four week's leave every year.[10]
Kindly confirm your acceptance to this offer immediately.[15]

Thanking you,

Yours faithfully,

Provisional appointment letter

Dear Sir/Madam,

The management is pleased to appoint you as a Steno-Secretary in our company on the following terms and conditions:

1. You will be on probation for a period of three months on the expiry of which your services shall automatically stand terminated unless you are specifically confirmed in writing on or before the date mentioned.
2. Your services can also be terminated at any time during the probationary period without notice.
3. You will be paid a sum of ₹ 4,700 p.m. as consolidated salary.
4. You will abide by all the standing orders/rules & regulations of the company as may be in force from time to time which inter-alia provide that:
   - (i) You will accept transfer anywhere in India and also to any concern/concerns in any section/plant/ deptt./unit under the same ownership/management.
   - (ii) You will not engage yourself in any outside work over and above your legitimate work in the company while you are on duty, on holidays or leave.
   - (iii) After confirmation, you will retire from services on completion of 55 years of age or after 30 years of service whichever occurs earlier, unless the management in its discretion for special reason permit you to continue thereafter.
5.
   - i) In case you absent yourself from duty without prior permission or proper leave, you shall be deemed to have voluntarily abandoned your service.
   - ii) If and when the information furnished by you in your application regarding your qualifications, experience, employment and last salary drawn etc. is found incorrect or untrue, you will be terminated from service without any notice or compensation.
6. Your services shall be terminated without notice and without assigning any reason due to loss of confidence, gross negligence, inefficiency of work or any other wilful misconduct on your part.
7. In case you leave/abandon your service during the aforesaid period, fifteen days' salary shall be deducted from your salary or Management reserves the right to recover the same.

If you accept and agree to the above terms and conditions of your appointment, please sign the duplicate copy of this letter of appointment as token of your acceptance.

Thanking you,

Yours faithfully,

Confirmation letter

Dear Sir/Madam,

The management is pleased to confirm your appointment as Steno-Secretary in our company on the following terms and conditions:

1. You will be paid a sum of ₹ 5,800/- (Five Thousand Eight Hundred Only) per month as salary from October 1, 2017.
2. Your services can be terminated by giving one month notice by either side, without assigning any reason whatsoever.
3. You will abide by all the standing orders/rules & regulations of the company as may be in force from time to time.
4. Your services can be transferred to anywhere in India and also to any concern/concerns in any shift/section/plant/deptt./unit under the same ownership/management or on deputation to any other firm.
5. While in the employment of the company you will not engage yourself in any other business, occupation or profession whether part time or full time without the written permission of the company.
6. Your services can be terminated without notice and without assigning any reason due to loss of confidence, gross negligence, inefficiency in work or any other wilful misconduct on your part.
7. You will retire from service in the Company on completion of 58 years of age or after 30 years of service, whichever occurs earlier.
8. In case you absent yourself from duty without prior permission or proper leave, you shall be deemed to have voluntarily abandoned your service.
9. The rights in any order, contracts or jobs secured by you or in any process/discovery/invention or copyright of writings/exposures/recordings etc. made during the course of employment with us shall belong to the Company.

If you accept and agree to the above terms and conditions of your appointment please sign the duplicate copy of this letter of appointment as taken of your acceptance.

Thanking you,

Yours faithfully,

Letters Taking up References

Starting of the letter

1. Mr. Kamal Kishore has applied to us for the post of Office Superintendent and we would be grateful if you could furnish us with details about his character and abilities.
2. Mr. Nand Lal of your office has applied for a peon's job in our office. He has given your name as referee in this regard.
3. Mr. Kamalakar Shastri has applied for the post of Steno-Secretary in this office and has referred us to you for any information regarding his character and abilities.
4. Mr. Ram Lal, presently employed by you as a sub-editor has applied for a similar job in our paper.
5. Mr. Kamal Kishore, an artist in your organisation has applied for the post of an illustrator in our agency.
6. Mr. Shyam Bihari Aggarwal, a translator in your organisation, has applied for the post of a Senior Translator (from Hindi to English) in our company.

Ask for specific information

7. We shall be grateful if you could let us know whether you found his work satisfactory.
8. We shall feel obliged if could say how good and fast he is at illustration.
9. In our impression he is a good translator, but we are not sure whether he is capable of taking the full charge of the translation department.
10. He appears to be fluent in both the languages. But we want to be sure if he is the right candidate for this job.
11. We shall be grateful if you would answer the following questions about his character and abilities:
    - i. Is he conscientious, intelligent and trustworthy?
    - ii. Is his health satisfactory?
    - iii. Does he get on well with his colleagues?
    - iv. Are his shorthand and typewriting speeds satisfactory?
    - v. Is he efficient in tabulating and statistical work?
    - vi. Is his output satisfactory ?
    - vii. Is he capable of producing good letters from dictated notes?

Close

12. I shall be most grateful for any information you could give me in this regard.
13. We shall, of course, regard as strictly confidential any information you give us.
14. We shall treat as strictly confidential any information you are kind enough to give us.
15. We shall very much appreciate any information you give us. It will, of course, be treated as strictly confidential.

(Letter taking up references)

Dear Sir,

Mr. Shyam Bihari Aggarwal, a Translator in your organistion has applied for the post of Senior Translator (from Hindi to English) in our company.[6] In our impression he is a good translator, but we are not sure whether he is capable of taking the full charge of the translation department.[9] We shall very much appreciate any information you could give us. It will, of course, be treated as strictly confidential.[15]

Thanking you,

Yours faithfully,

Replies to Reference Enquiries

Starting of the letter

1. Please refer to your letter of 8th August enquiring about Mr. Sushil Chandra who has applied in your firm for the post of Assistant.
2. In reply to your enquiry regarding Mr. Arun Mehta, I am pleased to say that he has been employed with me for the past three years and I have found him an intelligent and industrious young man.
3. In response to your enquiry about Mr. Madan Mohan, we are pleased to state that we have always found him trustworthy and reliable.
4. This is in response to your enquiry concerning Mr. Krishna Chandra who has applied for the post of Store Keeper in your office.
5. In response to your enquiry of 9th November, I wish to state that Mr. Anil Kumar is a man of high morals and integrity.
6. I am pleased to be able to reply favourably in response to your enquiry regarding Mr. Kamlakar Shastri.
7. I am replying to your inquiries of 8th April regarding Mr. Ram Lal.
8. Mr. Kishore Bhimani about whom you enquire has been employed by my company for the past 10 years.

9. He came to us from Creative Advertising where he had been employed as a junior artist.
10. This young man was a member of our proof reading department from November 1, 1995 to July 31, 2017.

Refer to Specific Qualities

11. He is an excellent translator and can translate from Hindi to English and vice versa competently. He is a reliable and steady worker and bears an excellent character.
12. Apart from subbing he has also been doing reporting assisgnments and I am happy to say that he has always had a nose for news.
13. With us he has been mainly doing pasting jobs as we don't have any illustration work. However, I gather that he is a very fine illustrator and the right candidate for the job in your agency.
14. We released him because his work fell below the standards that we normally required. It is, however, possible that he may do well in a different set-up.
15. He was always unpunctual and had a disturbing influence on other members of the staff. With a little self-discipline he might do well but from my own personal experience I cannot recommend him to you.

Close

16. We feel that he would be an asset to any organisation and wish him all the best.
17. I shall be very sorry to lose his services, but realise that his abilities demand wider scope than I can provide.
18. I can recommend him to you with every confidence knowing that if you appointed him he would serve you well.
19. So, I am sorry I cannot conscientiously recommend her.

(Reply letter to reference enquiries)

Dear Sir,
I am pleased to be able to reply favourably in response to your enquiry regarding Mr. Kamlakar Shastri.[6] He is an excellent translator and can translate from Hindi to English and vice versa competently. He is a reliable and steady worker and bears an excellent character.[11] I shall be very sorry to lose his services but realise that his abilities demand wider scope than I can provide.[17]

Thanking you,
Yours faithfully,

Letters Instituting Domestic Enquiry

Start the letter in this way

1. It has been reported to the management that you misbehaved with the head clerk Shri Ram Niwas on 3.00 p.m. on 12th October, 2017.
2. Shri R.N. Sharma has made a complaint in writing that on 15.11.2017 you refused to obey his orders and threatened him with violence in the presence of other staff.
3. It has been observed that you have been late in coming to office at least eight to ten days every month and also absent yourself many times without proper leave or information.
4. We understand that the file of our client M/s. Indo-Arab trading Co. has been misplaced by you and is not traceable so far.
5. Inspite of many verbal warnings given to you from time to time, you have been grossly negligent and inefficient in your work.

Inform about the time, place and name of the enquiry officer

6. The management has decided to hold a domestic enquiry into this incident.
7. Shri. Vimal Ahuja, our Personnel Manager, will hold the enquiry on 25.11.2017 in his room on the complaint of Mr. R.N. Sharma.
8. Please note an enquiry into your conduct will be held on 15th March, 2017 in the Committee Room. Shri V.N. Das shall be the Enquiry Officer.
9. You are requested to appear before the Enquiry Officer at the place and time mentioned above.
10. Please note that you should come with all oral and documentary evidence on which you wish to rely for your defence.
11. You will remain suspended pending the completion of enquiry against you.

Impress about the need to attend the Enquiry

12. It is in your own interest to attend the enquiry at the place and time given.
13. In case you willingly absent yourself from the enquiry, it shall proceed in your absence.

(Letter instituting domestic enquiry)

Dear Sir,

Shri R.N. Sharma has made a complaint in writing that on 15.11.2017 you refused to obey his orders and threatened him with violence in the presence of other staff.[2]

The management has decided to hold a domestic enquiry into this incident.[6] Shri Vimal Ahuja, our Personnel Manager will hold the inquiry on 25.11.2017 in his room on the complaint of Mr. R.N. Sharma.[7]

You are requested to appear before the Enquiry Officer at the place and time mentioned above.[9] Please note that you should come with all oral and documentary evidence on which you wish to rely for your defence.[10]

You will remain suspended pending the completion of enquiry against you.[11]

Thanking you,

Yours faithfully,

Letter Informing Result of Enquiry

Introduction

1. Shri R.N. Sharma had complained in writing that you refused to obey his orders and also threatened him with violence in the presence of other staff.
2. An important file of our client M/s. Indo-Arab Trading Co. had been misplaced by you resulting in loss to the firm.
3. You had been verbally warned many times regarding gross negligence and inefficiency in your work.

Mention about the enquiry instituted

4. The management had decided to institute a domestic enquiry into this incident.
5. It was decided to hold an enquiry into your conduct.
6. Shri Vimal Ahuja, our Personnel Manager was appointed the Enquiry Officer to hold an enquiry on 25.11.2017 in his room.
7. You attended the enquiry at the stipulated time and place and produced oral and documentary evidence in your defence.
8. The Enquiry Officer has held you guilty of the charges levelled against you.
9. In his report the Enquiry Officer has held you guilty of gross misconduct and recommended your dismissal.
10. You have been exonerated of all charges against you.

Now state the action proposed

11. The management has agreed with the findings of the Enquiry Officer and have decided to terminate your services.
12. However, the management has decided to take a lenient view of your misconduct in view of your excellent past record, and has decided to withhold your annual increment for the next two years.
13. You are hereby warned to be more efficient and careful in your work.

(Letter informing result of enquiry)

Dear Sir,

Shri R.N. Sharma had complained in writing that you refused to obey his orders and also threatened him with violence in the presence of other staff.[1] The management had decided to institute a domestic enquiry into this incident.[4] Shri Vimal Ahuja, our Personnel Manager was appointed the Enquiry Officer to hold the enquiry on 25.11.2017 in his room.[6] You attended the enquiry at the stipulated time and place and produced oral and documentary evidence in your defence.[7]

In his report, the Enquiry Officer has held you guilty of gross misconduct and recommended your dismissal.[9] However, the management has decided to take a lenient view of your misconduct in view of your excellent past record, and has decided to withhold your annual increment for the next two years.[12]

Thanking you,

Yours faithfully,

Letters Terminating Employment

Start by giving reasons

1. As you are aware the re-organisation of our office has become a subject of investigation by a firm of management consultants.
2. I regret to inform you that on account of heavy recession in the business, we have to resort to retrenchment of the staff.
3. Further to the talk you had with Mr. Vijay Vohra yesterday, I regret to inform you that your services will not be required by the company after the end of this month.
4. And so, we shall not be requiring your services anymore.

Middle part of the letter

5. I hope you will soon settle down well somewhere else and I extend my best wishes.
6. We have been quite satisfied with your services and hope you will soon find another suitable position.

Close

7. We wish you all success for the future.

(Letter regarding termination of employment)

Dear Sir,

I regret to inform you that on account of heavy recession in the business, we have to resort to retrenchment of the staff.[2] And so, we shall not be requiring your services anymore.[4] We have been quite satisfied with your services and hope you will soon find another suitable position.[6] We wish you all success for the future.[7]

Thanking you,

Yours faithfully,

SECTION - IV

Legal Templates

1. Power of Attorney

Power of Attorney : Power of Attorney (POA) is nothing but a simple document which lists out the powers that you want to share with the POA holder. It is primarily used by NRI (Non-resident Indians) to manage their property of India.

For example, if you have bought an apartment in India and your can't visit personally to take the possession, or sign in the registrar office for registration in your name, you can share these rights with any of your family member or a friend by issuing a registered power of attorney.

Note: Please note that it is now mandatory to have the POA registered specifically for property matters. You would have also heard the same from your builder/developer, asking for a registered POA to sign on your behalf.

Template

WHEREAS I/We, [Executant1 e.g., Anil Gupta] and [Executant2, e.g. Pooja Gupta], presently residing at [YOUR CURRENT RESIDENCE ADDRESS (write outside India address if you are not in India - e.g. , 123 river rd, MA, USA] and [BUILDER/COMPANY NAME WITH ADDRESS - e.g. M/S UNITECH Pvt Ltd., New Delhi] (herein referred to as 'Company/ Corporation'). I/We jointly approached company/corporation to purchase an apartment, and company/corporation agreed to sell the apartment number [EXACT FLAT NUMBER - e.g. A101] in the [PROJECT NAME AND ADDRESS e.g. ABC Project, Sector 11, Gurgaon, Haryana]. The apartment has the size of [AREA e.g. 1200] sq. Ft. with [NUMBER e.g. 1] open car parking at the rate of INR [PURCHASE PRICE] per Sq. Ft.

Now, I/We the above described as [Executant1 e.g. Anil Gupta] and [Executant2 e.g. Pooja Gupta] do hereby appoint, nominate and substitute [NAME OF POA HOLDER e.g. ABC SHARMA] resident of [POA HOLDER's ADDRESS IN INDIA - e.g. 111, old road, Delhi - 110006] as and to be my/our true and lawful attorney, for me/our in my/our name and on my/our behalf to do the following acts:

1. To sign, execute any deed for receiving the possession of the said apartment decribed above on my/our behalf and to execute any other document necessary to accomplish the aforesaid purpose.
2. To represent me/us in the office of [BUIDER/COMPANY NAME WITH ADDRESS - e.g. M/s UNITECH Pvt Ltd., New Delhi] to make payment of the balance sale price and all the amounts due and payable under the said agreement, to sign and deliver any letter, document and/or representation in connection with the possession of said apartment.

3. To represent me/us and sign on our behalf in the office of the sub-registrar for the purpose of registering the property and pay the requisite stamp duty to government.

4. To represent me/us for the purpose of renting out the apartment, receive the rent and sign the necessary document with the [PROJECT NAME] RWA (Resident welfare association) as applicable.

And I/us do hereby agree and undertake to ratify, confirm and be bound by what me/our said attorney shall or purport to do or cause to be done by virtue of those present as if the same have been done by me/us personally.

Witnees 1 Name and signature [ ]

Witnees 2 Name and signature [ ]

Executant 1 Passport size picture [ ]

Executant 1 Name and signature [ ]

Executant 2 Passport size picture [ ]

2. Charge-sheet

Charge sheet is basically the letter claiming the reason regarding certain misconduct or any other unprofessional behaviour performed by the employee in the organization. And employee need to give the clarification regarding the act for which charge sheet is given to him. Charge sheet is issued to an employee when an employee is involved in any type of misconduct or for his bad behaviour with the office colleagues or if the employee is involved in any kind of theft of the company's property or if he/she is being in a habit of getting absent from his duties or if he/she is not performing good then a charge sheet is issued to the employee for which he has to give an explanation for the charges which are imposed against him and if the employee neglects the charge sheet then a serious action is taken against him which can result as termination of the employee from the organization.

Template

Dated: __________

To

Mr. / Mrs. __________

Following are the charges against you:

After observing you for a long time we have found in your attendance record that you are in habit of absenting yourself from your duties without any information and sanction of leave. Your absenteeism has increased a lot from last 1 years.

Month	Dates	No. of days of unauthorized absence
XXX	XXX	XXX
XXX	XXX	XXX

You have been advised many times to improve your attendance record and not to indulge in unauthorized absence from your office. But despite these pieces of advice/reprimands and assurance given to you, you have not shown any improvement in your attendance. We have observed that you have become habitual of being absent from your duties which also affects the work of company. You need to give an explanation for this misconduct within 3 days and if we did not receive any explanation from you in the given time then we will presume that you do not have any explanation and the management wil be free to take any action in your case.

For ________________

(Authorized Signatory)

3. Promissory Note

Promissory note is a written promise to pay a debt. It is a financial instrument, in which one party (maker or issuer) promises in writing to pay a determinate sum of money to the other (the lender), either at a fixed, determinable future time or on demand of the payee subject to specific terms and conditions.

It is of different types-single/joint borrowers, payable on demand, payable in instalments or as lump sum, interest-bearing and interest-free.

Important Notes:

1. It is governed by Section 4 of the Negotiable Instruments Acts, 1881.
2. Pormissory Note executed in one State may be presented in another State in India with the stamp bearing on the promissory note. No additional stamp duty needs to be paid.
3. It should always be hand written. The agreement must state, in writing, the terms of instrument, extent of liability (amount), maker's and payee's name and the amount to be paid, among other things.
4. The promise to re-pay money and no other conditions should be mentioned in PN.
5. When a person issues a promissory note, he/she would have to stamp it as per the Indian Stamp Act and normally a revenue stamp is affixed on the PN signed by the promissory. You can use Re 1/- revenue stamp and get it cross signed by the borrower.
6. You may also execute the PN on a stamp paper if revenue stamps are not available.
7. Try to lend the money by cross A/c cheques. You can mention the cheque details in PN.
8. PN has a TIME validity. It is valid for only 3 years from the date of execution.
9. There is no limitation or ceiling with respect fo the amount.
10. If the borrower pays a part repayment then limitation of 3 years can be from either the date of execution or the last date of payment/acknowledgement whichever is later. The repayments are generally hand written on the back side of PN document (signed by both the parties).
11. PN is generally held by the Lender (Issuer). Once the loan is discharged or fully paid off, it should be cancelled and marked as "PAID IN FULL". And can be returned to the payee (borrower).
12. Witness signature is not required. But it is advisable to get it signed by a witness. (a person who is not a party of the note. You may consider getting it notarized as well but it is not mandatory).

Template

Promissory Note Providing for Interest

I, Shri____ S/o ____________________________ promise to pay Shri ____________________________ S/o ____________________ or order, on demand the some of ____ (Rupees ________________________________ only)with interest at the rate of________________ per cent mensem / annum from the date of these presents for value received.

Place:

Signature

Date:

4. Will

A will is a legal document by which a person expresses his/her wish as to how his/her property is to be distributed at death and names one or more persons, the executor, to manage the estate until its final distribution.

Template

I, Shri/Smt ________________ son / daughter / wife of Shri ________________,resident of __________________, by religion__________________, do hereby revoke all my previous Wills (or) Codicils and declare that this is my last Will, which I make on this ________ (Date)_____________. My Date of Birth is _______________

I declare that I am in good health and possess a sound mind. This Will is made by me without any persuasion or coercion and out of my own independent decision only.

I appoint Shri__________________ son/daughter of __________, resident of ____________ to be the executor of this Will. In the event Shri____________ were to predecease me, then Shri___________, will be the executor of this Will.

I bequeath the following assets to my Wife Smt...

1. My house is located at___________________(address).
2. Bank balance of my savings account no________________with ________________ (bank name & bank address).
3. My Bank fixed deposits in ___________ (bank name) bearing ______ (FD receipt nos).
4. The proceeds of my Term insurance policy__________ (Policy no) from_______ (insurance company name).
5. The contents of bank locker no_____, with bank_____, bank address______________.

I bequeath the following assets to my son Shri____________________.

1. Residential Plot no__________, located at_____________.
2. My car with registration no_______________.
3. My mutual fund investments with folio numbers_______________.
4. Any other asset not mentioned in this Will but of which I am the owner.

All the above assets are owned by me. No one else has rights on these properties.

Signature of Testator

(Full name)

Date: Place:

Witnesses

We hereby attest that this Will has been signed by Shri............as his last Will at .... (Place)......... in the joint presence of himself and us. The testator is in sound mind and made this Will without any coercion.

Signature of Witness (1)
(Name & Address)

Signature of Witness (2)
(Name & Address)

5. Board-resolution

(To be printed on organization letter head)

Template

A Board Resolution is a way of documenting a decision made by a company's Board of Directors or shareholders on behalf of the company.

CERTIFIED TRUE COPY OF THE RESOLUTION PASSED AT THE MEETING OF THE BOARD OF DIRECTORS OF (Company Name) ____________________ ____________ HELD ON (Date) ____________ AT (Address) ____________ ________________ RESOLVED THAT the company has decided to authorize, Mr. / Ms. ____________ and is hereby authorized to sign and submit all the necessary papers, letters, forms, etc to be submitted by the company in connection with "authorizing any of the personnel of the company (applicant) to procure Digital Certificate". The acts done and documents shall be binding on the company, until the same is withdrawn by giving written notice thereof.

Specimen Signatures of Authorised Signatory:

(Signature)

RESOLVED FURTHER THAT, a copy of the above resolution duly certified as true by designated director / authorised signatory of the company be furnished to Mudhra Limited and such other parties as may be required from time to time in connection with the above matter.

For the Organization,

(Seal & Signature)

Name: ________________________

Designation: ________________________Annexure II

Annexure II

6. Service-bond

Service Bond is basically an agreement which the company and the employee enter into which among the other terms contained therein states that in consideration of the training given to the employee and the money spent on the employee and the money spent on the employee in imparting such training, the employee will remain in the services of the company for a particular period.

(**Note:** *The service bond is to be executed on non-judicial stamp paper of appropriate value as per rules and regulations).*

Template

KNOW ALL MEN BY THESE PRESENTS THAT I ____________________________ S/o ________________ resident of ________________________________ working in (name of organization) _________________________________ as (designation) ________________________(referred to as the associate hereafter) do hereby bind myself and my heirs, executors and administrators to pay to the President of India (hereinafter called the Government) on demand the sum {equivalent to 110% (One hundred and ten percent)} of the expenditure incurred by the Department of Biotechnology on travel, associate award money, contingency grant etc., alongwith interest on the said amount at the prevailing government rates, compounded annually from the date of availing of grant, or, if payment is made in a country other than India, the equivalent of the said amount in the currency of that country converted at the official rate of exchange between that country and India AND TOGETHER WITH all costs between attorney and client and all charges & expenses that shall or may have been incurred by the Government.

WHEREAS I __________________________________ have been granted the Indo-Australian Career Boosting Gold Fellowships (IACBG-Fellowships) for the year 2015-16 by the Department of Biotechnology.

AND WHEREAS in the interest of the Government I have agreed to execute this bond with such conditions as hereunder written:

I will work in India for minimum 24 months* after availing and completing fellowship for a period of 12 months.

NOW THE CONDITION OF THE ABOVE WRITTEN OBLIGATION IS THAT in the event of my failing to comply with the terms and conditions of the Indo-Australian Career Boosting Gold Fellowships (IACBG-Fellowships) as annexed herewith, I shall be liable to pay, as bond money, a sum equivalent to 110% (One hundred and ten percent) of the expenditure incurred by DBT on travel, associate award money, contingency grant, etc., alongwith interest on the said amount at the prevailing government rates, compounded annually from the date of availing of grant.

AND upon my making such payment, the above written obligations shall be void and of no effect, otherwise, it shall be and remain in full force and virtue.

This Agreement shall in all respects be governed by the laws of India for the time being in force and the rights and liabilities hereunder shall, wherever necessary, be accordingly determined by the appropriate courts in India.

Signed and dated this ______________________________ day of ________________ Two thousand and ________________.

Signed and delivered by

____

(Signature, name and address)

* Varies according to the duration of fellowship minimum of 24 months are required for a fellowship of 12 months

In the presence of,

WITNESSES

ACCEPTED

1.

2.

For and on behalf of the President of India

WITNESSES

1.

2.

Head of the Department in case of Government employee/ Head of the Institution in case of others

Institutions Seal

* Strike out whichever is not applicable.

7. Agreement to Sell

Agreement to sell is a legal document through which a seller transfers or agrees to transfer the property in goods to the buyer for a price. Such an agreement may be absolute or conditional.

Template

This AGREEMENT TO SELL is executed at New Delhi, on this ____ day of __________ by and between; Sh. _______ S/o ______ R/o _____ hereinafter called "THE FIRST PARTY".

IN FAVOUR OF

Sh. _______ S/o______R/o______,hereinafter called "THE SECOND PARTY".

The expression of the terms the 'FIRST PARTY' and the 'SECOND PARTY' wherever they occur in the body of this Agreement to Sell, shall mean and include them, their legal heirs, successors, legal representatives, administrators, executors, transferee(s), beneficiary(ies), legatee(s),probatee(s), nominees and assignee(s).

AND WHEREAS the FIRST PARTY for his bonafide needs and requirements have agreed to sell, convey, transfer and assign to the SECOND PARTY and the SECOND PARTY has agreed to purchase alongwith proportionate, undivided, indivisible and impartible ownership rights in the said freehold land underneath the said building measuring ____ square yards, bearing No. ________, situated at ______________, with all rights, title and interest, easements, privileges and appurtenances thereto, with all fittings, fixtures, electricity and water connections, structure standing thereon, with all rights in common driveway, entrances, passages, staircase and other common facilities and amenities provided therein, hereinafter referred to as "THE SAID PORTION OF THE SAID PROPERTY" for a total sale

consideration of Rs. __________ (Rupees ____________________________________).

NOW THIS AGREEMENT TO SELL WITNESSETH AS UNDER :-

That in consideration of the sum of Rs. ________/- (Rupees _____________________), out of which a sum of Rs. ______________/- (Rupees __________________________), as advance money has been received by the FIRST PARTY from the SECOND PARTY, in the following manner;

the receipt of which the FIRST PARTY hereby admits and acknowledges and the remaining balance sum of Rs. _________/- (Rupees ____________________________), will be received by the FIRST PARTY from the SECOND PARTY, at the time of registration of the Sale Deed, the FIRST PARTY doth hereby agree to grant, convey, sell, transfer and assign all his rights, titles and interests in the said portion of the said property, fully described above, together with proportionate undivided, indivisible and impartible ownership rights in the freehold land underneath the said building to the SECOND PARTY, on the terms and conditions herein contained provided that nothing herein stated shall confer or deemed to have conferred upon the SECOND PARTY exclusively any right or title to the common driveway, passages, staircase, overhead water tanks, sewers, water meters and other common facilities to the exclusion of the FIRST PARTY and or the SECOND PARTY or owners or occupants of the other units of the said building.

That the actual physical vacant possession of the said portion of the said property will be delivered by the FIRST PARTY to the SECOND PARTY, at the time of the registration of the Sale Deed, after receiving the full consideration.

That on or before _____________, the FIRST PARTY will execute and get the Sale Deed of the said portion of the said property registered, in favour of the SECOND PARTY or his nominee/s, on receipt of the full and final balance amount, failing which either party shall be entitled to get the Sale Deed registered through the court of law by SPECIFIC PERFORMANCE OF THE CONTRACT, at the cost and expenses of the defaulting party.

That the FIRST PARTY hereby assures the SECOND PARTY that the FIRST PARTY has neither done nor been party to any act whereby the FIRST PARTY's rights and title to the said portion of the said property may in any way be impaired or whereby the FIRST PARTY may be prevented from transferring the said portion of the said property.

That the FIRST PARTY hereby declares and represents that the said portion of the said property is not subject matter of any HUF and that no part of the said portion of the said property is owned by any minor.

That the FIRST PARTY assures the SECOND PARTY that the said portion of the said property is free from all kinds of encumbrances such as prior Sale, Gift, Mortgage, Will, Trust, Exchange, Lease, legal flaw, claims, prior Agreement to Sell, Loan, Surety, Security, lien, court injunction, litigation, stay order, notices, charges, family or religious dispute, acquisition, attachment in the decree of any court, hypothecation, Income Tax or Wealth Tax attachment or any other registered or unregistered encumbrances whatsoever, and if it is ever proved otherwise, or if the whole or any part of the said portion of the said property is ever taken away or goes out from the possession of the SECOND PARTY on account of any legal defect in the ownership and title of the FIRST PARTY then the FIRST PARTY will be liable and responsible to make good the loss suffered by the SECOND PARTY and keep the SECOND PARTY saved, harmless and indemnified against all such losses and damages suffered by the SECOND PARTY.

That the house tax, water and electricity charges and other dues and demands if any payable in respect of the said portion of the said property shall be paid by the FIRST PARTY upto the date of handing over the possession and thereafter the SECOND PARTY will be responsible for the payment of the same.

That no common parts of the building shall be used by the SECOND PARTY or other owners/occupants of the said building for keeping/chaining pets, dogs, birds or for storage of cycles, motor cycles nor the common passage shall be blocked in any manner.

That the proportionate common maintenance charges will be paid by all the occupants/ owners of the said building in proportion of the area occupied by them.

That the SECOND PARTY shall have full right of access through staircase to the top terrace at all reasonable times to get the overhead tank repaired/cleaned etc. and to install T.V. Antenna. That the SECOND PARTY shall have, as a matter of right, right to use all entrances, passages, staircases and other common facilities as are available in the said building.

That a separate electric meter and water meter have been provided in the said building for the exclusive use of the owner(s)/occupants of the said portion of the said property.

That in the event of the building being damaged or not remaining in existence on any account whatsoever then the SECOND PARTY shall have the proportionate rights in the land alongwith other owners of the building and shall have the right to raise construction in proportion to the one as now being sold conveyed and being transferred under this Agreement to Sell.

That the SECOND PARTY have full right to nominate or assign this Agreement to Sell in favour of any person or persons, be it a firm, body corporate or association of person and the FIRST PARTY shall have no objection to it.

That pending completion of the sale, the FIRST PARTY neither shall enter into any agreement of sale in respect of the said property or any part thereof nor shall create any charges, mortgage, lien or any arrangement, in respect of the said property in any manner whatsoever.

That the photostat copies of all relevant documents in respect of the said property have been delivered by the FIRST PARTY to the SECOND PARTY.

That all the expenses of the Sale Deed viz. Stamp Duty, Registration charges, etc. shall be borne and paid by the SECOND PARTY.

That this transaction has taken place at New Delhi. As such, Delhi Courts shall have exclusive jurisdiction to entertain any dispute arising out of or in any way touching or concerning this Deed.

IN WITNESS WHEREOF, the FIRST PARTY and the SECOND PARTY have signed this AGREEMENT TO SELL at New Delhi, on the date first mentioned above in the presence of the following witnesses.

WITNESSES :-

1. FIRST PARTY.

2. SECOND PARTY.

8. Loan-agreement

A loan agreement is a contract between a borrower and the lender which regulates the mutual promises made each party.

Template

Loan Agreement between ________________________________

AND ________________________________

THIS AGREEMENT made and entered into at ________ this _____ day of 2017, ______ BETWEEN ______________________ hereinafter called "the Lender" AND ____________________________ hereinafter called "the Borrower" and reference to the parties hereto shall mean and include their respective heirs, executors, administrators and assigns;

WHEREAS the Borrower is in need of funds and hence has approached the Lender to grant her an interest-free loan of ₹_________/- (Rupees _______________________ only) for a period of _____ years;

AND WHEREAS the Lender has agreed to grant a loan to the Borrower, free of interest, as the Lender and the Borrower have known each other since several years;

AND WHEREAS the parties hereto are desirous of recording the terms and conditions of this loan in writing;

NOW THIS AGREEMENT WITNESSETH and it is hereby agreed by and between the parties hereto as under:-

1. The Borrower hereto, being in need of money, has requested the Lender to give her an interest-free loan of ₹ _____________/- (Rupees ____________________ only) to enable her to purchase a residential flat, to which the Lender has agreed.
2. The said loan is required by the Borrower for a period of _____ years, commencing from __/__/2017 and terminating on __/__/______.
3. The Borrower hereby agrees and undertakes to return the loan of ₹_____________/- (Rupees _______________________ only), in instalments, within the aforesaid period of _____ years and gives her personal guarantee for the same.
4. The terms and conditions of this Agreement are arrived at by the mutual consent of the parties hereto.

IN WITNESS WHEREOF the parties hereto have hereunto set and subscribed their respective hands the day and year first hereinabove written.

SIGNED AND DELIVERED by the within-

Named Lender in the presence of

SIGNED AND DELIVERED by the within-

Named Borrower in the presence of

9. Business-services Agreement

It is a contract entered into for a contractor to provide some form of task useful for the their employees in return for compensation. A service agreement can also be a feature offered along with a warrantee for a product for the manufacture to provide service or coverage of any costs of service in case the product malfunctions during a given period.

Template

AGREEMENT made at Mumbai this ____ day of _______ 2017 BETWEEN ________ situated at _______ (hereinafter referred to as "the Centre") of the One Part AND _______ a Company incorporated under _______________________ and having its corporate / registered office at __________________________a Company hereinafter called "the Client") (which expression should include its successors and assigns) of the Other Part;

AND WHEREAS the Centre is a member of _______________ Society, having its registered address at__________ and hereinafter referred to as the "said Society" and is in possession, use and occupation of the premises _______________, hereinafter referred to as the "said Premises".

AND WHEREAS the Centre is carrying on the business of providing office services in the name and style of ____________ at the said premises ____________ and for that purpose has made arrangements to render office facilities and services to persons who require such facilities for their business temporarily and on contract;

AND WHEREAS the client is carrying on the business of _____________ and is desirous of availing certain office facilities to enable it to more conveniently carry on its said business.

AND WHEREAS the Client has requested the Centre to grant to the Client such facilities;

AND WHEREAS Centre has agreed to grant the same on the terms and conditions mutually agreed upon;

AND WHEREAS the parties hereto are desirous of recording the said terms and conditions.

NOW THIS AGREEMENT WITNESSETH AS UNDER:

1. The Centre hereby agrees to grant to the Client certain office facilities in the said premises as set out herein to more conveniently carry on its said business in the name and style of ___________ and as incidental to such office services the Centre has permitted the Client to use until otherwise decided, a portion of the said premises and also to make available other ancillary office facilities, amenities, conveniences and services therein.
2. The Centre has agreed to render the following services to the Client:
   i. to occupy and use a portion of the Business Centre at the said premises for itself, its bonafide employees and visitors, for the purpose of carrying on the client's said business.

ii. to use furniture, fixtures and fittings provided in the said Centre.

iii. to avail of a peon's facility as may be reasonably required to attend to the needs of the Client.

iv. to avail the use of three telephone connections (two local and one with ISD facilities) in the Centre.

v. to avail the use of air-conditioner in the Centre.

vi. any further facilities which Centre at its discretion considers it necessary to provide to the Client.

vii. it is hereby expressly agreed and declared that save as otherwise herein expressly provided, the office services to be provided under this agreement, the Centre may at its sole discretion permit its other clients to avail of or share in common any of the said office services hereby agreed to be provided.

3. The Client further agrees and undertakes:

a. to take all reasonable and good care of the said Centre and furniture, fixtures and fittings therein as per separate list prepared and signed by the Centre and the Client) therein and not to cause any damage thereto or to any part thereof. To keep and maintain the fixtures and fittings in good order and condition, reasonable wear and tear or an act of God or for the reasons beyond the Control of the Client being excepted. In the event of any damage thereto or destruction thereof, save for reasons excepted as aforesaid, the Client shall at its own cost and expense immediately repair and/or replace the same or at the option of the Centre, the client pay the cost of such repair or replacement that may be carried out by the Centre.

b. to bring into the said Centre only office records and documents etc. but in any event no hazardous and inflammable items or things shall be brought into the office by the Client.

c. to use the said Centre only for commercial purpose as an office and in a lawful manner and in any event not to make any illegal use of the same and not to cause any disturbance, nuisance or annoyance to others in the said Centre.

d. In the event of the Client making use of the aforesaid facilities for any purpose other than confide commercial office purposes and the same resulting in any civil or criminal action, the Client shall keep Centre fully indemnified of and from and against all arise therefrom.

e. not to allow or permit any outsiders to use the premises or any part thereof.

f. to remove all their articles, belongings and things lying in the said Centre on expiry of the term of the arrangement or in the event of prior termination, upon the date of termination.

g. to observe and perform all the rules, regulations and bye-laws of the said Society wherein the center is situated, the client having made himself aware of all such rules, regulations and bye-laws and shall indemnify and keep indemnified the Centre against any loss or damage incurred by the Client for non-performance by the Client as aforesaid.

h. Not to do or suffer to be done anything in or around the said premises which is or is likely to cause prejudice to the rights and entitlements of the Centre as the member of the Society.

i. Not to make any structural or other alterations, modifications or additions in the said premises, except with the prior written consent of the Centre which shall not be unreasonably withheld.

j. Not to alter or change the original colour on the outer or inner wall of the said premises, except with the written consent of the Centre.

4. The Centre agrees to:

a. Keep the said Centre clean and tidy and provide electricity.

b. Provide a common peon facility entirely at its own discretion as may reasonably be required to attend to the needs of the Client.

c. Provide access to the NOC of the Centre's three telephone connections of which one shall have STD facility.

5. It is mutually agreed between the parties hereto as follows:

a. The term of this arrangement shall be for three months, commencing from the date of this agreement and the same shall be renewable for a further like terms, for a total period of 3 year commencing from the 1st day of April 2017 and ending on 31st March, 2020. Provided, however that the Centre may at its absolute discretion and without assigning any reason in that behalf refuse to grant any removal.

b. In consideration for the services to be rendered the Centre shall from time to time submit their Bill for quarterly Standard Services charges at the rate of ₹ ________/- (Rupees __________________ only) for the first four quarters, ₹____________ (Rupees ________________ only) for the next four quarters and ₹______________ (Rupees_____ _________ only) for the last four quarters. The Client shall also be liable to pay for the telephone rentals and the telephone calls made by the Client, electricity consumed by the Client and also other services specifically utilised by the Client on actual. These bills shall be paid by the Client within a week and in any event before demanding refund of the security deposit amount deposited by the Client with the Centre.

c. The arrangement herein is purely temporary and personal and not transferable under any circumstances and the Client shall not be entitled to assign or transfer the benefit of this arrangement to any other person/persons on any basis whatsoever.

d. No tenancy, leave and licence or any other protected rights whatsoever permitting the Client or its employees to come upon and use the said premises or any part thereof is created or intended or sought to be created by these presents and the parties hereto shall not plead any oral variation to the provisions thereof. The variation if any hereto shall not be valid, binding upon or enforceable against the parties hereto unless the same are duly recorded in writing in the form of supplemental agreement signed by both the parties hereto.

e. The Client shall be allowed to display its name board outside the premises at the place allotted by the Centre.

f. If the services charges/bills payable by the Client have been outstanding for two weeks from the date of receipt of the bill, the arrangement herein shall not be extended and thereupon on expiry of the two weeks, the Centre shall be entitled to prevent access to the Client and its employees into the said premises and every part thereof and allow the Client one day's time to remove its belongings. In the event of the Client refusing or neglecting to remove its belongings from the said premises, the Centre shall be entitled to open the premises or any part thereof allotted to the said Client using the original key in their possession and in the presence of witness remove the articles and things therein after making a list thereof. It is expressly agreed that the Centre shall not render itself liable for any civil or criminal action by so doing. This authority retained by the Centre and expressly agreed to by the Client is irrevocable and constitutes the basis for this agreement and the Client shall not be entitled to dispute, challenge or call into question the validity or reasonableness of this provision.

g. Any delay or indulgence by the Centre in enforcing the terms and conditions of this Agreement or any forbearance or giving of time to the Client shall not be construed as a waiver on the part of the Centre of any breach or non-observation and or non-compliance of any of the terms and conditions of this Agreement by the Client nor shall it in any manner prejudice the rights of the Centre against the Client.

h. All letters, receipts, notices or communications issued by the Centre or the Client and dispatched by Registered Post with Acknowledgement due or delivered by Hand Delivery to the address on the record of the other will be sufficient proof of receipt thereof by the other and shall be an effectual discharge on the part of the party forwarding the same and the same shall be deemed to have been received by the other party on the normal expiry period under post.

i. The Centre shall not be responsible or liable for any:

   1. Theft, loss, damage or destruction of any property of the Client or any person living in or visiting the said premises or in the said building from any cause whatsoever.

   2. for any personal or other injury caused to the person for the time being in the said premises on any account.

j. In the event of the Client committing any breach of the terms and conditions herein contained and failing within 7 (seven) days of the receipt of a notice in writing in that behalf given by the Centre to remedy or make good such breach the Centre shall be entitled to forthwith revoke and or terminate the arrangement and/or the permission granted and in such an event the provisions of clause 5(g) of this Agreement shall apply mutatis mutandis.

k. Each party shall bear and pay the fees of their respective legal representatives.

6. As security for the due performance of the provisions hereof the Client shall deposit with Centre an interest free security deposit of a sum of ₹____/- (Rupees ______). The said interest free security deposit, after deducting therefrom the amount of arrear or other dues if any from the Client shall be refunded by Centre to the Client without interest on the arrangement herein coming to an end, howsoever and whensoever, and upon the Client removing itself and all its belongings and things from the said premises.

7. The Centre shall be at liberty to terminate this Agreement or any renewal thereof by giving the Client three months notice in writing stating therein its desire to do so and on the expiry of such notice, and on the client removing itself, its employees and belongings from the said premises and otherwise performing its obligation under this agreement the Centre shall refund to the Client the interest free security deposit amount as contained in clause 6.

8. Upon the termination of this Agreement or sooner determination and upon the failure of the Client to remove itself, its employees and its belongings from the said premises. The Client shall be liable and hereby agrees to pay to the Centre liquidated damages of ₹_____________ (Rupees __________only) and compensation and/or manse profits of ₹__________ (Rupees____________) per day for the wrongful and unauthorised use of the said premises and the facilities provided therein. The Centre shall be entitled without prejudice to its other rights to forfeit the security deposit in the event of any breach on the part of the client.

9. It is further agreed and declared between the parties hereto that the permission hereby granted by the Centre to the Client to use a portion of the said premises is incidental to the availing of office facilities, amenities and services provided by the Business Centre to the Client and the Client shall not be entitled to avail other facilities separately as the arrangement is composite, impartibly and indivisible.

10. Any dispute between the parties hereto shall be referred to the sole arbitration of Mr_________________. Having his / its office at _______________and shall be subject to the provisions of the Arbitration and Conciliation Act, 1996.

IN WITNESS WHEREOF the parties hereto have hereunto set and subscribed their respective hands, the day and year first hereinabove written.

SIGNED AND DELIVERED by

__________________________)

as partner / proprietor of the Centre.)

in the presence of ______________)

SIGNED AND DELIVERED by the)

With in named _______________)

in the presence of______________)

10. Franchise-agreement

It is a legal contract between a frenchisor and franchisee. In it, well-established business consents to provide its brand, operational model, and required support to another party for them to set up and run a similar business in exchange for a fee and some share of the income generated are agreed to. It lays out the details of what duties each party needs to perform and what compensation they can expect.

Template

This AGREEMENT entered into on the_______________day of_____________, 2017 BETWEEN:

_______________________ Limited a Company incorporate under the Companies Act, 1956 or Companies Act, 2013, having its Registered Office at_______, represented herein by its______________ Shri____________(hereinafter referred to as the "XYZ Limited", which expression shall, whenever the context so requires or admits, mean and include its successors and assigns) of the ONE PART;

AND

M/s___________________ a Partnership Firm, having its place of Business at________ represented herein by its Partner Shri_________ (hereinafter referred to as the "AGENT", which expression shall, unless the context so requires or admits mean and include its Partners for the time being, their heirs, legal representatives, executors and permitted assigns) of the OTHER PART;

WHEREAS XYZ Limited is engaged inter alia in the business of marketing_________ products and are the owners of the trade name and trade mark "XYZ";

WHEREAS XYZ Limited is desirous of promoting________ products under its trade name and trade mark by setting up chain or retail outlets all over the country on its own and also by appointing stockist, retailers and franchises for the purpose of setting up of retail outlets;

WHEREAS the Agent has offered to set up one such Retail Outlet in the City of_______ and has represented to XYZ Limited that it is in a position to invest necessary capital and is also possessed of a suitable premises to set up and carry on the Retail Outlet and XYZ Limited has accepted the said offer;

NOW THIS AGREEMENT WITNESSETH AS FOLLOWS

That in consideration of the foregoing, the Company hereby appoint M/s Pustak Mahal as its Agent in the City of_________ upon the following terms and conditions:

1. The retail outlet for marketing______ products under the name and style of "XYZ" shall be set up and run in the Premises made available by the Agent, which premises is more fully described in the Schedule Premises". The premises will be made available free of cost or charges to XYZ Limited by the Agent during the subsistence of this Agreement.
2. The Agent will meet and bear the entire cost of furnishing and decorating the interior and exterior of the Schedule-Premises in accordance with the specifications and requirements of XYZ Limited, particularly touching upon the following aspects –

elevation, décor and interior design, selection of furniture, fitting, counters and stands, lighting system, illumination, mannequins, window display, air conditioning, fire fighting equipment, furnishings, flooring, etc. the cost of which is estimated to be of the order of ₹__________ (Rupees______________) He shall also provide necessary warehousing facilities and office space for the Company's representations.

3. The name of the Shop shall be promptly and clearly displayed as_________;

4. XYZ Limited will make available from time to time to the Agent________ products and shall be manufactured, sold or dealt in by XYZ Limited (hereinafter collectively referred to as "Stockist") and the Agent will take the Stocks on consignment and sell the same in retail at prices fixed from time to time by the XYZ Limited. The stocks shall at all times be the property of the XYZ Limited and the Agent shall only be entrusted the Stocks for the purpose of enabling their retail sale.

5. The Agent at his cost will employ necessary personnel to man and manage the Retail Outlet to the entire satisfaction of XYZ Limited.

THE AGENT COVENANTS WITH THE COMPANY AS FOLLOWS:

1. It shall duly and promptly pay the owner of the Schedule Premises rents and other charges and keep the lease subsisting and valid and ensure that the Schedule Premises is always available for running of the Retail Outlet.

2. That it shall not directly or indirectly or in Partnership or Association, with friends or relatives, or Companies engaged itself in business, which is same or similar to the one being carried on by XYZ Limited.

3. That it shall not sell, display or otherwise deal in any goods which are in any way similar to the goods sold or dealt in by XYZ Limited.

4. That it shall not use the Company's trade name and/or trademark in any manner other than that which is permitted by XYZ Limited.

5. That all sales effected by the Agent shall be strictly for cash only.

6. That it shall furnish to XYZ Limited at such intervals as they may required certified stocks statement of the stock of all goods held by the Agent giving full and correct particulars thereof.

7. That it shall remit each day the entire sale proceeds of the preceding day to the credit of the designated account of XYZ Limited, which may be indicated from time to time and shall forthwith sent intimation of such remittances to XYZ Limited.

8. That it shall not draw, accept or endorse any Bill on behalf of the XYZ Limited or in any way pledge the credit of XYZ Limited except with the previous written authorization of XYZ Limited.

9. That it shall be at all times responsible to XYZ Limited for any damage occasioned to the Stock either on account of the improper or negligent conduct on the part of the Agent, its servants or agents or for any reason whatsoever and shall make goods such loss to the XYZ Limited as and when demanded without demur.

10. That it shall furnish an irrevocable Bank Guarantee for a sum of ₹________ (Rupees________________) in favour of XYZ Limited covering the value of the Stocks held by it on consignment and that the said Bank Guarantee shall be enhanced from time to time as may be required by XYZ Limited to bring it in conformity with the value of the Stocks held by the Agent.
11. That it shall keep proper accounts of all Stocks received, sold, damaged and furnish to XYZ Limited each week full particulars of the Stocks and shall permit XYZ Limited, its agents and servants to inspect all Books of Account, Records and vouchers maintained in the Retail Outlet by it all reasonable times.
12. That it shall be responsible for any loss or damage sustained to the Stock while in the custody of the Agent.

DURATION: The duration of this Agreement shall be for a period of______________ years commencing from________. On the expiry of this period of earlier, the Agreement may be extended for such further period and on such terms as the parties may be mutually agreed in writing.

This Agreement is however terminable as follows:

a. by either party giving the other________ days notice in writing;
b. by XYZ Limited unilaterally without assigning any reasons
   i. if the agent is found guilty of misconduct, or
   ii. commits a breach of any of the provisions of the Agreement, or
   iii. is dissolved, or
   iv. any suit or other proceedings are instituted for its dissolution or winding up, or
   v. commits any act of bankruptcy,
   vi. suffers any execution or distress.

CONSIDERATION: In consideration of the foregoing, the Agent shall be entitled to a commission at the rate of______% of the net sale price realized by it in the Retail Outlet by sale of the Stocks. The expression net sale price shall mean the selling price of the Stocks excluding Sales Tax, local taxes and other levies imposed upon the sale or purchase of the Stocks and/or on the total turnover, packing and forwarding charges and gift wrapping charges. The commission shall be payable by XYZ Limited on or before the_________ Day of the succeeding month for which it is due upon receipt of the monthly statement of sales and realization of the sale proceeds.

ASSIGNMENT: This Agreement or the benefit therefrom shall not be assignable or transferable by the Agent in favour of anyone without prior written consent of the company.

SECURITY DEPOSIT: In order to ensure XYZ Limited the due performance of its obligations under this Agreement, the Agent has this day deposited a sum of ₹________ (Rupees______________) by Pay Order bearing No_________ dated______ drawn on________ Bank_______________ Branch_____________, in favour of XYZ Limited as Security Deposit. The said amount will be refundable upon the termination of this Agreement, free of interest, in the event of there being no outstanding claim against the Agent by XYZ Limited. XYZ Limited will however be entitled to appropriate and adjust and amounts which may be due to it from the Agent from out of the Security Deposit.

JURISDICTION: This Agreement is executed at______________City and it is hereby agreed that Court situated in______________. city alone will have exclusive jurisdiction over any matter arising under this Agreement to the execution of Courts situated in any part of the country.

SCHEDULE

Premises bearing No____________________ situated at____________________________ admeasuring and bounded as follows:

MEASUREMENTS

East to West:

North to South:

BOUNDARIES

ON THE EAST

WEST

NORTH

SOUTH

:

:

:

:

: By

: By

: By

: By

IN WITNESS WHEREOF the parties above named have executed these presents in the presence of the Witnesses attesting hereunder on the dates and place mentioned herein below:

Place:

Dated:

For XYZ Limited,

WITNESSES

1. ()

2. ()

Agent

11. Simple Compromise-agreement

It is legally biding document setting out the terms upon which the employer and employee agree to end the employment relationship. This will typically involve the employee agreeing not to bring any tribunal or court claims against the employer in exchange for an agreed sum of money or agreed reference.

Template

This Agreement of compromise made at ___________ on this ____ day of ____________, 2017 between A son of ______________ resident of _____________________ (hereinafter called Party No. 1) of the One Part and B son of _____________ resident of _____________________ (hereinafter called Party No. 2) of the Other Part.

WHEREAS, disputes and differences have arisen between the parties aforementioned regarding _______________________.

AND WHEREAS, the parties have agreed to settle their disputes and differences amicably between themselves without recourse to litigation and for that purpose are willing to abandon their claims in the manner hereinafter appearing.

NOW, This Deed Witnesseth That It Is Hereby Agreed As Follows:

1.

2.

IN WITNESS Whereof, the parties have hereunto set and subscribed their respective hands, the day, month and year first above written.

Signed and delivered by the Withinnamed A

Witnesses

1.

2.

Signed and delivered by the Withinnamed B

12. Deed of Family-settlement

Division of properties left by a deceased between son and daughters where son pays money to daughters.

Template

THIS DEED of family arrangement is made at .... on this .... day of............, 2017, between A son of Shri .... resident of .... (hereinafter called the FIRST PARTY) and Smt. B wife of Shri .... resident of .... (hereinafter called the SECOND PARTY) and Smt. C wife of Shri .... resident of .... (hereinafter called the THIRD PARTY) and Shri D .... son of .... resident of .... (hereinafter called the FOURTH PARTY).

WHEREAS by his will dated .... E son of late Shri .... resident of .... appointed the fourth party as the executors thereof and gave his movable and immovable assets unto his children the first party, second party and the third party in equal shares.

WHEREAS The said E died on .... and the executors obtained the probate of the said will from the .... District Court on ....

WHEREAS the executor has paid the funeral and testamentary expenses of the testator and all his debts which have come to his knowledge out of the estate of the testator.

WHEREAS The estate of the said E now in the hands of the executors consists of the immovable property described in the First Schedule hereunder written and the investments, particulars whereof are 1 described in the Second and Third Schedules hereunder written respectively.

WHEREAS the parties hereto of the first three parts are desirous that the first party shall receive the immovable property and the second party shall receive the investments specified in the Second Schedule hereunder written and that the third party shall receive the investments specified in the Third Schedule hereunder written as absolute owners.

NOW THIS DEED WITNESSETH AS FOLLOWS:

(1) The first party shall pay to each of the second and third parties, the sum of ₹. ....

(2) On the making of payment as aforesaid, the executors shall 3 assent to the vesting of the immovable property described in the First Schedule hereunder written in the first party as absolute owners.

(3) The executors shall transfer the investment specified in Second and Third Schedules to the second and third parties respectively and they will become the absolute owners of the said investments.

(4) It is expressly agreed by and between the parties hereto of the first three parts that they shall not claim any rights under the said will, save as hereinabove provided and they shall release and indemnity the executor from and against all actions, proceedings,

claims and demands in respect of the assent and transfers hereinbefore agreed to be made.

IN WITNESS WHEREOF the parties hereto have set and subscribed their hands to this writing, the day and year first hereinabove written.

The First Schedule above referred to;

(Description of immovable property)

The Second Schedule above referred to;

(Particulars of investments to be transferred to second party)

The Third Schedule above referred to;

(Particulars of investments to be transferred to third party)

Signed and delivered by the within-named first party

Signed and delivered by the within-named second party

Signed and delivered by the within-named third party

Signed and delivered by the within-named fourth party

WITNESSES:

1.

2.

13. Deed of Guarantee

A Deed of Guarantee is a document where one person agrees to be responsible for someone else's mortgage obligations if that person fails to carry out their own obligations.

Template

THIS DEED OF GUARANTEE executed on the day of Two Thousand and Seventeen:

BY:

(hereinafter referred to as the "FIRST PARTY", which expression shall, wherever the context so requires or admits, mean and include, his heirs, executors, administrators and assigns).

IN FAVOUR OF:

(Hereinafter referred to as the "SECOND PARTY", which expression shall, wherever the context so requires or admits, mean and include, its successors-in-title and assigns).

WITNESSES AS FOLLOWS:

I. WHEREAS by an Agreement dated ... .2017, the Second Party has arrived at an arrangement to contribute its effort and economic strength in the development being done by M/s.________________ of the Property bearingNo.________________________ in terms set out therein;

II. WHEREAS a copy of the said Agreement is hereto annexed and marked as Annexure 'A';

III. WHEREAS the First Party is one of the Partners/Directors of ________________ and apart from the assurances given by M/s.______________________________ the First Party herein has agreed to personally guarantee the performance and returns estimated of M/s.____ under the said Agreement, failing which the First Party will make good the amounts guaranteed hereunder and the Parties hereto are desirous of recording the terms of the guarantee;

IV. NOW THIS DEED OF GUARANTEE WITNESSES AS FOLLOWS:

1. In the premises aforesaid and at the request of the Second Party, the First Party hereby agrees with and guarantees the Second Party the payment assured to the Second Party under the Agreement dated______ 2017 by M/s.Pustak Mahal and in the event of the Second Party not receiving the amounts in terms of the Agreement dated_____ 2017, irrespective of any reasons from M/s. Pustak Mahal the First Party Mr.________________________ hereby irrevocably and unconditionally agrees and covenants to pay to the Second Party the amounts to be received by the Second Party in terms of the annexed Agreement or any part or parts thereof with interest thereon as aforesaid and as set out in the Agreement dated ... 2017 between the Second Party and M/s.Pustak Mahal upon demand in that behalf being made by the Second Party;

2. The First Party further agrees as follows:-

   a. A notice of demand issued by the Second Party or on its behalf stating that any of the sums under the annexed Agreement dated____ 2017 have become receivable, in terms of the said Agreement dated____ 2017 and that M/s.Pustak Mahal have failed or neglected in its assurances and failure of the Second Party receiving the said sum or any part thereof or any interest thereon as agreed, shall be conclusive and binding on the First Party as to that fact and without any further proof. The First Party shall make payment hereunder to the Second Party without any demur or default or without any recourse or reference to M/s.Pustak Mahal as the case may be.

b. The First Party further agrees to pay the amounts mentioned hereunder or any part thereof as the case may be, notwithstanding that there may be any dispute or difference between the Second Party and M/s_________ as to whether or not the said sums under the Agreement dated 2017 or any part thereof and interest thereon as aforesaid or any part thereof has or has not become due and receivable by the Second Party.

c. The First Party agrees that this Guarantee is in addition to and without prejudice to the existing security offered by and on behalf of M/s.________________________ to the Second Party and that all rights and remedies in respect thereof be reserved.

d. The First Party agrees that this guarantee shall be a continuing guarantee and shall not be considered as wholly or partially satisfied or exhausted by any part received by the Second Party or any settlement of account between the Second Party and M/s.____________________________.

e. The First Party agrees that this guarantee shall continue and be in force notwithstanding the discharge of M/s.__________________by operation of any law or insolvency /bankruptcy/winding up/ dissolution of M/s.________________________ and shall cease only on payment of amount guaranteed hereunder either by M/s._____________________________________ or the First Party herein.

f. The First Party shall have no right to the benefit of any other security that may be held by the Second Party until the Second Party receives all the amounts in respect of the monies and of all other claims under the said Agreement dated___ 2017 and on any account whatsoever arising out of the said Agreement dated_____2017, shall have been fully satisfied.

g. The First Party agrees that the Second Party under notice to the First Party, shall be at liberty to take other securities for the said monies due to the Second Party or any part thereof and to release or forbear to enforce all or any of the Second Party's remedies upon or under such securities and any collateral security or securities now held or be held by the Second Party and that no such release or forbearance as aforesaid shall have the effect of releasing the First Party from his liability or of prejudicing the Second Party's rights against the First Party under this Guarantee provided the notice mentioned herein above has been duly served on the First Party.

h. The First Party shall have no right to the benefit of any other security that may be held by the Second Party until the Second Party receives all the amounts in respect of the monies and of all other claims under the said Agreement dated____ 2017 and on any account whatsoever arising out of the said Agreement dated____ 2017 shall have been fully satisfied and in respect of the amounts from M/s._______________________; this Guarantee shall come to an end and in the event of the First Party paying under this Guarantee, the First Party shall be entitled to the security held by the Second Party at the time of total discharge.

3. The First Party agrees that demand for payment under this Guarantee shall be deemed to have been given to the First Party if made in writing and delivered at his address hereunder written and if sent by post shall be deemed to have been received by the Second Party 24 hours after posting thereof and in proving such services it shall be sufficient to prove that the letter containing the demand was properly addressed and put into post.

   NAME: MR. ____________________

Address for Notice:

4. It is agreed that this Guarantee shall be enforceable notwithstanding any change in the name of the Second Party company and it shall ensure for the benefit of any company with which the Second Party may become amalgamated or to which the Second Party may assign its rights.
5. It is agreed that this Guarantee shall remain in force until the performance assured by M/s.____ under the Agreement dated___ 2017 have been fulfilled and complied in terms thereof.
6. The First Party agrees that it shall not be discharged or released from this Guarantee by any arrangement made between the Second Party and M/s. ________________________ notice to him in writing with regards to any additional security given by M/s.____________ and/or M/s ____________________, or release of any security at present given or may be given in addition nor will the First Party be discharged or released from this Guarantee by any alterations in the obligations save and except the quantum and returns agreed to be paid by M/s. ________, to the Second Party undertaken by M/s.___________ or by any forbearance or waiver by the Second Party whether as to payment, time of performance or otherwise under notice to the First Party in writing. The First Party agrees that the reasons for such notice as set out in this Para is only for information and not to seek consent of the First Party.

IN WITNESS WHEREOF, the FIRST PARTY has executed this DEED OF GUARANTEE in the presence of the Witnesses attesting hereunder:

WITNESSES:

1)

FIRST PARTY

2)

14. Retainership-agreement

A retainership agreement is a work for hire contract. It falls between a one-time contract and full-time employment. Its distinguishing feature is that the employer pays in advance for work to be specified later addtional contracts regarding the performance of this work may also apply.

Template

THIS AGREEMENT is made at ______ this __________ day of ____________ 2017 between ______________________________ (Company's name) a company registered under the Companies Act, 1956, having its registered office at ______________________________ ________ hereinafter referred to as "the party of the first part" and ABC, an advocate/Firm of advocates or solicitors having his/their registered office at____________________, hereinafter referred to as "the party of the second part".

WHEREAS the party of the first part is a company and requires the assistance of solicitors and legal advisors for drafting notices to be issued to__________________, correspondence with the government departments/banks/ others, giving advice and solutions to internal problems of the company in accordance with the Companies Act, 1956 and the Articles of the company, etc.

AND WHEREAS the party of the first part has offered to appoint and retain the party of the second part to act for them as legal advisors and solicitors and the party of the second part have agreed to the said appointment and retainership.

AND WHEREAS the parties hereto have agreed to record the terms and conditions on which the party of the first part has agreed to appoint and retain the party of the second part to act for them as legal advisors and solicitors and the party of the second part has agreed to accept the said appointment and retainership.

NOW IT IS HEREBY AGREED BY AND BETWEEN THE PARTIES HERETO AS FOLLOWS:

1. The party of the first part hereby appoints and retains the party of the second part for drafting notices to be issued to_________________, correspondence with the government departments/banks/ others, giving advice and solutions to internal problems of the company in accordance with the Companies Act, 1956, Income Tax Act, 1961, Local laws relating to labour, P.F, ESI and the Articles of the company, etc___ and all ancillary and incidental matters.

2. The party of the first part shall pay to the party of the second part fees of ₹______ (Rupees_________ only) per month. The said fees will be in lieu of and in satisfaction of all professional charges and expenses including the office expenses of the party of the second part but excluding any out of pocket expenses and costs incurred in relation to the assignment.

3. The party of the first part shall also pay to the party of the second part all out of pocket expenses incurred by them in payment of travelling expenses, registration charges, etc. in respect of documents in relation to each transaction, etc.

4. The above fee quote is based on the assumption that there will be no material change in the scope. In the event of any material deviation in the foregoing assumption the parties hereto agree to re-assess and mutually revise the fee quote.
5. Invoices will be raised by the party of the second part on a monthly basis and will be payable within 15 days. A detailed narrative stating the nature of the work done will accompany the invoice. The invoice shall also include details of any out of pocket expenses and costs incurred in relation to the assignment.
6. The scope of the above services would not include any regulatory compliance (such as filings, etc. with statutory authorities, etc.), or providing substantive opinions or memoranda on any specific legal issue and the same will be charged separately.
7. This agreement will not extend to any litigation civil or criminal or arbitration whether arising out of any transaction entrusted to the party of the second part or otherwise. If any such matter of litigation or any legal proceedings in a court of law or tribunal or arbitrator is entrusted to them, the party of the second part will be entitled to charge fees according to their usual practice.
8. The party of the second part shall maintain full secrecy and shall not disclose any confidential matter or communication between the party of the first part and themselves to anybody else.
9. The party of the second part shall not act in any matter entrusted to them for any other party concerned or connected with such matter.
10. This agreement may be terminated by any party hereto by giving one month's prior notice to the other without assigning reason and on the expiry of the said period from receipt of the notice this agreement shall stand terminated except in respect of matters which are already entrusted to the party of the second part and are not completed.

IN WITNESS WHEREOF the parties hereto have put their hands the day and year first hereinabove written.

Signed by the concerned authority within-named)

___________ Company)

Rep.by its Managing Director)

Mr. ____________________)

In the presence of)

____________________)

Signed by the within-named)

____________________(retainers)

by its (concerned authority)

Ms. ____________________)

In the presence of)

____________________)

15. Partition-deed

A partition deed or agreement is a document that outlines in detail the rights and responsibilities of all parties to a business operation. It has the face of law and is designed to guide the partners in the conduct of the business.

Template

THIS DEED OF PARTITION made at ____________this ___________ day of 2017

(1) Sri____________, S/o______________, Age______ years, Occupation__________, Residing at_________________________, hereinafter referred to as the Party of the First Part.

(2) Sri______________________, S/o______________________, Age ________years, Occupation____________, Residing at_____________________________, hereinafter referred to as the Party of the Second Part.

(3) Sri_________________, S/o_____________, Age ________years, Occupation___________, Residing at_____________________________, hereinafter referred to as the Party of the Third Part.

(4) ___________________ etc.

WHEREAS:

1 (a) The parties hereto are the members and copartners of their joint and undivided Hindu Family and as such own immovable properties consisting of land and building thereon and situate at _________________and more particularly described in Schedule "A" hereunder written and each of the parties hereto is entitled to share in the Schedule "A" property.

(b) Parties to this partition have thrown their properties described in Schedule "A" in the common hatch pot and declared themselves as these properties are belonging to Joint Family property.

2. The parties desire to effect a partition of the said properties between themselves as they no longer desire to continue as members and copartners of their joint family property and desire to be separate in food, worship and estate.

3. The parties have agreed that the said Schedule "A" properties will be divided and partitioned in such a way that namely;

(a) The property described in the said First Schedule shall be allotted and belongs to the Party of the First Part exclusively.

(b) The property described in the said Second Schedule shall be allotted and belongs to the Party of the Second Part exclusively and,

(c) The property described in the said Third Schedule shall be allotted and belongs to the Party of the Third Part exclusively.

4. The parties hereto have proposed to effect and record the said partition in the manner following:

NOW THIS DEED WITNESSETH AS FOLLOW:

1. The parties have agreed that the said Schedule "A" properties will be divided and partitioned in such a way that namely;

   (a) The property described in the said First Schedule shall be allotted and belongs to the Party of the First Part exclusively,

   (b) The property described in the said Second Schedule shall be allotted and belongs to the Party of the Second Part exclusively and,

   (c) The property described in the said Third Schedule shall be allotted and belongs to the Party of the Third Part exclusively.

2. In consideration aforesaid, each of the parties hereto grant and release all his/her undivided share, right, title and interest in the property allotted to the other of them as aforesaid so as to constitute each party the sole and absolute owner of the property allotted to him/her freed and discharged from all rights, title, interest claims and demands of the other party hereto or concerning the same but subject to the payment of all taxes, rates, dues and duties and assessment payable to Government or Municipal Corporation or any other public body in respect thereof.

3. Each party covenants with the other that he/she has not done any act deed or thing whereby or by means whereof he/she is prevented from conveying and releasing the property to the other in the manner aforesaid.

4. Each party also covenants with the other that each party will execute and get registered, if necessary any deed, assurance or other document which may be required for fuller and more perfectly and effectually assuring the property, allotted to the other but at the cost and expenses of the other.

5. Each party hereto further covenants with the other that the latter will hereafter hold and stand possessed of the property allotted to him/her quietly and peacefully and enjoy the rents and profits thereof without any suit, interruption, claim or demand by the covenanting party, his/her heirs, executors administrators and assigns or any person claiming under him/her.

6. The original of the deed of partition will remain in the custody of the Party of the First Part and the duplicate copy hereof will remain in the custody of the Party of the Other Part.

7. And it is further agreed and declared that the title deeds relating to the properties and which are common to both of them and which are set out in the ____________Schedule hereunder written shall remain with the Party of the First Part who has agreed to give a covenant for production in favour of the Party of the ___________Part.

SCHEDULE "A"

(Details of Undivided properties belong to Joint Family)

Sl. No.	Description of the Property	Property standing in the name of
1		
2		
3		
4 etc.		

FIRST SCHEDULE

(Property allotted to the share of Sri ______________________________First part)

SECOND SCHEDULE

(Property allotted to the share of Sri ______________________________Second part)

THIRD SCHEDULE

(Property allotted to the share of Sri ______________________________Third part)

WITNESS:

1. FIRST PARTY

2. SECOND PARTY

3. THIRD PARTY

Etc.

16. Deed of Gift of Immovable Property

It is defined as the transfer of certain existing movable and immovable property made voluntarily and without consideration, by one person (donor) to another (donee) and is accepted by or on behalf of the donee.

Template

This Deed Of Gift is made at______ this______ day of 2017 between Mr. A of______ hereinafter referred to as 'the Donor' of the One Part and Mr. B of______ hereinafter referred to as 'the DONEE', of the Other Part.

WHEREAS the Donor is seized and possessed of the land and premises situated at______ and more particularly described in the Schedule hereunder written.

AND WHEREAS the DONEE is related to the Donor as______.

AND WHEREAS the Donor desires to grant the said land and premises to the DONEE as gift in consideration of natural love and affection as hereinafter mentioned

AND WHEREAS the DONEE has agreed to accept the gift as is evidenced by his executing these presents.

AND WHEREAS the market value of the said property is estimated to be ₹______.

NOW, this Deed Witnesseth that the Donor without any monetary consideration and in consideration of natural love and affection, which the Donor bears to the DONEE, doth hereby grant and transfer by way of gift the said land and premises situated at______ and more particularly described in the Schedule hereunder written together with all and singular the buildings and structures thereon and all the things permanently attached thereto or standing thereon and all the liberties, privileges casements and advantages appurtenant thereto and all the estate, right, title, interest, use, Inheritance, possession, benefit, claims and demand whatsoever of the Donor To Have And To Hold the same unto and to the use of the DONEE absolutely but subject to the payment of all taxes, rates, assessments, dues and duties now and hereafter chargeable thereon to the Government or Municipality or other Local Authority.

AND he the Donor doth hereby covenants with the DONEE;

a. That the Donor now has in himself, good right, full power and absolute authority to grant the said piece of land and other the premises hereby granted as gift in the manner aforesaid.

b. The DONEE may at all times hereafter peaceably and quietly enter upon, occupy, possess and enjoy the said piece of land and premises and receive the rents, Issues, and profits and rents thereof and every part thereof to and for his own use and benefit without any suit, lawful eviction, interruption, claim or demand whatsoever from or by the Donor or his heirs, executors, administrators and assigns or any person or persons lawfully claiming or to claim by, from, under or in trust for the Donor.

c. That the said land and premises are free and clear and freely and clearly and absolutely and forever released and discharged or otherwise by the Donor and well and sufficiently saved, kept harmless and Indemnified of and from and against all former and other estate, titles, charges and encumbrances whatsoever, had made, executed, occasioned or suffered by the Donor or by any other person or persons lawfully claiming or to claim by, from, under or in trust for the Donor.

d. And Further that the Donor and all persons having or lawfully claiming any estate or Interest whatsoever to the said land and premises or any part thereof from under or in trust for the Donor or his heirs, executors, administrators and assigns or any of them shall and will from time to time and at all times hereafter at the request and cost of the DONEE do and execute or cause to be done and executed all such further and other acts, deeds, things, conveyances and assurances in law whatsoever for better and more perfectly assuring the said land and premises and every part thereof unto and to the use of the DONEE in the manner aforesaid as by the DONEE, his heirs, executors, administrators and assigns or counsel in law shall be reasonably required.

IN WITNESS,WHEROF, the Donor as well as the DONEE (by way of acceptance of the said gift) have put their respective hands the day and year first hereinabove written.

THE SCHEDULE ABOVE REFERRED TO

Signed and Delivered by the within-named Donor______ in the presence of______.

Signed by within-named DONEE_______ in the presence of

1_____________

2_____________

Draft of Deed of Gift of Moveable Property

I, Mr______. residing at______ do hereby make a gift of the ornaments and jewellery specified in the schedule hereinunder written to my daughter Miss______ in consideration of natural love and affection on the occasion of her marriage.

SCHEDULE

SIGNED

DONOR

Witnesses.

1_____________

2_____________

Accepted

DONEE

17. Copyright-licence Agreement

This agreement is used when a person who owns the copyright in creative contract wishes to give permission to another person to use their contract (visual, text, music, film, etc.) in a particular way. It needs to be tailored to suit the needs of the specific case.

Template

This Copyright Licence Agreement (this "Agreement") is made effective as of [DATE] between [PROPERTY OWNER], of [ADDRESS], [CITY], [ZIP CODE] and [LICENSED PROPERTY USER], of [ADDRESS], [CITY], [ZIP CODE].

This Agreement shall be governed by the laws of [STATE]. This Agreement will commence on the [EFFECTIVE DATE] and continue until the [TERMINATION DATE] or until either party provides written notice of termination to the other party with a 30 days notice.

In this Agreement, the party granting the right to use the licensed property, [OWNER], will be referred to as the "Owner" and the party who is receiving the right to use the licensed property, [USER], will be referred to as the "User."

1. Owner owns all proprietary rights in and to the copyrightable and/or copyrighted works described in this Agreement. The copyrighted works will collectively be referred to as "Work."
2. Owner owns all rights in and to the Work and retains all rights to the Work, which are not transferred herein, and retains all common law copyrights and all federal copyrights which have been, or which may be, granted by the Library of Congress.
3. Owner desires to obtain, and Licensor has agreed to grant, a licence authorizing the use of the Work by Licensee in accordance with the terms and conditions of this Agreement.

The parties agree to abide by the terms as follows:

I. GRANT OF LICENCE. Owner owns [PROPERTY TO BE LICENSED] ("Property"). In accordance with this Agreement, Owner grants User a non-exclusive licence to Use or Sell [HIGHLIGHT THE TERMS THAT APPLY] the Property. Owner retains title and ownership of the Property. User will own all rights to materials, products or other works (the Work) created by User in connection with this licence. This grant of licence applies only to the following described geographical area:

PandaTip: This is where you will want to describe the geographical area where the licence applies.

II. RIGHTS AND OBLIGATIONS. User shall be the sole owner of the Work and all proprietary rights in and to the Work; however, such ownership shall not include ownership of the copyright in and to the Property or any other rights to the Property not specifically granted in this Agreement.

III. PAYMENT. User agrees to pay Owner a royalty which shall be calculated as follows:

PandaTip: You will want to identify how the royalty should be calculated.

The royalty will be paid by [DATE ROYALTY PAID].

IV. MODIFICATIONS. Unless the prior written approval of Owner is obtained, User may not modify or change the Property in any manner. Licensee shall not use Licensed property for any purpose that is unlawful or prohibited by these Terms of the Agreement.

V. DEFAULTS ON AGREEMENT. If User fails to abide by the obligations of this Agreement, including the obligation to make a royalty payment when due, Owner shall have the option to cancel this Agreement by providing 30 days written notice to User. User shall have the option of taking corrective action to cure the default to prevent the termination of this Agreement if said corrective action is enacted prior to the end of the time period stated in the previous sentence. There must be no other defaults during such time period or Owner will have the option to cancel this Agreement, despite previous corrective action.

VI. WARRANTIES. Neither party makes any warranties with respect to the use, sale or other transfer of the Property by the other party or by any third party, and User accepts the product "AS IS." In no event will Owner be liable for direct, indirect, special, incidental, or consequential damages, that are in any way related to the Property.

VII. TRANSFER OF RIGHTS. Neither party shall have the right to assign its interests in this Agreement to any other party, unless the prior written consent of the other party is obtained.

VIII. INDEMNIFICATION. Each party shall indemnify and hold the other harmless for any losses, claims, damages, awards, penalties, or injuries incurred by any third party, including reasonable attorney's fees, which arise from any alleged breach of such indemnifying party's representations and warranties made under this Agreement, provided that the indemnifying party is promptly notified of any such claims. The indemnifying party shall have the sole right to defend such claims at its own expense. The other party shall provide, at the indemnifying party's expense, such assistance in investigating and defending such claims as the indemnifying party may reasonably request. This indemnity will survive the termination of this Agreement.

IX. AMENDMENT. This Agreement may be modified or amended, only if the amendment is made in writing and is signed by both parties.

X. TERMINATION. This Agreement may be terminated by either party by providing 30 days written notice to the other party. This Agreement shall terminate automatically on [TERMINATION DATE].

i. Upon termination or expiration of this Agreement, Licensee User shall cease reproducing, advertising, marketing and distributing the Work as soon as is commercially feasible. Licensee shall have the right to fill existing orders and to sell off existing copies of the Work then in stock. Owner will have the right to verify the existence and validity of the existing orders and existing copies of the Work then in stock upon reasonable notice to Licensee.

ii. Termination or expiration of this Agreement shall not extinguish any of Licensee's or Copyright Owner's obligations under this Agreement including, but not limited to the obligation to pay royalties which by their terms continue after the date of termination or expiration.

XI. SEVERABILITY. If any provision of this Agreement shall be held to be invalid or unenforceable for any reason, the remaining provisions shall continue to be valid and enforceable. If a court finds that any provision of this Agreement is invalid or unenforceable, but that by limiting such provision it would become valid or enforceable, then such provision shall be deemed to be written, construed, and enforced as so limited.

This Agreement contains the entire agreement of the parties and there are no other promises or conditions in any other agreement whether oral or written. This Agreement supersedes any prior written or oral agreements between the parties.

The following signatures make this Agreement effective as of the date first written above.

OWNER

____ ____________________

[NAME], [TITLE] [BUSINESS NAME 1] DATE

LICENSEE/USER

____ ____________________

[NAME], [TITLE] [BUSINESS NAME 2] DATE

18. Irrevocable Power of Attorney

(To be stamped as a General Power of Attorney)

It is a document used in some business transactions. Irrevocable a durable power of attorney are typically given to give someone the authority to make decissions on your behalf in the event of an accident.

Template

THIS POWER OF ATTORNEY granted at this____________ day of____________ 2017 by 'A Limited' a company within the meaning of the Companies Act, 1956, and having its registered office at___________ (hereinafter referred to as 'the Borrower' which expression shall, unless excluded by or repugnant to the context include its successors and assigns) in favour of____________ a corporation constituted by____________ and having its Head office at____________ (hereinafter referred to as "the LENDER", which expression shall, unless excluded by or repugnant to the context, include its successors and assigns).

1. WHEREAS by an Agreement dated the____________ day of____________ 2017 (hereinafter referred to as "the said Agreement") made between the 'Borrower' and the 'Lender'. 'Lender' has agreed to grant the 'Borrower' financial assistance by way of a term of ₹______ (Rupees____________) (hereinafter referred to as "the financial assistance") for the purposes and on the terms and conditions set out therein.
2. 'Lender' has stipulated, inter alia, that if so required by 'Lender' at any time, the 'Borrower' shall secure Lender's loan of ₹______ (Rupees____________) together with interest, commitment charge, additional interest by way of liquidated damages, costs, charges, expenses and other moneys payable by the Borrower to Lender under the said Agreement by a registered legal mortgage in English form of all the properties of the Borrower immovable and movable, present and future and other assets, including uncalled capital and the charge in favour of the Lender to rank pari passu with the charge or charges created and/or to be created by the Borrower in favour of the Lender, AND the charge of Lender on movables to be subject to the charge or charges created and/or to be created by the Borrower in favour of its bankers on stocks of raw-materials, semi-finished and finished goods and consumable stores and book debts and such other movables as may be permitted by Lender in writing to secure borrowings for working capital requirements.
3. Lender has also stipulated that the Borrower shall, for the aforesaid purpose, execute an undertaking in favour of the Lender and shall simultaneously with the execution of such undertaking, grant an irrevocable power of attorney to the Lender, being these presents, authorising the Lender to execute in favour of itself a first legal mortgage in English form for and on behalf of the Borrower in the event of the Borrower failing, when required by the Lender, to duly execute and register a first legal mortgage in English form of all its immovable and movable properties as aforesaid.
4. The Lender has called upon the Borrower to execute these presents which the Borrower has agreed to do in the manner hereinafter expressed.

NOW THIS DEED WITNESSETH THAT in consideration of the Lender having sanctioned the said financial assistance to the Borrower, the Borrower hereby irrevocably appoints the Lender to be the true and lawful attorney of the Borrower in the name and for and on behalf of the Borrower to do, execute and perform the following acts, deeds and things, namely:

(i) To make, execute, sign, seal and deliver in favour of the Lender, at the expense of the Borrower, in all respects, a first legal mortgage in English form of all its immovable and movable properties, present and future, including lands, hereditaments and premises and fixed plants and machinery and uncalled capital agreed to be mortgaged to the Lender, with all such covenants, conditions, provisions, and stipulations, as may, in the absolute discretion of the Lender, be deemed necessary or expedient and in particular granting in favour of the Lender a right to take over the management of the Borrower, a right to appoint a receiver of the undertaking of the Borrower and a right to sell the Borrower's properties without intervention of the Court, for the purposes of securing to the Lender all the moneys payable by the Borrowers under the said Agreement, as aforesaid, the charge of the Lender to rank pari passu with the charge or charges created and/or to be created by the Borrower in favour of the Lenders for the purposes and in the manner mentioned therein. PROVIDED THAT the charge of the Lender on movables shall be subject to the charge or charges created and/or to be created by the Borrower in favour of its bankers on its stocks of raw materials, semi-finished and finished goods and consumable stores and book debts and such other movables as may be permitted by the Lenders in writing to secure borrowings for working capital requirements.

(ii) To investigate or cause to be investigated, at the expense of the Borrower in all respects, the Borrowers' title to the immovable properties agreed to be mortgaged by the Borrower to the Lender and to take all steps to make out title to the said properties to the satisfaction of the Lender as and when required by the Lender.

(iii) To apply for and obtain necessary clearance certificates under Section 230A of the Income Tax Act, 1961.

(iv) To do or cause to be done all such acts, deeds and things as may be necessary or proper for the effectual completion and registration of the said mortgage.

(v) AND GENERALLY to do or cause to be done every other act, matter or thing which the LENDER may deem necessary or expedient for the purposes of or in relation to these present.

(vi) The Borrower hereby agrees to deposit in advance with the Lenders sufficient sums to cover the expenses to be incurred on investigation of title, stamp duty and registration charges and other miscellaneous expenses for the purpose of and in connection with the execution and registration of the said mortgage deed in English form. In the event of failure on the part of the Borrower to deposit sufficient amounts with the Lenders, the Lenders may, but shall not be obliged to, incur the expenditure for the said purposes and the Borrower shall, on receipt of notice of demand from the Lenders, reimburse the same to the Lenders together with interest at the rate stipulated by the Lender from the date of payment by the Lender.

(vii) The Borrower hereby agrees that all or any of the powers hereby conferred upon the Lender may be exercised by any officer or officers of the Lender nominated by the Lender in that behalf.

(viii) AND the Borrower does hereby declare that all and every receipts, documents, deeds, matters and things which shall by the Lender or by any of its officers appointed by the Lender in that behalf, be made, executed or done for the aforesaid purposes by virtue of these presents shall be as good, valid and effectual to all intents and purposes whatsoever as if the same had been made, executed or done by the Borrower in its own name and person. The Borrower hereby agrees to ratify and confirm all that the Lender or any of its officers appointed by the Lender in that behalf shall do or cause to be done in or concerning the premises by virtue of this power of attorney.

(ix) AND the Borrower does hereby declare that this Power of attorney shall be irrevocable.

IN WITNESS WHEREOF the Borrower company has caused its Common Seal to be hereunto affixed the day and year first hereinafter written.

The Common Seal of the Borrower Company was hereunto affixed pursuant

to the resolution of its Board of Directors passed on the____________ in

the presence of Shri____________ Director and Shri____________

Director who have signed these presents in token thereof.

SECTION - V

Business English Vocabalary

Classified Vocabulary

Abbreviations and Acronyms

Word	Meaning
@	at
a/c	account
AGM	annual general meeting
a.m.	ante meridiem (before noon)
a/o	account of (on behalf of)
AOB	any other business
ASAP	as soon as possible
ATM	automated teller machine (cash dispenser)
attn	for the attention of
approx	approximately
cc	copy to
CEO	chief executive officer
c/o	care of (on letters: at the address of)
Co	company
cm	centimetre
COD	cash on delivery
dept	department
e.g.	exempli gratia (for example)
EGM	extraordinary general meeting
ETA	estimated time of arrival
etc	et cetera (and so on)
GDP	gross domestic product
GNP	gross national product
GMT	Greenwich mean time (time in London)
GST	Goods and services tax
i.e.	id est (meaning : 'that is')
Inc	incorporated
IOU	I owe you
IPO	initial public offer
Jr	junior
K	thousand
lb	pound (weight)
£	pound (money/currency)

Ltd	limited
mo	month
N/A	not applicable
NB	Nota Bene (it is important to note)
no	number
PA	personal assistant
p.a.	per annum (per year)
Plc	public limited company
pls	please
p.m.	post meridiem (after noon)
p.p.	per pro (used before signing in a person's absence)
PR	public relations
p.s.	post scriptum
PTO	please turn over
p.w.	per week
qty	quantity
R & D	research and development
re	with reference to
ROI	return on investment
RSVP	**r**epondez **s**'il **v**ous **p**lait (please reply)
s.a.e.	stamped addressed envelope
VAT	value added tax
VIP	very important person

Employment – Jobs

Word	Meaning
assessment	Evaluation of one's abilities
background	Education - qualifications - experience
bonus	Additional payment to an employee as an incentive or reward
curriculum vitae	Summary of one's education and experience to date; resume
dismiss	Discharge from employment (to fire, to sack, to let go)
employee	Person who works for a firm or company.
employer	Person or firm who employs people.
fire	To dismiss from a job.

fringe benefits	Advantages offered in addition to salary (life insurance, retirement scheme, company car, etc.). Also called 'perks', abbreviation for 'perquisites'.
hire	Employ or take on personnel in a company.
interview	Oral examination of a candidate for employment.
make redundant	Dismiss for economic reasons.
maternity leave	Period of absence for a female employee when having a baby.
notice	Advance warning of intention to leave one's job - to give or hand in one's resignation.
personnel	People who work for a firm or company (employees).
personnel officer	Manager responsible for recruitment, training and welfare of personnel (employees).
promotion	Advancement in rank or position in a company.
prospects	Opportunities for success or promotion in a career.
recruit	Look for and hire personnel.
resign	Leave a job voluntariily.
retire	Leave employment because of age.
sick leave	Absence because of illness - to be on sick leave.
staff	People who work for a firm or department; employees.
strength	Strong characteristic or particular ability.
strike	To go on strike : to stop working in protest against something.
take on	Employ or hire.
trainee	Person being trained for a job e.g. a trainee salesman.
training course	A course of study to prepare for a job e.g. a computer course.
unemployment benefits	Payments made by the state to an unemployed person.
vacancy	A position to be filled.
weakness	A lack of ability or a shortcoming in character.

Investments – Stock Market

Word	Meaning
Bid	The price a buyer is willing to offer for shares in a company.
Blue Chip Stocks	Stocks of leading companies with a reputation for stable growth and earnings.

Bond	Certificate issued by companies and governments to their lenders.
Capital	Money and other property of companies used in transacting the business.
Capital stock	All shares representing ownership of a company.
Commodities	Products such as agricultural products and natural resources (wood, oil and metals) that are traded on a separate, authorized commodities exchange.
Dividend	A portion of a company's earnings which is paid to the shareholders/stockholders on a quarterly or annual basis.
Equity	The value of stocks and shares; the net value of mortgaged property.
Equities	Stocks and shares which represent a portion of the capital of a company.
Futures	Contracts to buy or sell securities at a future date.
Insider	All those who have access to inside information concerning the company.
Insider dealing / trading	Buying or selling with the help of information known only to those connected with the business.
IPO	Initial Public Offering - selling part of a company on the stock market.
Issue	Put into circulation a number of a company's shares for sale.
Liabilities	The debts and obligations of a company or an individual.
Mortgage	Agreement by which a bank or building society lends money for the purchase of property, such as a house or apartment. The property is the security for the loan.
Mutual fund	Savings fund that uses cash from a pool of savers to buy securities such as stock, bonds or real estate.
Option	The right to buy and sell certain securities at a specified price and period of time.
Par value	Nominal face value.
Penny stock	Shares selling at less than $1 a share.
Portfolio	Various types of securities held by an individual or institution.
Securities	Transferable certificates showing ownership of stocks, bonds, shares, options, etc.
Share	The capital of a company is divided into shares which entitle the owner, or shareholder, to a proportion of the profits.
Share certificate	Certificate representing the number of shares owned by an investor.
Shareholder	Owner of shares.

Speculator	Someone who buys and sells stocks and shares in the hope of making a profit through changes in their value.
Stock	Shares (portion of the capital of a business company) held by an investor.
Stockbroker	A licensed professional who buys and sells stocks and shares for clients in exchange for a fee called a 'commission'.
Stockholder	Person who owns stocks and shares.
Trader	Investor who holds stocks and securities for a short time (minutes, hours or days) with the objective of making profit from short-term gains in the market. Investment is generally based on stock price rather than on an evaluation of the company.
Trading session	Period during which the Stock Exchange is open for trading.
Venture capital	Money raised by companies to finance new ventures in exchange for percentage ownership.
Yield	Return on investment shown as a percentage.

Marketing – Sales

Word	Meaning
after sales service	Service that continues after the sale of a product (maintenance, etc.)
agent	Person or company that acts for another and provides a specified service.
B2B e-commerce	Business to business e-commerce : use of commercial networks, online product catalogues and other online resources to obtain better prices and reach new customers.
B2C e-commerce	Business to consumer e-commerce : online sale of goods and services directly to consumers.
benchmarking	Comparing one's products to those of competitors in order to improve quality and performance.
buyer	1) Any person who makes a purchase. 2) A person employed to choose and buy stock for a company.
cash refund offer	Offer to pay back part of the purchase price of a product to customers who send a "proof of purchase" to the manufacturer.
chain store	Two or more shops or outlets that have the same owner and sell similar lines of merchandise.

client	A person who buys services or advice from a lawyer, an accountant or other professional.
close	Finalize a sale or deal.
convenience store	Small shop located near a residential area that opens long hours, seven days a week.
coupon	Certificate that gives customers a saving when they purchase a specific product.
deal	A business transaction.
department store	A large shop or store that carries a wide variety of product lines.
direct investment	Entering a foreign market by setting up assembly or manufacturing facilities in that country.
discount	A reduction in price.
e-commerce	Buying and selling by electronic means, primarily on the internet.
e-marketing	Promotion of products and services over the internet.
extranet	Network that connects a company with its suppliers and distributors
follow-up	Maintain contact after the sale to ensure customer satisfaction.
franchise	Association between a manufacturer or wholesaler (franchiser) and an independent business person (franchisee) who buys the right to own and operate a unit in the franchise system.
guarantee	A promise that product will be repaired or replaced if faulty.
intranet	A network that connects people to each other within a company.
joint venture	A way of entering a foreign market by joining with a foreign company to manufacture or market a product or service.
market leader	The company with the largest market share in an industry.
mark up	Percentage of the price added to the cost to reach a selling price.
opinion leader	Person with a reference, who, because of competence, knowledge, or other characteristics, exerts influence on others.
packaging	Designing and producing the container or wrapper for a product.
product line	A group of products that are closely related.
prospect	A potential customer.
representative	A person who represents and sells for a company.
retail	To sell in small quantities, as in a shop, directly to customers.
shopping centre	Group of shops developed and managed as a unit.
telephone marketing	Using the telephone to sell directly to customers.

trade fair	An exhibition at which companies in a specific industry can show or demonstrate their products.
viral marketing	The internet version of word-of-mouth marketing - email messages that customers pass on to friends.
wholesale	To sell goods and services to those buying for resale (e.g. a shop) or for business use.

Money – Finance

Word	Meaning
A.T.M.	Automated Teller Machine; cash dispenser
banknote	Piece of paper money.
bitcoin	Digital currency which allows payments to be sent from one party to another without going through a financial institution.
borrow	Obtain money which must be returned.
broke (to be)	To have no money.
budget	Amount of money available or needed for a specific use.
cash	Coins or bank notes (not cheques); actual money paid, not credit.
cash dispenser	Automatic machine from which a bank customer can withdraw money.
cashier	A person dealing with cash transactions in a bank, shop, etc.
cheque	Written order to a pay the stated amount from one's account.
coin	A piece of metal used as money.
currency	The money used in a country.
debt	Money owed by one person to another.
deposit	Sum or money payable as a first instalment on a purchase; Money placed in an account in a bank.
donate	Giving money, especially to charity; make a donation.
exchange rate	The rate at which one currency can be exchanged for another.
fee	Payment made to a professional person (doctor, lawyer, etc.).
interest	Money paid for borrowing or investing money.
invest	To put money into a business, property, etc. in order to earn interest or profit.

legal tender	Currency that cannot legally be refused as payment.
lend	Give or allow the use of money which must be returned, usually with interest.
loan	Sum of money to be returned with interest.
owe	To be in debt to someone; to owe money to somebody.
petty cash	Small amount of cash available for everyday expenses.
receipt	Written statement that money has been paid.
refund	Pay back money received; reimburse.
tip	Small sum of money given to a waiter, taxi driver, tec.
withdraw	Take money from a bank account.

Telephone

Useful telephone vocabulary and phrases in English.

Making contact	▪ Hello / Good morning / Good afternoon ... ▪ This is John Brown speaking ▪ Could I speak to .... please? ▪ I'd like to speak to .... ▪ I'm trying to contact ....
Giving more information	▪ I'm calling from Tokyo / Paris / New York / Sydney ... ▪ I'm calling on behalf of Mr. X ...
Taking a call	▪ X speaking. ▪ Can I help you?
Asking for a name / information	▪ Who's calling please? ▪ Who's speaking? ▪ Where are you calling from? ▪ Are you sure you have the right number / name?
Asking the caller to wait	▪ Hold the line please. ▪ Could you hold on please? ▪ Just a moment please.
Connecting	▪ Thank you for holding. ▪ The line's free now ... I'll put you through. ▪ I'll connect you now / I'm connecting you now.

Giving negative information	▪ I'm afraid the line's engaged. Could you call back later? ▪ I'm afraid he's in a meeting at the moment. ▪ I'm sorry. He's out of the office today. / He isn't in at the moment. ▪ I'm afraid we don't have Mr./Mrs./Ms/Miss. ... here ▪ I'm sorry. There's nobody here by that name. ▪ Sorry. I think you've dialled the wrong number./ I'm afraid you've got the wrong number.
Telephone problems	▪ The line is very bad ... Could you speak up please? ▪ Could you repeat that please? ▪ I'm afraid I can't hear you. ▪ Sorry. I didn't catch that. Could you say it again please?
Leaving / Taking a message	▪ Can I leave / take a message? ▪ Would you like to leave a message? ▪ Could you give him/her a message? ▪ Could you ask him/her to call me back? ▪ Could you tell him/her that I called? ▪ Could you give me your name please? ▪ Could you spell that please? ▪ What's your number please?

General Business Vocabulary

A

a.a.r	against all risks
absorb higher costs	to accept without raising prices
absorb	to take in or cancel out
abundant	plentiful
academic	relating to scholarly learning
academic	scholarly, literary
acceptance of the draft	a bill signed to indicate agreement with its terms acceptance or immediately upon acceptance
accomplish	perform
accumulate	to heap up
acquainted with	aware of
acquire	gain, get, obtain
acumen	sharpness and accuracy
acute	sharp
adapted	altered to suit, made to fit
adequate	sufficient

adjustment	alteration
adopt	to take idea
adore	to worship
adversely affected	made worse
advertising media	forms of publicity
aesthetic	appreciating the beauty
affluent	wealthy
after sight	after acceptance, from date bill is accepted
ahead of schedule	before the appointed time
ailment	illness
alacrity	readiness
alert	vigilant
alive	keen
all essential facts	all the necessary information
all round	general, applying to all goods
alternative	a choice of something different
alternative	choice between two things
amalgamate	join together
amend	change for betterment
anticipation	expectation
apologise	regret
appreciated	highly valued
appreciative	showing gratitude
approach	method
appropriate quarter	concerned people
appropriate	proper
appropriate	suited to the occasion, suitable
approval	agreement, consent
arbitration	settlement of disputes by independent persons
article	substance
assess	to estimate value
assets	property
assurance	a firm promise, word of honour
assured	satisfied, confident
astounding	surprising
astray	on wrong path
at maturity	when payment becomes due
at our disposal	for our use
auspicious	favourable
automatic	self-regulating
availability	state of being available

B

background	upbringing, training
banish	drive away
bank transfer	a direct transfer of funds by one bank to another
bankruptcy	inability to pay one's debts
been let down	been treated badly
belongings	movable possessions
bereavement	loss by death
bestow	to give
beyond	at, on or to the farther side
blatant	rough
bond	a binding agreement
bonded store	warehouse for goods liable to customs duty
brochure	a small book or pamphlet
bronchitis	inflammation of windpipe tubes
bulk cargoes	those not packed but loaded loose
buying motive	reason for buying
by instalments	in separate lots
by separate post	by another post

C

c i f Kolkata port named	price covers charges for insurance and transport to the port named
c i f values	values covering cost, insurance and freight
calamity	a disastrous event
captivate	to charm
car-ferry	transportation of cars over narrow water
cargo capacity	maximum amount that can be carried
carriage paid	sender pays for transport
cash against documents	payment made upon delivery of shipping documents
ceaseless	continuous
celebrate	to rejoice on an occasion
celebration offer	an offer to mark the occasion
celestial	of the sky / of heaven
certificate of origin duties	a document entitling importer to preferential customs duties
check our standing	enquire as to our position in business
cherish	to hold as dear
christening	giving a name
clear your account	to pay the balance owing
clearing agent	one who deals with the goods when they arrive
come to light	been discovered
commence	to start

commission house	a commission agency organised as a firm or company
commitment	engagement to carry out certain duties, obligation accepted or undertaken
committing	entrusting
compensate	to make some allowance in return
compensation	an amount that makes up the loss
compensation	making up for
compliment slip	a short printed greetings
compliment	praise
complimentary reference	a few words of praise
comply with	carry out, observe
comprehension	the power to understand
comprehensive	having a wide scope
concert	musical entertainment
concession	a privilege or favour granted, a benefit of some kind
concisely	in a few words
conclusive	final
condolence	sympathy with another's sorrow
conferred	granted
confidence	full trust
confine	restrict
confirm	to state or verify as correct
conform to	to be modelled on
congenial	agreeable
conscientious	careful to do the right thing
conscious	aware
consecutive	unbroken, running together
consequently	as a result
consideration	legal term for "something given"
consignee	the one to whom the goods are sent
consignor	the one who sends the goods
constancy	permanency
constituency	area sending a representative
constitution	structure
consultant	a professional adviser
contended	satisfied
contents	listing of matter that a book contains
contest	to debate
contract	agreement
contribute	to give help, money, etc.
convalescence	gain health after illness
conventional	according to custom

conviction	a strong belief
cordial	hearty
cosy	warm and comfortable
counter offer	an alternative to another person's offer
counter proposal	an alternative to someone's proposal
countermanded	cancelled
couriers	travelling attendants
courteous	polite, considerate
courtesy	polite behaviour
covenant	a clause in a deed (a sealed contract)
cover note	a document giving temporary insurance cover pending issue of policy
cover	the protection provided by insurance
covering letter	a letter enclosing documents
craftsmanship	expert skill in making things
credit standing	financial position
creditable	bringing credit
credit-worthy	believed to be financially sound
crockery	earthenware vessels, plates, etc.
crucial	decisive
current demand	demand at the present time
currently advertised	announced at the present time
currently	at the present time
cut losses	to reduce losses

D

D/A terms	documents against acceptance
D/P terms	documents against payment
damp	humid
deadline	the final date for payment
debenture	a bond bearing interest
debit	an entry of a sum owing
dedicate	to devote
defer payment	to pay later
defer	delay, postpone
deferred rebate	a discount to be allowed later
deferred	delayed
deliberately incurred	done intentionally
delicate	soft, not strong
delighted	pleased
demolition	breaking up, destruction
demonstrate	to show how the machines work
dereliction	neglect of duty

destination	place, point aimed at
deterioration	becoming worse
devaluation	reduction in value
deviate	turn away
diagnose	to determine the nature
diligent	hard working
diminished	lessened, reduced
disappointed	frustrated
discharge	to release
disclaiming	refusing to be responsible for
discount bills	to obtain payment on bills of exchange before the due date at a figure below face value
discretion	freedom of action
dispel any suspicion	to remove doubt
dispense with	to do without
dispose of the consignment	sell the goods
dispute	to contest, to oppose
distasteful	unpleasant
distinction	excellence
distinguished	prominent
distress	pain, difficulty
dividend	profit divided to share-holders
document	reliable paper
domiciled in London	marked as payable in London
draft	a bill of exchange before (or requiring) acceptance
draw on us	send a draft bill of exchange for acceptance
drawee	the person on whom a bill of exchange is drawn
drawer (of a cheque)	the party making the payment
duplicate	an exact copy duplicating
durable	long lasting
duration	time, period

E

eager	strongly desirous
earnest	sincere, serious
effectively	successfully, with good results
efficient	fit, capable
elaborate	complicated
elate	to make highly spirited
election manifesto	public declaration of principles and policies by a ruler, political party
embarrass	cause mental discomfort

en route for	on the way to
endorse	sign on the back
enhance	to increase
ensuing	coming near after
ensures	secures, makes certain
entail	make necessary
entail	to impose
enterprise	activities
enterprise	difficult undertaking
entertainment	amusement
entire	full
entrust	to trust
environment	surroundings
equipment	things needed for a purpose
establish	set up
establish	to fix firmly
esteem	good opinion
esteem	to respect greatly
exaggerate	overstate
exaltation	elevation
exceedingly	very much
exchange control	official controls in the foreign exchange market
exclusive	with the exclusion of all others
executives	management staff
exhilarate	to make joyous
expedite	to speed up
expel	to drive out
explore	to enquire thoroughly exporter's consent
express consent	permission clearly stated
extend	to enlarge
extensive	wide ranging, considerable
extent	range
extinguisher	an appliance for putting out fires
extraordinary	exceptional
extremely	in the utmost degree
exuberate	to abound
exult	to rejoice exceedingly

F

f o r Kanpur	price covers all charges to Kanpur including loading on to train
f o r values	values cover cost of placing goods on board.

factor — one of a number of causes, an agent who deals in his own name and has possession of the goods he has required to sell
fancied — imagined
favourable comment — a few words of praise
favourably — in a favourable manner
felicitate — to congratulate
fervour — earnestness
festival — public celebration
fiance — a betrothed person
fiercely — cruelly
firm conditions — a condition that cannot be varied
firm order — a definite order
first priority — attention before all else
flatter — to praise insincerely
flexible — capable of adjustment
flourishing — prospering
fluent — smooth and ready in speech
forge — to fabricate
forgive — to pardon
formalities — usual or established practices of transacting business
forthcoming — about to happen
forthcoming — available, ready for collection, about to be held
forwarding agents — agents who arrange for transportation of goods
fountain-head — source
fragile — easily broken
fragrance — sweet smell
freight rates — transport charges
freight — the charge made for transporting goods
frequent — occurring often
frighten — to fill with terror
furnish — to equip

G

gaiety — cheerfulness
garbage — rubbish
gay — full of fun
generous — unselfish
genuine — true
gesture — expressive movement
glorious — splendid
gone astray — been lost in transit
gorgeous — magnificent

gratified	pleased
gratitude	thankfulness
grief	deep sorrow
grievance	cause for complaint
gross proceeds	taking before deduction of expenses
grossly	very much, considerably
grudge	ill will
gruff	rough
guaranteed fast colour	guaranteed; not to fade
guarantor	on who agrees to answer for another's debts

H

habitual	customary
hardware	articles of iron, copper, etc.
harmonious	in agreement
harsh	disagreeable
haunt	appear repeatedly
hold our own	maintain our position in the market
honour cheques	to accept and pay out on cheques
honoured	paid when due
household effects	furniture, etc.
hover	remain in one place

I

identical	the very same
immaterial	of no importance
impact	strong impression
impertinent	inapplicable, rude
impression	influence
in full settlement	in complete discharge of the debt
in proportion to	according to
in the field	as an outside representative
in the long run	in the end, eventually
in triplicate	three copies required
inadequate	insufficient
incur	to be responsible for
incur	to bring on oneself
indent	to order goods (especially from abroad), an order especially from abroad
indispensable	absolutely necessary
indistinct	not clear
individual items	items of one kind only
individually examined	each inspected separately

inducement to buy	reason for buying
inevitable	unavoidable
inflation	a rise in the general level of prices
initial cover	the value insured at the beginning
initial publicity	advertising in the early stages
initially	at the beginning
insertions	separate inclusions
inspire customer confidence	encourage a feeling of security
inspire	to bring influence to bear
installation	act of putting apparatus in position
insulation	covering used to retain heat
insurance cover	protection from loss
interrupted	discontinuous
intimate	close
intrusion	an unwelcome act
invariable	unchangeable
investigation	a detailed enquiry
irrespective of their	apart from their total worth; aggregate value
irrevocable credit	a credit that cannot be cancelled without the
irrevocable	cannot be altered or cancelled
irritable	easily annoyed

J

jubilant	shouting with joy
justify	prove to be right

K

keenly	in a keen manner

L

lag behind	to follow slowly
laid professionally	laid by an expert
lavish	profuse, abundant, generous
lax	not strict
leisurely	without haste
let them down	failed in our duty
level headed	having sound common sense
liabilities	responsibilities
liberal	generous, plentiful
limp	not stiff
lines	items
linguist	a person skilled in foreign languages
liquidator	an official appointed to conduct the proceedings for closing down a business

litter	scattered rubbish
livelihood	means of living
load factor	the number of seats occupied
lofty	high
loneliness	isolation
lucrative	profitable

M

magnificent	splendid
maintenance	upkeep, support
manuscript	a document written by hand
maritime	relating to sea
marvellous	astonishing
mass produced	made in large quantities
materialise	to take material shape
maternity	related to child birth
matrimonial	connected with marriage
may not materialize	may not be fulfilled
meagre	scanty
media	methods of advertising
merchandise	articles of commerce
merchandising	trading
merit	worth
meritorious	praise-worthy
minimum	smallest amount
mirthful	jovial
misbehaviour	misconduct
miscreant	villain
mishap	unlucky accident
modify	alter, reorganize
moisture	dampness
monotonous	unchanging
monsoon	rainy season
more competitive	less expensive
mutual arrangement	both parties in agreement

N

neglect	pay no attention
negligence	carelessness
negotiable security	a document representing money, which transfers a secure title to a person who takes it honestly
neighbourhood	adjoining area
nominal	small, inconsiderable

normally	usually
notary public	usually a solicitor specially authorized to witness deeds and other important documents
notify	inform, to make known

O

obnoxious	very disagreeable
obsolescent	becoming out of date
obsolete	no longer used, out of date
obstruct	to block up
obvious	clear
on a sliding scale	varying with the quantity bought
on account	in part payment
on approval	for inspection and return if not wanted
on consignment	for sale on exporter's behalf
on time	punctually
open account terms	credit terms with periodic settlements
opportunities	good chances
opportunity	a good chance
option	the right to accept or refuse
oral notification	a verbal message
outstanding balance	the amount still owing
outstanding	remaining unpaid
over trading	trading especially buying on credit, beyond one's means
overall cost	total cost
overdraft	an amount withdrawn in excess of balance held
overdrawn	withdrawn in excess of balance available
overdue	remaining unpaid, in arrears
overhead	the general expenses of a business
oversight	mistake, omission
overwhelming	cover completely

P

pangs	sharp sudden feelings
particular	special
passing away	death
passing phase	a temporary state of affairs
passionate	with strong feeling
payment on account	part payment
payments on invoice	payment due as invoices are presented
pensive	thoughtful
performance	notable action
periodical	issued at regular intervals

perquisites	casual profit
PhD degree	the degree of Doctorate of Philosophy
pilferage	small thefts
pilgrimage	journey to a sacred place
pledge	promise
possess	own
post retirement	after retirement
potentiality	latent capacity
praiseworthy	laudable
precaution	a protective step taken in advance
preface	introductory statement placed in a book
prefer	to select
preliminary examination	a general first examination
preliminary negotiations	earlier discussions as to terms
preliminary	introductory
premium	the payment made for insurance
prestige	influence, reputation
prior to	before
privilege	special benefit
probation	period of trial
proceedings	going out, going ahead
procure	to obtain with effort
proforma invoice	an invoice sent for information only
project	scheme
prolong	extend
prolonged	lasting a long time
promissory note	a signed promise to pay stated sum of money on a certain date
promote	help to increase
prompted	encouraged, persuaded
promptly	without delay
properties	houses or other buildings
property	premises
proportions	dimensions
proposal form	a written request for insurance cover
prosaic	dull
prospect	expectation
prospective customer	person who may be expected to buy
prospective employer	the possible future employer
prospective	expected, hoped for
prospects	chances of success
provision	a term or condition in an agreement
provisional reservation	subject to confirmation

provisionally	temporarily, liable to be revised
puddle	small dirty pool of rain water
punctual	in time
push your business	engage in energetic selling
push your products	use active selling methods

Q

quarrel	a dispute
quarterly	every quarter of the year
query	a question
quickly spotted	promptly noticed

R

radiant	shining
rally	to assemble
range	representative collection
rash statement	a statement made recklessly
read between the lines	to gather the true meaning
ready sale	a quick sale
real property	land and buildings
rear	back part
reassuring	creating confidence
rebate	a refund, an allowance
rebate	discount
recent	not long before
reciprocate	to return a similar service or favour
rectify	to put right
recur	occur again, are repeated
rediscounting	to discount a bill which is to obtain payment for it before the due date, at a figure below face value
redundant	surplus to requirements
reference sample	a piece taken from the cloth supplied
references	names of persons who may be referred to
reflected	included, covered by
regularly	properly
reject	refuse
rejection	refusal to accept
relative importance	importance in relation to one another
relax	cause to become less rigid
relevant	pertaining to purpose
relieve	to lessen pain or distress
relocated	transferred to other positions
reluctantly compelled	forced unwillingly

reluctantly	unwillingly
reluctantly	with regret
remarkable	attracting attention
reminiscence	recollection
remit	to send money
remittance	a payment (or sum of money) sent
remunerative	profitable
repeat order	successive order for similar goods
representative selection	a selection covering all types
reprimand	rebuke officially
reputable	of good standing or reputation
requirement	need
requisite	required
requisites	things needed
resent	take offence at
reservation fee	the charge for booking a seat
resort to	to turn to, to engage in
resource	means
resources	financial position or means
respectively	relating to each in turn
response	reply
restraint	reserve, free from exaggeration, careful control
revealed	showed, disclosed
revive	to restore
revocable	can be altered or cancelled
reward	something given or received in return for service or merit
rid yourself	free yourself
ripe age	mature age
rippling	flowing in small waves
round off	finish off neatly
routine request	requests of an everyday kind
rung	step of a ladder

S

sagacity	soundness of judgement
sales promotion programmes	schemes for increasing sales
sales talk	complimentary references to the goods
salvage	items that can be recovered
saviour	deliverer
scheduled	according to a programme
scheduled	listed
scold	to rebuke
searching enquiries	a thorough investigation

secured	safe, guaranteed
security	bonds, certificates or other property pledged to cover a debt
selling point	a benefit claimed for a product
sentiments	feelings
serge	a strong twilled (i.e., diagonally lined) cloth
settlement	payment, completion by payment
sewage	waste matter carried in sewers
shirk	to avoid
shower	fall of rain
sight draft	a bill of exchange payable at a fixed time from
sixty days' sight	for payment within sixty days of acceptance
sliding scale	varying with quantity
smallest of margins	a very small profit
solace	comfortable in grief
sole charge	in complete control
sole representatives	the only agents
sole	exclusive, the one and only
solemn	serious looking
special concession	special discounts or other advantages
specialist	a person devoted to one branch of an occupation
specification	a detailed description of material used
speculate	guess, form opinion
spirits	courage
splendid	glorious
sprightly	lively
standard goods	goods not made especially to order
standardized	made to the same size and pattern
standing credit	a credit of fixed amount
standing order	an order to make certain payments at stated times
standing	status, established reputation
statistician	a person skilled in statistics or the study of facts
steep	rising or falling sharply
stenciling	typing on special paper to produce a master for
stereo	three dimensional
stunned	astounded
subject to	reduced by
substantial	considerable in amount
substitutes	goods that take the place of others
suitability	suitableness
supersede	take the place of something else
supplementary	additional
surroundings	environment

sustain	to uphold
syndicates	groups formed for a common purpose

T

tabulate	arrange in a list
tampered with	improperly interfered with
tapped	used for drawing water
tariff	a list of charges
temper	state or condition of mind
tenor of a draft	the period for which a bill of exchange is drawn
terrible	frightful
territory	region or country
testimonial	certificate
testimony	evidence
time basis	charged according to the time taken
to have recourse to law	to take legal action
to realize on our assets	to sell assets in order to raise cash
to the point	relating to the matter dealt with
toilet	a room for dressing self cleaning
token	sign
trade reference	names of traders who may be referred to
tragic	mournful
trample	to tread
transact	conduct, carry on
transit shed	a shed through which goods pass
transit	conveyance
treks	paths
tremendous	astonishingly large
trends	general tendencies
tribute	expression of regard or appreciation
tribute	praise
turnover	total sales
twine	twisted threads
typing pool	a centralized typing system

U

ultimate	last, basic
ultimately	finally
undergo	experience, pass through
undertaking	a promise
undisputed	without dispute
universally acknowledged	accepted by everyone
unqualified	clear, complete

unrivalled	without equal, second to none
unsolicited	not asked for
upkeep	act or cost of support
upliftment	rise
urge	to press urgently

V

vacuum	empty space
valid	hold good, legally binding or in order
valuable	of great value
velveteens	imitation velvet fabrics
venture	an undertaking to which risk is attached, the voyage and its risks
venture	to take risk
verify the claims	to prove the truth of statements made
vice	bad habit
vicinity	nearness, closeness
vigilant	watchful
virtual	being in fact
vital	essential
vital	pertaining to life
void	empty, vacant
voluntarily	of one's own free will
vulgarize	make common or coarse

W

waive	forego, go without
warrant	to guarantee
wastage	loss by waste
well behaved	of good behaviour
well found	based on sound reasons
well-being	welfare
with restraint	without exaggeration
withdraw	to draw back
without notice	no previous advice is necessary
without question	without raising any objection
working capital	the capital needed to keep a business running
worn threadbare	become dull and wearisome
worsen	to get or make worse Job Applications

SECTION - VI

English Thesaurus

English Thesaurus

of over 3300

Alternative & Relative Words

A

aback *(adv.)* back, behind, rearward; suddenly, unexpectedly

abandon *(v.)* forgo, forswear, quit, relinquish; forsake, leave, resign, vacate

abase *(v.)* debase, degrade, disgrace, dishonor, humiliate

abate *(v.)* decline, decrease, diminish, ease, ebb, fade, lower, moderate, slacken, relieve, slow

abbreviate *(v.)* abridge, condense, contract, cut, reduce, shorten, truncate

abdicate *(v.)* abandon, cede, disavow, disclaim, disown, relinquish, renounce, resign, secede

abdomen *(n.)* belly, breadbasket, gut, paunch, potbelly, stomach, tummy

abduct *(v.)* capture, kidnap, seize, shanghai

aberrant *(adj.)* divergent, errant, irregular, straying; abnormal, peculiar, queer, strange, unnatural, unusual, weird

abhor *(v.)* despise, detest, disgust, hate, loathe

ability *(n.)* aptitude, bent, capability, capacity, competence, dexterity, expertise, facility, faculty, knack, proficiency, qualification, skill, talent

abjure *(v.)* forswear, recall, renounce, retract, withdraw

ablaze *(adj.)* aflame, blazing, fiery, flaming; ardent, eager, excited, exhilarated, intense

able *(adj.)* competent, efficient, fit, qualified; accomplished, adroit, dexterous, expert, gifted, ingenious, proficient, talented

abnormal *(adj.)* aberrant, anomalous, deviant, irregular, odd, peculiar, unnatural

abode *(n.)* domicile, dwelling, habitat, house, residence

abolish *(v.)* abrogate, annul, cancel, eliminate, end, eradicate, erase, extinguish, nullify, obliterate

abominable *(adj.)* abhorrent, contemptible, despicable, detestable, disgusting, hateful, horrible, loathsome, offensive, repugnant

aboriginal *(adj.)* domestic, indigenous, local, native, original, primitive

abort *(v.)* annul, cancel, destroy, fail, interrupt, miscarry, nullify, scrap, stop, terminate

abound *(v.)* overflow, pour, swarm, swell, teem

about *(adv.)* referencing, regarding; almost, around, close, near, nigh

above *(adv.)* atop, beyond, over, overhead; preeminent, superior, surpassing

abreast *(adj.)*, *(adv.)* against, aligned; apprised, familiar

abrupt *(adj.)* quick, sharp, unexpected; blunt, boorish, brusque, hasty, impatient, rude

abscond *(v.)* depart, escape, flee

absence *(n.)* dearth, deficiency, need, want; nonattendance, truancy

absentee *(n.)* defector, delinquent, deserter, fugitive, escapee, runaway, truant

absolute *(adj.)* certain, definite, faultless, ideal, sure, unconditional, unquestionable, whole

absolve *(v.)* acquit, clear, discharge, excuse, exonerate, forgive, free, justify, liberate, pardon, release

absorb *(v.)* amalgamate, assimilate, consume, devour, engulf; engage, employ, occupy; grasp, learn, sense

abstain *(v.)* avoid, decline, eschew, forgo, refrain, shun

abstract *(adj.)* conceptual, ideal, hypothetical; apart, separate, special, unrelated; complicated, deep, difficult, obscure

abstruse *(adj.)* complex, difficult, intricate, involved

absurd *(adj.)* foolish, inane, irrational, ludicrous, preposterous, ridiculous, silly

abundant *(adj.)* abounding, copious, flowing, fruitful, opulent, plentiful, prodigal, profuse, prolific, teeming

abuse *(n.)* misuse, defilement, desecration, mistreatment, profanation, subversion, violation

abyss *(n.)* chasm, gorge, gulf, hole, perdition

academic *(adj.)* collegiate, erudite, learned, lettered, literary, scholastic, schooled; established, formalistic; speculative

academy *(n.)* college, conservatory, school

accede *(v.)* acquiesce, agree, allow, assent, comply, consent, grant, permit, sanction

accelerate *(v.)* hasten, expedite, quicken, throttle

accept *(v.)* embrace, take, welcome, affirm, hold, maintain, appreciate, conclude

accessible *(adj.)* approachable, attainable, available, convenient, obtainable, reachable

accessory *(n.)* abettor, accomplice, extra, add-on

accident *(n.)* casualty, misadventure, misfortune, wreck; coincidence, fortune

acclaim *(n.)* accolades, applause, approval, jubilation, plaudits, praise
acclimatize *(v.)* acclimate, adapt, adjust, conform
accolade *(n.)* acknowledgement, esteem, praise, tribute
accommodate *(v.)* fit, harmonize, reconcile, contain, have, hold
accompany *(v.)* chaperon, escort, follow, join, see, show, usher; complement, complete, enhance, supplement
accomplice *(n.)* accessory, affiliate, associate, confederate, conspirator, partner
accomplish *(v.)* achieve, attain, complete, do, effect, execute, fulfill, make, manage, perform, realize
accord *(n.)* agreement, conformity, consent, harmony, peace, unanimity
account *(n.)* anecdote, chronicle, description, explanation, journal, narration, recital, report, story, tale consideration, grounds, motive
accumulate *(v.)* accrue, amass, collect, cumulate, gather, heap, garner, increase, stockpile, store
accusation *(n.)* allegation, charge, complaint, denunciation, indictment, insinuation, slur, smear
accustom *(v.)* familiarize, habituate, inure, season
ace *(n.)* champion, expert, master, specialist
acerbic *(adj.)* bitter, harsh, rough, sharp, sour
ache *(n.)* agony, pain, pang, spasm, twinge
achieve *(v.)* accomplish, fulfill, finish, reach, attain, gain, get, realize, secure
acid *(adj.)* biting, cutting, sarcastic, sardonic, satirical, scornful, sharp, vitriolic
acknowledge *(v.)* admit, agree, allow, appreciate, approve, avow, concede, confess, confirm, declare, endorse, grant, ratify, recognize, reply, respond
acme *(n.)* apex, peak, summit, top, zenith
acquaint *(v.)* inform, accustom, advise, familiarize, reconnoiter, introduce, present
acquiesce *(v.)* assent, accede, accept, agree, bend, comply, concur, consent, rest, submit, yield
acquire *(v.)* attain, earn, gain, get, obtain, procure, secure
acrid *(adj.)* astringent, biting, bitter, caustic, harsh
acropolis *(n.)* bastion, citadel, blockhouse, fort, fortification, redoubt, stronghold
act *(n.)* accomplishment, deed, feat, performance; law, order, resolution, statute, writ
action *(n.)* activity, maneuver, movement, performance; exercise, conduct, response
active *(adj.)* animated, busy, dynamic, energetic, functioning, industrious, lively, living, mobile, moving, operative, spirited, tireless, working
actor *(n.)* artist, entertainer, impersonator, performer, player, thespian, trouper
actual *(adj.)* certain, definite, genuine, sure, true; concrete, material, real, tangible
actuate *(v.)* drive, impel, move, propel, push
acumen *(n.)* cleverness, discernment, insight, intelligence, keenness, sagacity, shrewdness
acute *(adj.)* keen, sharp; critical, crucial, intense, serious; astute, clever, discerning, ingenious, intelligent, keen, penetrating
adage *(n.)* cliché, maxim, motto, proverb, saying, slogan
adamant *(adj.)* firm, fixed, insistent, obstinate, resolute, set, steadfast, stubborn, unbending, unyielding
adapt *(v.)* acclimatize, accustom, adjust, conform, fashion, fit, modify, reconcile, shape, tailor
add *(v.)* annex, append, attach, augment, connect, supplement, unite; compute, figure, increase, sum, tally, total
addict *(n.)* buff, devotee, fan, hound, junkie, lover
add-on *(n.)* improvement, modernization, supplement
address *(n.)* discourse, lecture, oration, sermon; dwelling, house, lodging, residence
adept *(adj.)* able, capable, competent, expert, proficient, skilled
adequate *(adj.)* ample, enough, satisfactory, suitable
adhere *(v.)* attach, cleave, cling, fasten, hold; comply, follow, heed, obey
adjacent *(adj.)* abutting, adjoining, bordering, close, contiguous, near, nearby, neighbouring, touching
adjourn *(v.)* defer, discontinue, dissolve, recess, postpone, suspend
adjure *(v.)* ask, appeal, beg, beseech, entreat, implore, petition, plead, request, supplicate, urge
adjust *(v.)* adapt, alter, calibrate, correct, modify, regulate, tune
administer *(v.)* control, direct, execute, oversee, supervise; distribute, give, parcel
admire *(v.)* esteem, honour, regard, respect, revere, venerate

admit *(v.)* allow, grant, permit; concede, confess, disclose, divulge, expose, reveal
admonish *(v.)* caution, counsel, exhort, reprove, warn
adolescence *(n.)* puberty, pubescence, teens, youth
adopt *(v.)* assume, embrace, espouse, utilize; approve, confirm, endorse, sanction
adoration *(n.)* devotion, idolatry, veneration, worship
adorn *(v.)* beautify, bedeck, decorate, embellish, garnish, festoon, ornament, trim
adult *(adj.)* developed, grown, mature, ripe
adulteration *(n.)* contamination, pollution, taint
adulterer *(n.)* debaucher, lecher, libertine, philanderer, rake, reprobate
advance *(v.)* go, move, proceed, update, upgrade; introduce, propose, present, suggest; encourage, foster, propound; lend
advantage *(n.)* benefit, edge, gain, leverage, profit
adventure *(n.)* undertaking, experience, exploit
advent *(n.)* appearance, arrival, coming
adverse *(adj.)* antagonistic, conflicting, contrary, detrimental, hostile, negative, unfavourable, unfriendly
advertise *(v.)* broadcast, communicate, divulge, exhibit, expose, proclaim, promote, publicize, show
advice *(n.)* counsel, guidance, lesson, suggestion
advocacy *(n.)* adoption, belief, espousal, promotion
advocate *(v.)* advance, bolster, champion, further, promote, recommend, support
aesthetic, aesthetical *(adj.)* artistic, discriminating, elegant, pleasing, polished, refined, tasteful
affable *(adj.)* agreeable, amiable, civil, cordial, courteous, friendly, gracious, obliging, pleasant, sociable
affair (n.) business, circumstance, pursuit; liaison, relationship, rendezvous, tryst; event, function, party
affect *(v.)* alter, change, modify, sway, stir, transform; assume, dissemble, fake, feign
affection *(n.)* devotion, fondness, friendship, liking, love, regard, respect, tenderness, warmth
affidavit *(n.)* affirmation, deposition, oath, testimony
affiliate*(n.)* agent, associate, colleague, partner
affiliation *(n.)* alliance, association, coalition, confederation, connection, federation, pact, union
affinity *(n.)* affection, closeness, fondness; correspondence, likeness, resemblance
affirm *(v.)* assert, claim, maintain, state, swear, testify; approve, endorse, ratify
affix *(v.)* add, append, attach, bind, connect, fasten
afflict *(v.)* ail, beset, distress, hurt, torment
affluence*(n.)* abundance, prosperity, wealth
afford *(v.)* allow, grant, permit, provide, sustain
affront *(v.)* insult, abuse, offend, provoke, slight
afoot *(adj.)* hiking, marching; brewing, happening, hatching, progressing
aforementioned *(adj.)* earlier, former, preceding, prior
afraid *(adj.)* anxious, apprehensive, disquieted, fearful, frightened, scared, shocked, terrified
after *(adj.)*, (ad*v.)* afterward, following, later, subsequent, consequence, outcome, result
age *(n.)* eon, epoch, era, generation, time; adolescence, adulthood, childhood, infancy
agenda *(n.)* aims, goals, program, calendar, list, plan
agent *(n.)* ambassador, attorney, broker, factor, intermediary, proxy, surrogate; agency, cause, instrument, means, method, vehicle
aggrandize *(v.)* amplify, expand, extend, increase; boast, exaggerate, extol, praise
aggravate *(v.)* deepen, exacerbate, heighten, increase, intensify
aggregate *(adj.)* combined, complete, entire, total
aggressor *(n.)* attacker, intruder, invader, trespasser
aghast *(adj.)* appalled, astonished, horrified, shocked
agile *(adj.)* brisk, deft, lithe, lively, nimble, sprightly, vigorous; clever, keen, smart
agitate *(v.)* chum, mix, toss, tumble; discomfit, disquiet, fluster, perturb, ruffle, trouble, upset; argue, dispute
agnostic *(n.)* doubter, non-believer, skeptic, cynic scoffer
agog *(adj.)* anxious, breathless, eager, enthusiastic
agony *(n.)* anguish, distress, misery, pain, suffering, torment, torture
agree *(v.)* accede, acquiesce, allow, assent, concede; correspond, equal, harmonize, match, suit; contract, resolve, settle
agreement *(n.)* bargain, compact, contract, deal, pact, settlement, understanding; compromise, harmony, peace, unity
ahead *(adj.), (adv.)* before, earlier, preceding
aid *(n.)* backing, charity, help, relief, support; aide, assistant, colleague, supporter

alert *(adj.)* ready, aware, attentive, intelligent, wary
alien *(adj.)* different, foreign, strange, unfamiliar
allay *(v.)* calm, alleviate, ease, soothe, lessen
allege *(v.)* assert, attest, declare
alleviate *(v.)* abate, ease, relieve, lessen, soften
alliance *(n.)* union, treaty, marriage
allow *(v.)* approve, grant, let, permit, sanction
alms *(n.)* charity, dole, donation
aloof *(adj.)* cool, detached, distant, reserved
alter *(v.)* change, modify, adjust
altruism *(n.)* benevolence, charity, kindness
amateur *(n.)* beginner, neophyte, novice
amaze *(v.)* astonish, dumfound, stupefy, surprise
ambitious *(adj.)* determined, industrious, intent
ambivalent *(adj.)* uncertain, wavering
amend *(v.)* improve, change, correct
amiss *(adj.)* wrong, faulty, erroneous, imperfect, awry
among (*prep.*) amid, amongst, amidst
amount *(n.)* sum, product; expense, output, outlay; bulk, mass, number
ample *(adj.)* sufficient, plenty, adequate, enough
amuse *(v.)* entertain, divert, cheer, enliven
analyze *(v.)* dissect, examine, investigate
anarchy *(n.)* disorder, turmoil, chaos
ancestor *(n.)* forebear, progenitor, forefather
anchor *(n.)* tie, mooring, support, host
anger *(n.)* ire, wrath, rage, fury, exasperation, irritation
anguish *(n.)* pain, wretchedness, agony
animate *(v.)* activate, vitalize, arouse, energize
annex *(v.)* add, incorporate, append, attach, affix
annoy *(v.)* bother, irritate, pester, trouble
annul *(v.)* invalidate, repeal, revoke, cancel
answer *(v.)* respond, retort, acknowledge, refute, react, rebut; solve, elucidate, clarify
anticipate *(v.)* expect, forecast, predict, assume, await
anxiety *(n.)* concern, trouble, misgiving
apathetic *(adj.)* unemotional, unconcerned, indifferent
appall *(v.)* horrify, amaze, dismay, shock
apparel *(n.)* clothes, attire, suit, dress
apparition *(n.)* ghost, phantom, spirit
appeal *(v.)* beg, urge, petition; attract, interest, engage, tempt
appear *(v.)* emerge, rise, loom, arrive, recur, materialize, show; seem, resemble
appease *(v.)* satisfy, do, serve
appendix *(n.)* supplement, attachment, index, addition
appetite *(n.)* hunger, thirst, craving, longing, desire
applaud *(v.)* approve, cheer, clap, acclaim, praise
appoint *(v.)* name, select, designate, delegate
appreciate *(v.)* acknowledge, honour, praise, admire
apprehension *(n.)* foreboding, trepidation, dread, misgiving, fear
apprentice *(n.)* beginner, student, learner
apprise *(v.)* notify, teach, warn
approach *(n.)* avenue, path, entrance, gate, method, programme, procedure
appropriate *(adj.)* suitable, proper, suited, fitting
approval *(n.)* esteem, favour, admiration; sanction, endorsement, consent, permission
approximate *(adj.)* inexact, imprecise, close
apropos *(adj.)* applicable, appropriate, befitting
aptitude *(n.)* ability, capability, competence, capacity
archaic *(adj.)* antiquated, old, obsolete
ardent *(adj.)* fervent, impassioned, zealous, passionate, enthusiastic
argue *(v.)* dispute, contend, wrangle, bicker, debate
arid *(adj.)* parched, desert, dried, dry, barren
aristocracy *(n.)* nobility, elite, gentry, patricians
aroma *(n.)* smell, fragrance, perfume, odour
arrange *(v.)* order, regulate, systematize, organize
arrival *(n.)* entrance, appearance, landing, visitor, guest, traveller
arrogance *(n.)* insolence, audacity, haughtiness, pride
article *(n.)* writing, essay, editorial, commentary, item, object, substance, commodity, thing
articulate *(v.)* speak, enunciate, pronounce, verbalize; combine, connect, link
artifact *(n.)* antique, heirloom, relic
artistic *(adj.)* imaginative, creative, accomplished, cultured, sensitive, elegant, harmonious
ascend *(v.)* soar, rise, climb, scale
aspect *(n.)* appearance, looks, countenance, face, features, view, perspective, regard, slant, viewpoint
aspiration *(n.)* desire, inclination, ambition
assailant *(n.)* antagonist, foe, enemy, opponent
assassin *(n.)* murderer, slayer, butcher, killer
assault *(n.)* attack, charge, advance, onslaught
assemble *(v.)* convoke, convene, mobilize, gather, collect, construct, erect, join, unite

assent *(n.)* approval, permission, agreement
assert *(v.)* state, say, affirm, declare
asset *(n.)* property, holdings, possessions, capital
assign *(v.)* allocate, allot, earmark; appoint, commission, name, select, deputize, charge, elect
assist *(v.)* aid, support, serve, help
associate *(n.)* comrade, peer, colleague, friend, ally, henchman, confederate, collaborator, teammate
association *(n.)* relationship, friendship, camaraderie, membership, community, recollection, impression, remembrance, organization, union, club
assume *(v.)* suppose, theorize, presuppose, postulate, hypothesize, guess, conjecture, deem, imagine, surmise, opine, estimate, speculate, deduce, infer
assurance *(n.)* guaranty, support, pledge, promise; confidence, conviction, trust, certainty, faith
assure *(v.)* guarantee, aver, attest, convince, prove, persuade, induce
astonishment *(n.)* amazement, bewilderment, wonder
astute *(adj.)* perceptive, shrewd
athletic *(adj.)* hardy, robust, vigorous, powerful
atone *(v.)* compensate, pay
atrocious *(adj.)* cruel, offensive, appalling, horrible
attach *(v.)* adhere, join, connect, append, add; attribute, associate, impute, ascribe, give
attack *(n.)* assault, raid, onslaught, offensive, siege, invasion, incursion; slander, denunciation, blame, illness, seizure, breakdown, relapse
attain *(v.)* achieve, accomplish, arrive, reach, gain
attempt *(v.)* endeavour, strike, venture, try, ratify, affirm, endorse
attention *(n.)* regard, vigilance, heed, alertness, diligence, thoroughness, recognition
attitude *(n.)* air, demeanour, disposition, inclination, nature, temperament, mood, viewpoint
attract *(v.)* draw, pull, drag, bring; allure, entice, lure, charm, fascinate
audacious *(adj.)* bold, daring, shameless
audience *(n.)* interview, spectators, witness, patrons
augment *(v.)* increase, enlarge, expand, magnify
authentic *(adj.)* genuine, real, true, actual
author *(n.)* writer, journalist, columnist, playwright, poet, novelist, essayist
automatic *(adj.)* computerized, self-regulating, automated, involuntary, instinctive, spontaneous, intuitive
auxiliary *(adj.)* subsidiary, secondary, subordinate; supplementary, reserve, supplemental, spare, extra
avarice *(n.)* acquisitiveness, greed, stinginess, meanness
average *(adj.)* ordinary, medium, common
aversion *(n.)* abhorrence, disgust, dislike, loathing
awake *(adj.)* alert, attentive, vigilant; conscious
award *(n.)* citation, honour, scholarship, prize, judgement
awareness *(n.)* discernment, alertness, keenness, attentiveness, perception, apprehension, appreciation
awesome *(adj.)* striking, moving, exalted, grand

B

babble *(n.)* chatter, jabber, twaddle, nonsense
backlog *(n.)* queue, reserve, accumulation, accretion
baggage *(n.)* luggage, gear, trunk, valise, suitcase,
bait *(v.)* entice, attract, draw, fascinate; provoke, torment, anger, nag, bother
balance *(v.)* equalize, even, compensate, adjust, coordinate, equate, match, harmonize
balcony *(n.)* gallery, verandah, terrace
balm *(n.)* salve, lotion, dressing, medicine; comfort, relief, refreshment, remedy
banal *(adj.)* dull, trite, hackneyed, prosaic, trite
bandit *(n.)* highwayman, thief, brigand, robber
banish *(v.)* exile, deport, expel, expatriate, ostracize, outlaw, extradite, isolate
bankrupt *(adj.)* failed, broke, ruined, insolvent
barbarian *(n.)* savage, brute, beast
bare *(adj.)* bald, naked, unadorned, simple, modest; barren, void, unfurnished
bargain *(n.)* agreement, pact, compact, contract, deal; discount, reduction, steal, giveaway
barrier *(n.)* obstruction, hindrance, obstacle, hurdle, restriction, restraint, impediment, barricade
bashful *(adj.)* retiring, reserved, timid, modest, shy
basis *(n.)* foundation, justification, explanation, background, source, authority, principle, grounds
bask *(v.)* relax, enjoy, wallow
beam *(v.)* radiate, glitter, glare; grin, laugh, smirk
bear *(v.)* tolerate, undergo, endure, support, sustain
beastly *(adj.)* brutal, savage, coarse, depraved, loathsome, vile, foul, base, disgusting, vulgar

beat *(v.)* bash, pulsate, pound, thump, pulse, throb; overcome, conquer, defeat
bedlam *(n.)* pandemonium, clamour, confusion, noise
befall *(v.)* occur, happen, transpire
begin *(v.)* initiate, start, inaugurate, launch, mount, create, institute, introduce, originate, found, establish, commence, arise
behaviour *(n.)* conduct, performance, ways, manner
belief *(n.)* opinion, feeling, conviction
believe *(v.)* trust, accept, think
belligerent *(adj.)* warlike, pugnacious, hostile
beloved *(adj.)* cherished, loved, adored, worshipped, idolized, precious, prized, treasured, favoured
benefit *(v.)* help, aid, serve, profit
benevolence *(n.)* altruism, charity, kindness
bequeath *(v.)* grant, give, endow, bestow
beseech *(v.)* ask, implore, beg, solicit
best *(adj.), (adv.)* first, greatest, finest, incomparable, unrivalled, unequalled, inimitable, foremost
bestow *(v.)* bequeath, present, offer, give, endow
betray *(v.)* delude, trick, deceive, divulge, disclose
bewilder *(v.)* confound, disconcert, puzzle, confuse
bewitch *(v.)* charm, enchant, fascinate, captivate
bias *(n.)* prejudice, partiality, preference, inclination
bind *(v.)* attach, adhere, fasten; oblige, compel, force; shackle, fetter, leash, restrict, hitch, yoke, tether; join, unite, connect
biography *(n.)* memoir, journal, autobiography, life
bite *(n.)* taste, morsel, nibble
bitter *(adj.)* acrid, astringent, intense, harsh, severe; sarcastic, acrimonious, caustic, biting
bizarre *(adj.)* unusual, unexpected, fantastic, grotesque
blame *(v.)* charge, condemn, denounce, disparage
blatant *(adj.)* clear, obvious, plain
blemish *(n.)* flaw, defect, stain, imperfection, dent
blind *(adj.)* unseeing, unaware; closed, obstructed, blocked; accidental, unplanned, aimless
blithe *(adj.)* gay, lighthearted, vivacious
block *(n.)* chunk, slab, cake, clod, hunk; barrier, obstruction, hindrance, bar, obstacle
bloom *(n.)* blossom, floweret, glow, blush, flush
blotch *(n.)* stain, blemish, mark, patch
blow *(v.)* blast, fan; flutter, waft, whisk, flap, wave, buffet; pipe, toot, waste, squander; miss, flounder, miscarry
bluff *(n.)* hill, cliff, precipice, steep, mountain; deception, trick, ruse, delusion
blunt *(adj.)* dull, unsharpened, unpointed, round; abrupt, brusque, curt, bluff, rude
boast *(n.)* brag, pretension, self-satisfaction, bravado
body *(n.)* fuselage, hull, skeleton; society, organization; collection, reservoir, supply, variety; anatomy, physique, figure, build, corpse, cadaver, carcass, mummy, remains
bog *(n.)* marsh, swamp, wetlands
boisterous *(adj.)* rowdy, uproarious, noisy, loud, rude
bold *(adj.)* daring, courageous, intrepid, fearless, audacious, presumptuous, strong, clear, plain, definite
bombastic *(adj.)* high-sounding, pompous
bond *(n.)* attachment, connection, affiliation, friendship, debenture, security, warranty, certificate; surety, guaranty, warrant
boost *(n.)* assistance, aid, help; addition, advance, hike
border *(n.)* edge, hem, end, trim, decoration, fringe, margin, boundary, frontier, outpost, perimeter
boredom *(n.)* apathy, doldrums, listlessness, monotony, tedium, indifference
borrow *(v.)* take, sponge, bum, beg, chisel, mooch
bottom *(n.)* underside, base, foot; depths, bed, floor impertinence, audacity
boulevard *(n.)* street, avenue, highway, road
bound *(v.)* leap, spring, vault, jump; ricochet, recoil; limit, restrict, confine, circumscribe
boundary *(n.)* border, rim, bounds, extremity, periphery, extent, limit
bounteous *(adj.)* abundant, lavish, plentiful
bow *(v.)* stoop, yield, submit, surrender, acquiesce, capitulate
boycott *(v.)* ostracize, avoid, strike
brackish *(adj.)* salty, disagreeable, tainted
brain *(n.)* intellect, genius, mentality; scholar, egg-head, intellectual
brand *(n.)* mark, scar, welt, earmark, trademark
brave *(adj.)* fearless, daring, dauntless, valiant, intrepid, bold, unafraid
brawl *(v.)* fight, quarrel, squabble
breach *(n.)* break, opening, rupture, violation, infringement, transgression, crime

break *(n.)* fracture, split, rupture; pause, intermission, interim; accident, opportunity
breathe *(v.)* respire, inhale, exhale, gasp, pant
brevity *(n.)* conciseness, shortness, terseness
bribe *(v.)* corrupt, influence, entice, tempt
bridge *(n.)* structure, connection, bond, tie, joint
bright *(adj.)* quick-witted, intelligent, clever, alert; clear, sunny, fair; lively, cheerful, vivacious, luminous, lustrous, sparkling, illuminated
brilliant *(adj.)* sparkling, shining, dazzling, gleaming, bright, talented, profound, intelligent
brim *(n.)* rim, margin, border, edge
brisk *(adj.)* keen, invigorating, stimulating, active
bristle *(n.)* hair, fibre, quill, point
broad *(adj.)* cosmopolitan, cultivated, experienced, cultured; large, extensive, spacious, expansive, roomy, tolerant, progressive, unbiased, liberal
brochure *(n.)* handout, circular, pamphlet, folder
broken *(adj.)* busted, faulty, fractured, shattered, smashed, damaged, cracked; irregular, incoherent
brood *(v.)* pine, grieve, fret, sulk, mope, muse, worry
browse *(v.)* skim, peruse, scan, inspect, examine
brush *(v.)* clean, sweep, whisk, wipe; stroke, smooth, graze
brutal *(adj.)* pitiless, harsh, unmerciful, cruel
budge *(v.)* stir, shift, move
budget *(n.)* projection, estimate, allocation, plan, funds
buffoon *(n.)* clown, jester, fool, jerk
bulge *(n.)* swelling, protuberance, bump, prominence
bull *(n.)* steer, calf, ox, cow; nonsense, balder, dash, rubbish, trash
bully *(n.)* ruffian, rowdy, tough, rascal
bunch *(n.)* cluster, clump, group, sheaf, tuft, shock, bundle, knot, collection
bungalow *(n.)* cottage, house, lodge
bunk *(n.)* berth, cot, pallet; rubbish, rot, hogwash, nonsense
burden *(v.)* hinder, encumber, hamper, strain, load, tax, try, trouble, oppress
burglar *(n.)* thief, housebreaker, robber, criminal
burial *(n.)* interment, funeral, entombment
burlesque *(v.)* imitate, mock, satirize
burly *(adj.)* strong, muscular, hefty
burn *(v.)* ignite, kindle, incinerate, blaze, scorch
burst *(v.)* explode, erupt, rupture, disintegrate; break, crack, split, fracture, destroy
butcher *(v.)* slaughter, slay, kill; ruin, mutilate, spoil, botch, destroy
buzz *(v.)* hum, drone, whirr

C

cabin *(n.)* house, cottage, hut, home, shelter
cacophony *(n.)* dissonance, noise, din, racket
cafe *(n.)* coffeehouse, restaurant, cafeteria, lunchroom
cajole *(v.)* appeal, wheedle, coax, beguile
calculate *(n.)* count, measure, reckon, enumerate, determine, forecast, weigh, gauge, compute, cipher
callous *(adj.)* heartless, indifferent, unfeeling, hardened, insensitive
camouflage *(v.)* conceal, cover, veil, disguise, hide
cancel *(v.)* invalidate, rescind, repeal, retract, void
candid *(adj.)* sincere, open, frank, honest
canny *(adj.)* cautious, watchful, shrewd
capable *(adj.)* proficient, competent, able, intelligent
capsize *(v.)* overturn, invert, tip over, upset
captivate *(v.)* attract, charm, fascinate, bewitch
capture *(v.)* take, hold, seize, apprehend, arrest
care *(n.)* concern, regard, precaution, wariness, vigilance, custody, keeping, watch
career *(n.)* work, occupation, vocation, job, profession
caress *(v.)* touch, love, embrace, cuddle, pat
caricature *(v.)* mimic, ridicule, satirize
carnal *(adj.)* fleshly, worldly, sensuous, lewd
carnival *(n.)* merrymaking, festival, fair, entertainment
carry *(v.)* convey, transfer, cart, take, bring, haul, transfer, relay, support, bear, sustain, shoulder
cast *(n.)* facsimile, replica, copy; actors, players, company, troupe; appearance, aspect
caste *(n.)* position, status, birth
catalogue *(n.)* register, directory, index, classification
cause *(n.)* condition, circumstances; goal, motive, foundation, basis, reason
caution *(n.)* discretion, care, heed, prudence, warning
cavil *(v.)* criticize, object, complain

cede *(v.)* relinquish, surrender, yield
celebrate *(v.)* commemorate, observe, consecrate, honour, rejoice, revel
celibate *(adj.)* unmarried, abstaining, single, pure
cemetery *(n.)* churchyard, necropolis, catacomb, tomb, vault, crypt, sepulcher, graveyard, mortuary
censor *(n.)* restrict, suppress, withhold, expurgate
census *(n.)* count, enumeration, tabulation, tally
center *(n.)* middle, nucleus, core, heart; hub, metropolis, plaza, mart; essence
cerebral *(adj.)* brainy, intelligent
ceremony *(n.)* function, commemoration, celebration, rite, observance, ritual, formality, custom, tradition
certain *(adj.)* assured, positive, untroubled, confident, conclusive, incontrovertible, irrefutable, true, unmistakable; fixed, settled, concluded, definite
certificate *(n.)* document, warrant, credentials, certification, document, warranty, guarantee
cessation *(n.)* ending, stopping
challenge *(v.)* compete, defy, denounce, invite, dare, threaten, question, dispute, enquire, ask, doubt
champion *(n.)* conqueror, victor, hero
chance *(v.)* risk, venture, stake, hazard, wager, jeopardize, speculate
change *(v.)* make different, vary, alter, transform, changeable, turn; become different, evolve, transform, adapt, moderate, adjust; displace, supplant, transpose; undress, disrobe
chant *(n.)* recitation, chorus, incantation
character *(n.)* symbol, mark, sign, figure, emblem; temperament, nature, attribute, characteristic; crank, nut, oddball, weirdo
charge *(v.)* price, cost, blame, attack, assail, assault, invade
chase *(v.)* pursue, trail, track, seek, hunt
chastise *(v.)* scold, discipline, spank, punish
cheap *(adj.)* inexpensive, competitive, reasonable, economical; shoddy, poor
check *(v.)* control, bridle, repress, inhibit, neutralize, restrain; examine, review, monitor, investigate circumspect
cheer *(v.)* hearten, console, brighten, comfort, encourage, help; applaud, shout, salute, support, yell
chest *(n.)* breast, thorax, bosom, peritoneum, ribs; box, case, coffer, cabinet, strongbox, crate
chide *(v.)* scold, reprimand, lecture
chore *(n.)* task, routine, errand, job
chunk *(n.)* lump, piece, mass, part
churn *(v.)* stir, beat, mix, agitate
circular *(adj.)* spherical, cyclical, globular, round
circumvent *(v.)* avoid, bypass, dodge, elude, evade
clamour *(n.)* outcry, din, discord, noise, uproar
clandestine *(adj.)* covert, furtive, secret, sly
clasp *(n.)* fastener, buckle, pin, clamp
classify *(u.)* arrange, order, pigeonhole, organize, categorize, label, catalogue, tag, sort, index
clean *(adj.), (adv.)* pure, unadulterated, undefiled, spotless, cleansed; clear-cut, sharp, readable; complete, entire, total, absolute
clear *(adj.), (adv.)* obvious, explicit, plain, manifest; transparent, translucent; unclouded, sunny, bright, fair; exonerated, absolved
clever *(adj.)* skillful, apt, expert, adroit, able; intelligent, smart, bright, shrewd
cliche *(n.)* slogan, banality, triviality, motto
climax *(n.)* crisis, peak, culmination, zenith, summit
clog *(v.)* obstruct, impede, seal, close, hinder
close *(v.)* conclude, finish, terminate; seal, shut, clog, block, bar, dam, cork; come together, connect, meet, unite, agree, join; shut, slam, fasten, bolt, clench, bar, shutter, lock
clot *(v.)* thicken, coagulate, set, lump
clumsy *(adj.)* ungainly, gawky, inexpert, awkward
clutter *(n.)* disarray, jumble, disorder, confusion
coalition *(n.)* union, group, association, faction
coarse *(adj.)* rough, unrefined, crude; vulgar, low, common, base, obscene, rude
coax *(v.)* cajole, wheedle, inveigle, influence, urge
coerce *(v.)* force, compel, impel, constrain
cognizance *(n.)* knowledge, awareness, understanding
coincide *(v.)* correspond, match, agree
cold *(adj.)* windy, cool, freezing, frosty, frigid, nippy, brisk, numbing, raw; unfriendly, indifferent, reserved
collapse *(v.)* drop, deflate, fall, fail
collect *(v.)* consolidate, amass, accumulate, concentrate; congregate, assemble, flock, gather
collide *(v.)* hit, strike, crash, clash, disagree, oppose
colossal *(adj.)* large, huge, enormous, immense
combat *(n.)* conflict, battle, struggle, warfare, fight

comic, comical *(adj.)* funny, silly, humorous, ironic
commemorate *(v.)* honour, solemnize, memorialize
commensurate *(adj.)* equivalent, comparable
commentary *(n.)* criticism, analysis, interpretation
commission *(n.)* authority, license, permission; committee, representatives, board; payment, fee
commit *(v.)* perpetrate, complete, perform; entrust, delegate, promise, charge, employ, dispatch
commotion *(n.)* disturbance, tumult, uproar
communicate *(v.)* impart, inform, tell, confer, talk, converse, chat, write
compact *(adj.)* small, light, dense
companion *(n.)* comrade, escort, chaperon, bodyguard
compare *(v.)* relate, associate, link, correlate; examine, contrast, weigh, analyze
compassion *(n.)* concern, sympathy, pity
compel *(v.)* force, enforce, constrain, coerce
compete *(v.)* strive, struggle, oppose, clash, encounter
compile *(v.)* gather, collect, assemble, accumulate
complacent *(adj.)* self-satisfied, egotistic, happy, smug
complex *(adj.)* combined, compounded; convoluted, intricate, complicated, tortuous, knotty
complexion *(n.)* colouration, tinge, cast, pigmentation
complicate *(v.)* snarl, confound, jumble, tangle
composure *(n.)* self-control, calmness, poise, aplomb
comprehend *(v.)* understand, grasp, discern, perceive
compulsory *(adj.)* obligatory, requisite, necessary
conceal *(v.)* cover, screen, secrete, hide
concede *(v.)* acknowledge, grant, yield, admit, allow
conceit *(n.)* arrogance, narcissism, vanity
concern *(v.)* relate, influence; bother, worry
conclude *(v.)* close, terminate, finish, complete, achieve; deduce, presume, reason, gather, assume
concoct *(v.)* make, devise, plot, hatch
condemn *(v.)* doom, sentence, damn, convict, punish
condition *(n.)* stipulation, provision; tone, shape; circumstance, situation, position, status; limitation, restriction, qualification, restraint; illness, ailment, infirmity
conduct *(n.)* behaviour, deportment, demeanour, manner
conference *(n.)* meeting, discussion, gathering
confess *(v.)* acknowledge, own, concede, admit
confidant *(n.)* friend, adherent, companion
confident *(adj.)* assured, fearless, dauntless, bold
confirm *(v.)* ratify, affirm, settle, approve, endorse; prove, validate, verify, authenticate, explain
confound *(v.)* bewilder, befuddle, puzzle, perplex, fluster, embarrass, disconcert, baffle, mystify
congenial *(adj.)* friendly, compatible, harmonious
connoisseur *(n.)* critic, expert, judge
connotation *(n.)* implication, meaning, insinuation
conscience *(n.)* duty, morals, shame
consent *(v.)* accede, acquiesce, agree, allow, approve
conservative *(adj.)* cautious, reserved, conventional
considerable *(adj.)* important, noteworthy, significant; substantial, abundant, lavish, bountiful
consistent *(adj.)* constant, rational, regular
console *(v.)* comfort, cheer, gladden, encourage
conspicuous *(adj.)* obvious, striking, prominent, flagrant, noticeable
conspiracy *(n.)* plan, intrigue, collusion, connivance
constitute *(v.)* develop, create, establish; make up, frame, compound, compose
constraint *(n.)* coercion, compulsion, pressure; shyness, bashfulness, restraint, reserve
construct *(v.)* build, erect, make, fabricate, create
consumer *(n.)* user, customer, shopper, buyer
contagious *(adj.)* communicable, infectious, spreading, epidemic, deadly, endemic, catching
contemplate *(v.)* study, ponder, consider, muse, think
contempt *(n.)* disdain, disrespect, scorn, derision
contest *(n.)* competition, trial, match, challenge, game
continue *(v.)* endure, persevere, progress; renew, reinstate, reestablish
contract *(v.)* pledge, bargain, stipulate, obligate; diminish, shrink, recede, condense, compress, decrease; catch, get, incur
contrary *(adj.)* antagonistic, hostile, counter; contradictory, unpropitious; willful, headstrong, stubborn
contrive *(v.)* create, devise, scheme, improvise, invent

controversy *(n.)* contention, debate, quarrel, difference
convenient *(adj.)* accessible, available, handy, close
conventional *(adj.)* accepted, customary, typical, commonplace, traditional, formal
converse *(v.)* speak, talk, visit
convey *(v.)* transport, transfer, communicate, send
convict *(n.)* captive, felon, criminal, prisoner
convince *(v.)* persuade, establish, satisfy, teach
cooperate *(v.)* conspire, participate, agree
copy *(v.)* mimic, ape; reproduce, duplicate, counterfeit, forge, depict, portray
corporeal *(adj.)* material, tangible, physical
corpse *(n.)* body, carcass, remains, cadaver
correspond *(v.)* compare, match, resemble, conform; communicate, write, reply, answer
corrupt *(adj.)* immoral, underhanded, fraudulent, crooked, nefarious, unscrupulous, shady, dishonest
costly *(adj.)* expensive, splendid, precious
council *(n.)* group, cabinet, directorate, committee
counsel *(n.)* advice, guidance, instruction, suggestion; adviser, lawyer, attorney, barrister
countenance *(n.)* appearance, aspect, face, features
counter *(v.)* react, respond, oppose, restrict
counter *(n.)* board, shelf, ledge, bench, table
countless *(adj.)* innumerable, incalculable, infinite
coup *(n.)* feat, achievement, exploit
courage *(n.)* valour, boldness, spirit, audacity, mettle, stoutheartedness, gallantry, daring, spunk, strength
courteous *(adj.)* well-mannered, courtly, affable, polite
cover *(v.)* envelop, enshroud, encase; shield, screen, house, shelter; mask, disguise; embrace, comprise, incorporate; traverse, cross; drench, engulf; recount, narrate, relate, broadcast, record
coy *(adj.)* shy, demur, evasive, bashful, humble
craft *(n.)* occupation, career, work, job; proficiency, competence, aptitude, ability
cramp *(n.)* spasm, crick, pang, pain
crank *(n.)* bracket, bend, arm, handle; eccentric, character, complainer, grouch
crate *(n.)* box, carton, cage, container, package
craving *(n.)* need, longing, yearning, desire
create *(v.)* originate, build, fashion, shape, fabricate
creative *(adj.)* imaginative, inventive, artistic, original
credibility *(n.)* likelihood, probability, chance
creed *(n.)* belief, doctrine, dogma, faith
creep *(v.)* slither, writhe, crawl
crevice *(n.)* crack, chasm, cleft, slit, gap
crime *(n.)* transgression, wrongdoing, offense, violation
crisis *(n.)* plight, predicament, trauma, pickle
critic *(n.)* reviewer, commentator, analyst, examiner; detractor, complainer, mud-slinger
criticize *(v.)* evaluate, study, analyze, examine; chastise, reprove, reprimand, blame
crook *(n.)* criminal, swindler, thief, rogue; notch, fork, angle, bend
crop *(v.)* trim, cut, clip
cross *(v.)* intersect, divide, traverse, span; mingle, mix
crucial *(adj.)* critical, decisive, climatic, deciding; severe, trying, taxing, hard, difficult
crush *(v.)* subdue, defeat, overwhelm, annihilate; smash, pulverize, powder, grind
cry *(v.)* weep, sob, wail, sorrow, grieve
cuddle *(v.)* embrace, snuggle, huddle, nestle
cue *(n.)* signal, hint, prompt
culminate *(v.)* finish, close, end
culture *(n.)* convention, custom, mores; breeding, gentility, manners
cunning *(adj.)* sly, crafty, clever, skillful, ingenious
curious *(adj.)* inquisitive, interested, enquiring, questioning; strange, odd, rare, queer, unique
current *(adj.)* prevailing, contemporary, fashionable
current *(n.)* drift, flow, tide
custodian *(n.)* caretaker, attendant, gatekeeper
cut *(v.)* shorten, curtail, lessen, decrease; separate, cleave; cross, intersect, pass
cynic *(n.)* skeptic, mocker, scoffer, detractor, critic

D

dainty *(adj.)* delicate, fragile, petite, airy, lacy, cute
danger *(n.)* risk, peril, jeopardy, threat, menace
dangle *(v.)* hang, droop, sway, suspend
dare *(v.)* undertake, endeavour, hazard, risk, try; defy, confront, oppose, brave, challenge, face
dark *(adj.)* sinister, evil, gloomy, dismal, immoral, corrupt; unlit, dim, shadowy, somber, indistinct, dusky, murky, gloomy, obscure, shady, hazy
dart *(n.)* missile, barb, arrow, weapon

dash *(v.)* race, sprint, speed, hurry, run; smash, dampen, dismay, dispirit

date *(n.)* appointment, rendezvous, engagement, call, visit; companion, partner, friend, lover

dazzle *(v.)* blind, amaze, awe, astonish

deal *(n.)* agreement, pledge, pact, contract

debate *(v.)* discuss, contend, contest, dispute, argue

debris *(n.)* remains, rubble, rubbish, wreckage, trash

debt *(n.)* obligation, liability, mortgage, note

deceit *(n.)* misrepresentation, trickery, fraud, duplicity, deception, dishonesty

decent *(adj.)* seemly, respectable, nice, proper, ethical, virtuous, trustworthy, upright, good

decipher *(v.)* interpret, decode, translate, explain, solve

declare *(v.)* state, assert, tell, affirm, maintain, testify, certify, contend, allege, profess, swear

decorate *(v.)* adorn, beautify, renovate, brighten, enhance, embellish, elaborate

decrease *(v.)* lessen, diminish, decline, subside, shrink, reduce, check, curb, restrain, blunt, curtail

decree *(n.)* proclamation, edict, pronouncement, declaration, judgement

dedicate *(v.)* devote, apportion, assign

deed *(n.)* act, commission, accomplishment; document, release, agreement, charter, title

defeat *(v.)* conquer, overcome, vanquish, subdue, overthrow, crush, overwhelm, repulse, decimate

defend *(v.)* protect, shield, shelter, screen; justify, plead, alibi, endorse, recommend, support

defense *(n.)* resistance, protection, security, backing; denial, alibi, explanation, justification, proof

defiance *(n.)* insubordination, rebellion, insurgence, disobedience

deficit *(n.)* shortage, paucity, deficiency, lack

define *(v.)* limit, bound, confine, circumscribe, edge; describe, designate, characterize, represent, exemplify, explain, name

definite *(adj.)* exact, fixed, precise, positive, decisive, specific, categorical; clear, sharp, distinct, unmistakable, obvious, plain; sure, certain

deform *(v.)* damage, disfigure, deface, injure

degrade *(v.)* disgrace, debase, demote, discredit, diminish, humble

degree *(n.)* gradation, size, dimension, gauge; extent, quality, potency, proportion, intensity, scope; doctorate

deify *(v.)* exalt, idealize, worship

deity *(n.)* god, divinity, divine, celestial

delay *(v.)* postpone, defer, deter, impede, detain, check, curb, procrastinate, suspend, interrupt

delegate *(n.)* legate, emissary, proxy, deputy, minister, ambassador, agent, representative

deliberate *(adj.)* intentional, conscious, studied, planned, willful, considered, calculated, intended, purposeful, premeditated, designed, unhurried

delicate *(adj.)* fine, dainty, fragile, frail, subtle, tactful; susceptible, feeble, weak

delight *(n.)* enjoyment, joy, pleasure, happiness

delight *(v.)* fascinate, amuse, please, entertain

delirious *(adj.)* demented, crazy, irrational, insane

deliver *(v.)* produce, provide; liberate, save; pass, remit, give; present, address; allot, dispense

delude *(v.)* mislead, deceive, fool, trick

deluge *(v.)* flood, overwhelm, overrun

demented *(adj.)* crazy, bemused, unbalanced, insane

demonstrate *(v.)* prove, show, confirm; illustrate, exhibit, manifest, parade, display

demoralize *(v.)* dishearten, confuse, weaken, unman, enfeeble, discourage

denounce *(v.)* condemn, accuse, charge, blame, revile, reproach, rebuke, scorn, reprimand

deny *(v.)* contradict, disagree, disavow, disclaim, repudiate, controvert, renounce

depart *(v.)* leave, go, quit, withdraw

dependent *(adj.)* poor, immature, clinging, conditional

depict *(v.)* represent, picture, portray

deplorable *(adj.)* tragic, distressing, dreadful

depress *(v.)* squash, flatten; dismay, dampen, sadden, deject, oppress, discourage

deprive *(v.)* strip, despoil, divest, seize

deranged *(adj.)* disturbed, demented, crazy, insane

derelict *(adj.)* abandoned, negligent, delinquent

deride *(v.)* mock, ridicule, scorn, jeer

derivation *(n.)* root, source, beginning, origin

derive *(v.)* obtain, determine, conclude, assume

derivative *(adj.)* borrowed, learned, copied

derogatory *(adj.)* disparaging, belittling, faultfinding, detracting, critical, sarcastic

descent *(n.)* drop, sinking, reduction, tumble, decline, fall; slide, inclination; extraction, origin, lineage, family

describe *(v.)* recount, portray, depict, picture, specify, illustrate, name, define, explain
desert *(n.)* waste, wastelands, wilderness
desert *(v.)* abandon, defect, leave
deserve *(v.)* merit, earn, rate
design *(n.)* plan, schematic, rendering, pattern, layout, diagram, drawing, sketch, blueprint, plan
desire *(n.)* aspiration, longing, craving, lust, wish, mania, hunger, yearning, hankering, itch, passion
desolate *(adj.)* forsaken, dreary, deserted, uninhabited, abandoned, isolated, disconsolate, forlorn
despair *(n.)* hopelessness, depression, discouragement, desperation, gloom
despicable *(adj.)* detestable, contemptible, abject, base
destiny *(n.)* fate, future, fortune, doom
destitute *(adj.)* lacking, impoverished, poverty, penniless, poor
destroy *(v.)* ruin, demolish, raze, eradicate, annihilate, obliterate, extinguish, finish
detach *(v.)* disconnect, remove, separate, divide
detect *(v.)* distinguish, recognize, identify, discover
deter *(v.)* discourage, caution, dissuade, prevent, warn
detest *(v.)* dislike, loathe, abhor, despise, hate
devastate *(v.)* ravage, sack, pillage, destroy
develop *(v.)* enlarge, expand, extend, promote, cultivate, intensify; grow, mature, evolve; unfold, disclose, unravel, uncover, explain
deviate *(v.)* deflect, digress, wander, stray, differ
device *(n.)* apparatus, instrument, contrivance, mechanism, appliance, contraption, implement, utensil, gadget; artifice, scheme, design, dodge, trick, ruse, plan, technique
devoid *(adj.)* lacking, empty, void
devote *(v.)* assign, apply, consecrate, bless, dedicate
devour *(v.)* eat, gulp, swallow, gorge, absorb
diabolical *(adj.)* fiendish, wicked, tricky
dialect *(n.)* idiom, jargon, cant, vernacular, patois
diatribe *(n.)* tirade, denunciation
dictator *(n.)* ruler, autocrat, despot, tyrant, oppressor
die *(v.)* expire, perish, succumb, croak; fade, ebb, wither, decay, weaken, vanish
difference *(n.)* deviation, departure, exception; divergence, opposition, dissimilarity, diversity, departure, differentiation, contrast
difficult *(adj.)* strenuous, exacting, arduous, laboured, demanding, onerous, challenging, exacting, formidable; involved, perplexing, puzzling, mystifying, bewildering, profound, complicated, deep, ambiguous, obscure
diffident *(adj.)* shy, insecure, reserved
digest *(v.)* summarize, recap; absorb, consume; learn, study
dignity *(n.)* poise, bearing, air, stateliness, splendour, majesty, class, pride
digress *(v.)* stray, deviate, wander
dilemma *(n.)* predicament, quandary, difficulty
diligence *(n.)* earnestness, perseverance, industry, vigour, carefulness, intensity, attention, care
dilute *(v.)* thin, weaken, add, mix, reduce
dingy *(adj.)* drab, dirty, grimy, muddy, soiled
diplomat *(n.)* ambassador, consul, minister, legate, emissary, envoy, agent, representative, statesman
dire *(adj.)* serious, desperate, dreadful, terrible, horrible, frightful
disability *(n.)* feebleness, incapacity, injury, weakness
disadvantage *(n.)* obstacle, restraint, inconvenience, drawback, weakness
disagree *(v.)* differ, dissent, object, oppose, quarrel
disappear *(v.)* fade, die, escape, evaporate, vanish
disappoint *(v.)* dissatisfy, disillusion, frustrate, mis carry, thwart, foil, baffle
disapprove *(v.)* condemn, chastise, reprove, denounce
disaster *(n.)* calamity, mishap, debacle, misadventure, defeat, failure, tragedy, cataclysm, catastrophe
disburse *(v.)* pay, expend, use, contribute, spend
discard *(v.)* reject, expel, dispossess, relinquish
discharge *(v.)* remove, unpack, empty; release, liberate, free, fire
discipline *(v.)* train, control; punish, chastise, correct
disclose *(v.)* reveal, confess, publish
discomfort *(n.)* annoyance, uneasiness, trouble, displeasure, embarrassment
disconnect *(v.)* detach, separate, disengage, cut, divide
discontinue *(v.)* stop, end, finish, close, cease
discord *(n.)* conflict, strife, contention, disagreement

discourse *(v.)* converse, write, speak
discover *(v.)* invent, ascertain, detect, recognize, determine, observe, uncover, find, learn
discreet *(adj.)* prudent, cautious, discerning, reserved, wary, watchful, circumspect, politic, diplomatic
discrepancy *(n.)* variance, inconsistency, conflict
discrete *(adj.)* unconnected, distinctive, separate
discretion *(n.)* caution, wariness, prudence, tact
discriminate *(v.)* differentiate, separate, distinguish
discuss *(v.)* talk, argue, debate, dispute, confer, reason
disease *(n.)* sickness, malady, ailment, illness
disfigure *(v.)* deface, mar, mutilate, damage, hurt
disgraceful *(adj.)* dishonorable, disreputable, shocking, offensive, shameful
disguise *(n.)* mask, costume, masquerade, facade
disgust *(v.)* offend, repel, revolt, nauseate, sicken, shock, upset, disturb
disheveled *(adj.)* untidy, rumpled, unkempt
dishonour *(n.)* shame, ignominy, abasement, disgrace
disinclined *(adj.)* hesitant, reluctant, unwilling
dislike *(v.)* detest, deplore, abhor, hate, abominate, loathe, despise, scorn
dismal *(adj.)* dreary, bleak, gloomy, melancholy, desolate, morbid, ghastly, gruesome, cheerless, dusky, dingy, murky, bleak, somber, creepy, spooky
dismantle *(v.)* disassemble, undo, demolish, ruin, raze, destroy
dismiss *(v.)* reject, repudiate, disperse, expel, abolish, dispossess, exile, expatriate, banish, deport
disparage *(v.)* discredit, belittle, dismiss
dispatch *(v.)* transmit, express, forward; finish, conclude, kill
dispense *(v.)* distribute, apportion, assign, allocate
disperse *(v.)* scatter, separate, disband
display *(n.)* exhibition, exhibit, presentation, demonstration, performance, parade, pageant
disposed *(adj.)* prone, inclined, apt, likely
disprove *(v.)* refute, invalidate, deny
dispute *(n.)* conflict, squabble, disturbance, feud
disrespect *(n.)* discourtesy, insolence, irreverence
disrupt *(v.)* intrude, obstruct, break, interrupt
disseminate *(v.)* scatter, spread, sow, propagate, broadcast, distribute
dissent *(v.)* disagree, refuse, contradict, differ, oppose
dissident *(adj.)* hostile, opposed, disagreeing
dissolve *(v.)* liquefy, evaporate, disintegrate, disappear
distant *(adj.)* aloof, afar, abroad, removed
distinct *(adj.)* perceptible, clear, sharp, enunciated, audible, lucid, plain, obvious, clear, definite; discrete, separate, disunited
distinguish *(v.)* discern, detect, notice, discover; honour, celebrate, acknowledge, admire, praise
distort *(v.)* alter, misinterpret, misconstrue
distract *(v.)* detract, amuse, entertain, mislead
distraught *(adj.)* troubled, distressed
distress *(n.)* pain, anxiety, worry, sorrow, wretchedness, suffering, ordeal, anguish, grief, trouble
distribute *(v.)* disburse, dispense, issue, allocate
district *(n.)* area, neighborhood, community, vicinity
distrust *(v.)* mistrust, suspect, disbelieve, doubt
disturb *(v.)* trouble, worry, perplex, startle, alarm, arouse, depress, distress, provoke, irritate, harass
diverge *(v.)* radiate, veer, swerve, deviate
diverse *(adj.)* dissimilar, assorted, different, distinct
divine *(adj.)* godlike, sacred, hallowed, consecrated, anointed, sanctified, ordained, revered, venerated
divulge *(v.)* reveal, disclose, impart, confess, expose
docile *(adj.)* submissive, meek, mild, tractable, pliant, willing, obliging, manageable, tame, obedient
doctor *(n.)* physician, surgeon, intern, veterinarian, chiropractor, homeopath, osteopath, healer, quack, anesthetist, dentist, pediatrician, gynecologist, oculist, obstetrician, psychiatrist, psychologist, pathologist, dermatologist, endocrinologist, urologist, hematologist
doctrine *(n.)* policy, conviction, tradition, canon
dogmatic *(adj.)* authoritarian, dictatorial, stubborn intolerant, opinionated, domineering, tyrannical
domain *(n.)* territory, dominion, field, specialty, area
domestic *(adj.)* indigenous, native, homemade
dominant *(adj.)* commanding, authoritative, assertive, aggressive, powerful
donate *(v.)* contribute, grant, bestow, bequeath, dis tribute, give, provide
donor *(n.)* benefactor, contributor, patron, philanthropist, giver

dote *(v.)* adore, pet, admire, love
doubt *(n.)* uncertainty, skepticism, mistrust, suspicion, misgiving, apprehension
douse *(v.)* immerse, wet, submerge, drench, soak
drab *(adj.)* dismal, dingy, colourless, dreary, dull
drag *(n.)* impedance, restraint, hindrance, burden, impediment, barrier; tiresome, bother, annoyance, hang-up, nuisance
drag *(v.)* haul, move, transport, draw; dawdle, loiter, pause; crawl, delay
drama *(n.)* play, production, dramatization, show, melodrama, tragicomedy, opera, mystery
drastic *(adj.)* extreme, extravagant, exorbitant, radical
draw *(v.)* drag, attract, lug, tow, haul; sketch, outline, trace, depict
drawback *(n.)* disadvantage, shortcoming, hindrance
dread *(n.)* awe, horror, terror, fear
drift *(n.)* tendency, bent, trend, inclination, impulse, bias, leaning, disposition
drink *(v.)* swallow, gulp, sip, guzzle
drive *(n.)* trip, outing, airing, tour, excursion, jaunt, spin, journey; driveway, approach, avenue, boulevard, road; energy, effort, enthusiasm, vigour, impulse
drop *(n.)* speck, dash, dab, bit; fall, tumble, reduction, decrease, slump, lowering
drowsy *(adj.)* sleepy, sluggish, languid, indolent, lazy
dry *(adj.)* parched, desiccated, barren, dehydrated, drained; uninteresting, tedious, dull; sarcastic, cynical, biting, funny
dubious *(adj.)* indecisive, perplexed, hesitant, uncertain, questionable; ambiguous, indefinite, unclear, obscure
due *(adj.)* expected; deserved; unsatisfied, outstanding, unpaid
dumb *(adj.)* simple-minded, dull, stupid
dumfound *(v.)* astonish, shock, startle
dungeon *(n.)* cell, vault, prison
durable *(adj.)* strong, form, enduring, permanent
duress *(n.)* threat, coercion, compulsion, control, pressure, restraint
duty *(n.)* obligation, liability, burden, responsibility
dwell *(v.)* reside, live, inhabit, stay, lodge, settle, remain, continue, occupy
dynamic *(adj.)* forceful, intense, energetic, compelling, vigorous, magnetic, electric, effective, influential, charismatic, active, powerful
dynasty *(n.)* succession, sovereignty

E

eager *(adj.)* impatient, anxious, keen, fervent, zealous, intent
early *(adj.), (adv.)* primitive, premature, preceding, unexpected, punctual
earn *(v.)* deserve, win, merit; gain, obtain, attain, get, procure, realize, acquire, secure
earnest *(adj.)* serious, intense, important, ardent, zealous, warm, enthusiastic
earthly *(adj.)* human, mortal, global, mundane
earthy *(adj.)* coarse, dull, crude, unrefined, natural
eat *(v.)* devour, chew, swallow, feast, dine, gorge, feed; erode, corrode, waste, rust, spill
ebb *(v.)* decline, recede, subside, decrease
eccentric *(adj.)* unconventional, odd, queer, strange, unusual
eclipse *(v.)* darken, diminish, obscure
economic *(adj.)* business, financial, commercial
ecstasy *(n.)* joy, rapture, delight, happiness
edible *(adj.)* palatable, good, delicious, satisfying, savoury, tasty, nutritious, digestible
educate *(v.)* teach, train, inform, refine, tutor, instruct
effect *(n.)* conclusion, consequence, outcome, result
effect *(v.)* produce, cause, make, begun
effervescent *(adj.)* bubbly, lively, vivacious
effort *(n.)* attempt, undertaking, struggle, try, venture
egotism *(n.)* conceit, vanity, pride, self-love, arrogance, overconfidence, haughtiness
egregious *(adj.)* bad, outrageous, shocking
eject *(v.)* discard, reject, oust, evict
elaborate *(adj.)* gaudy, decorated, showy, dressy, flowery, flashy, ornate; intricate, complicated, involved, complex
elect *(v.)* choose, name, select
elegance *(n.)* taste, cultivation, polish, splendour, beauty, gracefulness, magnificence, courtliness, charm, sophistication, style
element *(n.)* substance, component, portion, particle, detail, part
elevate *(v.)* lift, hoist, heave, tilt; advance, appoint, further

eligible *(adj.)* qualified, suitable, fit, usable
eloquence *(n.)* fluency, wit, wittiness, expressiveness, diction, articulation, delivery, poise
elude *(v.)* evade, escape, dodge, shun, avoid
elusive *(adj.)* fleeting, fugitive, temporary
embargo *(n.)* restriction, prohibition, impediment, restraint
embarrass *(v.)* distress, disconcert, chagrin, confound, trouble, disturb, fluster, shame
embezzle *(v.)* thieve, forge, pilfer, steal
embrace *(v.)* hug, enfold, squeeze, grip
emerge *(v.)* rise, arrive, appear, form, evolve
emigrant *(n.)* exile, expatriate, colonist, migrant, pilgrim, refugee
eminence *(n.)* standing, prominence, distinction, fame
emissary *(n.)* intermediary, ambassador, consul, agent
emotion *(n.)* excitement, sentiment, passion
emphatic *(adj.)* definite, assured, strong, determined, forceful, earnest, positive, dynamic
employ *(v.)* operate, manipulate, apply; contract, procure, hire
emulate *(v.)* imitate, equal, compete, follow
encompass *(v.)* include, encircle, gird, surround
encounter *(n.)* meeting, interview, rendezvous, appointment; conflict, clash, collision, fight
encourage *(v.)* support, inspire, cheer, praise, fortify, help, aid, reassure, reinforce, back, strengthen
endeavour (v.) effort, undertaking, venture
endorse *(v.)* countersign, underwrite, subscribe, notarize; approve, sanction, acknowledge
endurable *(adj.)* tolerable, supportable, bearable
engross *(v.)* absorb, busy, fill, occupy
enhance *(v.)* embellish, magnify, amplify, increase
enigma *(n.)* problem, riddle, parable, puzzle
enlighten *(v.)* inform, divulge, acquaint, teach, tell
enormous *(adj.)* monstrous, immense, huge, large
enterprise *(v.)* undertaking, endeavour, affair, business
entertain *(v.)* cheer, delight, beguile, charm, captivate, stimulate, distract, indulge; invite, welcome
enthusiasm *(v.)* excitement, interest, fervour, ardour, eagerness, zeal
entrance *(n.)* access, entry, passage, approach, admittance, introduction, debut, enrolment
envelop *(v.)* encompass, contain, hide, surround, wrap
envelope *(n.)* pouch, pocket, container, wrapper
envy *(v.)* covet, crave, yearn, hanker
equilibrium *(n.)* balance, stability, symmetry
equipment *(n.)* tools, implements, utensils, apparatus, devices, tackle, machinery, fittings
equivalent *(adj.)* equal, corresponding, commensurate, comparable, similar
eradicate *(v.)* destroy, eliminate, exterminate
erect *(v.)* construct, fabricate, build
erratic *(adj.)* wandering, rambling, roving; eccentric, queer, unusual; deviating, inconsistent, unpredictable, irregular
erroneous *(adj.)* inaccurate, incorrect, untrue, false
erudite *(adj.)* scholarly, learned, cultured
erupt *(v.)* eject, emit, explode
escape *(n.)* flight, retreat, evasion, avoidance
escape *(v.)* elude, avoid, flee, evade, disappear, vanish
escort *(n.)* guide, attendant, guard, companion
espouse *(v.)* marry, advocate, adopt, uphold, support
essence *(n.)* pith, core, kernel, gist, nature, basis, substance, nucleus, germ
establish *(v.)* institute, organize, erect, build; verify, authenticate, confirm; fix, stabilize
ethical *(adj.)* moral, humane, respectable, decent, honest, noble
etiquette *(n.)* conduct, manners, behaviour
euphoria *(n.)* relaxation, health, well-being, happiness
evade *(v.)* avoid, dodge, shun, elude, baffle, conceal, deceive, veil, hide
event *(n.)* occasion, incident, occurrence, happening, affair, function, situation
evolve *(v.)* unfold, emerge, develop, grow
exact *(adj.)* accurate, precise, correct, perfect, definite; clear, sharp, distinct
exaggerate *(v.)* overstate, misrepresent, falsify, magnify, amplify, heighten, intensify, distort, stretch, overdo, elaborate, colour, fabricate
examine *(v.)* inspect, analyze, scrutinize, explore, probe; question, interrogate
exasperate *(v.)* annoy, irritate, provoke
exceed *(v.)* excel, outdo , surpass
excel *(v.)* surpass, transcend, exceed

excess *(n.)* profusion, surplus; prodigality, dissipation, intemperance, greed, waste
excite *(v.)* provoke, stimulate, inflame, arouse, stir, provoke, incite
exclaim *(v.)* shout, call, yell
exclude *(v.)* except, reject, ban, bar
execute *(v.)* perform, act, do, effect
exempt *(adj.)* privileged, excused, unrestricted
exhaust *(v.)* debilitate, tire, weaken, weary; deplete, use
exhort *(v.)* entreat, beg, urge
exist *(v.)* live, survive, be, endure
exotic *(adj.)* foreign, imported, extrinsic; peculiar, strange, different, fascinating, unusual
expand *(v.)* extend, augment, dilate, grow
expanse *(n.)* extent, reach, area, space, span, spread, scope, range
expect *(v.)* anticipate, await, hope; require, demand, exact; assume, presume, suppose, suspect
expedient *(adj.)* convenient, profitable, practical
expedite *(v.)* speed, quicken, advance
expel *(v.)* eject, dislodge, evict; dismiss, suspend, discharge, oust
expenditure *(n.)* outgo, payment, expense
experience *(n.)* background, skill, knowledge, practice, maturity, judgement, know-how
experience *(v.)* undergo, feel, endure
expert *(adj.)* skillful, practised, proficient, able
explain *(v.)* interpret, elucidate, illustrate, clarify, illuminate, expound, teach, demonstrate, define
explicit *(adj.)* clear, definite, understandable
exploit *(n.)* deed, venture, escapade, achievement
exploit *(v.)* utilize, employ, use
explore *(v.)* examine, search, hunt, seek
explosion *(n.)* detonation, blast, burst, discharge
expose *(v.)* uncover, disclose, reveal, unmask, unfold; endanger, imperil
express *(v.)* declare, tell, signify, utter
expulsion *(n.)* ejection, suspension, purge, removal
exquisite *(adj.)* fine, scrupulous, precise, dainty
extend *(v.)* enlarge, lengthen, increase, reach, continue, spread
extent *(n.)* span, space, area, expanse, bulk; scope, reach, range, magnitude, intensity
exterior *(adj.)* outer, outlying, outermost, outside
exterminate *(v.)* annihilate, eradicate, destroy
extinguish *(v.)* smother, choke, douse, stifle
extort *(v.)* extract, wrench, force, steal
extra *(adj.)* additional, other, spare, reserve, supple, auxiliary, added, more
extract *(v.)* derive, secure, obtain
extraneous *(adj.)* foreign; incidental, redundant
extraordinary *(adj.)* unusual, remarkable, curious, amazing
extravagance *(n.)* excess, lavishness, improvidence, waste
extravagant *(adj.)* lavish, prodigal, immoderate, wasteful
extreme *(adj.)* outermost, utmost, immoderate, excessive, outrageous, preposterous, exaggerated
exuberance *(n.)* fervour, eagerness, exhilaration, zeal
eye *(n.)* perception, taste, discrimination; focus, core, heart, kernel, nub

F

fable *(n.)* story, allegory, tale, parable
fabric *(n.)* cloth, textile, stuff, material, goods
fabricate *(v.)* construct, erect, make, form, build, manufacture, devise; misrepresent, contrive
fabulous *(adj.)* fictitious, remarkable, amazing, immense, unusual
facade *(n.)* face, appearance, look, front
facet *(n.)* surface, aspect, face, side, plane
facetious *(adj.)* humorous, whimsical, ridiculous, funny
facile *(adj.)* easy, simple, obvious, apparent, fluent
facilitate *(v.)* promote, aid, simplify, help
facsimile *(n.)* copy, duplicate, reproduction, mirror
fact *(n.)* certainty, truth, actuality, reality, evidence, action, deed, happening, occurrence, act, episode, incident
faculty *(n.)* ability, aptitude, peculiarity, strength, forte; instructors, mentors, professors, tutors, lecturers, advisers, scholars, fellows
fad *(n.)* fancy, style, craze, fashion, eccentricity, innovation, vogue, fashion
fade *(v.)* bleach, blanch, dim, vanish; diminish, hush, quiet, sink, decrease
failure *(n.)* fiasco, miscarriage, breakdown, stoppage, collapse, downfall, flop, washout; incompetent, underachiever, dropout, dud
faint *(adj.)* faltering, shaky, dizzy, weak, vague, thin, hazy, indistinct, dull; subdued, low, soft, quiet, muffled, hushed

fair *(adj.)* just, forthright, impartial, scrupulous, honest, decent, honourable, righteous, reasonable, even-handed, principled, trustworthy; ordinary, mediocre, commonplace; pleasant, clear, sunny, bright, calm, placid, tranquil, favourable, balmy

fair *(n.)* exposition, carnival, bazaar, festival, market

faith *(n.)* trust, confidence, credence, assurance, acceptance, conviction, sureness, reliance; belief, creed, doctrine, dogma, tenet, revelation, credo, gospel, canon, theology

fake *(adj.)* pretended, fraudulent, bogus, false

fall *(v.)* drop, decline, sink, topple, settle, droop, stumble, trip, plunge, descend, totter, recede, ebb, diminish, flop; yield, surrender, succumb, resign, capitulate

fallacy *(n.)* inconsistency, mistake, ambiguity, paradox, miscalculation, quirk, flaw, heresy, error

false *(adj.)* unfaithful, treacherous, disloyal, deceitful, unscrupulous, untrustworthy; spurious, fanciful, deceptive, fallacious, misleading, erroneous, inaccurate, fraudulent, fabricated, bogus

fame *(n.)* renown, glory, distinction, eminence, esteem, name, note, greatness, rank, position, standing, preeminence, regard, popularity

familiar *(adj.)* everyday, customary, accustomed, common, ordinary, informal, commonplace

family *(n.)* household, relatives, clan, relations, tribe, dynasty, descendants, forbears, heirs, genealogy, descent, parentage, extraction, kinship, lineage

famine *(n.)* starvation, want, misery, hunger

famous *(adj.)* known, renowned, eminent, foremost, famed, celebrated, noted, prominent, reputable, renowned, notable, notorious

fan *(n.)* supporter, follower, amateur, devotee

fancy *(adj.)* elaborate, ornamental, intricate, elegant, embellished, rich, adorned, ostentatious, gaudy, showy, baroque, lavish, ornate

fantastic *(adj.)* fanciful, whimsical, capricious, strange, odd, queer, quaint, peculiar, outlandish, wonderful, exotic, ludicrous

fantasy *(n.)* illusion, flight, figment, fiction

farce *(n.)* satire, travesty, burlesque

farewell *(n.)* goodbye, valediction, parting, departure

farsighted *(adj.)* aware, perceptive, sagacious

fascinate *(v.)* charm, captivate, entrance, enchant, bewitch, enrapture, delight, please, attract, lure, seduce, entice, intoxicate, tantalize

fashion *(n.)* manner, custom, convention, vogue, mode, usage, observance, style, craze

fasten *(v.)* lock, fix, tie, lace, close, bind, tighten, attach, secure, anchor, grip, clasp, clamp, pin, nail, tack, bolt, rivet, set, weld, cement, glue

fat *(adj.)* portly, stout, obese, corpulent, fleshy, plump, bulky, heavy

fatal *(adj.)* mortal, lethal, deadly

fate *(n.)* destiny, fortune, luck, doom

father *(n.)* parent, sire, progenitor, procreator, forebear, ancestor; originator, founder, inventor, author; pastor, ecclesiastic, parson

fatigue *(n.)* weariness, exhaustion, lassitude

fault *(n.)* wrongdoing, transgression, crime, impropriety, misconduct, malpractice, failing; error, defect, blunder, mistake, accountability, blame

favour *(v.)* indulge, prefer, pick, choose, value, prize, esteem

favourite *(adj.)* beloved, favoured, preferred, adored

favouritism *(n.)* bias, partiality, inequity, inclination

fear *(n.)* dread, fright, dismay, awe, anxiety, foreboding, concern, alarm

feasible *(adj.)* expedient, worthwhile, convenient, practicable, possible, attainable

feast *(n.)* banquet, entertainment, festival, fiesta, barbeque, picnic, dinner

feat *(n.)* deed, act, effort, achievement

feeble *(adj.)* weak, faint, fragile, puny

feel *(v.)* touch, caress, fondle, paw, grasp; experience, sense, perceive; believe, consider, hold, think

feign *(v.)* pretend, dissemble, imagine, fabricate

fellow *(n.)* youth, chap, lad, boy, stripling, apprentice, adolescent, juvenile, youngster, kid; associate, member, peer, colleague, friend

felony *(n.)* crime, misconduct, offense, transgression

feminine *(adj.)* soft, delicate, gentle, ladylike, matronly, maidenly, tender, womanly

ferment *(v.)* effervesce, foam, froth, bubble, seethe, fizz, work, ripen, rise

ferocious *(adj.)* savage, fierce, wild

fertile *(adj.)* productive, inventive, fruitful, rich, productive, fat, teeming, yielding, flowering

fervent *(adj.)* zealous, eager, ardent, enthusiastic
fervour *(n.)* ardour, enthusiasm, zeal
festival *(n.)* celebration, festivity, gala, carnival
feast *(v.)* get, retrieve, carry
fetish *(n.)* fixation, craze, mania, obsession
fetus *(n.)* embryo, organism, child
feud *(n.)* quarrel, strife, bickering, fight
fickle *(adj.)* inconstant, capricious, whimsical, mercurial, changing
fiction *(n.)* novel, tale, romance, story
fidelity *(n.)* faithfulness, loyalty, devotion
fiend *(n.)* barbarian, brute, beast, devil; fan, monomaniac
fierce *(n.)* ferocious, savage, wild, untamed, brutal, monstrous, vicious, dangerous, violent, threatening
fight *(n.)* struggle, battle, strife, contention, feud, quarrel, dispute, confrontation, brawl, bickering, wrangling, argument, debate, conflict, clash, scuffle, engagement
figure *(n.)* design, statue, shape, structure; body, frame, development, build, posture, attitude, pose, carriage; total, number; value, worth
file *(v.)* abrade, rasp, scrape, finish; classify, index, categorize, catalogue, register, list
filth *(n.)* dirt, contamination, pollution, muck, slop, squalor, grime, garbage, sludge
finance *(n.)* business, commerce, economics
find *(v.)* discover, detect, notice, perceive, discern, uncover, expose
fine *(adj.)* precise, accurate, definite; thin, subtle; powdery, granular
fine *(n.)* punishment, penalty, damage, forfeit
finish *(v.)* perfect, achieve; wax, stain, cover, paint; cease, close, end, stop
fire *(n.)* burning, flame, blaze, embers, sparks, glow, warmth, combustion, conflagration
firm *(adj.)* stable, solid, rooted, immovable, fastened, motionless, secured; solid, dense, compact, impenetrable, impervious, rigid, hardened, inflexible, unyielding; determined, steadfast, resolute, constant
first *(adj.)* beginning, original, primary, prime, initial, earliest, introductory
fishy *(adj.)* improbable, dubious, implausible, unlikely
fixture *(n.)* equipment, convenience, appliance, machine, device, equipment
fizzle *(n.)* disappointment, fiasco, defeat, failure
flabby *(adj.)* soft, yielding, limp, tender, fat
flair *(n.)* talent, aptitude, gift, ability
flamboyant*(adj.)* bombastic, ostentatious, ornate
flame *(n.)* blaze, flare, flash, fire
flatter *(v.)* adulate, glorify, praise
flaunt *(v.)* display, vaunt, brandish, boast
flavour *(n.)* taste, tang, relish
flaw *(n.)* defect, imperfection, stain, blemish
fleck *(n.)* spot, mite, dot, bit
flee *(v.)* run, desert, escape, retreat
flexible *(adj.)* limber, lithe, supple, elastic, malleable, pliable, tractable
flicker *(v.)* sparkle, twinkle, glitter, flash, shine
flimsy *(adj.)* thin, weak, slight, infirm, frail, insubstantial, fragile, decrepit
flippant *(adj.)* pert, frivolous, impudent, saucy, rude
flock *(n.)* congregation, group, pack, litter, herd
flood *(v.)* inundate, swamp, overflow, deluge, submerge, immerse
floor *(n.)* tiles, planking, carpet, rug, story, landing, basement
flourish *(v.)* thrive, increase, wax, succeed, adorn; wave
fluctuate *(v.)* waver, vacillate, falter, hesitate
fluent *(adj.)* eloquent, glib, smooth, verbose, chatty, articulate, persuasive, silver-tongued
flutter *(v.)* flap, ripple, wiggle, wave
focus *(v.)* attract, converge, convene, centre; clear: adjust, detail, sharpen
foe *(n.)* enemy, opponent, antagonist, adversary
foible *(n.)* failing, weakness, defect, fault
foliage *(n.)* leaves, greenery
folk *(n.)* people, race, nation, community, tribe, society, population, settlement, clan, confederation
follow *(v.)* ensue, postdate, succeed; imitate, conform, copy, mirror, reflect, mimic; observe, heed, regard, watch, comply; understand, comprehend, catch, realize; result, happen, ensue
foment *(v.)* encourage, incite, stimulate
fond *(adj.)* loving, enamoured, attached, affectionate
food *(n.)* nutriment, refreshment, edibles, comestibles, provisions, stores, sustenance, rations, board, cuisine, nourishment, fare
fool *(n.)* nitwit, simpleton, dunce, oaf, ninny, nincompoop, dolt, buffoon, blockhead, clown

foothold *(n.)* ledge, footing, niche, step
forbear *(v.)* abstain, stop, pause, cease
forbid *(v.)* prohibit, debar, restrain, inhibit, preclude, oppose, obstruct, bar, prevent, outlaw, disallow
force *(v.)* compel, coerce, press, drive, make, impel, oblige, require, demand, command, impose, exact
forceful *(adj.)* commanding, dominant, powerful
forecast *(n.)* prognosis, divination, foresight, prophecy
forefather *(n.)* ancestor, progenitor, forebear, father, parent, sire, forerunner, predecessor, originator, precursor, procreator, patriarch, founder, kinsman
foreign *(adj.)* alien, remote, exotic, strange, distant, different, alien, imported, borrowed, abroad
foreman *(n.)* overseer, manager, supervisor, superintendent, head, boss
foretell *(v.)* prophesy, predict, divine, foresee, forebode, augur, portend, foreshadow
forethought *(n.)* provision, planning, foresight
forever *(adv.)* always, everlastingly, perpetually, eternally, endlessly, forevermore
forewarn *(v.)* admonish, alarm, warm
forfeit *(v.)* lose, sacrifice, relinquish, abandon
forge *(v.)* counterfeit, falsify, fabricate, feign, imitate, copy, duplicate, reproduce
forget *(v.)* neglect, overlook, ignore, slight, disregard, skip, exclude
forgive *(v.)* pardon, overlook, excuse, exonerate
forgo *(v.)* quit, relinquish, waive, abandon
form *(n.)* figure, appearance, arrangement, configuration, formation, structure, contour, profile, silhouette; manner, mode, custom, method; model, mould; document, chart, questionnaire, application
formal *(adj.)* regular, orderly, precise, set; polite, reserved, distant, stiff, conventional
formality *(n.)* decorum, etiquette, correctness, behaviour
former *(adj.)* earlier, previous, foregoing, preceding
formula *(n.)* equation, recipe, directions, method
forsake *(v.)* desert, abandon, leave, quit
fortify *(v.)* strengthen, barricade, entrench, buttress
fortitude *(n.)* strength, firmness, valour, fearlessness, determination
fortune *(n.)* chance, luck, fate, uncertainty; wealth, riches, possessions, inheritance, estate
fossil *(n.)* remains, specimen, skeleton, relic
foul *(adj.)* filthy, impure, disgusting, nasty, vulgar, coarse, offensive; unfair, inequitable, unjust
foundation *(n.)* basis, reason, justification, authority; footing, pier, groundwork, bed, substructure, underpinning; institution, organization, endowment, institute, society, charity
fraction *(n.)* fragment, section, portion, part, division
fracture *(n.)* rupture, shattering, breach, dislocation, shearing, separating
fragile *(adj.)* frail, brittle, delicate, dainty, weak
fragment *(n.)* piece, scrap, remnant, bit
fragrance *(n.)* perfume, aroma, smell
frame *(n.)* skeleton, framework, scaffolding, support; border, margin, fringe, hem, trim, outline
franchise *(n.)* right, privilege, licence
fraternity *(n.)* society, brotherhood, fellowship
fraud *(n.)* deceit, trickery, duplicity, guile, deception
freedom *(n.)* liberty, independence, sovereignty, autonomy; privilege, immunity, license, indulgence, latitude
freeze *(v.)* solidify, congeal, harden; control, seal, terminate, immobilize
freight *(n.)* cargo, load, encumbrance, consignment, goods, tonnage
frenzy *(n.)* excitement, rage, craze, furor, insanity
frequent *(adj.)* habitual, customary, intermittent, periodic, commonplace; regular, repeated, recurrent, incessant, continual
fresh *(adj.)* new, green, recent, current, late, untried; unsalted, uncured, unspoiled, uncontaminated, preserved; colorful, vivid, bright; cool, clear, pure, clean, refreshed, rested, restored, relaxed, reinvigorated, revived; untrained, untried, unskilled
fret *(v.)* worry, irritate, agitate, vex, bother
friction *(n.)* attrition, abrasion, erosion, grinding; trouble, animosity, quarrel, discontent, hatred
friend *(n.)* schoolmate, playmate, roommate, companion, intimate, confidant, comrade, fellow, pal, chum, crony, buddy
fright *(n.)* fear, panic, terror, dread, horror, shock
frivolous *(adj.)* unimportant, slight, trifling, superficial, petty, trivial
frontier *(n.)* boundary, wilderness, hinterland
froth *(n.)* foam, bubbles, fizz, effervescence, lather
frugal *(adj.)* thrifty, economical, sparing, saving, parsimonious, careful

fruitful *(adj.)* prolific, productive, fecund, fertile
fry *(v.)* saute, sear, singe, brown, pan-fry
full *(adj.)* saturated, crammed, packed, stuffed, jammed, glutted, gorged, loaded; abundant, copious, ample, plentiful, sufficient, adequate, lavish, extravagant, profuse
fumble *(v.)* mishandle, bungle, mismanage, botch
fund *(n.)* money, capital, endowment, gift
funeral *(n.)* interment, burial, entombment, requiem
funny *(adj.)* comic, laughable, comical, whimsical, amusing, entertaining, diverting, humorous, witty, jocular, droll; suspicious, curious, unusual, odd
furious *(adj.)* raging, enraged, fierce, angry
furor *(n.)* tumult, excitement, stir, disturbance
fury *(n.)* rage, anger, wrath
fuss *(n.)* quarrel, complaint, bother, disturbance, stir
futile *(adj.)* useless, vain, fruitless, hopeless, impractical, unsuccessful, purposeless, ineffective, ineffectual, unproductive, empty, hollow
future *(adj.)* impending, imminent, destined, fated, prospective, expected, approaching, ultimate
fuzz *(n.)* nap, fluff, fur, hair

G

gab *(vi.)* talk, chatter, gossip, jabber, babble
gadget *(n.)* device, contrivance, object, contraption
gaiety *(n.)* merriment, jollity, mirth, exhilaration
gain *(v.)* augment, expand, enlarge, grow; progress, overtake; attain, realize, reach, succeed
gait *(n.)* walk, step, pace, carriage, movement
gallant *(adj.)* noble, brave, courteous, bold, courageous, intrepid
gallop *(v.)* leap, run, spring, bound, hurdle, swing, stride, lope, amble, trot
gamble *(v.)* bet, wager, plunge, speculate, risk, chance
game *(n.)* sport, play, recreation; fish, fowl, quarry, prey, wildlife
gangster *(n.)* criminal, gunman, racketeer
gap *(n.)* cleft, rift, hole; break, recess, pause; pass, chasm, hollow, ravine, gorge, canyon, gully, gulch
garish *(adj.)* showy, gaudy, ostentatious, ornate
gasp *(v.)* gulp, pant, puff, wheeze, blow, snort
gather *(v.)* collect, aggregate, amass, accumulate, assemble, conclude, deduce, assume; assemble, meet
gaudy *(adj.)* showy, flashy, tawdry, ornate
gauge *(v.)* measure, check, calibrate, calculate
gazette *(n.)* journal, newspaper, periodical
gem *(n.)* stone, jewel, bauble, ornament
general *(adj.)* broad, universal, extensive, ecumenical, ubiquitous; usual, customary, prevailing; indefinite, uncertain, imprecise, vague
generous *(adj.)* bountiful, lavish, profuse, prodigal, magnanimous
genesis *(n.)* generation, creation, beginning
genial *(adj.)* cordial, kind, warmhearted, friendly
genius *(n.)* talent, intellect, intelligence, gift, aptitude, astuteness, acumen, capability
genuine *(adj.)* authentic, actual, original, unaffected, reliable, staunch, trustworthy, certain, valid, positive, frank
germ *(n.)* microbe, bacterium, micro-organism, virus, parasite, bug
gesture *(n.)* movement, indication, intimation, sign
ghastly *(adj.)* terrifying, hideous, horrible, frightening, repulsive, disgusting, abhorrent, offensive
ghost *(n.)* spirit, apparition, vision, specter, phantom, spook, devil
gibberish *(n.)* jargon, chatter, claptrap, nonsense
gibe *(v.)* sneer, mock, taunt
giddy *(adj.)* high, towering, lofty, steep
giggle *(v.)* laugh, titter, chuckle, snicker
gimmick *(n.)* device, stratagem, catch, method, trick
girdle *(n.)* belt, cinch, sash, underwear
girl *(n.)* schoolgirl, lass, woman, lassie, damsel, maid, maiden
glance *(v.)* see, peep, glimpse
glare *(v.)* light, beam, glow, radiate; pierce, glower
glide *(v.)* float, drift, waft, skim, fly, flit, soar
glimmer *(n.)* view, flash, impression, sight
glitter *(n.)* luster, brilliancy, sparkle, shimmer, gleam
globule *(n.)* drop, particle, bubble
gloomy *(adj.)* dreary, depressing, discouraging, dismal, murky
glory *(n.)* grandeur, majesty, brilliance
gluttony *(n.)* voracity, edacity, intemperance, greed
gnaw *(v.)* tear, crunch, champ, masticate, bite, chew
good for nothing *(n.)* loafer, vagabond, vagrant
goodness *(n.)* decency, morality, honesty, virtue
gorge *(n.)* chasm, abyss, crevasse, ravine

gorgeous *(adj.)* beautiful, dazzling, superb, sumptuous, impressive, grand

gory *(adj.)* blood-soaked, bloodstained, offensive

gossip *(n.)* scandal, meddling, hearsay, slander, defamation; snoop, meddler, tattler, scandalmonger, muckraker, backbiter

gossip *(v.)* tattle, chat, report, blab, babble, repeat

govern *(v.)* rule, administer, oversee, supervise, dictate, tyrannize

grab *(v.)* seize, clutch, grasp, take

grace *(n.)* charm, nimbleness, agility, poise, dexterity, symmetry, balance, style, harmony; mercy, forgiveness, love, charity

grade *(n.)* rank; class, category, classification; incline, gradient, slant, inclination, pitch, ascen escent, ramp, climb, elevation, height, hill; fill, causeway, dike, dam

gradual *(adj.)* creeping, regular, continuous, regulated

grand *(adj.)* splendid, stately, dignified, regal, noble, illustrious, august, majestic, overwhelming

grant *(n.)* gift, boon, reward, present, allowance, stipend, donation, endowment, bequest

graph *(n.)* diagram, chart, design, plan

graphic *(adj.)* illustrated, visual, sketched, pictured; clear, picturesque, comprehensible, striking, expressive, eloquent, poetic

grasp *(n.)* grip, hold, clutch, cinch

grate *(v.)* rub, rasp, grind, abrade

grateful *(adj.)* thankful, appreciative, pleased, obliged

gratify *(v.)* please, satisfy, delight

gratuity *(n.)* present, tip, reward, bonus

grave *(adj.)* important, momentous, consequential, critical; somber, solemn, serious, sober

grave *(n.)* vault, sepulcher, tomb, crypt, mausoleum, catacomb

gravity *(n.)* importance, seriousness, significance

great *(adj.)* large, numerous, big, commanding, vast; exceptional, surpassing, transcendent; grand, majestic, exalted, famous, renowned, celebrated, distinguished, noted

greedy *(adj.)* avid, grasping, rapacious, selfish, miserly, intemperate, mercenary, covetous

greet *(v.)* hail, welcome, address, recognize, embrace, nod, acknowledge, bow

gregarious *(adj.)* companionable, friendly

grievance *(n.)* hardship, injury, complaint, objection

grieve *(v.)* lament, bewail, regret, sorrow, mourn

grim *(adj.)* gloomy, sulky, morose, glum; austere, strict, harsh, severe; implacable, inexorable

grimace *(n.)* smirk, smile, sneer

grin *(v.)* smirk, simper, beam, smile

grind *(v.)* crush, powder, mill, granulate, crumble

grit *(n.)* pluck, courage; sand, dust

groan *(n.)* moan, sob, grunt, cry

groceries *(n.)* food, edibles, comestibles, foodstuffs

groove *(n.)* furrow, rut, channel, trench, depression, gutter, ditch

gross *(adj.)* total, entire; corpulent, obese, huge; obscene, indecent, lewd, coarse, shameful

grotesque *(adj.)* ludicrous, odd, bizarre, malformed, ugly, distorted, deformed

grouch *(n.)* complainer, grumbler, growler, bear, sorehead, crab, crank, bellyacher

group *(n.)* assemblage, cluster, crowd; collection, accumulation, assortment, combination; organization, association, club, society

grow *(v.)* increase, expand, swell, wax, thrive, enlarge, multiply, flourish; become, develop, evolve, progress, age, ripen, blossom, mature; cultivate, raise, tend, foster, produce, plant, breed

growl *(v.)* snarl, grumble, bark, grunt, cry

grudge *(n.)* enmity, spite, rancor, animosity, hatred

gruesome *(adj.)* horrible, ghastly, grim, grisly, frightful

gruff *(adj.)* bluff, churlish, harsh, grating, hoarse

grumble *(v.)* complain, growl, whine, protest, fuss

grumpy *(adj.)* sullen, grouchy, cantankerous, irritable

grunt *(v.)* snort, groan, mutter, grumble

guarantee *(n.)* surety, promise, bond

guaranty *(n.)* warranty, contract, certificate

guard *(n.)* sentry, sentinel, watchman

guardian *(n.)* protector, overseer, trustee, custodian, keeper, defender, supervisor, baby-sitter

guess *(v.)* estimate, presume, infer, speculate, imagine, surmise, theorize, venture, suppose, presume

guest *(n.)* visitor, caller, patron, client

guilt *(n.)* blame, error, fault, liability, weakness, failing

guise *(n.)* appearance, disguise, mode, semblance

gulf *(n.)* chasm, abyss, abysm, depth, ravine, bay, inlet, sound, cove

gullible *(adj.)* innocent, trustful, simple, naive

gulp *(v.)* swallow, gasp, swig

guru *(n.)* teacher, instructor, mentor

gust *(n.)* blast, burst, blow, breeze, wind

gusto *(n.)* enjoyment, zest, zeal, fervour, ardour

gymnasium *(n.)* arena, coliseum, ring, rink, pit, gym

gymnast *(n.)* acrobat, tumbler, jumper, athlete

gypsy *(n.)* wanderer, tramp, vagrant, traveller

H

habit *(n.)* custom, mode, practice, fashion, manner; addiction, fixation

hackneyed *(adj.)* commonplace, trite, state

hag *(n.)* crone, shrew, ogress, hellcat, fishwife, witch

halfway *(adj.)* partial, midway, incomplete, partially, imperfectly, insufficiently, moderately, middling

halfway *(adv.)* half, partly, midway

hall *(n.)* public room, chamber, assembly, arena, ballroom, church, clubhouse, salon, lounge, gymnasium, amphitheater, gallery; foyer, corridor, hallway

hallmark *(n.)* label, endorsement, seal, emblem

hallucination *(n.)* delusion, vision, dream

halt *(n.)* stop, cessation, break, pause

hamlet *(n.)* town, village

hand *(n.)* helper, worker, labourer; calligraphy, script; applause

handicap *(n.)* disadvantage, obstacle, impediment, affliction, hindrance, disorder, injury

handle *(v.)* check, examine, feel, manage, operate, use, work, deal

handsome *(adj.)* attractive, impressive, stately, robust, well-dressed, slick, beautiful

hand-to-mouth *(adj.)* marginal, minimal, borderline

handy *(adj.)* near, nearby; dexterous, able, useful, beneficial, advantageous, gainful, helpful, profitable, usable

hang-out *(n.)* bar, joint, hole, headquarters, room

hang-up *(n.)* problem, predicament, difficulty

haphazard *(adj.)* accidental, random, offhand, casual, slipshod, reckless, irregular, unplanned, aimless

happy*(adv.)* joyously, gladly, cheerily, gaily, merrily, brightly, blissfully, cheerfully, gleefully

happy *(adj.)* joyous, merry, mirthful, gay, laughing, contented, genial, satisfied, cheery, jolly, sparkling, blissful, exhilarated, pleased, gratified, ecstatic, overjoyed, radiant, smiling, elated

happy-go-lucky *(adj.)* easygoing, unconcerned, thoughtless, irresponsible

harass *(v.)* annoy, attack, tease, vex, irritate, bother

harbour *(n.)* refuge, port, pier, inlet, wharf, dock

harbour *(v.)* shelter, secure, defend, lodge; consider, cherish, regard

hard *(adj.)* compact, unyielding, solid, impermeable, tough, dense, firm; difficult, arduous, tricky, trying, tedious, complex, abstract, puzzling, troublesome, laborious; cruel, perverse, unrelenting, vengeful; severe, harsh, exacting, grim

hardheaded *(adj.)* willful, stubborn, headstrong

hardly *(adv.)* scarcely, barely, imperceptibly, infrequently, somewhat, rarely, slightly, sparsely

hardship *(n.)* trial, sorrow, worry, difficulty, grief

hardy *(adj.)* tough, resistant, solid, staunch, seasoned, fit, acclimatized, rugged, robust, hearty, hale, vigorous, powerful, sturdy, solid, substantial, strong

hark, harden *(v.)* listen, heed, infliction, impairment, damage; evil, wickedness, outrage, abuse

harmonious *(adj.)* harmonic, tuneful, musical, melodic; congruous, agreeable, corresponding, suitable, adapted, similar, like, cooperative, friendly, conforming, balanced, symmetrical

harp *(v.)* carp, nag, repeat, pester, complain

harrow *(v.)* torment, distress, harass

harsh *(adj.)* rough, severe, discordant, jangling, cacophonous, grating, dissonant, creaking, clashing, jarring, clamorous, hoarse, rasping, screeching, ear splitting, tuneless, shrill

harvest *(n.)* crops, yield, fruit, grain, produce, vegetable

hassle *(n.)* dispute, squabble, struggle, bother

haste *(n.)* speed, dispatch, precipitation, rashness, impetuousness, foolhardiness, recklessness, hastiness, carelessness, heedlessness

hat *(n.)* headgear, headpiece, helmet, chapeau, bonnet, cap, derby, sombrero, topper, bowler, panama, beret, turban, hood, cowl, beret
hatch *(v.)* produce, originate, bear
hate *(n.)* dislike, animosity, enmity, hatred
haughty *(adj.)* disdainful, arrogant, proud, egotistic
haul *(n.)* tug, lift; distance, voyage, trip; spoils, take, find, booty
haunt *(v.)* frequent, habituate, visit; obsess, torment, possess, trouble, hound, terrify, plague, vex, harass, worry, frighten, annoy, bother, disturb
have *(v.)* keep, retain, use, maintain, control, treasure, hold, possess; beget, produce
haven *(n.)* harbour, port, refuge, shelter
havoc *(n.)* destruction, confusion, devastation, plunder
hazard *(n.)* chance, risk, peril, jeopardy, danger
haze *(n.)* fog, mist, smog, cloudiness
head *(n.)* skull, scalp, crown, bean, leader, chief, commander, officer, ruler; top, summit, peak, crest; front, start, source, origin; intelligence, brain, foresight, ingenuity, judgement
headache *(n.)* pain, migraine, neuralgia; problem, mess, difficulty, trouble
heal *(v.)* cure, restore, renew, regenerate, remedy, rejuvenate, medicate, revive, rehabilitate, resuscitate, help, ameliorate
health *(n.)* vigour, wholeness, healthfulness, fitness, bloom, hardiness, stamina, energy, strength
heap *(v.)* pile, add, lump, load, pack
hear *(v.)* listen, attend, catch, apprehend, eavesdrop, perceive, overhear; try, judge, examine, referee
hearsay *(n.)* rumour, scandal, report, gossip
heartache *(n.)* sorrow, pain, despair, anguish, grief
hearty *(adj.)* warm, zealous, sincere, cheery, cheerful, jovial, animated, ardent, genial, enthusiastic, genuine, passionate, intense, exuberant, devout, unfeigned, fervent, responsive, friendly
heat *(n.)* warmth, fever, fervour, ardour, passion, excitement, desire
heave *(v.)* throw, toss, move, rock, bob, pitch, lurch, roll, reel, sway, throb, slosh
heavy *(adj.)* weighty, ponderous, huge, stout, dense, substantial, hefty, large; burdensome, troublesome, oppressive, vexatious, difficult, disturbing, onerous; dull, listless, slow, apathetic, indifferent; gloomy, dejected, cloudy, overcast, dark, dismal
hectic *(adj.)* frantic, unsettled, boisterous, restless
hector *(v.)* bully, annoy, tease, vex
heed *(n.)* notice, care, note, regard
heinous *(adj.)* hateful, atrocious, wicked
heir *(n.)* inheritor, successor, descendent, heiress, beneficiary, inheritor, prince
heirloom *(n.)* legacy, inheritance, bequest, gift, antique
heist *(n.)* robbery, burglary
help *(n.)* assistance, advice, comfort, aid, support, gift, charity, encouragement, subsidy, service, relief, endowment, cooperation, guidance; aid, representative, assistant, faculty, staff; relief, maintenance, sustenance, nourishment, remedy
hem *(n.)* border, skirting, edging, edge, fringe, rim
henpeck *(v.)* nag, bully, suppress, intimidate, bother
herd *(n.)* flock, group, drove, pack, brood, swarm, lot, bevy, covey, gaggle, nest, brood, flight, school, clan
hereditary *(adj.)* inherited, genetic, paternal
heresy *(n.)* dissent, nonconformity, dissidence, sectarianism, schism, unorthodoxy, secularism
heritage *(n.)* legacy, birthright, ancestry, dowry, share, endowment, status, heredity; culture, custom, fashion, system
hermit *(n.)* ascetic, recluse, monk, loner
hero *(n.)* champion, model, conqueror, god, martyr, warrior, saint, star, knight-errant
hesitant *(adj.)* doubtful, skeptical, irresolute, uncertain, slow, delaying, wavering, dawdling, lazy
hex *(n.)* spell, curse
hiatus *(n.)* break, pause, space, gap
hidden *(adj.)* secluded, private, covert, concealed, occult, masked, screened, veiled, clouded, obscured, disguised, unseen, camouflaged, shrouded, shadowy, clandestine, cloistered, surreptitious
hide *(n.)* skin, pelt, rawhide, fur, leather
hide *(v.)* conceal, shroud, curtain, veil, camouflage, cover, mask, cloak, screen, suppress, withhold, shield, secrete, hoard, closet, obscure, disguise
hideous *(adj.)* frightful, shocking, revolting, hateful, ghastly, grisly, ugly
hierarchy *(n.)* government, authority, ministry, regime
highway *(n.)* roadway, parkway, freeway, turnpike
hike *(v.)* tramp, tour, explore, travel, walk; raise, lift, advance, increase

hilarious *(adj.)* gay, merry, funny, amusing, lively, witty, entertaining

hinder *(v.)* stop, impede, obstruct, check, retard, fetter, block, thwart, bar, clog, encumber, burden, inhibit, shackle, interrupt, arrest, curb, oppose, deter, hamper, frustrate, intercept, prohibit, stall, slow, down, smother, disappoint, spoil, gag, annul

hint *(n.)* allusion, mention, inkling, implication, reference, observation, notice, tip, clue, omen, scent, notion, taste, suspicion, innuendo, sign, impression, indication, suggestion

hire *(v.)* engage, secure, enlist, appoint, delegate, authorize, retain, commission, empower, select, pick, contract, procure

history *(n.)* account, annals, records, archives, chronicle, writings, evidence, record

hit *(n.)* blow, slap, rap, punch; success, favourite, sellout, knockout

hitch *(n.)* loop, noose, tie; difficult, obstacle, hindrance, block

hoard *(v.)* amass, acquire, keep, accumulate, save

hoary *(adj.)* white, old, aged, grey-haired

hoax *(n.)* trick, fabrication, deceit, deception, lie

hobby *(n.)* pursuit, avocation, pastime, diversion, interest, activity, pursuit, sport, amusement, craft

hodgepodge *(n.)* mixture, jumble, combination, mess

hokum *(n.)* nonsense, trickery, chicanery

hold *(v.)* possess, keep, retain, have, accept; support, sustain, brace, buttress, prop; grasp, grip, clutch, embrace, squeeze, hug, seize; imprison, enclose, restrain; resist, persevere, continue, endure; adhere, cling, fasten, stick

hole *(n.)* cavity, perforation, puncture, slot, eyelet, split, tear, cleft, opening, fissure, gap, gash, rift, rupture, aperture, breach, crater, gorge, hollow, chasm, crevasse, burrow, den, lair; difficulty, impasse, tangle, mess, crisis, emergency

holiday *(n.)* festival, fiesta, carnival, jubilee, anniversary, celebration

holocaust *(n.)* loss, fire, destruction

holy *(adj.)* devout, pious, righteous, moral, just, good, angelic, godly, reverent, venerable, humble, saintly, innocent, godlike, saintlike, faultless, chaste, upright, virtuous, dedicated, devoted, spiritual, religious

homage *(n.)* loyalty, worship, respect, adoration, deference, devotion, reverence

home *(n.)* residence, habitation, abode, lodging, quarters, domicile, shelter; orphanage, sanitarium, hospital

homogenize *(v.)* blend, combine, integrate

honesty *(n.)* fidelity, scrupulousness, candour, openness, morality, goodness, virtue

honour *(n.)* distinction, recognition, attention, reputation, tribute, integrity

hood *(n.)* cowl, shawl, bonnet, veil, capuchin, mantle, cover; criminal, gangster, crook

hoodlum *(n.)* rowdy, thug, gangster, crook, criminal

hook *(v.)* curve, angle, crook, arch; catch, pin, secure, fasten

hoot *(n.)* howl, whoop, boo, cry

hope *(n.)* expectation, anticipation; purpose, wish, goal

horde *(n.)* crowd, swarm, pack, throng, gathering

horrible *(adj.)* repulsive, dreadful, disgusting, terrible, frightful, shameful, shocking, awful

horrid *(adj.)* shocking, hideous, disturbing, shameful, offensive, pitiful

horticulture *(n.)* cultivation, agriculture, farming

hospital *(n.)* clinic, infirmary, sanitarium, dispensary

hostile *(adj.)* unfriendly, antagonistic, hateful, opposed

hot *(adj.)* fiery, flaming, blazing, baking, roasting, scorching, blistering, searing, sizzling, broiling, scalding, parching; aroused, furious, ill-tempered, indignant, angry

hotel *(n.)* motel, lodging, inn, hostel, resort, tavern

hound *(v.)* bully, pester, badger, provoke, annoy

house *(n.)* home, habitation, dwelling, residence; family, line, tradition, ancestry; congress, council, parliament

housekeeper *(n.)* caretaker, servant, domestic

hover *(v.)* remain, wait, float, linger

howl *(v.)* cry, wail, bawl, lament, yell

hub *(n.)* centre, core, middle, focus, heart

hubbub *(n.)* uproar, bustle, noise, racket

hue *(n.)* colour, tint, value, dye

hug *(v.)* embrace, hold, squeeze, clasp, press, cling, clutch, envelop, enfold, nestle, cuddle

huge *(adj.)* large, tremendous, enormous, immense

humane *(adj.)* merciful, kind, benevolent, sympathetic, understanding, compassionate, kindhearted, tenderhearted, forgiving, charitable, tender, generous, lenient, altruistic, philanthropic, magnanimous, unselfish, warmhearted

humble *(adj.)* submissive, gentle, diffident, retiring, bashful, shy, timid, reserved, deferential, mild, withdrawn, hesitant, fearful, tentative, obedient, passive, tame, restrained, subdued; modest, seemly, becoming, homespun, servile, insignificant, plain, common, homely, simple

humid *(adj.)* moist, damp, stuffy, sticky, muggy

humiliate *(v.)* humble, shame, debase, chasten, mortify, degrade, dishonour, demean, conquer, vanquish, disgrace, embarrass

humour *(n.)* comedy, entertainment, amusement, jesting, witticism, banter, joke, mirth; disposition, wittiness, gaiety, playfulness

hunch *(n.)* intuition, notion, feeling, premonition, instinct, anticipation, clue, foreboding, portent, apprehension, misgiving, qualm, suspicion, inkling

hunger *(n.)* longing, yearning, lust, want

hunk *(n.)* lump, chunk, mass, clod, slice, morsel

hunt *(v.)* pursue, follow, stalk, hound, trail, seek, track, chase; search, probe, seek

hurdle *(n.)* obstacle, barricade, blockade, barrier

hurrah *(v.)* applaud, cheer, approve

hurry *(v.)* scurry, scuttle, dash, sprint, rush, scoot, dart, spring, speed, fly, bustle, race; urge, drive, push, spur, goad

hurt *(v.)* injure, cut, bruise, slap, abuse, flog, whip, torture, stab, harm, wound, lacerate, bite, burn, punch, pinch, scourge, lash, cane, switch; harm, maltreat, injure, spoil, damage, destroy; pain, ache, throb, sting

hush *(v.)* calm, soothe, quiet, silence, gag, stifle

husky *(adj.)* rough, throaty, growling, gruff; muscular, sinewy, strapping

hustle *(v.)* rush, push, hurry, race, run, speed

hygiene *(n.)* health, sanitation, cleanliness

hyperbole *(n.)* metaphor, exaggeration

hypnotize *(v.)* mesmerize, fascinate, captivate, stupefy, soothe, anesthetize

hypocrisy *(n.)* pretense, affectation, bigotry, sanctimony, dishonesty, lie

hysteria, hysterics *(n.)* neurosis, emotionalism, delirium, agitation, confusion, excitement, nervousness

I

icon *(n.)* image, picture, idol, hero

iconoclast *(n.)* dissenter, rebel, radical

idea *(n.)* belief, theory, hypothesis, assumption, conjecture, notion, thought; whimsy, whim, fantasy

ideal *(adj.)* typical, model, archetypal; perfect, best, theoretical, supreme, fitting, excellent

ideal *(n.)* concept, paragon, goal, prototype, model

identical *(adj.)* same, alike, twin, indistinguishable

identity *(n.)* characteristics, identification, individuality, uniqueness, name

idiom *(n.)* expression, usage, jargon

idiot *(n.)* simpleton, nincompoop, booby, fool

idle *(adj.)* unemployed, unoccupied, uncultivated, motionless, inert, resting

idol *(n.)* image, icon, god

ignite *(v.)* fire, light, enkindle, burn

ignoble *(adj.)* mean, dishonorable, low, base

ignorance *(n.)* incomprehension, incapacity, inexperience, illiteracy, simplicity, shallowness

ill *(adj.)* harmful, evil, noxious, unfavourable; unwell, unhealthy, ailing

illegal *(adj.)* unlawful, illicit, banned, outlawed, unauthorized, unlicensed, illegitimate, prohibited, forbidden

illegible *(adj.)* unreadable, faint, unintelligible, confused, obscure

illicit *(adj.)* unlawful, prohibited, unauthorized, illegal

illiteracy *(n.)* ignorance, stupidity, idiocy

illogical *(adj.)* irrational, unreasonable, absurd, fallacious, incorrect, inconsistent, unscientific, contradictory, unsound, implausible

illuminate *(v.)* lighten, illumine, decorate, light; illustrate, explain, interpret, elucidate

illusion *(n.)* deception, fancy, hallucination, mirage, apparition, delusion, trick, dream

illustrate *(v.)* explain, picture, portray, depict

image *(n.)* idol, representation, effigy, form, drawing, portrait, photograph, replica, picture; conception, perception, thought, idea

imagery *(n.)* metaphor, representation, comparison

imaginary *(adj.)* fancied, illusory, visionary, dreamy, hypothetical, theoretical, imagined, hallucinatory, whimsical, fabulous, nonexistent, mythological, legendary, fictitious, unreal

imbalance *(n.)* unevenness, inequality, irregularity
imbecilic *(adj.)* foolish, silly, jerk
imbibe *(v.)* ingest, gorge, guzzle, drink, swallow
imitate *(v.)* impersonate, mirror, mime, ape, simulate, parody; duplicate, counterfeit, falsify, reproduce; simulate, parallel
immaculate *(adj.)* pure, unsoiled, unsullied, spotless, stainless, bright, clean
immaterial *(adj.)* unimportant, insignificant, irrelevant
immature *(adj.)* childish, youthful, sophomoric, naive
immediate *(adj.)* now, next, prompt, following
immense *(adj.)* large, gigantic, tremendous, enormous
immerse *(v.)* plunge, involve, submerge, douse, steep, soak, drench, dunk, souse
immigrant *(n.)* outsider, newcomer, alien
imminent *(adj.)* impending, approaching, coming
immobility *(n.)* firm, fixed, motionless
immoral *(adj.)* sinful, corrupt, shameless, bad
immovable *(adj.)* solid, stable, fixed, firm
immune *(adj.)* exempt, free, insusceptible, privileged, excused, safe
impact *(n.)* shock, impression, contact, collision
impair *(v.)* diminish, spoil, injure, hurt, break, damage
impart *(v.)* bestow, grant, present, allow; announce, divulge, admit, reveal
impartial *(adj.)* unbiased, disinterested, equal, fair
impasse *(n.)* deadlock, standstill, cessation, pause
impatient *(adj.)* anxious, eager, feverish, restless
impeach *(v.)* charge, arraign, denounce, indict, discredit, reprimand, blame, incriminate, try
impeccable *(adj.)* flawless, perfect, exact, precise
impede *(v.)* hinder, obstruct, slow
impel *(v.)* drive, force, urge
imperfect *(adj.)* flawed, incomplete, deficient, faulty
imperious *(adj.)* haughty, arrogant, bossy
impersonate *(v.)* portray, mimic, represent, imitate
impervious *(adj.)* impassable, impermeable, impenetrable, watertight
impetuous *(adj.)* hasty, impulsive, rash
impinge *(v.)* encroach, infringe, strike, touch
implement *(n.)* tool, instrument, appliance, utensil
implicit *(adj.)* implied, certain, absolute, accurate, inevitable
imply *(v.)* indicate, intimate, suggest, hint, implicate, signify, mean, indicate
import *(n.)* meaning, signification, value, worth
important *(adj.)* significant, momentous, essential, critical, primary, foremost, marked, valuable, crucial, vital, serious, consequential; well-known, influential, famous
impose *(v.)* force, presume, burden, compel
impossible *(adj.)* inconceivable, vain, unattainable, unworkable, futile, hopeless
imposture *(n.)* fraud, deceiver, pretender, charlatan
impotent *(adj.)* powerless, inept, infirm, unable; barren, frigid, unproductive
impoverish *(v.)* bankrupt, exhaust, destroy
impregnate *(v.)* fill, pervade, soak, infuse; conceive, reproduce, fertilize
impress *(v.)* indent, emboss, imprint, dent, stamp; affect, dazzle, stir, fascinate
imprint *(n.)* banner, trademark, emblem, signature; dent, indentation
improbable *(adj.)* doubtful, unlikely, uncertain
improve *(v.)* update, refine, enrich, enhance, augment
impudent *(adj.)* bold, insolent, rude
impulse *(n.)* surge, pulsation, beat; urge, stimulus, whim, caprice, spontaneity, notion, inclination, disposition
impute *(v.)* ascribe, assign, charge
inaccessible *(adj.)* distant, rare, remote, separated
inaccurate *(adj.)* incorrect, inexact, fallacious, mistaken, wrong
inadequacy *(n.)* inferiority, weakness, defect, flaw, drawback, shortcoming, blemish, lack
inane *(adj.)* senseless, pointless, foolish, silly
inapt *(adj.)* unfit, unsuitable, ill-suited
inaugurate *(v.)* induct, begin, introduce, initiate
incantation *(n.)* chant, charm, recitation, supplication
incarcerate *(v.)* confine, imprison, detain
incarnate *(adj.)* bodily, manifest, personified
incense *(n.)* scent, fragrance, essence, perfume
incentive *(n.)* motive, spur, inducement, impetus, enticement, temptation, inspiration, encouragement, reason
incessant *(adj.)* continual, ceaseless, constant
incident *(n.)* occurrence, happening, episode, event

incise *(v.)* cut, engrave, dissect, chop, split, divide
incite *(v.)* rouse, stir, stimulate, provoke, spur
incline *(v.)* tilt, bow, nod; prefer, favour
include *(v.)* contain, embrace, involve, incorporate, constitute, intellect, insert
incoherent *(adj.)* disorganized, muddled, muffled
income *(n.)* revenue, earnings, salary, wages, profit, dividends, proceeds, receipts, commission
incompetent *(adj.)* incapable, unfit, unskilled
incongruous *(adj.)* inconsistent, contradictory
incorrigible *(adj.)* bad, difficult, unreformed
increase *(n.)* growth, addition, development, spread, enlargement, expansion, escalation
incredible *(adj.)* unbelievable, improbable, ridiculous
incumbent *(adj.)* binding, obligatory, required
incursion *(n.)* inroad, invasion, foray
indecision *(n.)* hesitation, doubt, uncertainty
indelible *(adj.)* ingrained, enduring, strong, permanent
index *(v.)* list, catalogue, alphabetize, arrange, tabulate
indicate *(v.)* symbolize, betoken, intimate, mean; show, name, point
indifferent *(adj.)* unconcerned, cool, unemotional, unsympathetic, heartless, unresponsive, unfeeling, nonchalant, impassive, detached, callous, stony, remote, reserved, distant, arrogant, unmoved
indirect *(adj.)* devious, roundabout, tortuous, twisting, devious, sinister, rambling, oblique
individual *(adj.)* personal, particular, solitary, distinctive, personalized, sole, private
indomitable *(adj.)* invincible, unconquerable, resolute
induce *(v.)* begin, cause, effect, persuade, produce
infidelity *(n.)* unfaithfulness, adultery
infirm *(adj.)* sickly, weak, frail
inflame *(v.)* arouse, incense, disturb, excite; hurt, redden, swell; burn, kindle, scorch, ignite
inflate *(v.)* expand, swell, bloat, widen; magnify, overestimate, raise
inflection *(n.)* tone, enunciation, intonation, accent
inflict *(v.)* impose, administer, deliver, strike, cause
influence *(n.)* power, authority, control, command esteem, prominence, prestige, reputation
inform *(v.)* tell, betray, instruct, relate, teach
informal *(adj.)* casual, intimate, relaxed
infringe *(v.)* encroach, trespass, transgress, meddle
infuse *(v.)* fill, inspire; steep
ingenious *(adj.)* able, clever, cunning, gifted, intelligent, original, resourceful, shrewd, skillful
ingrain *(v.)* imbue, fix, instill, teach
ingredient *(n.)* component, constituent, element
inhabit *(v.)* dwell, occupy, reside, stay
inherent *(adj.)* inborn, inbred, inherited, innate, intrinsic, native, natural
inherit *(v.)* acquire, receive, succeed, get
inhibit *(v.)* check, restrain, repress, frustrate, hinder
inhuman *(adj.)* mean, heartless, cruel, fierce, ruthless
inequity *(n.)* crime, evil, injustice, sin, wickedness
initiate *(n.)* beginner, learner, novice
injure *(v.)* harm, damage, wound, hurt
inkling *(n.)* hint, indication, notion, innuendo, suspicion, suggestion
inmate *(n.)* occupant, patient, convict, prisoner
innate *(adj.)* inborn, native, inherent
innocence *(n.)* honesty, simplicity, purity, naivete, chastity, ignorance, virtue
innovation *(n.)* change, newness, addition
innuendo *(n.)* hint, insinuation, aside, intimation
inopportune *(adj.)* disadvantageous, ill-timed, inappropriate, awkward, untimely
inquisitive *(adj.)* curious, questioning, meddling, analytical, snoopy, nosy, interested
insane *(adj.)* demented, crazed, frenzied, lunatic, psychotic, raving, deluded, possessed, idiotic, stupid
insatiate *(adj.)* ravenous, voracious
inscribe *(v.)* address, carve, dedicate, engrave, write
insecure *(adj.)* anxious, vague, uncertain, troubled
insert *(v.)* introduce, place, inject, include
insidious *(adj.)* treacherous, deceitful, harmful
insincere *(adj.)* deceitful, pretentious, shifty, dishonest, false, hypocritical, sly
insipid *(adj.)* dull, flat, tasteless, uninteresting
insolent *(adj.)* disrespectful, insulting, rude
insolvent *(adj.)* bankrupt, broke, failed, ruined
inspire *(v.)* encourage, enthuse, fire, invigorate, motivate, stimulate
install *(v.)* establish, introduce, inaugurate
instant *(adj.)* momentary, quick, pressing, current

instill *(v.)* infuse, indoctrinate, implant, teach
instinct *(n.)* impulse, sense, intuition, feeling
institute *(n.)* establishment, organization, body, centre
instruct *(v.)* inform, teach, order, direct, educate
instrument *(n.)* utensil, apparatus, implement, device, tool; deed, document
insular *(adj.)* detached, isolated, narrow, provincial
insurance *(n.)* security, indemnity, assurance, warrant
insure *(v.)* secure, warrant, protect, guarantee
intact *(adj.)* entire, whole, together
intangible *(adj.)* indefinite, uncertain, vague
integral *(adj.)* whole, entire, essential
intellect *(n.)* understanding, intelligence, mentality
intend *(v.)* purpose, aspire, aim, indicate, signify, denote
intense *(adj.)* deep, profound, heightened, vivid, impassioned, exaggerated, violent, excessive, keen, piercing, cutting, severe
intensity *(n.)* concentration, strength, power, fervour, passion, ardour, severity, depth, magnitude
intent *(adj.)* fixed, absorbed, focused
intent *(n.)* design, plan, aim
intercept *(v.)* obstruct, ambush, block, hijack
interest *(n.)* attention, excitement, curiosity, enthusiasm; claim, right, stake
interior *(adj.)* within, inside, inland, inner, internal, inward, central, inside
interlope *(v.)* interfere, intrude, meddle
intermediate *(adj.)* intervening, medium, intermediary, median, central, middle
intermediate *(adj.)* interval, interim, recess
intermix *(v.)* mix, mingle
intermittent *(adj.)* cyclic, recurring, periodic, recurrent, changing, irregular
intern *(v.)* detain, imprison, hold
intern *(n.)* train, apprentice, tutor
interpret *(v.)* translate, explain, render, delineate, define, describe
interrogate *(v.)* question, ask, examine
interrupt *(v.)* intervene, interfere, infringe
intersperse *(v.)* scatter, strew, sprinkle
intervene *(v.)* intercede, mediate, negotiate, reconcile
interview *(n.)* meeting, audience, conference
intimate *(adj.)* close, trusted, secret, special
intimate *(v.)* hint, allude, suggest
intimidate *(v.)* frighten, threaten, alarm
intolerant *(adj.)* dogmatic, bigoted, prejudiced
intoxicate *(v.)* inebriate, muddle, befuddle
intricacy *(n.)* elaborateness, complexity, difficulty
intrigue *(v.)* plot, scheme, delight, please, attract, charm, entertain, fascinate
intrinsic *(adj.)* essential, inborn, inherent
introduce *(v.)* advance, offer, propose, acquaint; add, enter, include
introvert *(n.)* loner, recluse
intrude *(v.)* encroach, trespass, interfere, meddle
invade *(v.)* attack, intrude. infringe, trespass, interfere
invaluable *(adj.)* priceless, expensive, dear, valuable
invective *(n.)* railing, abusive, tirade
invent *(v.)* create, discover, originate, devise, fashion, form, design, improvise, contrive, build
investigate *(v.)* enquire, review, examine, study
invigorate *(v.)* animate, energize, enliven, excite, exhilarate, freshen, stimulate
invincible *(adj.)* impregnable, invulnerable, powerful, strong, unconquerable
inviolate *(adj.)* hallowed, holy, intact, pure, sacred
invoice *(n.)* notice, statement, bill, receipt
invoke *(v.)* implore, solicit, summon
involve *(v.)* associate, commit, connect, comprise, connect, entangle, implicate, include, link
iota *(n.)* jot, particle, trace, scrap, grain, bit, speck
irascible *(adj.)* irritable, temperamental, testy, touchy
irate *(adj.)* enraged, furious, incensed, angry
irk *(v.)* vex, annoy, harass, disturb, bother
irony *(n.)* satire, ridicule, mockery, derision, sarcasm
irrevocable *(adj.)* permanent, indelible, inevitable
irritable *(adj.)* cranky, testy, touchy, huffy, peevish, petulant, surly, moody, churlish, grouchy, grumpy
island *(n.)* isle, bar, archipelago
isolate *(v.)* detach, insulate, confine, seclude, divide
itemize *(v.)* list, catalogue, enumerate, number, detail

J

jab *(v.)* poke, punch, hit, blow
jacket *(n.)* coat, tunic, jerkin, cape
jackpot *(n.)* bonanza, winnings, luck, profit, success
jaded *(adj.)* cold, impassive, indifferent, nonchalant, world-weary
jam *(n.)* conserve, marmalade, jelly; trouble, dilemma, problem, difficulty
jargon *(n.)* idiom, vernacular, colloquialism, localism, dialect, slang
jaunt *(n.)* excursion, trip, tour, journey, walk
jealous *(adj.)* envious, possessive, resentful
jeer *(v.)* deride, insult, mock, ridicule, taunt
jeopardize *(v.)* endanger, imperil, expose, venture, risk
jerk *(n.)* twitch, tic, shake, quiver; scamp, scoundrel, fool, rascal
jest *(v.)* joke, tease, mock, sneer
jewel *(n.)* prize, bauble, gem, trinket
jiggle *(v.)* shake, twitch, wiggle, jerk
jingle *(n.)* rhyme, verse, clangour
job *(n.)* employment, situation, position, calling, vocation, career, pursuit, business, profession, trade; task, assignment, undertaking, project, chore, errand, duty
jocular *(adj.)* comic, frolicsome, funny, witty
join *(v.)* unite, blend, combine, connect, couple, attach, link, fuse, entwine, associate
joke *(v.)* jest, quip, banter, laugh, play, frolic, wisecrack
jolt *(n.)* bump, bounce, blow, jerk, surprise, shock, surprise
jostle *(v.)* push, elbow, nudge
jot *(v.)* write, note, scribble, record
journal *(n.)* diary, chronicle, record; periodical, publication, newspaper, magazine, daily
journalist *(n.)* columnist, commentator, reporter
journey *(n.)* trip, tour, excursion, jaunt, travel
jovial *(adj.)* affable, amiable, merry, happy
jubilee *(n.)* anniversary, celebration, festival
judge *(n.)* moderator, arbiter, referee, umpire; analyst, critic, expert, specialist
judge *(v.)* hear, decide, adjudicate, rule
juice *(n.)* sap, extract, fluid, liquid
jumble *(n.)* clutter, mess, hodgepodge, confusion
junction *(n.)* joining, coupling, joint, union; crossroads, crossing, intersection
jungle *(n.)* tangle, wilderness, undergrowth, forest
junk *(n.)* scrap, waste, garbage, filth, trash
jurisdiction *(n.)* authority, range, province, scope, domain, extent, empire, sovereignty
just *(adj.)* precisely, exactly, correctly, perfectly, accurate; hardly, barely, scarcely; only, merely, simply, plainly; fair, impartial, equal, righteous
jut *(adj.)* extend, bulge, project
juvenile *(adj.)* childish, youthful, adolescent, teenage
juxtapose *(v.)* compare, contrast, match

K

keepsake *(n.)* memento, token, remembrance, reminder
kernel *(n.)* seed, grain, core, nut, germ
kettle *(n.)* vessel, cauldron, saucepan, stewpot, pot
kid *(n.)* child, son, daughter, boy, girl
kid *(v.)* mock, tease, joke
kidnap *(v.)* abduct, capture, shanghai
killjoy *(n.)* grouch, sourpuss, spoilsport
kiln *(n.)* dryer, oast, oven
kind *(adj.)* accommodating, agreeable, charitable, compassionate, considerate, generous, kindhearted, loving, obliging, sensitive, tactful, tender
kind *(n.)* classification, species, genus; type, sort, variety, description, denomination, designation
kindle *(v.)* fire, excite, light, ignite
kingdom *(n.)* realm, domain, country, empire, diligence, strain, stress, effort, dominions, territory
kinship *(n.)* affiliation, relationship, connection, alliance, family
knack *(n.)* dexterity, trick, skill, faculty, ability
knead *(v.)* work, shape, twist, press
knickknack *(n.)* bric-a-brac, ornament, trifle, bauble, trinket, showpiece, gewgaw
knife *(n.)* blade, dagger, stiletto, lancet, machete, scalpel, dirk
knit *(v.)* unite, join, intermingle, affiliate
knob *(n.)* bulge, protuberance, node, bump; handle, doorknob, latch
knot *(n.)* bond, tie, cinch, hitch, splice, group
knowledge *(n.)* information, learning, wisdom, enlightenment, expertise, awareness

L

label *(v.)* identify, mark, name, specify

labour *(n.)* work, activity, toil, operation, employment, undertaking, energy, industry, diligence, strain, stress, effort

lacerate *(v.)* tear, wound, cut, rip

lack *(n.)* deficiency, scarcity, insufficiency, inadequacy; need, privation, poverty, distress

laconic *(adj.)* concise, curt, succinct, terse

ladle *(n.)* spoon, skimmer, scoop

lady *(n.)* woman, female, matron, gentlewoman

lame *(adj.)* halt, unpaired, handicapped, limping

lament *(v.)* grieve, deplore, bemoan

lampoon *(v.)* satirize, burlesque, ridicule

land *(n.)* property, estate, tract, ranch, farm, lot; country, province, region, nation

landscape *(n.)* countryside, scenery, panorama, view

language *(n.)* expression, tongue, word, sign, signal, gesture, vocabulary, diction, dialect, idiom, vernacular, speech, jargon

lanky *(adj.)* lean, rangy, thin

lantern *(n.)* light, torch, lamp

lapse *(v.)* pass, void, slip, deteriorate, decline, weaken

larceny *(n.)* theft, burglary, thievery, robbery, crime

lascivious *(adj.)* bawdy, carnal, immoral, lewd, lurid, sensual, sexual

lass *(n.)* girl, woman, lady, damsel, maiden

lassitude *(adj.)* weariness, listlessness, fatigue

lasting *(adj.)* enduring, abiding, constant, permanent

latent *(adj.)* potential, undeveloped, dormant

lather *(n.)* foam, froth, bubbles

latitude *(n.)* freedom, degree, measure

latter *(adj.)* after, following, late, last, recent

laud *(v.)* glorify, honour, praise

laugh *(v.)* chuckle, snicker, titter, chortle, cackle, guffaw, giggle

lavatory *(n.)* basin, privy, bathroom, washroom, toilet

lavish *(adj.)* profuse, extravagant, generous, unsparing, plentiful

lawful *(adj.)* legal, legitimate, decreed, permitted, constitutional; legislated, enacted, official, enforced, protected, legitimized, established

lawyer *(n.)* attorney, solicitor, jurist, defender, counsel, solicitor, barrister, advocate

laxity *(n.)* slackness, negligence

layout *(n.)* arrangement, design, organization, plan

leave *(n.)* departure, farewell, consent, vacation

lazy *(adj.)* indolent, idle, sluggish, apathetic, loafing, flagging, slothful, lethargic

leader *(n.)* guide, conductor, director, manager, officer, captain, master, ruler, boss

leaflet *(n.)* brochure, handbill, circular, pamphlet reprimand

league *(n.)* union, alliance, group, unit, organization

leap *(v.)* jump, bound, spring, vault, bounce

learn *(v.)* acquire, read, master, ascertain, determine, unearth, hear, memorize, study

lethal *(adj.)* deadly, fatal, mortal, malignant, harmful

lethargy *(n.)* stupor, dullness, drowsiness

letter *(n.)* message, memo, note, memorandum, epistle, line, mail; symbol, character, type

leverage *(n.)* power, purchase; lift, hold, support

leviathan *(n.)* monster, beast, mammoth

levity *(n.)* flippancy, frivolity, silliness

lewd *(adj.)* smutty, indecent, sensual; wanton, lascivious, licentious, lecherous, dissolute, debauched, corrupt, depraved, vulgar

lexicon *(n.)* dictionary, vocabulary, glossary

liable *(adj.)* accountable, answerable, exposed, obliged; apt, inclined, likely, tending

liaison *(n.)* agent, connection, emissary, proxy; affair, intrigue, romance, tryst

liar *(n.)* deceiver, perjurer, falsifier, fibber

liberal *(adj.)* progressive, broad-minded, nonconformist, permissive, radical, tolerant; generous: indulgent, lavish, magnanimous

libertine *(n.)* lecher, pervert, rake, rouge

liberty *(n.)* emancipation, enfranchisement, rescue, freedom; leave, relaxation, rest, leisure, recreation; privilege, permission, decision, selection; rights, freedom, independence

license *(n.)* consent, authorization, permission, sanction; permit, certificate, registration; freedom, looseness, excess, immoderation, latitude

licit *(adj.)* authorized, lawful, sanctioned

lid *(n.)* cover, cap, top, roof, hood

lie *(v.)* falsify, prevaricate, deceive, misinform, exaggerate, distort, concoct, misrepresent, dissemble, delude; prostrate, recline, retire, rest, sleep

life *(n.)* being, entity, presence, consciousness, vitality; biography, story, memoir; duration, lifetime, span, generation, season, cycle; excitement, zeal

lift *(v.)* elevate, raise, hoist; steal, filch, pilfer

light *(adj.)* illuminated, radiant, luminous, bright; vivid, colourful, rich, clear; slight, frivolous, trivial, unimportant; lively, spirited, animated, active; ethereal, airy, fluffy, downy, dainty, thin, sheer, insubstantial, graceful

light-headed *(adj.)* inane, fickle, frivolous, silly; tired, delirious, dizzy, weak

light-hearted *(adj.)* gay, joyous, cheerful, happy

like *(v.)* enjoy, relish, savour, fancy; admire, esteem, approve; prefer, choose, desire, fancy

likely *(adj.)* probable, conceivable, rational, plausible, apt, tending, prone, liable

limb *(n.)* branch, arm, bough, offshoot; appendage, arm, leg, part

limit *(n.)* boundary, frontier, border, extent, extremity

limp *(adj.)* weak, pliant, flaccid, flabby, pliable, slack, loose, flimsy

line *(n.)* border, limit, boundary, edge, row, rank, file, order, arrangement, sequence, column, groove, profession, career, vocation; cord, filament; descent, pedigree, lineage, family, heredity

linear *(adj.)* successive, direct, straight

linger *(v.)* remain, loiter, tarry, lag, delay, dawdle, wait

lingerie *(n.)* underwear, dainties, unmentionables

linguist *(n.)* lexicographer, translator, grammarian

link *(n.)* loop, ring, coupling; seam, weld, intersection, fastening, splice, articulation, joint

liquid *(adj.)* watery, molten, moist, aqueous, liquefied, dissolved, melted, thawed, wet; running, splashing, thin, moving, viscous, fluid, juicy

list *(v.)* catalogue, register, tally, inventory, index; pitch, slant, incline

listen *(v.)* hear, heed, attend, overhear

litany *(n.)* form, ritual, recital, list

literacy *(n.)* scholarship, education, knowledge

literal *(adj.)* actually, exactly, strictly, verbatim

literate *(adj.)* lettered, learned, scholarly, educated

lithograph *(n.)* print, copy

litter *(n.)* debris, mess, jumble, hodgepodge, trash, clutter; brood, piglets, puppies, kittens, offspring

little *(adj.)* small, diminutive, tiny, wee, slight, miniature, puny; inadequate, inconsiderable, insufficient; shallow, petty, superficial, frivolous, trivial; base, weak, shallow, mean, petty

live *(v.)* exist, subsist, survive, breathe, be; relish, savour, experience; dwell, inhabit, abide; continue, remain, survive, endure, last

livelihood *(n.)* job, career, means, subsistence

lively *(adj.)* active, animated, brisk, energetic, spirited, vigorous, vivacious

load *(n.)* cargo, capacity, bundle; responsibility, charge, obligation, trust, duty

loan *(v.)* lend, provide, advance

loath *(adj.)* disinclined, unwilling, opposed

loathe *(v.)* detest, dislike, hate

lobby *(n.)* entryway, antechamber, foyer, hall, vestibule

locale *(n.)* vicinity, territory, district, area, region

locate *(v.)* discover, find, establish, determine, place, settle, inhabit, dwell

lodge *(n.)* retreat, inn, hostel, hotel, motel, resort, cabin, cottage; society, club, fraternity

lodge *(v.)* shelter, board, harbour, quarter; place: fix, leave, deposit, embed

logic *(n.)* reasoning, deduction, induction, thought

logy *(adj.)* lethargic, sluggish, dull

loiter *(v.)* linger, dawdle, idle, tarry, wait

lonely *(adj.)* abandoned, homesick, forlorn, deserted, lonesome, soiitary, secluded

longing *(n.)* craving, yearning, pining, desire, wish

loom *(v.)* appear, rise, emerge; threaten, hulk, hover, approach

loop *(v.)* curve, encircle, connect, bend

loose *(adj.)* slack, free, careless; wanton, unrestrained, dissolute; unattached, disconnected, baggy, free; vague, random, obscure

loot *(n.)* plunder, spoils, take, booty

lopsided *(adj.)* uneven, unbalanced, tipped, irregular

lost *(adj.)* misplaced, mislaid, obscured, strayed, vanished; perplexed, puzzled; wasted, ruined

lotion *(n.)* cream, balm, salve, unguent, cosmetic

lounge *(n.)* sofa, couch, divan; room, bar, lobby, parlour, salon

love *(n.)* attachment, infatuation, rapture, ardour; respect, regard, admiration

lover *(n.)* suitor, sweetheart, admirer, escort, paramour, fiance, boyfriend, girlfriend, steady

low *(adj.)* crouched, sunken; muffled, hushed, quiet; sad, dejected, moody, blue; vulgar, base, mean, coarse; moderate, inexpensive, cheap
loyal *(adj.)* fair, true, dependable, firm, faithful
loyalty *(n.)* fidelity, allegiance, faithfulness, constancy, attachment, support, devotion
lucid *(adj.)* clear, obvious, unmistakable; bright, luminous; rational, normal
luck *(n.)* prosperity, wealth, windfall, blessings; fate, opportunity, break, accident
lucrative *(adj.)* profitable, fruitful, productive, gainful
ludicrous *(adj.)* absurd, ridiculous, laughable, farcical, incongruous
luggage *(n.)* baggage, trunks, bags, valises
lukewarm *(adj.)* cool, tepid, chilly
lull *(n.)* pause, hiatus, stillness, hush, silence
lull *(v.)* soothe, quiet, calm
luminous *(adj.)* lighted, glowing, radiant, bright
lump *(n.)* mass, clump, block, chunk, hunk
lunacy *(n.)* madness, dementia, mania; foolishness, silliness
lunge *(v.)* thrust, surge, bound, jump
lure *(v.)* entice, enchant, bewitch, allure
lurid *(adj.)* ghastly, gruesome, sensational
luscious *(adj.)* toothsome, palatable, delicious
lush *(adj.)* verdant, dense, grassy; rich, juicy, succulent; elaborate, extravagant, luxurious, ornamental, ornate
lust *(n.)* desire, appetite, passion, sensuality
luster *(n.)* brightness, radiance, glow, brilliance, light
luxurious *(adj.)* comfortable, affluent, expensive, rich
lyrical *(adj.)* melodious, sweet, rhythmical, poetic

M

machine *(n.)* contrivance, device, implement
macrocosm *(n.)* universe, world
made *(adj.)* fashioned, built, formed, manufactured
magazine *(n.)* periodical, journal, publication
magic *(n.)* occultism, wizardry, sorcery, divination, witchcraft, voodooism, soothsaying
magnanimous *(adj.)* charitable, noble, unselfish, forgiving, generous
magnate *(n.)* tycoon, mogul
magnetic *(adj.)* alluring, appealing, attractive, irresistible, captivating, fascinating, charming
magnificent *(adj.)* splendid, grand, exalted, majestic
magnify *(v.)* amplify, expand, increase, enlarge
magnitude *(n.)* extent, quantity; importance, greatness, consequence, significance
maim *(v.)* disfigure, mutilate, disable, damage, hurt
main *(adj.)* principal, chief, leading, dominant, foremost
maintain *(v.)* uphold, support, sustain, affirm, defend; state, attest, declare, say; preserve, keep, conserve, reserve, save, manage
majesty *(n.)* grandeur, nobility, greatness
make *(v.)* manufacture, construct, fabricate, assemble, fashion, produce, build, form; create, originate, generate, devise, conceive, invent; constrain, compel, coerce; wage, conduct, engage, prepare, ready, arrange, adjust, cook; earn, gain; reach, arrive
maladroit *(adj.)* awkward, bungling, clumsy, inept
malady *(n.)* affliction, ailment, disease, sickness
malice *(n.)* hatred, spite, animosity, resentment
malign *(v.)* vilify, defame, slander
mall *(n.)* market, shop, arcade
malodorous *(adj.)* stinking, fetid
mammoth *(adj.)* huge, large, colossal
manacle *(v.)* chain, handcuff, shackle
manage *(v.)* control, lead, oversee, mastermind, engineer, handle, supervise; contrive, accomplish, effect, achieve; endure, survive
mandatory *(adj.)* imperative, compulsory, obligatory
manoeuver *(v.)* plot, scheme, contrive, design, conspire
manger *(n.)* trough, tub, crib
mania *(n.)* craze, lunacy, madness, desire, obsession
manifest *(adj.)* apparent, clear, evident, obvious
manipulate *(v.)* control, shape, mould, form
mannequin *(n.)* model, dummy, display
manner *(n.)* conduct, deportment, demeanour, behaviour; custom, habit, use, way, practice
mansion *(n.)* house, villa, hall, estate, home
mantle *(n.)* cloak, blanket, role, job
manual *(n.)* handbook, guidebook, reference
manufacture *(v.)* make, fabricate, produce, build

manuscript *(n.)* book, paper, document, composition
mar *(v.)* damage, spoil, disfigure, harm, scratch, deface
margin *(n.)* edge, border, lip, shore, boundary
marine *(adj.)* nautical, maritime, oceanic
mark *(v.)* brand, imprint, label, identify, earmark; signify, denote, mean, characterize, qualify
market *(v.)* sell, trade, vend, exchange, barter
marry *(v.)* wed, espouse; join, unite, combine
marsh *(n.)* swamp, morass, bog, quagmire
martyr *(n.)* saint, victim, sufferer, offering, scapegoat
marvel *(v.)* wonder, awe, stare
mash *(v.)* crush, bruise, squash, pulverize, press
mask *(v.)* disguise, cloak, conceal, veil, hide
massacre *(v.)* slaughter, kill, exterminate, annihilate
massage *(v.)* rub, knead, stimulate, caress
massive *(adj.)* weighty, bulky, huge, cumbersome, large
master *(v.)* conquer, subdue, humble, succeed, overcome; understand, comprehend
match *(n.)* equal, peer, equivalent, counterpart, approximation; race, rivalry, competition
material *(adj.)* physical, real, tangible; essential
maternal *(adj.)* motherly, protective, nurturing
matrimony *(n.)* marriage, wedlock, union
matrix *(n.)* mould, die
matter *(n.)* substance, material, constituents, object, thing, element; subject, interest, focus, theme; affair, concern
mature *(adj.)* developed, ripe, grown, cultured
maudlin *(adj.)* tearful, sentimental, over-emotional
maxim *(n.)* saying, proverb, aphorism, adage, epithet
maximum *(adj.)* greatest, supreme, highest, best
mayhem *(n.)* crime, violence, chaos
maze *(n.)* labyrinth, tangle, convolution, intricacy
meager *(adj.)* lean, scanty, spare, wanting
mean *(adj.)* humble, servile, pitiful, vicious, contemptible, despicable, degenerate, unscrupulous; base, low, vulgar, common
mean *(v.)* signify, symbolize, imply, suggest, designate, denote
meander *(v.)* wander, wind, roam, flow, ramble
meaning *(n.)* sense, import, definition, implication, intent, connotation, context, significance
means *(n.)* machinery, method, system, agency; wealth, resources, substance, property
measure *(n.)* degree, dimension, capacity, weight, volume, distance, quantity, area, mass; rule, test, example, norm, criterion
mechanical *(adj.)* automated, programmed, automatic; stereotyped, unchanging, monotonous
medal *(n.)* badge, award, commemoration, decoration
meddle *(v.)* interfere, interlope, intervene, encroach
mediate *(v.)* arbitrate, negotiate, intervene
medication *(n.)* remedy, pill, vaccination
mediocre *(adj.)* middling, average, common, ordinary
meditation *(n.)* contemplation, reflection, thought
medley *(n.)* mixture, conglomeration, variety
meek *(adj.)* humble, unassuming, passive, docile
meet *(v.)* engage, battle, match, face; touch, coincide, join, intersect; assemble, gather, converge, congregate; satisfy, fulfill, suffice
melancholy *(adj.)* gloomy, depressed, dispirited, sad
mellow *(v.)* ripen, mature, age
melodramatic *(adj.)* artificial, sensational, exaggerated
memento *(n.)* keepsake, reminder, souvenir
memoir *(n.)* biography, autobiography, account
memorable *(adj.)* unforgettable, notable, significant, monumental, eventful, exceptional, singular
memorize *(v.)* retain, learn, remember
menace *(v.)* threaten, intimidate, portend
mend *(v.)* repair, patch, fix, aid, remedy, cure, correct
medial *(n.)* servant, domestic, maid, lackey
mental *(adj.)* thoughtful, rational, intellectual, subconscious, telepathic, psychic
mention *(v.)* remark, comment, infer, intimate, suggest
merchandise *(v.)* advertise, sell, trade, market
merciful *(adj.)* lenient, softhearted, mild, tolerant
mere *(adj.)* minor, insignificant, little
merit *(n.)* worth, excellence, honour, character, virtue
merriment *(n.)* mirth, joy, gaiety, happiness, humour
mesh *(v.)* engage, coincide, suit, agree, fit
mess *(n.)* confusion, disorder, jumble, clutter

message *(n.)* communication, tidings, information
metamorphosis *(n.)* transformation, change, conversion
metaphorical *(adj.)* figurative, symbolical, allegorical
method *(n.)* procedure, process, technique, system
meticulous *(adj.)* mindful, cautious, thorough
miff *(v.)* offend, annoy, upset
might *(n.)* power, ability, strength, force, sway
migrate *(v.)* move, emigrate, leave
mild *(adj.)* moderate, gentle, meek, temperate
militant *(adj.)* aggressive, warlike, belligerent
mimic *(v.)* imitate, copy, simulate, impersonate; mock, burlesque, caricature, ridicule
mind *(n.)* mentality, perception, judgement, wisdom, intellect; intention, inclination, determination
miniature *(adj.)* small, tiny, little, minute
minister *(n.)* clergyman, ambassador, delegate
minister *(v.)* attend, tend, help
minor *(adj.)* inferior, secondary, lesser, trivial
miracle *(n.)* marvel, revelation, wonder
mirage *(n.)* illusion, phantasm, hallucination, fantasy
mirth *(n.)* gaiety, laughter, frolic, jollity, fun
miscellaneous *(adj.)* diverse, unmatched, unlike; mixed, muddled, scattered, confused, disordered
mischievous *(adj.)* playful, roguish, naughty
miser *(n.)* niggard, skinflint, money-grubber
miserable *(adj.)* wretched, distressed, troubled
mislead *(v.)* delude, trick, beguile, dupe, misrepresent
miss *(n.)* failure, slip, blunder, mishap, mistake, deviation, woman, lass, maid, female, girl
mission *(n.)* purpose, charge, commission
missionary *(n.)* apostle, evangelist, messenger
mist *(n.)* vapour, cloud, rain, haze, fog
mistake *(v.)* err, blunder, misjudge, botch, bungle
mix *(v.)* blend, combine, mingle, stir, unite; confuse, jumble, tangle; associate, fraternize
moan *(v.)* groan, wail, whine
mob *(n.)* throng, crowd, rabble, multitude, horde
mobile *(adj.)* movable, loose, free
mock *(adj.)* imitation, counterfeit, sham
mode *(n.)* manner, fashion, method
model *(n.)* example, prototype, ideal; pattern, design, standard; poser, sitter, mannequin, nude
moderate *(adj.)* inexpensive, cheap, economical; modest, temperate, calm, reserved; tolerant, restrained, cautious; temperate, mild
modem *(adj.)* stylish, chic, smart, fashionable; contemporary, new, current, renovated, improved
modest *(adj.)* humble, unassuming, meek, diffident; plain, seemly, tasteful, unadorned, unaffected; moderate, reasonable, inexpensive, economical; proper, pure, chaste, seemly, decent; lowly, simple, unaffected
modify *(v.)* change, vary, alter
moist *(adj.)* wet, humid, dank, moistened, damp
mould *(n.)* form, matrix, shape, frame, pattern, cast, growth
molest *(v.)* harm, bother, annoy, irritate, badger
molten *(adj.)* melted, liquefied, flowing
moment *(n.)* time, instant, jiffy, importance, significance, note, consequence
momentum *(n.)* impetus, impulse, drive, energy
monetary *(adj.)* pecuniary, financial, fiscal
monologue *(n.)* speech, talk, discourse, address
monopoly *(n.)* trust, syndicate, cartel
monster *(n.)* chimera, werewolf; abnormality; criminal, rascal, savage
monument *(n.)* memorial, shrine, statue, monolith
mood *(n.)* state, condition, temper, humour, disposition
moot *(adj.)* disputable, arguable, debatable
moral *(adj.)* virtuous, proper, scrupulous, honourable, aboveboard, principled, chaste, noble
morale *(n.)* assurance, resolve, spirit, confidence
morbid *(adj.)* sickly, unhealthy, ailing; gloomy, melancholic, depressed
morning *(n.)* dawn, daybreak, cockcrow, sun-up
morose *(adj.)* surly, downcast, gloomy
morsel *(n.)* piece, bite, chunk, bit, part
mortal *(adj.)* malignant, lethal, deadly; human, transient, perishable, temporary
motel *(n.)* hotel, cabin, inn, resort
motif *(n.)* theme, melody, design
motion *(n.)* change, act, action, passage; suggestion, proposition, plan
motto *(n.)* maxim, adage, saw, aphorism, sentiment, slogan, catchword, axiom, proverb, saying
mound *(n.)* pile, heap, knoll, hill
mount *(v.)* ascend, rise, scale, clamber
mourn *(v.)* grieve, sorrow, bemoan, languish, pine
move *(v.)* arouse, stir, stimulate; impel, actuate; introduce, submit; go, walk, run, travel, progress, proceed, traverse

mow *(v.)* cut, scythe, reap, harvest
muddle *(v.)* confuse, disarrange, mix, jumble, snarl
muffler *(n.)* scarf, neckpiece, choker
mumble *(v.)* mutter, utter, murmur
munch *(v.)* chew, masticate, crunch, bite, eat
mundane *(adj.)* normal, ordinary, everyday
municipality *(n.)* community, district, village, town
murder *(n.)* homicide, carnage, slaying, butchery
murky *(adj.)* gloomy, dark, dim, dusky, dingy, dirty
muscular *(adj.)* brawny, powerful, husky, strong
museum *(n.)* collection, archives, treasury, depository
music *(n.)* melody, harmony, tune, air, strain
mutation *(n.)* change, modification, deviation
mute *(adj.)* speechless, silent, bewildered, unspoken
mutiny *(n.)* insurrection, revolt, resistance, revolution
mutter *(v.)* mumble, murmur, grumble, complain
myriad *(n.)* variable, innumerable, endless, multiple
mystical *(adj.)* occult, spiritual, mysterious, secret
myth *(n.)* legend, fable, saga, parable, tale, story

N

nab *(n.)* grab, take, snatch, seize
nag *(v.)* scold, vex, annoy, pester, bother
naive *(adj.)* unaffected, artless, innocent, unsophisticated, gullible, credulous, trusting, inexperienced
naked *(adj.)* uncovered, unclad, bare, exposed
name *(n.)* reputation, renown, fame; title, designation; star, hero, lion, celebrity
narrate *(v.)* tell, recite, describe, reveal, report
nasty *(adj.)* offensive, foul, gross, vulgar; indecent, immodest, smutty, lewd, sarcastic, mean
nation *(n.)* people, populace, community, society, state, realm, country, domain
natural *(adj.)* original, fundamental, inherited, native; characteristic, usual, customary, ingenuous, artless, spontaneous, real, actual, tangible, physical
naughty *(adj.)* mischievous, wayward, roguish
neat *(adj.)* tidy, trim, prim, spruce, dapper, orderly, precise; clever, dexterous, skillful, agile
necessary *(adj.)* essential, important, requisite, required, imperative, compulsory, mandatory
nefarious *(adj.)* vile, wicked, evil, foul, sinful
negative *(n.)* refusal, contradiction, disavowal, refutation, denial; picture, film, image, plate
neglect *(v.)* disregard, disdain, affront, ignore, spurn; evade, defer, procrastinate, postpone
negotiate *(v.)* bargain, mediate, conciliate, arbitrate
niche *(n.)* recess, cranny, position, vocation
night *(n.)* evening, nightfall, twilight, bedtime
nimble *(adj.)* light, quick, spry, active, graceful; alert, bright, clever, intelligent
noble *(adj.)* exalted, courtly, lordly, dignified, distinguished; meritorious, virtuous, refined, chivalrous; aristocratic, patrician; stately, impressive, imposing
noise *(n.)* sound, clamour, racket, fracas, din, uproar
nomad *(n.)* wanderer, migrant, vagabond, traveller
nominate *(v.)* name, appoint, propose, designate
nonchalant *(adj.)* casual, unconcerned, impassive, detached, indifferent; careless, negligent, trifling
nonsense *(n.)* inanity, trash, senselessness, fun, jest, absurdity
noose *(n.)* loop, hitch, lasso, rope
nostalgia *(n.)* longing, homesickness, wistfulness
nosy *(adj.)* snoopy, curious, inquisitive, interested
notch *(n.)* nick, indent, cut, dent, groove
noted *(adj.)* well-known, celebrated, notorious, famous
notice *(n.)* warning, notification, announcement, attention, interest
notion *(n.)* whim, fancy, idea, assumption
notorious *(adj.)* infamous, known, disreputable
nourish *(v.)* feed, encourage, sustain
novel *(adj.)* new, strange, odd, unique, unusual
novel *(n.)* story, tale, fiction, romance
novice *(n.)* beginner, neophyte, amateur
noxious *(adj.)* injurious, harmful, deadly
nudge *(v.)* poke, bump, tap, push, touch
nugget *(n.)* lump, ingot, chunk, rock
nuisance *(n.)* bother, annoyance, vexation, trouble; breach, infraction, affront
null *(adj.)* void, invalid, vain, unsanctioned
numb *(v.)* deaden, stupefy, paralyze, stun, dull
numerous *(adj.)* many, copious, diverse, infinite
nuptials *(n.)* wedding, marriage, matrimony
nurse *(v.)* tend, minister, aid, treat
nurture *(v.)* nourish, feed, sustain
nutritious *(adj.)* nourishing, wholesome, healthful

O

oath *(n.)* promise, vow, pledge; profanity, curse, swearword, blasphemy
obdurate *(n.)* stubborn, hardhearted, firm
obedient *(adj.)* dutiful, loyal, devoted, deferential, faithful; docile, submissive, compliant
obese *(adj.)* fat, corpulent, plump, stout
obey *(v.)* yield, conform, submit, serve comply
object *(n.)* article, gadget; goal, aim, objective
object *(v.)* disapprove, protest, dispute, complain
obligate *(v.)* bind, restrict, constrain, force
oblige *(v.)* accommodate, assist, aid, contribute, help; constrain, bind, force, compel, coerce
oblivion *(n.)* obscurity, void, emptiness, nothing
obnoxious *(adj.)* offensive, annoying, disagreeable
obscure *(adj.)* vague, indistinct, unclear, hazy, arcane
observant *(adj.)* alert, discerning, perceptive, bright
observe *(v.)* watch, scrutinize, see, notice; remark, note, mention; commemorate, dedicate, solemnize; comply, follow, obey
obsessed *(adj.)* haunted, beset, controlled, troubled
obsession *(n.)* fixation, fascination, passion, mania
obsolete *(adj.)* antiquated, archaic, out-of-date
obstacle *(n.)* hindrance, restriction, obstruction
obstruct *(v.)* block, interfere, bar, hinder, prevent
obtain *(v.)* get, take, acquire, seize, procure
obvious *(adj.)* apparent, perceptible, open, clear, intelligible, comprehensible, understandable
occasion *(n.)* event, occurrence, incident, happening
occult *(adj.)* hidden, mysterious, supernatural, secret
occupation *(n.)* vocation, employment, job, profession
occupy *(v.)* seize, conquer, invade, pervade, engage, absorb, engross, involve, fascinate
occur *(v.)* happen, transpire, befall
odd *(adj.)* unusual, unique, strange; single, sole, unpaired, unmatched, lone
odious *(adj.)* hateful, offensive, repulsive
odour *(n.)* smell, perfume, fragrance, bouquet
offense *(n.)* misdeed, crime, wrong, insult, injury, hurt
offer *(v.)* present, tender, propose, submit
offer *(n.)* proposal, submission, attempt
offhand *(adj.)* impromptu, informal, improvised
offspring *(n.)* child, progeny, issue, descendant, heir
ointment *(n.)* salve, lubricant, lotion, cream, balm
old *(adj.)* aged, elderly, venerable, seasoned, enfeebled; archaic, prehistoric, antique
omen *(n.)* warning, portent, augury, indication, sign
omit *(v.)* exclude, drop, skip, overlook, disregard
omnipotent *(adj.)* all-powerful, almighty
omnipresent *(adj.)* universal, pervasive, ubiquitous
once *(adj.), (adv.)* formerly, previously, earlier
only *(adj.)* solely, exclusively, entirely, totally; simply, barely, hardly; sole, single, isolated, unique
onset *(n.)* beginning, opening, start, origin
ooze *(v.)* leak, seep, exude, flow
opaque *(adj.)* dim, dusky, darkened, murky, gloomy
open *(adj.)* clear, divulged, revealed, unobstructed; free, public; unguarded, accessible; frank, plain, candid, straightforward
operate *(v.)* functional, work, serve, run, percolate; manipulate, conduct, administer
opinion *(n.)* belief, view, sentiment, conception
opponent *(n.)* rival, competitor, adversary, antagonist
oppose *(v.)* contradict, dispute, defy, confront, resist; fight, compete, encounter, assail, storm, clash
oppress *(v.)* harass, maltreat, abuse, bother
optimal *(adj.)* favourable, desirable, optimum
optimism *(n.)* faith, cheerfulness, confidence, enthusiasm, expectation, certainty
option *(n.)* choice, selection, alternative
opulence *(n.)* riches, wealth, affluence
oracle *(n.)* prophet, seer, sage, fortune teller
oral *(adj.)* spoken, vocal, verbal, uttered, voiced
ordain *(v.)* establish, install, appoint; destine, fate, consecrate, invest, bless
order *(n.)* arrange, plan, system, command, stipulation, mandate, injunction; class, kind, hierarchy, classification, progression, succession, series
order *(v.)* classify, organize, direct, instruct, require; buy, secure, request
ordinance *(n.)* law, direction, mandate
ordinary *(adj.)* usual, normal, common; average, mediocre, accepted, typical, characteristic
organise *(v.)* arrange, systematize, coordinate, classify; establish, build, found, plan, formulate
orientation *(n.)* familiarization, introduction
originate *(v.)* introduce, found, start, begin
ornament *(n.)* decoration, embellishment, adornment, beautification

ornate *(adj.)* showy, gaudy, adorned, embellished
orphan *(n.)* foundling, waif, stray
oust *(v.)* eject, expel, discharge, evict, dislodge
outbreak *(n.)* explosion, outburst, commotion, tumult; violence, mutiny, revolution
outburst *(n.)* discharge, eruption, outbreak
outcast *(n.)* exile, fugitive, vagabond, undesirable, refugee
outcome *(n.)* upshot, consequence, result
outcry *(n.)* complaint, clamour, objection
outfit *(v.)* supply, equip, provide
outlandish *(adj.)* foreign, grotesque, queer, rude
outlaw *(v.)* forbid, ban, banish, condemn
outlook *(n.)* viewpoint, scope, vision, prospect, likelihood, possibility, opportunity, probability
outrage *(v.)* offend, wrong, affront, insult
outright *(adj.)* unmitigated, unconditional, obvious
outside *(adj.)* outermost, external, outer
outskirts *(n.)* suburbs, limits, boundary, edge
outwit *(v.)* trick, bewilder, confuse, deceive
over *(adj.)* above, overhead, higher; beyond, past, farther; accomplished, finished
overcast *(adj.)* cloudy, gloomy, dark
overcome *(v.)* conquer, overwhelm, vanquish
overconfident *(n.)* reckless, impudent, heedless, rash
overdo *(v.)* amplify, overreach, exaggerate, enhance; tire, fatigue, exhaust, overtax
overdue *(adj.)* late, delayed, belated, tardy
overhaul *(v.)* recondition, modernize, renew, repair
overpower *(v.)* overwhelm, master, subjugate, defeat
overrate *(v.)* overvalue, magnify, exaggerate
oversee *(v.)* superintend, superwise, manage
oversight *(n.)* failure, overlooking, mistake, error
overt *(adj.)* apparent, open, obvious, public
overture *(n.)* suggestion, advance, tender, prelude, prologue, preface, introduction
overwhelm *(v.)* defeat, overcome, overthrow, conquer; bewilder, confound, confuse, surprise
own *(v.)* acknowledge, grant, admit, declare; possess, hold, have, enjoy, retain, keep

P

pace *(n.)* step, gait, movement, speed
pacify *(v.)* calm, soothe, conciliate, appease, placate
padding *(n.)* stuffing, wadding, waste, filling
pagan *(adj.)* heathen, unchristian, idolatrous
page *(n.)* leaf, sheet, folio, side, surface, recto, verso
page *(v.)* call, summon, seek
pageant *(n.)* parade, celebration, pomp
paint *(v.)* sketch, picture, depict; brush, swab, daub, cover, spread
palace *(n.)* manor, mansion, castle
palpitate *(v.)* tremble, quiver, pulsate
paltry *(adj.)* worthless, small, insignificant, trifling
pamper *(v.)* overindulge, spoil, pet, humour, gratify, coddle, please
pandemonium *(n.)* noise, disorder, uproar, anarchy, riot, confusion
pang *(n.)* pain, throb, sting, bite
panic *(n.)* dread, alarm, fright, fear
panorama *(n.)* view, spectacle, scenery, prospect
pant *(v.)* gasp, desire, wheeze, throb, palpitate
pantomime *(n.)* sign, charade, mime
pantry *(n.)* storage, provisions, storeroom, larder, cupboard, closet, room
pants *(n.)* trousers, breeches, slacks, jeans, overalls, cords, shorts, corduroys, pantaloons, chaps, knickers, bloomers, rompers
parable *(n.)* fable, allegory, moral, story, tale
parade *(v.)* march, demonstrate, display, exhibit
paradox *(n.)* mystery, enigma, ambiguity, puzzle
paraphernalia *(n.)* trappings, equipment, gear
parasite *(n.)* dependent, sponger, hanger-on, toady
parch *(v.)* scorch, dry, shrivel, desiccate, dehydrate
pardon *(v.)* exonerate, clear, absolve, reprieve, acquit, liberate, discharge, free, release, forgive, condone, overlook, exculpate, excuse
parental *(adj.)* paternal, maternal, familial, genetic
park *(n.)* plaza, square, lawn, green, promenade, tract, grounds, woodland, meadow
parody *(v.)* mimic, copy, caricature, imitate, joke
parole *(v.)* release, discharge, pardon, liberate, free
parson *(n.)* clergyman, cleric, preacher, minister
partial *(adj.)* incomplete, unfinished; prejudiced, unfair, influenced, biased, inclined
participate *(v.)* compete, play, strive, engage
particle *(n.)* jot, scrap, atom, molecule, fragment, piece, shred, bit, part
partition *(n.)* division, distribution, barrier, separation, wall, obstruction
partner *(n.)* associate, worker, ally, comrade

party *(n.)* affair, reception, gathering, function; group, company, crowd, assembly; organization, faction
passage *(n.)* journey, voyage, crossing, trek; passageway, entrance, hall; excerpt, section, portion, paragraph, quote
passenger *(n.)* traveller, commuter
passion *(n.)* feeling, craving, desire, emotion
passive *(adj.)* complacent, inert, lifeless, idle
passport *(n.)* pass, permit, visa, identification
password *(n.)* countersign, watchword, identification
past *(adj.)* former, preceding, foregoing, earlier
pastor *(n.)* priest, rector, clergyman, minister
pasture *(n.)* grass, grazing, meadow, field
pat *(v.)* tap, touch, stroke, pet, rub
patch *(n.)* piece, bit, scrap, spot
patch *(v.)* repair, darn, mend
path *(n.)* trail, way, track, byway
pathetic *(adj.)* sad, touching, affecting, moving, pitiful
pathos *(n.)* pity, sorrow, grief
patience *(n.)* forbearance, fortitude, composure, endurance, perseverance, persistence
patient *(adj.)* submissive, forbearing, unruffled, imperturbable, passive, persevering, calm
patriarch *(n.)* ruler, master, ancestor, chief
patriot *(n.)* statesman, nationalist, loyalist, chauvinist
pattern *(n.)* model, original, guide, copy
pause *(v.)* stop, halt, cease, interrupt, suspend; reflect, deliberate
payment *(n.)* reimbursement, restitution, refund, reparation; portion, part
peace *(n.)* pacification, conciliation, agreement; tranquillity, harmony, silence, stillness; composure, contentment
peak *(n.)* summit, zenith, height, summit
peculiar *(adj.)* unusual, wonderful, singular, outlandish, strange; unique, characteristic, eccentric
pedestal *(n.)* base, stand, foundation, support
peek *(n.)* sight, glimpse, glance, look, spy
peep *(v.)* chirp, twitter, squeak, chirrup
peeve *(v.)* irritate, annoy, anger, bother
penalize *(v.)* chasten, castigate, punish
penchant *(n.)* inclination, taste, bias
pendant *(n.)* locket, lavaliere, decoration, jewellery
pending *(adj.)* continuing, awaiting, undecided
penetrate *(v.)* pierce, perforate, puncture
perceive *(v.)* observe, note, look, notice; comprehend, sense, grasp
perch *(v.)* roost, land, rest, sit
peremptory *(adj.)* decisive, final, imperious, dictatorial
perforate *(v.)* bore, pierce, drill, slit, stab, penetrate
perform *(v.)* accomplish, do, achieve, fulfill, discharge, effect, complete, finish, realize; enact, show, exhibit, display, dramatize, execute
perfume *(n.)* scent, fragrance, aroma, odour
perilous *(adj.)* precarious, unsafe, dangerous
period *(n.)* epoch, era, age, end, limit, conclusion
periphery *(n.)* circumference, perimeter, border
perjury *(v.)* false statement, falsify, lie
permanent *(adj.)* fixed, enduring, abiding, continuing, lasting, imperishable, persevering, constant
permeate *(v.)* penetrate, pervade, saturate, fill
permission *(n.)* liberty, consent, license, authorization, approval, sanction, endorsement, affirmation
perpetrate *(v.)* perform, commit, act, do
perpetual *(adj.)* continual, unceasing, constant, endless; repetitious, repeating, recurrent
perplex *(v.)* puzzle, confound, bewilder, confuse
persecute *(v.)* oppress, harass, victimize, abuse
perseverance *(n.)* grit, resolution, pluck, determination
persist *(v.)* persevere, pursue, strive, continue, endure
person *(n.)* individual, being, character, personage
personal *(adj.)* private, secret, confidential; individual, peculiar, particular, special
personify *(v.)* represent, symbolize, exemplify
personnel *(n.)* employees, workers, group, staff
perspective *(n.)* view, vista, aspect, attitude, outlook
persuade *(v.)* influence, induce, convince, cajole
pertain *(v.)* belong, relate, refer, concern
perturb *(v.)* disturb, pester, worry, irritate, bother
pervade *(v.)* penetrate, spread, suffuse, permeate
perverse *(adj.)* deviant, wayward, delinquent, bad
pervert *(u.)* corrupt, ruin, vitiate, divert

pessimism *(n.)* unhappiness, gloom, sadness
pester *(v.)* annoy, harass, provoke, bother
petition *(n.)* request, prayer, supplication, appeal
petrified *(adj.)* stone, hardened, mineralized, firm
petty *(adj.)* small, contemptible, insignificant, frivolous, trivial, unimportant
phantasm *(n.)* vision, illusion, specter
phenomenal *(adj.)* extraordinary, unique, remarkable
philanthropic *(adj.)* benevolent, humanitarian, kind
phlegmatic *(adj.)* calm, sluggish, indifferent
phobia *(n.)* avoidance, aversion, hatred, resentment
phony *(adj.)* affected, imitation, artificial, false
physical *(adj.)* material, corporeal, visible, tangible, palpable, substantial, real
physique *(n.)* structure, build, constitution, body
pick *(v.)* choose, select, separate; gather, pluck, pull
picture *(n.)* view, photograph, image, portrait; description, depiction, portrayal
picturesque *(adj.)* charming, pictorial, scenic, graphic, striking, arresting, quaint
piece *(n.)* part, portion, share, section
pierce *(v.)* penetrate, stab, probe
piety *(n.)* reverence, devotion, devoutness, veneration, grace
pile *(n.)* heap, collection, mass, quantity
pilgrim *(n.)* traveller, wayfarer, wanderer, sojourner
pill *(n.)* tablet, capsule, pellet, medicine, drug
pillage *(v.)* plunder, loot, rob, destroy, steal
pillow *(n.)* cushion, pad, support, headrest
pinnacle *(n.)* apex, zenith, crest, summit, climax
pious *(adj.)* reverent, devout, divine, holy, religious
piracy *(n.)* robbery, theft, pillage, holdup
pitch *(n.)* slant, incline, angle, grade; throw, toss, hurl, cast; frequency, tone, sound
pith *(n.)* centre, essence, heart, core
pity *(n.)* compassion, charity, tenderness, kindliness, benevolence, clemency, humanity, sympathy
pivot *(v.)* turn, whirl, swivel, rotate
place *(n.)* position, point, spot; locality, locus, site, area, region; status, position
plague *(n.)* pestilence, illness, epidemic
plain *(adj.)* obvious, open, manifest, clear, understandable; simple, unadorned, unpretentious, mod est; ordinary, everyday, commonplace; blunt, out spoken, candid, impolite, rude
plan *(n.)* design, scheme, project, idea, undertaking, plot, conspiracy, strategy, arrangement, layout, disposition, order
plateau *(n.)* tableland, elevation, hill
plausible *(adj.)* convincing, probable, credible, likely
player *(n.)* athlete, contestant, actor, performer
playful *(adj.)* joking, whimsical, comical, funny
playwright *(n.)* writer, author, tragedian
plea *(n.)* appeal, request, supplication, pleading
pleasant *(adj.)* affable, agreeable, obliging, charming, gracious, amiable, polite, civil, cordial, sociable
please *(v.)* gratify, delight, satisfy
pleasure *(n.)* enjoyment, delight, happiness, amuse ment, preference; desire
pledge *(n.)* security, surety, guarantee, agreement
plentiful *(adj.)* bountiful, prolific, profuse, lavish, extravagant, copious, abundant, abounding
plenty *(n.)* abundance, lavishness, deluge, torrent, bounty, profusion, avalanche
plight *(n.)* condition, dilemma, state
plump *(adj.)* obese, stout, fleshy, fat
plunge *(v.)* cast, fall, rush, dive, jump
poach *(v.)* steal, filch, pilfer, smuggle
poetic *(adj.)* lyrical, romantic, imaginative
poetry *(n.)* verse, rhythm, rhyme, poesy
poignant *(adj.)* penetrating, moving, touching
point *(v.)* indicate, show, name, denote; direct, guide, steer, influence, lead
pointless *(adj.)* prosaic, trivial, unnecessary; ineffective, useless, impotent, incompetent, weak
poise *(n.)* carriage, bearing, grace, composure, dignity
poisonous *(adj.)* noxious, venomous, toxic, harmful
poke *(v.)* jab, punch, crowd, push,
polish *(v.)* smooth, burnish, finish, shine
polite *(adj.)* polished, mannerly, amiable, gracious, cordial, diplomatic, civil, sociable, respectful
pollute *(v.)* soil, defile, stain, dirty
pompous *(adj.)* pretentious, arrogant, haughty, proud
ponder *(v.)* meditate, think, deliberate, consider
poor *(adj.)* indigent, penniless, destitute, needy, starved, beggared, broke, weak, puny, feeble, infirm; mediocre, shoddy, deficient, cheap, flimsy
poppycock *(n.)* drivel, nonsense, gibberish

populace *(n.)* people, multitudes, masses, people
popular *(adj.)* liked, favourite, beloved, celebrated, admired, famous, widespread
porous *(adj.)* absorbent, pervious, permeable
portable *(adj.)* movable, transportable, transferable
portend *(v.)* foretell, predict, herald
portion *(n.)* part, scrap, fragment, piece; allotment, share, quota
portray *(v.)* draw, describe, depict, characterize
pose *(n.)* position, attitude, affectation, pretense
posh *(adj.)* rich, smart, comfortable
position *(n.)* location, whereabouts, bearings; view, belief; job, office, occupation; status, rank; posture, carriage, bearing
positive *(adj.)* decisive, clear, emphatic, assertive, resolute, certain, confident, sure
possess *(v.)* have, hold, own, occupy, control, maintain
possibility *(n.)* plausibility, feasibility, chance, hazard, hope, prospect
post *(n.)* column, pillar, pedestal, upright, mast
posterior *(adj.)* subsequent, after, succeeding, next, following, later; behind, back
posterity *(n.)* eternity, descendants, children, offspring
postpone *(v.)* defer, delay, suspend, retard, withhold, shelve, adjourn, pause
postscript *(n.)* appendix, addition, supplement
posture *(n.)* pose, carriage, aspect, presence; feeling, sentiment, disposition
potable *(adj.)* clean, fresh, unpolluted
potency *(n.)* power, energy, vigour; authority: influence, control, dominion, command
pouch *(n.)* bag, sack, receptacle, container
pounce *(v.)* seize, spring, attack, bound, surge, jump
poverty *(n.)* want, privation, insolvency; lack, shortage, inadequacy, scarcity
power *(n.)* vigour, stamina, authority, jurisdiction, dominion, dominance, control, supremacy; compulsion, coercion, horsepower, potential, dynamism
practical *(adj.)* useful, feasible, workable, rational, utilitarian, serviceable, efficient, effective
practice *(n.)* usage, mode, manner, fashion, exercise, rehearsal, system
pragmatic *(adj.)* logical, sensible, practical, realistic
praise *(v.)* commend, applaud, acclaim, endorse, eulogize, compliment, celebrate, honour, glorify, extol, congratulate
prank *(n.)* trick, antic, game, escapade, caper, joke
preach *(v.)* lecture, teach, sermonize, discourse, exhort, moralize, talk, harangue, inform, address
precarious *(adj.)* uncertain, unsafe, risky, doubtful, dubious, dangerous
precede *(v.)* lead, antedate, preface, introduce, herald, forerun
precious *(adj.)* valuable, costly, expensive; beloved, cherished, prized; delicate, fragile, dainty
precipice *(n.)* cliff, crag, bluff, hill, mountain
precise *(adj.)* exact, accurate, definite, careful
predecessor *(n.)* forerunner, antecedent, ancestor
predicament *(n.)* difficulty, strait, plight, scrape, circumstance, mess, pinch, crisis
predict *(v.)* foretell, prophesy, prognosticate, divine
predominant *(adj.)* supreme, almighty, powerful; first, transcendent, surpassing, superlative, principal
preeminent *(adj.)* distinguished, eminent, outstanding
preface *(v.)* introduce, commence, precede, begin
preference *(n.)* choice, election, option, selection, pick
prehistoric *(adj.)* ancient, primitive, antiquated, old
prejudice *(n.)* bias, inclination, partiality
preliminary *(adj.)* preparatory, preceding, introductory
prelude *(n.)* introduction, preamble, prologue, preface
premature *(adj.)* rash, precipitate, untimely, early
premise *(n.)* supposition, assumption, proposition
premium *(adj.)* excellent, select, prime, superior
premonition *(n.)* foreboding, portent, sign, warning
preparation *(n.)* rehearsal, anticipation, build-up; preparedness, readiness, fitness, training, mixture, compound, medicine
prerequisite *(n.)* requirement, necessity, essential
prerogative *(n.)* privilege, advantage, exemption, right
presence *(n.)* occupancy, residence, inhabitancy; nearness, closeness; appearance, behaviour
preserve *(v.)* guard, protect, shield; keep, process, cure
preside *(v.)* officiate, direct, lead, control, manage

pressure *(n.)* tension, burden, stress, squeeze
prestige *(n.)* influence, reputation, fame, esteem
presume *(v.)* believe, consider, suppose, assume
pretend *(v.)* feign, affect, imitate, simulate, represent
pretty *(adj.)* attractive, lovely, beautiful; pleasant, delightful, cheerful, pleasing
prevalent *(adj.)* prevailing, common, widespread
prevent *(v.)* preclude, block, stop, thwart, halt, impede, check, frustrate, obstruct, inhibit, restrain, hinder
previous *(adj.)* former, antecedent, prior, preceding
prick *(v.)* pierce, stick, cut, hurt, puncture
pride *(n.)* egotism, haughtiness, disdain, condescension
prim *(adj.)* exact, stiff, formal, demure, decorous, polite, proper, precise
primp *(v.)* dress, prepare, paint, powder
principal *(adj.)* chief, leading, first, main, foremost, preeminent, dominant, prevailing
prior *(adj.)* before, antecedent, foregoing, preceding
prisoner *(n.)* captive, convict, detainee, hostage
privacy *(n.)* seclusion, solitude, isolation, aloofness, separation, concealment, secrecy
privilege *(n.)* right, perquisite, prerogative, indulgence, affluence
probable *(adj.)* likely, seeming, presumable, feasible, plausible
procedure *(n.)* fashion, mode, method, system, order
proceed *(v.)* move, progress, continue, advance
process *(n.)* operations, means, manner, method
prod *(v.)* provoke, crowd, shove, push
product *(n.)* result, output, outcome
profanity *(n.)* irreverence, abuse, cursing, swearing
profession *(n.)* career, occupation, calling, avocation, vocation, position; declaration, vow, oath
professor *(n.)* teacher, educator, instructor, lecturer
proficiency *(n.)* learning, skill, knowledge, ability
profit *(n.)* gain, return, proceeds. remuneration
profound *(adj.)* scholarly, learned, sagacious, intellectual, great, intense
progress *(n.)* headway, impetus, motion, improvement, advancement, development, growth
prohibit *(v.)* forbid, interdict, obstruct, prevent, ban
project *(n.)* plan, scheme, outline, design
prominent *(adj.)* famous, notable, leading, distinguished, striking, noticeable
promiscuous *(adj.)* indiscriminate, unrestricted, lewd, wanton, loose, immoral
promote *(v.)* further, encourage, help, aid, assist, support, back, champion, advocate, bolster, nourish, nurture, subsidize, boost, advance
prompt *(adj.)* timely, precise, punctual
prone *(adj.)* disposed, inclined, predisposed, likely
pronounced *(adj.)* noticeable, clear, definite, obvious
pronouncement *(n.)* report, declaration, statement
proof *(n.)* verification, confirmation, substantiation, corroboration, testimony
propensity *(n.)* talent, capacity, ability, inclination
prophecy *(n.)* prediction, forecast, prognostication
prophet *(n.)* seer, oracle, soothsayer, astrologer
proponent *(n.)* defender, advocate, champion, protector
propose *(v.)* offer, recommend, submit, volunteer
propriety *(n.)* accordance, compatibility, congruity, modesty, dignity, pleasantness
prospect *(n.)* expectation, promise, outlook, possibility
prosper *(v.)* thrive, flourish, flower, succeed
protection *(n.)* shield, screen, shelter, defense, safeguard, security, guaranty
protest *(n.)* meeting, rally, demonstration, dissent
proud *(adj.)* stately, distinguished; vain, vainglorious, haughty, arrogant
provide *(v.)* furnish, equip, outfit, stock, supply
provision *(v.)* requirement, stipulation, prerequisite
provoke *(v.)* vex, irritate, aggravate, bother, incite, stir, rouse, arouse, cause, make, produce, begin
proxy *(n.)* agent, broker, representative, delegate
prudent *(adj.)* careful, cautious, circumspect, wary, discreet; practical, sensible, wise, discerning
pry *(v.)* snoop, spy, nose, enquire, meddle
pseudo *(adj.)* imitation, quasi, sham, false
publish *(v.)* distribute, print, issue; advertise, announce, promulgate, proclaim
pudgy *(adj.)* fat, chubby, chunky, stout
pulpy *(adj.)* soft, smooth, thick, fleshy
pun *(n.)* witticism, quip, joke
punctual *(adj.)* prompt, precise, exact, meticulous
puny *(adj.)* small, feeble, inferior, diminutive, weak

pure *(adj.)* unimixed, unadulterated, simple, clear, undiluted, clear, immaculate, germ-free, sterilized, sanitary, refined; chaste, virginal, continent, celibate; absolute, sheer, utter, complete

purge *(v.)* cleanse, evacuate, eliminate

purpose *(n.)* aim, intention, end, goal, mission, objective, expectation, intent, aspiration

putrid *(adj.)* rotten, corrupt, putrefied, decayed

puzzle *(v.)* perplex, obscure, bewilder, complicate, confuse, wonder, marvel, surprise, astonish

Q

quaint *(adj.)* odd, strange, fanciful, whimsical

quake *(v.)* tremble, shake, quiver, move, rock

quality *(n.)* attribute, trait, endowment, condition, character, nature, essence; grade, class, merit, worth, excellence, variety, rank

qualm *(n.)* scruple, suspicion, doubt, uncertainty

quarrel *(v.)* dispute, wrangle, contend, squabble, clash, bicker, contest, disagree, argue, feud

queasy *(adj.)* squeamish, sick, uneasy, uncomfortable

queer *(adj.)* odd, peculiar, strange, curious

quiet *(adj.)* silent, calm, peaceful, hushed, muffled, noiseless, still, reserved, reticent

quirk *(n.)* whim, caprice, fancy, peculiarity

quiver *(v.)* vibrate, shudder, wave, shiver, tremble

quote *(v.)* excerpt, extract, say, repeat; price, request, demand, value

R

rabble *(n.)* crowd, mob, masses, riffraff, people

rabid *(adj.)* fanatical, obsessed, zealous; insane, deranged, mad

racket *(n.)* uproar, clatter, din, disturbance, noise, conspiracy, scheme, corruption, crime, theft

radial *(adj.)* branched, outspread, spreading

radiant *(adj.)* shining, luminous, radiating, bright

radical *(adj.)* fundamental, original, primitive, native, organic; extreme, progressive, militant, seditious, riotous, rebellious, revolutionary, heretical

raft *(n.)* flatboat, barge, float, catamaran, boat

rage *(n.)* fury, frenzy, tantrum, uproar, storm, out burst; fad, fashion, style, mode, vogue, craze, mania

ragged *(adj.)* tattered, frayed, frazzled, threadbare

raid *(n.)* attack, invasion, foray, assault, roundup

rain *(v.)* pour, drizzle, shower, sprinkle, mist, storm

raise *(v.)* lift, elevate, hoist, boost; rear, breed, cultivate, produce; erect, construct, build

rake *(n.)* rascal, lecher, drunkard, scoundrel

ramble *(v.)* saunter, stroll, roam, wander; drift, stray, diverge, meander, digress

rampant *(adj.)* raging, uncontrolled, violent, turbulent, tumultuous, unruly, unrestrained

rancid *(adj.)* unpleasant, tainted, stale, bad, rotten

random *(adj.)* aimless, haphazard, casual, unpredictable, irregular

rank *(n.)* row, column, file, string, line; eminence, position, distinction, standing, status, ancestry

ransack *(v.)* search, rummage, scour, seek; loot, pillage, plunder, ravish, strip, rifle

rant *(v.)* rave, fume, rail, rage, yell

rapid *(adj.)* swift, speedy, accelerated, hurried, fast

rapt *(adj.)* awed, transported, entranced, enchanted

rapture *(n.)* delight, ecstasy, pleasure, satisfaction

rare *(adj.)* exceptional, singular, extraordinary, unusual; scarce, expensive, precious, select, superlative, excellent

rascal *(n.)* scoundrel, rogue, rake, knave, cad, scalawag, reprobate, miscreant

rash *(adj.)* hasty, impetuous, impulsive, foolish, heedless, foolhardy, brash

rational *(adj.)* logical, stable, thoughtful, sensible, impartial, objective, sober; intelligent, sensible, wise; responsible

rattle *(v.)* disconcert, bother, unnerve, confuse, disturb, embarrass

raucous *(adj.)* hoarse, harsh, loud, gruff, rough

ravage *(v.)* pillage, devastate, despoil, plunder, sack

rave *(v.)* talk, babble, gabble, jabber; rage, storm, splutter, rail, rant

ravenous *(adj.)* voracious, starved, hungry

raw *(adj.)* natural, crude, rough; immature, inexperienced; cold, biting, windy, bleak; chafed, bruised

react *(v.)* respond, reciprocate, behave, answer

ready *(adj.)* prepared, alert, handy, expectant, available; eager, willing, ardent, zealous

real *(adj.)* authentic, original; existing, actual, substantive, tangible

realism *(n.)* authenticity, naturalness, actuality, reality

realize *(v.)* fulfil, complete, accomplish; recognize, apprehend, discern; obtain, receive, get
realm *(n.)* kingdom, province, domain, sphere
rear *(n.)* back, hindmost, tail, posterior, rump, butt
reason *(n.)* intelligence, sanity; logic, speculation, rationalism, analysis; motive, end, rationale, aim, mind, brain, mentality, intellect
reassure *(v.)* console, comfort, encourage, guarantee
rebel *(n.)* revolutionary, agitator, insurgent, mutineer, nonconformist
rebound *(v.)* recoil, reflect, ricochet, bounce
rebuke *(v.)* chide, reprove, condemn, reprimand
recede *(v.)* retreat, shrink, ebb, lower, abate, decline, decrease, fall
receipt *(n.)* acquisition, receiving, acceptance, arrival; voucher, acknowledgment, notice, stub
recent *(adj.)* modern, fresh, novel, contemporary
reception *(n.)* gathering, party, soiree, entertainment
receptive *(adj.)* alert, perceptive, observant
recess *(n.)* nook, cell, cubicle; intermission, interlude
recipient *(n.)* receiver, beneficiary, heir
recite *(v.)* render, enact, dramatize, interpret, soliloquize, narrate, recount
reckless *(adj.)* heedless, thoughtless, wild, rash
reclaim *(v.)* recover, redeem, regain, mend, improve
recognize *(v.)* place, recall, remember, acknowledge, appreciate, realize
recommend *(v.)* commend, praise, endorse, suggest, prescribe, urge, advise
reconcile *(v.)* adjust, adapt, arrange, regulate
record *(n.)* document, manuscript, account, history, deed; disk, phonograph
recover *(v.)* salvage, redeem, rescue, reclaim; convalesce, heal, mend, revive, recuperate
recreation *(n.)* pastime, amusement, relaxation
recuperate *(v.)* recover, convalesce, heal
recur *(v.)* return, reappear, happen, repeat
redeem *(v.)* recover, repay, purchase, atone, compensate; save, liberate, free, deliver, rescue
redemption *(n.)* regeneration, salvation, rebirth, rescue
redress *(n.)* compensation, payment, reparation
redundant *(adj.)* superfluous, wordy, verbose, dull
referee *(n.)* arbitrator, umpire, conciliator, judge
refine *(v.)* strain, filter, clean, separate; improve, better, clarify, explain
reflect *(v.)* ponder, contemplate, concentrate, weigh, consider, think
reform *(n.)* reformation, betterment, improvement
refrain *(v.)* avoid, cease, forbear, abstain
refuge *(n.)* shelter, sanctuary, retreat, haven
refund *(n.)* return, reimbursement, repayment, remuneration, compensation, rebate, settlement
refuse *(v.)* reject, decline, rebuff, spurn, deny
refute *(v.)* disprove, answer, deny
regard *(n.)* look, gaze, glance; estimation, appreciation, affection, admiration
regard *(v.)* observe, notice, mark; consider, view, think; respect, esteem, value, admire
region *(n.)* territory, area, realm, locale, domain, sphere
regret *(n.)* remorse, compunction, repentance, qualm, grief, pain, anxiety, sorrow
regret *(v.)* mourn, lament, rue, repent, grieve, sorrow
regular *(adj.)* customary, conventional, usual; orderly, methodical, precise, systematic, organized, consistent, rhythmic, periodic, measured
regulate *(v.)* control, rule, legislate, direct, govern, manage; adjust, adapt, standardize, rectify, correct
rehabilitate *(v.)* restore, reinstate, change, reestablish
reign *(v.)* rule, govern, manage
reimburse *(v.)* repay, compensate, refund
reinforce *(v.)* encourage, strengthen, support, boost
reject *(v.)* refuse, repudiate, decline, renounce, deny; discard, expel, eliminate
rejuvenate *(v.)* reinvigorate, refresh, strengthen
relapse *(v.)* backslide, revert, regress, deteriorate, degenerate, weaken, sink
relate *(v.)* tell, recount, recite, retell, describe, report; connect, associate, correlate, compare
relax *(v.)* slacken, repose, recline, unbend, rest
release *(v.)* liberate, acquit, loose, free
relevance *(n.)* connection, pertinence, importance
reliable *(adj.)* unimpeachable, trustworthy, reputable, irrefutable, incontestable, dependable, unfailing
relic *(n.)* vestige, trace, heirloom, antique, keepsake, memento, token

relief *(n.)* softening, alleviation, comforting; aid, assistance, support, help, succor; relaxation, comfort, contentment, restfulness
religion *(n.)* faith, belief, persuasion, theology, doctrine, communion, piety
relish *(v.)* fancy, like, enjoy
reluctance *(n.)* unwillingness, disinclination, qualm, hesitation, doubt
remark *(v.)* say, state, speak, mention, observe
remarkable *(adj.)* exceptional, extraordinary, unusual
remedy *(v.)* help, aid, heal, counteract, repair, cure
remnant *(n.)* remainder, residue, leavings, dregs
remorse *(n.)* anguish, guilt, compunction, contrition, grief, regret
remote *(adj.)* distant, removed, secluded, isolated; ancient, aged, old; separated, unrelated, irrelevant
rendition *(n.)* interpretation, translation, version
renew *(v.)* refresh, regenerate, rehabilitate, invigorate, restore, freshen, stimulate
renounce *(v.)* disown, disavow, deny, discard
renovate *(v.)* remake, rehabilitate, renew
repair *(v.)* restore, fix, correct, refurbish, mend
repel *(v.)* rebuff, resist, oppose, repulse, offend
repentance *(n.)* sorrow, remorse, self-reproach, regret, guilt, penitence
replenish *(v.)* refill, restock, renew
replica *(n.)* copy, likeness, model, duplicate, imitation, reproduction
represent *(v.)* depict, render, portray, enact, symbolize, describe; imitate, substitute, impersonate
repress *(v.)* check, restrain, control, curb, hinder
reprieve *(n.)* delay, respite, suspension
reprimand *(v.)* reprove, rebuke, chide, reproach, denounce, criticize, scold
reproach *(v.)* censure, upbraid, condemn, scold, blame
repudiate *(v.)* reject, retract, repeal, revoke, abandon
repulsive *(adj.)* offensive, disgusting, odious, forbidding, horrid
reputable *(adj.)* distinguished, celebrated, honourable, trustworthy, honest, worthy, brave, noble
request *(v.)* ask, solicit, beseech, entreat, sue, beg
rescue *(v.)* save, recover, redeem, salvage, retrieve; free, deliver, liberate, release
resemblance *(n.)* likeness, correspondence, coincidence, similarity
resentment *(n.)* annoyance, irritation, anger
reservoir *(n.)* supply, store, reserve, pool, cistern
residue *(n.)* remainder, leavings, scraps, shavings
resilient *(adj.)* rebounding, elastic, springy, flexible
resist *(v.)* oppose, endure, bear, persist, suffer, abide, persevere, last, repel
resolve *(v.)* decide, determine, conclude, decree
resource *(n.)* reserve, support, means, stratagem
resourceful *(adj.)* ingenious, capable, active, intelligent
respect *(n.)* regard, relation, esteem, honour, admiration
respite *(n.)* delay, postponement, reprieve, pause
respond *(v.)* reply, rejoin, acknowledge, answer
responsible *(adj.)* accountable, liable, obligated, obliged, pledged, bound, answerable; reliable, capable, dutiful, dependable, competent
rest *(n.)* repose, quiet, slumber, peacefulness, relaxation, doze, nap, respite; residue, surplus, remnant, balance; intermission, interval, inactivity, pause, recess
restless *(adj.)* fidgety, jumpy, nervous, uneasy, agitated, unsettled, restive, impatient, jittery
restrain *(v.)* curb, bridle, rein, regulate, muzzle, inhibit, deter, hamper, restrict, gag, limit, contain, check
restrict *(v.)* limit, circumscribe, contract, shorten
result *(n.)* consequence, outcome, aftermath, upshot, settlement, determination, payoff, end
resurrection *(n.)* transformation, rebirth, renewal
retard *(v.)* hinder, postpone, delay, impede
retort *(n.)* reply, counter, repartee, response, answer
retraction *(n.)* denial, revocation, cancellation
retreat *(n.)* refuge, sanctuary, port, haven, resort
retribution *(n.)* punishment, reprisal, retaliation
retrieve *(v.)* recover, regain, reclaim
return *(v.)* reappear, recur, repeat, revive, rebound; restore, replace; reply, respond, retort; repay, reimburse, recompense, refund; interest, profit
reveal *(v.)* disclose, publish, betray, announce, declare, show
revenge *(n.)* retaliation, reprisal, retribution
revenue *(n.)* income, return, earnings, yield, receipts, proceeds, profits
reverence *(n.)* veneration, respect, admiration, regard, esteem, adoration, praise

review *(v.)* correct, criticize, revise; examine, analyze, check
revise *(v.)* improve, correct, reconsider, rewrite, edit, change, modify
revoke *(v.)* annul, reverse, recall, retract, cancel
revolve *(v.)* roll, spin, rotate, twirl, turn
rich *(adj.)* wealthy, moneyed, affluent; luxurious, magnificent, resplendent, lavish, ornate, splendid, elegant; fertile, lush, fruitful, luxuriant
riches *(n.)* wealth, fortune, possessions, money
ricochet *(v.)* carom, rebound, reflect, bounce
riddle *(n.)* enigma, puzzle, dilemma, complexity
ridicule *(v.)* mock, gibe, scoff, sneer, taunt, mimic, deride, scorn, caricature, satirize
righteous *(adj.)* virtuous, just, honorable, exemplary, noble, trustworthy, ethical, impartial; religious, devout, pious, saintly, angelic, devoted, reverent, spiritual, holy
rigid *(adj.)* stiff, unyielding, inflexible, solid, firm; strict, exact, rigorous, severe; fixed, set, unmoving, definite, determined
rim *(n.)* margin, edge, border, verge, brim, lip, brink
ring *(n.)* circle, circlet, girdle, jewellery, band, signet, bracelet; group, party, bloc, faction, group, gang, band; sound, clangor, jangle
riot *(n.)* uproar, tumult, confusion, disorder, disturbance, protest
ripen *(v.)* develop, evolve, advance, grow
risk *(n.)* hazard, peril, jeopardy; contingency, prospect, uncertainty
rival *(n.)* competitor, antagonist, opponent
rival *(v.)* approach, match, equal
rivalry *(n.)* competition, contention, opposition, dispute
rob *(v.)* burglarize, plunder, defraud, cheat, pilfer, filch, embezzle, pillage, sack, loot
robust *(adj.)* vigorous, husky, hale, hearty, sound
rogue *(n.)* knave, outlaw, miscreant, criminal
romantic *(adj.)* poetic, fanciful, chivalrous, courtly
rooted *(adj.)* grounded, based, fixed, firm
rot *(n.)* decay, decomposition, corruption, disintegration, nonsense, trash, silliness, foolishness
rotate *(v.)* turn, twist, wheel, revolve, move
rotten *(adj.)* spoiled, putrefying, decaying, rancid; unsound, defective, impaired, weak; corrupt, contaminated, polluted, tainted, defiled, dirty
rough *(adj.)* uneven, irregular, bumpy, jagged, coarse; severe, harsh, strict, stem; crude, boorish, uncivil, uncultivated, rude; turbulent, buffeting, stormy, tumultuous; unfinished, incomplete, imperfect; approximate, inexact, uncertain
rouse *(v.)* waken, arouse, raise, awaken; stimulate, urge, stir, provoke, animate, excite
routine *(adj.)* usual, customary, conventional, habitual
rove *(v.)* walk, meander, wander, roam
rowdy *(adj.)* noisy, rebellious, mischievous, unruly
royal *(adj.)* regale, imperial, sovereign, supreme, noble; stately, dignified, majestic, courtly, aristocratic, lordly, imposing, resplendent
rubbish *(n.)* waste, debris, nonsense, litter, trash
rude *(adj.)* boorish, brutish, uncouth, vulgar, harsh, gruff, abusive, brazen, audacious, hostile, insensitive, rough, violent; coarse, unrefined, unpolished, crude; primitive, ignorant, barbarous
rugged *(adj.)* rough, uneven, hilly, broken, mountainous; strong, vigorous, hale, sturdy, hardy, healthy
ruin *(v.)* destroy, demolish, wreck, ravage; impoverish, beggar
rule *(v.)* govern, control, dictate, manage, regulate
rumble *(n.)* reverberation, resounding, roll, noise
rumour *(n.)* report, gossip, tidings, hearsay, tale
rumple *(v.)* wrinkle, crumple, crush, fold
rupture *(v.)* break, burst, crack, tear
rural *(adj.)* country, rustic, agrarian, suburban
ruthless *(adj.)* cruel, savage, brutal, merciless, fiendish, unmerciful, ferocious, vengeful, barbarous

S

sabotage *(v.)* subvert, undermine, attack, destroy
sacrifice *(n.)* tribute, atonement; loss, discount, deduction, reduction
sad *(adj.)* unhappy, downcast, gloomy, sorrowful, glum, dispirited, depressed, melancholy, blue; pitiable, disheartening, discouraging, dreary, disquieting
saint *(n.)* paragon, martyr, altruist, believer
salute *(v.)* greet, recognize, praise
salvage *(v.)* save, retrieve, recover, regain
sanction *(v.)* approve, confirm, authorize, countenance

sanctuary *(n.)* church, shrine, temple; shelter, refuge, asylum, resort, haven
sane *(adj.)* rational, normal, lucid, sober, sound, balanced, sensible, reasonable, wise
sanitary *(adj.)* hygienic, wholesome, sterile, healthful
sarcastic *(adj.)* scornful, mocking, ironical, satirical, taunting, derisive, sneering, snickering, cynical
satire *(n.)* irony, sarcasm, mockery, ridicule, caricature
saturate *(v.)* soak, overfill, drench, steep, immerse
savage *(adj.)* primitive, crude, simple; cruel, barbarous, inhuman, brutal; wild, untamed, uncivilized, uncultured, uncontrolled
savor *(v.)* partake, enjoy, relish, appreciate, like
scaffold *(n.)* platform, gallows, framework, structure, block, gibbet
scald *(v.)* burn, steam, char, blanch, parboil
scamper *(v.)* hasten, speed, haste, hurry, run
scanty *(adj.)* scarce, meager, small, inadequate, thin, skimpy, sparse, diminutive
scare *(v.)* panic, terrify, alarm, frighten
scene *(n.)* occurrence, spectacle, view, display
scent *(v.)* smell, perfume, odour, fragrance, redolence
scholarly *(adj.)* erudite, cultured, studious, learned
scoff *(v.)* mock, deride, jeer, ridicule
scorching *(adj.)* fiery, searing, sweltering, burning, hot
scorn *(v.)* refuse, despise, disdain
scoundrel *(n.)* rogue, scamp, villain, rascal
scowl *(v.)* frown, glower, disapprove, grimace
scramble *(v.)* mix, combine, blend, beat; climb, clamber, push, struggle
scrap *(n.)* trash, junk, waste, cuttings, chips; bit, fragment, particle, piece, morsel; fight, quarrel, brawl, squabble
scratch *(v.)* wound, hurt, cut, mark, injure, scar
scrub *(v.)* rub, cleanse, scour, clean, wash
scrupulous *(adj.)* exact, punctilious, strict, careful
scrutinize *(v.)* examine, view, study, stare, watch
scuffle *(n.)* struggle, shuffle, strife, fight
seam *(n.)* joint, union, stitching, closure, suture
seasonal *(adj.)* periodically, biennial, annual, yearly
secede *(v.)* withdraw, retract, leave, retreat
seclusion *(n.)* solitude, aloofness, privacy, retirement, retreat, concealment
secrecy *(n.)* hiding, seclusion, privacy, mystery, dark, darkness, isolation, reticence, stealth
secrete *(v.)* hide, conceal, cover, disguise; emit, discharge, produce, exude
secure *(adj.)* safe, guarded, defended; assured, determined, confident
sediment *(n.)* dregs, silt, grounds, residue
seek *(v.)* search, delve, dig, ransack, look, sniff, prowl
seethe *(v.)* boil, simmer, stew
seize *(v.)* grasp, take, catch, grab, clutch, snatch
seldom *(adv.)* rarely, infrequently, occasionally, un commonly, scarcely, hardly
select *(v.)* pick, decide, elect, choose
sell *(v.)* market, vend, barter, exchange, trade, bargain, peddle, retail, wholesale, contract, retail
sellout *(n.)* betrayal, deception, deal, trick
semblance *(n.)* resemblance, aspect, appearance
senile *(adj.)* aged, infirm, feeble, old, sick
senior *(adj.)* older, elder, higher, superior
sensation *(n.)* consciousness, perception, feeling
sense *(n.)* sensation, feeling, touch, sight, hearing, taste, smell; intellect, perception, reason, cleverness, knowledge, thought; reasonableness, judg ment, discretion, fairness; tact, understanding
sensitive *(adj.)* tender, delicate, sore, painful; touchy, tense, nervous, irritable, unstable
sensuous *(adj.)* passionate, physical, exciting, sensual, gratifying, hedonistic
sentiment *(n.)* feeling, emotion, opinion, thought
sentry *(n.)* sentinel, watch, protector, watchmen
sequel *(n.)* continuation, progression, sequence, series
sequence *(n.)* succession, order, continuity, progression, flow; arrangement, distribution, classification; series, chain, string, array
serene *(adj.)* calm, unruffled, tranquil, composed, sedate, placid
sermon *(n.)* discourse, lesson, doctrine, lecture
service *(v.)* maintain, sustain, repair
setback *(n.)* hindrance, check, delay, difficulty
settle *(v.)* prove, establish, verify; finish, end, achieve; locate, reside, dwell, colonize
sever *(v.)* separate, part, split, cleave, cut, divide
severe *(adj.)* exacting, inflexible, harsh, cruel, oppressive, rigid, rigorous, difficult, oppressive, relentless

sew *(v.)* join, fasten, stitch, tack, bind, piece, baste
sewage *(n.)* excrement, offal, waste, residue
shabby *(adj.)* threadbare, worn, ragged, faded, dilapidated, deteriorated, seedy
shadow *(adj.)* slight, inconsiderable, superficial; silly, trifling, inane, frivolous, petty, foolish
sham *(adj.)* pretended, false, misleading, untrue
shame *(v.)* humiliate, mortify, dishonour, disgrace
shape *(n.)* form, contour, configuration; pattern, frame, mould; condition, fitness, health
shatter *(v.)* break, sliver, split, burst
sheath *(n.)* scabbard, case, covering
sheer *(adj.)* abrupt, steep, precipitous, perpendicular; transparent, delicate, fine
shine *(v.)* radiate, glitter, sparkle, twinkle, glimmer, glow, blaze; reflect, glisten, gleam, mirror; polish, scour, brush, burnish, wax
shiver *(v.)* shake, tremble, vibrate, quiver
shore *(n.)* coast, beach, seaside, bank; support, prop, buttress, strut
shortage *(n.)* lack, deficiency, failure, dearth, shortfall
shove *(v.)* push, nudge, jostle, press
showy *(adj.)* conspicuous, flamboyant, pretentious
shred *(n.)* strip, fragment, splinter, rag
shrewd *(adj.)* cunning, sharp, keen, intelligent, canny, crafty, cagey
shrine *(n.)* temple, altar, church, sanctuary
shrivel *(v.)* wither, shrink, decrease
shroud *(v.)* hide, cover, conceal, obscure, veil, screen
shudder *(v.)* tremble, shake, shiver, quiver
shun *(v.)* avoid, ignore, eschew, evade
shy *(adj.)* timid, reserved, distrustful, suspicious
siege *(n.)* attack, assault, onslaught, blockade
sieve *(v.)* strain, purify, filter
sigh *(n.)* moan, groan, gasp, cry
signify *(v.)* mean, indicate, communicate, denote, imply, intimate, portend
silence *(n.)* serenity, hush, tranquillity, quiet
silly *(adj.)* foolish, imprudent, ridiculous, absurd, inane, frivolous
simple *(adj.)* unaffected, plain, clear, unadorned, uncomplicated, bare, innocent, artless
simplify *(v.)* clarify, explain, elucidate, interpret
sincere *(adj.)* honest, genuine, earnest, faithful
sinister *(adj.)* ominous, menacing, base, bad, evil
sink *(v.)* submerge, depress, fall, lower, droop
sip *(v.)* drink, imbibe, taste, sample, savour
situation *(n.)* circumstances, predicament, state, job, trade, status, station, rank
skeleton *(n.)* bones, framework, outline, structure
skeptic *(n.)* doubter, cynic, unbeliever, agnostic
skid *(v.)* slip, slide, swerve, veer, glide
skill *(n.)* dexterity, ability, expertise, competence, talent; occupation, craft, vocation, trade, job
skin *(v.)* strip, peel, husk, scale, scalp
skinny *(adj.)* thin, lean, bony, gaunt, emaciated
skirmish *(n.)* scuffle, scrimmage, engagement, combat
slack *(adj.)* lax, loose, lazy, indolent, sluggish, slow
slander *(n.)* gossip, libel, scandal, misrepresentation
slang *(n.)* jargon, lingo, dialect, colloquialism
slap *(v.)* smack, strike, hit, spank, cuff, buffet
slaughter *(n.)* slaying, bloodshed, carnage, massacre
sleazy *(adj.)* flimsy, shoddy, cheap, trashy, rundown
slender *(adj.)* thin, slim, slight, spare, fragile, flimsy
slight *(v.)* disregard, insult, snub, neglect, overlook
slime *(n.)* mire, muck, mud, ooze
slit *(v.)* cut, gash, slash, rip, slice, split, tear, pierce
sloppy *(adj.)* careless, lax, untidy, messy, disorderly
sluggish *(adj.)* languid, lethargic, indolent, slothful
slumber *(v.)* sleep, rest, nap, doze, snooze
slur *(n.)* insult, innuendo, slight, affront, blemish
sly *(adj.)* cunning, wily, deceitful, deceptive, tricky, shifty, evasive, elusive, shrewd, clever, calculating, treacherous, shady, slick, smooth, slippery
smash *(v.)* break, shatter, crush, pound, destroy, demolish, wreck, ruin
smear *(v.)* slander, libel, sully, slur; smudge, daub, plaster, spread, apply
smell *(n.)* odour, aroma, fragrance, scent, stench, stink
smirk *(n.)* sneer, leer, grimace
smooth *(adj.)* level, flat, flush, polished, sleek, uniform; suave, glib, polite, courteous
smother *(v.)* suffocate, stifle, asphyxiate, strangle, subdue, suppress
smudge *(n.)* smear, blot, blur, stain, blemish, streak
smug *(adj.)* conceited, egotistical, satisfied
snare *(v.)* catch, entangle, trap, trick, lure
sneak *(v.)* lurk, prowl, creep, slink, steal
sneer *(v.)* criticize, deride, ridicule, scoff, gibe, taunt

snip *(v.)* clip, pare, cut, lop, nip, slice, slit
snivel *(v.)* weep, whine, bawl, bemoan, blubber
snobbery *(n.)* contempt, arrogance, insolence
soak *(v.)* steep, saturate, douse, permeate, infuse
sob *(v.)* cry, moan, weep, wail, lament, whimper, bewail
social *(adj.)* genial, pleasant, polite, civil, pleasant
society *(n.)* fellowship, association, brotherhood, fraternity, club; community, civilization, people, nation
soggy *(adj.)* saturated, damp, wet, soaked, sodden
sojourn *(n.)* stay, visit, stopover, vacation, abide
solace *(v.)* comfort, console, soothe, cheer, relieve, assuage, allay, soften, mitigate
solemn *(adj.)* sacred, grave, serious, grim, imposing
solicit *(v.)* supplicate, beg, implore, urge, request, ask, enquire, question, proposition
solid *(adj.)* whole, regular, unbroken, firm, substantial, sound, hard, stable, dense, stout
solidify *(v.)* harden, crystallize, set, coagulate, congeal
solitary *(adj.)* single, sole, individual, singular, isolated, lonely, remote, separate
solitude *(n.)* isolation, seclusion, privacy
somber *(adj.)* dull, gloomy, dark, dim, drab, dismal, depressing, dreary, melancholy
sonorous *(adj.)* resonant, reverberating, vibrant
sooty *(adj.)* blackened, dirty, grimy, dingy, filthy
soothe *(v.)* calm, comfort, ease, quiet, refresh, soften, alleviate, assuage, mitigate
soothsayer *(n.)* prognosticator, diviner, oracle, prophet, astrologer, seer, mystic
sophisticated *(adj.)* worldly, refined, cultured
sorcery *(n.)* magic, witchcraft, alchemy, enchantment
sore *(adj.)* sensitive, raw, tender, painful, inflamed
sorrow *(n.)* grief, affliction, anguish, remorse, misery, sadness, woe, trouble, affliction
sorry *(adj.)* regretful, repentant, apologetic
sort *(v.)* order, arrange, classify, distribute, assort
soul *(n.)* spirit, essence, ghost, being
source *(n.)* origin, beginning, inception, cause, root
souvenir *(n.)* keepsake, token, memento, relic, trophy
space *(n.)* room, area, gap, expanse, distance, interval
spad *(n.)* distance, measure, length, extent, stretch
spare *(adj.)* thin, gaunt, slight, emaciated; excess, additional
sparse *(adj.)* meager, inadequate, scanty, thin, spare
spasm *(n.)* convulsion, fit, contortion, seizure
spatter *(v.)* splash, slosh, spray, shower, speckle
special *(adj.)* specific, certain, particular, designated, unique, distinctive, uncommon, unusual
specify *(v.)* stipulate, designate, cite, name, define
specious *(adj.)* deceptive, misleading, false
speck *(n.)* bit, particle, trace, grain, iota
spectacle *(n.)* sight, show, demonstration, wonder
specter *(n.)* ghost, spook, phantom, spirit, apparition
speculate *(v.)* consider, theorize, contemplate, consider, infer
speech *(n.)* language, oration, communication
speedy *(adj.)* quick, fast, hasty, brisk, swift, hurried
sphere *(n.)* globe, orb, shell, planet; province, realm, environment
spirit *(n.)* ghost, apparition, phantom, specter; vivacity, vigour, zeal, ardour; significance, meaning, sense
spiteful *(adj.)* vindictive, malicious, cruel, malevolent, nasty
spleen *(n.)* anger, petulance, wrath, rancour
splendid *(adj.)* grand, magnificent, impressive, dazzling
spoil *(v.)* decay, ruin, damage, decompose, putrefy
sporadic *(adj.)* occasional, infrequent, scattered
sprawl *(v.)* recline, lounge, relax, slouch
spring *(v.)* bound, leap, issue, jump, hop, vault
sprout *(v.)* germinate, bud, burgeon, grow, develop
spurious *(adj.)* false, fake, deceptive, phony, feigned
spurn *(v.)* reject, shun, slight, snub, scorn, disdain
spurt *(v.)* burst, gush, spout, issue, spring
squabble *(v.)* wrangle, quarrel, bicker, argue, feud
squalor *(n.)* filth, poverty, misery
squeamish *(adj.)* queasy, modest, prudish, finicky
squeeze *(v.)* compress, crush, squash, press, pinch
squirm *(v.)* wriggle, writhe, fidget, twist, shift
stab *(n.)* wound, cut, puncture, thrust
staff *(n.)* personnel, employees, crew, cast
stagnant *(adj.)* inert, stale, dirty, filthy, fetid
stalwart *(adj.)* stout, sturdy, strong, rugged, robust, vigorous, bold, gallant, steadfast, formidable
stamina *(n.)* endurance, strength, vigour, vitality, power
stammer *(v.)* sputter, falter, stumble, hesitate, stutter

staple *(adj.)* basic, necessary, essential, fundamental
stark *(adj.)* simple, desolate, dreary, grim, harsh
startle *(v.)* surprise, alarm, scare, frighten, disturb
state *(n.)* country, nation, condition, situation, circumstances, status, position, standing, station
stately *(adj.)* majestic, dignified, regal, grand, elegant
stationary *(adj.)* fixed, static, permanent, rooted, stable
statue *(n.)* sculpture, image, icon, figurine
stature *(n.)* height, bulk, build, status, standing
status *(n.)* state, condition, position, rank, standing
statute *(n.)* law, decree, act, bill, rule, ordinance, edict
steadfast *(adj.)* resolute, unwavering, constant, faithful, dependable, firm
steep *(adj.)* precipitous, sheer, abrupt
steer *(v.)* guide, direct, pilot, conduct, lead, navigate
stereotype *(v.)* classify, categorize, typecast, label
stem *(adj.)* severe, rigid, hard, strict, austere, rigorous
stiff *(adj.)* rigid, formal, inflexible, firm, stubborn, obstinate, unyielding, formal, uncompromising, severe
stiffen *(v.)* harden, congeal, thicken, coagulate
stigma *(n.)* disgrace, shame, infamy, blemish, blot, stain, taint
stigmatize *(v.)* disgrace, discredit, dishonour, defame, shame, brand, humiliate
stingy *(adj.)* niggardly, miserly, tight, closefisted
stipulate *(v.)* specify, determine, designate, indicate
stir *(n.)* tumult, bustle, excitement, commotion, disorder, uproar, furor, agitation, fuss
stockpile *(n.)* reserve, supply, deposit, hoard, store
stoic *(n.)* impassive, apathetic, indifferent, nonchalant, composed, poised
stolid *(adj.)* impassive, unemotional, dispassionate, indifferent, imperturbable
stomach *(n.)* belly, paunch, abdomen
stoop *(v.)* bend, bow, crouch
story *(n.)* tale, anecdote, yam, parable, fable, legend, report, account; level, floor
stout *(adj.)* plump, portly, heavy, bulky, corpulent; resolute, brave, courageous, bold, fearless, indomitable, firm, strong, robust, hardy
straight *(adj.)* direct, honest, fair, just, virtuous, open
strain *(n.)* effort, exertion, force, pressure, anxiety, tension, stress
strange *(adj.)* unusual, abnormal, bizarre, peculiar, extraordinary, outlandish, unfamiliar, unknown
stratagem *(n.)* trick, deception, wile, scheme, plan, contrivance, device
stray *(v.)* wander, drift, roam, deviate, digress
streamer *(n.)* flag, banner, pennant, standard, ensign
strength *(n.)* power, force, might
strenuous *(adj.)* vigorous, spirited, laborious
strident *(adj.)* raucous, shrill, harsh, piercing
strife *(n.)* conflict, fight, discord, clash
stringent *(adj.)* strict, harsh, severe
stroll *(v.)* walk, saunter, meander, wander, roam
struggle *(n.)* battle, clash, conflict, exertion, endeavour
stubborn *(adj.)* obstinate, headstrong, stiff, resolute, inflexible, intractable
stupendous *(adj.)* amazing, astounding, marvelous, extraordinary, incredible, spectacular, wondrous
stupor *(n.)* daze, trance, numbness, lethargy
sturdy *(adj.)* robust, rugged, stalwart, strong, muscular, firm, indomitable, stout
stylish *(adj.)* fashionable, chic, smart, modish
suave *(adj.)* sophisticated, smooth, cultured, worldly
subjective *(adj.)* biased, prejudiced, individual
subjugate *(v.)* conquer, enslave, subdue, defeat
submerge *(v.)* immerse, engulf, plunge, sink
submit *(v.)* comply, obey; suggest, volunteer, propose, present, tender
subordinate *(adj.)* inferior, lower, junior, subservient
subsequent *(adj.)* following, ensuing, succeeding, later, after
subservient *(adj.)* subordinate, servile, deferential
subsidy *(n.)* endowment, allowance, grant, bequest
substantial *(adj.)* plentiful, abundant, ample, considerable, wealthy, affluent, influential, valuable
subterfuge *(n.)* ploy, scheme, stratagem, device, expedient, deceit
subtle *(adj.)* delicate, understated, refined, elusive, deceptive, inferred, insinuated, artful, insidious
subtract *(v.)* deduct, decrease, diminish, lessen, lower

succession *(n.)* sequence, order, continuation
succinct *(adj.)* brief, concise, terse, abbreviated
succour *(n.)* aid, help, sustenance, assistance
succumb *(v.)* submit, concede, relent, capitulate, collapse, fail
suffer *(v.)* endure, tolerate, bear, undergo, agonize
suffuse *(v.)* saturate, pervade, soak, impregnate
suitor *(n.)* wooer, admirer, gallant, beau
sulk *(v.)* pout, scowl, frown, glower
summary *(n.)* condensation, digest, abridgment, brief
summit *(n.)* peak, pinnacle, apex, crown, culmination
summon *(v.)* call, invite, invoke, request, petition
sumptuous *(adj.)* luxurious, elegant, lavish, opulent
sundry *(adj.)* various, several, divers
supersede *(v.)* replace, supplant, succeed
supplant *(v.)* replace, displace, succeed, supersede
supply *(v.)* equip, stock, replenish
support *(n.)* aid, assistance, help, relief, succour; brace, prop, column, buttress, strut
suppress *(v.)* overpower, repress, curb, quell, crush; bury, cover
surcharge *(n.)* tax, duty, surtax, tariff, levy, toll
surface *(n.)* rise, appear, emerge
surmise *(v.)* speculate, guess, infer, imagine, suppose
surmount *(v.)* conquer, transcend, hurdle, overcome
surplus *(n.)* excess, abundance, remainder, residue
surrender *(v.)* submit, abandon, capitulate, yield
surrogate *(adj.)* substitute, backup, alternative
survey *(n.)* poll, study, review, outline, critique
survival *(n.)* subsistence, continuation, durability
suspect *(v.)* mistrust, doubt; suppose, imagine, conjecture
suspend *(v.)* postpone, delay, defer, interrupt
suspense *(n.)* apprehension, indecision, anxiety
suspicion *(n.)* skepticism, misgiving, mistrust, cynicism, notion, impression
swagger *(v.)* strut, prance, boast, brag, gloat
swallow *(v.)* drink, eat, gulp, consume, devour
swamp *(n.)* marsh, mire, morass, slough
swarm *(n.)* horde, mass, flock, multitude, host
swear *(v.)* declare, testify, affirm; damn, curse
sweet *(adj.)* luscious, aromatic, fragrant, clean, fresh, melodious, harmonious, mellow
swift *(adj.)* fast, rapid, expeditious, fleet, prompt, quick
swindle *(v.)* trick, deceive, dupe, defraud, victimize
switch *(v.)* swap, trade, exchange, replace, substitute
sycophant *(n.)* flatterer, flunky, parasite, toady
sylvan *(adj.)* picturesque, pastoral, idyllic
symbolize *(v.)* signify, connote, mean, represent
sympathize *(v.)* commiserate, console, pity
synopsis *(n.)* summary, abridgment, condensation
systematic *(adj.)* methodical, orderly, precise, regular

T

tabloid *(n.)* newspaper, periodical, publication
taboo *(adj.)* forbidden, banned, prohibited
tacit *(adj.)* implied, understood, assumed, inferred
taciturn *(adj.)* reserved, quiet, reticent
tag *(v.)* label, ticket, designate, identify
tailor *(v.)* customize, adapt, adjust, conform
tale *(n.)* narrative, account; fib, lie
talisman *(n.)* amulet, charm
talk *(n.)* conversation, dialogue, discourse, speech
tame *(adj.)* docile, gentle, obedient
tame *(v.)* domesticate, train
tamper *(v.)* alter, change, meddle, damage
tangible *(adj.)* material, corporeal, tactile, discernible, evident, actual, real, genuine
tantamount *(adj.)* equivalent, parallel, identical
tarnish *(n.)* blemish, blot, stain, taint
taste *(n.)* partiality, liking, bias, preference
taunt *(v.)* insult, jeer, mock, provoke
tavern *(n.)* bar, saloon, pub, cafe, inn, lodge
tawdry *(adj.)* cheap, sleazy, flashy, ostentatious
tease *(v.)* annoy, taunt, torment, harass, irritate, vex
tedious *(adj.)* monotonous, tiresome, dull, boring
tell *(v.)* recount, describe, report, speak, mention, explain, reveal, declare, divulge
temper *(n.)* disposition, temperament, humour, composure, poise
temperament *(n.)* disposition, attitude, mood, emotion, nature, character
temperate *(adj.)* calm, composed, cool, reasonable
tenable *(adj.)* defensible, justifiable, maintainable
tenant *(n.)* renter, leaseholder, inhabitant
tender *(adj.)* fragile, frail; sympathetic, kindhearted, considerate

tenet *(n.)* belief, conviction, dogma, creed, doctrine
tenuous *(adj.)* fine, narrow, insubstantial, flimsy, feeble
tepid *(adj.)* lukewarm, indifferent, halfhearted, languid
terminate *(v.)* complete, conclude, eliminate, cancel
terminology *(n.)* vocabulary, language, jargon
terrible *(adj.)* frightful, appalling, dreadful, horrible, horrendous, disastrous, disturbing, extreme
terrific *(adj.)* splendid, marvelous, wonderful, outstanding, super
terror *(n.)* fright, horror, alarm, dismay, consternation
terse *(adj.)* brief, succinct, concise, precise, curt
test *(n.)* inspection, experiment, examination, quiz
testy *(adj.)* irritable, cranky, grouchy, edgy, short-tempered, touchy, peevish
theorem *(n.)* principle, hypothesis, postulate, premise
theory *(n.)* conjecture, speculation, rationale, explanation, view, conception, outlook
therapeutic *(adj.)* restorative, curative, recuperative, remedial, corrective
thesis *(n.)* opinion, contention, argument, assumption, assertion, hypothesis
thick *(adj.)* abundant, dense, packed, crowded
thin *(adj.)* lean, gaunt, scanty, meager, scarce
think *(v.)* contemplate, meditate, consider, remember, recall, recollect, believe, suppose
thirst *(n.)* longing, desire, yearning, eagerness
thoroughfare *(n.)* artery, highway, expressway, boulevard, concourse, freeway
thought *(v.)* concept, conviction, notion, opinion, theory, hypothesis, supposition
threadbare *(adj)* worn, shabby, tattered, frayed, seedy
threaten *(v.)* endanger, menace, terrorize, scare
thrift *(n.)* economy, husbandry, conservation
thrive *(v.)* flourish, succeed, increase, grow
throng *(n.)* mass, multitude, horde, swarm, host, assemblage, crowd
through *(adj.)* completed, done, finished
thrust *(v.)* shove, plunge, jab, push
thug *(n.)* hoodlum, goon, gangster, criminal
tiara *(n.)* crown, diadem, coronet
tie *(n.)* rope, band, strap, cord, necktie, bow, scarf, cravat, choker, connection, relation, bond, link, knot, draw, deadlock, stalemate
tiff *(n.)* quarrel, dispute, disagreement, scrap, spat
tighten *(v.)* squeeze, compress, constrict, clench
time *(n.)* age, epoch, generation, cycle; interval, duration, span, rhythm, tempo, beat, cadence
timid *(adj.)* shy, retiring, fearful, withdrawn, reticent, indecisive, vacillating
timorous *(adj.)* timid, fearful, apprehensive, anxious, scared, afraid
tinker *(v.)* dabble, putter, potter, trifle
tiny *(adj.)* small, diminutive, minute, microscopic
tirade *(n.)* harangue, denunciation, outburst
title *(n.)* designation, name, appellation, epithet; interest, holding, ownership
titter *(v.)* laugh, giggle, snicker, chuckle
token *(adj.)* nominal, superficial, minimal
token *(n.)* symbol, mark, sign, note
tolerable *(adj.)* endurable, sufferable, bearable; adequate, decent, average
tolerant *(adj.)* unprejudiced, moderate, merciful
tomb *(n.)* grave, vault, crypt, sepulcher, mausoleum
tonic *(adj.)* refresher, restorative, stimulant
topical *(adj.)* local, isolated, provincial, regional
torment *(n.)* anguish, suffering, distress, misery
torpid *(adj.)* inactive, inert, lethargic, sluggish, motionless, dormant, hibernating
torpor *(n.)* idleness, inactivity, indolence, sluggishness
torrent *(n.)* cloudburst, deluge, flood
tortuous *(adj.)* winding, serpentine, twisted, snaky, crooked, bent
toss *(v.)* throw, fling, pitch, cast, hurl, chuck
totter *(v.)* stumble, falter, weave, reel, lurch
tough *(adj.)* rugged, hardy, durable, sturdy, unyielding, incorrigible
tourist *(n.)* visitor, sightseer, wayfarer
tournament *(n.)* competition, rivalry, contest, match, event, series
toxic *(adj.)* poisonous, deadly, lethal, virulent
trace *(n.)* vestige, indication, hint, suggestion
track *(v.)* hunt, trail, pursue, trace
tragedy *(n.)* disaster, calamity, catastrophe, affliction, suffering, tribulation
trait *(n.)* characteristic, quality, property, attribute, mannerism, habit
tramp *(n.)* vagabond, vagrant, gypsy
tranquil *(adj.)* peaceful, serene, placid, still, pleasant, cool, restful

transform *(v.)* alter, transfigure, convert, change
transgress *(n.)* overstep, infringe, violate, trespass
translate *(v.)* reword, explain, interpret, decipher
translucent *(adj.)* transparent, clear, limpid
transparent *(adj.)* translucent, diaphanous, lucid, clear, thin, sheer
transpire *(v.)* happen, occur, ensue, result
transpose *(v.)* switch, swap, exchange, transfer
trap *(n.)* snare, trick, stratagem, manoeuver, artifice
traumatic *(adj.)* alarming, upsetting, frightful
travesty *(n.)* parody, satire, spoof, burlesque, lampoon, farce
treacherous *(adj.)* unfaithful, deceitful, deceptive, insidious, disloyal, treasonous, unstable
treatise *(n.)* dissertation, thesis, essay, discourse
treaty *(n.)* agreement, settlement, covenant, pact
tribulation *(n.)* distress, suffering, hardship
tribute *(n.)* accolade, homage, recognition, applause
trinket *(n.)* bauble, adornment, decoration, ornament
triumph *(v.)* prevail, conquer, overwhelm, overpower, win, revel
trivial *(adj.)* insignificant, inconsequential, unimportant, irrelevant, frivolous
trophy *(n.)* award, citation, medal
trot *(v.)* canter, jog, lope, amble
trouble *(n.)* calamity, distress, misfortune, tribulation, worry, stress
trough *(n.)* channel, furrow, rut, crater, ditch
truculent *(adj.)* fierce, mean, malevolent, pugnacious, belligerent, contentious, hostile
trunk *(n.)* chest, strongbox, coffer, case
try *(v.)* endeavour, strive, test, examine
tryst *(n.)* meeting, rendezvous, assignation
tumble *(v.)* fall, slip, descend, decline, totter, drop
tumult *(n.)* disorder, commotion, turmoil, melee, agitation, ferment
turbulent *(adj.)* violent, blustery, disorderly
turmoil *(n.)* chaos, commotion, disorder, tumult,
turpitude *(n.)* depravity, baseness, perversion, vileness, evil, sinfulness, corruption
tussle *(v.)* scuffle, grapple, struggle, brawl
tweak *(v.)* nip, pinch, grasp, squeeze, pull, twist
twinge *(n.)* twitch, tingle, spasm, crick, stitch, throb
twirl *(v.)* twist, gyrate, turn, rotate, pivot
typify *(v.)* represent, personify, epitomize, exemplify, illustrate
tyrannical *(adj.)* oppressive, despotic, arbitrary, domineering, unjust, cruel

U

ubiquity *(n.)* prevalence, pervasiveness, commonness, omnipresence, universality
ulterior *(adj.)* concealed, shrouded, obscured
ultimate *(adj.)* extreme, final, decisive, concluding, eventual, maximum, utmost, preeminent
unassuming *(adj.)* modest, unpretentious, humble, simple, plain, diffident
unauthorized *(adj.)* unsanctioned, prohibited, illicit, forbidden, banned
unbalanced *(adj.)* unstable, maladjusted, biased, untrustworthy, treacherous
unbend *(v.)* relax, rest, soften, ease, relent
unbiased *(adj.)* impartial, objective, neutral, unprejudiced, tolerant, disinterested
uncanny *(adj.)* strange, odd, weird, mysterious, eerie
unceasing *(adj.)* continual, incessant, chronic, perpetual, persistent
uncivilized *(adj.)* primitive, barbarous, crude, uncouth
uncommon *(adj.)* exceptional, extraordinary, unique, remarkable, rare, scarce
unconditional *(adj.)* absolute, certain, unrestricted
unconscious *(adj.)* senseless, oblivious, benumbed
uncouth *(adj.)* rude, ill-mannered, vulgar, crass
underestimate *(v.)* misjudge, miscalculate, slight
undergo *(v.)* endure, tolerate, suffer, bear, abide
undermine *(v.)* weaken, erode, corrode, decay, threaten
underrate *(v.)* devaluate, lessen, downgrade, depreciate
understand *(v.)* comprehend, grasp, perceive, discern, interpret, hear, accept, conclude
underwrite *(v.)* guarantee, support, endorse
undo *(v.)* cancel, efface, erase, expunge, obliterate
undulate *(v.)* wave, surge, heave, flap, pulsate
uneasy *(adj.)* restless, perplexed, troubled, apprehensive, fidgety, nervous, jittery, uncomfortable
unequal *(adj.)* disparate, unlike, uneven, odd
unfathomable *(adj.)* incomprehensible, enigmatic, mysterious, inscrutable, profound, baffling, puzzling
uniform *(adj.)* regular, routine, normal, unwavering, invariable, consistent, steady

unify *(v.)* combine, integrate, consolidate, compact, concentrate, arrange, blend, integrate, synthesize

unintentional *(adj.)* involuntary, accidental, inadvertent, unplanned, unconscious

unique *(adj.)* singular, particular, peerless, unrivalled, unequalled, matchless, unusual, uncommon, odd, peculiar, rare

unison *(n.)* coincidence, agreement, concord

unity *(n.)* union, harmony, agreement, concert, unison, concord, rapport, congruity

unjust *(adj.)* unfair, partial, prejudiced, biased, inequitable, shabby, undeserved, unjustified, unmerited

unkempt *(adj.)* disorderly, disheveled, messy, tousled, untidy, crude, vulgar

unnerve *(v.)* upset, unsettle, aggravate, fluster, discourage, disconcert

unprecedented *(adj.)* unparalleled, unique, unequal, unusual, uncommon, untoward

unravel *(v.)* explain, elucidate, clarify, justify, resolve, interpret, solve, untangle, unwind, disengage

unveil *(v.)* reveal, show, expose, divulge, announce

upheaval *(n.)* eruption, earthquake, volcano, outbreak, explosion, outburst

uphold *(v.)* maintain, support, champion, sustain, endorse, sanction, bolster, help

upright *(adj.)* upstanding, honest, good, outstanding, moral, ethical, principled, just, righteous, pure, true

uproar *(n.)* clamour, commotion, disturbance, furor, hubbub, melee

uproot *(v.)* remove, transport, liquidate, excavate, extirpate, eradicate, eliminate, dislodge

upset *(adj.)* irritated, worried, uneasy, shaky, troubled, unsettled, disturbed, aggravated, concerned, perturbed, disconcerted

urban *(adj.)* city, metropolitan, civic

urbane *(adj.)* suave, poised, polished, refined, smooth, elegant, gracious, courteous

urchin *(n.)* waif, stray, foundling, orphan, ragamuffin, child, infant

urge *(n.)* drive, desire, impulse, craving, passion, push, influence, stimulus, impulse

urgent *(adj.)* pressing, compelling, demanding, driving, forcing, imperative, anxious, insistent

usable *(adj.)* useful, employable, applicable, functional, serviceable

useful *(adj.)* beneficial, helpful, effective, practical, functional, handy

usual *(adj.)* common, customary, ordinary, familiar

usurp *(v.)* capture, commandeer, appropriate, assume, seize

utensil *(n.)* instrument, device, implement, gadget

utmost *(adj.)* ultimate, maximum, maximal, entire, greatest, undiminished, unlimited

utopian *(adj.)* idealistic, ideological, visionary, perfect, ideal, fanciful, theoretical

utter *(adj.)* complete, entire, total, unconditional, unqualified, thorough

utterance *(n.)* assertion, declaration, enunciation, proclamation, pronouncement

V

vacant *(adj.)* empty, uninhabited, abandoned, deserted, expressionless, vapid

vacation *(n.)* holiday, furlough, respite, sabbatical

vaccinate *(v.)* immunize, inoculate, inject

vacillate *(v.)* waver, hesitate, fluctuate, alternate, sway, falter

vacuum *(n.)* void, emptiness, vacuity, nothingness

vagrant *(n.)* beggar, tramp, hobo, idler, loafer

vague *(adj.)* obscure, indistinct, indefinite, imprecise, unspecified, uncertain, loose, unclear

valet *(n.)* servant, attendant, butler, steward

valour *(n.)* bravery, courage, boldness, spirit

valuable *(adj.)* expensive, precious, rare, priceless, useful, beneficial, profitable, serviceable

vandalism *(n.)* defacement, damage, mutilation, dis figuration, marring, spoiling

vanish *(v.)* disappear, depart, evaporate, fade, dissolve, exit

vanity *(n.)* conceit, pretension, self-esteem, pride, folly, arrogance

vanquish *(v.)* conquer, overwhelm, overpower, defeat, quell, quash, subdue, suppress, subjugate, crush

vapour *(n.)* fog, haze, mist, gas, smog, condensation

variance *(n.)* difference, divergence, discrepancy, incongruity, disagreement, discord

variety *(n.)* category, group, classification, division

varnish *(v.)* embellish, disguise, mask, veil, falsify
vault *(n.)* crypt, tomb, mausoleum, sepulcher
vaunt *(v.)* boast, gloat, brag, strut, swagger, flaunt
vehement *(adj.)* fervent, energetic, impassioned
vehicle *(n.)* conveyance, medium, means, agency, instrumentality
velocity *(n.)* speed, swiftness, quickness
venerate *(v.)* admire, worship, revere, esteem, respect
vengeful *(adj.)* vindictive, unforgiving, unrelenting, spiteful, rancorous, intractable, malicious
venial *(adj.)* excusable, justifiable, forgivable
venom *(n.)* bitterness, virulence, malice, anger, contempt, spitefulness, malevolence, hate
vent *(v.)* express, air, assert, verbalize, articulate, expound, release, unleash, discharge
venture *(n.)* undertaking, enterprise, adventure, investment, speculation, endeavour, attempt
venture *(v.)* chance, wager, risk, gamble, hazard, dare, plunge, imperil, jeopardize, endanger
veracious *(adj.)* truthful, accurate, precise, honest, sincere, trustworthy, righteous
veracity *(n.)* truth, honesty, sincerity, accuracy, precision, exactness, correctness
verandah *(n.)* terrace, porch, deck, patio, courtyard
verbal *(adj.)* oral, spoken, stated
verdict *(n.)* decision, judgement, ruling, adjudication, decree, determination, sentence
verge *(n.)* edge, brink, border, limit, margin, rim, brim
verify *(v.)* confirm, prove, authenticate, corroborate substantiate, validate
vernacular *(adj.)* native, indigenous, regional, informal, colloquial, everyday, ordinary, familiar
versatile *(adj.)* flexible, pliable, adaptable, tractable, all-round, resourceful
versed *(adj.)* experienced, seasoned, competent, adept, capable, skilled, practiced, trained
vertical *(adj.)* erect, upright, perpendicular, plumb
vestige *(n.)* trace, indication, shred, fragment, remainder, hint, suggestion
veteran *(adj.)* experienced, seasoned, skilled, versed
vex *(v.)* annoy, harass, irk, bother, disturb, irritate, plague, torment, agitate
vibrate *(v.)* shake, flutter, tremble, quiver, undulate, fluctuate, oscillate, reverberate
vicinity *(n.)* area, locality, neighbourhood, environment, proximity, nearness
vicious *(adj.)* immoral, base, degenerate, vile, depraved, reprehensible, wrong, malicious, malevolent, spiteful, malignant, unruly
victim *(n.)* casualty, dupe, gull, prey, sucker, fool
victor *(n.)* winner, champion, vanquisher, conqueror
vigilant *(adj.)* watchful, alert, observant, attentive, careful, wary
vigour *(n.)* strength, power, potency, stamina, energy, endurance, vitality, soundness
vile *(adj.)* evil, depraved, wretched, repulsive, contemptible, revolting, disgusting, offensive, vulgar
village *(n.)* town, community, hamlet, municipality
villain *(n.)* miscreant, cad, rascal, rogue, scoundrel
vindicate *(v.)* exonerate, acquit, absolve, clear, defend, justify, support, uphold, corroborate, assert
vintage *(adj.)* classic, antique, old, excellent
violation *(n.)* transgression, infringement, breach, debasement, assault, outrage
violent *(adj.)* intense, fierce, furious, rough, vicious, brutal, barbarous, savage, fierce
virgin *(n.)* pure, undefiled, unsullied, unadulterated, unmixed, fresh, unspoiled
virile *(adj.)* vibrant, strong, forceful, vigorous, robust, masculine
virtue *(n.)* integrity, justice, temperance, purity, decency, merit, distinction, excellence
virulent *(adj.)* malignant, venomous, poisonous; bitter, malicious, antagonistic
virus *(n.)* infection, disease, germ, microbe
visa *(n.)* endorsement, permit, authorization
visage *(n.)* countenance, appearance, aspect
visible *(adj.)* discernible, perceptible, perceivable, obvious, apparent, clear, evident, conspicuous
visibility *(n.)* distinctness, perceptibility, prominence, clarity
visitor *(n.)* guest, caller, company
vista *(n.)* view, perspective, prospect, outlook
vital *(adj.)* essential, necessary, important, critical, requisite; vigorous, lively, energetic, active
vivacious *(adj.)* lively, animated, brisk, spirited, sprightly, energetic, spry
vivid *(adj.)* shining, intense, lucid, lively, spirited, energetic, vivacious, realistic, picturesque, distinct, graphic, striking, clear, discernible

vocabulary *(n.)* lexicon, glossary, dictionary
vocal *(adj.)* spoken, oral, expressed, articulated, verbalized; outspoken, open, honest, assertive, candid, blunt, frank
vociferous *(adj.)* noisy, boisterous, uproarious, blatant, loud, ranting
vogue *(n.)* fashion, style, custom, trend, fad, popularity, acceptance, rage
volatile *(adj.)* explosive, unstable, fickle, erratic, frivolous, passing, transient, ephemeral
volume *(n.)* book, manuscript; size, magnitude, bulk; loudness, intensity, strength
voluntary *(adj.)* willing, disposed, inclined, prone, deliberate, intended, intentional, planned, willful
volunteer *(v.)* offer, extend, render, submit, tender, propose, suggest, recommend
voluptuous *(adj.)* sensual, indulgent, carnal, erotic, lustful, licentious
voracious *(adj.)* greedy, insatiable, ravenous, hungry, rapacious, grasping
vouch *(v.)* certify, attest, swear, state, assure
vow *(v.)* swear, promise, assure, attest, certify, affirm, pledge
voyage *(n.)* journey, excursion, trip, tour
vulgar *(adj.)* coarse, tasteless, gross, crude, unrefined
vulgarity *(n.)* obscenity, rudeness, indelicacy, coarseness, crassness, impropriety, immodesty
vulnerable *(adj.)* unprotected, unguarded, defenseless, exposed, susceptible, unsafe

W

waft *(v.)* float, hover, drift, skim, flit, flutter
wager *(v.)* bet, stake, risk, gamble, hazard
waif *(n.)* stray, foundling, orphan, urchin, ragamuffin
wad *(v.)* lament, bemoan, sob, whine, mourn
waive *(v.)* forgo, sacrifice, relinquish, renounce, resign, postpone, defer, shelve, table
wand *(n.)* baton, staff, stick, scepter
wander *(v.)* roam, drift, ramble, meander, rove, range, stroll, saunter, digress, stray, veer
wanton *(adj.)* malicious, hateful, spiteful, reckless, wilful, unruly; lewd, lascivious, lustful, dissolute
ward *(n.)* child, minor, orphan; district, territory, precinct, parish
warm *(adj.)* gracious, amiable, pleasant, kind, intimate, amicable, sympathetic, close
warrant *(v.)* certify, approve, authorize, sanction
wash *(v.)* clean, cleanse, scrub, swab, bathe
watch *(v.)* observe, view, see, regard, scrutinize, inspect, guard, patrol, protect
waver *(v.)* fluctuate, vacillate, hesitate
wax *(v.)* increase, grow, enlarge, expand, flourish
waylay *(v.)* ambush, assail, lurk, trap
wealth *(n.)* riches, affluence, assets, abundance
weary *(adj.)* tired, exhausted, drained, fatigued
weary *(v.)* harass, annoy, bother, badger, pester, irk, vex, distress
weigh *(v.)* consider, contemplate, ponder, study
weird *(adj.)* mysterious, eerie, spooky, uncanny, unnatural, ghostly, puzzling, arcane
well *(adj.)* healthy, strong, hardy, robust, fit, sound
whereabouts *(n.)* location, position, situation, locale, place, spot, site
whimper *(v.)* cry, whine, sniffle, snivel, weep
whimsical *(adj.)* capricious, fanciful, playful, impulsive
whine *(v.)* cry, complain, grumble, snivel, whimper
wholesome *(adj.)* nourishing, healthy, nutritious, beneficial, advantageous, good
wicked *(adj.)* evil, corrupt, vile, immoral, nefarious
wild *(adj.)* untamed, uncivilized, unrestrained
wile *(n.)* trickery, deception, deceit, artifice, ruse
wilt *(v.)* droop, wither, shrivel, decay, slump
wince *(v.)* flinch, recoil, cringe, falter, twitch
windfall *(n.)* blessing, godsend, boon, bonanza
winnow *(v.)* sift, separate, sieve, extract, eliminate
winsome *(adj.)* winning, beautiful, charming, captivating, lovely, cute, engaging, comely, delightful
wisdom *(n.)* sagacity, understanding, discretion, insight, tact, intelligence, knowledge
wish *(v.)* crave, yearn, want, need; direct, order, bid, instruct; request, beg, entreat, solicit
wistful *(adj.)* melancholy, longing, yearning, sentimental, nostalgic, wishful, plaintive
witchcraft *(n.)* sorcery, wizardry, divination, magic
wither *(v.)* shrivel, wilt, shrink, atrophy, languish
withstand *(v.)* oppose, defy, confront, resist, endure
witness *(n.)* spectator, bystander, onlooker, eyewitness, observer
witticism *(n.)* quip, jest, pun, gag, joke, wisecrack
wizard *(n.)* magician, conjurer, soothsayer, sorcerer

woeful *(adj.)* mournful, sad, sorrowful, doleful

wonder *(v.)* question, ponder, doubt, speculate; marvel, gape, stare

wonderful *(adj.)* extraordinary, marvelous, astounding, awesome, remarkable, excellent, superb

woo *(v.)* court, charm, pursue, cultivate, entice, entreat, seek

worry *(n.)* anxiety, apprehension, fear, disquiet, uneasiness, misgiving

worship *(n.)* adoration, devotion, reverence, veneration, praise, idolize

worth *(n.)* value, importance, quality, excellence

wrangle *(v.)* dispute, bicker, quarrel, squabble

wrap *(v.)* enfold, envelop, swathe, bandage, swaddle, cover

wrath *(n.)* anger, fury, ire, irritation, resentment

wreak *(v.)* perpetrate, do, perform, commit

wreath *(n.)* garland, bouquet, decoration

wreckage *(n.)* remains, debris, wreck

wretch *(n.)* miscreant, rogue, villain, rascal, brute

wrinkle *(n.)* fold, crease, pucker, furrow, ridge

writ *(n.)* law, decree, order, edict

write *(v.)* inscribe, scrawl, sign, compose, record

wrong *(adj.)* immoral, evil, false, inaccurate, improper

wrong *(v.)* harm, abuse, oppress, maltreat, dishonour

Y

yardstick *(n.)* measure, standard, scale, guide, gauge, model, norm

yearning *(n.)* longing, craving, desire, want, wish

yell *(v.)* cheer, root, shout, call, holler, scream

yield *(v.)* surrender, abdicate, cede, concede, resign, grant, acquiesce, give

yoke *(n.)* couple, harness, join, link, attach, connect

youth *(n.)* immaturity, adolescence, minority

Z

zany *(adj.)* crazy, funny, silly, nonsensical, wacky

zeal *(n.)* enthusiasm, fervour, passion, spirit, ardour

zealot *(n.)* fanatic, devotee, partisan

zealous *(adj.)* enthusiastic, eager, fervent, passionate, spirited, ardent, earnest

zenith *(n.)* top, peak, crest, elevation

zest *(n.)* relish, enthusiasm, gusto, enjoyment, delight, keenness

Books on English Improvement

Big Size 18.5 x 24 cm
Pages over 392 0004 R

Big Size 18.5 x 24 cm
Pages over 264
8722 F

Big Size 18.5 x 24 cm
Pages over 368 0007 R

Big Size 18.5 x 24 cm
Pages 384 0001 R

Big Size 18.5 x 24 cm
Pages 360
0014 R

Big Size 18.5 x 24 cm
Pages 256
0010 R

12 S
0008 R Big Size 18.5 x 24 cm
Pages 388

Big Size 18.5 x 24 cm
Pages 384 0002 R

Big Size 18.5 x 24 cm
Pages 264 9694 J

Big Size 18.5 x 24 cm
Pages 352 1234 S

1232 A - Assamese-Hindi
1233 B - Hindi-Assamese
1215 S - Hindi-Tamil
1217 S - Hindi-Telugu
1218 S - Hindi-Bangla
1219 S - Hindi-Gujarati
1216 S - Hindi Kannada
1236 A - Malayalam-Arabic
1221 S - Tamil-Hindi
1223 S - Telugu-Hindi
1224 S - Bangla-Hindi
1225 S - Gujarati-Hindi
1222 S - Kannada-Hindi
1128 B - Hindi-Arabic
1220 S - Malayalam-Hindi
1214 S - Hindi-Malayalam

glish-Hindi, English-Tamil, English-Kannada
glish-Telugu, English-Urdu, English-Assamese
glish-Bangla, English-Odia, English-Malayalam
glish-Marathi, English-Gujarati

Over 1200 Entries
All in Colours

Size 13.5 x 19.5 cm
Pages 464

Size 14 x 21.5 cm
Pages 584

Size 13.5 x 19.5 cm
Pages 576

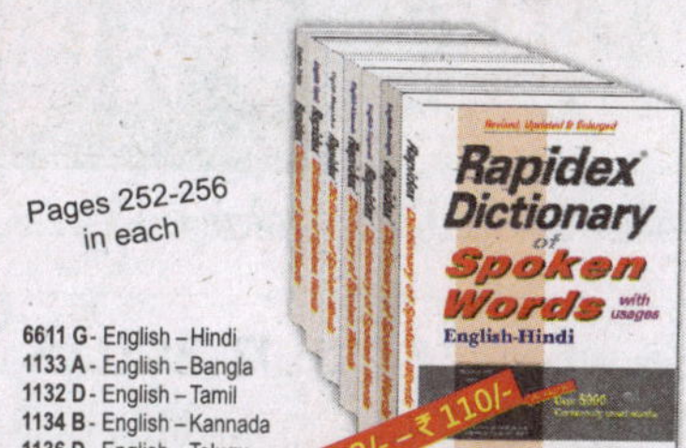

Pages 252-256 in each

6611 G- English – Hindi
1133 A - English – Bangla
1132 D - English – Tamil
1134 B - English – Kannada
1136 D - English – Telugu
1137 A - English – Gujarati
1135 C - English – Malayalam

6607 L

English-Hindi, English- Marathi
English-Odia, English-Kannada
English-Tamil, English-Telugu
English-Nepali, English-Assamese
English-Bangla

अंग्रेज़ी के 10000 से अधिक शब्द
हर शब्द के अनेक अर्थ
अर्थानुसार प्रयोग

Compact Size 10.2x12.7 cm
Pages 384 in each

English-Hindi, English-Marathi,
English-Odia, English-Kannada,
English-Tamil, English-Telugu,
English-Nepali, English-Bangla
English to Punjabi & Hindi,
English-Assamese

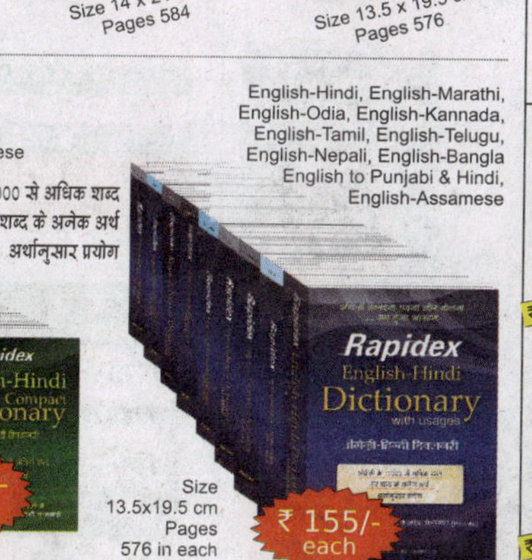

Size 13.5x19.5 cm
Pages 576 in each

Page 256 (with CD) Page 310
Page 316 Page 344

4 Books of English Learning Library

Full Set packed in a Slipcase ₹ 600/-

POPULAR SCIENCE

9825 E • ₹ 175/-

2215 S • ₹ 165/- Available in Hindi also. Contains: 10 Projects

2214 S • ₹ 165/- Available in Hindi also. FREE Tutorial CD

New — HOW THINGS WORK?

8702 B • ₹ 150/-

Projects in Instrumentation for Engineering Students

8733 D • ₹ 195/-

Mini & Major ELECTRONICS PROJECTS for Engineering Students

9660 K • ₹ 295/-

9412 C • ₹ 120/-

6678 D • ₹ 250/-

6679 A • ₹ 150/-

QUIZ BOOKS

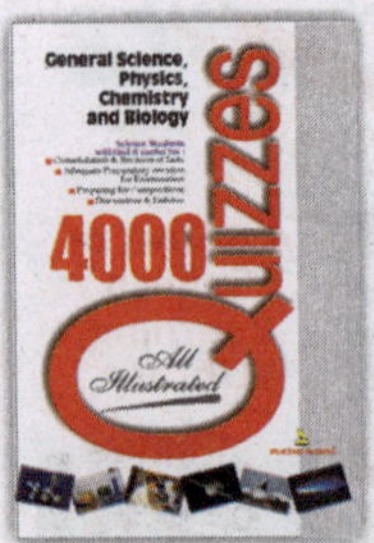

8965 D • ₹ 150/-

7726 K • ₹ 120/-

7723 F • ₹ 100/-

7727 L • ₹ 120/-

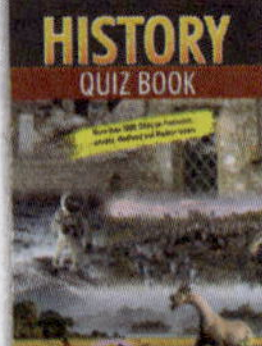

7753 G • ₹ 150/-

7725 B • ₹ 100/-

7722 E • ₹ 120/-

NEW RELEASES

8767 C • Rs. 120/-

0019 R • Rs. 160/-

8762 P • Rs. 140/-

8764 T • Rs. 160/-

Set Code: 4514 S

- Over 900 Illustrations
- Over 800 Pages
- 890 Articles
- Four Volumes

Set 4 Vols.: ₹ 780/-
Each Vol.: ₹ 195/-

Available in Hindi & English both

MISCELLANEOUS

Big Size 18.5 x 24 cm Pages 232

101 Wonders of the World

9495 R • ₹ 175/-

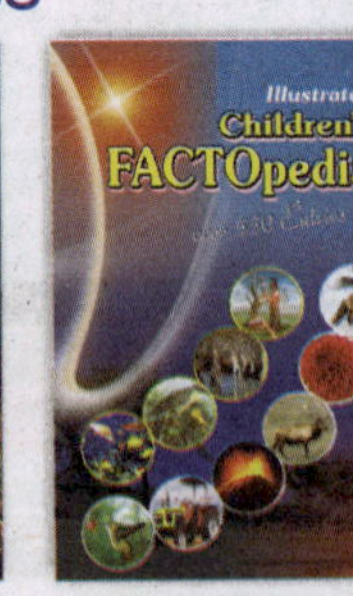

9496 A • Rs. 120/

HOMEOPATHY, AYURDEDA

8887 D • ₹ 295/-

8944 D • ₹ 250/-

8923 D • ₹ 250/-

9446 B • ₹ 15

HERBAL CURE

8010 D • ₹ 96/-

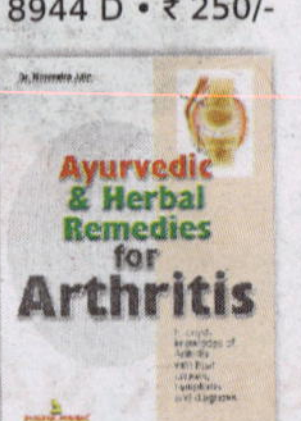

9094 E • ₹ 96/-

8270 B • ₹ 195/-

8948 A • ₹ 12

SELF-IMPROVEMENT

New

698 R • ₹ 195/- 9498 C • ₹ 180/- 9490 H • ₹ 175/- 9464 R • ₹ 80/- 9096 B • ₹ 150/- 5614 E • ₹ 150/- 4008 J • ₹ 150/- 9026 D • ₹ 120/- 9786 M • ₹ 195/-

491 J • ₹ 100/- 8885 D • ₹ 150/- 9081 D • ₹ 150/- 9091 B • ₹ 120/- 9060 B • ₹ 195/- 9684 F • ₹ 195/- 9449 A • ₹ 195/- 9788 R • ₹ 195/-

MANAGEMENT/JOB/CARRIER/BUSINESS & PROFESSION

All Time Bestsellers

9461 K • ₹ 150/- 5338 A • ₹ 135/- (with CD) 8979 A • ₹ 135/- 9406 B • ₹ 150/- 9682 D • ₹ 120/- 8729 T • ₹ 120/-

New

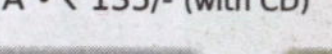

8716 T • ₹ 160/- 9313 D • ₹ 150/- 5623 B • ₹ 250/- 9439 L • ₹ 150/- 5441 D • ₹ 195/- HB 8883 D • ₹ 150/- 8735 F • ₹ 150/-

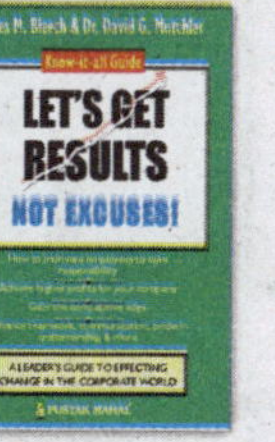

4018 D • ₹ 150/- 9079 B • ₹ 195/- 4005 E • ₹ 195/- 5643 B • ₹ 120/- 9431 C • ₹ 175/- 9697 P • ₹ 195/- 9763 P • Rs. 195/-

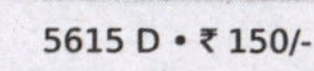

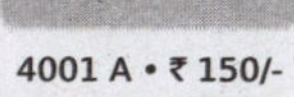
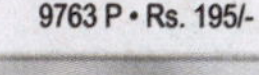

5618 D • ₹ 120/- 5640 C • ₹ 120/- 5615 D • ₹ 150/- 9672 G • ₹ 150/- 4001 A • ₹ 150/- 5646 A • ₹ 225/- 4017 D • ₹ 150/-

PERSONALITY DEVELOPMENT

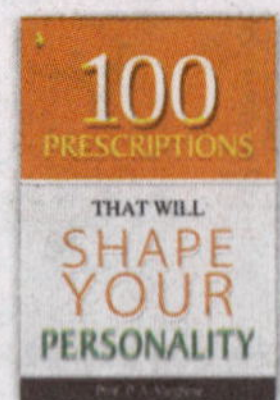

9748 E • ₹ 195/- 9666 A • ₹ 150/- 9678 R • ₹ 195/-

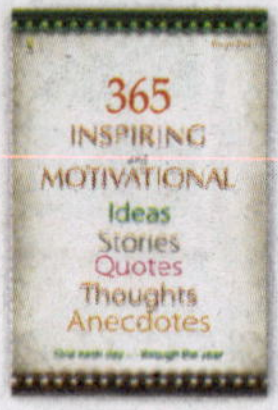

9670 E • ₹ 240/- 9696 M • ₹ 220/- 9070 B • ₹ 195/-

9430 B • ₹ 165/- 5642 A • ₹ 150/- 9450 B • ₹ 195/-

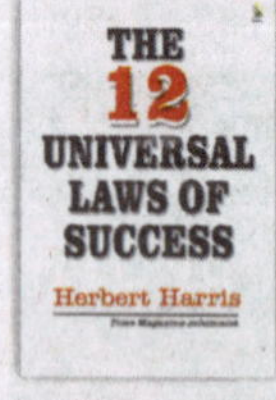

9088 C • ₹ 195/- 9668 C • ₹ 150/- 9455 C • ₹ 150/-

5639 B • ₹ 80/- 9667 B • ₹ 150/- 8966 E • ₹ 100/-

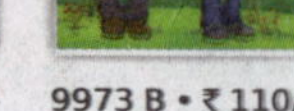

9981 B • ₹ 96/- 8868 D • ₹ 120/- 9973 B • ₹ 110/-

MEMORY DEVELOPMENT / STUDENT DEVELOPMENT / STRESS MANAGEMENT

9090 A • ₹ 220/- 5622 A • ₹ 120/- 9071 D • ₹ 165/- 8731 B • ₹ 100/-

2241 J • ₹ 100/- 94441 S • ₹ 160/- 8710 K • ₹ 140/-

9652 D • ₹ 120/- 8962 A • ₹ 150/- 9654 D • ₹ 100/-

9487 E • ₹ 150/- 9466 T • ₹ 96/- 9089 D • ₹ 135/-

4016 D • ₹ 160/- 4009 K • ₹ 150/- 8997 B • ₹ 120/-

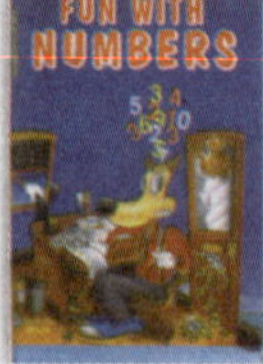

4010 L • ₹ 100/- 9787 P • ₹ 100/- 2244 D • ₹ 80/-

PARENTING

9906 J • ₹ 250/- (HB) 8261 D • ₹ 180/-

9674 J • ₹ 220/- 9784 J • ₹ 150/-

9594 K • ₹ 80/- 8917 D • ₹ 120/-

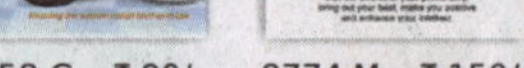

9458 G • ₹ 80/- 8774 M • ₹ 150/-

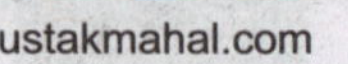

9065 A • ₹ 80/- 9994 E • ₹ 120/-

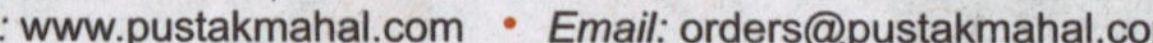

ALTERNATIVE THERAPIES

8882 F • ₹ 215/-

8983 E • ₹ 100/-

9935 F • ₹ 120/-

8889 D • ₹ 100/-

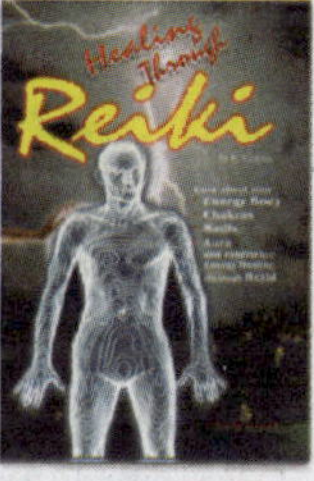

8842 D • ₹ 120/-

8941 A • ₹ 100/-

COMMON AILMENTS & DISEASES

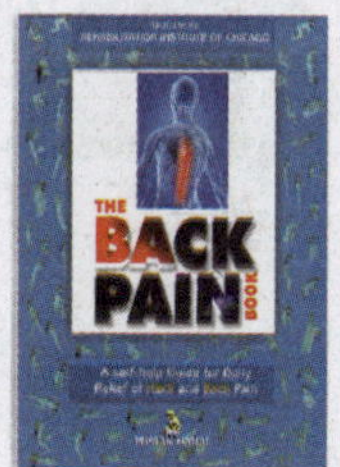

8891 D • ₹ 120/-

8281 A • ₹ 100/-

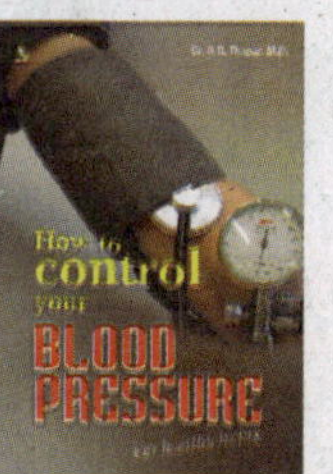

8094 D • ₹ 120/-

8888 D • ₹ 96/-

8908 D • ₹ 120/-

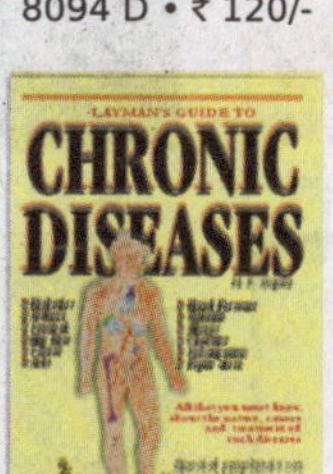

8848 D • ₹ 150/-

GENERAL HEALTH

8747 D • ₹ 150/-

9075 C • ₹ 225/-

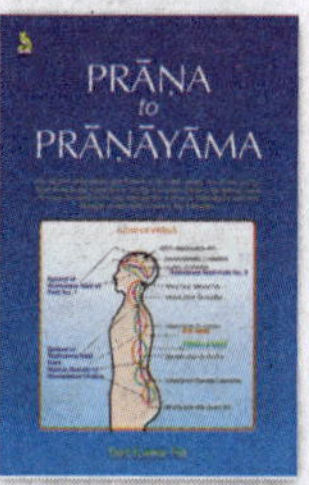

8773 K • ₹ 195/-

8859 G • ₹ 80/-

8877 A • ₹ 150/-

9940 D • ₹ 150/-

8870 D • ₹ 100/-

9950 B • ₹ 120/-

8847 M • ₹ 100/-

SLIMMING & FITNESS

8277 B • ₹ 120/-

8875 K • ₹ 120/-

9445 A • ₹ 150/-

DIET & NUTRITION

8276 A • ₹ 96/-

9941 D • ₹ 100/-

8904 D • ₹ 150/-

8985 B • ₹ 150/-

8968 G • ₹ 120/-

8271 C • ₹ 96/-

9037 D • ₹ 150/-

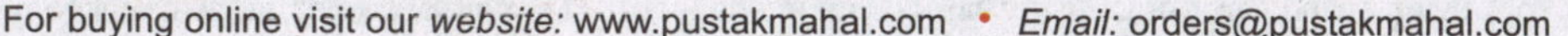

HINDOOLOGY / RELIGION / SPIRITUAL BOOKS

9873 C • ₹ 60/-

9770 E • ₹ 150/-

4179 A • ₹ 295/- (HB)

4138 B Rs. 250

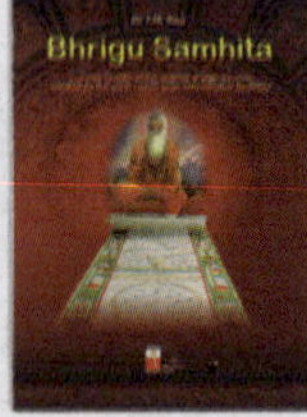

4177 B • ₹ 250/-

9997 C • ₹ 80/-

4181 C • ₹ 195/-

9984 E • ₹ 399/- (HB)

4130 B • ₹ 120/-

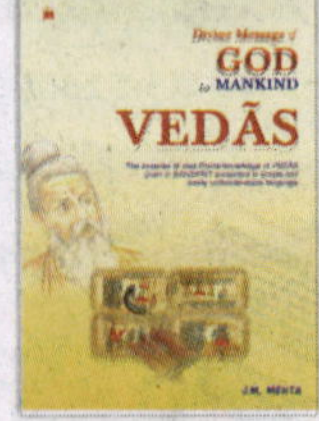

9811 P • ₹ 120/-

9585 A • ₹ 96/-

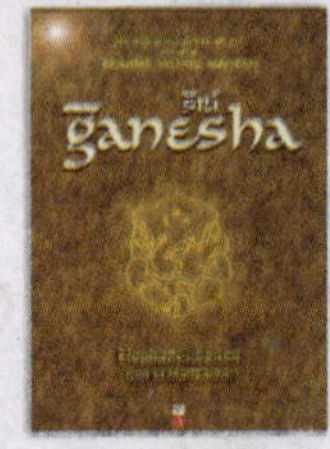

9508 D • ₹ 95/-

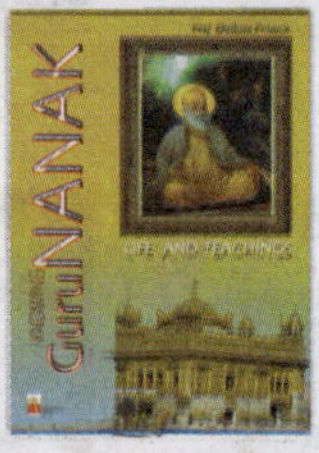

9989 D • ₹ 96/-

4183 A • ₹ 350/- (HB)

9504 D • ₹ 100/-

9540 D • ₹ 150/-

9513 A • ₹ 195/-

4126 B • ₹ 96/-

9812 R • ₹ 120/-

9504 D • ₹ 100/-

4124 A • ₹ 120/-

4190 C • ₹ 160/-

9509 A • ₹ 150/-

4152 B • ₹ 96/-

4188 A • ₹ 160/-

4132 D • ₹ 100/-

9987 E • ₹ 150/-

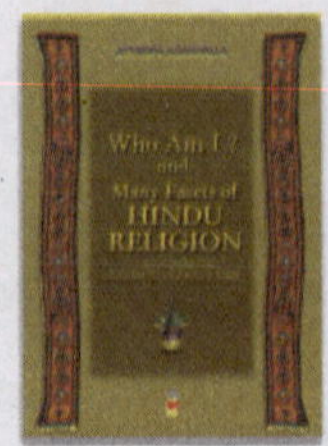
9520 D • ₹ 120/-

4134 B • ₹ 80/-

4182 D • ₹ 96/-

9405 A • ₹ 195/-

COMPUTERS

7712 K • ₹ 165/-

7711 J • ₹ 120/-

9768 C • ₹ 175/-

7766 A • ₹ 120/-

HOME MAKING / GRILLS & RAILINGS

3111 E • ₹ 175/-

3107 F • ₹ 88/-

3106 E • ₹ 100/-

3105 D • ₹ 100/-

3108 G • ₹ 150/-

3104 M • ₹ 100/-

ASTROLOGY / VASTU / HYPNOTISM / PAMISTRY

9871 A • ₹ 395/-

9693 H • ₹ 195/-

9671 F • ₹ 195/-

2127 D • ₹ 250/-

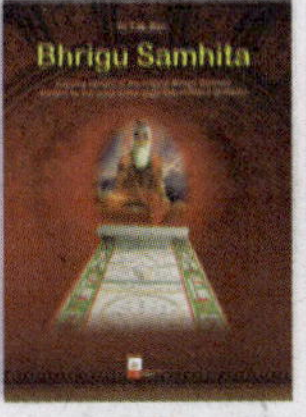
4177 C • ₹ 295/-

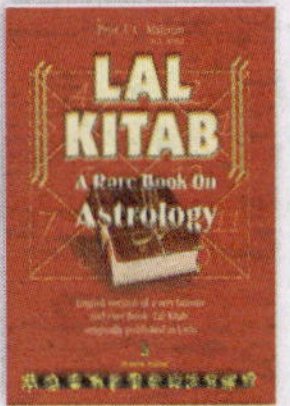
9086 A • ₹ 350/-HB

2116 D • ₹ 150/- 8259 D • ₹ 88/- 2109 F • ₹ 150/- 2112 D • ₹ 150/- 3110 B • ₹ 120/- 2133 B • ₹ 96/-

8899 D • ₹ 195/- 8925 D • ₹ 96/- 9432 D • ₹ 150/- 2120 D • ₹ 150/- 2109 F • ₹ 100/-

ENGLISH IMPROVEMENT

97540 D • ₹ 175/-

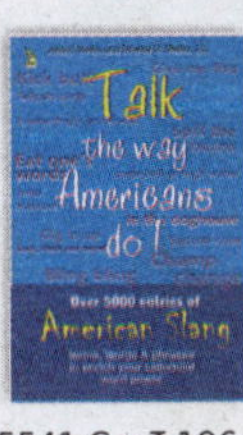

5541 C • ₹ 196/-

6651 E • ₹ 220/-

9448 D • ₹ 195/-

9056 A • ₹ 150/-

5538 D • ₹ 100/-

PERSON & PERSONALITIES

9669 D • ₹ 120/-

9825 E • ₹ 175/-

2113 D • ₹ 195/-

9764 R • ₹ 100/-

8991 D • ₹ 120/-

BODY / BEAUTY CARE

8093 D • ₹ 150/-

9986 B • ₹ 150/-

8971 B • ₹ 120/-.

9922 F • ₹ 120/-

8865 F • ₹ 120/-

JOKES HUMOUR & SATIRE

2342 C • ₹ 100/- 2343 D • ₹ 100/-

2318 A • ₹ 96/- 2319 B • ₹ 96/-

YOGA & MEDITATION

9453 A • ₹ 250/-

9087 B • ₹ 195/-

8741 N • ₹ 195/-

8743 R • ₹ 225/-

8269 A • ₹ 195/-

9998 D • ₹ 150/-

8901 D • ₹ 150/-

9958 S • ₹ 160/-

8939 D • ₹ 96/-

SAYING/QUOTATIONS/ PROVERBS

9474 F • ₹ 170/-

9789 A • ₹ 150/-

8999 D • ₹ 80/-

9953 A • ₹ 100/-

8947 E • ₹ 100/-

8890 D • ₹ 150/-

5512 A • ₹ 150/-

8963 B • ₹ 80/-

9425 A • ₹ 60/-

FUN, FACTS, MAGIC & MYSTERIES

9484 B • ₹ 150/- 2275 D • ₹ 120/- 9479 M • ₹. 120/- 9470 B • ₹ 100/-

2208 M • ₹ 100/- 9816 D • ₹ 100/- 2247 F • ₹ 100/- 2250 A • ₹ 140/-

2211 F • ₹ 100/- 9457 E • ₹ 150/- 2237 M • ₹ 100/- 2335 A • ₹ 80/-

2243 L • ₹ 100/- 9775 M • ₹ 100/- 9985 A • ₹ 80/- 5110 A • ₹ 80/-

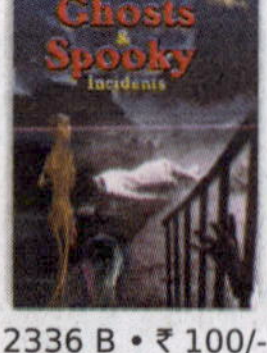

2337 C • ₹ 100/- 2336 B • ₹ 100/- 2331 C • ₹ 100/- 9977 B • ₹ 100/-

FICTION

William Shakespeare — Set Price ₹ 297/- ₹ 99/- Each Volume

3 Books • 15 Plays

Sherlock Holmes — Set Price ₹ 495/- ₹ 99/- Each Volume

5 Books • 25 Stories

All-time favourite world famous
25 ENGLISH CLASSICS for Children

Set Price ₹ 495/- ₹ 99/- Each Volume

5 Books • 25 Stories

Volume 1
1. The Adventure of Silas Marner 2. Alice's Adventures in Wonderland 3. Gulliver's Travels 4. Black Beauty 5. Treasure Island

Volume 2
1. Around the World in 80 Days 2. Frankenstein 3. Heidi 4. The Hound of the Baskervilles 5. The Invisible Man

Volume 3
1. Great Expectations 2. Jane Eyre 3. Jungle Book 4. Oliver Twist 5. The Three Musketeers

Volume 4
1. The Man in the Iron Mask 2. The Call of the Wild 3. David Copperfield 4. The Secret Garden 5. The War of the Worlds

Volume 5
1. A Tale of Two Cities 2. 20,000 Leagues under the Sea 3. King Solomon's Mines 4. Little Women 5. The Merry Adventures of Robin Hood

By MUNSHI PREMCHAND

9592 H • ₹ 195/- Pages 272

9512 D • ₹ 250/- Pages 352

9820 H • ₹ 150/- Pages 208

WORLD FAMOUS SERIES

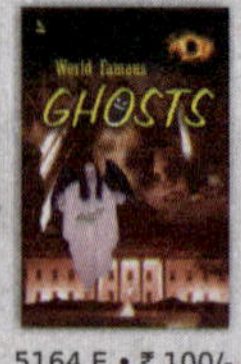

9472 D • ₹ 100/- 5164 E • ₹ 100/- 9483 A • Rs. 100/- 51107 • ₹ 100/- 9766 A • Rs. 100/- 9489 G • Rs. 100/- 9761 M • Rs. 120/-

World Famous Mysterious Objects
True Stories of Mowglis and other Wild Childrens
World Famous Treasures (Lost and Found)
World Famous WARs & Battles
True Stories of Mystic Places
World Famous Adventures
World Famous Military Operations
World Famous Spy Scandals
World Famous Spies & Spymasters
World Famous Crooks & Con Men
True Stories 81 Weird Humans
True Stories of Great Explorers
World Famous Strange Mysteries
and many more.......

LOVE, ROMANCE & SEX

9602 B • Rs. 125/- 8260 D • Rs. 96/- 8266 D • Rs. 80/- 8278 C • Rs. 120/- 8916 D • Rs. 120/-

MORAL, WISDOM & FAIRY TALES

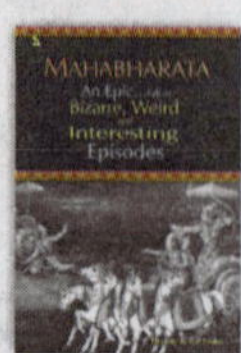

9677 P • Rs. 150/- 9486 D • Rs. 250/- 8967 F • Rs. 80/- 9077 E • Rs.120/- 9563 N • Rs. 125/- 2289 D • ₹ 96/-